D0464329

Schott's Almanac

2008

All knowledge is of itself of some value.
There is nothing so minute or inconsiderable,
that I would not rather know it than not.
— SAMUEL JOHNSON (1709–84)

Published by Bloomsbury Publishing Plc., 36 Soho Square, London, W1D 3QY, UK

www.benschott.com

1 2 3 4 5 6 7 8 9 10

The paper this book is printed on is certified by the © 1996 Forest Stewardship Council A.C. (FSC). It is ancient-forest friendly. The printer holds FSC chain of custody SGS-COC-2061

ISBN 978-0-7475-8469-8

A CIP catalogue record for this book is available from the British Library.
Designed & typeset by BEN SCHOTT
Printed in Great Britain by
CLAYS Ltd, ST IVES Plc.

Also by BEN SCHOTT

Schott's Original Miscellany
Schott's Food & Drink Miscellany
Schott's Sporting, Gaming, & Idling Miscellany
Schott's Miscellany Diary (with Smythson of Bond St.)
American and German editions of *Schott's Almanac 2008* are also available

Schott's Almanac

2008

· The book of things past and the song of the future ·

Conceived, edited, and designed by

BEN SCHOTT

UK & Series Editor · Claire Cock-Starkey

US Editor · Bess Lovejoy
German Editor · Alexander Weber
Researcher · James Matthews

BLOOMSBURY

Preface

A calendar, a calendar! look in the almanack;
find out moonshine, find out moonshine.
— A Midsummer Night's Dream, III i

Completely revised and updated, *Schott's Almanac 2008* picks up from where the 2007 edition left off, to create a seamless biography of the year. ❦ In his 2007 MacTaggart Lecture, Jeremy Paxman said of television journalism, 'there comes a point where the frenzy has to be put to one side, the rolling story halted, so that we can make sense of things'. Though a book, *Schott's Almanac* aspires to follow the Paxman prescription of 'assessing, filtering, separating the froth from what matters', to offer an informative, selective, and entertaining analysis of the year. ❦ The C21st almanac is necessarily different from some of its distinguished predecessors [see p.6], which were published in times when the year was defined by considerations astronomical, ecclesiastical, or aristocratic. By exploring high art and pop culture, geopolitics and gossip, scientific discovery and sporting achievement, *Schott's Almanac* endeavours to describe the year as it is lived, in all its complexity.

— *Schott's* is an almanac written to be read.

THE ALMANAC'S YEAR

In order to be as inclusive as possible, the *Schott's Almanac* year runs until mid-September.

Data cited in *Schott's Almanac* are taken from the latest sources available at the time of writing.

ERRORS & OMISSIONS

Every effort has been taken to ensure that the information contained within *Schott's Almanac* is both accurate and up-to-date, and grateful acknowledgement is made to the various sources used. However, as Goethe once said: 'error is to truth as sleep is to waking'. Consequently, the author would be pleased to be informed of any errors, inaccuracies, or omissions that might help improve future editions.

Please send all comments or suggestions to the author, care of:

Bloomsbury Publishing Plc, 36 Soho Square, London, W1D 3QY
or email *editor@schottsalmanac.com*

The author is grateful to the readers who sent in comments on the 2007 edition. Notable corrections and clarifications are included in the Errata section on p.352.

Contents

EARLY ALMANACS OF NOTE

Solomon Jarchi	*c.*1150
Peter de Dacia	*c.*1300
Walter de Elvendene	1327
John Somers (Oxford)	1380
Nicholas de Lynna	1386
Purbach	1150–1461
After the invention of printing	
Gutenberg (at Mainz)	1457
Regiomontanus (at Nuremberg)	1474
Zainer (at Ulm)	1478
Richard Pynson	1497
Stoffler (in Venice)	1499
Poor Robin's Almanack	1652
Francis Moore's Almanack	1698–1713
Almanach de Gotha	1764
Whitaker's Almanack	1868

ALMANAC vs ALMANACK

The spelling and etymology of 'almanac' are the subject of some dispute. The *Oxford English Dictionary* notes the very early use of 'almanac' by Roger Bacon in 1267, though Chaucer used 'almenak' in *c.*1391; and Shakespeare, 'almanack' in 1590. Variations include almanach(e), amminick, almanacke, &c. A number of etymologies for *almanac* have been suggested: that it comes from the Arabic *al* [the] *mana(h)* [reckoning or diary]; that it comes from the Anglo-Saxon *al-moan-heed*, 'to wit, the regard or observations of all the moons', or from the Anglo-Saxon *al-monath* [all the months]; or that it is linked to the Latin for sundial, *manachus*. In 1838, *Murphy's Almanac* made the bold prediction that 20 January that year would be 'Fair, prob. lowest deg. of winter temp'. When, on the day, this actually turned out to be true, *Murphy's Almanac* became a best seller.

SYMBOLS & ABBREVIATIONS

>	greater than
≥	greater than or equal to
<	less than
≤	less than or equal to
♂	male/men
♀	female/women
c.	*circa*, meaning around or roughly
km	kilometre
m	metre
mi	mile
'/"	feet/inches
C	Century (e.g. C20th)
ONS	Office of National Statistics
Crown ©	Crown Copyright

Throughout the *Almanac*, some figures may not add to totals because of rounding.

'AVERAGES'

With the following list of values: 10, 10, 20, 30, 30, 30, 40, 50, 70, 100 = 390

MEAN or AVERAGE	the sum divided by the number of values	39
MODE	the most popular value	30
MEDIAN	the 'middle' value of a range, here: (30+30)/2	30
RANGE	the difference between the highest & lowest values	90

Chronicle

Days and months are itinerants on an eternal journey;
the years that pass by are also travellers. — MATUSO BASHÓ (1644–94)

SOME AWARDS OF NOTE

TIME Magazine Person of the Year [2006]
'YOU'
'for seizing the reins of the global media, for founding and framing the new digital democracy, for working for nothing and beating the pros at their own game'

Tipperary International Peace Prize .... Most Rev. Dr the Lord Robin Eames
Woodrow Wilson Award for Public Service .. Dr Kenneth Cooper [CEO Cooper Inst.]
Robert Burns Humanitarian Award .... Adi Roche
Australian of the Year .... Professor Tim Flannery [scientist & writer]
BP Portrait Award .... Paul Emsley, for *Michael Simpson*
Car of the Year [*What Car?*] .... Vauxhall Corsa
Prison Officer of the Year [HM Prison Service] .... Pam Chalk [HMP Wealstun]
International Engine of the Year .... BMW 3-litre Twin Turbo (335i)
International Wine Challenge · champion red .... Bald Hills Pinot Noir 2005
– champion white .... Beaune Clos des Mouches Premier Cru 2005
Charity of the Year [Charity Awards] .... Storybook Dads
GQ Woman of the Year .... Tracey Emin
Barrister of the Year [*The Lawyer*] .... Laurence Rabinowitz QC, One Essex Court
Day Nursery of the Year .... Rossett House, Wrexham
Annual Ernest Hemingway Look-Alike Award .... Larry Austin, USA
Slimmer of the Year .... Sarah Chivers [lost 76kg · 12st]
Pet Slimmer of the Year .... Willie the cat [lost 2kg · 4·4lb]
Chess Club of the Year .... West Nottingham Chess Club
Rears of the Year .... ♂ Lee Mead · ♀ Siân Lloyd
Pier of the Year .... Southend
Sexiest Hollywood Pensioner [LOVEFiLM] .... ♂ Jack Nicholson · ♀ Helen Mirren
Gay of the Year [2006, *Boyz Magazine*] .... George Michael
Celebrity Mum of the Year .... Katie Price (aka Jordan)
Best British Cuppa [UK Tea Council] .... Peacocks Tearoom, Ely, Cambridgeshire

PLAIN ENGLISH CAMPAIGN · 2006

Supermodel Naomi Campbell won the PEC's 'Foot in Mouth Award' for this gem:

'I love England, especially the food.
There's nothing I like more than a lovely bowl of pasta.'

MISC. LISTS OF 2007

POLITEST CITIES
according to Somerfield
Glasgow · Sheffield
Cardiff · Aberdeen
Leeds · London
Bristol · Newcastle
Birmingham · Liverpool

TOP ART HEROES
Among 18–25s, according to Arts Award
Walt Disney
Peter Kay
Banksy
Leonardo da Vinci
Bob Marley

BRAND AFFINITY
According to Marketing

Loved	*Loathed*
Google	Pot Noodle
Tesco	QVC
Nokia	Novon
eBay	McDonald's
Persil	Tiny
Dell	Fiat

THE UK'S FAVOURITE WORDS
According to BT
Love · Serendipity
Family · Sunshine
Chocolate · Smile
Antidisestablishmentarian
Holiday · Hope · Happy

MADAME TUSSAUDS
New waxworks for 2007 in the London Museum
Kylie Minogue
(Kylie's fourth incarnation, and Madame Tussauds' first ever 'scented' figure)
Kate Moss
Shah Rukh Khan
Justin Timberlake

THINGS TO BAN FROM SHOPPING CENTRES
According to G4S

Skateboards &c.	46%
Veils &c. [p.290]	41%
Ball games	37%
Hooded tops	31%
Heelys [see p.203]	30%
Religious icons	19%
Groups of youths	16%
Offensive T-shirts	13%

MOST POWERFUL CELEBRITIES
As ranked by Forbes
Oprah Winfrey
Tiger Woods · Madonna
Rolling Stones
Brad Pitt · Johnny Depp
Elton John · Tom Cruise
Jay-Z · Steven Spielberg

BRITAIN'S MOST POPULAR SHOPS
According to Which?

1	John Lewis
2	Waitrose
3	Marks & Spencer
4	Local electricals
=	Waterstone's
=	Body Shop
7	Aldi
8	Lidl
=	Jessops
10	Ikea

MOST ADMIRED MEN
According to Esquire
Gordon Ramsay
Stephen Hawking
Ray Mears
Daniel Craig
Ricky Gervais
Pete Doherty was the least admired – followed by Russell Brand and David Beckham.

2008 WORDS

The following words celebrate anniversaries in 2008, based upon the earliest cited use traced by the venerable *Oxford English Dictionary*:

{1508} *voluptuousness* (being voluptuous) {1608} *monarchizer* (one who advocates monarchy) · *sugar-plum* (something given as a sop) · *wenchless* (without wenches) {1708} *auctioneer* (one who conducts auctions) · *dendrology* (the study of trees) · *stakeholder* (one who keeps stake money secure) {1808} *barium* (the element) · *Falstaffian* (resembling Shakespeare's Falstaff) · *gas-light* (the light of a gas lamp) · *hoax* (a naughty deception) · *koala* (the marsupial) · *piano-player* (a pianist) · {1908} *bejesus* (an Anglo-Irish oath) · *dead man's handle* (the control of an electric train) · *strap-hang* (to hold on to train or bus straps) {1958} *Afro-Caribbean* · *bootstrap* (computer initiation) · *doner kebab* (the Turkish dish) · *Gedankenexperiment* (a thought experiment) · *nanosecond* (one thousand-millionth of a second) · *sheepshagger* (one who…) {1998} *Bluetooth* (radio technology) · *chav* (member of the urban underclass)

SOME SURVEY RESULTS OF 2006–07

%	*result (of British adults, unless stated)*	*source & month*
99	of Glaswegians claimed always to offer a seat to pregnant women	[Somerfield; Feb]
91	claim to recycle newspapers and cardboard	[*Sunday Mirror*/ICM; Mar]
82	claim to recycle glass and plastic	[*Sunday Mirror*/ICM; Mar]
76	claim to recycle cans and tins	[*Sunday Mirror*/ICM; Mar]
76	of consumers had moved their business because of poor service	[BSI; May]
74	reported paying more in tax than 10 years ago	[*The Daily Politics*/Populus; Feb]
69	keep in touch with at least one childhood friend	[Children's Society; Jun]
64	of working families rely on grandparents for free childminding	[Skipton/YouGov; Jul]
56	admitted to pretending they had prepared ready-meals or takeaways	[IGD; May]
55	do not have a will	[AXA/ICM; Jan]
54	of doctors said morale in the NHS was 'poor' or 'terrible'	[*Hospital Doctor*; Apr]
51	of Scots approve of Scotland becoming independent	[*Daily Mail*/ICM; Jan]
51	of CEOs have made a conference call wearing a bathrobe, or less	[Avaya; Jul]
48	of English approve of Scotland becoming independent	[*Daily Mail*/ICM; Jan]
48	do not trust television very much at all	[Edinburgh TV Festival/YouGov; Aug]
47	think [news] broadcasts often fail to reflect their views	[BBC/Ipsos; Oct 06]
47	of workers spend some time working not in their office	[Microsoft/The Future Lab; Jan]
46	think their vote has virtually no impact on decisions in Westminster	[ICM; Jan]
43	would do more to halt climate change if other people did more, too	[Ip. MORI; Jul]
41	of women said email was vital to their lives	[ICM; June]
40	of St Patrick's Day revellers knew who the saint was	[Manchester Irish Festival; Mar]
38	of men said email was vital to their lives	[ICM; June]
36	are regularly saving for their retirement	[Aviva; Apr]
36	of Londoners have never set foot on a farm	[Linking Environment & Farming; Jun]
30	keep an object at home to use against intruders	[Cornhill Direct; Jul]
30	of Scots would share a toothbrush with their partner	[British Dental Health Fdtn; May]
29	would take a loved one's 'penalty points' to save their driving licence	[Churchill; Jun]
29	think Britain does not and never did need nuclear weapons [see p.264]	[Populus; Feb]
29	of women have been physically hurt by a partner	[*This Morning*/YouGov; Jan]
25	of domestic wireless networks are unsecured	[moneysupermarket.com; Apr]
25	of all dogs in Northern Ireland are obese	[PDSA; Jul]
18	think human activity does not have significant effect on the climate	[Ip. MORI; Jul]
18	said they had no sex education while at school	[Family Planning Assoc./NOP; Feb]
18	of consumers have avoided a company because of its ethical behaviour	[Populus; Mar]
17	do not feel safe in their homes at night	[Cornhill Direct; Jul]
14	were under the influence of drugs or alcohol when they first had sex	[Durex; Jul]
14	would be uncomfortable seeing a gay GP	[Stonewall/YouGov; Jun]
13	of pensioners said they were lonely and rarely left the house	[Help the Aged; Mar]
12	brushed their teeth only a few times a week, or never	[Dental Health Fdtn; May]
11	think Jews have too much influence in UK politics	[*Jewish Chronicle*/YouGov; Jan]
6	of car drivers are completely uninsured	[uSwitch; Jul]
5	would emigrate to escape the British taxman	[MRI Overseas Property; Mar]
5	are living in their 'dream home'	[Alliance & Leicester; Jul]
3	never purchase supermarket 'own brand' products	[*Retail Week*/ICM; Jan]
2	had a better opinion of Jade Goody after *Celebrity Big Bro.*	[*News of the World*/ICM; Jan]

WORDS OF THE YEAR

SMEATONATOR · John Smeaton – hero baggage handler who 'assisted' police in the Glasgow airport attack [see p.29].

SURGE · description of Bush's deployment of an extra 21,500 troops to Iraq – part of his NEW WAY FORWARD.

PANSURGENCY · global terror threat, defined by the US National War College as a strategy to 'incite worldwide insurgencies to overthrow Western ideals and replace them with a new world order under radical views of Islam'.

PUMPING PARTY · (illegal) gatherings where plastic surgeons give 'back street' injections of silicone, botox, &c.

CHATTY PACKAGING · faux-friendly marketing blurb that aspires to a casual, cheeky, and personal tone.

SUBSIDARIAT · *Daily Mail* editor Paul Dacre's term for loss-making media organisations subsidised by profitable parent companies (*Times*, *Guardian*), or by the tax payer (BBC).

HABs · Husbands And Boyfriends: male equivalent of Wives And Girlfriends. *Also* SCRUMMIES – rugby WAGs.

MIS-LIT · Misery Literature, recounting abuse, degradation, or harm.

WE'RE IN JAIL, DUDE · exclamation by one of the US pilots involved in the 'friendly fire' death of Matty Hull.

BLARNEY ARMY · Irish cricket fans.

URBAN CHILD SOLDIERS · inner-city children involved with guns and gangs. *Also* GUN-MINDING · asking someone (often one under-age) to hold a weapon.

NO KNICKER GIRLS · *Heat*'s term for girls (Paris, Britney, Lindsay, &c.) photographed 'going commando'.

GERIATRIC LIFERS · prisoners who will remain in jail well into old age, as a result of mandatory minimum terms.

RETAIL JAILS *or* TESCO JAILS · 'short-term holding facilities' in malls or other areas of 'high-volume' offending.

NEET · those (especially the young) Not in Education, Employment, or Training.

ONESICKMANSHIP · game played by hypochondriacal men during a woman's menstrual cycle. *Also* BEERIODS · male periods (caused by alcoholic excess). *Also* MOOBS · man boobs. *Also* MITS · man tits. *Also* THE MALE MENOPAUNCH · the dreaded beer-gut of middle age. *Also* MANCATION · an all-male holiday. *Also* BROMANCE · platonic male-only relationships. *Also* MANBAND · an older, more mature, or reformed, boyband.

TOMBSTONING · the reckless pastime of jumping off high rocks into water.

CHOKING GAME · sometimes fatal playground auto-asphyxiation 'game'.

WOM · Word Of Mouth marketing.

RUPPIES · Retired Urban People.

KEYSTONE SPOOKS · pejorative term for the security services.

PHILANTHROPRENEURS · sponsors of non-profit ventures; often young tech billionaires. *Also* FILMANTHROPISTS · philanthropists who finance socially aware films. *Also* MINIGARCH · not quite an oligarch (annual income ≤$50m).

WORDS OF THE YEAR cont.

GROUP-RELATED · a supposedly less glamorous alternative to 'gang-related'.

PAY-AS-YOU-THROW · charging for rubbish disposal by quantity [see p.13].

SHEDQUARTERS · the 'home office'.

SWISHING · swapping, not shopping.

MABAs · Middle-Aged British Artists; Tracey Emin's description of what were once the Young British Artists (YBAs).

FERAL BEAST · the modern media which 'just tears people and reputations to bits', as defined by Tony Blair during a speech in which he also called the *Independent* a VIEWSPAPER.

COUGARS · women of a certain age who prey on younger men.

SCREWFACE · a scowl of disrespect.

SHAMBO · a 'sacred' bull that was put down after testing positive for bovine TB – causing controversy between Hindus and health officials in Wales.

MASSTIGE · retail marriage of mass and prestige (e.g. *Viktor & Rolf* for H&M).

TORTURE PORN · misogynist (horror) films that frequently depict sexualised violence against women. *Also* GORNO · excessively violent films (e.g. *Hostel*).

VULTURE FUNDS · companies that buy cheap the debt of poor countries, and then sue for the full sum, plus interest.

SARKONAUTES · supporters of French President Nicolas Sarkozy.

CHRISTIANISM · analogue of Islamism.

PITCH BEAST · animals used in advertising: usually cute, like penguins.

9818783 · Paris Hilton's inmate number during her brief incarceration [see p.119].

FREDALO · see p.296.

FED-EX · nickname for Kevin Federline after his divorce from Britney Spears.

PEERENTS · parents who aspire to be like their children's peers.

5 S's · graduated escalation of force, said to be part of the US military's Iraq rules of engagement: *Shout; Show weapon; Shove; Shoot to warn; Shoot to kill.*

NASHI ['*Ours*' in Russian] · a jingoistic, pro-Putin Russian youth movement. Nashi claims to be anti-Fascist, though its thuggish record has led some to warn of the threat from NASHISM [see p.32].

BURQINI · full-length swimsuit for Muslim women [see p.290]. MANKINI · louche male swimsuit, à la Borat.

HEDGE HOGS · wealthy (greedy) hedge fund managers.

CHILD DECOYS · children (and sometimes women) used by insurgents in Iraq to deflect the attention of the security forces away from car bombs.

MOREGEOISIE · consumers who strive to acquire more than others.

STUNT EATING · eating for media attention: [1] by celebrities, to disprove allegations of anorexia; [2] by officials, to reassure consumers about the safety of a food (e.g. poultry, post-avian flu); [3] by authors, to promote special diets.

WORDS OF THE YEAR cont.

BECLOWN · to embarrass oneself by pontificating out of ignorance.

BULLY TV · shows that glorify bullies: *The Apprentice*, *The Weakest Link*, &c.

GLAMPING · glamorous camping.

GHOST FLIGHTS · empty aircraft flown only to keep key airport 'runway slots'.

NEWPEAT · a TV episode edited to include previously unseen material.

WATER NEUTRAL · ensuring water use is sustainable and recyclable.

SLURB · suburban area with poor housing (a mixture of SLum and subURB).

GLOCAL *and* GLOCALIZATION · when global companies aspire to respect local customs and sensitivities.

RED CELL TEAMS · security analysts who imagine novel forms of terrorism.

GORACLE · fan nickname for Al Gore. *Conversely* AL BORE · derisive reference to Gore's ECO-VANGELISM.

THE MOTHER OF ALL TARGETS · Prince Harry, who was said to have been targeted by insurgents as he planned to join his regiment in Iraq.

POVERTARIAN · one who works in the 'poverty industry'.

BULLYCIDE · the suicide of a child who has been bullied or harassed to death. *Also* E-THUGS · cyber-bullies.

DARK TOURISM · travel to places associated with death, destruction, poverty, or tragedy. *Also* SLUM TOURISM.

REXY · neologism for 'sexy anorexia' – supposedly coined by supermodel Kate Moss. *Also* MANOREXIA · anorexia in men. *Also* AGEOREXIA · ageorexia is to age, as anorexia is to weight.

GREY FEVER · urban hay fever.

PROSTITOTS · children who are dressed in sexually inappropriate clothing.

SUPERFOODS · foods with a 'health halo' [see p.221].

LOCAVORES · those who eat only locally grown food.

SECURITY THEATRE · the pretence of (airport) security.

72ed · Jihadi slang for death; a reference to the number of virgins that martyrs believe will greet them in Paradise.

AGFLATION · inflation in agriculture prices and, therefore, food.

RICHISTAN · the bubble of wealth the über-rich inhabit. *Also* BIZARRISTAN · Turkmenistan under (now dead) President Niyazov. *Also* OUTSOURCISTAN · areas dependent on outsourced contracts.

SANDWICH GENERATION · those caring for young children and elderly parents at the same time.

PROSUMERS · professional consumers who contribute to the design or manufacture of the products they buy.

SAGA LOUTS · binge-drinking OAPs.

CLIMATE CANARIES · those people and environments likely to be the first affected by global warming.

OBJECT OF THE YEAR: THE LIGHT BULB

After 127 years in the spotlight, incandescent light bulbs may soon fade into history, as a host of initiatives seek to turn lighting eco-friendly. In February 2007, Australia announced that stricter energy standards would ban incandescent bulbs by 2010, forcing consumers to buy alternatives, like compact fluorescent light bulbs (CFLs). Australia's Environment Minister said, 'if the whole world switched to these bulbs today, we would reduce our consumption of electricity by an amount equal to five times Australia's annual consumption of electricity'. For a country that refused to sign the Kyoto Protocol, Australia's nationwide ban was dramatic and bold, but it was not made in isolation. In November 2006, Wal-Mart announced a campaign to sell 100m CFLs by 2008. In January 2007, a Bill was proposed to ban the sale of incandescents in California by 2012. In February 2007, similar legislation was proposed in a number of other US states. In March 2007, Philips announced it would phase out incandescents by 2016. In the same month, the EU discussed a ban on such bulbs by 2010. In April 2007, Canada imposed a federal ban on incandescents from 2012. ❦ Although dozens of people played a part in the invention of the light bulb (including Joseph Swan and Humphrey Davy), history's laurels rest on the head of Thomas Edison, not least because of his US Patent #223898, filed 27/1/1880. In fundamental design, the modern incandescent – with its finely coiled filament set within an inert-gas-filled glass bulb – differs little from those pioneered in the C19th. And, despite a range of modifications, incandescents still emit only 5% of the energy they consume as light; the rest is wasted as heat. CFLs are filled with a gas that emits UV light when excited by electricity. In turn, this UV light causes the bulb's interior coating to emit light visible to the human eye. Compared to incandescents, CFLs are 4× more efficient, last up to 10× longer, consume 50–80% less energy, and produce 75% less heat. And, although CFLs are currently more expensive to buy, the US Dept of Energy claims that >$30 in electricity can be saved over the lifetime of *each* bulb. ❦ While the cost and energy-saving arguments for CFLs are powerful, public acceptance has been hindered by a sense that the quality of light CFLs emit is insufficiently 'soothing' or 'natural' – the so-called 'wife test'. Furthermore, because CFLs contain mercury, the safe disposal of spent or broken bulbs can be more complex and expensive. As the obligation to use CFLs becomes more widespread, it is clear that their price, quality, and ease of safe disposal will all have to improve. Indeed, they are likely to face competition from other forms of eco-lighting, such as light emitting diodes (LEDs). ❦ The demise of incandescents is part of a series of low-level 'eco-hardships' which are (more or less) consumer-approved or even consumer-driven. Other eco-hardships include removing 'standby' modes from appliances; charging for plastic bags (or banning them altogether, as in San Francisco); charging for the collection of (unrecyclable) waste; pricing drivers off congested roads; encouraging people to turn down domestic thermostats; &c. It remains to be seen, however, whether these individual acts can have an aggregate effect sufficient to counter environmental damage at an industrial and governmental level.

SIGNIFICA · 2007

Some (in)significa(nt) footnotes to the year. ❦ The Human Genome Organisation announced that genes given unusual names, such as 'lunatic fringe', 'faint sausage', and 'mothers against decapentaplegia (MAD)', would be renamed in order to avoid awkward doctor–patient conversations, should the genes be linked to defects. ❦ A Tennessee man running for Senate legally changed his middle name to 'None of the Above', in a bid to appeal to disenchanted voters. ❦ According to *New Scientist*, all of the gold mined in history (193,000 tonnes) would fit inside a cube with sides 22 metres long. ❦ A *60 Minutes* investigation discovered that Saddam Hussein, Zacarias Moussaoui, and 14 of the (dead) 9/11 hijackers were still barred from travel by the federal 'No Fly' list. ❦ Mitch Daniels, George W. Bush's first budget director, tried (and failed) to get the Office of Management and Budget to use *You Can't Always Get What You Want* by the Rolling Stones as its hold music. ❦ Barbie's full name is Barbara Millicent Roberts, and she apparently owns 38 pets, including cats, dogs, horses, a panda, a lion cub, and a zebra. ❦ A pearl earring lost by Marlene Dietrich 73 years ago was found by workmen when they drained a lake under the Big Dipper ride at Blackpool Pleasure Beach. The workmen also recovered three sets of false teeth, a glass eye, a toupée, a bra, and *c*.£350 in (very) loose change. ❦ According to the US Census Bureau, more people are injured each year by wheelchairs than lawn mowers. ❦ A Portuguese aristocrat bequeathed his entire fortune to 70 strangers picked at random from a telephone directory. A close friend suggested he wanted to 'create confusion'. ❦ A couple from Michigan received packages in the post containing a liver and a human ear, instead of the table legs they had bid for on eBay. ❦ Research by Bosch indicated that the average British woman will vacuum a distance of 7,300 miles over the course of her lifetime; men will vacuum only 850 miles. ❦ Marvel Comics killed off Captain America in the last instalment of the comic; the 'pinnacle of human perfection' was shot three times by a sniper. ❦ The equivalent of 3,000 swimming pools of water are pumped out of London Underground tunnels each day. ❦ Three schoolgirls were suspended from John Jay High School, New York, for saying the word 'vagina' during a reading of Eve Ensler's *The Vagina Monologues*. ❦ Beijing announced plans to replace poorly translated English road signs in advance of the 2008 Summer Olympics, depriving the city of such classics as: '*To take notice of safe: the slippery are very crafty*', and '*Show mercy to the slender grass*'. ❦ The US Postal Service removed clocks in 37,000 post offices nationwide, in an effort to persuade 'people to focus on the postal service and not the clock'. ❦ 171 Swiss soldiers accidentally invaded Liechtenstein during a night-training exercise; the government of Liechtenstein admitted they had not noticed. ❦ To introduce 'highly charged storylines' in a 'dynamic new environment', Postman Pat left the village of Greendale after he was promoted to run the Special Delivery service. ❦ Colonel Muammar Gaddafi called for every Italian (all 59m of them) to undergo DNA testing, to ascertain if any were descendants of the 3,500 Libyans deported to Italy in 1911. Gaddafi promised full Libyan citizenship to all descendants. ❦ James Doohan (Scotty from *Star Trek*) had his last wish fulfilled, when his cremated remains were blasted into orbit in a capsule with the ashes of 200 other Earthlings.

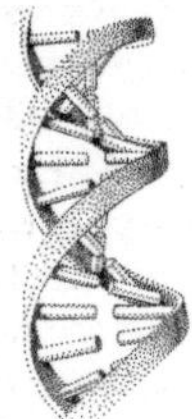

SIGNIFICA · 2007 cont.

The capsule eventually fell to Earth, and was found three weeks later in New Mexico. ❦ The cocktail of choice for Princes William and Harry was reported to be the 'Treasure Chest' – half a litre of vodka and a bottle of champagne poured into a wooden box filled with juice, ice cubes, and chopped fruit. ❦ Hyperinflation in Zimbabwe became so rampant [see p.28] that golfers habitually paid for their drinks before they set off on a round because, by the time they reached the 19th hole, the prices had gone up. ❦ The Japanese island of Iwo Jima reverted to its original name, Iwo To. Both names are written using the same two Japanese characters – and both mean Sulphur Island – but they are pronounced differently. ❦ According to Halifax Home Insurance, the number of windows broken in the UK rises by 20% during the Wimbledon fortnight, as youngsters around the country attempt to emulate their tennis heroes. ❦ Mika Brzezinski, a news anchor on MSNBC's *Morning Joe*, repeatedly refused to read a story about Paris Hilton's release from jail. Ms Brzezinski crumpled her script into a ball, tried to burn it, and eventually put it through a paper shredder. ❦ A German performance-art student dressed as one of China's 2,000-year-old terracotta warriors, and posed among the statues for several minutes before being discovered by police. ❦ In an effort to improve civic order, Beijing began celebrating 'Queuing Day' on the 11th of each month. Those who waited patiently in line were rewarded with long-stemmed roses. ❦ According to police forensic scientists, the shoe print most frequently found at British crime scenes is the Nike Air Max 95; the criminals' second choice of footwear is the Reebok Classic. ❦ Former Roswell Airbase press officer Lieutenant Walter Haut, who spent much of his career denying conspiracy theories, left a sworn affidavit to be opened after his death. In the statement, Haut asserted that the 'weather balloon claim' was a cover story for a crashed UFO and 'small humanoid extraterrestrials'. ❦ Belgian TV channel RTBF hoaxed people into believing that, following a unilateral declaration of independence by Flanders, Belgium had split. The station interrupted its programming with the spoof newsflash at 8·21pm, but was forced to broadcast the message '*This is fiction*' at 8·50pm, following widespread viewer panic. ❦ A Moscow exhibition of gifts presented to Russian leaders 1921–90 featured a 1930s portrait of Lenin made entirely from human hair. ❦ Waltzing was added to the national curriculum in China, in an effort to combat child obesity. ❦ In an attempt to break the world record, Brazilian Claudio Paulo Pinto stretched his eyeballs 0·3" out of their sockets (sadly, he failed; the world record is 0·43"). ❦ According to the charity Campaign Against Living Miserably, 100,000 years of human life are lost each year in Britain due to male suicide. ❦ On his retirement, Tony Blair was presented with a steel-string acoustic guitar by Labour MPs and peers. ❦ The Ministry of Defence revealed that convoys of nuclear material in Britain had encountered 67 safety incidents 2000–07; luckily, none were 'serious security failures'. ❦ President Bush invited incoming House Speaker Nancy Pelosi for lunch at the White House. They dined on pasta salad as a tribute to Pelosi's Italian heritage, and ate a dessert ominously called 'chocolate freedom'. ❦ The widening of the M6 will cost £1,000 an inch: the 51-mile stretch of road will total £2·9bn, twice Britain's yearly aid budget to Africa. ❦

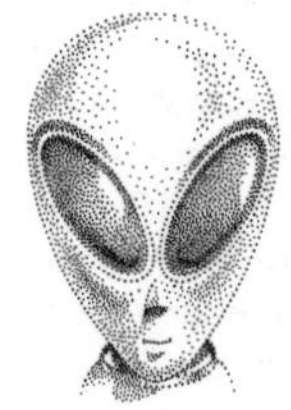

BLAIR TO BROWN

Tony Blair announced his retirement as leader of the Labour party on Thursday 10 May 2007: a week after Labour's poor election results [see p.21], and a day after the start of power sharing in Northern Ireland [see p.30]. Having informed his Cabinet earlier in the day, Blair told a meeting of party activists in Sedgefield that he would tender his resignation as PM to the Queen on 27 June. In a speech that vacillated between confident and defensive, Blair attempted to define his decade in power:

I have been Prime Minister of this country for just over 10 years. In this job, in the world today, that is long enough, for me but more especially for the country. Sometimes the only way you conquer the pull of power is to set it down. ... So 1997 was a moment for a new beginning ... Expectations were so high. Too high. Too high in a way for either of us. ... But go back to 1997. Think back. No, really, think back. ... There is only one Government since 1945 that can say all of the following: more jobs, fewer unemployed, better health and education results, lower crime; and economic growth in every quarter – this one. ... Think about the culture of Britain in 2007. I don't just mean our arts that are thriving. I mean our values. The minimum wage. Paid holidays as a right. ... Equality for gay people. Or look at the debates that reverberate round the world today. ... Britain is not a follower. It is a leader. ... I don't think Northern Ireland would have been changed unless Britain had changed. ... What I had to learn, however, as PM was what putting the country first really meant. ... It means doing what you genuinely believe to be right. ... Then came the utterly unanticipated and dramatic. September 11th 2001 and the death of 3,000 or more on the streets of New York. I decided we should stand shoulder to shoulder with our oldest ally. I did so out of belief. So Afghanistan and then Iraq. The latter, bitterly controversial. Removing Saddam and his sons from power, as with removing the Taleban, was over with relative ease. But the blowback since, from global terrorism and those elements that support it, has been fierce and unrelenting and costly. ... For me, I think we must see it through. ... But I ask you to accept one thing. Hand on heart, I did what I thought was right. I may have been wrong. That's your call. But believe one thing if nothing else. I did what I thought was right for our country. ... This country is a blessed nation. The British are special. The world knows it. In our innermost thoughts, we know it. This is the greatest nation on Earth. It has been an honour to serve it. I give my thanks to you, the British people, for the times I have succeeded, and my apologies to you for the times I have fallen short. Good luck.

The following day, Friday 11 May, Gordon Brown launched his bid to succeed as Labour leader and PM. While heaping praise on Tony Blair ('[he] led our country for ten years with distinction, with courage, passion, and insight') he signalled a substantial shift in substance and style ('I have never believed presentation should be a substitute for policy. I do not believe politics is about celebrity'). Responding to fears that a 'coronation' would be damaging, Brown said he welcomed a contest for the leadership. This challenge was answered by the left-wing MP John McDonnell who pledged to 'rescue this Labour government from itself'. However, on 18 May, Labour announced that Brown had received 313 nominations, making it 'mathematically impossible' for another candidate to get the 45 nominations required to stand. Brown said he was 'truly humbled' by the support of so many MPs. Yet, the absence of any vote for the leadership drew some criticism, as did the unprecedented six-week interregnum before prime ministerial power was transferred.

BLAIR TO BROWN cont.

Criss-crossing the globe (in what John Major called 'the longest farewell tour since Dame Nellie Melba') Blair visited a host of countries (including America, Iraq, and Africa), concluding with a meeting with the Pope (fuelling speculation that Blair might convert to Catholicism after resignation). Meanwhile, the curious limbo between Blair and Brown saw the government face a range of problems, including the collapse of a new system for junior doctor training; the postponement of controversial Home Information Packs [HIPs]; the absconding of several men under anti-terror control orders; the controversial BAE decision; and tough negotiations over the EU's constitution-replacing treaty. ❦ Brown's accession to party leader was rubber-stamped at a conference in Manchester on 24 June [at which his party deputy was elected, see below]. After a warm, if brief, introduction by Blair ('he has all the qualities to mark him out as a great Prime Minister'), Brown took to the stage and said, 'I will endeavour to justify every day and in every act the trust you have placed in me ... Leadership is an awesome responsibility'. ❦ Prime Ministerial power was transferred on 27 June. After his final PMQs (which ended with a [stage-managed?] standing ovation), Blair was driven to the Palace to resign. Ten minutes later, the Queen invited Brown to form a government. At just before 3pm, Brown arrived at No. 10 and declared 'this will be a new government with new priorities'. Quoting his school motto, he said 'I will try my utmost. This is my promise to all of the people of Britain. And now let the work of change begin'. ❦ As Blair resigned as an MP to become a Middle East envoy [see p.29], Brown set about appointing his first Cabinet [see p.251].

Deputy Leadership Election · 24·6·2007

After Brown succeeded Blair without a single vote cast, the election of Labour's deputy leader was seen as a proxy vote for the direction of the party. Six candidates (ranging from Blairite to 'old Labour') faced a series of hustings to convince the electorate of MPs & MEPs, Labour members, and levy-paying members of affiliated unions.

Candidate	*1st round %*	*2nd round*	*3rd round*	*4th round*	*5th round*
Hazel Blears	11·77				
Peter Hain	15·32	16·42			
Hilary Benn	16·40	18·22	22·33		
Jon Cruddas	19·39	20·39	23·89	30·06	
Alan Johnson	18·16	23·74	27·90	36·35	49·56
HARRIET HARMAN	18·93	21·23	25·88	33·58	50·43

Harman's 0·87% victory over bookies' favourite Johnson was widely attributed to her left-leaning position – notably, she expressed regret at voting for the Iraq invasion, and appeared to say that Labour should apologise for the war. Despite her mandate, Brown swiftly ended the tradition of party deputy becoming deputy PM; indeed his first Cabinet was notable for having no deputy PM at all. Harman was made Party Chairman and given a Cabinet seat as Leader of the Commons [see p.251].

BAROMETER OF IRAQI OPINION 2004–07

Below is a picture of the decline of Iraq – from three polls of >2,000 Iraqis across all 18 provinces, by D3 Systems for the BBC, ABC News, ARD TV, and *USA Today*:

Overall, how would you say things in your life are going these days?

(%)	'07	'05	'04
Very good	8	22	13
Quite good	31	49	57
Quite bad	32	18	14
Very bad	28	11	15
Refused/DK	–	1	1

Compared to the time before the war, how are things overall in your life?

(%)	'07	'05	'04
Much better	14	21	22
Somewhat better	29	31	35
About the same	22	19	23
Somewhat worse	28	19	13
Much worse	8	10	6
Refused/DK	–	1	2

What is the single biggest problematic issue you face these days?

(%)	'07	'05	'04
Security	48	18	25
Political/military	13	–	2
Economic	17	15	21
Social	22	16	18
Personal issues	1	7	4
Other	–	4	2
No problems	–	31	18
No opinion	–	9	8

From today's perspective, and all things considered, what do you think about the US-led coalition forces invasion of Iraq in spring 2003?

(%)	'07	'05	'04
Absolutely right	22	19	20
Somewhat right	25	28	29
Somewhat wrong	19	17	13
Absolutely wrong	34	33	26
Refused/DK	–	4	13

Do you support the presence of coalition forces in Iraq?

(%)	'07	'05	'04
Strongly support	6	13	13
Somewhat support	16	19	26
Somewhat oppose	32	21	20
Strongly oppose	46	44	31
Refused/DK	–	3	10

The % of those who in the last year (March '06–March '07) have ...

Avoided leaving their home	78
Not sent their children to school	68
Avoided police stations, &c.	80
Avoided crowded areas, markets	83
Avoided coalition forces	91
Avoided travel	83
Avoided going to/seeking work	72
Watched what they told others	85

Conditions where you live (%2004→%2007)	*very good*	*quite good*	*quite bad*	*very bad*	*net decline 2004–07*
Electricity supply	8→2	27→11	28→37	37→51	45% *worse*
Clean water	20→9	31→22	22→35	26→34	41% *worse*
Medical care	17→8	34→23	24→35	22→34	43% *worse*
Availability of jobs	7→3	19→17	23→44	46→35	16% *worse*
Security situation	20→17	29→30	21→21	29→32	5% *worse*
Local schools	37→12	35→31	15→35	11→21	59% *worse*

IRAQ CONFLICT · FATALITIES TO DATE

MONTH	US TROOP FATALITIES BY CAUSE OF DEATH								COALITION FATALITIES		IRAQI CIVILIAN FATALITIES	
	IEDs	*Car bombs*	*Mortars*	*RPGs*	*Helicopter*	*Hostile fire*	*Non-hostile*	*All*	*UK*	*Other*	*Min*	*Max*
MAR '03	0	0	0	0	8	50	7	65	27	0	2,077	3,972
APR	0	0	3	4	8	41	18	74	6	0	2,647	3,433
MAY	0	0	0	0	7	6	24	37	4	1	499	540
JUN	0	0	0	4	0	14	12	30	6	0	541	572
JUL	4	0	0	9	0	15	20	48	1	0	593	632
AUG	7	0	0	2	0	7	19	35	6	2	735	780
SEP	5	0	2	2	1	9	12	31	1	1	525	542
OCT	13	0	4	2	0	14	11	44	1	2	461	484
NOV	20	0	1	1	39	8	13	82	1	27	433	459
DEC	18	1	2	0	0	4	15	40	0	8	504	523
JAN '04	20	3	4	1	14	4	1	47	5	0	541	561
FEB	9	0	2	0	2	3	4	20	1	2	560	578
MAR	19	0	4	0	0	12	17	52	0	0	917	951
APR	16	10	7	13	2	78	9	135	0	5	1,166	1,225
MAY	21	2	12	2	0	25	18	80	0	4	541	610
JUN	12	2	7	1	0	15	5	42	1	7	746	827
JUL	17	2	7	2	0	16	10	54	1	3	682	745
AUG	16	0	2	4	2	33	9	66	4	5	742	810
SEP	15	11	4	2	0	37	11	80	3	4	809	895
OCT	12	19	2	4	2	19	5	63	2	2	830	895
NOV	18	6	4	4	0	93	12	137	4	0	1,353	1,522
DEC	14	2	1	0	2	41	12	72	1	3	806	884
JAN '05	29	3	3	8	33	11	20	107	10	10	949	996
FEB	25	1	1	0	0	15	16	58	0	2	1,116	1,152
MAR	13	7	1	0	0	10	4	35	1	3	646	735
APR	20	7	5	2	0	12	6	52	0	0	852	974
MAY	33	10	6	2	2	14	13	80	2	6	1,030	1,187
JUN	36	8	2	3	2	18	9	78	1	4	1,077	1,203
JUL	36	2	3	0	0	4	9	54	3	1	1,355	1,411
AUG	40	7	1	0	0	27	10	85	0	0	1,982	2,118
SEP	37	0	2	0	0	3	7	49	3	0	1,163	1,264
OCT	57	2	7	0	0	11	19	96	2	1	982	1,115
NOV	40	6	0	0	2	24	12	84	1	1	1,008	1,171
DEC	42	3	2	1	2	9	9	68	0	0	854	942
JAN '06	24	3	0	1	13	10	11	62	2	0	1,320	1,407
FEB	36	2	1	0	0	7	9	55	3	0	1,386	1,442
MAR	12	1	3	1	0	9	5	31	0	2	1,594	1,713
APR	45	1	1	1	2	15	11	76	1	5	1,486	1,590
MAY	36	2	0	0	4	17	10	69	9	1	1,925	2,083
JUN	33	0	1	0	0	23	4	61	0	2	2,280	2,422
JUL	21	3	0	1	0	13	5	43	1	2	2,853	3,061
AUG	29	0	0	0	2	29	5	65	1	0	2,500	2,685
SEP	29	4	1	1	0	26	10	71	3	2	2,121	2,345
OCT	52	0	0	1	0	46	6	105	2	2	2,646	2,887
NOV	38	0	0	0	2	22	8	70	6	2	2,755	2,916
DEC	72	0	1	1	5	26	10	115	1	2	2,549	2,654
JAN '07	34	0	1	0	14	30	5	84	3	0	2,376	2,475
FEB	25	2	0	0	9	33	10	79	3	1	2,235	2,367
MAR	51	0	2	0	0	19	10	82	1	0	2,285	2,415
APR *troop 'surge'*	60	0	1	1	0	34	8	104	12	1	2,480	2,590
MAY	82	0	0	0	2	37	6	127	3	2	2,643	2,770
JUN	57	0	0	4	0	31	8	100	7	0	1,997	2,092
JUL	46	0	2	1	1	19	11	80	8	1	2,500	2,600
AUG	32	0	0	4	19	19	9	84	4	0	1,800	2,011
%	39·5	3·5	3·1	2·4	5·4	31·2	14·9	…	…	…	…	…
TOTAL	1,478	132	115	90	201	1,167	559	3,743	168	129	75,453	83,233

[US troop source: Brookings Institution; at end 8/07. Helicopter losses include hostile and non-hostile deaths. Key: Improvised Explosive Devices; Rocket Propelled Grenades. UK & other coalition deaths source: icasualties.org, at end 8/07. Iraqi civilian deaths source: Iraq Body Count, at 28/8/07: figures for April–August 2007 are provisional.]

VIRGINIA TECH MASSACRE

On 16 April 2007, 23-year-old Seung-Hui Cho went on the deadliest 'shooting spree' in US history. He shot to death 32 and wounded 17 students and staff at the Virginia Polytechnic Institute and State University, where he was a senior, before committing suicide. This massacre, the latest in a long line of campus killings, catalysed international shock and revulsion, and prompted US introspection and debate over campus security, mental health care, the privacy of data, and gun laws.

Born in 1984 in Seoul, South Korea, Cho emigrated to the United States with his family aged 8. According to reports, Cho grew up a frail, shy, uncommunicative 'loner', with emotional and mental health problems. After being bullied at school, Cho enrolled at Virginia Tech in 2003 as a business information technology major, later switching to English. According to a state mental health report, while Cho did nothing to attract disciplinary attention in his first two years, his behaviour from autumn 2005 involved 'a significant number of incidents … in which other students and faculty members perceived or experienced his actions … as extremely odd, frightening and/or threatening'. At the insistence of a teacher, Cho was removed from some classes for one-on-one tuition. And, on a number of occasions, Cho was warned by authorities for harassing and stalking female students. After one such warning, on 13/12/2005, Cho expressed suicidal thoughts to a roommate and was subsequently detained for a night at a psychiatric hospital. The next day, a judge concurred with an independent evaluation that Cho did not pose an imminent danger to himself or others, and ordered follow-up outpatient treatment. From then, apart from some relatively minor infractions, Cho attracted no further official attention until his attack 16 months later. ❦ At *c.*07:15 on 16 April 2007, Cho murdered 2 students in a nearby dorm before returning to his room to change clothes. At 09:01 he mailed a package to *NBC News* containing a 'multimedia manifesto' of text, photos, and video 'explaining' his attack. At 09:26, university officials sent the first in a series of emails warning students of the incident. At 09:40, Cho entered the classroom building Norris Hall and chained shut the doors. In *c.*11 minutes, Cho had fired 174 rounds with two semi-automatic pistols (purchased just months earlier), killing 30 and wounding 17, before shooting himself at 09:51. ❦ Two days later, NBC controversially aired parts of Cho's disturbing and incoherent 'manifesto'. Railing against the 'rich' and 'debauched', Cho compared himself to Christ and said, 'you forced me into a corner and gave me only one option'. ❦ On 23 April, Virginia Tech held a remembrance service for Cho's victims. Federal, state, and school inquiries were launched, and officials vowed to explore the causes of the tragedy. In June, after it was revealed that Cho's mental health treatment should have prevented him buying guns, the House legislated to improve nationwide background checks. ❦ VA Tech's President, Charles W. Steger, vowed, 'to the extent that rational conclusions can be drawn from irrational violence … we will learn and the world will learn from this'.

ELECTIONS 2007

Elections on 3 May for the Scottish Parliament, the Welsh Assembly, and English and Scottish councils were the greatest test of public opinion since the 2005 general election – and the electorate's final chance to comment on the decade of New Labour. Expectations were dampened by a wave of pre-vote spin – not least by Tony Blair who beseeched voters not to give him 'a kicking one last time on my way out of the door'. Overall, the results could be summed thus: *no meltdown* for Labour (even with just 27% of the vote); *no breakthrough* for Cameron's Tories (who, despite a 41% share, failed to make headway in key northern seats); and *no comfort* for the Liberal Democrats (nor for the leadership of Menzies Campbell). The best performances were achieved by the two main nationalist parties who did well enough to upset Labour's control, but failed to secure the breakthroughs for which they were hoping. ❦ In Wales, Plaid Cymru gains ensured that Labour did not control the Senedd, but after weeks of negotiation failed to create a workable coalition, Rhodri Morgan was re-appointed First Minister of a minority Labour government on 25 May. ❦ In Scotland, a tightly fought election was marred by confusion and anger over voting papers and an electronic counting system that saw *c.*140,000 ballots rejected. Ultimately the SNP secured an historic 1-seat victory over Labour to become the largest party in the Parliament. On 16 May, Alex Salmond became the first Nationalist First Minister of Scotland; he was elected 49 to 46 after he received backing from the two Green MSPs, and the Tories and Lib Dems abstained. In forming a minority government, Salmond accepted that he would have to appeal for support 'policy by policy' across the divided chamber.

ENGLISH LOCAL ELECTIONS	COUNCILLORS		COUNCILS	
	net ±	*total*	*net ±*	*total*
Conservative	+911	5,315	+39	165
Labour	–505	1,877	–8	34
Liberal Democrats	–246	2,171	–4	23
Other	–162	1,112	0	5
No Overall Control	NA	NA	–27	85

SCOTTISH PARLIAMENT	*Constituency*	*Region*	*total*	*seats ±*
Scottish Nationalist Party	21	26	47	+20
Labour	37	9	46	–4
Conservative	4	13	17	–1
Liberal Democrat	11	5	16	–1
Green	0	2	2	–5
Others	0	1	1	–2

[In council elections, Labour secured 2 councils, Independents 3, and 27 had no overall control.]

WELSH ASSEMBLY	*Constituency*	*Region*	*total*	*seats ±*
Labour	24	2	26	–4
Plaid Cymru	7	8	15	+3
Conservatives	5	7	12	+1
Liberal Democrats	3	3	6	0
Others	1	0	1	0

CLIMATE CHANGE · EXPERT OPINION

The near-unanimity of expert opinion on the reality of global warming (and mankind's effect on it) was confirmed in 2006–07 by a series of reports. In late 2006, a UK government review by Nicholas Stern stated that 'the scientific evidence is now overwhelming: climate change presents very serious global risks, and it demands an urgent global response'. Stern predicted that, without action, there was a >75% chance of global temperatures rising 2–3°C by 2057, and a 50% chance of a 5°C rise. The impact of this would be more flooding and extreme weather, a decline in food supply, the extinction of ≤40% of species, and the displacement of millions. In the worst scenario, the global economy could shrink by 20%. 'All countries will be affected', Stern predicted, yet 'the most vulnerable – the poorest countries and populations – will suffer earliest and most, even though they have contributed least to … climate change'. Stern calculated it would cost 1% of global GDP to stabilise emissions (with a low-carbon route that could strengthen the world economy), and concluded, 'there is still time to avoid the worst impacts of climate change'. ❦ In a series of reports in 2007, the Intergovernmental Panel on Climate Change (IPCC) stated it was >90% certain that human activity, not least the burning of fossil fuels, caused global warming. And the panel made some disheartening predictions for the C21st:

Warmer & fewer cold days & nights over most land areas	probability >99%
Warmer & more frequent hot days & nights over most land areas	>99%
Frequency of warm spells/heat waves increases over most land areas	>90%
Frequency of heavy precipitation events increases over most areas	>90%
Area affected by droughts increases	>66%
Intense tropical cyclone activity increases	>66%
Increased incidence of extreme high sea level (not tsunamis)	>66%

Composed of hundreds of world experts, the IPCC is respected and influential. However, because IPCC reports are approved line-by-line by 113 governments, it was alleged that some of the panel's bolder findings were diluted, or even excised, at the insistence of China, America, India, &c. That said, the director of the UN Environment Programme claimed the IPCC's 2007 reports 'may go down in history as the day when the question mark was removed from … whether climate change has anything to do with human activities'. Curiously, as the scientific consensus becomes unequivocal, 56% of Britons still think that experts remain divided over whether human activity is contributing to global warming [7/07, Ipsos Mori]. It seems that certain groups have a vested interest in nurturing the seeds of doubt – an echo, perhaps, of the 'debate' linking smoking and cancer. ❦ Governments that have hitherto resisted 'eco-vangelism' may increasingly be influenced by national security. Already, the world has been given a taste of the unrest caused by extreme weather (Katrina), desertification (Nigeria), displacement (Darfur, Tuvalu), water wars (Bolivia), heavy precipitation (2007 floods), and pandemics (SARS, avian flu). As the US Center for Naval Analyses stated in April 2007, climate change 'poses a serious threat to America's national security', 'acts as a threat multiplier for instability in some of the most volatile regions of the world', and 'will add to tensions even in stable regions of the world'. Also in April, at Britain's behest, the UN Security Council held its first-ever debate on the security threat of global warming. It is unlikely to be the last.

CLIMATE CHANGE · BRITISH PUBLIC OPINION

The charts below give a snapshot of current British opinion on climate change:

81% are concerned about climate change †	34% think global warming will present a threat to them in their lifetime ‡	77% think human activities contribute to global warming ‡
58% think that climate change has caused their local weather to change †	73% think the seasons are not arriving at the same time of year as they used to †	81% are concerned about the impact of climate change on children †
80% have installed some energy efficient light bulbs [see p.13] †	61% think the state should tax 4-wheel drive cars more heavily †	89% claim to switch off lights when leaving a room †
77% think the UK is too reliant on foreign oil †	60% think the UK's dependence on foreign oil threatens its national security †	79% think the government should do more to tackle global warming †
57% do not know which political leader to trust on the environment †	68% believe they have personally seen evidence of climate change §	22% believe that the issue of climate change has been exaggerated §
70% believe that if no change is made, the world will experience a major eco-crisis soon §	9% think climate change is mainly caused by natural processes §	46% think the world community will find a solution to climate change §
77% would like Britain to ban incandescent light bulbs [see p.13] §	21% support eco-taxes on flying §	14% support eco-taxes on petrol §
15% think they can have no personal impact on climate change §	54% say they would do more to be green, if others did more also §	49% would support a 'bin tax' for the disposal of unrecyclable rubbish *
38% would support further 'green taxes' on airline travel to deter flyers *	42% tend not to use eco-friendly products because of their perceived cost ∞	70% wanted climate change claims to be proven by independent bodies ∞
61% could not name anyone they admired on the issue of climate change ∞	52% would prefer to do business with eco-friendly companies ∞	27% do not believe the claims made by energy efficient products and services ∞

[Key to sources: † = GMI World Environment Review, May 2007 · ‡ = Harris Poll, April 2007 · § = Ipsos MORI Social Research Institute, 2007 · * = *Sunday Mirror*/ICM, March 2007 · ∞ = Consumers Int., June 2007]

HARRY POTTER-MANIA

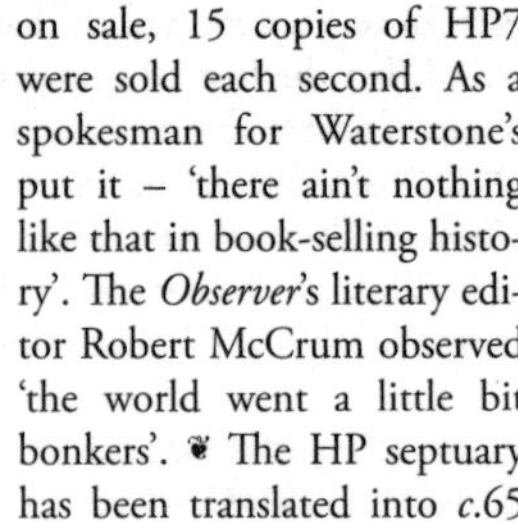

J.K. Rowling

The publication of the 7th (and supposedly final) instalment of J.K. Rowling's Harry Potter series – *Harry Potter & the Deathly Hallows* – was accompanied by an unprecedented avalanche of media coverage. Papers around the world dedicated reams of newsprint to 'HP7', and thousands of Potter themed websites quivered with anticipation. A late-night post on *TheLeakyCauldron.org* gushed, 'we're about 25 minutes away from receiving the book, here in Naperville, Ill. It's just about starting to feel real, guys ... Living through this time together has been a privilege and an honour for all of us'. However, the prelude to the strictly embargoed launch at midnight on 21 July 2007, was not without controversy. Days before the book's official release, photographs purportedly of every page of HP7 were circulated online. The *New York Times* and *Baltimore Sun* provoked reader outrage (and a denunciation from Rowling) by publishing 'embargo-busting' reviews of HP7 days before the launch. And Rowling's US publisher, Scholastic, threatened legal action against two companies for shipping copies of HP7 early. In Israel, Orthodox Jews denounced bookshops that planned to open on the Sabbath to sell HP7. In Britain, independent booksellers were squeezed as the big chains and supermarkets fought a price war that saw the £17·99 book sold at a loss for many retailers, for as little as £5. (The supermarket chain Asda apologised unreservedly after accusing the publisher, Bloomsbury, of 'profiteering'.) In the end, as with the launch of previous HP books, such incidents and accidents served only to stoke the fires of anticipation for the moment of official publication. Shops in >90 countries opened their doors at 00:01 GMT (05:01 GMT in the US) to hordes of children and adults – many dressed as characters from the series. According to press reports, in the first few hours on sale, 15 copies of HP7 were sold each second. As a spokesman for Waterstone's put it – 'there ain't nothing like that in book-selling history'. The *Observer*'s literary editor Robert McCrum observed 'the world went a little bit bonkers'. ❦ The HP septuary has been translated into *c*.65 languages (including Latin and Khmer), has sold >330m copies, and has inspired 5 blockbusting movies. Its royalties have catapulted Rowling from penury to a wealth estimated by *Forbes* in 2007 at *c*.$1bn. Predictably, some critics have derided Rowling's plots, prose, and profits – notably asserting that her series does little to encourage children to read beyond its pages. As Harold Bloom asked in a vitriolic *Wall Street Journal* review in 2000, 'Is it better that they read Rowling than not read at all? Will they advance from Rowling to more difficult pleasures?' To the latter question, Bloom thought not – yet a 2005 Waterstone's survey found that 84% of British teachers said HP had a positive impact on children's reading abilities, and 67% said HP helped turn non-readers into readers. ❦ If HP7 is the last in the series (Rowling mischievously warned, 'never say never'), it remains to be seen whether the books' legacy can be as lasting as their initial impact has been spectacular. On the day *Deathly Hallows* was published, a Google search for 'Harry Potter' elicited 167m results; in comparison, a search for 'Jesus Christ' elicited just 8·4m.

THE SMOKING BAN

By 1 July 2007, a ban on smoking in workplaces and enclosed public spaces was in force across the UK. England was the last to impose the ban (in July 2007), following the lead of Wales and N Ireland (April 2007), and Scotland (March 2006). The law applies to anything that can be smoked – including cigarettes, pipes, cigars, herbal cigarettes, and water-pipes such as hookahs. Individuals flouting the ban face a £50 on-the-spot fine; companies can be fined up to £2,500. By September 2007, some beneficial consequences of the ban had already been reported. Glasgow University revealed that the first 10 months of the Scottish ban had seen a 17% fall in the number of people admitted to hospital suffering from heart attacks. And, according to AC Nielsen data, in the first month of the English ban, cigarette sales in England fell by 6·9%. It remains to be seen whether such positive effects will be enduring, and whether the pub and bar trade will be negatively affected in the way some have predicted. The table below charts some of the many smoking bans in place worldwide:

Country	*date of ban*	*smoking banned in*
Belgium	2007	restaurants & bars serving food
Bhutan	2005	all public places (sale of tobacco banned in 2004)
Cuba	2005	workplaces
Denmark	2007	restaurants, bars, & clubs
France	2007	workplaces, public transport
Ireland	2004	all workplaces – the first such nationwide ban
Italy	2005	enclosed public spaces, cafés, restaurants
Netherlands	2004	workplaces, public transport (indoor public spaces from 07·08)
New Zealand	2004	indoor public places inc. bars & restaurants
Norway	2004	public buildings, cafés, bars, & restaurants
Spain	2006	workplaces, public transport
USA	varies	18 States currently have bans of some sort

A June 2007 survey by the Campaign for Real Ale, revealed that 840,000 people who never normally frequent pubs would do so after the UK ban. ❦ In N Korea, a smoking ban of sorts was imposed after doctors advised the country's leader Kim Jong-il to quit. Since July 2007, smoking has been banned in Kim's home, his office, and any public space he might visit. ❦ In England, Wales, & N Ireland, actors may smoke on-stage at the discretion of the local council 'where the artistic integrity of a performance makes it appropriate for a person to smoke'. These rules do not apply in Scotland, where any 'lit substance' is prohibited on-stage. ❦ In July 2007, police reportedly 'had a word' with former Lib Dem leader Charles Kennedy after he was allegedly caught smoking out of a window on a train. ❦ Borders bookshop reported that the ban had inspired a 260% rise in the sale of books devoted to kicking the habit. ❦ Rolling Stones Keith Richards and Ronnie Wood avoided any sanction after lighting up while performing at the O2 Arena, London. ❦ In August 2007, Ciao Surveys reported that *c.*30% of smokers said they now smoked less when out in bars and pubs, and 1·8% had quit smoking altogether; 30% of smokers and 90% of non-smokers were in favour of the ban; and almost all non-smokers and 66% of smokers said pubs were 'nicer places' since the ban. 61% of smokers complained that pubs now reeked of other unwelcome smells, such as stale beer and body odour. ❦ The British Academy of Cosmetic Dentistry reported in 9/07 that demand for tooth-whitening had increased by 12% since the ban. [Sources: BBC, WHO, *Times*, *Guardian*, &c.]

2007 FLOODS · UNITED KINGDOM & SOUTH ASIA

Torrential rain across the UK in June caused severe flooding in the Midlands, Yorkshire, Lincolnshire, and N Ireland. In Hull alone, *c*.7,000 homes suffered water damage, and the city council was criticised for failing to insure public buildings. The government pledged £2·1m in aid but, on 4 July, Hull council claimed it was 'the forgotten city', hinting at a north–south divide that some saw reflected in the media's coverage. ❦ On 20 July, heavy rain caused swathes of Oxfordshire, Berkshire, and Worcestershire to succumb to rising water. On 21 July, parts of the M5 were shut, prompting the RAF to launch its largest-ever peacetime operation, to rescue stranded drivers. In Gloucestershire, 350,000 were left without running water, 48,000 without electricity, and *c*.2,000 were forced to seek emergency shelter. (The dominant media image was of Tewkesbury, made an island by the swollen Severn and Avon.) ❦ The scale of the disaster, in which 7 died, prompted questions about the preparedness of local and national government and the adequacy of flood defences. As the rains abated and the waters receded, Flood Recovery Minister John Healey announced the damage was likely to total £2·7bn, and the Environment Agency warned that £1bn a year was required to update infrastructure. And the consequences of the floods threatened to ripple into 2008, as economists warned of inflationary pressures on food prices and insurance premiums. In August, the Met Office confirmed that the UK had experienced the wettest summer since records began, leaving many to wonder if this supposedly 1-in-150-year disaster was in fact a taste of things to come.

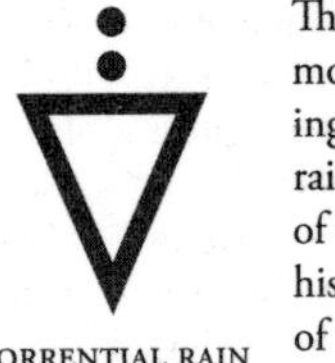

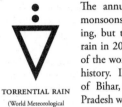

TORRENTIAL RAIN
(World Meteorological Organization symbol)

By 3 August 2007, *c*.20m people across India, Nepal, Bangladesh, and Bhutan had been displaced by flooding. Weeks of heavier-than-usual monsoon rains caused rivers to burst, fields to flood, and valuable crops to be destroyed. The annual June–September monsoons often cause flooding, but the sheer volume of rain in 2007 resulted in some of the worst damage in recent history. In India, the states of Bihar, Assam, and Uttar Pradesh were the most severely affected – 1,100 died, *c*.12m were made homeless, and many villages were submerged 6ft under water. Bangladesh reported that *c*.60% of the country was submerged, 5m were displaced, and >64 had died. In the highlands of Nepal and Bhutan, landslides killed many and caused extensive damage. By 10 August, the number of people affected across S Asia was estimated at 30m, and the total killed ranged from 500–3,000. As the rains eased, waterborne diseases became the major threat. Aid agencies distributed mosquito nets, food packages, and water purification kits in an effort to contain the spread of disease. Yet, in Bangladesh, 50,000 became ill after consuming contaminated food and drink, and in India doctors struggled to cope with outbreaks of diarrhoea. On 13 August, Oxfam released a report entitled *Sink or Swim: Why Disaster Risk Reduction is Central to Surviving Floods in South Asia*. Poorly designed embankments and badly maintained defences were blamed for hampering the natural flow of water, and Oxfam's Ashvin Dayal concluded, 'This year's flood is a wake-up call for south Asia's governments, current flood policies are not working and in some cases are exacerbating the problem'.

OTHER MAJOR STORIES IN BRIEF

Alexander Litvinenko

On 23/11/06, ex-KGB agent Alexander Litvinenko died in a London hospital. It soon emerged that his body contained a 'major dose' of the lethally radioactive element Polonium-210 – traces of which were later found at dozens of locations and in hundreds of people [see p.182]. The subsequent imbroglio, as macabre as it was complex, shed light on tensions between Russia and the West [see p.??]. In a letter he purportedly wrote while dying, Litvinenko accused President Putin of playing a part in his death. A number of sources alleged that Litvinenko had been targeted for betraying Russia. On 6/12/06, after far-reaching inquiries, the British police announced that they were treating Litvinenko's death as murder. On 22/5/07, the British announced there was sufficient evidence to charge the former KGB officer Andrei Lugovoi with deliberate poisoning, and to request his extradition from Russia. Lugovoi vigorously denied the charges, and accused the British of themselves killing Litvinenko who, he claimed, was a British spy. On 5/7, Russia refused Britain's extradition request, citing Article 61·1 of its Constitution. Britain responded on 16/7 by expelling 4 Russian diplomats. Russia countered three days later by expelling an equal number of British personnel, and threatening to end co-operation on visa applications and counter-terrorism. ❦ At the time of writing, tensions between Britain and Russia were still high, though both countries saw the need to get over what Putin called a 'mini crisis'. However, Britain remained determined to prosecute whoever was responsible for what was, in effect, the deployment of a Weapon of Mass Destruction on British soil – albeit in nano-quantities.

Celebrity Big Brother & 'Racism'

The fifth series of *Celebrity Big Brother* began on 3/1/07 with 14 'B' and 'C-list' names, including Jermaine Jackson, Leo Sayer, and Dirk Benedict. However, public and media attention quickly focused on the interactions between Bollywood star Shilpa Shetty and fellow housemates Jade Goody, Danielle Lloyd, and Jo O'Meara – which some alleged descended into racist bullying, including disparaging remarks about Indian cooking and a reference to Shetty as 'Shilpa Poppadom'. These incidents prompted an unprecedented >44,500 complaints to the watchdog Ofcom, and sparked a torrent of press coverage, questions in the Commons, Anglo–Indian diplomatic tensions, and even police investigations. Finally, after 26 days, Shetty won the contest with 63% of the public vote. ❦ A 24/5 Ofcom report concluded that Channel 4 had made 'serious editorial misjudgments' and had breached the Broadcasting Code three times. C4 was required to broadcast Ofcom's findings before the next series of *Big Brother*, and the channel instigated a number of voluntary reforms. ❦ On 7/6, during the 2007 non-celebrity version of *Big Brother*, one of the contestants was evicted from the house for saying the word 'nigger' [see p.116].

Bob Woolmer

On 18/3/07, a day after Pakistan lost to Ireland and dropped out of the Cricket World Cup, Pakistan's coach, Bob Woolmer, was found unconscious in his hotel room in Kingston, Jamaica. He was declared dead in hospital some hours later. On 20/3, the Jamaican police announced that they were treating the death as suspicious, despite no signs of a struggle or of theft. On 22/3,

OTHER MAJOR STORIES IN BRIEF cont.

having questioned and fingerprinted the Pakistan squad, the police announced they were treating the death as murder. Over the following weeks, a whirlwind of conspiracies alleged everything from suicide and assault to strangulation and poisoning – some even hinted at the involvement of an international match-fixing cartel. Finally, on 12/6, the Jamaican police rejected early post mortem findings and declared that Woolmer had, in fact, died of natural causes.

Iran Hostage Crisis

On 23/3/07, 15 British sailors and Marines were seized at gunpoint by Iranian forces, after boarding a merchant ship in the northern Arabian Gulf. The exact location of the vessels in relation to the Shatt al-Arab median line that divides Iraqi and Iranian waters was the subject of heated disagreement: both countries claimed the other had crossed into its waters. Over the following days and weeks, intense diplomatic negotiations attempted to secure the release of the naval personnel. In retaliation for what they called an 'illegal act', the British government suspended bilateral contracts with Iran, and the EU called for the sailors' 'immediate release'. (The UN Security Council refused to 'deplore' Iran's action, expressing only 'grave concern'.) British outrage intensified when Iranian media broadcast interviews with the hostages, in which they 'admitted' to being in Iranian waters. However, on 4/4, a day after the Foreign Sec. warned against hopes of a 'swift solution', President Ahmadinejad announced that he would release the hostages as a 'gift' to the people of Britain. The naval personnel returned home the next day, only to become embroiled in a controversy about selling their stories to the media.

Zimbabwe's Stagflation

The catastrophic state of Zimbabwe's economy under the brutal kleptocracy of President Robert Mugabe spiralled out of control in 2007. Sustained stagflation resulted in unemployment of >80%, food and fuel shortages, and hyperinflation that rose faster than it could be tracked. In June, the US ambassador to Zimbabwe, Christopher Dell, told the *Guardian,* 'I believe inflation will hit 1·5m% [*sic*] by the end of 2007, if not before'. Dell said that Zimbabwe's government was 'committing regime change on itself'. Mugabe, who is standing for re-election in 2008, blamed British 'tricks, dishonesty, and hypocrisy' for his country's plight. In August it became clear that Mugabe's bizarre edict to shopkeepers to simply slash prices (on pain of arrest) had only exacerbated shortages and panic. 3m Zimbabweans are thought to have fled the country (*c.*23% of the population), and the UN estimated that >4m would require food aid during 2008.

Hamas vs *Fatah*

The simmering violence between the secular Fatah and the Islamist Hamas – which began after Yasser Arafat's death in 2005, and worsened after the 2006 Palestinian elections – descended into all-out conflict in mid-2007. From 10/6/07, Hamas launched a series of successful attacks on Fatah positions in Gaza, and four days later, Hamas had control of the Gaza Strip. In response, Palestinian President (and Fatah leader) Mahmoud Abbas dissolved the elected unity government, declared a state of emergency, and announced that Gaza and the West Bank would be ruled by decree through an appointed government led by PM Salam Fayyad. The reality, however, was a Hamas-led

OTHER MAJOR STORIES IN BRIEF cont.

Gaza and a Fatah-led West Bank. Israel, which had stood back during the fighting, sought to isolate Hamas by closing the checkpoints into Gaza, and signalled its support for Abbas by releasing hundreds of Palestinian prisoners and millions of dollars of frozen tax receipts. While expressing concern for the residents of Gaza, many in the international community, including the US and EU, sought to bolster Abbas by pledging millions in aid. At the time of writing, tensions in the region remained high. Although Hamas (which seeks Israel's destruction) had hoped to improve its reputation by securing the release of kidnapped BBC reporter Alan Johnston, it seemed that the international focus was on securing Fatah in the West Bank, while further isolating Hamas in Gaza.

Blair as Middle East Envoy

Within hours of resigning as PM [see p.17] Tony Blair was appointed envoy to the Quartet – a group (EU, US, UN, Russia) working for Middle East peace. While some welcomed Blair's appointment (including the Palestinian Authority), others (including Hamas) were more sceptical, citing Blair's ties with America, his role in the Iraq war, and his reluctance to restrain Israel during its 2005 war with Lebanon. A number of commentators questioned whether Blair's reputation in the region might dent his credibility as an honest broker, noting also that the Quartet's narrow brief limited his remit to economic and infrastructural reconstruction, rather than political negotiation.

UK Terror Attacks

Within days of Gordon Brown replacing Blair as PM, Britain experienced a series of attempted terror attacks. In London, on 29/6/07, two car bombs (one parked outside a busy nightclub) containing gas cylinders, nails, and petrol failed to detonate and were defused by police. The next day, two men drove a burning car containing gas cylinders into the main doors of Glasgow's international airport. The car failed to explode, no bystanders were injured, and two men were arrested. The police stated that they believed the three attacks were linked, and the UK's terror alert was raised to 'Critical'. ❦ At the time of writing 3 men (all foreign-born doctors working in the National Health Service) had been charged and were awaiting trial. One of those allegedly involved in the Glasgow attack died in hospital from his burns.

'Cash for Honours'

On 20/7/07, the Crown Prosecution Service (CPS) announced that no charges would be brought following a 16-month Met Police inquiry into allegations that political honours had been granted in return for political party contributions. The CPS stated 'there is insufficient evidence to provide a realistic prospect of conviction against any individual for any offence in relation to this matter'. During the investigation (which reportedly cost *c.*£1m) the police interviewed 136 people, including Tony Blair 3 times, and arrested 4 people, all of whom had denied any wrongdoing.

Darfur

On 31/7/07, the UN passed Resolution 1769, authorising 26,000 UN and African Union (AU) peacekeepers to join the 7,000 AU troops already in the Sudanese province of Darfur. It was envisaged that the first wave of troops would deploy in 10/07, with the full force in place by early 2008. ❦ Darfur

OTHER MAJOR STORIES IN BRIEF cont.

has been in crisis since at least 2003, when black African rebels attacked government targets in protest at their poor treatment. In response, Sudanese forces, in cahoots (it is alleged) with the Arab Janjaweed militia, launched a genocidal campaign of repression, ethnic cleansing, and human rights abuse, resulting in >200,000 deaths and the displacement of *c*.2·5m. ❦ At Sudan's insistence, Resolution 1769 stopped short of authorising sanctions, ensured the new force was mainly (entirely?) African, and prohibited the pursuit of suspected war criminals. ❦ At the time of writing, optimism about the UN's initiative was balanced by a host of doubts: Would even the world's largest peacekeeping force be sufficient for an area the size of France, with few roads and little infrastructure? Would the troops be properly trained, funded, and equipped, and would they be adequately mandated to protect civilians and aid workers? Would those countries with economic and military ties to Sudan (China and Russia) support the peace? Would the Darfurian rebel groups cease their internecine fighting? Would Sudan co-operate fully with the UN force? And, axiomatically, would there be a peace in Darfur to keep?

Northern Ireland Power Sharing

On 5/8/07, Ian Paisley (DUP) was sworn in as First Minister of the Northern Ireland Assembly, and Martin McGuinness (Sinn Féin) as his Deputy in the new power-sharing executive. Upon taking office, Paisley said, 'I believe we're starting on a road which will bring us back to peace and prosperity'. McGuinness responded, 'We must overcome the difficulties which we face in order to achieve our goals and seize the opportunities that exist'. Greeting the return to devolved government, Tony Blair said, 'Look back and we see centuries marked by conflict, hardship, even hatred among the people of these islands; look forward and we see the chance to shake off those heavy chains of history'.

Madeleine McCann

3-year-old Madeleine McCann was allegedly abducted from her bed at a holiday resort in Praia da Luz, Portugal, between 9:30–10pm on 3/5/07. It was reported that her parents, Gerry and Kate, were dining that evening at a nearby restaurant, but were checking on their children regularly. The resulting manhunt dominated the British media for the following months, attracting support from a wealth of celebrities and politicians – including the Pope. While the McCanns faced some criticism for leaving their daughter alone (and, harshly, for 'milking' the media's relentless coverage), they were praised also for their dignity, stoicism, and passion. ❦ At the time of writing, despite intense speculation over a range of suspects and considerable police activity, no conclusive news of Madeleine had been heard. In a dramatic turn of events, on 7–8/9, after being questioned by Portuguese police, Madeleine's parents were declared 'arguido' – a status in Portuguese law under which the two are treated as suspects, with additional legal rights, although neither had been arrested or charged, and both vigorously denied any wrongdoing. Gerry & Kate returned to the UK on 9/9, in the full glare of the world's media, vowing to clear their names and continue the hunt for their daughter.

Subprime

In the US, subprime loans are made to those with poor (or no) credit history,

OTHER MAJOR STORIES IN BRIEF cont.

in return for higher interest rates, fees, and penalties. A range of subprime lending exists (from loans to credit cards), but the most dominant form has been mortgages, and it was this segment which hit 'meltdown' in 2006–07. Buoyed by rising house prices, lenders over-estimated the sums that could safely be lent. Keen to get on the housing ladder, borrowers 'over-stated' how much they earned. And, as loans came off their initial low rates, and house prices weakened, many could not afford their repayments or to refinance their debt, and the incidence of delinquency, default, and foreclosure rocketed. In early 2007, a number of major US lenders collapsed. This had a domino effect both on market confidence and on those hedge funds and investment banks around the world with subprime exposure – often in the form of complex 'bundles' of debt. In August, world markets reacted with such volatility that many Central Banks injected millions into the market to avoid a 'credit crunch'. The Chairman of the Fed warned the crisis could cost $50–$100bn, and was forced to cut the Fed's interbank 'discount' rate. CNN Money estimated that *c.*2·4m Americans could lose their homes. At the time of writing, the 'violent correction' in the US subprime market had spilled out into the world's 'real economies'. In August, the FTSE, along with other markets, saw haphazard trading, and, as credit became tighter, banks became less willing to lend to each other. The Bank of England (BOE) expressed concern, and increased its reserves for banks struggling with liquidity. On 14/9, the BOE provided an emergency loan to Northern Rock, prompting a 'run' on that bank in which >£2bn was withdrawn amidst scenes of panic. On 17/9, the Chancellor Alistair Darling said the Treasury would underwrite all deposits in Northern Rock – an unprecedented move that calmed savers and the markets. On 19/9, the US Fed cut a key interest rate by 0·5% in an attempt to boost confidence and stability.

Home Information Packs (HIP)

From 1/8/07, sellers of 4-bedroom homes in England and Wales had to provide a HIP for their property (on 10/9, the scheme was extended to 3-bedroom properties). HIPs must contain a range of documents, including an Energy Performance Certificate (EPC), a sale statement, standard property searches, evidence of title, and lease details, where relevant. The aim of HIPs was to speed up sales, and pre-empt an EU directive requiring all property sales after 2009 to include an EPC. However, the cost of compiling HIPs (*c.*£300–£600), coupled with a lack of qualified EPC inspectors, has led some to question whether HIPs will help or hinder sales.

Foot And Mouth (F&M)

F&M was confirmed on a farm in Guilford, Surrey, on 3/8/07 – prompting a cull of animals on the farm, and a national ban on the movement of livestock. Suspicions that the outbreak was linked to the nearby animal research laboratory at Pirbright were confirmed by an official report on 7/9, which blamed 'defective drainage'. The last restrictions on animal movements were lifted on 8/9 – but farmers were shocked when 2 new F&M cases were reported just days later. Farming's woes deepened on 22/9, when the UK's first-ever case of Bluetongue disease was confirmed in Suffolk. At the time of writing, new restrictions on animal movement were in force, and anxiety was high.

PERSON OF THE YEAR: VLADIMIR PUTIN

Much of the recent posturing between Putin and the West has been decidedly reminiscent of the Cold War, not least: Moscow's objections to the US defence shield, and its threat to target missiles at Europe; the 'gas supply wars' with Ukraine and Belarus; withdrawal from the Conventional Forces in Europe Treaty; oil-related territorial shenanigans under the North Pole; Russia's resumption of long-range bomber patrols; disruption to Russian language BBC World Service broadcasts; and the Litvinenko affair [see p.27]. In July 2007, the *Economist* noted that 'Russia is no longer exporting a rival ideology … nor fighting proxy wars with America around the globe'. However, Russia remains armed with the world's largest known gas reserves, strong political and economic influence over an archipelago of marginalised states, an Armageddonic nuclear arsenal, and a permanent seat (and veto) on the UN Security Council. Thus, whether the issue is terrorism, climate change, energy security, nuclear proliferation, Palestine, Iraq, Iran, Kosovo, or Darfur – Putin's Russia cannot be ignored. ❦ Vladimir Vladimirovich Putin was born in 1952 to working-class parents. He studied law at Leningrad University, where he was recruited by the KGB in 1975. After two years as a low-level spook, Putin was sent to Moscow for elite training. In 1985, he was assigned to the KGB office in Dresden, where he reportedly worked with the Stasi to gather Western technology secrets. In 1990, after the fall of the Berlin Wall, Putin was recalled to assist the rector of Leningrad University – a thinly veiled KGB cover. Over the next few years, Putin climbed the political ladder in (the renamed) St Petersburg, before he was summoned to Moscow in 1996. In a vertiginous rise, Putin became Boris Yeltsin's deputy Chief of Staff in 1997, and head of the Federal Security Service in 1998. In 1999, Putin was appointed Secretary of the Security Council (March), PM (August), and Acting President (December). In March 2000, Putin was elected President – despite being as unknown to most Russians as he was to the rest of the world. ❦ The West welcomed Putin's early advocacy of democratic and economic reforms as much as his stylistic differences from the haphazard Yeltsin. Yet, by 2003, this optimism was overshadowed by Putin's quasi-Soviet clampdown on media freedoms and opposition protests, and his pursuit of foreign investors and Russia's newly minted oligarchs. Although he opposed the Iraq invasion, Putin used Bush's 'war on terror' to justify his Chechnya policy, and cited Guantánamo Bay to rebuff criticisms of his record on human rights. ❦ Putin has exploited Russia's petro-dollars (and US unpopularity) to renegotiate what he sees as the parlous deals Russia made as the Soviet Union collapsed. As he told al-Jazeera, 'Russia knows its worth. We will work towards creating a multipolar world … but Russia does have enough potential to influence the formation of the new world order'. ❦ Since Russia's constitution forbids 3 consecutive presidential terms, Putin must step down in 2008. Despite hinting he would like to stay on (and an approval rating of *c*.80%), few believe Putin will actually rewrite the law to do so. That said, aged just 55, it is implausible that he will simply fade into the background.

SCHEMATIC · WORLD EVENTS OF NOTE · 2006–07

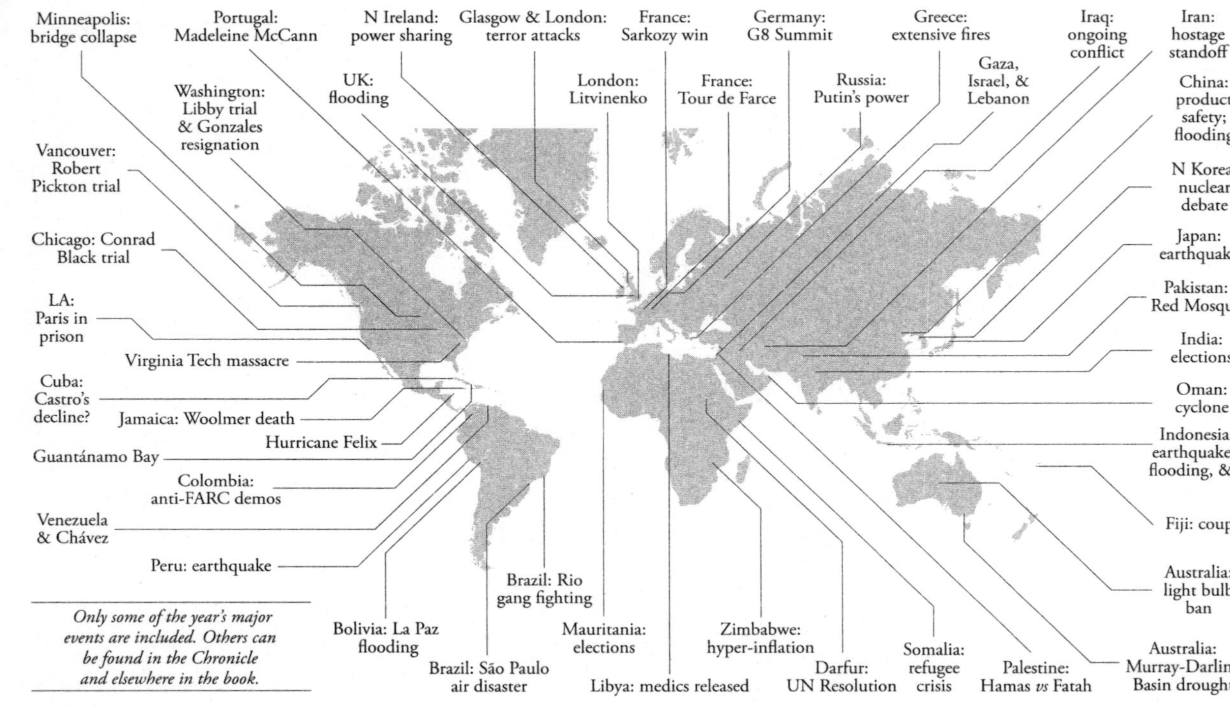
Minneapolis: bridge collapse
Portugal: Madeleine McCann
N Ireland: power sharing
Glasgow & London: terror attacks
France: Sarkozy win
Germany: G8 Summit
Greece: extensive fires
Iraq: ongoing conflict
Iran: hostage standoff
Washington: Libby trial & Gonzales resignation
UK: flooding
London: Litvinenko
France: Tour de Farce
Russia: Putin's power
Gaza, Israel, & Lebanon
China: product safety; flooding
Vancouver: Robert Pickton trial
N Korea: nuclear debate
Chicago: Conrad Black trial
Japan: earthquake
LA: Paris in prison
Pakistan: Red Mosque
Virginia Tech massacre
India: elections
Cuba: Castro's decline?
Oman: cyclone
Jamaica: Woolmer death
Hurricane Felix
Indonesia: earthquakes, flooding, &c.
Guantánamo Bay
Colombia: anti-FARC demos
Venezuela & Chávez
Fiji: coup
Peru: earthquake
Australia: light bulb ban
Brazil: Rio gang fighting
Only some of the year's major events are included. Others can be found in the Chronicle and elsewhere in the book.
Bolivia: La Paz flooding
Mauritania: elections
Zimbabwe: hyper-inflation
Somalia: refugee crisis
Australia: Murray-Darling Basin drought
Brazil: São Paulo air disaster
Libya: medics released
Darfur: UN Resolution
Palestine: Hamas *vs* Fatah

IN BRIEF · SEPTEMBER – OCTOBER 2006

The daily chronicle below picks up from the 2007 edition of Schott's Almanac.

SEPTEMBER 2006 · {23} >35 died in a car bomb attack in Baghdad. ❦ A leaked French secret services memo claimed that Osama bin Laden died of typhoid in August 2006. ❦ 20,000–50,000 people congregated in Budapest's main square, calling for the resignation of PM Ferenc Gyurcsány. ❦ RIP @ 84, composer Sir Malcolm Arnold. {24} Europe won the Ryder Cup, beating America 18½–9½. {25} A 5-month-old baby died after being attacked by 2 Rottweilers that belonged to his family. ❦ Bloomberg reported that Cherie Blair called Gordon Brown a 'liar' as she watched him give his keynote speech to the Labour party conference; Cherie denied the charge. {26} Japan's parliament elected conservative Shinzo Abe as PM. {28} The Chief Inspector of Prisons released a damning report on Pentonville, describing the jail as 'overrun with cockroaches'. {30} A plane crashed in the Amazon rainforest, Brazil, killing all 155 passengers.

Cherie Blair

OCTOBER · {1} 8 died and >60 were injured in gun fights between rival factions in Gaza; the attacks began when government workers complained about unpaid wages. ❦ In his opening speech to the Conservative party conference, David Cameron refused to commit to tax cuts, angering many delegates. {2} 32-year-old gunman Charles Carl Roberts burst into an Amish school in Pennsylvania; he released all the boys before shooting 12 girls, killing 3 immediately and leaving 9 seriously wounded; he then killed himself (2 girls later died from their injuries). ❦ Russia reacted angrily to the Georgian government arrest of 4 alleged Russian spies in Tbilisi. {3} N Korea announced it would conduct nuclear tests at some point in the future. ❦ Tesco announced its half-year profits had risen 10·3%, to £1·09bn. ❦ The US offered to return to Britain 9 British residents held at Guantánamo Bay; the British government refused the offer because the prisoners had no legal right of residence. ❦ Russia imposed economic sanctions on Georgia, despite the release of the alleged Russian spies; the US urged calm. {4} The Independent Monitoring Cmsn reported that the IRA had significantly changed, did not want to return to violence, and no longer had the capacity to launch a sustained terror campaign. ❦ An entire brigade of Iraqi police was removed from duty in Baghdad after they were suspected of being involved with sectarian death squads. {6} Jack Straw became embroiled in a row after reporting that he asked Muslim women to consider removing their veils at his surgery [see p.290]. {7} A US medic testified that US marines in Hamdaniya had forced an Iraqi civilian into a hole before shooting him repeatedly in the head. {9} N Korea announced it had performed a successful nuclear weapons test, prompting international condemnation and calls for UN sanctions. ❦ RIP @ 27, 3-times snooker Masters champion Paul Hunter. ❦ Google bought YouTube for $1·65bn. ❦ Danny and Rickie Preddie were sentenced to 8 years in youth custody for the 2000 manslaughter of Damilola Taylor. {10}

It was such a visible statement of separation and of difference.
– JACK STRAW on the veil

IN BRIEF · OCTOBER 2006

The government announced that British soldiers on dangerous operations for >6 months would receive a bonus to pay off their tax bills. {11} Investigations continued into N Korea's nuclear test claims, after indications that the blast was smaller than initially thought. ❦ A report by the Bloomberg School of Public Health estimated that 655,000 Iraqis had been killed since the 2003 invasion [see p.19]. {12} Home Office data revealed that >1,000 crimes were committed by 'tagged' criminals released early from prison. {13} Head of the Army, Sir Richard Dannatt, told reporters that the presence of British armed forces in Iraq was aggravating the security situation and that they should 'get out some time soon'. ❦ A British man, Dhiren Barot, pleaded guilty to plotting to plant a 'dirty bomb' in a planned series of attacks across the UK. {14} The UN Security Council voted unanimously to impose economic and weapons sanctions on N Korea, though the sanctions did not carry the threat of military action [see p.63]. {15} Israeli police said they had enough evidence to charge President Moshe Katsav with rape and wire-tapping. ❦ In Iraq, >10 died in car bombs in Baghdad, and 40 bodies were found dumped in Balad. {16} It emerged that 2 male terror suspects under 'control orders' had gone on the run; the Home Office said the public was not at risk. ❦ US intelligence confirmed that N Korea had indeed carried out nuclear tests. ❦ >100 died in Sri Lanka after Tamil Tigers rammed a military convoy with a truck bomb. ❦ Madonna was granted interim custody of a year-old Malawian boy she hoped to adopt; aid workers vowed to thwart her plans, alleging that she had bypassed Malawi's adoption rules. {17} 2 died and >60 were injured when 2 metro trains collided in Rome. ❦ The population of America reached 300m. ❦ Iceland announced it would resume commercial whaling. {18} 9 US soldiers were killed in Iraq; 4 in a roadside bomb in Baghdad. {19} 2 children and a British Royal Marine died when a suicide bomber attacked a Nato vehicle in Helmand, Afghanistan. ❦ *c.*41 died in a wave of sectarian attacks across Iraq. {20} Clare Short announced she would resign the Labour whip and sit as an independent MP. {21} Paul Smith, a British oil-worker taken hostage in Nigeria who had reportedly died of malaria, turned up alive and well. {22} A senior US State Dept official said the US had shown 'arrogance and stupidity' in Iraq. ❦ Israel admitted using phosphorus shells against Lebanon during the 2006 war. ❦ Michael Schumacher retired from Formula One at the close of the season; Fernando Alonso won the World Championship for a 2nd year. {23} A referendum in Panama backed a $5·2bn expansion of the Panama Canal to allow passage of the largest ships. ❦ Jeffrey Skilling was sentenced to 24 years in jail for his part in the Enron fraud. {24} Home Sec. John Reid announced plans to restrict the number of Romanians and Bulgarians allowed to work in GB when the two countries joined the EU in 2007. {26} 2 British children were found dead in a villa in Corfu; their father and his partner were found comatose alongside; it was speculated the family had been poisoned. ❦ Local officials said that scores of civilians had been killed in Nato raids in S Afghanistan; Nato admitted

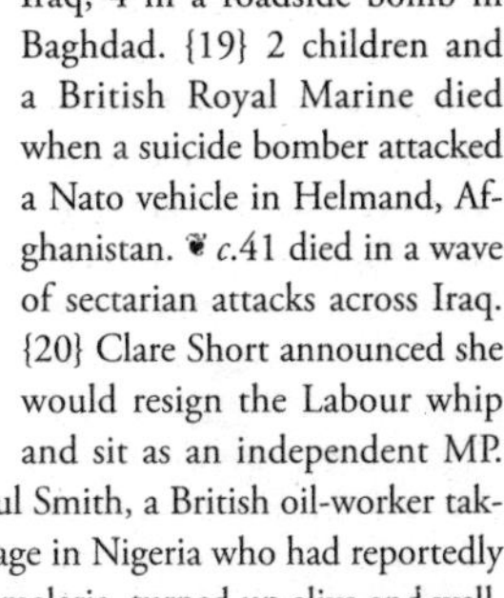

Kim Jong-il

I know he will be very happy in America. – YOHANE BANDA (father of Madonna's adopted son)

IN BRIEF · OCTOBER – NOVEMBER 2006

>12 deaths. {28} Tests concluded that the 2 children in Corfu died of carbon monoxide poisoning; 4 hotel staff faced charges of negligence. {30} The Stern Review into climate change [see p.22]. ❦ >29 died and >50 were injured in a bomb attack on Shia labourers queuing for work in Baghdad. {31} A parliamentary vote calling for an immediate inquiry into the Iraq war was defeated by 25. ❦ Network Rail admitted a series of safety breaches that contributed to the Ladbroke Grove rail crash that killed 31; the company faced an unlimited fine. ❦ RIP @ 90, former PM and President of S Africa, P.W. Botha [see p.55].

NOVEMBER · {1} America warned of mounting evidence that Iran, Syria, and Hezbollah were plotting to overthrow the Lebanese government. {3} The National Audit Office reported that Britain's armed forces had a personnel deficit of >5,000. ❦ British Airways announced that additional security after the August 2006 transatlantic terror alert cost them £100m. ❦ 83 corpses were found during a 36-hour period in Baghdad; some showed signs of torture. {4} >7 Palestinians, including a 12-year-old girl, died in Israeli raids in Gaza. ❦ >22,000 joined a rally in London to highlight climate change. {5} Saddam Hussein was sentenced to death; the British government welcomed the verdict. ❦ England suffered a record 41–20 defeat to the All Blacks at Twickenham. {7} Londoner Dhiren Barot was jailed for life for plotting to detonate a series of bombs in London and the US. ❦ Americans went to the polls for the midterm elections. {8} Democrats swept the US midterms, winning 233 House seats and 51 Senate seats for their first bicameral majority in 6 years. ❦ >18 died and >40 wounded after Israeli shelling in Gaza. ❦ Suicide bombers killed >42 at an army training camp in Pakistan. {9} The Bank of England raised interest rates to 5% [see p.237]. {10} The head of MI5 warned that the agency was tracking 30 known terror plots and keeping 1,600 suspects under surveillance. ❦ RIP @ 87, Jack Palance. ❦ Palestinian PM Ismail Haniya offered to resign in return for the lifting of the West's aid boycott. {11} America vetoed a draft UN resolution to condemn Israel for an attack on Gaza that killed 18 civilians. {12} 4 British soldiers died and 3 were injured when their boat was attacked near Basra. ❦ RIP @ 27, Desert Orchid [see p.55]. {13} Blair called for Iran and Syria to co-operate in plans to bring peace to Iraq and the Middle East. {14} 100 men were kidnapped from an Iraqi research institute in Baghdad; all were released by midnight. {15} UK unemployment hit its highest level for 7 years, increasing 27,000 to 1·71m. ❦ After striking a plea bargain to avoid the death penalty, a US soldier admitted that he and 3 other servicemen raped a 14-year-old Iraqi girl in Mahmudiya, before murdering the rest of her family. {16} The death sentence of a British man, Mirza Tahir Hussain, held in Pakistan for 18 years on charges of murder, was commuted to life in prison after pleas from Blair and Prince Charles. ❦ Joseph Kabila was named the winner of presidential elections in DR Congo. {17} Pakistan's interior minister announced that Mirza Tahir Hussain had been released from prison. ❦ Ségolène

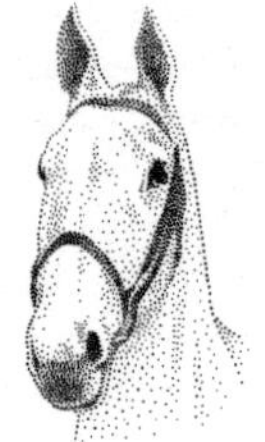
Desert Orchid

Maybe this will help alleviate the pain of the widows and the orphans.
– NOURI MALIKI, Iraqi PM

IN BRIEF · NOVEMBER – DECEMBER 2006

Royal was selected to be France's socialist presidential candidate. ❦ The Dutch Cabinet supported a plan to ban women from wearing the burqa in public. ❦ Ofcom announced regulations to ban junk-food adverts during TV programmes aimed at <16s; the ruling would come into force by end of 1/07. {18} Gordon Brown made his first visit to Iraq. ❦ The African Union announced that the Sudanese government and the Janjaweed had launched attacks on Darfur, killing >70. {19} Former KGB agent and critic of Vladimir Putin, Alexander Litvinenko, was reported to have been poisoned in London during a meeting about the death of Russian journalist Anna Politkovskaya [see p.27]. {20} The Kremlin dismissed claims that they were behind the poisoning of Litvinenko, whose condition had deteriorated. {21} Anti-Syrian Christian leader Pierre Gemayel was murdered in Lebanon. ❦ RIP @ 81, Robert Altman [see p.55]. {22} A British oil-worker held captive in Nigeria was killed and an Italian injured during a botched rescue attempt. ❦ Patricia Hewitt was interviewed by police as a witness in the 'cash-for-peerages' investigation [see p.29]. {23} >144 died and >200 injured in a series of attacks in Baghdad's Sadr City. ❦ RIP @ 58, journalist Nick Clarke [see p.55]. {24} Litvinenko died in hospital [see p.27]. ❦ Convicted Loyalist killer Michael Stone burst into Stormont carrying explosives and a handgun; he was arrested at the scene. {25} A Gaza cease-fire was agreed between Israel and the Palestinians. {26} Investigations into the death of Litvinenko were stepped up; British officers flew to Moscow, and those who had been in the same restaurants or bars as Litvinenko were asked to come forward for radiation testing. ❦ Blair expressed his 'deep sorrow' for Britain's role in the slave trade; he stopped short of issuing the full apology many had called for ahead of the 2007 bicentenary of the abolition of slavery. {27} Australia thrashed England by 227 runs in the first Ashes Test in Brisbane [see p.309]. {28} Michael Grade resigned as BBC Chairman to become head of ITV. ❦ RIP @ 79, DJ Alan 'Fluff' Freeman [see p.55]. ❦ Donnel Carty and Delano Brown were sentenced to life for the 2006 murder of lawyer Tom ap Rhys Pryce. {29} Widespread disturbances took place at Harmondsworth immigration detention centre. ❦ RIP @ 72, anti-smoking guru Allen Carr [see p.55]. ❦ Andy Robinson resigned as England rugby coach after his team lost 8 of their last 9 matches. {30} BA grounded 3 planes after traces of radiation linked to the poisoning of Litvinenko were found; the planes underwent tests and *c.*33,000 passengers who flew the London–Moscow route were traced. ❦ Gordon Brown and his wife Sarah revealed that their youngest son, Fraser, had cystic fibrosis. ❦ Fijian military chief Cmdr Frank Bainimarama threatened to launch a coup if his demands to scrap controversial legislation were not met by 1/12.

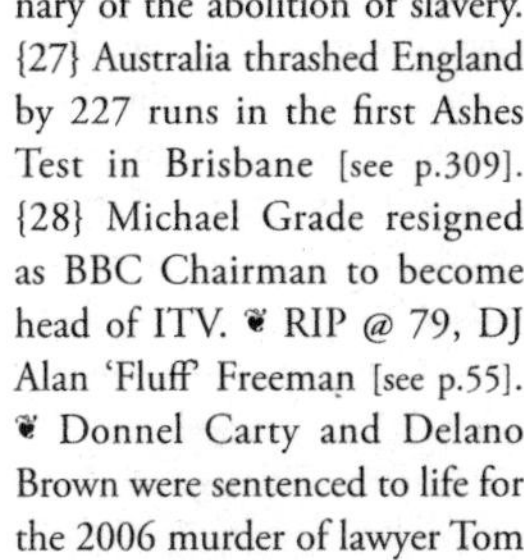
A. Litvinenko

It is hard to believe what would now be a crime against humanity was legal at the time. – TONY BLAIR on slavery

DECEMBER · {1} >146 died in the Philippines after a typhoon caused a mudslide. ❦ Thousands of Lebanese rallied in support of Hezbollah and pro-Syrian allies, and called for the Lebanese government to resign. {2} Fidel Castro missed a military parade in honour of his 80th birthday,

IN BRIEF · DECEMBER 2006

exacerbating speculation over his health. {3} 2 firefighters died in a blaze at a fireworks factory in E Sussex. {4} Venezuelan President Chávez secured a 3rd term in office. ❦ US Ambassador to the UN, John Bolton, announced he would step down. ❦ Blair announced that the government would renew Trident [see p.264]. {5} Bainimarama said he had seized control of Fiji. {6} >6 died in a suicide attack in S Afghanistan. ❦ The long-awaited Iraq Study Group's report into America's Iraq policy was published; it advised that current military strategy was untenable and that dialogue with Syria and Iran was advisable. ❦ The latest pictures from NASA's Mars Global Surveyor provided evidence that water may have 'recently' flowed on Mars [see p.191]. {7} >150 houses were damaged and 6 people injured after a freak tornado hit Kensal Rise, NW London. ❦ Fiji was suspended from the Commonwealth [see p.271]. ❦ Police investigating the murder of a prostitute in Suffolk found a second body, raising fears of a serial killer. {10} Augusto Pinochet died @ 91 [see p.55]. ❦ The murdered body of a 3rd prostitute was found in Suffolk. {11} Gunmen in Gaza killed the 3 children of Baha Balousheh, an intelligence officer with links to Fatah; reprisals were feared. ❦ 2 more women were reported missing in Suffolk; police warned prostitutes to stay off the streets. {12} >57 died and hundreds injured when a car bomb and suicide bomber simultaneously attacked a busy square in Baghdad. ❦ 2 more women were found dead in Suffolk, taking the total to 5. ❦ Ethiopia's former Marxist leader, Mengistu Haile Mariam, was found guilty of genocide *in absentia*; the former leader lives in exile in Zimbabwe. ❦ There were calls for Ehud Olmert to resign, after he accidentally confirmed that Israel had nuclear weapons. {14} The official UK police report into the death of Princess Diana concluded her death was a 'tragic accident' and dismissed the many conspiracy theories. ❦ Blair was interviewed by police in the 'cash-for-honours' investigation; the PM was neither cautioned nor accompanied by a lawyer. {15} Clashes broke out between Fatah and Hamas in Gaza, after Fatah was accused of trying to assassinate PM Ismail Haniya. {16} Leona Lewis beat Ray Quinn in the *X Factor* final [see p.126]. {17} Blair held talks with Palestinian leaders and the Israeli PM, in an effort to re-start the peace process. {18} Australia regained the Ashes on the final day of the 3rd Test in Perth [see p.309]. ❦ Cuban officials assured US envoys that Castro did not have terminal cancer. ❦ A 37-year-old man was arrested on suspicion of the murder of 5 female prostitutes in Suffolk. ❦ Fatah and Hamas announced a truce. {19} A second man was arrested in connection with the Suffolk murders. ❦ 5 Bulgarian nurses and a Palestinian doctor were sentenced to death after being accused of deliberately infecting children in a Libyan hospital with HIV. ❦ RIP @ 95, Joseph Barbera. {20} BA cancelled hundreds of domestic flights after heavy fog blanketed much of Britain. {21} RIP @ 66, Saparmurat Niyazov, eccentric President of Turkmenistan. ❦ A 48-year-old man was charged with murdering 5 prostitutes in Suffolk; another man was released on bail. ❦ The leader of the Union of Islamic Courts (UIC), which controls much of Somalia,

Hugo Chávez

It's a huge occasion for me and the team. To win the Ashes back the way we have done. – RICKY PONTING

IN BRIEF · DECEMBER 2006 – JANUARY 2007

claimed the UIC was at war with Ethiopia. {22} 8 US marines were charged with the deaths of 24 Iraqi civilians in Haditha. {23} The UN Sec Council voted to pass a resolution imposing sanctions on Iran over its nuclear programme [see p.63]. {24} Ethiopia admitted that its troops were fighting the UIC in Somalia. ❦ RIP @ 81, comedian Charlie Drake. {25} RIP @ 73, soul-singer James Brown [see p.55]. ❦ In her Christmas message, the Queen called for a better inter-generational understanding [see p.276]. ❦ John Prescott had his Christmas dinner in hospital after he was diagnosed with kidney stones. {26} Iraq's Court of Appeal upheld the death sentence on Hussein. ❦ >260 died when an oil pipeline in Lagos exploded after being punctured by thieves. {27} RIP @ 93, former US president Gerald Ford. {28} 6 died when a helicopter crashed into the sea off Morecambe Bay, Lancashire. {30} Saddam Hussein was hanged in Baghdad. Mobile phone footage of his death was leaked, and an outcry erupted over taunts directed at him during his execution. ❦ 19 were injured in an ETA bomb attack on Barajas airport; the Spanish government suspended all dialogue with the group. {31} 3 died in a series of bombs in Bangkok, Thailand, thought to have been planted by opponents of the military government. ❦ Many New Year's Eve firework parties and concerts were cancelled as gales swept across Britain. ❦ The 3,000th US soldier was killed in Iraq.

John Prescott

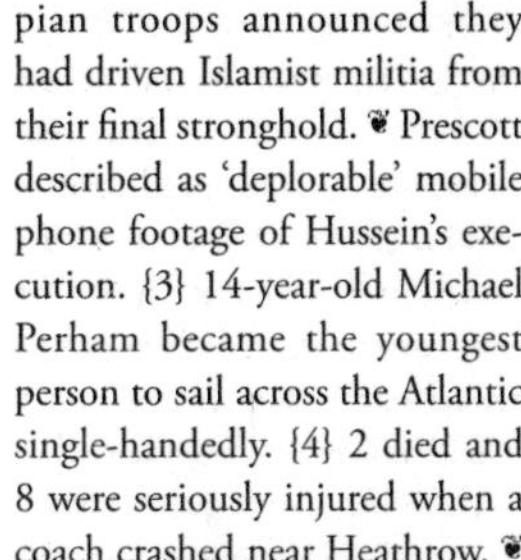

He was dramatic to the end, dying on Christmas Day.
– JESSE JACKSON on James Brown

JANUARY 2007 · {1} Romania and Bulgaria joined the EU [see p.268]. ❦ 5-year-old Ellie Lawrenson was mauled to death by a pit-bull at her grandmother's home in Merseyside. ❦ An Indonesian aircraft went missing near Sulawesi, with 102 people on board. ❦ The government announced the legal age to buy tobacco would rise to 18 in October 2007. {2} Somali government and Ethiopian troops announced they had driven Islamist militia from their final stronghold. ❦ Prescott described as 'deplorable' mobile phone footage of Hussein's execution. {3} 14-year-old Michael Perham became the youngest person to sail across the Atlantic single-handedly. {4} 2 died and 8 were seriously injured when a coach crashed near Heathrow. ❦ The Met Office warned that, as a result of global warming and El Niño, 2007 was likely to be the hottest on record [see p.74]. ❦ Nancy Pelosi was sworn in as the first female speaker of the US House of Representatives. {7} Blair and Brown both criticised the manner of Hussein's execution. ❦ RIP @ 77, Magnus Magnusson [see p.56]. {8} Labour backbenchers expressed anger after it emerged that Cabinet Minister Ruth Kelly sent one of her children to private school. ❦ Russia cut gas supplies to Poland, Germany, and Ukraine in a dispute over payment with neighbouring Belarus. ❦ A German court sentenced Moroccan Mounir al-Motassadek to 15 years in jail for aiding the 9/11 attacks. {9} America carried out air strikes on Islamist fighters in Somalia, who they accused of having links to al-Qaeda. ❦ RIP @ 53, David Ervine, leader of Progressive Unionists. {10} The Home Office was criticised after it was revealed that the details of 27,529 Britons who had committed crimes abroad had not been entered into a national database, thereby allowing

IN BRIEF · JANUARY 2007

them to work with vulnerable people. {11} Bush announced he would send an extra 21,500 troops to Iraq. ❦ A leaked government memo revealed that the NHS was not on track to meet its targets for combating MRSA [see p.105]. ❦ Nato announced it had killed 150 Taleban fighters in E Afghanistan. ❦ David Beckham revealed he was leaving Real Madrid for LA Galaxy. {12} Terrorists fired a rocket into the US Embassy in Athens, Greece; no one was hurt. {15} 2 of Saddam Hussein's key aides were hanged in Baghdad; Barzan al-Tikriti and Awad Hamad al-Bandar were executed for the murder of 148 Shias in the 1980s. ❦ The trial of the 6 men accused of masterminding the failed 21 July London bomb attacks opened at Woolwich Crown Court. {16} A UN human rights official stated that 34,452 Iraqi civilians had been killed during 2006 – a figure nearly 3 times higher than previous estimates [see p.19]. ❦ >70 died when car bombs exploded at Baghdad University; the majority of those killed were female students on their way home. ❦ >21,000 complaints were made about alleged racism during *Celebrity Big Brother*; concerns grew that Indian actress Shilpa Shetty was being subjected to racist bullying by fellow contestants [see p.27]. {18} 4 died after storms battered the UK. ❦ The Carphone Warehouse suspended its sponsorship of *Celebrity Big Brother*. {19} Concerns were raised by US, Japan, and Australia after it was reported that China had conducted a missile test in space. ❦ Downing St aid Ruth Turner was arrested in connection with the 'cash-for-honours' investigation; she denied any wrongdoing and was released on bail without charge. The CPS has since announced that no one will face charges following the investigation [see p.29]. ❦ Jade Goody was voted out of *Celebrity Big Brother*, amidst a public outcry over alleged racist bullying. {20} John Reid announced the Home Office might be split, creating one dept for justice and another for security. ❦ Hillary Clinton joined the race for the Democratic presidential nomination. {21} Coastguards warned that 200 tons of oil had leaked from the *MSC Napoli* after it beached off Beer Head, Devon. ❦ 25 US troops died in Iraq, as a further 3,000 were drafted in to boost numbers. {22} >130 died in attacks across Iraq. ❦ Coastguards began pumping oil from the stricken *MSC Napoli*. ❦ Channel 4 executives ordered a review of *Celebrity Big Brother*, but declined to take the series off air. {23} Hundreds of scavengers descended on Beer Head to seize booty washed ashore from the *MSC Napoli*. ❦ 5 men were arrested across Britain in relation to suspected terror offences. ❦ Pro-Hezbollah protesters blockaded the streets of Beirut in an attempt to unseat the ruling administration. {24} In his State of the Union address Bush warned that failure in Iraq would have 'grievous' consequences. {26} Prison overcrowding hit the news after a sex offender was spared jail when a judge followed the Home Sec's plea to keep all but the most serious offenders out of prison. ❦ The Royal Editor of the *News of the World*, Clive Goodman, was jailed for 4 months for plotting to intercept Royal phone messages. {27} Tens of thousands protested in Washington demanding US troops withdraw from Iraq. {28} >250 Iraqi militants were killed after fighting

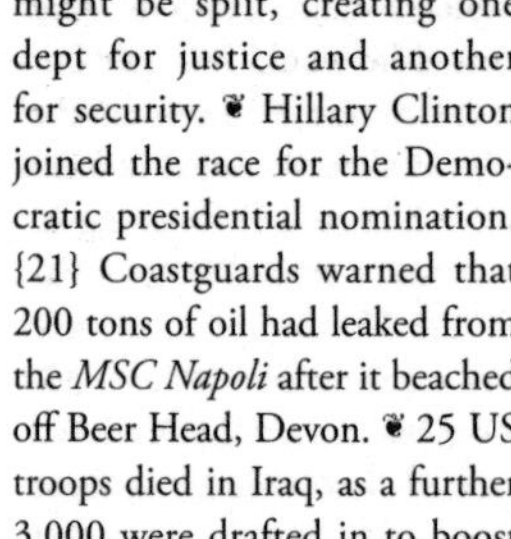

Hillary Clinton

I am proud to have played for two of the biggest clubs in football.
– DAVID BECKHAM

IN BRIEF · JANUARY – FEBRUARY 2007

with Iraqi and US troops around Najaf. ❦ Sinn Féin voted to support a police force in N Ireland for the first time, raising hopes that power-sharing could be re-established. ❦ Shilpa Shetty won *Celebrity Big Brother* [see p.27]. {29} Beleaguered Home Sec John Reid insisted he would not quit but would continue to reform the Home Office. ❦ 3 died in Eilat in the first suicide bombing in Israel since April 2006. ❦ Fatah and Hamas agreed a truce after fighting had killed >30. {30} The Casino Advisory Panel selected Manchester to host Britain's first 'super-casino'. {31} Lord Levy was re-arrested in relation to the 'cash-for-honours' inquiry; he denied any wrongdoing and was released on bail without charge. The CPS has since announced that no one will face charges following the investigation [see p.29]. ❦ 8 suspected terrorists were arrested in Birmingham; it was later alleged they were plotting to kidnap and murder a Muslim British soldier.

Shilpa Shetty

FEBRUARY · {1} It emerged that Tony Blair had been interviewed by police for a second time in relation to the 'cash-for-honours' inquiry; the police had embargoed the news for a week for 'operational reasons'. ❦ >58 died and hundreds were injured in a double suicide attack in Hilla, Iraq. {2} Community leaders in Birmingham urged calm, 2 days after local men were arrested on suspicion of terror offences. ❦ Fresh fighting erupted between Fatah and Hamas in Gaza, breaking the recently agreed truce; *c.*10 died. ❦ The Intergovernmental Panel on Climate Change reported [see p.22]. ❦ >20 died and >340,000 were made homeless after flash floods in Jakarta, Indonesia. ❦ >19 died when a tornado struck Florida. {3} It was confirmed that the Asian strain of bird flu had killed 2,600 turkeys at a Bernard Matthews farm in Suffolk; thousands of birds were culled as a precaution. ❦ >130 died when a lorry bomb was detonated at a busy market in Baghdad. {4} 16-year-old James Andre Smartt-Ford was shot dead at an ice rink in Streatham, London. {5} A British soldier was killed by a roadside bomb near Basra. ❦ A female worker sustained hand injuries when a letter bomb exploded at the London HQ of Capita. {6} The *Sun* obtained a video recording from the cockpit of a US fighter plane at the centre of the friendly-fire incident in 2003 which killed Lance Corporal Matty Hull; the video reportedly showed US soldiers weeping after realising their error. The British coroner had been refused access to the tape by US authorities. ❦ The cull of 159,000 birds at the Bernard Matthews farm in Suffolk was completed. ❦ A 15-year-old boy was murdered in his bed in Peckham, London. ❦ A 2nd letter bomb injured 2 workers at Vantis in Wokingham. {7} 2 of the 9 men arrested in an anti-terror operation in Birmingham were released without charge. ❦ A parcel bomb exploded at the DVLA offices in Swansea, injuring a worker; police warned that a disgruntled motorist might be targeting motoring-related companies. {8} RIP @ 39, *Playboy* model Anna Nicole Smith [see p.56]. ❦ Fatah and Hamas signed a deal to create a unified Palestinian government, but stopped short of recognising Israel. ❦ The UK was blanketed by the heaviest

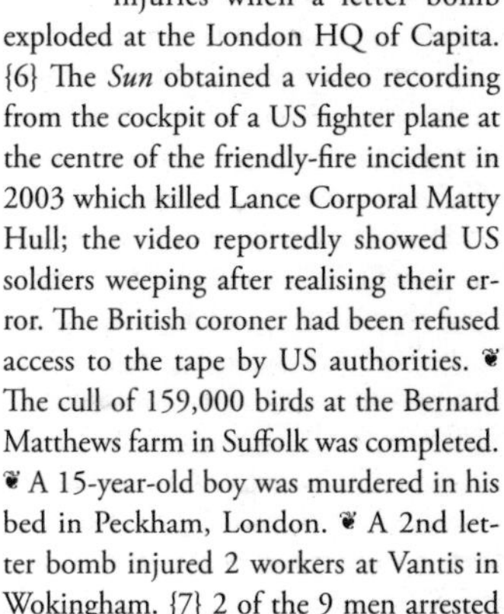

It is our turn to make this agreement work and to make this agreement stick.
– KHALED MESHAAL, Hamas

IN BRIEF · FEBRUARY – MARCH 2007

snowfall in 11 years. {9} A 36-year-old Birmingham man was charged with plotting to kidnap and kill a British soldier; 4 others were charged with supplying equipment and funding terrorism. {10} Senator Barack Obama announced he was a candidate for the Democratic presidential nomination. ❦ A new biography of David Cameron alleged that he smoked cannabis as a schoolboy at Eton; Cameron refused to comment. {11} The US military accused Iran of supplying insurgents in Iraq with sophisticated roadside bombs. ❦ Dame Helen Mirren won the best actress Bafta for her portrayal of the Queen. {12} >70 died when 3 bombs exploded in Baghdad. {13} After talks in Beijing, N Korea agreed to close its main nuclear reactor in return for fuel aid. ❦ 2 bombs exploded in Lebanon, killing 2 and injuring >20. ❦ 3 young men were arrested after a 2-year-old girl, Casey Leigh Mullen, was found murdered. ❦ The Independent Police Complaints Cmsn ordered the Metropolitan Police to apologise to the 2 men arrested in the Forest Gate 'anti-terror' raid in 6/06. {14} 11 died in a bus bomb in Iran, aimed at the Revolutionary Guard. ❦ A 15-year-old boy was shot dead in his home in Clapham, S London. ❦ The Brit Awards were broadcast live [see p.138]. ❦ A 21-year-old Leeds man was charged with the rape and murder of his 2-year-old niece, Casey Leigh Mullen. {15} The trial began in Spain of 29 accused of involvement in the 2004 Madrid bombs which killed 191. {17} A suicide bomber killed >15 in Quetta, Pakistan. {18} >60 died in 3 separate car bombs in Shia areas of Baghdad. {19} >65 died when a bomb exploded on a train travelling from India to Pakistan; it was thought the blast was an attempt to disrupt peace talks. ❦ A Cambridgeshire man was arrested in connection with the recent spate of letter bombs. {21} Blair announced the withdrawal of 1,600 troops from Iraq. ❦ It was announced that Prince Harry's regiment would be deployed to Iraq. {22} A report by the IAEA indicated that Iran had ignored the latest UN deadline and was extending uranium enrichment. {23} An elderly woman was killed and 5 were injured after a train derailed in Cumbria. ❦ It was announced that >1,000 extra British troops would be sent to Afghanistan. {24} A faulty set of points was blamed for causing the Cumbria rail crash; Network Rail promised to check >700 other points. {25} The 79th Academy Awards were held [see p.150]. {26} Cleric Abu Qatada lost his appeal against deportation to Jordan. ❦ A UN court cleared Serbia of genocide during the Bosnian war, but ruled that it had failed to stop the Srebrenica massacre. {27} Charles Clarke and Alan Milburn sent an email to Labour MPs, calling for an 'open debate' on the party's future – a move interpreted as an attempt to find a challenger to Gordon Brown. {28} Drivers across the southeast complained that contaminated petrol had damaged their cars.

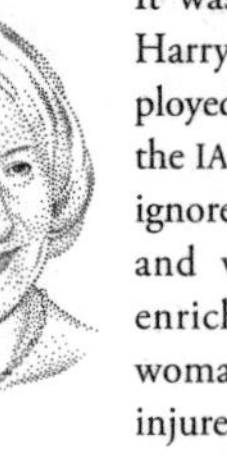
Helen Mirren

One thing I'm convinced of… is that people want something new.
– BARACK OBAMA

MARCH · {2} The High Court ruled that a jury should hear the 2 inquests into the death of Diana and Dodi. ❦ The Attorney-General obtained an injunction preventing the BBC from broadcasting a story about the 'cash-for-honours' probe. ❦ 5 British embassy staff and their rela-

IN BRIEF · MARCH 2007

tives were kidnapped during a sightseeing trip in Ethiopia. ❦ 14 Iraqi policemen were found dead in Baghdad. {3} Supermarkets cleared their pumps of contaminated petrol. {4} 2 UK soldiers were killed in S Afghanistan. {5} A schoolgirl died after being swept away by a river in Dartmoor. ❦ ITV announced they would suspend premium-rate phone competitions, pending an investigation into a number of scandals [see p.127]. {6} A 6·3 earthquake hit Sumatra, killing >70. ❦ 9 US soldiers died in 2 bomb attacks in N Iraq. {7} 22 died after a plane burst into flames on landing at Yogyakarta airport, Indonesia; 118 survived. ❦ N Ireland went to the polls to elect the new Stormont Assembly. ❦ MPs voted in favour of a 100% elected House of Lords [see p.255]. {8} RIP @ 71, John Inman [see p.56]. ❦ Conservative MP Patrick Mercer resigned his frontbench post, after remarks he made about ethnic minority soldiers were criticised. {9} The Democratic Unionist Party came top of N Ireland's elections, taking 36 of 108 seats. ❦ The police announced that no charges would be brought over the *Celebrity Big Brother* racism row. {11} Zimbabwe opposition leader Morgan Tsvangirai was arrested while attempting to hold a political rally. {12} BBC correspondent Alan Johnston was feared kidnapped in Gaza. ❦ 4 Britons held in Ethiopia for 12 days were released. {14} RIP @ 65, *Avengers* actor Gareth Hunt. ❦ Tsvangirai was taken to intensive care after suffering injuries whilst in police custody. ❦ The government won a vote to renew Trident, despite the rebellion of 95 Labour MPs [see p.264]. ❦ A vicar was found stabbed to death outside his church

Ismail Haniya

It is critical that our viewers have absolute confidence in the services that we offer. – JOHN CRESSWELL, ITV

in S Wales. ❦ The BBC apologised after it emerged that *Blue Peter* had faked a competition [see p.127]. {15} Angelina Jolie adopted a Vietnamese boy [see p.115]. ❦ After months of negotiations, Palestinian PM Ismail Haniya revealed a national unity cabinet. ❦ Culture Sec Tessa Jowell announced that the bill for the 2012 Olympics had risen to £9·35bn. ❦ The trial of media mogul Conrad Black opened in Chicago; he was accused of racketeering, fraud, and tax evasion. {16} A coroner ruled that the killing of Lance Corporal Matty Hull by US soldiers in a 'friendly fire' incident in Iraq was unlawful. ❦ Sally Clark, the solicitor wrongly accused of murdering her 2 baby sons, died aged 42. ❦ 11 Iraqi detainees escaped from a UK-run military prison near Basra. {17} The new Wembley Stadium opened for the first time, to host a community event. {18} 15-year-old Adam Regis was stabbed to death in E London. ❦ It was announced that Pakistan cricket coach Bob Woolmer had died the day after his team was knocked out of the Cricket World Cup [see p.27]. ❦ Zimbabwean opposition MP Nelson Chamisa was beaten with metal bars and prevented from leaving the country; the African Union urged Mugabe to respect human rights. {19} ITN revealed the names of 16 US troops they asserted were present when reporter Terry Lloyd was unlawfully killed in S Iraq. {20} Former Iraqi VP, Taha Yassin Ramadan, was hanged for his part in the murder of Shias in the 1980s. ❦ The US and EU agreed to maintain sanctions against the Palestinians until the Palestinians recognised Israel and renounced violence. ❦ Ministers agreed that schools could ban

IN BRIEF · MARCH – APRIL 2007

children from wearing a full-face veil on security, safety, or learning grounds [see p.290]. {21} Jamaican police announced that the death of Bob Woolmer was being treated as suspicious [see p.27]. ❦ Gordon Brown's 11th Budget [see p.228]. ❦ 2 British soldiers were killed in an accident on a nuclear submarine in the Arctic. ❦ 4 were arrested in connection with the death of Adam Regis. {22} 3 men were arrested in connection with 7/7 London bombings. {23} Jamaican police announced they were treating Woolmer's death as murder, after a pathologist asserted Woolmer had been strangled. ❦ 72 died in an explosion at a weapons depot in Mozambique. ❦ 15 British naval personnel were captured at gunpoint by Iranian forces, who accused them of entering Iranian waters [see p.28]. {24} The UN voted to increase sanctions against Iran over its nuclear programme. {25} Blair denounced Iran's holding of UK naval personnel as 'unjustified and wrong'. {27} 50 died and >125 injured when 2 truck bombs exploded in Talafar, N Iraq. {28} Iranian state TV broadcast pictures of captured Leading Seaman Faye Turney 'apologising' for trespassing in Iranian waters; the Iranian Foreign Minister said she would be released shortly. ❦ 22-year-old English woman Lindsay Ann Hawker was found dead in a bath full of sand on the balcony of a Tokyo apartment. {29} Southern African leaders nominated S African President Thabo Mbeki to mediate between Robert Mugabe and Zimbabwean opposition parties. {30} ❦ Network Rail was fined £4m for safety breaches that contributed to the 1999 Paddington rail crash in which 31 died. {31} Confidential papers released by the Treasury reportedly indicated that Gordon Brown had been forewarned that measures in his 1997 Budget would create a pension shortfall.

M. Ahmadinejad

APRIL · {1} ❦ British resident Bisher al-Rawi returned to the UK after 5 years in Guantánamo Bay. ❦ Foreign Sec Margaret Beckett sent a diplomatic note to Iran, requesting the release of the 15 naval personnel. {2} A ban on smoking in enclosed public spaces came into force in Wales [see p.25]. ❦ EMI announced it would remove digital 'locks' from its downloadable music [see p.142]. ❦ A British soldier died while on patrol in Basra. {3} A French TGV train set a new speed record of 356mph. ❦ Brian 'The Milkman' Wright was jailed for 30 years after police smashed his drug-smuggling empire. {4} In a surprise move, Iranian President Ahmadinejad announced all 15 British naval personnel would be released immediately, as a 'gift' to Britain. ❦ Violence marred Manchester Utd's match against AS Roma at the Stadio Olimpico; 11 Man Utd fans were taken to hospital. {5} The freed naval personnel returned to the UK and were reunited with their families. ❦ 4 British soldiers were killed by a roadside bomb near Basra. ❦ 3 men were charged in connection with the 7/7 London bombings. {6} A pregnant 22-year-old, Krystal Hart, was found shot dead at her flat in Clapham, London; police speculated her death may have involved a parking dispute. {7} >40 died in sectarian fighting in NW Pakistan. {8} The MoD sparked controversy by permitting the freed naval personnel to sell their stories to the media. {9} The

Captured personnel being paraded and manipulated in this way doesn't fool anyone. – TONY BLAIR

IN BRIEF · APRIL 2007

MoD reversed their decision over the selling of stories; Faye Turney and Arthur Batchelor had already sold their accounts to the press. ❦ Ahmadinejad announced that Iran could produce uranium on an industrial scale. ❦ A 40-year-old man was charged with the murder of Krystal Hart. {10} Somerset introduced a pilot scheme that allowed parents to ascertain if any convicted paedophiles lived in their area. {12} 23 died in blasts in the Algerian capital; al-Qaeda claimed responsibility. ❦ RIP @ 84, writer Kurt Vonnegut. ❦ A bomb exploded in the Iraqi parliament's café, killing >8 (2 were MPs). ❦ World Bank President Paul Wolfowitz issued a statement apologising for 'mistakes' made when his romantic partner was given a pay rise and promotion by the Bank in 2005. {14} It was reported that Prince William had split from his long-term girlfriend Kate Middleton [see p.275]. ❦ >36 died in a suicide car bomb attack in Karbala, Iraq. ❦ Silver Birch won the Grand National. ❦ Russian chess champion Garry Kasparov was arrested in Moscow for attempting to organise an anti-Kremlin rally. {15} 2 British soldiers died in a mid-air helicopter collision N of Baghdad. ❦ According to reports, a Palestinian group claimed to have killed kidnapped Alan Johnston; the BBC stressed the story had not been verified. ❦ Cameron said Defence Sec Des Browne should consider resigning over his decision to allow naval personnel to sell their stories. ❦ The World Bank's Oversight Cmte expressed 'great concern' over the Wolfowitz controversy; Wolfowitz said he intended to remain in his post. {16} 32 were murdered by a student in a shooting at Virginia Tech; it was the deadliest shooting in US history [see p.20]. ❦ Defence Sec Browne apologised for allowing the naval personnel to sell their stories, and launched an inquiry into the Iranian incident. {17} £1 became worth >$2 for the first time since 1992. {18} England slunk out of the Cricket World Cup after a lacklustre performance against S Africa [see p.296]. ❦ >200 died in sectarian violence across Baghdad. {19} A US TV station broadcast footage from the 'media manifesto' sent to them by Virginia Tech gunman on the morning of the massacre. ❦ 2 British soldiers were killed and 3 injured in SE Iraq. ❦ Bernard Matthews received *c.*£600,000 in compensation for the healthy turkeys culled during the bird flu outbreak in Suffolk. ❦ Duncan Fletcher resigned as England's cricket coach after a disappointing World Cup. {20} The police handed their file on the 'cash-for-honours' investigation to the Crown Prosecution Service. {21} Arabic TV aired a video of a 12-year-old Afghan boy beheading a man said to have been spying for America. {22} The London Marathon was run [see p.299]. {23} A BBC Panorama investigation alleged that GMTV had defrauded its viewers out of thousands of pounds in a phone-in competition scandal; in response GMTV sacked their phone-in provider [see p.127]. ❦ RIP @ 76, Boris Yeltsin [see p.56]. ❦ Umaru Yar'Adua won Nigeria's presidential elections with 70% of the vote; EU observers called the election a 'charade'. ❦ A 22-year-old male runner taken ill after completing the London Marathon died in hospital. {24} Japanese businessman Joji Obara was cleared of raping and killing British air hostess

Prince William

> *The university was struck today with a tragedy of monumental proportions.*
> – VA Tech Pres. CHARLES STEGER

IN BRIEF · APRIL – MAY 2007

Lucie Blackman; he was convicted of the rape of 9 other women and jailed for life. ❦ 9 US soldiers were killed in a suicide attack on their base in N Iraq. ❦ Separatists attacked a Chinese-run oil facility in Ethiopia, killing 65 Ethiopians and 9 Chinese. {25} RIP @ 61, Alan Ball. ❦ The trial of Phil Spector opened in Los Angeles. ❦ Boris Yeltsin was buried in Moscow. {27} RIP @ 80, Mstislav Rostropovich [see p.56]. {28} A 4·3 earthquake struck the Kent coast damaging many houses and cutting off electricity to the area. ❦ A car bomb killed >55 in Karbala, Iraq. {29} Australia won the Cricket World Cup [see p.296]. {30} A smoking ban came into force in N Ireland [see p.25]. ❦ 5 men were jailed for life for their part in a plot to blow up a UK nightclub and shopping centre with a fertiliser bomb. ❦ Nato-led troops killed >100 Taleban fighters in a major offensive in, Afghanistan.

Nicolas Sarkozy

MAY · {1} MI5 faced a parliamentary inquiry after it was revealed that, in the course of the 'fertiliser bomb plot' investigation, agents tailed two of the 7/7 bombers but failed to follow up the lead. ❦ The Interior Ministry of Iraq announced that Abu Ayyub al-Masri, the alleged leader of al-Qaeda in Iraq, had been killed during a battle between insurgents. ❦ >30 were arrested across UK, Belgium, and the Netherlands in connection with animal rights extremism. ❦ A 17-year-old boy was arrested after allegedly shooting his 12-year-old sister; she later died in hospital. ❦ >30 civilians died during a Nato offensive in W Afghanistan. {2} Bush vetoed a bill that tied Iraq war funding to a timetable for troop withdrawal. ❦ Blair rejected calls for an independent inquiry into the 7/7 London bombings. ❦ Israeli PM Olmert faced calls to resign after a critical report into the Lebanon war was released. {3} Voters across England, Wales, and Scotland went to the polls [see p.21]. ❦ The Ulster Volunteer Force announced it was renouncing violence and would disband from midnight. ❦ 3-year-old British girl Madeleine McCann was reported missing from a holiday apartment in Praia da Luz, Portugal – she was reportedly snatched from her bed while her parents ate at a nearby restaurant. {4} The Scottish National Party became Scotland's largest party [see p.21]. ❦ Kate and Gerry McCann, the parents of missing Madeleine, made an emotional appeal for her return. ❦ Charles Clarke announced he would not challenge Brown for the Labour leadership. {5} Portuguese police announced they had identified a suspect in the abduction of Madeleine. ❦ A Kenyan plane carrying 144 people, including 5 Britons, crashed in Cameroon. {6} Nicolas Sarkozy won the French Presidency with 53% of the vote. ❦ Home Sec John Reid announced he would resign from the Cabinet when Blair left. ❦ A Baghdad car bomb killed 33. ❦ Manchester Utd secured the Premiership title after Chelsea failed to beat Arsenal [see p.304]. {7} 6 died in one of the worst-ever crashes on the M25; 5 of the dead were from the same stag party. ❦ The Queen met Bush at the White House. ❦ RIP @ 86, former Speaker of the Commons, Lord Weatherill. {8} Devolution returned to N Ireland; Ian Paisley and Martin McGuinness took their pledges

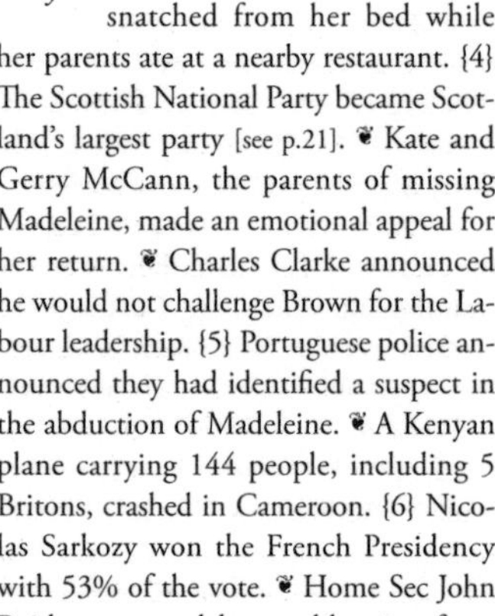

We have been moved by the enormous willingness of people to … help find Madeleine. – GERRY MCCANN

IN BRIEF · MAY 2007

of office [see p.30]. ❦ Portuguese police said they could not be sure Madeleine was still alive. ❦ John Higgins beat Mark Selby in an epic World Championship Snooker final at the Crucible [see p.317]. ❦ RIP @ 48, Isabella Blow [see p.56]. {9} 4 were arrested in connection with 7/7 London bombings, including the widow of one of the bombers. {10} Blair announced he would step down as PM on 27/6 [see p.16]. ❦ The Bank of England raised interest rates to 5·5% [see p.237]. {11} Brown launched his leadership campaign. ❦ The Independent Police Complaints Cmsn announced that 11 police officers involved in the shooting of Jean Charles de Menezes would not face disciplinary action. {12} Gerry McCann paid tribute to Madeleine at a church service in Praia da Luz, on the occasion of her 4th birthday. ❦ Serbia won the Eurovision Song Contest amid controversy about E European 'block voting' [see p.140]. ❦ Political factions clashed in Pakistan; 34 died and >120 were injured. {13} Nato announced it had killed Mullah Dadullah, the Taleban's military leader in Afghanistan. {14} A 21-year-old man was stabbed to death in Merseyside, in what police called a 'targeted, racially motivated' murder. ❦ Palestinian Interior Minister Hani Qawasmi resigned over the growing factional violence in Gaza; Egypt attempted to broker a peace deal. {15} 7 died after Hamas ambushed a group of pro-Fatah soldiers. ❦ 4 held in relation to the 7/7 bombings were released without charge. ❦ A man treated as a suspect in the search for Madeleine claimed he was an innocent scapegoat; Portuguese police admitted they had insufficient evidence to charge him. {16} Sarkozy was sworn in as President of France. ❦ It was announced that Prince Harry would not serve in Iraq because of security threats. ❦ Brown secured the backing of 308 MPs, seeing off any leadership challenge [see p.16]. ❦ >17 died in Gaza in fighting between Fatah, Hamas, and Israel. {17} Estonia alleged that Russia had been launching cyber-attacks on Estonian websites since a Soviet war memorial in Tallinn was moved in late April. {18} Channel Five won the rights to Aussie soap *Neighbours* after the BBC withdrew from the bidding. {19} Chelsea beat Manchester Utd in the first FA Cup Final at the new Wembley Stadium [see p.306]. {20} >40 died as Lebanese soldiers clashed with Palestinian refugees. {21} A fire destroyed much of the *Cutty Sark*; arson was suspected. ❦ A British soldier was killed in Iraq after his convoy was ambushed near Basra. {22} >24 died when a car bomb exploded in a Baghdad market. ❦ The CPS announced it had enough evidence to charge former KGB officer Andrei Lugovoi with the murder of Litvinenko; British representatives asked Russia to begin extradition. ❦ Ruth Kelly delayed the introduction of Home Information Packs until August [see p.31]. {23} Thousands of Palestinians fled from the Nahr al-Bared refugee camp, where Lebanese soldiers and Fatah al-Islam fighters had clashed. ❦ 3 suspected terrorists held under 'control orders' went on the run. ❦ AC Milan beat Liverpool 2–1 in the Champions League final [see p.305]. {24} Israel took captive 30 Hamas officials, including the Education Minister, claiming they supported the firing of rockets into Israel. {26} 4 Palestinians died in Israeli

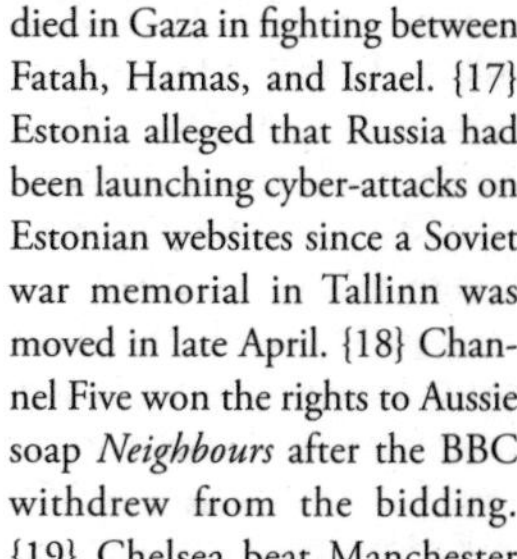
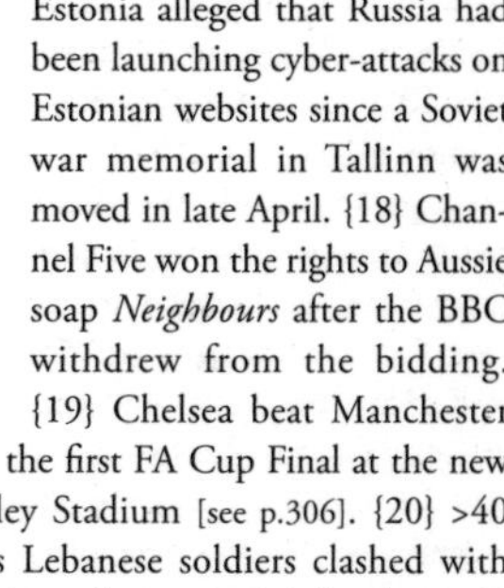

Prince Harry

I will hire serious lawyers in London in order to defend my honest name.
– ANDREI LUGOVOI

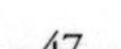

IN BRIEF · MAY – JUNE 2007

air strikes on Gaza. {28} A British soldier was killed in Helmand. {29} 5 Britons were kidnapped in Baghdad; the financial analyst and his bodyguards were seized by a group of men in Iraqi police uniform. ❦ Bush appointed Robert Zoellick to replace Wolfowitz as head of the World Bank. {31} Lugovoi claimed the UK secret services were responsible for Litvinenko's poisoning. ❦ 7 died, including 1 British soldier, when a Nato helicopter was shot down by the Taleban in Helmand. ❦ Former *News of the World* editor, Andy Coulson, was appointed as Director of Communications for the Conservative Party.

2012 London Olympic logo

JUNE · {1} A video was released on the internet by the Army of Islam, showing pictures of Johnston and demanding the release of Abu Qatada. ❦ Fighting between Islamic militants and the Lebanese army in Nahr al-Bared intensified, killing 14. {2} After 15 attempts, Frankie Dettori finally won the Derby, riding *Authorized.* {3} Putin threatened to aim missiles at European targets if America persisted with its controversial E European missile shield. ❦ John Prescott was admitted to hospital with a suspected chest infection. {4} The war crimes trial of ex-leader of Liberia Charles Taylor opened in The Hague. ❦ Paris Hilton began a 23-day prison sentence in LA for violating parole on her drink-driving conviction. ❦ The logo for the 2012 London Olympics was unveiled; within hours >8,000 had signed a petition condemning the design. {5} 8 died and >40 injured in a train crash in S Australia. ❦ It was announced that John Prescott was suffering from pneumonia and had been moved to a high-dependency unit. ❦ Former aide to Dick Cheney, Lewis Libby, was sentenced to 30 months in jail for perjury and obstructing justice. ❦ The G8 Summit opened in Heiligendamm, Germany, amid growing tensions between Russia and the West. {7} Contestant Emily Parr was evicted from the '*Big Brother* house' after using the word 'nigger'; she said she meant no offence. ❦ A British soldier was shot dead during a patrol in S Iraq. ❦ At the G8 Summit, Merkel announced a new agreement to tackle climate change. ❦ Paris Hilton was released from jail for medical reasons after serving just 3 days.

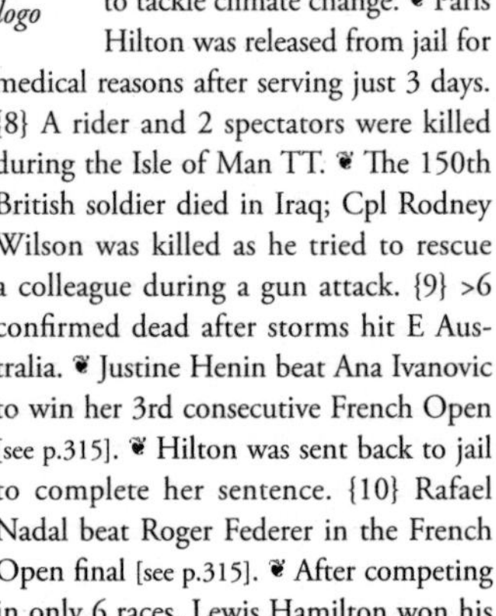

{8} A rider and 2 spectators were killed during the Isle of Man TT. ❦ The 150th British soldier died in Iraq; Cpl Rodney Wilson was killed as he tried to rescue a colleague during a gun attack. {9} >6 confirmed dead after storms hit E Australia. ❦ Justine Henin beat Ana Ivanovic to win her 3rd consecutive French Open [see p.315]. ❦ Hilton was sent back to jail to complete her sentence. {10} Rafael Nadal beat Roger Federer in the French Open final [see p.315]. ❦ After competing in only 6 races, Lewis Hamilton won his first Grand Prix in Montreal [see p.316]. {11} A policeman was stabbed to death and 2 others suffered stab injuries during an incident in Luton. {12} 7 Afghan policemen were killed by US soldiers during a 'friendly fire' incident in Nangarhar. ❦ Jamaican police announced that Bob Woolmer had, in fact, died of natural causes [see p.27]. ❦ Blair attacked the media during a speech [see p.11]. {13} Fighting between Hamas and Fatah escalated in Gaza, as the factions struggled for control; 80 people have been killed so far.

> *My sons and I are relieved to be officially informed that Bob died of natural causes.* – GILL WOOLMER

IN BRIEF · JUNE 2007

❦ Palestinian President Abbas dismissed the Hamas-led coalition and declared a state of emergency in the Palestinian Authority. ❦ Michael Barrymore and 2 other men were arrested in connection with the 2001 death of Stuart Lubbock. ❦ RIP @ 88, Kurt Waldheim, former UN Sec Gen [see p.56]. {14} Bertie Ahern was re-elected as Irish Taoiseach after securing a coalition. {15} Hamas took full control of Gaza. ❦ Barrymore was released from police custody without charge. ❦ Flooding caused chaos across GB; >40 flood warnings were issued [see p.26]. {16} Ian Botham and Salman Rushdie received knighthoods in the Queen's Birthday Honours [see p.279]. {17} 10,000 took part in a ceremony on Horse Guard's Parade to mark the 25th anniversary of the Falklands conflict. ❦ Palestinian President Abbas swore in a new emergency government, excluding members of Hamas; America announced it would restore aid to the region. ❦ RIP @ 62, designer Gianfranco Ferre. {18} Police smashed a British-run internet paedophile ring, rescuing 31 children from abuse. ❦ Protests were held in Pakistan against Rushdie's knighthood; a Pakistani minister claimed the honour might inspire terrorists. ❦ RIP @ 76, Bernard Manning [see p.57]. ❦ 7 children were killed in Paktika, Afghanistan, after a US-led attack on a suspected al-Qaeda hideout. ❦ Michael Vaughan announced he was stepping down as England's one-day cricket captain. {19} It was mooted that some non-violent prisoners might be released from jail early to stem overcrowding; the prison population in England and Wales hit >81,000 [see p.108]. ❦ 2 separate inquiries into the kidnapping of the 15 British Navy personnel reported that, although mistakes had been made, no individual should be singled out for blame. ❦ >78 died in a truck bombing near a Shia mosque in Baghdad. {20} RIP @ 82, Piara Khabra, the oldest serving MP. ❦ The 152nd British soldier to be killed in Iraq died near Basra. {22} Attorney-General Lord Goldsmith announced he would stand down with Blair. ❦ Nato's Sec Gen Jaap de Hoop Scheffer announced an investigation into the death of 25 Afghan civilians in a Nato air strike in Helmand; Afghan President Karzai warned that further civilian deaths might turn Afghans against Nato. {23} Blair announced a new European Treaty had been agreed that allowed the UK to opt out of the charter on human and social rights, and to continue to have an independent foreign policy. ❦ Thierry Henry announced he was leaving Arsenal for Barcelona. ❦ A 16-year-old boy was stabbed to death after a street fight with up to 40 youths in Beckenham, Kent. {24} Harriet Harman was voted Deputy Leader of the Labour party [see p.17]. ❦ 6 UN peacekeepers died in Lebanon after their vehicle was hit by an IED. ❦ Ali Hassan al-Majid (aka 'Chemical Ali') was sentenced to death by a court in Baghdad for the genocide of 180,000 Kurds in 1988. {25} A man died in Hull after being trapped in a flooded drain, after torrential rain fell over much of Britain. ❦ Wimbledon started [see p.314]. {26} Hundreds were evacuated from their S Yorkshire homes after fears that a reservoir was about to burst its banks; in Sheffield, a 68-year-old man and a 13-year-old boy died in severe flooding. ❦ The US Dept

Salman Rushdie

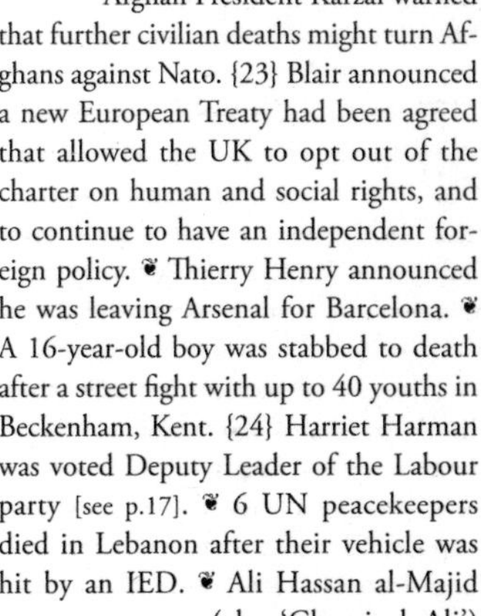

River levels are dropping and obviously a massive clean up is under way.
– DAVID ROOKE, Environment Agency

IN BRIEF · JUNE – JULY 2007

of Justice announced it would investigate BAE over allegations of corruption in a deal with Saudi Arabia. {26} Tory MP Quentin Davies defected to Labour. {27} A teenager was stabbed to death in Islington, London. ❦ At Buckingham Palace, the Queen asked Gordon Brown to form a government [see p.17]. ❦ Floods in Sheffield and Worcestershire continued to wreak havoc; a 5th person died after becoming trapped in a car. ❦ Blair was appointed envoy to the Middle East hours after resigning as an MP [see p.29]. {28} 3 British soldiers were killed and one was seriously injured when a roadside bomb exploded near Basra. ❦ Brown unveiled his first Cabinet [see p.251]. ❦ Abdelbaset Ali Mohmed al-Megrahi, the man jailed for the Lockerbie bombing, was granted leave to launch a new appeal. ❦ Tim Henman was knocked out of Wimbledon by Feliciano Lopez in a 5-set thriller [see p.314]. {29} Two car bombs were discovered in central London; they were defused by police [see p.29]. ❦ 800,000 in Pakistan were displaced by a cyclone; floods hit coastal regions in Balochistan province. ❦ The US Supreme Court agreed to hear an appeal by Guantánamo Bay captives who wished to challenge their detention. {29} 2 men rammed a burning car into the terminal building at Glasgow airport; both were arrested at the scene [see p.29]. ❦ 2 were arrested on the M6 in connection with the 'terror' incidents in London and Glasgow. The UK threat level was raised to 'Critical'. ❦ Israel launched air strikes on Gaza, killing 7 Palestinians. ❦ Amidst scenes of technophile excitement, Apple's much anticipated iPhone went on sale in the US.

Alan Johnston

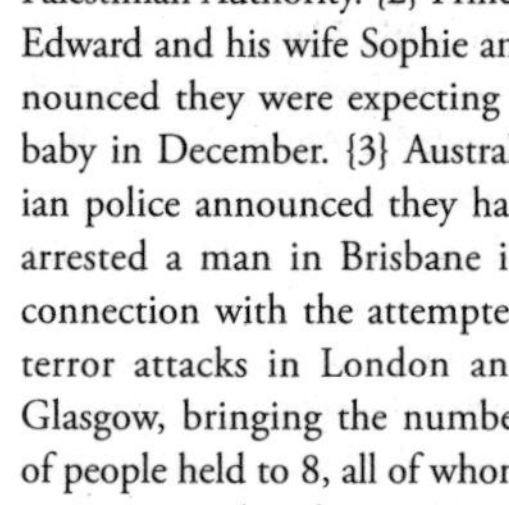

JULY · {1} The smoking ban came into force in England [see p.25]. ❦ Princes William and Harry hosted a concert to mark the 10th anniversary of the death of their mother. ❦ Israel released millions of dollars of funds to the Palestinian Authority. {2} Prince Edward and his wife Sophie announced they were expecting a baby in December. {3} Australian police announced they had arrested a man in Brisbane in connection with the attempted terror attacks in London and Glasgow, bringing the number of people held to 8, all of whom were reported to have connections to the NHS. ❦ President Bush commuted the jail sentence of I. Lewis Libby (a former aide to Dick Cheney) who was earlier convicted of perjury. ❦ >16 died when Pakistani troops clashed with Islamists at Islamabad's Red Mosque; leaders of the mosque had been campaigning for Sharia law to be imposed. Hundreds of militants and students remained inside the mosque, many of whom refused to leave. {4} Alan Johnston was released after 114 days of captivity in Gaza. ❦ The terror threat was reduced from 'Critical' to 'Severe'. ❦ 15 died in a car bomb at a checkpoint in Ramadi, Iraq. ❦ The leader of the Red Mosque in Islamabad, Maulana Abdul Aziz, was caught trying to escape disguised in a burqa; >700 students surrendered and left the mosque as the siege continued. {5} RIP @ 80, George Melly [see p.57]. ❦ A 3-year-old British girl was kidnapped by gunmen in Nigeria. ❦ The Bank of England raised interest rates to 5·75% [see p.237]. {6} More doctors were arrested by police in Australia in connection with the London and Glasgow terror plots. ❦ An

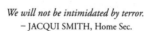

We will not be intimidated by terror.
– JACQUI SMITH, Home Sec.

IN BRIEF · JULY 2007

Iraqi doctor was charged with conspiracy to cause explosions at Glasgow airport. ❦ The insurance industry announced that claims relating to the floods in parts of England and Wales could total *c.*£1·5bn. ❦ The Labour party in Wales voted by a large majority to form a coalition with Plaid Cymru. {7} >105 died when a truck bomb exploded in Amirli, N Iraq. ❦ A series of Live Earth concerts were held around the world to raise awareness of climate change. ❦ Alan Johnston was reunited with his family in the UK. ❦ Venus Williams beat Marion Bartoli to secure her 4th Wimbledon title [see p.314]. {8} After 4 days of captivity, kidnappers in Nigeria freed the 3-year-old British girl unharmed. ❦ Roger Federer beat Rafael Nadal to win his 5th consecutive Wimbledon title [see p.314]. {9} Muktar Ibrahim, Yassin Omar, Ramzi Mohammed, and Hussain Osman were found guilty of conspiring to carry out suicide bomb attacks in London on 21/7/05; 2 other men faced a re-trial. {10} Pakistani troops stormed the Red Mosque in Islamabad: >50 militants and 8 soldiers died; *c.*50 women and children were rescued. ❦ Ayman al-Zawahiri, al-Qaeda's 2nd in command, warned the UK could be targeted over the decision to honour Rushdie [see p.279]. {11} The 4 men convicted of the 21/7 London bomb plot were sentenced to life in prison with a minimum tariff of 40 years. {12} RIP @ 65, Nigel Dempster. {13} 2 16-year-old London girls were charged with drug smuggling after they were arrested at Accra airport in Ghana, allegedly carrying cocaine worth £300,000; the girls claimed they had been 'set up', and said they were innocent. ❦ Media tycoon Conrad Black was found guilty of fraud, but was cleared of racketeering and tax evasion; Black announced he would appeal. ❦ The IAEA and Iran came to an agreement over the inspection of key Iranian nuclear sites.

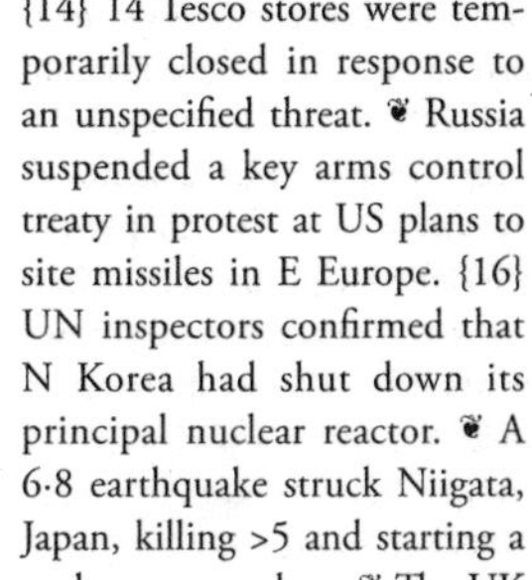
Jacqui Smith

{14} 14 Tesco stores were temporarily closed in response to an unspecified threat. ❦ Russia suspended a key arms control treaty in protest at US plans to site missiles in E Europe. {16} UN inspectors confirmed that N Korea had shut down its principal nuclear reactor. ❦ A 6·8 earthquake struck Niigata, Japan, killing >5 and starting a fire at a nuclear power plant. ❦ The UK expelled 4 Russian diplomats in response to Russia's refusal to extradite Lugovoi [see p.27]. ❦ Boris Johnson announced he would stand to run as the Tory candidate for London mayor. ❦ Police raided Newcastle, Rangers, and Portsmouth football clubs in connection with an inquiry into corruption. {17} Japan admitted a number of small nuclear leaks had occurred as a result of the 16/7 earthquake. {18} >200 died when a plane crashed in São Paulo, Brazil. ❦ Metronet, the company responsible for the upkeep of much of London's tube network, went into administration. ❦ The BBC announced it was suspending all phone-in competitions [see p.127]. ❦ Russia expelled 4 British embassy staff. {19} Home Sec. Jacqui Smith admitted she had smoked cannabis as a student; a host of other Labour MPs made similar admissions. {20} The CPS announced that no one would face charges as a result of the 'cash-for-honours' investigation [see p.29]. ❦ 3 RAF servicemen were killed near Basra. ❦ Israel began the release of >250 Palestinian prisoners

I will take very special memories of this final.
– ROGER FEDERER

IN BRIEF · JULY – AUGUST 2007

in a gesture of goodwill to Fatah. ❦ In by-elections, Labour held Sedgefield and Ealing Southall, albeit with reduced majorities; the Tories were pushed into 3rd place by the Lib Dems in both polls. ❦ Flash floods across central England and Wales left many people homeless [see p.26]. {21} Pratibha Patil was elected India's first female president. ❦ The final book in the Harry Potter septuary was released at midnight [see p.24]. {22} Continued flooding left >150,000 homes in Gloucestershire without fresh water; power was threatened across the region. ❦ Recep Tayyip Erdogan was re-elected as Turkey's PM; opponents warned his former Islamism may threaten Turkey's secular traditions. ❦ 2 Tory MPs called for a vote of no confidence in David Cameron's leadership. ❦ Negotiations began in an attempt to release 23 S Korean aid workers kidnapped by the Taleban in Ghazni, Afghanistan. ❦ Padraig Harrington won the Open [see p.311]. {24} The flood waters began to recede in some areas of central and W England and power was restored to 48,000 homes. ❦ 6 Bulgarian medics, imprisoned by Libya for 8 years for allegedly infecting Libyan children with HIV, were released and returned to Bulgaria where they were pardoned. ❦ Authorities in Hungary announced that >500 had died in a week-long heatwave. {25} >50 died and >135 were injured when 2 bombs exploded amid groups of Iraqis celebrating their national team's victory in football's Asian Cup. ❦ The Taleban killed one of the 23 S Korean hostages held in Afghanistan, as mediators continued to negotiate. ❦ Tour de France leader Michael Rasmussen was sacked by his team and removed from the Tour [see p.302]. {26} >340,000 remained without fresh tap-water in Gloucestershire, despite an easing of the flooding. ❦ A father and son died after succumbing to petrol fumes as they attempted to pump out a flooded Rugby club in Gloucestershire. {27} An Indian doctor held in Australia in relation to the Glasgow terrorist attacks was released without charge after police admitted 'a mistake has been made'. ❦ After months of legal wrangling, Shambo, a sacred bull with bovine TB, was taken from its home at a multi-faith temple in Carmarthenshire and slaughtered. ❦ >13 died when a suicide bomber struck near the Red Mosque in Islamabad, Pakistan. {28} Police found the body of 19-year-old Mitchell Taylor under flood water in Tewkesbury; he had been missing since 21/7. {29} RIP @ 67, Mike Reid [see p.??]. ❦ Spaniard Alberto Contador won the 2007 Tour de France [see p.302]. {30} RIP @ 89 Ingmar Bergman. ❦ Brown and Bush held their first formal talks, in the US. ❦ >650 died in central China after devastating storms. {31} A 2nd S Korean hostage was killed by the Taleban. ❦ The British Army ended operations in N Ireland after 38 years. ❦ RIP @ 94 Michelangelo Antonioni. ❦ The UN Security Council voted to send 26,000 peacekeeping troops to Darfur [see p.29].

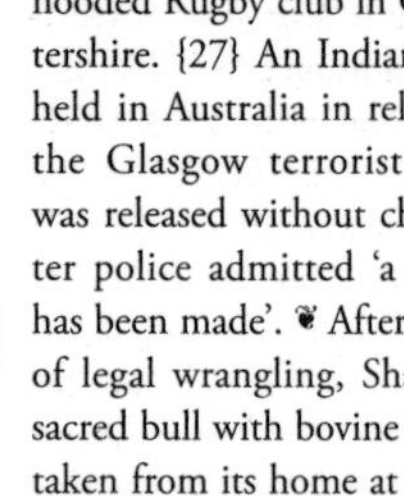
David Cameron

When I finished one chapter near the end I absolutely howled.
– J.K. ROWLING

AUGUST · {1} BA was fined a total of £270m after allegedly 'fixing' the price of fuel surcharges. {2} Kafeel Ahmed, the man seriously burned during the attack on Glasgow airport, died of his injuries. ❦ 13 died when a motorway bridge over

IN BRIEF · AUGUST 2007

the Mississippi River in Minneapolis collapsed. ❦ Actor Chris Langham was found guilty of downloading child pornography. ❦ Russia asserted her claim to the Arctic by planting a flag on the seabed 4,200m below the North Pole. {3} Foot and mouth disease was discovered in cattle on a Surrey farm; a total ban on all livestock movement was imposed. ❦ >20m were displaced and >200 died in monsoon flooding across N India, Bangladesh, and Nepal [see p.26]. {4} Brown cancelled his holiday in Dorset to attend meetings about the Surrey foot and mouth outbreak. {5} Defra revealed that the strain of foot and mouth disease found in Surrey was identical to that produced at a nearby animal disease research site at Pirbright. {6} BAA won a High Court injunction to prevent a small number of climate change pressure groups from protesting at Heathrow, but failed to get the wide-ranging ban on protests they had wanted. ❦ A further 100 cattle were culled after more cases of foot and mouth were discovered in the Surrey exclusion zone; the Health and Safety Executive announced it was likely the infection had come from a nearby research site. ❦ Media speculation over the fate of Madeleine McCann reignited after it was reported that blood splatters had been found in the girl's room in Praia da Luz. ❦ The UN warned that millions were at risk from disease after devastating floods across S Asia. {8} 2 British soldiers were killed when an IED exploded next to their patrol in Basra. {10} Global stock markets experienced another volatile day after concerns about the state of the US subprime housing market [see p.30]. ❦ RIP @ 57, Tony Wilson, Manchester music impresario. {12} A motorcyclist, Gerry Tobin, was shot dead while riding home from a biker festival on the M40 in Warwickshire. ❦ 47-year-old Garry Newlove died after being attacked by a group of youths in Warrington. ❦ Karl Rove announced he would step down as George W. Bush's senior adviser. {14} 3 teenagers were charged with the murder of Garry Newlove. ❦ N Korean state media reported that hundreds of people had died in floods across the country. ❦ >200 killed in N Iraq in attacks aimed at the Yazidi sect. ❦ Mattel recalled *c.*18m Chinese-made toys, after concerns were raised about lead paint and loose parts. ❦ The Taleban released 2 female S Korean hostages; 19 remained in captivity. {15} >450 died after an 8·0 quake struck SW Peru. ❦ Jack McConnell announced he would step down as the leader of the Scottish Labour party. {16} A-Level results improved again; 25·3% gained an A grade. {17} RIP @ 94, journalist Bill Deedes. {18} A man died, 5 were injured and 2 were missing after a fire ravaged a hotel in Newquay, Cornwall. ❦ Rescuers found 127 bodies in a collapsed church in Pisco, Peru, one of the towns hit by the earthquake. ❦ Restrictions on the movement of cattle were eased. {19} Climate change protestors camping near Heathrow began 24 hours of direct action; a number were arrested. {20} Jamaica was hit by Category 4 hurricane Dean. {21} Wendy Alexander was elected leader of Scotland's Labour party. {22} 14 US soldiers died when their Black Hawk helicopter crashed in N Iraq. ❦ 11-year-old Rhys Jones died after he was shot in the neck in a suspected gang

Mahmoud Abbas

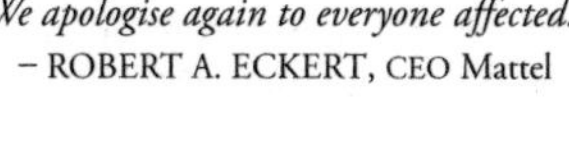

We apologise again to everyone affected.
– ROBERT A. ECKERT, CEO Mattel

IN BRIEF · AUGUST – SEPTEMBER 2007

related incident in Croxteth, Liverpool. ❦ 4 men were arrested in connection with the murder of Gerry Tobin. {23} GCSE results were released; 63·3% got grades C–A*. ❦ Henman announced he would retire after the Davis Cup [see p.315]. {24} 3 British soldiers were killed in Afghanistan by suspected US 'friendly fire'. ❦ >15 died in S Greece as a result of extensive wildfires. ❦ C4 announced they would 'rest' the next series of *Celebrity Big Brother*. {25} 7 were questioned over the murder of Rhys Jones. ❦ The Greek PM announced a state of emergency, after >200 wildfires killed >47, and threatened thousands of homes; arson was suspected in many blazes. {26} The Duchess of Cornwall pulled out of a memorial service for Diana, Princess of Wales. {27} US Attorney General Alberto Gonzales resigned amidst ongoing controversy relating to his dismissal of 8 US attorneys. {28} Former Islamist Abdullah Gul was sworn in as Turkey's new president. {29} The Taleban freed 12 of the 19 S Korean hostages they were holding in Afghanistan. ❦ A 15-year-old boy was arrested on suspicion of murdering Rhys Jones. ❦ 20,000 prison staff walked out in a surprise strike. ❦ Radical cleric Moqtada Sadr announced he would freeze the activities of his Mehdi militia for 6 months. ❦ 3 men were shot dead, 2 women were injured, and a 3-year-old girl survived unscathed after a 'targeted' attack on a family in Bishop's Stortford. {30} The Taleban released the final 7 S Korean hostages, ending a 6-week ordeal. {31} The 10th anniversary of the death of Princess Diana was marked by memorial services around the country. ❦ 2 men were arrested for the murder of 3 men in Bishop's Stortford. ❦ Brian Belo won *Big Brother 8* [see p.116].

Duchess of Cornwall

SEPTEMBER · {2} The 550 British troops posted in Basra Palace began withdrawal, leaving the post in the hands of Iraqi soldiers. ❦ US negotiators announced that N Korea would end its nuclear programme by the end of 2007 in return for economic aid. ❦ The Lebanese government announced it had gained full control of the Nahr al-Bared refugee camp, ending months of fighting. {3} RIP @ 43, Jane Tomlinson [see p.57]. {5} 3 men were arrested in Germany, suspected of planning a terrorist attack on a US military base in Ramstein and on Frankfurt airport. ❦ >21 reported dead after hurricane Felix hit Nicaragua. ❦ RIP @ 71, Luciano Pavarotti [see p.57]. {7} Portuguese police named Madeleine McCann's mother and father, Kate and Gerry, as 'arguido' suspects [see p.30]. ❦ A new video of Osama bin Laden emerged in which he encouraged America to convert to Islam. ❦ The Rugby World Cup began in France. {9} Former Pakistani PM Nawaz Sharif returned to Pakistan after 7 years in exile; on landing he was deported to Saudi Arabia. {10} RIP @ 64, Anita Roddick [see p.57]. {11} >69 Israeli soldiers were killed after a rocket fired from Gaza hit their camp in Zikkim. {12} A new case of foot and mouth was identified at a farm in Surrey [see p.31]. ❦ An 8·4 earthquake struck Sumatra, Indonesia, killing 9.

I'm looking forward to taking a step back from the tennis life and spending time with my family. – TIM HENMAN

The daily chronicle will continue in the 2009 edition of Schott's Almanac.

SOME GREAT LIVES IN BRIEF

PIETER WILLEM BOTHA
12·1·1916–31·10·2006 (90)

As PM and President of South Africa from 1978–89, P.W. Botha maintained apartheid, ordered murderous attacks on political opponents, and attempted to destabilise neighbouring countries. The so-called Great Crocodile refused even to appear before the Truth & Reconciliation Commission. His death was little mourned.

DESERT ORCHID
11·4·1979–13·11·2006 (27)

The grey gelding 'Dessie' was one of the most popular horses of his time, alongside Arkle and Red Rum. During his career (1983–91), Dessie won 34 of 70 starts, including the King George VI chase four times, and the 1989 Cheltenham Gold Cup – voted the 'race of the century' by the *Racing Post*.

ROBERT ALTMAN
20·2·1925–20·11·2006 (81)

Altman's unique style of film directing tended to be somewhat hit (*M*A*S*H*, *Nashville*, *The Player*, *Gosford Park*) and miss (*Quintet*, *Popeye*, *Prêt-à-Porter*). Yet by creating ambitious narrative tapestries and allowing his actors to improvise, Altman's 'pursuit of the imperfect moment' ensured his films were never ignored.

NICK CLARKE
9·6·1948–23·11·2006 (58)

Credited with one of the finest voices in broadcasting, Clarke spent more than 30 years as a BBC journalist, earning the accolade of 'national treasure'. As presenter of Radio 4's *The World At One* from 1994, Clarke proved that an interviewer could be dogged and incisive without ever descending to arrogance or aggression. In the words of PM Tony Blair, Clarke was 'a true professional'.

ALAN 'FLUFF' FREEMAN
6·7·1927–27·11·2006 (79)

Born in Australia, Fluff (a nickname born in a sweater-in-the-wash incident) came to epitomise a breed of eccentric British DJ – mocked by Harry Enfield's 'Smashey & Nicey', but always loved by the public. With his assured style and idiosyncratic turn of phrase (*'not 'arf pop-pickers'*) Fluff was firmly established in the roll-call of 'radio royalty'.

ALLEN CARR
2·9·1934–29·11·2006 (72)

From an unhappy accountant with a 100-a-day cigarette habit, Carr turned himself into the world's most successful and wealthy anti-smoking campaigner. His Easyway method persuaded smokers that cigarettes were the *cause* not the *cure* for their stress. On being diagnosed with the lung cancer that eventually killed him, Carr remarked that his illness was 'a price worth paying' for the millions of smokers he had helped to quit.

AUGUSTO PINOCHET
25·11·1915–10·12·2006 (91)

General Pinochet presided over a brutal regime during which >3,000 Chileans were executed and many thousands were tortured or 'disappeared'. Claiming to be saving Chile from communism, Pinochet implemented harsh economic reforms that, despite a recession in the 1980s, were ultimately successful in making Chile one of the wealthiest Latin American states. The (disputed) ill-health of his old age saved Pinochet from standing trial for the human rights abuses many alleged he had instigated.

JAMES BROWN
3·5·1933–25·12·2006 (73)

Brown's role in creating funk, fathering disco, and supplying the beat for rap

SOME GREAT LIVES IN BRIEF cont.

and R&B truly earned him his many (self-appointed) titles – not least 'The Godfather of Soul'. A chequered personal life and time in prison dampened neither the spirit nor the appeal of this Black American icon – 'The Hardest Working Man in Show Business'.

MAGNUS MAGNUSSON
12·10·1929–7·1·2007 (77)

Magnusson's talents as a journalist, editor, archaeologist, ornithologist, author, translator, and historian were overshadowed by his 25-year long chairmanship of *Mastermind*. Magnusson will remain in the public memory firing questions in clipped tones (Iceland via Edinburgh and Oxford) to contestants cowering in the famous black chair – and for his catchphrase, 'I've started, so I'll finish'.

ANNA NICOLE SMITH
28·11·1967–8·2·2007 (39)

A model, actress, stripper, and reality TV star, Smith was 'famous for being infamous'. Her life vacillated between oddity (her marriage to an oil billionaire 60 years her senior) and tragedy (the death of her 20-year-old son). A paternity 'tug of love' over her 5-month-old daughter ensured that Smith remained in the headlines long after her untimely death from a drug overdose.

JOHN INMAN
28·6·1935–8·3·2007 (71)

The only thing to compete with Mrs Slocombe's 'pussy' in the innuendo-heavy department store sit-com *Are You Being Served* was John Inman (as Mr Humphries), mincing towards a customer, trilling his catchphrase, 'I'm free!'. Viewers across the world lapped up Inman's camp stylings – first honed in rep and later flaunted as one of Britain's best-loved pantomime dames.

BORIS YELTSIN
1·2·1931–23·4·2007 (76)

Russia's first elected President, Yeltsin rose to power as a populist reformer, but left a troubled legacy. After helping to orchestrate the dissolution of the Soviet Union, his economic 'shock therapy' led to rapidly declining living conditions, and a 1993 political crisis. After the disastrous invasion of Chechnya in 1994 and a second term marked by failing health, he handed power to Putin on New Year's Eve 1999 [see p.32].

MSTISLAV ROSTROPOVICH
27·3·1927–27·4·2007 (80)

Widely acclaimed as the greatest cellist since Pablo Casals, Rostropovich combined musical excellence with a deep commitment to humanitarian causes. Exiled from the Soviet Union in 1974, Rostropovich went to America until the Cold War thaw allowed him to re-establish relations with his homeland.

ISABELLA BLOW
19·11·1958–7·5·2007 (48)

One of fashion's genuine iconoclasts, Blow worked for a host of magazines, and with many of the industry's most respected names. Revolving around style and the stylish, her life was eccentric, aristocratic, creative, generous, impoverished, and, finally, suicidally tragic. Blow is credited with 'discovering' a constellation of stars, including Philip Treacy, Stella Tennant, Sophie Dahl, and Alexander McQueen.

KURT WALDHEIM
21·12·1918–14·6·2007 (88)

Waldheim's distinguished career as an Austrian diplomat and then UN Secretary-General (1972–82) ended in ignominy, when his previously denied wartime service in the German army

SOME GREAT LIVES IN BRIEF cont.

was exposed. Despite a number of allegations against him, Waldheim was elected Austrian President in 1985. Yet, ostracism by the international community made his position untenable, and he did not seek re-election in 1992. Three years later, on the basis of his war record, he was denied entry into the US to celebrate the UN's 50th anniversary.

BERNARD MANNING
13·8·1930–18·6·2007 (76)

Manning defended his racist humour, claiming he was an equal opportunity bigot. All creeds and colours were fair game to the 18-stone comic who rose from the northern clubs to become one of Britain's wealthiest performers. Manning refused to joke about mothers-in-law, death, or the disabled, and was horrified to be accused of using the word 'wog'. He maintained, however, that 'nigger' and 'coon' were historically respectable.

GEORGE MELLY
17·8·1926–5·7·2007 (80)

Decked out in bold fedoras, eye-watering ties, and howling zoot suits, 'Goodtime George' personified an irrepressible sliver of bawdy and bohemian jazz excess. He combined his career as a singer with a portfolio of interests including journalism, film, fly-fishing, and (Surrealist) art – living a hedonistic life of loucheness and excess every bit as colourful as his sartorial armour.

MIKE REID
19·1·1940–29·7·2007 (67)

A Hackney-born lad who had served time in Brixton and worked as a stunt man, Reid was ideally qualified to play the gruff wheeler-dealer Frank Butcher in *EastEnders* – and Doug 'The Head' Denovitz in Guy Ritchie's *Snatch*. Reid began his showbiz career as a stand-up – an apprenticeship that taught him his trademark combination of toughness and fatalism.

JANE TOMLINSON
21·2·1964–3·9·2007 (43)

An 'ordinary housewife' from Leeds, Tomlinson turned her terminal cancer into the catalyst for one of the most remarkable individual fund-raising efforts. Undertaking the kind of sporting challenges that would fell a fit twenty-something (including the first marathon run whilst on chemotherapy), Tomlinson raised >£1·5m for charity – earning herself the *Sunday Times* Sportswoman of the Year, the BBC's Helen Rollason Award, the CBE, and the admiration of millions.

LUCIANO PAVAROTTI
12·10·1935–6·9·2007 (71)

One of opera's greatest tenors, Pavarotti was, according to Decca, 'the most popular classical artist in the history of the recording industry'. It was entirely fitting that Pavarotti, who as a youth had a talent for football, achieved the zenith of his fame during the 1990 World Cup. As one of the Three Tenors (alongside José Carreras and Placido Domingo), 'Big Lucy' (as the 20-stone singer was known) brought arias like *Nessun dorma* out of the opera house into the streets – via the terraces.

ANITA RODDICK
23·10·1942–10·09·2007 (64)

Driven by campaigning zeal and a deep concern for the environment, Roddick became one of Britain's most successful businesswomen. She started the enthusiastically green and ethical chain *Body Shop* in 1976 – which, thirty years later, was sold to L'Oréal for £652m.

The World

You never enjoy the world aright, till the sea itself floweth in your veins, till you are clothed with the heavens, and crowned with the stars: and perceive yourself to be the sole heir of the whole world, and more than so, because men are in it who are every one sole heirs as well as you.
— THOMAS TRAHERNE (*c.*1637–74)

ASYLUM LEVELS & TRENDS · 2006

In 2006, the United States became the most popular destination for asylum seekers – receiving an estimated 51,500 applications. Figures from the United Nations High Commissioner for Refugees (UNHCR), released in March 2007, revealed the industrialised countries that received the largest share of asylum applications:

Country (%)	*2005*	*2006*
United States	14·4	17·0
France	14·7	10·1
UK	9·1	9·2
Sweden	5·2	8·0
Canada	5·8	7·6
Germany	8·5	7·0
Netherlands	3·7	4·8

In 2006, the top nationalities applying for asylum in the United Kingdom were:

Nationality	*applicants*
Eritrean	2,725
Iranian	2,675
Afghan	2,650
Somalian	2,155
Zimbabwean	2,095
Chinese	1,970
Pakistani	1,805
Iraqi	1,305
Nigerian	940
Sudanese	755

[Source: UNHCR]

INTERNATIONAL DEVELOPMENT & AID

Organisation for Economic Co-operation and Development (OECD) figures show that development aid has fallen by 5·1% since 2005, to $103·9bn in 2006. This fall in aid was due to the exceptionally high levels donated in 2005, mainly in the form of debt relief for countries such as Iraq and Nigeria. The US was the largest donor in 2006. As before, only 5 of the 22 major donors managed to hit the UN target of giving 0·70% of their Gross National Income to Overseas Development Aid:

Country	ODA $m	% GNI
Australia	2,128	0·30
Canada	3,713	0·30
Denmark	2,234	0·80
France	10,448	0·47
Germany	10,351	0·36
Ireland	997	0·53
Japan	11,608	0·25
Luxembourg	291	0·89
Netherlands	5,452	0·81
Norway	2,946	0·89
Spain	3,801	0·32
Sweden	3,967	1·03
UK	12,607	0·52
US	22,739	0·17

[Provisional figures, 2006]

THE DOOMSDAY CLOCK

In 1947, the *Bulletin of the Atomic Scientists* established its 'Doomsday Clock' – the hands of which move to and from midnight (the figurative end of civilisation), as the threat of nuclear devastation ebbs and flows. In 2007, the clock hit '5 minutes to midnight', reflecting the growing threat of nuclear proliferation and, significantly, the new threats posed by climate change. Below are the time changes since the clock was established at '7 minutes to midnight'.

-7 (1947) The Doomsday Clock appears on the cover of the *Bulletin of the Atomic Scientists* for the first time, in the wake of the Hiroshima and Nagasaki bombs.

-3 (1949) President Truman tells the American public that, despite official denials, the Soviets have tested their first nuclear device, thereby starting the arms race.

-2 (1953) International security is thrown into disarray, as the US and the Soviets test thermonuclear hydrogen bombs within months of each other during 1952–53.

-7 (1960) A number of political and scientific interactions signal that the US and the Soviets are keen to avoid confrontation and quell diplomatic hostilities.

-12 (1963) The US and the Soviets sign the Partial Test Ban Treaty ending all atmospheric testing, and signalling an awareness of the risks of nuclear conflict.

-7 (1968) France and China both develop nuclear weapons; regional wars include the US and Vietnam, India and Pakistan, and Israel with its Arab neighbours.

-10 (1969) Tensions are reduced when most of the world's nations sign the Nuclear Non-Proliferation Treaty – significantly not India, Pakistan, nor Israel.

-12 (1972) The US and the Soviets sign the Strategic Arms Limitation Treaty and the Anti-Ballistic Missile Treaty, signalling a slowing of the arms race.

-9 (1974) India tests its first nuclear device, bringing the bomb to South Asia. Both the US and the Soviets appear to be modernising their nuclear arsenals.

-7 (1980) Some promising moves towards disarmament fail to end the superpowers' reliance on nuclear weapons as an integral part of their national security.

-4 (1981) The Soviet invasion of Afghanistan hardens the US nuclear position; Carter pulls the US from the Moscow Olympics; Reagan vows to win the Cold War.

-3 (1984) US–Soviet relations sink to a low as negotiations all but cease. The US pursues a space-based anti-ballistic capability, raising fears of a new arms race.

-6 (1988) The US and the Soviets sign the historic Intermediate-Range Nuclear Forces Treaty, banning for the first time a whole category of nuclear weapons.

-10 (1990) The risk of nuclear war diminishes with the collapse of the Soviet Union, the fall of the Berlin Wall in 1989, and the end of the Cold War.

-17 (1991) The Cold War's end; Strategic Arms Reduction Treaty, and unilateral measures lower tensions and cast doubt on the reliance on nuclear weapons.

-14 (1995) Hopes fade for a Cold War peace dividend as US hawks view Russia with suspicion; concern grows over unsecured nukes in the former Soviet Union.

-9 (1998) India and Pakistan stage nuclear tests within weeks of each other; Russia and the US still maintain 7,000 warheads ready to fire within 15 minutes.

-7 (2002) Concern grows about terrorist groups acquiring unsecured nuclear material; the US expresses a more dogmatic attitude to nuclear proliferation.

-5 (2007) US & Russia stand ready to attack; N Korea conducts tests; Iran threatens to acquire a nuclear bomb; damage to ecosystems is causing environmental crises.

[Source: *Bulletin of the Atomic Scientists*]

INTERNATIONAL OPINIONS ON TORTURE

A BBC World Service survey published in October 2006 suggested that nearly one third of people around the world supported some use of torture. 27,000 people in 25 countries were asked which of two statements was closest to their opinion:

'Terrorists pose such an extreme threat that governments should now be allowed to use some degree of torture if it may gain information that saves innocent lives'

'Clear rules against torture should be maintained because any use of torture is immoral and will weaken international human rights'

Internationally, 59% of respondents opposed torture under any circumstances, and 29% considered some degree of torture acceptable. Below is a country breakdown:

Country	*against all torture*	*allow some torture*	*don't know*
Australia	75%	22	3
Canada	74	22	4
China	49	37	13
Egypt	65	25	9
France	75	19	6
Germany	71	21	7
Great Britain	72	24	4
India	23	32	45
Indonesia	51	40	8
Iraq	55	42	1
Israel	48	43	9
Italy	81	14	6
Russia	43	37	19
Turkey	62	24	14
USA	58	36	7

[Source: BBC/Globescan/PIPA · Some figures do not add up to 100% due to rounding]

THE DEATH PENALTY

Amnesty International's annual Death Penalty Statistics, released in April 2007, indicated a 25% fall in executions and death sentences around the world in 2006. During 2006, the Philippines abolished the death penalty for ordinary crimes, and both Georgia and Moldova removed death penalty provisions from their constitutions. However, more than 1,591 people were executed in 25 countries in 2006; 3,861 death sentences were passed in 55 countries; and more than 20,000 prisoners were held on 'death row'. Since 1990, >45 countries have abolished the death penalty, though it is still in force in 69 states. Below is Amnesty International's estimate of the countries that executed the greatest number of people during 2006:

China....... 1,010	Pakistan 82	Sudan...........65	Saudi Arabia....39
Iran........... 177	Iraq.............65	USA............53	Yemen..........30

EXTRAORDINARY RENDITION

In November 2006, a group of MEPs, led by the Italian socialist Giovanni Claudio Fava, produced a draft report into 'extraordinary rendition' – whereby suspected terrorists are airlifted by secret CIA flights to countries that use torture. The report alleged that a number of European governments knew of this illegal transfer but resisted attempts to investigate its extent. Poland was accused of allowing CIA agents to run a secret detention centre (or 'black site') on its soil. The report alleged that Britain allowed the stopover of 170 CIA flights – roughly 100 more than had been previously admitted by MPs. The report called for all those European countries that had not already done so to launch independent investigations into all CIA stopovers, and it named 10 countries that allegedly co-operated with CIA flights:

Country	*No. of CIA stopovers*
Germany	336
Britain	170
Ireland	147
Portugal	91
Spain	68
Greece	64
Cyprus	57
Italy	46
Romania	21
Poland	11

[Source: Draft Report: On the Alleged Use of European Countries by the CIA for the Transportation and Illegal Detention of Prisoners (2006/220 (INI))] · In February 2007, the EU Parliament voted to pass a slightly watered-down version of the report: 382 MEPs voted for, 256 against, and 74 abstained. In June 2007, the Association of Chief Police Officers announced its investigations had uncovered no evidence that the CIA had used British airports for extraordinary rendition flights. At the same time, the first criminal trial over an alleged case of extraordinary rendition opened in Italy. 26 Americans and 6 Italians were accused of the 2003 kidnap of a Muslim cleric in Italy, from where he was allegedly transported to Egypt to be tortured. Due to constitutional complications with the evidence, the trial was adjourned at the end of June 2007 to be heard by a higher court at a later date.

GLOBAL FREEDOM

The US pressure group Freedom House annually compiles a *Freedom in the World Survey*, classifying countries by the political rights and civil liberties their citizens enjoy. Countries are judged to be: FREE, PARTLY FREE, or NOT FREE. The following countries were classified by *freedomhouse.org* as still being NOT FREE in 2007:

Algeria · Angola · Azerbaijan · Belarus · Bhutan · Brunei · Burma · Cambodia
Cameroon · Chad · China · Congo (Brazzaville) · Congo (Kinshasa)
Côte d'Ivoire · Cuba · Egypt · Equatorial Guinea · Eritrea · Guinea · Iran · Iraq
Kazakhstan · Laos · Libya · Maldives · North Korea · Oman · Pakistan · Qatar
Russia · Rwanda · Saudi Arabia · Somalia · Sudan · Swaziland · Syria · Tajikistan
Thailand · Togo · Tunisia · Turkmenistan · UAE · Uzbekistan · Vietnam · Zimbabwe

The Economist Intelligence Unit released a Global Peace Index in May 2007, that ranked 121 countries according to factors such as levels of organised crime, violence, and military expenditure. The top three most peaceful countries were judged to be Norway, New Zealand, and Denmark. The three countries languishing at the bottom of the index were Iraq, Sudan, and Israel. The UK was placed at 49 – and the USA was judged to be the 96th most peaceful country.

SIGNIFICANT ONGOING CONFLICTS

The Quaker lobby group Friends Committee on National Legislation (FCNL) classifies a significant ongoing conflict as one in which at least 1,000 have been killed. As of January 2007, the FCNL and the Centre for Defense Information reported there were fifteen significant ongoing armed conflicts in the world – they are:

Middle East	*began*
US global 'war on terror' *&* 'terrorists with global reach'	2001
Iraq government and allies *&* Iraqi and foreign resistance	2003
Israel *&* Hamas, Hezbollah, Islamic Jihad, &c.	1975
Asia	
Afghanistan: Kabul government *&* al-Qaeda and Taleban	1978
India *&* Assam (ULFA) insurgents, &c.	1986
Sri Lanka *&* Tamil Eelam	1978; 2002
Philippines *&* New People's Army	1969
Latin America	
Colombia *&* National Liberation Army (ELN)	1978
Colombia *&* Revolutionary Armed Forces of Colombia (FARC)	1978
Europe	
Russia *&* Chechnya	1994; 1996
Africa	
Democratic Republic of Congo *&* indigenous insurgents	1997
Nigeria: ethnic and religious communal violence	1970
Somalia: Somaliland, Puntland, and other factions	1978; 2005
Sudan *&* Sudan Liberation and Justice and Equality Movements	2003
Uganda *&* Lord's Army	1986

[Source: Center for Defense Information, as at 1 January 2007]

THE UN SECURITY COUNCIL

The United Nations Security Council (UNSC) has a mandate under the 1945 United Nations Charter to maintain international peace and security. The Council held its first meeting in London in January 1946, and has been in continuous session ever since – a representative of each of the member nations is present at the UN's headquarters at all times. The Council has five permanent members: China, France, the Russian Federation, the UK, and the US. Alongside these serve ten non-permanent members, who are elected for 2-year terms by the UN General Assembly. In 2007–08, the non-permanent members were: Belgium, Congo, Ghana, Indonesia, Italy, Panama, Peru, Qatar, Slovakia, and South Africa. The 1-month Presidency of the Security Council rotates among members of the Council, according to the English alphabetical order of country names. Each Council member may cast one vote. For a resolution [see p.63] to be passed, at least nine of the fifteen must vote 'yes'. All permanent members of the Council must vote in the affirmative for substantive matters to pass, giving each member a veto. The United Nations Charter states that all members are obliged to accept and enforce decisions made by the Security Council – it is the only UN body which has such powers.

UN SECURITY COUNCIL RESOLUTIONS OF NOTE

Year	*resolution number*	*called for*
1947	27	an immediate cessation of hostilities between troops from the Netherlands and the Republic of Indonesia
1948	50	a cessation of hostilities in Palestine, without prejudice to the rights, claims, and position of either Arabs or Jews
1950	82	North Korea to cease hostilities against the Republic of Korea and withdraw to the 38th parallel
1956	118	the operation of the Suez Canal to be insulated from the politics of any country
1963	181	the government of South Africa to abandon the policies of apartheid and release all political prisoners
1967	242	withdrawal of Israel from the occupied territories, in exchange for a peace settlement
1973	338	a cease-fire between Israeli and Arab forces to end the Yom Kippur War
1974	353	Turkey to respect the independence of Cyprus and the withdrawal of all troops of every nationality
1982	502	an immediate cessation of hostilities and the withdrawal of all Argentine troops from the Falklands
1982	514	Iran and Iraq to suspend hostilities and withdraw to internationally recognised borders
1990	660	the immediate withdrawal of all occupying Iraqi forces from Kuwait
1994	955	the establishment of an international tribunal to bring to justice those who committed atrocities in Rwanda
1998	1172	India and Pakistan to cease the development of nuclear weapons
1999	1244	Kosovo to be placed under transitional UN administration, and a Nato-led peacekeeping force to be deployed
1999	1264	the establishment of a multinational force to restore peace and security in East Timor
1999	1267	the Taleban in Afghanistan to stop supporting terrorism, and surrender Osama bin Laden
2001	1373	condemnation of the 9/11 attacks and for countries to work together to prevent terrorist acts
2002	1441	Iraq to comply with all previous calls for disarmament, and disclose and surrender all WMD
2003	1515	the Roadmap to a permanent two-state solution to the Israeli–Palestinian conflict to be adhered to
2004	1556	the Sudanese government to disband the Janjaweed, and bring to justice those who committed atrocities in Darfur
2006	1701	full cessation of hostilities between Israel and Hezbollah in Lebanon
2006	1718	sanctions to be imposed against North Korea, in response to their nuclear test
2006	1737	Iran to suspend nuclear activities, sanctions imposed to prevent the supply of nuclear-related technology to Iran
2007	1769	a peace-keeping force of 20,000 military personnel be deployed to the Darfur region of Sudan [see p.29]

NOBEL PEACE PRIZE

The 2006 Nobel Peace Prize was awarded in equal parts to the GRAMEEN BANK and its founder and managing director, MUHAMMAD YUNUS (1940–)

for their efforts to create economic and social development from below

Muhammad Yunus was born in Chittagong, Bangladesh, in 1940. He was a Fulbright Scholar at Vanderbilt University, where he earned his PhD in economics in 1969, and later joined the Chittagong University Economics Department. Before founding Grameen Bank, Yunus developed a form of village government and a system of co-operative farming, both of which were later adopted by the Bangladeshi government. ❦ Grameen Bank was founded as an independent bank by government legislation in 1983. Grameen (meaning 'village' or 'rural' in Bengali) offers small, collateral-free loans to the 'poorest of the poor' in rural Bangladesh. The bank's philosophy deems credit a basic human right, and challenges the traditional wisdom that the poor are not 'creditworthy'. Loans are offered alongside institutional support, such as weekly meetings for groups of borrowers. The bank has so far disbursed over $5·3bn to *c.*6.67m borrowers and, unlike most Third World banks, it lends almost exclusively to women. The bank claims repayment rates are *c.*98%. ❦ Yunus became frustrated with teaching economic theories during the 1974 Bangladesh famine, in which hundreds of thousands died. He began an 'action research' project in the nearby village of Jobra, where he interviewed villagers about the 'real-life economics' of their existence. In Jobra, Yunus and his students discovered that many were so poor they had to depend on usurious middlemen for the materials of their trade, leaving them with only the basics of survival. Sickened, Yunus loaned the villagers enough money ($27) to buy their own materials and cut out the middlemen. All the loans were repaid, and Yunus' generosity grew into a full-fledged business plan, which expanded to other villages with the help of Bangladesh's Central Bank. As of May 2006, Grameen had 2,247 branches, covering >86% of the villages in Bangladesh. Grameen is non-profit: 90% of the bank's shares are owned by its borrowers, the balance is held by the government. Yunus claims that within 5 years, 50% of Grameen's borrowers have escaped poverty, in that they now possess, among other essentials, clean drinking water, warm clothes in winter, mosquito netting in summer, a sanitary latrine, a house with a tin roof, schooling for children, and ≥$75 in savings. ❦ Grameen has catalysed what some call a 'microfinance revolution'. Over 250 institutions in *c.*100 countries have reportedly established microcredit programmes based on the Grameen model. In the last decade, organisations have expanded the idea of microcredit to include profit-making commercial ventures. Recently, foundations established by tech billionaires (like the Michael and Susan Dell Foundation, the Bill and Melinda Gates Foundation, and Google.org) have contributed major microfinance funding. Yet only time will tell whether microcredit can eradicate poverty, as Yunus earnestly believes.

Muhammad Yunus

CHILD WELL-BEING

The well-being of children in 21 industrialised nations was ranked by a UNICEF report published in February 2007. The study used more than 40 indicators to assess children including: their relationship with their parents; rates of teenage pregnancy; drugs use; and levels of literacy. The Netherlands rated top overall, and the UK languished in most areas, coming in the bottom third of results for five out of the six main categories [see p.93]. The overall and category rankings are laid out below:

overall rank		*material well-being*	*health & safety*	*educational well-being*	*behaviours & risks*	*subjective well-being*	*family & friends*
1st	Netherlands	10th	2nd	6th	3rd	1st	3rd
2nd	Sweden	1st	1st	5th	1st	7th	15th
3rd	Denmark	4th	4th	8th	6th	12th	9th
4th	Finland	3rd	3rd	4th	7th	11th	17th
5th	Spain	12th	6th	15th	5th	2nd	8th
6th	Switzerland	5th	9th	14th	12th	6th	4th
7th	Norway	2nd	8th	11th	13th	8th	10th
8th	Italy	14th	5th	20th	10th	10th	1st
9th	Ireland	19th	19th	7th	4th	5th	7th
10th	Belgium	7th	16th	1st	19th	16th	5th
11th	Germany	13th	11th	10th	11th	9th	13th
12th	Canada	6th	13th	2nd	17th	15th	18th
13th	Greece	15th	18th	16th	8th	3rd	11th
14th	Poland	21st	15th	3rd	2nd	19th	14th
15th	Czech Rep.	11th	10th	9th	9th	17th	19th
16th	France	9th	7th	18th	14th	18th	12th
17th	Portugal	16th	14th	21st	15th	14th	2nd
18th	Austria	8th	20th	19th	16th	4th	16th
19th	Hungary	20th	17th	13th	18th	13th	6th
20th	USA	17th	21st	12th	20th	—	20th
21st	UK	18th	12th	17th	21st	20th	21st

[Source: UNICEF, *Report Card 7: An Overview of Child Well-being in Rich Countries*, 2007]

SAKHAROV PRIZE

Presented by the European Union since 1988, the Sakharov Prize for Freedom of Thought aims to reward individuals who challenge oppression and campaign for human rights. It is named in honour of Soviet physicist Andrei Sakharov (1921–89), who helped to develop the hydrogen bomb but later won the Nobel Peace Prize for his work campaigning against nuclear weapons. In 2006, the €50,000 prize was awarded to leader of the Belarusian opposition ALIAKSANDR MILINKEVICH, for his fight to bring democracy to his country despite an oppressive political climate.

THE FBI'S MOST WANTED

Fugitive [as at 17·9·07]	*allegation*	*reward*
Osama bin Laden	terrorism	$25,000,000
Diego Montoya (captured 10·9·07)	drug running	$5,000,000
James J. Bulger	murder; racketeering	$1,000,000
Victor Manuel Gerena	armed robbery	$1,000,000
Robert William Fisher	murder; arson	$100,000
Alexis Flores	kidnapping; murder	$100,000
Glen Stewart Godwin	murder; prison escape	$100,000
Jorge Alberto Lopez-Orozco	murder	$100,000
Emigdio Preciado Jr	attempted murder; assault	$100,000
Jon Savarino Schillaci	sexual assault; child pornography	$100,000

WORLD DEATH WATCH

In 2006, the World Health Organisation forecast the leading causes of death in 2030, based on 2002 statistics. Overall trends show a shift from communicable, maternal, and nutritional diseases towards non-communicable illnesses – although AIDS is predicted to become the 3rd worst killer after heart disease and stroke.

2002 actual causes of death		*2030 predicted causes of death*
Ischemic heart disease	1	ischemic heart disease
Cerebrovascular disease (stroke)	2	cerebrovascular disease
Lower respiratory infections	3	HIV/AIDS
HIV/AIDS	4	COPD†
COPD†	5	lower respiratory infections
Perinatal conditions	6	trachea, bronchus, lung cancer
Diarrheal diseases	7	diabetes
Tuberculosis	8	road traffic accidents
Trachea, bronchus, lung cancer	9	perinatal conditions
Road traffic accidents	10	stomach cancer

The WHO also predicts that in 2030 1·1m people worldwide will die from self-inflicted injuries, 0·8m from violence, and 0·3m from war. † Chronic obstructive pulmonary disease; a group of lung diseases primarily caused by smoking. Projections according to a baseline scenario. [Source: WHO, 2006]

SUICIDE RATES WORLDWIDE

suicides per million pop.					
Japan	20·3	Poland	13·6	Canada	10·6
Korea	18·7	New Zealand	12·0	Germany	10·3
France	15·1	Australia	11·1	USA	10·2
		Ireland	11·1	UK	6·3

[Source: OECD. Figures are the most recent available: data from Germany are 2004; Poland and Japan, 2003; UK, USA, Ireland, France, Korea, Australia, and Canada, 2002; and New Zealand, 2000.]

WORLD'S TEN WORST DICTATORS

American magazine *Parade* annually publishes a list of the world's worst dictators, based on their record of human rights abuse. The 2007 top ten ('06 rank in brackets):

No.	*Dictator*	*age*	*country*	*years' reign*	*facial hair?*
1 (1)	Omar al-Bashir	63	Sudan	18	goatee†
2 (2)	Kim Jong-il	64	North Korea	13	none
3 (9)	Sayyid Ali Khamenei	67	Iran	18	bushy beard
4 (6)	Hu Jintao	64	China	5	none
5 (7)	King Abdullah	83	Saudi Arabia	12	cavalier beard
6 (3)	Than Shwe	74	Burma	15	none
7 (4)	Robert Mugabe	82	Zimbabwe	27	Hitler-esque
8 (5)	Islam Karimov	69	Uzbekistan	18	none
9 (11)	Muammar al-Qaddafi	64	Libya	38	none
10 (16)	Bashar al-Assad	41	Syria	7	moustache

† 'A beard trimmed in the form of a tuft hanging from the chin, resembling that of a he-goat' [*OED*].

PRIVACY RANKINGS

In November 2006, the human rights organisation Privacy International ranked 36 countries on their record of protecting privacy. Scores were awarded in 13 categories including: constitutional protections; extent of visual surveillance; law enforcement's access to data; communications interception; workplace monitoring; and data sharing provisions. Category scores were averaged to create an overall country score, which Privacy International characterised using the following scale:

4·1–5·0 .... consistently upholds human rights standards
3·6–4·0 .... significant protections and safeguards
3·1–3·5 .... adequate safeguards against abuse
2·6–3·0 .... some safeguards but weakened protections
2·1–2·5 .... systemic failure to uphold safeguards
1·6–2·0 .... extensive surveillance societies
1·1–1·5 .... endemic surveillance societies

Germany ranked at the top of the scale (3·9), while Malaysia and China were tied at the bottom (1·3). Below were the overall scores for some other countries of note:

Canada	3·6	New Zealand	2·5	USA	2·0
France	2·9	Australia	2·4	UK	1·5†
Ireland	2·5	Israel	2·2	Russia	1·4

† According to the Privacy International report, 'the current privacy picture in the UK is decidedly grim'. The UK ranked lower than any other EU country, scoring alongside Russia, Singapore, Malaysia, and China as an 'endemic surveillance society'. Yet the UK did receive middling marks in the democratic safeguards category, which looked at public consultation processes and accountability.

2006 GLOBAL HUNGER INDEX

In October 2006, the International Food Policy Research Institute released its 2006 Global Hunger Index (GHI), which ranked levels of hunger in 94 'developing' and 22 'transitional' countries. Three indicators were used to rank the countries on a 0–100 scale: the proportion of people who are food-energy deficient; infant mortality rates; and the prevalence of underweight children under five years old. Twelve countries with values exceeding 30 displayed 'extremely alarming' rates of hunger:

Country	*hunger level*
Burundi	42·70
Eritrea	40·37
Congo DR	37·60
Ethiopia	36·70
Sierra Leone	35·20
Niger	33·43
Angola	32·17
Liberia	32·00
Zambia	31·77
Comoros	30·81
Cambodia	30·73
Tajikistan	30·25

[Data from 2003]

The GHI was calculated in 1981, 1992, 1997, and (most recently) 2003. As conditions have improved, so too have the rankings of a number of countries, including Mozambique, Ghana, and Guatemala.

THE WORLD'S FATTEST COUNTRIES

According to the World Health Organisation, there are 1·6bn overweight adults worldwide – a figure that is predicted to swell by 40% in the next decade. *Forbes* compiled a list of the countries with the highest percentage of overweight adults†:

	Country	*%*
1	Nauru‡	94·5
2	Micronesia	91·1
3	Cook Islands	90·9
4	Tonga	90·8
5	Niue	81·7
6	Samoa	80·4
7	Palau	78·4
8	Kuwait	74·2
9	USA	74·1
10	Kiribati	73·6
(28	UK	63·8)

† Adults with a Body Mass Index >25 [see p.103]. ‡ Island republic on a coral atoll halfway between Australia and Hawaii. Figures based on latest WHO estimates. [Source: Forbes.com, February 2007]

CLIMATE CHANGE & GLOBAL MIGRATION

Christian Aid warned that an estimated 1bn people will be displaced by 2050 because of the effects of climate change and a developing migration crisis. Their report, *Human Tide: The Real Migration Crisis*, released to mark Christian Aid Week in May 2007, revealed that 155m people are currently displaced by conflicts, natural disasters, and the effects of large-scale development projects (like dams and plantations). This figure is likely to grow dramatically as the effects of climate change are felt, and the causes of internal displacement are magnified. The countries worst affected by mass displacement are often those least able to cope, and security experts warn that future conflicts are likely to develop over competition for scarce resources. Christian Aid identified 6 countries currently experiencing serious levels of internal displacement which, as a result, are at greatest risk from a future migration crisis. They are: SUDAN, COLOMBIA, UGANDA, SRI LANKA, BURMA, and MALI.

BIG GAME HUNTING & CONSERVATION

A study by the conservation biologist Dr Peter Lindsey, published in *Biological Conservation* in January 2007, suggested that big game hunting may be good for conservation. When managed properly, hunting provides economic motivation for the local population to protect the environment and combat poaching. Trophy hunting is a growing market in southern Africa, annually contributing $28·5m to Namibia, $27·6m to Tanzania, and $100m to South Africa. The table below reveals some of the animals available to hunt in Namibia, and their trophy cost in 2007:

Animal	*trophy cost (US$)*
Jackal	100
Baboon	110
Ostrich	310
Springbok	350
Impala	520
Blue Wildebeest	800
Hartmann Zebra	1,000
Black Wildebeest	1,100
Giraffe	2,500
Leopard	3,400
Cheetah	3,400

[Source: Kowas Adventure Safaris, Namibia] · In 2003, Marco Festa-Bianchet, a wildlife biologist at Univ. of Sherbrooke, Quebec, reported in *Nature* that hunting of bighorn sheep in Canada may have harmed the gene pool. The research suggested that since hunters generally targeted animals with the largest horns or antlers, the sheep with the best genes were threatened. Due to pressure from hunting, bighorn sheep in Alberta, Canada, were increasingly found to have smaller horns and poorer genes.

EUROPEAN MAMMAL ASSESSMENT

The results of the first assessment of European mammals, undertaken by the World Conservation Union (IUCN) for the European Commission, was published in May 2007. The report indicated that 15% of all mammal species in Europe are under threat of extinction, mainly as a result of habitat degradation. 27% of Europe's mammals have declining populations, 32% are stable, and just 8% have increasing populations. Below is a summary of mammal species by category of threat in 2007:

IUCN red list threat category	*no. species Europe*	*no. species marine*	*no. species total*
Extinct	2	0	2
Extinct in the Wild	0	0	0
Regionally Extinct	0	1	1
Critically Endangered	3	2	5
Endangered	7	2	9
Vulnerable	19	2	21
Near Threatened	20	1	21
Least Concern	146	7	153

Critically endangered species in Europe include: the Iberian Lynx (found only in isolated locations in Spain; only 84–143 animals remain); the Bavarian Pine Vole (endemic to the northeastern Alps; less than 50 specimens have ever been collected); the European Mink (under greatest threat from the more ferocious American Mink); and the Mediterranean Monk Seal (just 350–450 animals survive).

OCEANIC DEAD ZONES

Oceanic 'dead zones' are regions of low oxygen in which most fish and plants cannot survive. While some dead zones occur naturally, pollution has caused their number to double in every decade since the 1960s. New dead zones are formed when pollution encourages blooms of algae that die and fall to the seabed; there they are consumed by bacteria which choke the water's supply of oxygen. While some fast-swimming fish can escape dead zones, bottom-dwellers like shellfish frequently die. A number of species face extinction if dead zones continue to spread. In October 2006, the UN Environmental Programme estimated there may be 200 dead zones worldwide, up from 149 in 2004. Newly detected zones announced in October 2006 include:

Archipelago Sea	Finland
Elefsis Bay	Greece
Fosu Lagoon	Ghana
Mersey Estuary	United Kingdom
Mondego River	Portugal
Montevideo Bay	Uruguay
Paracas Bay	Peru

[Source: UNEP, 2006]

As of autumn 2006, the Census of Marine Life had counted *c*.75,000 species of marine mammals living in the world's oceans – including *c*.16,000 species of fish. 2006 discoveries of note included the 'Jurassic shrimp', thought to have died out 50 million years ago; a species of 'hairy crab' named *kiwa hirsuta*; and 8 million herring swimming in a school the size of Manhattan, discovered off New Jersey.

ENERGY WASTE

The Energy Saving Trust (EST) warned that if current levels of energy wastage continue, Britons will have released an extra 43m tonnes of carbon dioxide into the atmosphere by 2010. An EST report, released in October 2006, named the UK as the most wasteful of Europe's most populous countries, ahead of Italy, France, Spain, and Germany. The EST survey showed that Britons confessed to committing 32 energy wasteful actions a week, the most common of which are listed below:

71%	leave appliances on standby
67%	boil more water than needed
65%	leave chargers plugged in
63%	forget to turn lights off
48%	use a car for short journeys
44%	wash clothes at 60°C
32%	leave the engine running when their car is stationary
27%	over-rev their car engine
15%	wash clothes at 90°C

TOP TEN RECIPIENTS OF UK AID

The top 10 beneficiaries of UK aid, according to latest figures from the OECD:

Nigeria	$1,164m
Iraq	$796m
India	$535m
Bangladesh	$232m
Zambia	$224m
Afghanistan	$222m
Tanzania	$217m
Ghana	$192m
Congo DR	$189m
Sudan	$157m

[Source: OECD, 2005. In 2005, the UK's net Official Development Assistance budget increased 36·6% since 2004, to $10,767m.]

CO_2 & CLIMATE CHANGE

The 2007 Climate Change Performance Index (CCPI), produced by GermanWatch (an independent, non-profit, non-governmental organisation), showed that *c*.65% of all global carbon dioxide (CO_2) emissions come from just 10 countries – they are:

Country	*% global CO_2 emissions*
USA	21·82
China	17·94
Russia	5·75
Japan	4·57
India	4·15
Germany	3·19
Canada	2·07
UK	2·02
South Korea	1·74
Italy	1·74

The CCPI ranked 56 industrialised countries by comparing their environmental policies and emissions. According to the 2007 index, the best and worst nations are:

The best climate change records		*The worst climate change records*	
1 Sweden	6 Argentina	56 Saudi Arabia	51 Canada
2 UK	7 Hungary	55 Malaysia	50 Thailand
3 Denmark	8 Brazil	54 China	49 Iran
4 Malta	9 India	53 USA	48 South Korea
5 Germany	10 Switzerland	52 Kazakhstan	47 Australia

In April 2007, the Center for Naval Analyses produced a report entitled 'National Security and the Threat of Climate Change', which warned the US government that global warming should be considered a threat to national security. The study indicated that climate change could cause large-scale migrations, increase the spread of disease, and cause conflict over scarce resources. Marc Levy, a researcher at New York's Columbia University, supported these findings using data on the availability of water and the incidence of civil war. His research suggested that when rainfall is particularly low, the risk of low-level conflict developing into civil war roughly doubles in the following year.

WORLD ECOLOGICAL DEBT DAY

The US think tank Global Footprint Network regularly assesses the date on which human consumption outstrips the Earth's ability to supply resources sustainably. By living beyond its environmental means, mankind is placing such pressure on the Earth's resources that this so-called 'ecological debt day' is falling ever earlier:

Year	*debt day*
1987	19 December
1990	7 December
1995	21 November
2000	1 November
2005	11 October
2006	9 October

[Source: Global Footprint Network/NEF]

BRITISH SPECIES AT RISK

The number of species in Britain classed as endangered has almost doubled since 1994, according to a 2007 report by UK Biodiversity Action Plan. 1,149 plants, birds, and mammals (such as the skylark, dormouse, and red squirrel) are currently under threat. The report blamed damaging farming techniques and rural planning.

KÖPPEN'S CLIMATIC CLASSIFICATION SYSTEM

In *c.*1900, Russian-born climatologist Wladimir Köppen (1846–1940) developed a system to classify world climates. Köppen's classification system has been updated over the years, but it is usually broken down into the following five categories:

	Category	specifications
A	Tropical humid	*rainy climate, no winter, coolest month >18°C*
B	Dry	*arid climate*
C	Warmer temperate	*rainy, coolest month >0°C but <18°C, warmest >10°C*
D	Colder temperate	*rainy, severe winter, coldest month <0°C, warmest >10°C*
E	Polar	*polar climate, no warm season, warmest month <10°C*

Some examples: [A]: Brazil, Indonesia, Thailand · [B]: Yemen, Libya, most of Australia · [C]: UK, Spain, Hong Kong · [D]: Norway, most of Canada, Latvia · [E]: Greenland, parts of Chile, parts of Russia. ❦ By 2100, many of the world's climates will have disappeared due to the effects of global warming, according to a study published in the *Proceedings of the National Academy of Sciences* in March 2007. Researchers indicated that, as the world heats up, many climates will be lost, replaced by new ones with higher temperatures and greater rainfall. Shifting climate zones are likely to have the greatest impact on endangered animals that depend on the Arctic ice, such as polar bears and ring seals.

MAMMALS AT RISK

In January 2007, the Zoological Society of London created the EDGE project to conserve the most genetically unique mammals that usually receive little or no conservation attention. Each year, the project implements research for ten different species considered to be at risk. The species earmarked for research in 2007 were:

1	Yangtze River (Baiji) dolphin	6	Slender loris
2	Long-beaked echidna	7	Hirola
3	Hispaniolan solenodon	8	Golden-rumped elephant shrew
4	Bactrian camel	9	Kitti's hog-nosed bat
5	Pygmy hippopotamus	10	Long-eared jerboa

GLOBAL ENVIRONMENTAL CITIZEN PRIZE

Prince Charles accepted the 2006 Global Environmental Citizen Prize from Harvard Medical School's Center for Health and the Global Environment in January 2007. Awarded since 2001, the prize rewards outstanding achievement in raising awareness of global environmental change. Previous winners include:

2005	Al Gore	2003	Jane Goodall	2001	Edward O. Wilson
2004	Bill Moyers	2002	Harrison Ford		

The Prince was branded a hypocrite by some environmental campaigners for flying with a 20-strong entourage to New York to collect the prize, when he could have accepted it via a video-link.

GROWING & SHRINKING FORESTS

Many forests have expanded in size between 1990–2005, according to a November 2006 report in the *Proceedings of the National Academy of Sciences*. 22 of the 50 countries investigated by Pekka Kauppi at the University of Helsinki had a growing tree population. The greatest improvements were seen in China and the western industrialised states, whereas Brazil and Indonesia persisted in their ruthless clearing of forests. Kauppi's study proposed a relationship between 'wealth and woods', suggesting that countries with an annual per capita GNP ≥$4,600 usually had a tree population that was stable or increasing. In contrast, countries with lower annual per capita GNPs tended to continue clearing forests – an act likely to accelerate the greenhouse effect. Below are the areas with growing and shrinking forests:

Growing forests	*Shrinking forests*
USA · Western Europe	Indonesia · Brazil
China · India	Nigeria · Philippines

IPODS, KIM, & COGNAC

In the wake of North Korea's first nuclear test in October 2006, a number of countries, including America and Japan, applied sanctions halting the export of a range of luxury goods to Kim Jong-il's poverty-stricken state. Below are some of the items from which the dictator and his friends will (theoretically) have to abstain:

Swiss watches · works of art · Cognac · cigarettes · sporting goods† · diamonds
musical instruments‡ · Sony PlayStations · MP3-players (iPods &c.)§
gemstones · luxury cars · caviar · tuna steaks · fountain pens

† Kim is a sports fan and owns a basketball inscribed with Michael Jordan's signature (a gift from former US Secretary of State Madeleine Albright). ‡ Kim's new wife, Kim Ok, is said to be a devoted pianist. § Despite the sanctions, the illegal trade of consumer electronics and DVDs is highly likely; Kim's video collection is said to include >20,000 titles. He is rumoured to be a fan of James Bond and Godzilla, and to have a soft spot for Whitney Houston's emetic film *The Bodyguard* (1992).

WORLD'S TOP TEN RIVERS AT RISK

Pollution, climate change, and shipping are pushing many rivers towards crisis, according to a 2007 WWF report, which listed the river systems at greatest risk:

River system	*key risk*
Danube	shipping
Ganges	water extraction
Indus	climate change
La Plata	27 proposed dams
Mekong	over-fishing
Murray-Darling	invasive species
Nile	climate change
Rio Grande	water extraction
Salween	16 proposed dams
Yangtze	pollution

[Source: WWF *Rivers at Risk*, Mar 2007] In June 2007, researchers in Brazil asserted that the Amazon was 105km longer than the Nile.

UK'S HOTTEST YEAR

Figures released in January 2007 by the Met Office, in conjunction with the University of East Anglia, revealed that 2006 was the hottest year on record – with a mean temperature of 9·7°C across the United Kingdom. Central England Temperature (CET) figures† showed that several other records were broken in 2006: July was the warmest month ever recorded, with an average temperature of 19·7°C; September was the hottest ever, with an average temperature of 16·8°C; and autumn was the warmest on record, with an average temperature of 12·6°C. The Met Office figures below show the UK's warmest years on record since 1914:

Year	*mean temp.* °C	Year	°C	Year	°C
2006	9·73	2003	9·51	2002	9·48
		2004	9·48	2005	9·46

The chart below illustrates the mean average air temperatures, and the maximum and minimum average monthly temperatures, for the years between 1970–2005:

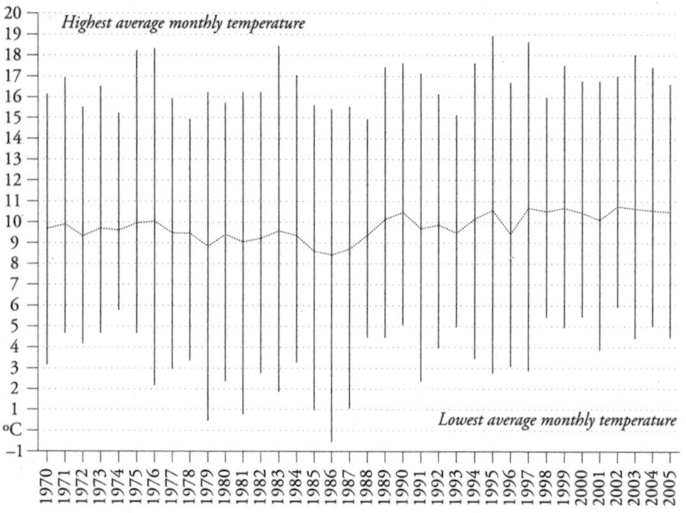

[Source: Met Office · DfT] † Readings taken since 1659 within the triangle formed by Bristol, London, and Lancashire. ❦ According to the European Climate Support Network, autumn 2006 was the warmest on record in Belgium, Denmark, Germany, Netherlands, Switzerland, and the UK. ❦ In January 2007, the Met Office predicted that 2007 was likely to be the globe's hottest year on record, and warned that climate change was to blame. ❦ America's National Oceanic and Atmospheric Administration (NOAA) reported in March 2007 that winter in the northern hemisphere had been the warmest since records began 125 years ago. NOAA maintained that the weather trend was not evidence of man-made global warming. ❦ The Woodland Trust declared spring 'the new summer' in April 2007, because events that usually occur in May (e.g. the flowering of hawthorn and return of migrating swifts) had occurred by mid-April. The Met Office later confirmed it had been the hottest April since records began, May–July however, were the wettest months in England & Wales since 1766.

THE CLASSICAL PLANETS

symbol	name	diameter	no. of moons	surface gravity	rings?	distance from Sun	mean temp	day length
		km		m/s²		×10⁶ km	°C	hours
☿	Mercury	4,879	0	3·7	N	57·9	167	4,222·6
♀	Venus	12,104	0	8·9	N	108·2	457	2,802·0
⊕	Earth	12,756	1	9·8	N	149·6	15	24·0
♂	Mars	6,794	2	3·7	N	227·9	–63	24·6
♃	Jupiter	142,984	63	23·1	Y	778·4	–110	9·9
♄	Saturn	120,536	60	9·0	Y	1,426·7	–140	10·7
♅	Uranus	51,118	27	8·7	Y	2,871·0	–195	17·2
♆	Neptune	49,532	13	11·0	Y	4,498·3	–200	16·1

In June 2007, non-planet Pluto suffered a further blow when astronomers revealed Eris had a greater diameter. Consequently, Pluto could no longer claim even to be the largest of the dwarf planets.

CLASSICAL PLANETARY MNEMONIC

M	V	E	M	J	S	U	N
any	ery	ducated	en	ustify	tealing	nique	inth
ercury	*enus*	*arth*	*ars*	*upiter*	*aturn*	*ranus*	*eptune*

THE CONTINENTS

Continent	*area km²*	*est. population*	*population density*
Asia	44,579,000	3,959m	88·8
Africa	30,065,000	910m	30·3
North America	24,256,000	331m	13·6
South America	17,819,000	561m	31·5
Antarctica	13,209,000	(a scientist or two)	—
Europe	9,938,000	729m	73·4
Australia	7,687,000	33m	4·3

THE OCEANS

Oceans make up *c.*70% of the globe's surface. The five oceans are detailed below:

Ocean	*area km²*	*greatest known depth at*	*depth*
Pacific	155,557,000	Mariana Trench	10,924m
Atlantic	76,762,000	Puerto Rico Trench	8,605m
Indian	68,556,000	Java Trench	7,258m
Southern	20,327,000	South Sandwich Trench	7,235m
Arctic	14,056,000	Fram Basin	4,665m

A WORLD OF SUPERLATIVES

Highest city	La Paz, Bolivia	3,636m
Highest mountain	Everest, Nepal/Tibet	8,850m
Highest volcano	Ojos del Salado, Chile	6,908m
Highest dam	Rogun, Tajikistan	335m
Highest waterfall	Angel Falls, Venezuela	979m
Biggest waterfall (volume)	Inga, Dem. Rep. of Congo	43,000m^3/s
Lowest point	Dead Sea, Israel/Jordan	–400m
Deepest point	Challenger Deep, Mariana Trench	–11,033m
Deepest ocean	Pacific	average depth –4,300m
Deepest freshwater lake	Baikal, Russia	1,637m
Largest lake	Caspian Sea	370,886km^2
Largest desert	Sahara	9,065,000km^2
Largest island	Greenland	2,166,086km^2
Largest country	Russia	17,075,400km^2
Largest population	China	1·3bn
Largest monolith	Uluru, Australia	345m high; 9·4km base
Largest landmass	Eurasia	54,745,500km^2
Largest river (volume)	Amazon	28bn gal/min
Largest peninsula	Arabian	2,590,000km^2
Largest rain forest	Amazon, South America	1·2bn acres
Largest forest	Northern Russia	2·7bn acres
Largest atoll	Kwajalein, Marshall Islands	16km^2
Largest glacier	Vatnajökull, Iceland	8,100km^2
Largest concrete artichoke	Castroville, USA	6m×4m
Largest archipelago	Indonesia	17,508 islands
Largest lake in a lake	Manitou, on an island in Lake Huron	104km^2
Largest city by area	Mount Isa, Australia	40,977km^2
Smallest country	Vatican City	0·44km^2
Smallest population	Vatican City	821 people
Smallest republic	Republic of Nauru	21km^2
Longest coastline	Canada	202,080km
Longest mountain range	Andes	8,900km
Longest suspension bridge	Akashi-Kaikyo, Japan	1,990m
Longest rail tunnel	Seikan, Japan	53km
Longest road tunnel	Lærdal, Norway	24·5km
Longest river	Nile [see p.73]	6,695km
Tallest inhabited building	Dubai Tower, UAE	512m
Tallest structure	KVLY-TV Mast, USA	629m
Most land borders	China & Russia	14 countries
Most populated urban area	Tokyo, Japan	35·2m
Most remote settlement	Tristan da Cunha	2,334km from neighbours
Least populous capital city	San Marino, San Marino	pop. 4,482
Warmest sea	Red Sea	Average temp. *c.*25°C
Longest bay	Bay of Bengal	1,850km
Largest banknote	Brobdingnagian bills, Philippines	14"×8½"

Unsurprisingly, a degree of uncertainty and debate surrounds some of these entries and their specifications.

POPULATION BY CONTINENT

Year	*World*	*Africa*	*N America*	*S America*	*Asia*	*Europe*	*Oceania*
Millions							
1980	4,447	472	371	242	2,645	694	23
1990	5,274	626	424	296	3,181	721	27
2000	6,073	801	486	348	3,678	730	31
2010	6,838	998	540	393	4,148	726	35
2020	7,608	1,220	594	431	4,610	715	38
2030	8,296	1,461	645	461	4,991	696	41
2040	8,897	1,719	692	481	5,291	671	43
2050	9,404	1,990	734	490	5,505	640	45
Percentage distribution							
1980	100%	10·6	8·4	5·4	59·5	15·6	0·5
2000	100%	13·2	8·0	5·7	60·6	12·0	0·5
2050	100%	21·2	7·8	5·2	58·5	6·8	0·5

WORLD BIRTH & DEATH RATES

Births	*time unit*	*deaths*	*change*
133,201,704	*per* YEAR	55,490,538	+77,711,166
11,100,142	*per* MONTH	4,624,212	+6,475,931
364,936	*per* DAY	152,029	+212,907
15,206	*per* HOUR	6,335	+8,871
253	*per* MINUTE	106	+148
4·2	*per* SECOND	1·8	+2·5

[Source: US Census Bureau, 2007 · Figures may not add up to totals because of rounding]

URBAN POPULATION

Tabulated below are the percentages of the urban population in various regions:

Region	*% of population in urban areas · 1975*	*2005*	*2030 (est.)*
Africa	25·3	38·3	50·7
Asia	24·0	39·8	54·1
Europe	66·0	72·2	78·3
Latin America & Caribbean	61·2	77·4	84·3
North America	73·8	80·7	86·7
Oceania	71·7	70·8	73·8
World	37·3	48·7	59·9

[Source: United Nations Department of Economic and Social Affairs, 2005]

MEGACITIES

The term 'megacity' is used by the UN for cities or metropolitan areas with >10m people. Below are the largest megacities (2003), with their estimated 2015 populations:

Megacity	*country*	*pop. 2003 (m)*	*est. pop. 2015*
Tokyo	Japan	35·0	36·2
New York	USA	21·2	22·8
Seoul-Inchon	South Korea	20·3	24·7
Mexico City	Mexico	18·7	20·6
São Paulo	Brazil	17·9	20·0
Mumbai	India	17·4	22·6
Los Angeles	USA	16·4	17·6
Delhi	India	14·1	20·9
Manila, Quezon City	Philippines	13·9	16·8
Calcutta	India	13·8	16·8

[Source: Münchener Rück, 2005]

MISS EARTH

22-year-old Hil Yesenia Hernandez Escobar from Chile was crowned Miss Earth in a ceremony in Manila in November 2006. The beauty pageant has ecological ambitions, with the winning beauty travelling the world for a year to 'actively promote and get involved in the preservation of the environment and the protection of Mother Earth'. In addition to posing in skimpy swimsuits, contestants are judged planting young trees. The official theme song '*Woman of the Earth*' represents one of the highlights of the award ceremony; it includes the following powerful lyrics:

I am a woman of the earth, Spreading love and joy, fun and laughter
Woman of the earth, Making miracles forever after

THE NEW SEVEN WORLD WONDERS

The New 7 Wonders Foundation is a privately funded group that organised the selection of a new list of world wonders. Since 2001, more than 100 million people worldwide have voted online and by telephone for their favourite global landmarks. The new list was announced on 07·07·07 to a worldwide television audience of 1·6bn people in 170 countries. The seven new wonders the public selected were:

Chichén Itzá, Mexico	Great Wall, China	Taj Mahal, India
Christ Redeemer, Brazil	Machu Picchu, Peru	The Giza pyramids were given
Colosseum, Italy	Petra, Jordan	'honorary wonder' status

The 7 ancient wonders: pyramids of Egypt, colossus of Rhodes, hanging gardens of Babylon, mausoleum of Halicarnassus, statue of Zeus at Olympia, temple of Artemis at Ephesus, pharos of Alexandria.

DEVELOPMENT INDEX

The UN Human Development Index annually ranks 177 countries by health, life expectancy, income, education, and environment. The 2006 ranking was:

Most developed	*Least developed*
1 .... Norway	177 .... Niger
2 .... Iceland	176 .... Sierra Leone
3 .... Australia	175 .... Mali
4 .... Ireland	174 ... Burkina Faso
5 .... Sweden	173 .. Guinea-Bissau
6 .... Canada	172 .. C African Rep
7 .... Japan	171 .... Chad
8 .... USA	170 .... Ethiopia
9 ...... Switzerland	169 .... Burundi
10 ..... Netherlands	168 ... Mozambique

FAILED STATES

Research organisation Fund for Peace, in association with *Foreign Policy*, annually compiles an index of failed states. Twelve social, economic, military, and political factors are used to rank the states most vulnerable to 'violent internal conflict and societal deterioration'. The most failing states in 2007 were:

1 .... Sudan	8 .... Afghanistan
2 .... Iraq	9 .... Guinea
3 .... Somalia	10. C African Rep
4 ..... Zimbabwe	11 .... Haiti
5 .... Chad	12 .... Pakistan
6 .... Ivory Coast	13 ...... N Korea
7 ..... DR Congo	14 .... Burma

NOTES TO THE GAZETTEER

The gazetteer on the following pages is designed to allow comparisons to be made between countries around the world. As might be expected, some of the data are tentative and open to debate. A range of sources has been consulted, including the CIA's *World Factbook*, Amnesty International, HM Revenue and Customs, &c.

Size km²	*sum of all land and water areas delimited by international boundaries and coastlines*
Population	*July 2007 estimate*
Flying time	*approximate actual travelling time from London Heathrow to capital city; will vary depending on route and connecting flight, as well as direction travelled, &c.*
GMT	*based on capital city; varies across some countries; varies with daylight saving*
Life expectancy at birth	*in years; 2007 estimate*
Infant mortality	*deaths of infants <1, per 1,000 live births, per year; 2007 estimate*
Median age	*in years; 2007 estimate*
Birth & death rates	*average per 1,000 persons in the population at midyear; 2007 estimate*
Fertility rate	*average theoretical number of children per woman; 2007 estimate*
HIV rate	*percentage of adults (15–49) living with HIV/AIDS; mainly 2003 estimate*
Literacy rate	*%; definition (especially of target age) varies; mainly 2003 estimate*
Exchange rate	*spot rate at 30·6·07*
GDP per capita	*($) GDP on purchasing power parity basis/population; from 2006*
Inflation	*annual % change in consumer prices; years vary, from 2006*
Unemployment	*% of labour force without jobs; years vary, generally from 2006*
Voting age	*voting age; (U)niversal; (C)ompulsory for at least one election; *=entitlement varies*
Military service	*age, length of service, sex and/or religion required to serve vary*
Death penalty	*(N) no death penalty; (N*) death penalty not used in practice; (Y) death penalty for common crimes; (Y*) death penalty for exceptional crimes only*
National Day	*some countries have more than one; not all are universally recognised*

GAZETTEER · ALGERIA – SOUTH KOREA · [1/4]

Country	Size (km²)	Population (m)	Capital city	Phone access code	Phone country code	Flying time (h)	GMT
United Kingdom	244,820	60·8	London	00	44	—	n/a
United States	9,826,630	301·1	Washington, DC	011	1	7h50	–5
Algeria	2,381,740	33·3	Algiers	00	213	2h45	+1
Argentina	2,766,890	40·3	Buenos Aires	00	54	15h45	–3
Australia	7,686,850	20·4	Canberra	0011	61	25h	+10
Austria	83,870	8·2	Vienna	00	43	2h20	+1
Belarus	207,600	9·7	Minsk	810	375	4h40	+2
Belgium	30,528	10·4	Brussels	00	32	1h	+1
Brazil	8,511,965	190·0	Brasilia	0014	55	16h	–3
Bulgaria	110,910	7·3	Sofia	00	359	3h	+2
Burma/Myanmar	678,500	47·4	Rangoon	00	95	13h	+6½
Cambodia	181,040	14·0	Phnom Penh	001	855	14h	+7
Canada	9,984,670	33·4	Ottawa	011	1	7h45	–5
Chile	756,950	16·3	Santiago	00	56	17h	–4
China	9,596,960	1·3bn	Beijing	00	86	10h	+8
Colombia	1,138,910	44·4	Bogota	009	57	13h	–5
Cuba	110,860	11·4	Havana	119	53	12h	–5
Czech Republic	78,866	10·2	Prague	00	420	1h50	+1
Denmark	43,094	5·5	Copenhagen	00	45	1h50	+1
Egypt	1,001,450	80·3	Cairo	00	20	4h45	+2
Estonia	45,226	1·3	Tallinn	00	372	4h	+2
Finland	338,145	5·2	Helsinki	00	358	3h	+2
France	547,030	60·9	Paris	00	33	50m	+1
Germany	357,021	82·4	Berlin	00	49	1h40	+1
Greece	131,940	10·7	Athens	00	30	3h45m	+2
Haiti	27,750	8·7	Port-au-Prince	00	509	20h30	–5
Hong Kong	1,092	7·0	—	001	852	12h	+8
Hungary	93,030	10·0	Budapest	00	36	2h25	+1
India	3,287,590	1·1bn	New Delhi	00	91	8h30	+5½
Indonesia	1,919,440	234·7	Jakarta	001	62	16h	+7
Iran	1,648,000	65·4	Tehran	00	98	6h	+3½
Iraq	437,072	27·5	Baghdad	00	964	14h30	+3
Ireland	70,280	4·1	Dublin	00	353	1h	0
Israel	20,770	6·4	Jerusalem/Tel Aviv	00	972	5h	+2
Italy	301,230	58·1	Rome	00	39	2h20	+1
Japan	377,835	127·4	Tokyo	010	81	11h30	+9
Jordan	92,300	6·1	Amman	00	962	6h	+2
Kazakhstan	2,717,300	15·3	Astana	810	7	8h15	+6
Kenya	582,650	36·9	Nairobi	000	254	8h20	+3
Korea, North	120,540	23·3	Pyongyang	00	850	13h45	+9
Korea, South	98,480	49·0	Seoul	001	82	11h	+9

GAZETTEER · KUWAIT – ZIMBABWE · [1/4]

Country	*Size (km²)*	*Population (m)*	*Capital city*	*Phone access code*	*Phone country code*	*Flying time (h)*	*GMT*
United Kingdom	244,820	60·8	London	00	44	—	n/a
United States	9,826,630	301·1	Washington, DC	011	1	7h50	–5
Kuwait	17,820	2·5	Kuwait City	00	965	6h	+3
Latvia	64,589	2·3	Riga	00	371	2h45	+2
Lebanon	10,400	3·9	Beirut	00	961	4h45	+2
Liberia	111,370	3·2	Monrovia	00	231	12h	0
Lithuania	65,200	3·6	Vilnius	00	370	4h	+2
Malaysia	329,750	24·8	Kuala Lumpur	00	60	12h25	+8
Mexico	1,972,550	108·7	Mexico City	00	52	11h15	–6
Monaco	1·95	32·7k	Monaco	00	377	2h	+1
Morocco	446,550	33·8	Rabat	00	212	5h45	0
Netherlands	41,526	16·6	Amsterdam	00	31	1h15	+1
New Zealand	268,680	4·1	Wellington	00	64	28h	+12
Nigeria	923,768	135·0	Abuja	009	234	6h15	+1
Norway	323,802	4·6	Oslo	00	47	2h	+1
Pakistan	803,940	164·7	Islamabad	00	92	10h	+5
Peru	1,285,220	28·7	Lima	00	51	15h15	–5
Philippines	300,000	91·1	Manila	00	63	15h	+8
Poland	312,685	38·5	Warsaw	00	48	2h20	+1
Portugal	92,391	10·6	Lisbon	00	351	2h30	0
Romania	237,500	22·3	Bucharest	00	40	3h15	+2
Russia	17,075,200	141·4	Moscow	810	7	4h	+3
Rwanda	26,338	9·9	Kigali	00	250	11h20	+2
Saudi Arabia	2,149,690	27·6	Riyadh	00	966	6h15	+3
Singapore	692·7	4·6	Singapore	001	65	12h45	+8
Slovakia	48,845	5·4	Bratislava	00	421	3h30	+1
Slovenia	20,273	2·0	Ljubljana	00	386	3h30	+1
Somalia	637,657	9·1	Mogadishu	00	252	12h45	+3
South Africa	1,219,912	44·0	Pretoria/Tshwane	00	27	11h	+2
Spain	504,782	40·4	Madrid	00	34	2h20	+1
Sudan	2,505,810	39·4	Khartoum	00	249	12h	+3
Sweden	449,964	9·0	Stockholm	00	46	2h30	+1
Switzerland	41,290	7·6	Bern	00	41	2h	+1
Syria	185,180	19·3	Damascus	00	963	6h30	+2
Taiwan	35,980	22·9	Taipei	002	886	14h30	+8
Thailand	514,000	65·1	Bangkok	001	66	14h20	+7
Turkey	780,580	71·2	Ankara	00	90	5h15	+2
Ukraine	603,700	46·3	Kiev/Kyiv	810	380	3h25	+2
Venezuela	912,050	26·0	Caracas	00	58	11h30	–4
Vietnam	329,560	85·3	Hanoi	00	84	13h45	+7
Zimbabwe	390,580	12·3	Harare	00	263	12h50	+2

GAZETTEER · ALGERIA – SOUTH KOREA · [2/4]

Country	*Male life expectancy*	*Female life expectancy*	*difference*	*Infant mortality*	*Median age*	*Birth rate*	*Death rate*	*Fertility rate*	*Adult HIV rate*	*Literacy*
United Kingdom	76·2	81·3	–5·1	5·0	39·6	10·7	10·1	1·7	0·2	99
United States	75·1	81·0	–5·9	6·4	36·6	14·2	8·3	2·1	0·6	99
Algeria	71·9	75·2	–3·3	28·8	25·5	17·1	4·6	1·9	0·1	70
Argentina	72·6	80·2	–7·6	14·3	29·9	16·5	7·6	2·1	0·7	97
Australia	77·7	83·6	–5·9	4·6	37·1	12·0	7·6	1·8	0·1	99
Austria	76·3	82·3	–6·0	4·5	41·3	8·7	9·8	1·4	0·3	98
Belarus	64·3	76·1	–11·8	6·6	38·2	9·5	14·0	1·2	0·3	100
Belgium	75·7	82·2	–6·5	4·6	41·1	10·3	10·3	1·6	0·2	99
Brazil	68·3	76·4	–8·1	27·6	28·6	16·3	6·2	1·9	0·7	89
Bulgaria	68·9	76·4	–7·5	19·2	40·9	9·6	14·3	1·4	0·1	98
Burma/Myanmar	60·3	64·8	–4·5	50·7	27·4	17·5	9·3	2·0	1·2	90
Cambodia	59·3	63·4	–4·1	58·5	21·3	25·5	8·2	3·1	2·6	74
Canada	77·0	83·9	–6·9	4·6	39·1	10·8	7·9	1·6	0·3	99
Chile	73·7	80·4	–6·7	8·4	30·7	15·0	5·9	2·0	0·3	96
China	71·1	74·8	–3·7	22·1	33·2	13·5	7·0	1·8	0·1	91
Colombia	68·4	76·2	–7·8	20·1	26·6	20·2	5·5	2·5	0·7	93
Cuba	74·8	79·4	–4·6	6·0	36·3	11·4	7·1	1·6	0·1	100
Czech Republic	73·1	79·9	–6·8	3·9	39·5	9·0	10·6	1·2	0·1	99
Denmark	75·6	80·4	–4·8	4·5	40·1	10·9	10·3	1·7	0·2	99
Egypt	69·0	74·2	–5·2	29·5	24·2	22·5	5·1	2·8	0·1	71
Estonia	66·9	78·1	–11·2	7·6	39·4	10·2	13·3	1·4	1·1	100
Finland	75·1	82·3	–7·2	3·5	41·6	10·4	9·9	1·7	0·1	100
France	77·3	84·0	–6·7	3·4	39·0	12·9	8·6	2·0	0·4	99
Germany	76·0	82·1	–6·1	4·1	43·0	8·2	10·7	1·4	0·1	99
Greece	76·8	82·1	–5·3	5·3	41·2	9·6	10·3	1·4	0·2	96
Haiti	55·3	58·7	–3·4	63·8	18·4	35·9	10·4	4·9	5·6	53
Hong Kong	79·0	84·6	–5·6	2·9	41·2	7·3	6·5	1·0	0·1	94
Hungary	68·7	77·4	–8·7	8·2	38·9	9·7	13·1	1·3	0·1	99
India	66·3	71·2	–4·9	34·6	24·8	22·7	6·6	2·8	0·9	61
Indonesia	67·7	72·8	–5·1	32·1	26·9	19·7	6·3	2·4	0·1	90
Iran	69·1	72·1	–3·0	38·1	25·8	16·6	5·7	1·7	0·1	77
Iraq	68·0	70·6	–2·6	47·0	20·0	31·4	5·3	4·1	0·1	74
Ireland	75·3	80·7	–5·4	5·2	34·3	14·4	7·8	1·9	0·1	99
Israel	77·4	81·8	–4·4	6·8	29·9	17·7	6·2	2·4	0·1	97
Italy	77·0	83·1	–6·1	5·7	42·5	8·5	10·5	1·3	0·5	98
Japan	78·7	85·6	–6·9	2·8	43·5	8·1	9·0	1·2	0·1	99
Jordan	76·0	81·2	–5·2	16·2	23·5	20·7	2·7	2·6	0·1	90
Kazakhstan	61·9	72·8	–10·9	27·4	29·1	16·2	9·4	1·9	0·2	100
Kenya	55·2	55·4	–0·2	57·4	18·6	38·9	11·0	4·8	6·7	85
Korea, North	69·2	74·8	–5·6	22·6	32·4	15·1	7·2	2·1	—	99
Korea, South	73·8	80·9	–7·1	6·1	35·8	9·9	6·0	1·3	0·1	98

GAZETTEER · KUWAIT – ZIMBABWE · [2/4]

Country	*Male life expectancy*	*Female life expectancy*	*difference*	*Infant mortality*	*Median age*	*Birth rate*	*Death rate*	*Fertility rate*	*Adult HIV rate*	*Literacy*
United Kingdom	76·2	81·3	–5·1	5·0	39·6	10·7	10·1	1·7	0·2	99
United States	75·1	81·0	–5·9	6·4	36·6	14·2	8·3	2·1	0·6	99
Kuwait	76·2	78·5	–2·3	9·5	26·0	22·0	2·4	2·9	0·1	93
Latvia	66·4	77·1	–10·7	9·2	39·6	9·4	13·6	1·3	0·6	100
Lebanon	70·7	75·8	–5·1	23·4	28·3	18·1	6·1	1·9	0·1	87
Liberia	38·9	41·9	–3·0	149·7	18·1	43·8	22·2	5·9	5·9	58
Lithuania	69·5	79·7	–10·2	6·7	38·6	8·9	11·1	1·2	0·1	100
Malaysia	70·0	75·6	–5·6	16·6	24·4	22·7	5·1	3·0	0·4	89
Mexico	72·8	78·6	–5·8	19·6	25·6	20·4	4·8	2·4	0·3	91
Monaco	76·0	83·8	–7·8	5·3	45·5	9·1	12·9	1·8	—	99
Morocco	68·9	73·7	–4·8	38·9	24·3	21·6	5·5	2·6	0·1	52
Netherlands	76·5	81·8	–5·3	4·9	39·7	10·7	8·7	1·7	0·2	99
New Zealand	76·0	82·1	–6·1	5·7	34·2	13·6	7·5	1·8	0·1	99
Nigeria	46·8	48·1	–1·3	95·5	18·7	40·2	16·7	5·5	5·4	68
Norway	77·0	82·5	–5·5	3·6	38·7	11·3	9·4	1·8	0·1	100
Pakistan	62·7	64·8	–2·1	68·8	20·9	27·5	8·0	3·7	0·1	50
Peru	68·3	72·0	–3·7	30·0	25·5	20·1	6·2	2·5	0·5	88
Philippines	67·6	73·5	–5·9	22·1	22·7	24·5	5·4	3·1	0·1	93
Poland	71·2	79·4	–8·2	7·1	37·3	9·9	9·9	1·3	0·1	100
Portugal	74·6	81·4	–6·8	4·9	38·8	10·6	10·6	1·5	0·4	93
Romania	68·4	75·6	–7·2	24·6	36·9	10·7	11·8	1·4	0·1	97
Russia	59·1	73·0	–13·9	11·1	38·2	10·9	16·0	1·4	1·1	99
Rwanda	47·9	50·2	–2·3	85·3	18·6	40·2	14·9	5·4	5·1	70
Saudi Arabia	73·8	78·0	–4·2	12·4	21·4	29·1	2·6	3·9	0·01	79
Singapore	79·2	84·6	–5·4	2·3	37·8	9·2	4·4	1·1	0·2	93
Slovakia	71·0	79·1	–8·1	7·1	36·1	10·7	9·5	1·3	0·1	100
Slovenia	72·8	80·5	–7·7	4·4	41·0	9·0	10·4	1·3	0·1	100
Somalia	47·1	50·7	–3·6	113·1	17·6	44·6	16·3	6·7	1·0	38
South Africa	43·2	41·7	1·5	59·4	24·3	17·9	22·5	2·2	21·5	86
Spain	76·5	83·3	–6·8	4·3	40·3	10·0	9·8	1·3	0·7	98
Sudan	48·2	50·0	–1·8	91·8	18·7	34·9	14·4	4·7	2·3	61
Sweden	78·4	83·0	–4·6	2·8	41·1	10·2	10·3	1·7	0·1	99
Switzerland	77·8	83·6	–5·8	4·3	40·4	9·7	8·5	1·4	0·4	99
Syria	69·3	72·0	–2·7	27·7	21·1	27·2	4·7	3·3	0·1	80
Taiwan	74·6	80·7	–6·1	5·5	35·5	9·0	6·5	1·1	—	96
Thailand	70·2	75·0	–4·8	18·9	32·4	13·7	7·1	1·6	1·5	93
Turkey	70·4	75·5	–5·1	38·3	28·6	16·4	6·0	1·9	0·1	87
Ukraine	62·2	74·0	–11·8	9·5	39·2	9·5	16·1	1·2	1·4	99
Venezuela	70·2	76·5	–6·3	22·5	24·9	21·2	5·1	2·6	0·7	93
Vietnam	68·3	74·1	–5·8	24·4	26·4	16·6	6·2	1·9	0·4	90
Zimbabwe	40·6	38·3	2·3	51·1	20·1	27·7	21·8	3·1	24·6	91

GAZETTEER · ALGERIA – SOUTH KOREA · [3/4]

Country	Currency	Currency code	£1 =	GDP per capita $	Inflation %	Unemployment %	Fiscal year end
United Kingdom	Pound=100 Pence	GBP	—	31,800	3·0	2·9	5 Apr
United States	Dollar=100 Cents	USD	2·0	44,000	2·5	4·8	30 Sep
Algeria	Dinar=100 Centimes	DZD	138·9	7,600	3·0	15·7	31 Dec
Argentina	Peso=10,000 Australes	ARS	6·1	15,200	9·8	8·7	31 Dec
Australia	Dollar=100 Cents	AUD	2·4	33,300	3·8	4·9	30 Jun
Austria	euro=100 cent	EUR	1·5	34,600	1·6	4·9	31 Dec
Belarus	Ruble=100 Kopecks	BYR	4,235·1	8,100	9·5	1·6	31 Dec
Belgium	euro=100 cent	EUR	1·5	33,000	2·1	8·1	31 Dec
Brazil	Real=100 Centavos	BRL	3·9	8,800	3·0	9·6	31 Dec
Bulgaria	Lev=100 Stotinki	BGL	2·9	10,700	6·5	9·6	31 Dec
Burma/Myanmar	Kyat=100 Pyas	MMK	12·7	1,800	21·4	10·2	31 Mar
Cambodia	Riel=100 Sen	KHR	7,907·1	2,700	5·0	2·5	31 Dec
Canada	Dollar=100 Cents	CAD	2·2	35,600	2·0	6·4	31 Mar
Chile	Peso=100 Centavos	CLP	1,030·3	12,700	2·6	7·8	31 Dec
China	Renminbi Yuan=100 Fen	CNY	15·1	7,700	1·5	4·2	31 Dec
Colombia	Peso=100 Centavos	COP	3,918·8	8,600	4·3	11·1	31 Dec
Cuba	Peso=100 Centavos	CUP/C	2·0	4,000	5·0	1·9	31 Dec
Czech Republic	Koruna=100 Haléru	CZK	41·3	21,900	2·7	8·4	31 Dec
Denmark	Krone=100 Øre	DKK	11·0	37,000	1·8	3·8	31 Dec
Egypt	Pound=100 Piastres	EGP	11·2	4,200	6·5	10·3	30 Jun
Estonia	Kroon=100 Sents	EEK	22·9	20,300	4·4	4·5	31 Dec
Finland	euro=100 cent	EUR	1·5	33,700	1·7	7·0	31 Dec
France	euro=100 cent	EUR	1·5	31,100	1·5	8·7	31 Dec
Germany	euro=100 cent	EUR	1·5	31,900	1·7	7·1	31 Dec
Greece	euro=100 cent	EUR	1·5	24,000	3·3	9·2	31 Dec
Haiti	Gourde=100 Centimes	HTG	71·4	1,800	14·4	*c.*65	30 Sep
Hong Kong	HK Dollar=100 Cents	HKD	15·6	37,300	2·2	4·9	31 Mar
Hungary	Forint=100 Fillér	HUF	367·0	17,600	3·7	7·4	31 Dec
India	Rupee=100 Paisa	INR	80·7	3,800	5·3	7·8	31 Mar
Indonesia	Rupiah=100 Sen	IDR	17,413·3	3,900	13·2	12·5	31 Dec
Iran	Rial(=100 Dinars)	IRR	18,272·1	8,700	15·8	15·0	20 Mar
Iraq	New Iraqi Dinar	NID	2,486·9	2,900	64·8	*c.*27·5	31 Dec
Ireland	euro=100 cent	EUR	1·5	44,500	3·9	4·3	31 Dec
Israel	Shekel=100 Agora	ILS	8·4	26,800	-0·1	8·3	31 Dec
Italy	euro=100 cent	EUR	1·5	30,200	2·3	7·0	31 Dec
Japan	Yen=100 Sen	JPY	241·5	33,100	0·3	4·1	31 Mar
Jordan	Dinar=1,000 Fils	JOD	1·4	5,100	6·3	15·4	31 Dec
Kazakhstan	Tenge=100 Tiyn	KZT	237·0	9,400	8·6	7·4	31 Dec
Kenya	Shilling=100 Cents	KES	131·9	1,200	10·5	40·0	30 Jun
Korea, North	NK Won=100 Chon	KPW	248·1	1,800	—	—	31 Dec
Korea, South	SK Won=100 Chon	KRW	1,852·8	24,500	2·2	3·3	31 Dec

GAZETTEER · KUWAIT – ZIMBABWE · [3/4]

Country	Currency	Currency code	£1 =	GDP per capita $	Inflation %	Unemployment %	Fiscal year end
United Kingdom	Pound=100 Pence	GBP	—	31,800	3·0	2·9	5 Apr
United States	Dollar=100 Cents	USD	2·0	44,000	2·5	4·8	30 Sep
Kuwait	Dinar=1,000 Fils	KWD	0·6	23,100	3·0	2·2	31 Mar
Latvia	Lats=100 Santims	LVL	1·0	16,000	6·8	6·5	31 Dec
Lebanon	Pound=100 Piastres	LBP	2,984·2	5,700	4·8	20·0	31 Dec
Liberia	Dollar=100 Cents	LRD	2·0	900	15·0	85·0	31 Dec
Lithuania	Litas=100 Centas	LTL	5·1	15,300	3·8	5·7	31 Dec
Malaysia	Ringgit=100 Sen	MYR	6·7	12,900	3·8	3·5	31 Dec
Mexico	Peso=100 Centavos	MXN	21·4	10,700	3·4	3·2	31 Dec
Monaco	euro=100 cent	EUR	1·5	30,000	1·9	—	31 Dec
Morocco	Dirham=100 centimes	MAD	16·4	4,600	2·8	7·7	31 Dec
Netherlands	euro=100 cent	EUR	1·5	32,100	1·4	5·5	31 Dec
New Zealand	Dollar=100 Cents	NZD	2·7	26,200	3·8	3·8	31 Mar
Nigeria	Naira=100 Kobo	NGN	252·0	1,500	10·5	5·8	31 Dec
Norway	Krone=100 Øre	NOK	12·0	46,300	2·3	3·5	31 Dec
Pakistan	Rupee=100 Paisa	PKR	120·0	2,600	7·9	6·5	30 Jun
Peru	New Sol=100 Cents	PEN	6·2	6,600	2·1	7·2	31 Dec
Philippines	Peso=100 Centavos	PHP	91·5	5,000	6·2	7·9	31 Dec
Poland	Zloty=100 Groszy	PLN	5·5	14,300	1·3	14·9	31 Dec
Portugal	euro=100 cent	EUR	1·5	19,800	2·5	7·6	31 Dec
Romania	New Leu=100 New Bani	RON	4·8	9,100	6·8	6·1	31 Dec
Russia	Ruble=100 Kopecks	RUR	51·0	12,200	9·8	6·6	31 Dec
Rwanda	Franc=100 Centimes	RWF	1,078·1	1,600	6·7	—	31 Dec
Saudi Arabia	Riyal=100 Halala	SAR	7·5	13,600	1·9	*c.*25	31 Dec
Singapore	Dollar=100 Cents	SGD	3·0	31,400	1·0	3·1	31 Mar
Slovakia	Koruna=100 Halierov	SKK	49·4	18,200	4·4	10·2	31 Dec
Slovenia	euro=100 cent	EUR	1·5	23,400	2·4	9·6	31 Dec
Somalia	Shilling=100 Cents	SOS	2,675·2	600	—	—	—
South Africa	Rand=100 Cents	ZAR	14·0	13,300	5·0	25·5	31 Mar
Spain	euro=100 cent	EUR	1·5	27,400	3·5	8·1	31 Dec
Sudan	Dinar=100 Piastres	SDD	395·9	2,400	9·0	18·7	31 Dec
Sweden	Krona=100 Øre	SEK	13·6	32,200	1·4	5·6	31 Dec
Switzerland	Franc=100 Centimes	CHF	2·4	34,000	1·2	3·3	31 Dec
Syria	Pound=100 Piastres	SYP	103·1	4,100	8·0	12·5	31 Dec
Taiwan	Dollar=100 Cents	TWD	66·5	29,500	1·0	3·9	30 Jun
Thailand	Baht=100 Satang	THB	68·9	9,200	5·1	2·1	30 Sep
Turkey	New Lira=100 New Kurus	TRY	2·6	9,000	9·8	10·2	31 Dec
Ukraine	Hryvena=100 Kopiykas	UAH	9·9	7,800	11·6	*c.*10	31 Dec
Venezuela	Bolívar=100 Centimos	VEB	4,239·4	7,200	15·8	8·9	31 Dec
Vietnam	Dong=100 Xu	VND	31,711·2	3,100	7·5	2·0	31 Dec
Zimbabwe	Dollar=100 Cents	ZWD	—	2,100	976·4	80·0	31 Dec

GAZETTEER · ALGERIA – SOUTH KOREA · [4/4]

Country	Voting age	Driving side	UN vehicle code	Internet country code	Military service	Death penalty	National Day
United Kingdom	18 U	L	GB	.uk	N	N	—
United States	18 U	R	USA	.us	N	Y	4 Jul
Algeria	18 U	R	DZ	.dz	Y	N*	1 Nov
Argentina	18 UC	R	RA	.ar	N	Y*	25 May
Australia	18 UC	L	AUS	.au	N	N	26 Jan
Austria	18 U	R	A	.at	Y	N	26 Oct
Belarus	18 U	R	BY	.by	Y	Y	3 Jul
Belgium	18 UC	R	B	.be	N	N	21 Jul
Brazil	16 U*	R	BR	.br	Y	Y*	7 Sep
Bulgaria	18 U	R	BG	.bg	Y	N	3 Mar
Burma/Myanmar	18 U	R	BUR	.mm	N	N*	4 Jan
Cambodia	18 U	R	K	.kh	Y	N	9 Nov
Canada	18 U	R	CDN	.ca	N	N	1 Jul
Chile	18 UC	R	RCH	.cl	Y	Y*	18 Sep
China	18 U	R	RC	.cn	Y	Y	1 Oct
Colombia	18 U	R	CO	.co	Y	N	20 Jul
Cuba	16 U	R	CU	.cu	N	Y	1 Jan
Czech Republic	18 U	R	CZ	.cz	N	N	28 Oct
Denmark	18 U	R	DK	.dk	Y	N	5 Jun
Egypt	18 UC	R	ET	.eg	Y	Y	23 Jul
Estonia	18 U	R	EST	.ee	Y	N	24 Feb
Finland	18 U	R	FIN	.fi	Y	N	6 Dec
France	18 U	R	F	.fr	N	N	14 Jul
Germany	18 U	R	D	.de	Y	N	3 Oct
Greece	18 UC	R	GR	.gr	Y	N	25 Mar
Haiti	18 U	R	RH	.ht	N	N	1 Jan
Hong Kong	18 U*	L	—	.hk	N	N	1 Oct
Hungary	18 U	R	H	.hu	N	N	20 Aug
India	18 U	L	IND	.in	N	Y	26 Jan
Indonesia	17 U*	L	RI	.id	Y	Y	17 Aug
Iran	18 U	R	IR	.ir	Y	Y	1 Apr
Iraq	18 U	R	IRQ	.iq	N	Y	17 Jul
Ireland	18 U	L	IRL	.ie	N	N	17 Mar
Israel	18 U	R	IL	.il	Y	Y*	14 May
Italy	18 U*	R	I	.it	N	N	2 Jun
Japan	20 U	L	J	.jp	N	Y	23 Dec
Jordan	18 U	R	HKJ	.jo	N	Y	25 May
Kazakhstan	18 U	R	KZ	.kz	Y	Y	16 Dec
Kenya	18 U	L	EAK	.ke	N	N*	12 Dec
Korea, North	17 U	R	—	.kp	N	Y	9 Sep
Korea, South	19 U	R	ROK	.kr	Y	Y	15 Aug

GAZETTEER · KUWAIT – ZIMBABWE · [4/4]

Country	Voting age	Driving side	UN vehicle code	Internet country code	Military service	Death penalty	National Day
United Kingdom	18 U	L	GB	.uk	N	N	—
United States	18 U	R	USA	.us	N	Y	4 Jul
Kuwait	16 U*	R	KWT	.kw	Y	Y	25 Feb
Latvia	18 U	R	LV	.lv	Y	Y*	18 Nov
Lebanon	21 C*	R	RL	.lb	Y	Y	22 Nov
Liberia	18 U	R	LB	.lr	N	N	26 Jul
Lithuania	18 U	R	LT	.lt	Y	N	16 Feb
Malaysia	21 U	L	MAL	.my	N	Y	31 Aug
Mexico	18 UC	R	MEX	.mx	Y	N	16 Sep
Monaco	18 U	R	MC	.mc	—	N	19 Nov
Morocco	18 U	R	MA	.ma	Y	N*	30 Jul
Netherlands	18 U	R	NL	.nl	N	N	30 Apr
New Zealand	18 U	L	NZ	.nz	N	N	6 Feb
Nigeria	18 U	R	WAN	.ng	N	Y	1 Oct
Norway	18 U	R	N	.no	Y	N	17 May
Pakistan	18 U	L	PK	.pk	N	Y	23 Mar
Peru	18 UC*	R	PE	.pe	Y	Y*	28 Jul
Philippines	18 U	R	RP	.ph	Y	N	12 Jun
Poland	18 U	R	PL	.pl	Y	N	3 May
Portugal	18 U	R	P	.pt	N	N	10 Jun
Romania	18 U	R	RO	.ro	N	N	1 Dec
Russia	18 U	R	RUS	.ru	Y	N*	12 Jun
Rwanda	18 U	R	RWA	.rw	N	Y	1 Jul
Saudi Arabia	21 C	R	SA	.sa	N	Y	23 Sep
Singapore	21 UC	L	SGP	.sg	Y	Y	9 Aug
Slovakia	18 U	R	SK	.sk	N	N	1 Sep
Slovenia	18 U*	R	SLO	.si	N	N	25 Jun
Somalia	18 U	R	SO	.so	N	Y	1 Jul
South Africa	18 U	L	ZA	.za	N	N	27 Apr
Spain	18 U	R	E	.es	N	N	12 Oct
Sudan	17 U	R	SUD	.sd	Y	Y	1 Jan
Sweden	18 U	R	S	.se	Y	N	6 Jun
Switzerland	18 U	R	CH	.ch	Y	N	1 Aug
Syria	18 U	R	SYR	.sy	Y	Y	17 Apr
Taiwan	20 U	R	—	.tw	Y	Y	10 Oct
Thailand	18 UC	L	T	.th	Y	Y	5 Dec
Turkey	18 U	R	TR	.tr	N	N	29 Oct
Ukraine	18 U	R	UA	.ua	Y	N	24 Aug
Venezuela	18 U	R	YV	.ve	Y	N	5 Jul
Vietnam	18 U	R	VN	.vn	Y	Y	2 Sep
Zimbabwe	18 U	L	ZW	.zw	N	Y	18 Apr

Society & Health

What is not good for the beehive, cannot be good for the bees.
— MARCUS AURELIUS (AD 121–180)

'CHEMICAL CASTRATION'

On 13 June 2007, the then Home Sec. John Reid announced that, as part of a review of child sex offences, he would explore 'developing the use of drug treatments alongside existing psychological treatments'. Reid stressed that any drug treatments would be voluntary ('because to succeed it relies on the co-operation of the offender'), and would not be a 'substitute for prison' for the worst offenders. Inevitably, the headlines following Reid's statement spoke of 'chemical castration'. ❦ A number of countries currently offer (or enforce) drug treatments to control the libido of sex offenders, including Italy, Hungary, France, Sweden, Germany, Denmark, the Czech Republic, and Canada. In the US, *c*.8 states allow chemical or surgical castration – for example, California requires high-risk sex offenders whose victims were under 13 years old to undergo drug treatment as a condition of their release from prison. ❦ A range of chemicals are used to reduce levels of testosterone, with the aim of diminishing sexual drive, desires, urges, and fantasies – including drugs usually prescribed for breast cancer, prostate cancer, depression, and birth control. Although reported rates of success vary and side effects can be severe, John Reid asserted that such drugs 'have been shown to be effective in reducing sexual drive and reducing offending, sometimes significantly'. ❦ In a fascinating 2007 article in the *Howard Journal*, Dr Karen Harrison of University of the West of England Law School examined the issues surrounding chemical castration. (Though she noted that this term 'has an ugly jarring sound to it', and suggested that all parties may be more amenable to drug therapies if terms like 'anti-hormone treatment' were used, that did not 'summon up images of pain and suffering'.) Citing a wealth of research, Harrison warned that drug therapy is likely only to work for a certain class of paedophile (those who are solely attracted to children). Furthermore, she cautioned that to be effective, drug therapy probably needs to be restricted to those with a genuine desire to change, and combined in a 'package of treatment' with psychotherapy or counselling. However, Harrison concluded by approvingly quoting Dr Fred Berlin: 'if legislation and punishment alone cannot fully solve the problem, medicine and science need to be called into action. And if society can be made safer by such means, why not use them?' ❦ With a change of PM and Home Sec. [see p.251], the status of government plans for 'chemical castration' is unclear. Yet it seems likely that public outrage over child abuser recidivism is likely to encourage the government to try whatever measures are available.

UK POPULATION FIGURES

(million)	1971	1981	1991	2001	2005	2011	2021
England	46·4	46·8	47·9	49·4	50·4	52·0	54·6
Wales	2·7	2·8	2·9	2·9	3·0	3·0	3·2
Scotland	5·2	5·2	5·1	5·1	5·1	5·1	5·1
N Ireland	1·5	1·5	1·6	1·7	1·7	1·8	1·8
UK	55·9	56·4	57·4	59·1	60·2	61·9	64·7

[Mid-year estimates for 1971–2005; 2005-based projections for 2011 & 2021 · Source: ONS]

UK BIRTHS & DEATHS

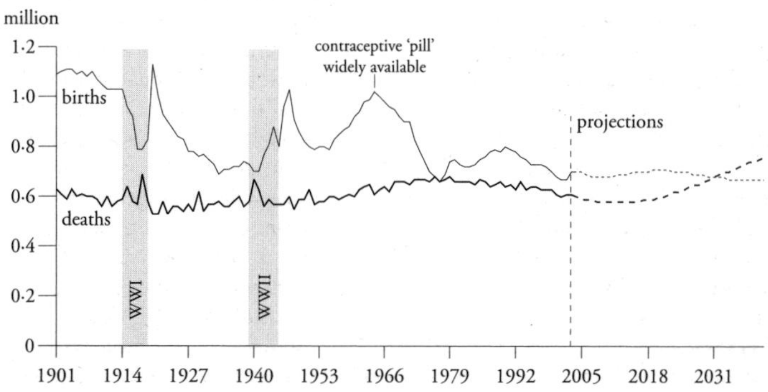

[Data for 1901–21 exclude Ireland. Data from 1981 exclude the non-residents of N Ireland. 2003-based projections for 2004–41. Source: Social Trends 35 · Crown ©]

UK FERTILITY RATE

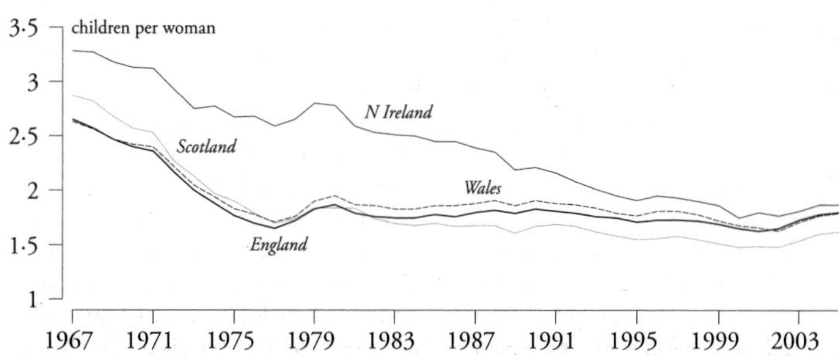

In 2007, the fertility rate in England hit 1·87 children per woman – its highest level since the 1980s. [Source: ONS, General Register Office for Scotland, N Ireland Statistics and Research Agency]

GB POPULATION BY ETHNIC GROUP

All White	91·9%	White British	88·2%
		White Irish	1·2%
		Other White	2·5%
All Asian or Asian British	4·1%	Indian	1·8%
		Pakistani	1·3%
		Bangladeshi	0·5%
		Other Asian	0·4%
All Black or Black British	2·0%	Black Caribbean	1·0%
		Black African	0·9%
		Other Black	0·2%
Mixed	1·2%		
Chinese	0·4%		
Other ethnic groups	0·4%		

[Source: Social Trends 2005 · Crown © Data from 2001 Census]

Tabulated below is the population of Great Britain by ethnic group and age, 2001:

Ethnicity	*age <16*	*16–64*	*>65*
White British	20%	63	17
White Irish	6	69	25
Other White	14	76	10
Mixed	50	47	3
Indian	23	71	7
Pakistani	35	61	4
Bangladeshi	38	58	3
Other Asian	24	71	5
Black Caribbean	20	69	11
Black African	30	68	2
Other Black	38	59	3
Chinese	19	76	5
Other ethnic groups	19	78	3

[Source: Social Trends 2007 · Crown © · Data from 2001 Census]

SOCIALISING WITH ETHNIC MINORITIES

70% of Britons had no close friends from within other ethnic groups, according to a November 2006 survey for the Cmsn for Racial Equality. The Mori poll asked how often Britons mixed socially outside their ethnic group, in various locations:

How often do you socialise with other ethnic groups	*≥ monthly*	*< monthly*
At home	30%	57%
At work, school, or college	49%	29%
Through hobbies or sports	32%	50%
Socially outside work	41%	44%
At the shops	62%	29%

OPINIONS OF BRITISH MUSLIMS

The propensity to fundamentalist belief amongst the younger generation of British Muslims was highlighted by *Living Apart Together* – a January 2007 report by the independent think tank Policy Exchange. According to the report, 36% of 16–24-year-old British Muslims believed that a Muslim who converted to another religion should be put to death; 19% of those ≥55 agreed. On the subject of identity, the report revealed that 86% of British Muslims reported that their religion was 'the most important thing' in their life. Despite this, 59% said they had more in common with non-Muslims in Britain than with Muslims abroad. 87% of Muslims disagreed with the statement '*I admire organisations like al-Qaeda that are prepared to fight against the West*', but there was a difference across age groups, as shown below:

% by age	16–24	25–34	35–44	45–54	>55
Agreed	13	6	6	2	3
Disagreed	80	88	87	89	92

Of British Muslims questioned, 84% agreed that 'on the whole, I feel I have been treated fairly in this society, regardless of my religious beliefs'. However many respondents felt they had been victims of religious discrimination in the past year:

Discrimination &c. in the past year	*% of British Muslims*
Been subject to violence because of your religion	6
Been stopped by police because you are a Muslim	9
Been subject to verbal abuse because of your religion	25
Felt that some non-Muslims were hostile because of your religion	30
Felt you were an object of suspicion because of your religion	31
None of these	52

The survey also explored how the general and Muslim populations saw the West:

'Many of the problems in the world today are a result of arrogant Western attitudes'

	agree	*disagree*	*don't know*
General population	30%	39	31
Muslim population	58%	35	7

A Gallup poll of London Muslims revealed that 69% identified strongly with their religion, and 57% identified strongly with Britain, suggesting that the former did not preclude the latter. The greatest difference between London Muslims and the general London public lay in attitudes to what was considered morally acceptable:

Is morally acceptable	*Muslims*	*others*
Sex outside marriage	11%	82%
Homosexual acts	4	66
Abortion	10	58
Death penalty	31	43
Suicide	4	38
Viewing pornography	4	29
Having an affair	5	18
Crimes of passion	3	2
'Honour' killings	3	1

[Source: Gallup, April 2007]

CHILDREN IN CARE & ADOPTION

60,300 children in England were being 'looked after' by the authorities, as of March 2006, according to the Department for Education and Skills [DfES]. The level of local authority care ranged from children's homes to care orders, but most children were in foster care. Below is a breakdown of 'looked after' children, by sex and age:

Sex		*Age*			
				5–9	11,500 (19%)
Male	33,400 (55%)	<1	2,900 (5%)	10–15	26,100 (43%)
Female	26,900 (45%)	1–4	8,500 (14%)	>16	11,300 (19%)

The data below show the number of 'looked after' children by type of placement:

Placement	*number*	*%*
Fostered	42,000	70
Children's home	6,600	11
With parents	5,300	9
Placed for adoption	2,900	5
Other	3,600	6

6% of all 'looked after' children were adopted in 2006; below is an age breakdown:

<1 *years old*	190 (5%)	5–9	900 (25%)	>16	20 (1%)
1–4	2,300 (64%)	10–15	180 (5%)	Average age at adoption: 4y1m	

Since 2000, >2,200 children have been adopted from abroad. According to DfES figures (for 2000–06), the most common countries of adoptee origin included:

Country	*no. adopted*
China	1,060
Russia	183
India	162
Guatemala	153
Thailand	137
USA	115
Cambodia	65
Vietnam	38
Romania	33

[Applications received by country 2000–4·10·06]

CHILDHOOD IMMUNISATION SCHEDULE

Age	immunisation	*injections*
2m	*diphtheria, tetanus, whooping cough, polio, Hib* [DTaP/IPV/Hib]	1
3m	*pneumococcal conjugate vaccine* [PCV]	1
	[DTaP/IPV/Hib] + *meningitis C* [MenC]	2
4m	[DTaP/IPV/Hib] + [MenC]	2
12m	[Hib/MenC] + [PCV]	2
13m	*measles, mumps, rubella* [MMR]	1
3y4m–5y	*diphtheria, tetanus, whooping cough, polio* [DTaP/IPV] + [PCV]	2
	measles, mumps, rubella [MMR]	1
13y–18y	*diphtheria, tetanus, polio* [Td/IPV]	1

(The above is only a guide and parents are strongly advised to consult medical professionals.) In March 2007, experts highlighted five additional vaccinations that might be considered for teenagers. The proposed vaccines were: human papilloma virus (HPV) to protect against cervical cancer; hepatitis B; whooping cough booster; chickenpox; and meningococcus (quad) against four types of meningitis.

MOST POPULAR NAMES · 2006

Below are the most popular names of 2006, from the Office of National Statistics:

Jack (no change from 2005)	*nickname for John*	1	*? feminine version of Oliver*	(+3) Olivia
Thomas (+1)	*Greek form of Aramaic for 'twin'*	2	*from the Latin Gratia*	(+5) Grace
Joshua (–1)	*Jehova saves*	3	*allegedly created by Shakespeare*	(–2) Jessica
Oliver (+1)	*? from Latin for 'olive tree'*	4	*from the gemstone*	(+11) Ruby
Harry (+4)	*nickname for Henry*	5	*from the Latin Aemilia*	(–3) Emily
James (–2)	*English form of Jacomus & Jacob*	6	*French form of Sophia*	(–3) Sophie
William (+1)	*from German for 'protector'*	7	*Greek for 'young green shoot'*	(–2) Chloe
Samuel (–1)	*from Hebrew for 'name of God'*	8	*from the Latin Lucia*	(–) Lucy
Daniel (–3)	*from Hebrew for 'God is my judge'*	9	*flower, symbol of purity*	(+7) Lily
Charlie (+2)	*pet form of Charles*	10	*shortened form of Eleanor, &c.*	(–4) Ellie

A *Times* analysis of the top 3,000 names indicated that if all the various spellings of the name were aggregated, Muhammad was the 2nd most popular name for a boy in Britain in 2006, after Jack. ❦ A survey of British birth certificates from the last 22 years (by findmypast.com) uncovered the influence of popular culture on many parents, resulting in: 2,614 Shakiras, 1,611 Britneys, 1,120 Keanus, 265 Beyoncés, 48 Didos, 39 Gazzas, 36 Arsenals, 27 Tupacs, 6 Gandalfs, 3 Snoops, and 2 Supermans.

CHILDREN'S WELL-BEING · UK

A UNICEF report [see p.65], released in February 2007, stated that the well-being of children in the UK was the lowest in the Western world. Below are some figures:

Children in the UK who ...	%
Reported low family affluence [2001]	15·3
Reported <10 books in their home [2003]	9·4
Rated their health as 'fair or poor' [2001]	22·6
Are overweight according to their BMI [2001]	15·8
'Liked school a lot' [2001]	19·0
Had parents that spend time talking to them several times/week [2000]	60·5
Found their peers 'kind and helpful' [2001]	43·3
Smoked cigarettes at least once a week [2001]	13·1
Had been drunk 2 or more times (11,13, & 15-year-olds) [2001]	30·8
Had used cannabis in the last 12 months (15-year-olds) [2001]	34·9
Had had sexual intercourse by age 15 [2001]	38·1
Aspired to low skilled work [2003]	35·3
Lived in a single-parent family [2001]	16·9
Ate round a table with their parents several times/week [2000]	66·7

[Source: UNICEF, *Report Card 7: an Overview of Child Well-being in Rich Countries*, 2007] · Figures released by the Department for Work and Pensions in March 2007 revealed that there had been a 200,000 rise in the number of UK children living in poverty. Relative poverty in this case is defined as those who earn less than 60% of the average income, including housing costs. A single person is considered 'in poverty' if they earn <£145 a week, and a couple with 2 children if they earn <£332.

EDUCATION KEY STAGES

The chart below illustrates the basic structure of the English education system:

Stage	*age*	*year*	test or qualification
FOUNDATION	3–4		
	4–5	reception	*foundation stage profile*
KEY STAGE 1	5–6	year 1	
	6–7	year 2	*tests in English & maths*
KEY STAGE 2	7–8	year 3	
	8–9	year 4	
	9–10	year 5	
	10–11	year 6	*tests in English, maths, & science*
KEY STAGE 3	11–12	year 7	
	12–13	year 8	
	13–14	year 9	*tests in English, maths, & science*
KEY STAGE 4	14–15	year 10	*some take* GCSEs
	15–16	year 11	*most take* GCSEs *or other*
post compulsory education/training	16–17	year 12	AS *or* A LEVELS *or other*
	17–18	year 13	A LEVELS *or other*
	18–19		

HOMEWORK TIME GUIDELINES

The DfES recommends the following time guidelines for children's homework:

Years (age)	*recommended time*
1 & 2 (6–7)	1 hour/week
3 & 4 (8–9)	1·5 hours/week
5 & 6 (10–11)	30 mins/day
7 & 8 (12–13)	45–90 mins/day
9 (14)	1–2 hours/day
10 & 11 (15–16)	1·5–2 hours/day

[Source: Department for Education. Research by DfES indicated that the average point score at Key Stage 3 increased in line with the number of evenings spent doing homework.]

PUBLIC EXPENDITURE ON EDUCATION

2003 figures from the Department for Education and Skills offer an international comparison of public expenditure on education, as a percentage of a country's GDP:

Country	*% GDP*
Denmark	8·3
Iceland	7·8
New Zealand	6·8
France	5·9
Mexico	5·8
Poland	5·8
USA	5·7
UK	5·4
Netherlands	5·1
Italy	4·9
Australia	4·8
Germany	4·7
Korea	4·6
Ireland	4·4
Spain	4·3
Japan	3·7
Turkey	3·7

According to DfES, in 2007–08 real terms public funding per school pupil in England was £4,730.

STUDENT LIFE

UNITE, the UK's largest provider of student accommodation, published its 2007 Student Experience Report in January 2007. >1,600 students from 20 universities participated in the study, which revealed that 59% think the best part of student life is the improvement of career prospects, and 47% think the worst part is having too little cash. Below is the breakdown of a day in the life of an average UK student:

Activity	*hours spent*				
Sleeping	7·1	Socialising (home)	1·7	Working	1·0
Lectures	3·4	Eating	1·4	Cleaning	0·9
Studying	2·8	Travelling	1·1	Sport	0·7
Socialising (out)	1·7	Bathing	1·1	[61% liked to sleep during their time off]	
		Other	1·1		

74% of all students were in debt, each owing an average of £7,798. (The average amount of debt across all UK students, including the 26% without any debts, was £5,760.) Of the 2006/07 intake of students: 74% had a government student loan, 41% had an overdraft, 19% owed money to their parents, and 16% had credit card debts. According to UNITE, the average student expenditure per term week was:

Expense	£				
Accommodation	62·80	Clothes	12·40	Films	2·90
All food	25·00	Travel	11·70	Internet access	2·90
Going out	18·90	Mobile phone	9·60	Cigarettes	2·80
Alcohol	16·20	Soft drinks	7·00	Music	2·40
		Toiletries	5·50	*Total*	180·10

Students were asked what problems they had brought to the community in which they lived: 67% said drunkenness; 67% noise; 44% anti-social behaviour; and 8% said they 'brought the area down'.

THE RUSSELL GROUP

Formed in 1994, the Russell Group is an association of twenty major research-led universities in the UK. Named after the Hotel Russell, where it first convened, the group aims to promote research excellence and attract the best staff and students to its institutions. In 2004/05, Russell Group universities won *c.*64% of the total quality-related research funding allocated by funding councils, and accounted for 56% of all doctorates awarded in the UK. The 20 Russell Group institutions are:

University of Birmingham · University of Bristol · University of Cambridge
Cardiff University · University of Edinburgh · University of Glasgow
Imperial College · King's College · University of Leeds · University of Liverpool
LSE · University of Manchester · Newcastle University · University of
Nottingham · Queen's University · University of Oxford · University of Sheffield
University of Southampton · University College London · University of Warwick

A PricewaterhouseCoopers' report, released in Feb. 2007, suggested that over their lifetime, someone with a degree in medicine was likely to earn £340,315 more than someone who had two A Levels.

DECLINING RATES OF MARRIAGE

In 2005, rates of marriage in England and Wales fell to their lowest level since records began in 1862. This fall came after a three-year rise that had bucked the overall trend of a long-term decline in marriages. There were 244,710 marriages in 2005, down from 273,070 in 2004 – the lowest annual number of weddings since 1896, when 242,764 unions were formed. Below are rates of marriage since 1862:

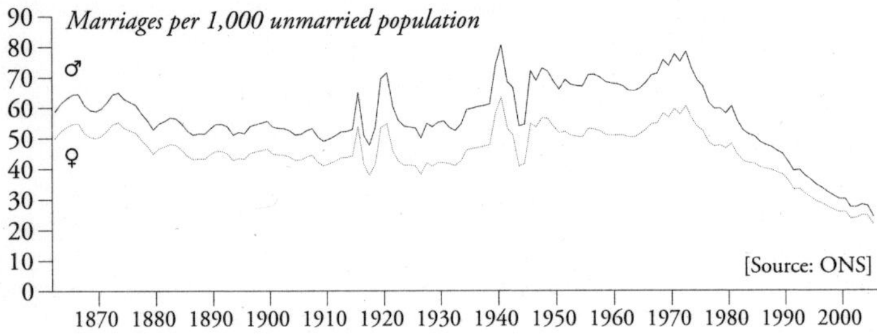

SHAM MARRIAGES

Laws introduced in February 2005 to prevent 'sham marriages' have been linked to the UK's declining rate of marriage. The new rules require those born outside the EU, who only have permission to remain in the UK for six months, to gain special permission from the Home Office to wed. This stipulation is currently being challenged by human rights lawyers, who claim it discriminates against immigrants. But the 76 Register Offices which process marriage applicants from immigrants have reported that, since the law came in, applications have fallen by *c*.60%. The Home Office data below reveal the number of 'suspect' marriages reported by registrars:

2001.........752 | 2002.......1,205 | 2003.......2,684 | 2004.......3,578

NUMBER OF CIVIL PARTNERSHIPS

Between December 2005 (when civil partnerships became legal) and September 2006, 15,672 same-sex couples registered their union in the United Kingdom. The number of UK civil partnerships formed each month is tabulated below by sex:

Month	♂–♂	♀–♀	*total*
December	1,286	667	1,953
January '06	1,305	529	1,834
February	1,004	578	1,582
March	884	564	1,448
April	955	590	1,545
May	813	563	1,376
June	821	618	1,439
July	918	675	1,593
August	791	680	1,471
September	795	636	1,431
TOTAL	9,572	6,100	15,672

[Source: ONS, General Register Office for Scotland, Northern Ireland Statistics & Research Agency]

REASONS FOR DIVORCE

26% of divorcees admitted to have harboured doubts about the solidity of their relationship as they walked down the aisle – according to research by insidedivorce.com in January 2007. The average length of a marriage before one of the parties decided that the relationship was not working was 7 years and 3 months; however, it generally took 10 years and 6 months before formal divorce proceedings began. Below are some of the reasons most commonly offered for divorce or separation:

Reason	%
Partner's infidelity	42
Abuse	34
Boredom	29
Lack of sex	22
Financial disagreements	22
Alcohol/drug abuse	22
Debt	17
Partner's career took priority	11
Hobbies (e.g. football)	8
Respondent's infidelity	8
Life changing event (e.g. family death)	7
Gambling	5
Too much focus on kids	5
Respondent's career took priority	4
'Empty nest syndrome'	3

On average, divorce cost £28,000, and 45% of those questioned admitted that they were poorer post-divorce (21% claimed to be richer). 45% reported that they felt relieved as a result of divorce; 38% were happier, and 23% were sadder. 60% of children with divorced parents were happy that their unhappy parents had split. ❦ Research by Grant Thornton, released in April 2007, indicated that a private detective was employed to uncover infidelity in 49% of the divorce cases handled by top lawyers.

FREQUENCY OF SEX

On average, Britons have sex 92 times a year, according to the latest Durex global sex survey. However, only 42% of Brits are satisfied with their sex life, and most spend 16 mins per 'session'. Below is a global breakdown of those who have sex weekly:

% having sex weekly	
Greece	87
Brazil	82
Russia	80
China	78
Spain	72
Switzerland	72
France	70
India	68
Germany	68
Netherlands	63
Australia	60
Canada	59
UK	55
USA	53
Japan	34

FAVOURITE FETISH

Results from a global survey into sexual fetishes indicated that feet and shoes are the most commonly cited kink. Researchers from the University of Bologna, writing in the *International Journal of Impotence Research*, monitored activity in fetish-related internet discussion groups to gather information on the sexual preferences of the general population. When discussing favourite body parts, 47% opted for feet and toes, compared to just 3% who favoured (the more mainstream) breasts. 64% of those asked to name their favourite object associated with the body claimed to be most turned on by shoes or boots, 12% by underwear, 7% by hair, and 5% by muscles. 150 of the *c.*5,000 people questioned admitted to having a passion for hearing aids.

ADULT LITERACY

Poor adult literacy costs Britain nearly £2bn each year in lost earnings, according to research led by Jean Gross for KPMG Foundation. The December 2006 report concluded that each child who left primary education with below-standard reading and writing would cost the state an extra £45,000–53,000 by the time they were 37 – as a result of consequent truancy, crime and depression. In 2001, the government created national standards for literacy – the framework of which is given below:

Level	*National curriculum* (NC) *equivalent*	*literacy (reading) skill*
Entry level 1	NC level 1	*understands short texts with repeated language patterns on familiar topics · can obtain information from common signs and symbols*
Entry level 2	7 years old NC level 2	*understands short straightforward texts on familiar topics · can obtain information from short documents, familiar sources, signs, and symbols*
Entry level 3	11 years old NC level 3–4	*understands short straightforward texts on familiar topics accurately and independently · can obtain information from everyday sources*
Level 1	GCSE grades D–G NC level 5	*understands short straightforward texts of varying length on a variety of topics accurately and independently · can obtain information from different sources*
Level 2	GCSE grades A–C NC levels 6–8	*understands a range of texts of varying complexity accurately and independently can obtain information of varying length and detail from different sources*

DfES figures (2002/03) show adult literacy levels for the population of England:

Level	*people (m)*	*%*
Entry level 1 or below	1·1	3
Entry level 2	0·6	2
Entry level 3	3·5	11
Level 1	12·6	40
Level 2 or above	14·1	44

Charted below are the rates of literacy, by education level, in England (2002/03):

Education level	*Entry level %*	*Level 1 %*	*Level 2+ %*
Degree or above	4	26	70
Other higher education	7	38	55
A Level or equivalent	10	43	48
5+ A*–C GCSE	12	46	42
NC level 1	18	52	30
Other	29	43	28
None	43	40	17

[Sources: Literacy Trust · DfES] A December 2006 report by the Get On literacy campaign indicated that millions of English adults would be unable to read the lyrics to their favourite karaoke classics. It was suggested that those performing Queen's *Don't Stop Me Now* would require Level 2 literacy skills.

ASYLUM DEMOGRAPHICS

Applications for asylum in the UK fell by 24% in 2005 (to 25,710), according to Home Office figures. Only an estimated 31% of applicants were granted asylum, 'humanitarian protection', or 'discretionary leave'. The nationalities most frequently seeking asylum were: Iranian, Somali, Eritrean, Chinese, and Afghan. The majority of principal applicants in 2005 were aged <35, and the majority (71%) were male. Below are the demographic characteristics of applicants for UK asylum in 2005:

% Males (18,345)	*age*	% Females (7,365)
–	0–4	–
1	5–9	1
4	10–14	3
24	15–19	19
19	20–24	19
22	25–29	22
14	30–34	15
8	35–39	9
4	40–44	5
2	45–49	3
1	50–54	1
–	55–59	1
1	≥60	2

CLASSES OF BRITISH NATIONALITY

The classes of British nationality, as defined by the British Nationality Act (1981):

BRITISH CITIZENSHIP · granted to those with a connection to the UK, Channel Islands, or Isle of Man. The only type of citizenship that confers automatic right of abode.

BRITISH DEPENDENT TERRITORIES CITIZENSHIP (BDTC) · for those connected with existing British Overseas Territories (BOT).

BRITISH OVERSEAS CITIZENSHIP · for citizens from former territories such as Malaysia and Kenya who have no connections to the UK or BOT.

BRITISH SUBJECT · applies only to those who, prior to 1983, were classed as 'British subjects without citizenship'; those with citizenship cannot be described as a 'subject'. The designation 'subject' cannot be passed by descent, and will become obsolete when the last British subject dies.

BRITISH NATIONALS (OVERSEAS) · created by Hong Kong Act (1985) and British Nationality (Hong Kong) Order (1986). BNOs are former BDTCs who applied for BNO status prior to the handover of Hong Kong to China.

BRITISH PROTECTED PERSON · status granted to people who come from Protectorates, Protected States, or Mandated Territories who, under the British Empire, enjoyed the 'protection' of the British Crown.

DRUGS & HARM

A two-year study by the Royal Society of Arts Cmsn on Illegal Drugs advised that drug addiction should be treated as an issue of health rather than of crime. The March 2007 report argued that the current drug classification system was unsuitable because some illegal substances cause little harm, whereas alcohol and tobacco, though legal, are known to pose serious health risks. The study suggested that an index of harm be used to replace the current system of drug classification – similar to the index below, produced by the Advisory Council on the Misuse of Drugs. This index was developed by independent experts in an attempt to create a more scientifically rigorous method of drug classification. A drug's harm rating is set by its impact in three core areas: the *physical harm* caused by the drug; the tendency of the drug to cause *dependence*; and the impact on *families and society*. Each element is scored on a scale of 0–3 (where 3 is the most harmful). The table below illustrates the score of a selection of drugs in each harm category:

Substance	*class*	*physical harm*	*dependence*	*social harm*	*overall harm*
Heroin	A	2·78	3·00	2·54	2·77
Cocaine	A	2·33	2·39	2·17	2·30
Barbiturates	B	2·23	2·01	2·00	2·08
Alcohol	–	1·40	1·93	2·21	1·85
Ketamine	–	2·00	1·54	1·69	1·74
Amphetamine	B	1·81	1·67	1·50	1·66
Tobacco	–	1·24	2·21	1·42	1·62
Cannabis	C	0·99	1·51	1·50	1·33
LSD	A	1·13	1·23	1·32	1·23
GHB	C	0·86	1·19	1·30	1·12
Ecstasy	A	1·05	1·13	1·09	1·09

60% of cannabis sold in Britain is grown locally, according to a DrugScope report released in March 2007. More than 1,500 cannabis farms have been closed by police in London over the past 2 years.

DRUG USE IN ENGLAND & WALES

Figures from the British Crime Survey (2005/06) show the proportion of adults (by age group) who reported having used illicit drugs at any point during their life:

Drug *age*	*16–19*	*20–24*	*25–29*	*30–34*	*35–44*	*45–54*	*55–59*	*all*
Cannabis (%)	35·1	44·4	46·7	40·1	28·5	18·8	11·1	29·8
Amphetamines	7·5	14·5	23·8	20·5	11·8	5·6	2·8	11·5
Any cocaine	6·5	14·5	15·2	10·4	6·4	2·4	1·1	7·3
Ecstasy	5·8	14·4	18·2	14·0	5·7	0·9	0·2	7·2
Opiates	0·4	1·1	1·9	1·2	0·9	0·5	0·3	0·9
All Class A	11·2	21·8	26·5	21·4	13·6	6·6	3·6	13·9
Any drug	40·4	49·0	51·6	45·8	34·2	23·4	15·4	34·9

[Source: British Crime Survey · UK Drug Policy Commission]

THE FAMILY

Long a topic of political debate, the family took centre stage in 2007, as all parties attempted to place it at the heart of their ideology. Gordon Brown called his last Budget 'a Budget for Britain's families, for fairness, and for the future'. A few days later, David Cameron declared that the Tories no longer stood just for the individual, 'now we stand for the family, for the neighbourhood – in a word, for society'. This appreciation of families as prerequisite for an ordered and prosperous state came at a time when the traditional family unit (married parents with one or more children) has never been more uncommon – as the following data indicate:

The *size of the average British household* has fallen from 2·9 people in 1971 to 2·4 in 2006. Below is a breakdown of the size of British households:

Household size (%)	*1971*	*2006*
One person	18	29
Two people	32	36
Three people	19	16
Four people	17	13
Five people	8	4
Six or more	6	2

Below is *household size by ethnic group*:

Group [GB, 2001]	*people per household*
Bangladeshi	4·5
Pakistani	4·1
Indian	3·3
Black African	2·7
Chinese	2·7
Mixed	2·5
White British	2·3
Black Caribbean	2·3

Below is a breakdown of British *people in households, by type and family*:

Household type (%)	*1971*	*2006*
One person	6	12
One family households		
· Couple		
— *no children*	19	25
— *dependent children*	52	37
— *non dep-child. only*	10	8
· Lone parent	4	12
Other households	9	5

Below are the *number of children (<16) of divorced parents* [England & Wales]:

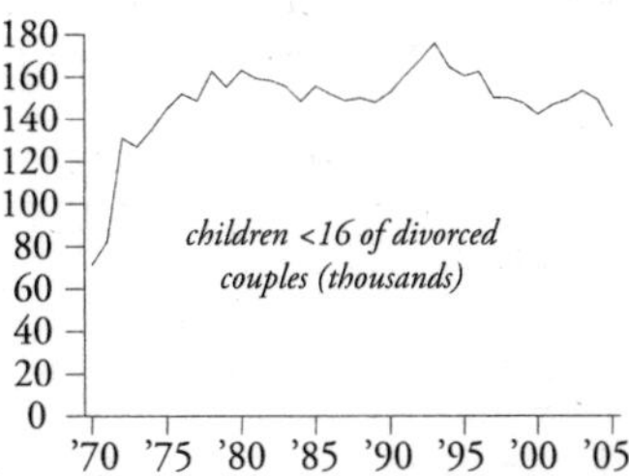

The percentage of children living in lone parent families has risen markedly between 1972–2006, as the data below illustrate:

Children in... (%)	*1972*	*2006*
Couple families	92	77
Lone mother families	6	22
Lone father families	1	2

Below are *UK births outside marriage, as a percentage of all births*:

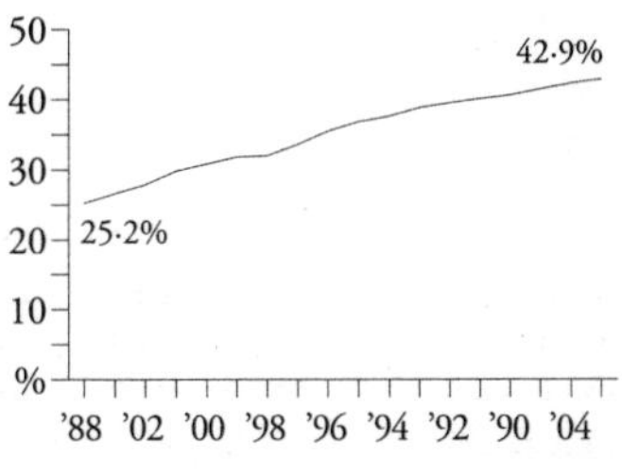

[Source: Social Trends 2007, Crown ©]

BREAST SIZES

A poll for bra company Triumph revealed that 57% of British women require at least a D-cup brassière. Below is a breakdown of European women, by bra cup-size:

% with bra size	A	B	C	≥ D
UK	6	19	18	57
Denmark	7	24	19	50
Netherlands	8	29	27	36
Belgium	9	35	28	28
France	7	38	29	26
Sweden	14	33	30	24
Greece	9	40	28	23
Austria	10	51	27	11
Italy	1	68	21	10

DOCTORS & NHS SPENDING

A survey by Doctors.net.uk for the *Daily Telegraph* in April 2007 asked doctors which treatments they believed the NHS should pay for. The results are below:

Should the NHS pay to treat	*% yes*	*% no*
Alcohol-related accidents or illness	55	45
Drug-related accidents or illness	56	44
All assisted fertility treatments	24	76
Elective Caesarean	62	38
Varicose veins	70	30
Vasectomy reversal	20	80
Gender reassignment	16	84
Drugs or treatments for slimming	43	38

COSMETIC SURGERY

More than 28,900 cosmetic surgery procedures were performed in the UK during 2006, according to the annual report of the British Association of Aesthetic Plastic Surgeons [BAAPS (!)]. 92% of all procedures were carried out on women. The use of liposuction as an 'effort free' method of weight loss was thought to explain the 90% rise in its popularity between 2005–06. The top procedures in 2006 were:

Procedure	*no.*	*% change*†
Breast augmentation	6,156	+9
Blepharoplasty[1]	5,065	+48
Liposuction	3,986	+90
Face/neck lift	3,281	+44
Breast reduction	3,219	+19
Abdominoplasty[2]	2,743	+47
Rhinoplasty[3]	2,678	+18
Otoplasty[4]	943	–20
Brow lift	868	+50

† between 2005–06 · [1] eyelid lift; [2] tummy tuck; [3] nose job; [4] ear tweak. [Source: BAAPS]

BODY IMAGE

51% of young women would consider paying for plastic surgery to improve their looks, according to a BBC Radio 1 survey of >25,000 men and women, mostly aged 17–34. When asked how they perceived their own weight, respondents answered:

Skinny	*slim*	*normal*	*overweight*	*fat*
3	22%	44%	25%	6%

The majority of men and women said that they preferred the curvaceous female form; 80% of men preferred the male body to be muscular. The survey also found:

% of respondents who admitted …	
They believe their body stops them getting a boyfriend	♀=53†
There was 'lots they would change' about their body	♀=50
Skipping a meal to lose weight	♀=43
Were OK with their appearance	♂=49
Would have breast enlargement	♀=36
Would have liposuction	♀=32
To being on a diet	♀=20 · ♂=10
Hating what they looked like	♀=10
Making themselves sick	♀=8
Using the Atkins diet	♀=1
They were 'size zero' [see p.176]	♀=<1

[Source: BBC Radio 1 Newsbeat, 1Xtra TXU, February 2007 · † girls aged 12–16]

OBESITY

According to the Health Survey for England (2001), 21% of men and 23% of women are obese. Obesity is measured by the Body Mass Index (BMI), derived by dividing weight (Kg) by the square of height (m). A BMI >30 defines one as obese. (Increasingly, medics are using abdominal girth calculations rather than the BMI to assess obesity.)

CLASS	*underweight*	*normal*	*overweight*	*obese*		
BMI	<18·5	18·5–24·9	25–29·9	class I 30–34·9	class II 35–39·9	class III >40
RISK	*varies*	*average*	*increased*	*moderate*	*severe*	*very severe*

PUBLIC EXPENDITURE ON HEALTH

2007 OECD Factbook figures reveal per capita public expenditure ($) on health:

Country	($) *1990*	*2004*
Australia	876	2,107
Canada	1,295	2,210
France	1,174	2,475
Germany	1,576	2,341
Hungary	530	917
Ireland	571	2,063
Italy	1,097	1,852
Japan	866	1,832
Luxembourg	1,427	4,603
Mexico	124	307
Netherlands	962	1,894
Sweden	1,428	2,399
UK	825	2,164
USA	1,093	2,727
OECD *average*	867	1,844

THE NHS

In 2006/07, the NHS reported:

Calls to NHS Direct	16,000 a day
Visits to GPs	900,000 a day
Visits to A&E	50,000 a day
Average inpatient wait	6·4 weeks
Average outpatient wait	3·3 weeks
No. of doctors	126,000
No. of qualified nurses	398,000
Total NHS workforce	1·3m
Wait in A&E <4 hours	96·8%
Emergency calls	6·3m
Emergency incidents	5·1m
Emergency patient journeys	3·6m

[Source: 2007 Chief Exec's Report to the NHS, and Department of Health statistics]

Prescriptions currently cost £6·85 per item. ❦ In May 2007, the Commonwealth Fund compared the health services of five countries, judging each on: quality of care, access, equity, and efficiency. The NHS was rated as the best, followed by Germany, Australia, New Zealand, Canada, and the USA.

FIVE-POINT NATIONAL TRIAGE SCALE

Triage systems are employed by medics to assess and sort patients according to the level of their injuries, allowing treatment to be provided on the basis of need rather than by time of arrival. A number of triage scales exist, but the majority of NHS casualty departments employ the five-point national triage scale, detailed below:

Level	*colour*	*label*	status
1	RED	Immediate resuscitation	*patients in need of immediate treatment for preservation of life*
2	ORANGE	Very urgent	*seriously ill or injured patients whose lives are not in immediate danger*
3	YELLOW	Urgent	*patients with serious problems but apparently stable condition*
4	GREEN	Standard	*standard cases without any immediate danger or distress*
5	BLUE	Non-urgent	*patients whose conditions are not true accidents or emergencies*

MOST SEARCHED-FOR AILMENTS

Below are the ailments most often searched for on the NHS Direct website during May–October 2006 – providing a glimpse into the health concerns of the nation:

Search	*number of searches*
Chickenpox	111,861
Pregnancy	108,639
Thrush	89,957
Diabetes	83,074
Irritable bowel syndrome	70,463
Back pain	68,560
Sciatica	63,016
Glandular fever	62,893
Kidney infection	61,745
Anaemia	61,731
Thyroid (underactive)	61,161
Shingles	60,184
Ringworm	59,564

HEALTHCARE & HANDWASHING

Deaths involving MRSA and *Clostridium difficile* have risen year on year between 2001–05, according to the NHS's latest Spring 2007 Health Statistics Quarterly.

Staphylococcus aureus is a bacterium that *c.*⅓ of people carry on their skin with no ill effects, although it can cause serious infections if it enters the body – particularly if an individual's immune system is weak, such as when they are in hospital. Meticillin-resistant *Staphylococcus aureus* (MRSA) are strains that have developed resistance to the most common antibiotics. First isolated in 1961 (when the antibiotic meticillin was introduced), the incidence of MRSA has increased since 1992. Between 2001–05, MRSA was mentioned on 1 in 500 death certificates in England & Wales. Between 2004–05, mentions of MRSA on death certificates increased by 39% – though this rise may in part be explained by an increase in awareness and reporting.

Clostridium difficile is a spore-forming anaerobic bacterium (i.e. one that does not grow in the presence of oxygen), which is the major cause of antibiotic-associated diarrhoea and colitis. Because *C. difficile* or *C. dif* (as it is abbreviated) is usually kept in check by 'healthy' intestinal bacteria, it tends to affect those who are being treated with broad spectrum antibiotics for a serious underlying condition. One of the groups most at risk from infection is the elderly in hospitals or care homes. First described in the 1930s, *C. difficile* was only recognised as the cause of diarrhoea and colitis following antibiotic treatment in the 1970s. Between 2001–05, *C. difficile* was mentioned on 1 in 250 death certificates in England and Wales.

Since MRSA and *C. difficile* are both spread by cross infection, hospital cleanliness and hand hygiene have become issues of concern. Doctors, nurses, auxiliaries, patients, and visitors are now encouraged to ensure their hands are washed (ideally with an alcohol rub) before and after each patient contact, using comprehensive handwashing guidelines, like the one below from the Royal College of Nursing:

1. Palm to palm.

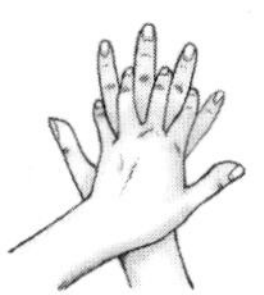

2. Right palm over left dorsum and left palm over right dorsum.

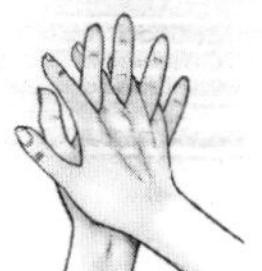

3. Palm to palm, fingers interlaced.

4. Backs of fingers to opposing palms with fingers interlocked.

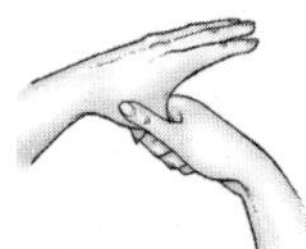

5. Rotational rubbing of right thumb clasped in left hand, and vice versa.

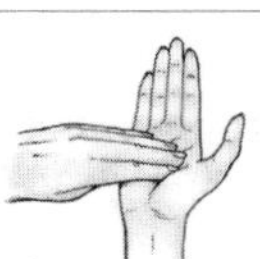

6. Rotational rubbing, backwards and forwards with clasped fingers of right hand in left palm and vice versa.

From 2008, guidelines will require those with patient contact to be 'bare below the elbow', banning jewellery, watches, and ties, and replacing the traditional 'white coat' with disposable plastic aprons.

SOME HEALTH STORIES OF NOTE

{OCT 2006} · A study by the University of Southern California indicated that becoming a mother at 50 posed no significant risk to health. ❦ Research published in the *American Journal of Medicine* suggested that a brisk 30-minute walk every day could help cut the risk of catching a cold. {NOV} · A long-term Norwegian study found that heavy smokers who halve their daily cigarette intake do not cut their risk of premature death; they concluded that the best course of action is to give up smoking entirely. ❦ A study from Woodend Hospital in Aberdeen suggested that (contrary to what your mother said) slouching at a 135° angle is better for your back than sitting upright. {DEC} · A Danish study that followed 420,000 people and took 21 years to complete concluded that there is no link between mobile phones and cancer. ❦ A New Zealand study warned parents not to let babies sleep in car seats unchecked, as the lack of head control in babies can lead to breathing difficulties. ❦ A study from the University of Toronto suggested that low levels of alcohol in the blood could help to protect the brain from the effects of head injury. {JAN 2007} · A study published in the *European Heart Journal* suggested that adding milk to tea might reduce the tea's health benefits. The researchers showed that black tea improved cardiovascular function, but some proteins contained in milk appeared to negate these positive effects. ❦ Researchers from the University of Illinois suggested that, to protect against prostate cancer, men should eat tomatoes and broccoli in combination. Both vegetables have been shown to have positive effects individually, but the study suggested they were even more effective at combating cancer when eaten together. ❦ An initial study at the University of North Carolina raised concerns that taking statins (drugs used to help lower cholesterol) could increase the risk of Parkinson's disease. ❦ Results from an American study published in the *Lancet* suggested that growing up near a major road or motorway could affect the development of children's lungs. The study indicated that children who lived up to 500m from a motorway had significantly lower lung volume and peak flow than those who lived over 1,500m away. ❦ A study by researchers from the University of Leeds indicated that pre-menopausal women who ate significant amounts of fibre reduced their risk of breast cancer by up to half. {FEB} · Research from Bristol University and the US National Institutes of Health indicated that mothers who ate a lot of fish when pregnant had children with greater communication and social skills. ❦ Harvard School of Public Health and the University of Athens suggested that men who take 30-minute siestas three times a week could cut their risk of heart disease by 37%. {MAR} · A study carried out at the University of Bristol revealed that there had been a 4·4% increase each year (since 1985) in the number of children diagnosed with type 1 diabetes. Researchers speculated that the fivefold increase in diagnoses was likely to have an environmental cause. ❦ A study published in the *Journal of Agriculture and Food Chemistry* indicated that drinking fruit juices like purple grape, cranberry, and apple is beneficial to health and can provide protection from chronic diseases. {APR} · A study of health

SOME HEALTH STORIES OF NOTE cont.

risks published in the journal *Public Health* suggested that breathing city air pollution could be more harmful than the fallout from an atom bomb. ❦ German researchers suggested that drinking cocoa before bedtime could help reduce blood pressure, and therefore cut the risk of heart attack. ❦ A team from Columbia University warned that eating too much bacon can damage the lungs. The study suggested that nitrates in meat were to blame for the high rates of chronic obstructive pulmonary disease amongst those who ate cured meats ≥14 times a month. ❦ Research published in the *Lancet* indicated that hormone replacement therapy significantly increased the risks of developing ovarian, breast, and womb cancer. {MAY} · Research presented at an Experimental Biology meeting suggested that eating pistachios could help reduce cholesterol. ❦ Following a review of 900 studies, researchers at the Silent Spring Institute, Massachusetts, proposed a list of chemicals in food and the environment that might contribute to breast cancer. The research indicated that at least 29 of the chemicals were widely produced in the US, including 10 food additives registered with the US Food and Drug Admin. ❦ Researchers at Sydney Children's Hospital suggested that many children are wrongly diagnosed as allergic to peanuts. The study revealed that of 84 children who showed a positive result for a standard pinprick test, only 67% were actually allergic when given peanuts to eat (in a controlled environment). ❦ Michigan University Medical School released the results of trials that suggested using creams containing vitamin A could reduce wrinkles. ❦ Research by Aberdeen University indicated that exposure to pesticides can increase the risk of developing Parkinson's disease. Being knocked unconscious in the boxing ring or during an accident also increased the risks. {JUN} · An analysis of 221 cases by the French Institute of Public Health, Epidemiology, & Development suggested that agricultural workers who had been exposed to high levels of pesticides had an elevated risk of developing a brain tumour. ❦ A study by the charity Education for Health suggested that roughly three-quarters of students who take hay fever medication will drop a grade in their exams over the summer. Yet, sufferers who refrain from taking drugs have a 40% risk of gaining a lower exam grade than expected. The study's authors called for exams to be taken before the hay fever season. ❦ Scientists writing in *Lancet Infectious Diseases* suggested that Echinacea can help to clear up a cold. The team of American researchers reviewed 14 previous studies into the remedy, and concluded that Echinacea might reduce the duration of a cold by an average of 1·4 days. {JUL} · Researchers at Imperial College London suggested that keeping cats can irritate the lungs and aggravate asthma. ❦ The European Food Safety Authority warned that Red 2G, a dye used in cheap sausages to keep them looking fresh, was potentially carcinogenic. {AUG} · Researchers from Hong Kong proposed that the Chinese tile game mahjong could trigger epileptic fits. {SEP} · A study in the *Journal of Human Hypertension* warned that many toddlers were suffering from high blood pressure due to too much salt in their diet.

PRISON POPULATION BY OFFENCE

The table below shows the percentage of male and female prisoners, by offence:

% ♂ *prisoners*	*offence*	% ♀ *prisoners*
26·4	violence against the person	17·7
12·3	sexual offences	1·3
11·5	robbery	8·1
12·7	burglary	6·7
5·5	theft and handling	13·2
2·8	fraud and forgery	6·7
16·8	drugs offences	34·3
3·1	motoring offences	0·8
8·5	other offences	10·5
0·5	offence not recorded	0·7
52,917	TOTAL (number)	3,085

[Source: National Offender Management Service, Oct 2006. Figures relate to prisoners given an immediate custodial sentence, and do not include those on remand.] According to estimates produced by the Centre for Crime and Justice Studies in May 2007, it 'could cost £49,220 a year to keep a criminal in jail'. This figure includes the cost of supporting the family of the offender. ❦ As of 10·8·07, the prison population was 80,708, the majority of whom (76,121) were male. ❦ According to the 2006/07 HMPS Annual Report: the escape rate was 0·01% of the prison population; the rate of self-inflicted deaths per 100,000 of the average prison population was 96·3; 7,675 prisoners completed drug treatment programmes; 24.1% of prisoners were held in overcrowded conditions; and the average prison officer took 11·6 sick days a year. ❦ As of March 2007, 73% of the prison population were white, 16% black, 7% Asian, 3% mixed race, and 1% were Chinese or other.

MURDER INVESTIGATION CATEGORIES

The Association of Chief Police Officers' 2006 *Murder Investigation Manual* categorises murders to determine the appropriate level of resources to be deployed.

Category A+	*A homicide or other major investigation where the public concern is such that normal staffing levels are not adequate to keep pace with the investigation.*
Category A	*A homicide or other major investigation which is of grave concern or where vulnerable members of the public are at risk, where the identity of the offender(s) is not apparent or the investigation and securing of evidence requires significant resource allocation.*
Category B	*A homicide or other major investigation where the identity of the offender(s) is not apparent, the continued risk to the public is low and the investigation or securing evidence can be achieved within normal force resourcing arrangements.*
Category C	*A homicide or other major investigation where the identity of the offender(s) is apparent from the outset and the investigation and/or securing of evidence can be achieved easily.*

FIRE STATISTICS · UK

The annual Fire Statistics report presents a detailed analysis of fires in the UK:

Year	*Fires*	*False Alarms*		*Chimney*	*Fatalities*		*Casualties*	
	(000s)	*(000s)*	*malicious*	*Fires*	*civilian*	*firefighter*	*civilian*	*firefighter*
2005	430·3	439·1	8·9%	2·3%	489	2	13,704	359
2004	443·0	449·6	11·0%	2·2%	504	3	14,181	398
2003	621·0	472·4	12·4%	1·9%	591	1	15,015	521
2002	519·4	477·1	14·1%	2·3%	561	1	16,030	565
2001	546·8	481·1	15·4%	3·0%	606	0	16,627	779
2000	476·5	460·5	16·1%	3·3%	613	0	16,960	686
1999	468·8	468·3	17·2%	3·5%	623	0	17,541	657
1998	409·7	456·6	18·4%	4·6%	656	0	17,517	681
1997	469·0	489·6	20·3%	4·7%	723	0	17,779	804
1996	532·2	489·7	22·5%	5·4%	706	3	17,348	873
1995	604·2	507·0	22·6%	4·2%	736	0	16,149	1,022

The figures below relate to 2005, the most recent year for which data are available:

DELIBERATE FIRES

In 2005, 79,700 deliberate primary fires were set: 10,400 of which were in dwellings, 14,000 in other buildings, and 47,800 in road vehicles. Overall, the incidence of deliberate fires in 2005 fell for the fourth consecutive year.

CAUSES OF DEATH

There were 491 fire-related deaths in 2005, the lowest on record since 1959. Below are the causes of these deaths:

Overcome by gas/smoke.......... 44%
Burns................................22
Burns & overcome by gas/smoke....19
Unspecified..........................10
Other..................................3

CHIMNEY FIRES

Chimney fires are those 'confined within the chimney structure', 'that did not involve casualties or rescues', and were 'attended by four or fewer appliances'. In 2005, there were 9,700 such fires, a fall from 9,800 in 2004. By comparison, in 1965 (the first year for which figures are available) there were 72,100.

SMOKE ALARMS

Smoke alarms were absent where fire started in 47% of dwelling fires in 2005 – accounting for 203 deaths and 4,800 casualties. Of all dwelling fires in 2005:

Smoke alarm absent............... 47%
Operated & raised alarm............35
Operated & did not raise alarm......5
Alarm failed..........................12

80% of households in England and Wales currently have working smoke alarms – compared with 8% in 1988.

TIME OF CALL

Below are the times of calls to the fire and rescue services for accidental and deliberate dwelling fires in 2005:

Call time (%)	*accidental*	*deliberate*
00:00–05:59	12	26
06:00–11:59	18	10
12:00–17:59	37	23
18:00–23:59	33	41

[Source: Fire Statistics UK 2005, Dept. for Communities & Local Govt. Crown ©]

POLICE ADVICE & INFORMATION

Advice and information gleaned from the Police National Legal Database (PNLD):

Spitting, if done deliberately, will constitute an assault; if accidental, it will not. ❦ The police do not have the authority to break into a house to help a trapped cat. In fact, 'it is more than likely that when the cat gets hungry it will leave the house the same way it got in'. ❦ The police are unlikely to take any action if your cat has been killed by a dog. Past court decisions have suggested it 'is the nature of a dog to kill and wound small animals'. ❦ Rent bailiffs must call between sunrise and sunset. 'Once a bailiff has gained peaceable entry once, they can use force to gain entry on any subsequent visit'. ❦ 'A "car cruise" is a gathering of large numbers of car enthusiasts who meet at car parks, where "boy racers" show off their customised vehicles'. ❦ The behaviour of youths who throw eggs at your window 'could' constitute harassment. ❦ You should contact your local council if you have an infestation of bees. ❦ 'Whilst there is no legal requirement to report a crime, there is a moral duty'. ❦ 'CS spray is not legal … it is a prohibited firearm'. ❦ 'A cyclist can commit the offence of dangerous cycling as opposed to dangerous driving'. ❦ 'It is an offence to ride a pedal cycle … whilst being unfit through drink or drugs'. ❦ 'If you set your dog onto an intruder and the person suffers injury then you may face prosecution and the court could order the dog to be kept under control or destroyed … if an intruder breaks in whilst you are out and is attacked by the dog then it is unlikely that you would face the need to defend a possible court order'. ❦ If the dog next door is constantly barking then you should 'speak to your neighbour about the problem as they may not be aware it is happening'. ❦ If there is a bat in your house you should 'close the door to the room, dim the lights, open all windows. This will give the bat a chance to find its own way out of the room'. ❦ 'It is an offence to cut down a hedge or tree intentionally or recklessly whilst there are birds nesting in it'. ❦ 'It is illegal to have any red lights to the front of a vehicle'. ❦ 'Although an unmarked police car can stop vehicles, a constable must be in uniform in order to carry out the stop … unless you are 100% certain it is the police, do not stop'. ❦ Exemptions to wearing a seat belt include: 'a licensed taxi whilst on duty' and 'a person involved in a procession organised by or on behalf of the Crown'. ❦ If stranded without money, the police may be able to help: 'A friend or family member must deposit some money at their nearest police station. When this has been done, that police station will contact the police station you are at and they will release the same amount of money to you'. ❦ Although 'the St George's flag has become a symbol of right-wing political parties … it does not automatically mean that a person who displays such a flag shares those views, they could be an avid football fan and/or very patriotic, which are two entirely different things'. ❦ You can pick wild flowers 'as long as you are keeping them for your own personal use and are not selling them. You cannot, however, pick the whole plant – that would be classed as theft'.

[Excerpted from askthe.police.uk]

BRITISH CRIME SURVEY 2007

The annual British Crime Survey (BCS) measures crime in England and Wales by interviewing people about crimes they have experienced in the past year, and their fear of crime. The BCS is widely seen as a useful partner to the police's recorded crime figures since, for a number of reasons, certain crimes often go unreported. Charted below are the changes in BCS and reported crimes from 2005/06–2006/07, which illustrate that crime in England and Wales has remained relatively stable†:

British Crime Survey	'05/'06–'06/'07
Vandalism	+10%
Domestic burglary	–1%
All vehicle thefts	–2%
Theft from the person	*no change*
Violent crime	+5%
All BCS crime	+3%

† Yet, 65% of people thought there was more crime in the country as a whole, and 41% thought that crime had increased in their local area.

Police Recorded Crime	'05/'06–'06/'07
Criminal damage	*no change*
Domestic burglary	–3%
Other burglary	–4%
Offences against vehicles	–4%
Other theft	–4%
Robbery	+3%
Violence against the person	–1%
Sexual offences	–7%
Drug offences	+9%
Total recorded crime	–2%

MIDDLE-CLASS CRIME

Research by Keele University suggested that petty crime amongst the middle classes is rife. The June 2007 study, by Professor Susanne Karstedt and Dr Stephen Farrall, indicated that 61% had committed a crime against their employer, the government, or a business. Those questioned admitted to the following misdemeanours:

Paid cash-in-hand to avoid tax	34%
Kept cash when 'over-changed'	32%
Purloined something from work	18%
Avoided paying TV licence	11%
Padded out an insurance claim	7%
Asked a bureaucrat friend to 'bend the rules'	6%
Misclaimed benefits	3%

GUN CRIME

According to a 2006 Home Office report on gun crime, an illegal firearm can be purchased in the UK for as little as £50. Below are the 'street' prices of various guns:

Weapon	*cost (£)*
Shotgun	50–200
Handgun (used)	150–200
Converted imitation	400–800
Handgun (unused)	1,000–1,400
Automatic weapon	800–4,000

Used weapons command a lower price, since they could be traced to previous crimes. Automatic weapons include: MAC-10 (£800–£2,000); Uzi (£950–£2,000); MAC-11 (£3,000); and Sterling submachine gun (£4,000). According to the report, ammunition varies in price and availability. A box of ·45 calibre bullets costs *c.*£3,000, while a single ·38 calibre bullet can be purchased for 50p.

VICTIMS OF VIOLENT CRIME

The British Crime Survey divides violent crime into four categories, based on the relationship between the victim and suspect. DOMESTIC VIOLENCE includes all violent incidents, except muggings, that involve partners, ex-partners, household members, or other relatives; MUGGING comprises robbery, attempted robbery, and snatch theft from the person; STRANGER VIOLENCE includes common assaults and woundings in which the victim did not know the offender; ACQUAINTANCE VIOLENCE comprises woundings and common assaults in which the victim knew one or more of the offenders at least by sight. The most recent BCS figures on violent crime (2003) suggest the crimes most likely to be experienced by age and gender:

Victim age	*domestic*	*mugging*	*stranger*	*acquaintance*
♀ 16–29	39%	16	16	29
♂ 16–29	8%	17	41	35
♀ 30–59	33%	14	19	33
♂ 30–59	10%	9	45	36

A report by the Violence Research Group at Cardiff University indicated that an estimated 369,000 people attended Accident and Emergency departments as a consequence of violence in 2005. The study examined A&E records from 29 hospitals across England and Wales, and discovered people were most likely to seek treatment at A&E for a violence-related injury on Saturdays or Sundays, in the months of May, July, October, and December. Those most likely to be victims of violence were males aged 18–30; 72·6% of those treated in A&E were male, and 27·4% female. Rates of injury resulting from violence are tabulated below, by age group:

Age group	*number*	*%*
0–10	445	1·2
11–17	5,794	16·7
18–30	16,028	46·1
31–50	10,494	30·3
>50	1,986	5·7

A further study by the Violence Research Group, published in the *British Medical Journal* in December 2006, indicated that assault injuries were most severe when the victim had been kicked. The study sampled 24,660 patients who reported injury from assault: 74·5% of the victims were male; 55·7% were injured with fists, 15·8% by another body part, and 7% with feet. Although attacks where a weapon was used were more likely to cause injury than where no weapon was involved, kicking was found to be the 'assault mechanism' that resulted in the most severe injuries.

SCOTLAND YARD'S MOST WANTED

Fugitive	*allegation*
Dwaine St Michael Israel	drugs
Ibrahim Adam	terrorism
Lamine Adam	terrorism
Saifullah 'Saffi' Siddiqi	murder
Noel F. Cunningham	armed robbery
Ayub Khan	murder
Sukhdip Singh Chhina	murder
James Francis Hurley	murder
Ibrahim Bangura	murder
Adrian Paul	triple shooting
James Walter 'Jimbles' Tomkins	murder
Youseff Ahmed Wahid	murder

[Source: Scotland Yard; as at 17·09·2007]

PROSTITUTION

A 2004 Home Office report estimated that *c.*80,000 people may be involved in prostitution in the UK. The 2001 National Survey of Sexual Attitudes and Lifestyles reported that across Britain 4·3% of men (aged 16–44) admitted to paying for sex in the previous 5 years; amongst men in London, the figure was 8·9%. In 2001, the Royal Economic Society reported that Britons spent *c.*£770m on prostitution each year (compared with £400m spent on cinema visits), calculating that legalising prostitution could raise tax revenues of £250m. ❦ Prostitution – payment for sexual services (usually through money or drugs) – is not specifically illegal in the UK, although a range of associated activities are, including: keeping a brothel, coercing another into prostitution for gain ('pimping'), loitering or soliciting, advertising the services of a prostitute in phone boxes, 'kerb crawling', and so on. ❦ For obvious reasons, accurate and comprehensive data relating to prostitution are difficult to acquire, though a number of studies have provided a snapshot of those involved:

*c.*85% of prostitutes reported a history of physical abuse in the family
*c.*45% reported a history of familial sexual abuse
30–60% of prostitutes had spent time in local authority care, foster homes, secure accommodation, or were known to the social services
80–95% of street-based prostitutes were addicted to heroin and/or crack cocaine

A 2004 analysis of 333 women involved in prostitution indicated the following:

Age	%	*Ethnic origin*	%	*Highest qualification*	%
16–20	16	White	83	None	66
21–30	62	Afro-Caribbean	11	GCSE	21
31–40	17	Pakistani	<1	Vocational	5
≥41	6	Asian	1	Further/higher	4
(Average age	25)	Other	5	Other	5

Of these women, 3% were married, 74% were single, and 20% cohabited with a 'boyfriend' or 'pimp'. Of the 49% who had one or more children, 65% did not live with them. 74% of these women had experienced physical violence, and 53% reported having been indecently assaulted or forced to have sex. ❦ The average age of the men who solicited these women was 35. 67% of these men were in full-time employment, and 12% were students. 47% of male clients were married, 58% were white Europeans, and 44% were owner-occupiers. ❦ The number of young people involved in prostitution in the UK is thought to be between 2,000–5,000, with a female to male ratio of 4:1. Although figures vary, *c.*50–75% of prostitutes were drawn into the 'trade' aged <18. In recent years, children involved in prostitution have been treated by the criminal justice system more as victims than perpetrators of crime. (For example, the Sexual Offences Act 2003 made the purchase of sexual services from a child a specific criminal offence for the first time.) And, increasingly, a similar approach is taken with the victims of kidnapping and global sex trafficking.

[Sources: *Paying the Price,* Home Office; *Tackling Street Prostitution,* Hester & Westmarland; *For Love or Money: Pimps & the management of sex work,* May, Haracopos, & Hough; & others.]

Media & Celebrity

If you have to tell them who you are, you aren't anybody.
— GREGORY PECK (1916–2003)

HELLO! vs OK! COVER STARS

Date	*Hello!*	*OK!*
02·01·07	Sharon & Ozzy Osbourne	Jordan & Peter Andre
09·01·07	Tina Hobley marries Oliver Wheeler	Victoria Beckham
16·01·07	Kate Middleton	Cheryl Cole
23·01·07	Siân Lloyd	David & Victoria Beckham
30·01·07	Victoria Beckham	Angelina Jolie
06·02·07	Katie Holmes	Sarah Harding
13·02·07	Sean 'P Diddy' Combs	Jade, Danielle, & Shilpa (*Celeb BB*)
20·02·07	Victoria Beckham, Emma Bunton, & Geri Halliwell	Shilpa Shetty
27·02·07	Prince William & Kate Middleton	Kerry Katona's wedding
06·03·07	Jemima Khan	Danielle Lloyd
13·03·07	Liz Hurley & Arun Nayar's English wedding	Victoria Beckham
20·03·07	Liz & Arun's Indian wedding	Kerry Katona & baby Heidi
27·03·07	Angelina Jolie & Pax Thien	Nadine Coyle & Jesse Metcalfe
03·04·07	Mel B, Coleen McLoughlin, & Charlotte Church	Jordan & Kerry
10·04·07	Coleen McLoughlin & Wayne Rooney	Sarah Harding
17·04·07	Prince Harry & Chelsy Davy	Victoria Beckham
24·04·07	Prince William & Kate Middleton	David & Victoria Beckham
01·05·07	Kate Middleton	Mel B & baby Angel
08·05·07	Sir Paul McCartney & Sabrina Guinness	Jordan & son Harvey
15·05·07	The Queen	Kerry Katona & daughters
22·05·07	Cameron Diaz, J-Lo, & Kate Moss	Jordan & Peter Andre
29·05·07	Coleen McLoughlin	Girls Aloud
05·06·07	Victoria Beckham	Brad Pitt & George Clooney
12·06·07	Kate Middleton	Jordan
19·06·07	Princes William & Harry	Victoria Beckham
26·06·07	Rod Stewart & Penny Lancaster	John Terry & Toni Poole
03·07·07	Myleene Klass & fiancé	Steven Gerrard marries Alex Curran
10·07·07	Princes William & Harry	Jordan
17·07·07	Michael Flatley & new son	Chantelle
24·07·07	Victoria Beckham	Eva Longoria marries Tony Parker
31·07·07	Rod Stewart & Penny Lancaster's wedding	Kerry Katona
07·08·07	Kate Middleton	Jordan, Peter, & baby Princess
14·08·07	Mel B	Big Brother's Chanelle & Charley
21·08·07	Summer's hottest couples	Holly Willoughby's wedding
28·08·07	Mel B	Jordan & Peter Andre
04·09·07	Princess Diana	Kerry Katona

SOME HATCHED, MATCHED, & DISPATCHED

HATCHED

Heidi Elizabeth *to*	Kerry Katona & Mark Croft
Eden & Savannah *to*	Marcia Cross & Tom Mahoney
Johan Riley Fyodor Taiwo *to*	Heidi Klum & Seal
Angel Iris *to*	Mel B & Eddie Murphy
Henry Daniel *to*	Julia Roberts & Danny Moder
Princess Tiaamii *to*	Katie Price & Peter Andre
Alexander Pete *to*	Naomi Watts & Liev Schreiber
Henry Lee *to*	Jack White & Karen Elson
Beau *to*	Emma Bunton & Jade Jones
Ava *to*	Myleene Klass & Graham Quinn

MATCHED

Michelle Heaton & Andy Scott-Lee	Hertfordshire
Tom Cruise & Katie Holmes	Bracciano, Italy
Matt Lucas & Kevin McGee	Home House, London
Kerry Katona & Mark Croft	Gretna Green
Elizabeth Hurley & Arun Nayar	Sudeley Castle, UK & Jodhpur, India
Amy Winehouse & Blake Fielder-Civil	Miami, USA
Rod Stewart & Penny Lancaster	Portofino, Italy
Steven Gerrard & Alex Curran	Cliveden House Hotel, Berkshire
Eva Longoria & Tony Parker	Paris, France
Mel B & Stephen Belafonte	Las Vegas, USA

DISPATCHED

Reese Witherspoon & Ryan Phillippe (*married for* 7 years)	separating
Britney Spears & Kevin Federline (2 years)	divorced
Pamela Anderson & Kid Rock (4 months)	filed for divorce
Dita Von Teese & Marilyn Manson (1 year)	filed for divorce
Chantelle & Preston (10 months)	separated
Sir Salman Rushdie & Padma Lakshmi (3 years)	filed for divorce

CELEBRITY ADOPTIONS

Celebrity	*adopted*	*year*	*from*
Sheryl Crow	Wyatt Steven	2007	USA
Angelina Jolie	Pax Thien, Zahara, Maddox	2007, 2005, 2002	Vietnam Ethiopia, Cambodia
Meg Ryan	Daisy	2006	China
Madonna	David	2006	Malawi
Ewan McGregor	undisclosed	2006	Mongolia
Sharon Stone	Quinn, Laird, Roan	2006, 2005, 2000	USA
Calista Flockhart	Liam	2001	USA
Nicole Kidman	Connor, Isabella	1995, 1993	USA
Michelle Pfeiffer	Claudia Rose	1993	USA

IACGMOOH

The sixth series of *I'm a Celebrity … Get Me Out of Here* was enlivened by the tall stories of David Gest – although ex-Busted star Matt Willis was eventually crowned *King of the Jungle.* The 'celebrities' left in the following order:

12th	Toby Anstis
11th	Scott Henshall
10th	Faith Brown
9th	Lauren Booth
8th	Phina Oruche
7th	Malandra Burrows
6th	Jan Leeming
5th	Dean Gaffney
4th	David Gest
3rd	Jason Donovan
2nd	Myleene Klass
WINNER	MATT WILLIS

QUOTES OF NOTE

DAVID GEST (*to Matt*) · You're not exactly the most beautiful person in the world. You could do a commercial for acne. MATT WILLIS (*in response*) I think it's all the beans I'm eating. Is that what happened to your face? ❦ PHINA ORUCHE · *(about Jan)* Jesus lift me out of this situation right now before … I kick this woman's head in. ❦ SCOTT HENSHALL · If a spider bites me that's fine, it's part of what we signed up for. But if another contestant sinks their teeth in … I think that's overstepping the mark. ❦

BIG BROTHER 8

In a bid to refresh the format BB8 opened with an all-female house. Men entered gradually and a modicum of interest was piqued by the on–off Chanelle and Ziggy romance. Viewing figures slumped to *c.*3·8m (compared to *c.*4·5m for BB7). Brian Belo won the £100,000 prize, with 60% of the vote.

Eviction order	
20. Emily (ejected)	10 = David
19. Lesley (quit)	9 Amy
18. Shabnam	8 Gerry
17. Seány	7 = Tracey
16. Billi	7 = Kara-Louise
15 Jonathan (quit)	6 Jonty
14. Laura	5 Carole
13. Nicky	4 Ziggy
12. Charley	3 Liam
11 Chanelle (quit)	2 = Sam
10 = Shanessa	2 = Amanda
	Winner BRIAN

QUOTES OF NOTE

EMILY · Are you pushing it out, you nigger?† ❦ SEÁNY · There's too much oestrogen in this house, and I think most of it is coming from Gerry. ❦ CHANELLE · I can't help it if I've got a natural curl to my hair. ❦ CHARLEY · People got chips on their shoulders. I can't help it if I'm the 'It Girl' from the house. ❦ BRIAN · Nicky, sort it out, love. You're at the stage where you sniff ashtrays and eat food out of a box. ❦

† This racial slur caused Emily to be ejected.

UNDESERVED CELEBRITY

In December 2006, *Arena* magazine asked its readers to vote for the personalities that least deserved their celebrity status. Below are the ten 'least worthy' stars:

1	Pete Doherty†	5	Tom Cruise	9	Graham Poll
2	Russell Brand	6	Gordon Ramsay	10	Peaches Geldof
3	Syed Ahmed	7	Johnny Borrell		
4	David Cameron	8	Jimmy Carr		

† Doherty took 38% of the votes

VANITY FAIR'S HOLLYWOOD · 2007

The stars featured on the cover of the 2007 *Vanity Fair* 'Hollywood issue' were:

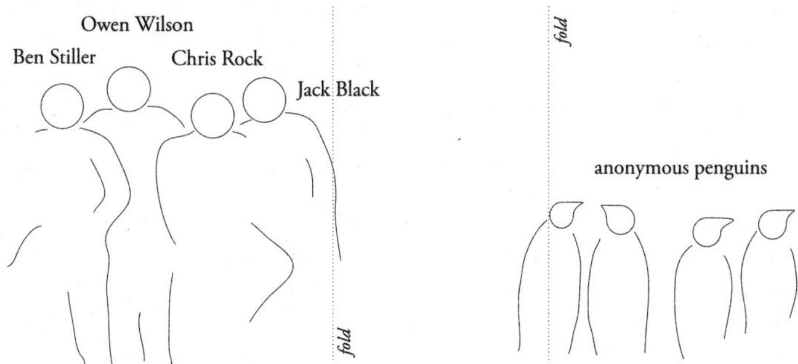

MAX CLIFFORD'S GUIDE TO FAME

In December 2006, the influential publicist and 'PR guru' Max Clifford gave Fame TV his advice for those in search of celebrity. His top tips for making it big were:

1	appear on a reality TV show	6	flaunt your body
2	enter a talent contest	7	date a Royal Family member
3	be abysmal on a talent show	8	make a home sex video
4	gain fame by association	9	be a success on MySpace
5	date a celebrity	10	be in right place at right time

SEXIEST MEN & WOMEN 2007

FHM's 'sexiest' women		*Cosmopolitan*'s 'most desirable' men
Jessica Alba	1	Orlando Bloom
Keeley Hazell	2	Wentworth Miller
Eva Longoria	3	Prince Harry
Adriana Lima	4	Prince William
Scarlett Johansson	5	Jude Law
Hayden Panettiere	6	Lewis Hamilton
Cheryl Tweedy	7	Robbie Williams
Angelina Jolie	8	Jason Orange
Emily Scott	9	Alex Zane
Elisha Cuthbert	10	Sam Branson

Readers of US *Maxim* voted Lindsay Lohan the hottest woman of 2007. *People* magazine named George Clooney Sexiest Man Alive for the 2nd time. Clooney quipped: 'This one's going to be hard for Brad (Pitt) since he's been Sexiest Man Alive twice. He's enjoyed that mantle. I'd say 'Sexiest Man Alive' to him and he'd go, 'Two-time.' So that's been taken away ... So Brad's going to be upset'.

MOST DESIRED CELEBRITIES

A September 2007 poll by *Yahoo! Personals* asked members of the public to name the unmarried celebrity they'd most like to date:

Most desired men	*Most desired women*
George Clooney	Jessica Alba
Matthew McConaughey	Jennifer Aniston
Kanye West	Queen Latifah
Andy Roddick	Jessica Simpson
Ricky Martin	Maria Sharapova

REHAB

In 2007 a rash of high-profile stars suffered particularly public meltdowns and were banished to rehab. Below is a summary of some celeb-attended rehab centres:

BETTY FORD CENTRE
Rancho Mirage, CA · *founded*: 1982
Treatment: Old-fashioned approach to detox based on the 12-step recovery programme. Clients perform chores, such as cleaning the toilets.
Cost: £19,700 for 90 days
Celeb clients: Elizabeth Taylor, Ozzy Osbourne, Drew Barrymore, Keith Urban, David Hasselhoff, Billy Joel.

PROMISES
Malibu, CA · *founded*: 1997
Treatment: Luxury spa-style centre with new-age treatments offered alongside addiction counselling.
Cost: £25,000 a month
Celeb clients: Mel Gibson, Charlie Sheen, Diana Ross, Britney Spears.

THE MEADOWS
Wickenburg, AZ · *founded*: 1976
Treatment: Desert-based centre that 'provides a path to personal completeness and integrity, for those seeking treatment for trauma and addictions'.
Cost: £2,000 a night
Celeb clients: Kate Moss, Robbie Williams, Tara Palmer-Tomkinson

THE PRIORY
Roehampton, London · *founded*: 1980
Treatment: Treats a plethora of problems from alcoholism to eating disorders through psychotherapy and cognitive behavioural therapy.
Cost: *c*.£2,500 a week
Celeb clients: Paula Yates, Jade Goody, Pete Doherty, Ronnie Wood

'*I always said I would die before I went to rehab*' – Lindsay Lohan · '*I was sent to a very humbling place called rehab*' – Britney Spears · '*They tried to make me go to rehab, I said no! no! no!*' – Amy Winehouse. [Sources: *Us Weekly; The Independent* · Costs are approximate and depend on treatment received.]

WORLD'S MOST ELIGIBLE WOMEN

Men's magazine *FHM* produced a list of the world's most eligible women in 2007:

1 ...... Kimberly Stewart
2 .... Carmen Electra
3 ...... Princess Beatrice†
4 .... Sarah Harding
5 ..... Scarlett Johansson
6 .... Lindsay Lohan
7 ...... Maria Sharapova
8 .... Paris Hilton
9 .... Keeley Hazell
10 ...... Keira Knightley

† 5th in line to the throne

CELEBRITY INTRIGUE

{SEP 2006} · 'Guerrilla artist' Banksy tampered with 500 copies of Paris Hilton's début album, doctoring images on the cover and including remixes of her songs, with titles such as 'Why Am I Famous?' and 'What Am I For?' {OCT} · Leaked documents purportedly from the divorce of Paul McCartney and Heather Mills suggested that Paul had attacked his wife with a broken wine glass – an allegation he vigorously denied. ❦ Naomi Campbell was arrested in London for an alleged attack on her counsellor; she denied the charge. {DEC} · Shortly after announcing her divorce from Kevin Federline, Britney Spears was repeatedly pictured (without underwear) enjoying bacchanalian nights out with Paris Hilton. After the media criticised her behaviour, Britney admitted on her website, 'I probably did take my new found freedom a little too far'. ❦ Lindsay Lohan disclosed that she had been attending Alcoholics Anonymous for the past year. ❦ Lib Dem MP Lembit Öpik (41) started dating one of the Cheeky Girls, Gabriela Irimia (23), after breaking off his engagement to TV presenter Siân Lloyd (48) . {FEB 2007} Robbie Williams checked into rehab on his 33rd birthday for his dependency on prescription drugs; the *Sun* reported he was consuming 36 double espressos, 20 cans of Red Bull, and 60 cigarettes a day. ❦ Britney Spears astonished onlookers by shaving off all her hair at a Los Angeles beauty salon. {APR} · Alec Baldwin apologised after a voicemail was leaked to the press in which he called his 11-year-old daughter 'a thoughtless little pig'. A remorseful Baldwin blamed his outburst on the pressures of 'parental alienation'. {MAY} Calum Best admitted he had a problem, after the *Sun* caught him in a 'drug-fuelled' dalliance with prostitutes. Best told the paper, 'I go out and get drunk, I get high on cocaine and I do stupid debauched things with the wrong women'. {JUN} · Paris Hilton spent 23 days in prison for violating parole after a drink-driving conviction. She was briefly released from jail on medical grounds, before a judge ordered her to complete her sentence. Hilton claimed that jail made her want to be a more responsible role model. {JUL} · Kate Moss reportedly left Pete Doherty and burned a collection of his letters after the *News of the World* alleged that Doherty had been unfaithful. Doherty again avoided jail after pleading guilty to the possession of crack cocaine and heroin. {AUG} · Amy Winehouse briefly attended rehab after reportedly overdosing on a combination of drugs. Shortly afterwards, after a reported spat with her husband at a London hotel, she was photographed with bloodied toes and he with a scratched face. Intense media interest in Amy's behaviour culminated in her in-laws calling for fans to consider boycotting her records until she sought help for drug addiction. ❦ American It-girl, Nicole Richie served just 82-minutes of her 4-day jail sentence for driving under the influence. ❦ Lindsay Lohan was sentenced to 1-day in jail for drugs and driving offences, after negotiating a plea bargain.

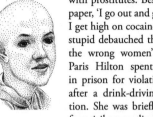

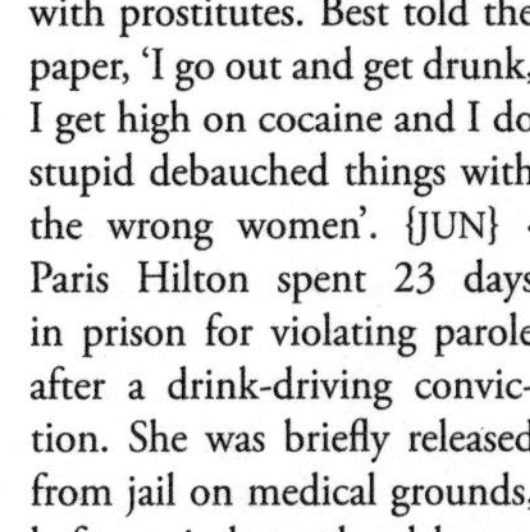

Britney Spears

Being in jail is by far the hardest thing I have ever done.
– PARIS HILTON

CELEBRITY IN QUOTES

CHRISTINA AGUILERA · I'm an ocean because I'm really deep. If you search deep enough, you can find exotic treasures. ❦ KATIE HOLMES · I knew I'd end up marrying Tom [Cruise] at some point. My medium said that years ago. ❦ NICOLE RICHIE · I've come to realise that it's not me who's weight-obsessed – it's America. ❦ NAOMI CAMPBELL · I don't have any more anger problems than anyone else – it's just that I am always in the public eye. ❦ LEONARDO DICAPRIO · I've been planted here to be a vessel for acting. ❦ SCARLETT JOHANSSON · I believe in plastic surgery. I don't want to become an old hag! ❦ HILARY SWANK · I love taking public transportation and being with people. When you start losing touch with people, you lose touch with life. ❦ JOHN TRAVOLTA · I have fame on the level of Elvis, but part of the reason I didn't go the same way was because of my [Scientology] beliefs. ❦ DREW BARRYMORE · Happy people are beautiful. They become like a mirror and they reflect that happiness. ❦ ORLANDO BLOOM · Everything else has begun to pall – the jet-setting, the nightclubs, the bachelor lifestyle; now I need some permanence and stability. ❦ KEVIN COSTNER · I'm always surprised when a film of mine is not good. ❦ EVA LONGORIA · I lost a lot of jobs because I was too pretty. ❦ PAUL McCARTNEY · I'll go on a bus and people will look at me a bit weird – you know, 'What's he doing on a bus?' Then they go, 'Well, he's on a bus', and I go, 'I'm on a bus'. ❦ JESSICA ALBA · Men's magazines have nipples, so why don't women have a magazine where men show their penises? ❦ VICTORIA BECKHAM · I always pose, it's just the look I have. ❦ SIENNA MILLER · I have a great relationship with wine. We have been together about 10 years and we just love each other. ❦ JUSTIN TIMBERLAKE · Sometimes I feel like a monkey in a zoo. ❦ KATIE HOLMES *on private jets* · It's like a bus, only quicker! ❦ LINDSAY LOHAN · I'm a sexual person. And once a month I'm a McDonald's person. ❦ BRUCE WILLIS · I don't bounce as well off the concrete floors as I used to. ❦ PARIS HILTON · I think every decade has an iconic blonde like Marilyn Monroe – and right now I'm that icon. ❦ AMY WINEHOUSE · It isn't exaggerated – I'm a terrible drunk.

MOST-DESIRED CELEB FEATURES

Each year plastic surgeons Toby G. Mayer and Richard W. Fleming poll their *c.*1,500 clients at the Beverly Hills Institute of Aesthetic & Reconstructive Surgery about the celebrity features they consider to be the most desirable. The 2007 list:

WOMEN		MEN	
Nose	*Jennifer Connelly, Jennifer Lopez*	Nose	*Jude Law, Leonardo DiCaprio*
Eyes	*Penélope Cruz, Cameron Diaz*	Eyes	*J. Timberlake, Patrick Dempsey*
Lips	*Kate Winslet, Scarlett Johansson*	Lips	*Ashton Kutcher, Brad Pitt*
Jaw/chin	*Sharon Stone, Katie Holmes*	Jaw/chin	*Matt Damon, Jeremy Piven*
Cheeks	*Keira Knightley, Cate Blanchett*	Cheeks	*George Clooney, Johnny Depp*
Body	*Beyoncé Knowles, Halle Berry*	Body	*Mark Wahlberg, Will Smith*
Skin	*Reese Witherspoon, Paris Hilton*	Skin	*Ryan Seacrest, Orlando Bloom*

TOP EARNING DEAD CELEBS

According to *Forbes* magazine's 2007 list of top-earning dead celebrities, grunge icon Kurt Cobain sensationally surpassed Elvis 'The Pelvis' Presley for the first time ever. Below is the full ranking of the thirteen icons resting in peace and plenty:

1	Kurt Cobain	6	Andy Warhol	11	J.R.R. Tolkien
2	Elvis Presley	7	Dr Seuss	12	George Harrison
3	Charles M. Schulz	8	Ray Charles	13	Bob Marley
4	John Lennon	9	Marilyn Monroe		
5	Albert Einstein	10	Johnny Cash		[all earned >$7m Oct 05–06]

10 MOST INFLUENTIAL PEOPLE WHO NEVER LIVED

Recognition, popularity, and persistence were the traits required for fictitious characters to enter Lazar, Karlan, and Salter's splendid book, *101 Most Influential People Who Never Lived*. Their top 10 imaginary, yet consequential, characters were:

1	Marlboro Man	6	Frankenstein's Monster
2	George Orwell's Big Brother	7	Siegfried
3	King Arthur	8	Sherlock Holmes
4	Santa Claus	9	Romeo & Juliet
5	Hamlet	10	Dr Jekyll & Mr Hyde

CELEBRITY LEGS

The following celebrities were judged to have the best and worst legs, according to a survey undertaken by hosiery manufacturer Pretty Polly in November 2006:

Best lallies	*Worst lallies*
Kelly Brook · Kate Moss	Victoria Beckham · Nicole Richie
Beyoncé · Cameron Diaz	Jade Goody · Nikki Grahame
Mischa Barton	Tara Palmer-Tomkinson

HOLLYWOOD'S WORST-DRESSED WOMEN

Former designer Richard Blackwell has issued his annual 'Worst Dressed Women List' for 47 years. In 2006, Paris Hilton and Britney Spears (nicknamed 'The Screamgirls' by Mr Blackwell) tied for number one. The rest of the 2006 top 10:

1	Britney Spears/Paris Hilton	6	Paula Abdul
2	Camilla Parker-Bowles	7	Sharon Stone
3	Lindsay Lohan	8	Tori Spelling
4	Christina Aguilera	9	Sandra Oh
5	Mariah Carey	10	Meryl Streep

MULTI-CHANNEL GROWTH

According to BARB the number of homes receiving multi-channel television are:

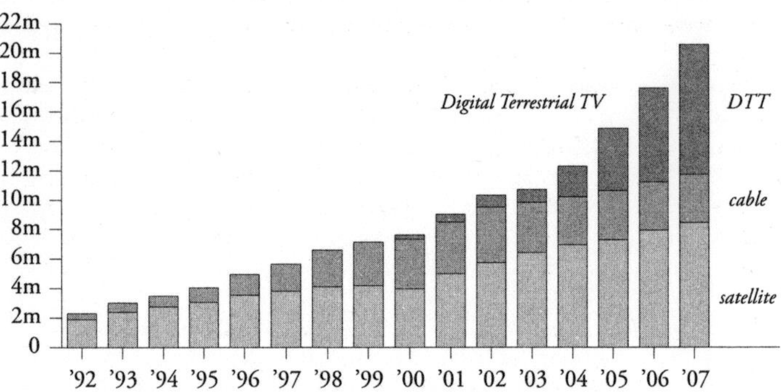

FAVOURITE DOCTOR WHO

Below are the most popular Doctors Who – according to *Doctor Who Magazine*:

David Tennant	28·2%	Peter Davison	5·7
Tom Baker	26·5	Sylvester McCoy	3·3
Christopher Eccleston	11·4	Colin Baker	2·8
Jon Pertwee	9·6	William Hartnell	2·4
Patrick Troughton	8·8	Paul McGann	1·4

BBC & IMPARTIALITY

In June 2007, the BBC Trust published *From Seesaw to Wagon Wheel* – a report on the impartiality of the Corporation. The title refers to the report's premise that current political and social debates tend to be multifaceted rather than polarised – the left/right, either/or *seesaw* replaced by the *wagon wheel* used in cricket coverage, 'where the wheel is not circular and has a shifting centre with spokes that go in all directions'. The report concluded that the BBC's tradition of impartiality needed to be strengthened and modified, to respond to the changing patterns of media consumption and the rapid rise of unregulated, sometimes user-generated, and often partisan broadcasts. The report recommended 12 guiding principles to safeguard impartiality, which it broadly defined as 'a mixture of accuracy, balance, context, distance, even-handedness, fairness, objectivity, open-mindedness, rigour, self-awareness, transparency ... truth ... breadth of view and completeness'.

The report raised specific concerns about the BBC's handling of single-issue campaigns, especially 'global, celebrity-driven mass entertainment in "a good cause"'. Singled out for comment were the 2005 Make Poverty History campaign (which Ofcom judged to be *political*) and the Live8 concerts.

CONSUMPTION OF NEWS

The Communications Act (2003) stipulates that Ofcom must set quotas for how much UK national/international and UK nations/regions news must be shown on Public Service Broadcast TV each week. The current quotas for news coverage are:

Channel / *Hours/week*	*national news (total)*	*national news (peak 18:00–22:30)*	*regional news (total)*	*regional news (peak)*
BBC 1	26h 28m	5h 16m	4h 25m	2h 16m
ITV1	7h 00m	2h 24m	5h 30m	2h 30m
GMTV	5h 00m	n/a	0h 45m	n/a
Channel 4	4h 00m	4h 00m	n/a	n/a
Five	7h 50m	1h 55m	n/a	n/a

Ofcom's *New News, Future News* report asked 'What is your main source of news?':

News source	*2002 %*	*2006 %*
Television	65	65
Newspapers	15	14
Radio	16	11
Internet	2	6
Word of mouth	1	1
Magazines	0	1

[Respondents ≥16]

Below is a breakdown of TV channels' share of news viewing from October 2006:

News on	*% viewing*
BBC 1	50·6
BBC 2	4·6
BBC24	5·2
ITV1	26·8
C4	4·5
Five	2·8
Sky News	4·9
Other	0·6

Ofcom asked which topics people would like to see *more of*, *about the same*, or *less of*:

Topic	*More*	*about the same*	*less*
Current events in region	46%	51	3
Human interest stories	42	49	9
Politics in region	33	53	13
Crime	33	51	15
Current events in UK	31	65	4
World politics/events	25	59	15
Consumer affairs	23	65	12
City/business news	20	66	12
UK-wide politics	19	61	20
Celebrity behaviour	13	46	41

Below is the public's perception of the impartiality of various news sources, 2002–06:

News source	*2002 %*	*2006 %*
BBC 1	77	54
ITV	60	41
Channel 4	44	19
Five	29	13
Sky News	22	24

[Source: Ofcom, *New News, Future News* · June 2007]

ADVERTISING EXPENDITURE · 2006

Below is a breakdown of UK advertising expenditure in 2006, by media and sector:

TV

Sector	expenditure (£m)
Entertainment	464·8
Finance	438·2
Food	411·9
Retail	384·5
Cosmetics	336·8

RADIO

Sector	expenditure (£m)
Motors	84·8
Entertainment	83·0
Retail	76·9
Govt/political	73·3
Finance	56·3

INTERNET

Sector	expenditure (£m)
Finance	100·8
Entertainment	62·6
Computers	44·1
Business/industry	42·8
Telecoms	40·4

PRESS

Sector	expenditure (£m)
Finance	355·6
Entertainment	318·0
Motors	304·7
Retail	280·0
Travel	254·7

OUTDOOR

Sector	expenditure (£m)
Entertainment	152·2
Telecoms	95·6
Motors	57·9
Retail	57·1
Drink	56·1

CINEMA

Sector	expenditure (£m)
Motors	28·2
Telecoms	23·3
Entertainment	20·9
Drink	18·1
Food	11·3

[Source: Nielsen Media Research 2007 ©]

MOST COMPLAINED-ABOUT ADVERTS

The Advertising Standards Authority's [ASA] 2006 annual report detailed the broadcast adverts which drew the most complaints. The worst eight adverts were:

GAY POLICE ASSOCIATION · An ad, deemed offensive to Christians, that used a Bible to highlight religion as a cause of homophobic attacks.
553 complaints · Upheld

HM REVENUE & CUSTOMS · Seen to represent all plumbers as tax-evaders by portraying one hiding under a sink.
271 complaints · Not upheld

DOLCE & GABBANA · Adverts criticised for glorifying and condoning knives and violence.
166 complaints · Upheld

MOTOROLA · Complaints about glamorising knife crime in an ad that used the punning tagline 'the cutting edge of technology'.
160 complaints · Not upheld

CARPHONE WAREHOUSE · A phone service that promised to be 'free forever' was deemed to be misleading.
145 complaints · Upheld

FRENCH CONNECTION · Concerns about a martial-arts fight that ended with a lesbian kiss.
127 complaints · Complaints not justified

CHANNEL 5 · Concerns over racism prompted by the tagline 'nothing good ever came out of America'.
99 complaints · Not upheld

KELLOGG'S · An ad in which a man rode upon a dog prompted some to fear it would encourage animal cruelty.
96 complaints · Not upheld

[Source: asa.org.uk]

FAVOURITE TV JINGLE

According to a June 2007 survey in the *Telegraph*, Britain's favourite TV jingles are:

#	*product*	TV jingle
1	Shake 'n' Vac	*Do the Shake and Vac, and put the freshness back*
2	R. Whites	*I'm a secret lemonade drinker*†
3	Wall's Cornetto	*Just one Cornetto*
4	Asda	*That's Asda price* [chink, chink]
5	Club biscuits	*If you like a lot of chocolate on your biscuit, join our club*
6	Sheila's Wheels	*For bonzer car insurance deals, girls get on to Sheila's Wheels*
7	Coco-Pops	*I'd rather have a bowl of Coco-Pops*
8	Fairy Liquid	*Mild, green, Fairy Liquid*
9	Heinz	*Beans meanz Heinz*
10	Um Bongo	*Um Bongo, Um Bongo, they drink it in the Congo*

† Written and performed by Ross McManus, featuring his son, Elvis Costello, on backing vocals.

OTHER TV AWARDS OF NOTE · 2006/07

Awards	*category*	*winner*
National TV Awards ['06]	Most popular actor	David Tennant · *Doctor Who*
	Most popular actress	Billie Piper · *Doctor Who*
	Most popular drama	*Doctor Who*
British Soap Awards	Best actor	Antony Cotton · *Coronation Street*
	Best actress	Kate Ford · *Coronation Street*
	Best soap	*Coronation Street*
Primetime Emmys	Actor in drama	James Spader · *Boston Legal*
	Actress in drama	Sally Field · *Brothers and Sisters*
	Outstanding drama	*The Sopranos*
Royal Television Society	Comedy drama	*The Royle Family: the Queen of Sheba*
	Features & factual entertainment	*The Apprentice*
	Soap	*Coronation Street*
	Drama series	*The Street*

CHILDREN'S TV VOICE-OVER ARTISTS

Below are the most popular voices from children's television, according to a poll to promote the BBC kids' series *Underground Ernie* – itself voiced by Gary Lineker.

Brian Cant	*Camberwick Green*; *Play School*; *Trumpton*
Oliver Postgate	*Bagpuss*; *The Clangers*; *Ivor the Engine*; *Noggin the Nog*
David Jason	*Angelmouse*; *Count Duckula*; *Danger Mouse*
Bernard Cribbins	*The Wombles*
Jim Henson	*Kermit the Frog*
Ray Brooks	*Mr Benn*
Ringo Starr	*Thomas the Tank Engine*
Kenneth Williams	*Willo the Wisp*
Sylvia Anderson	*Lady Penelope*

THE TV BAFTAS · 2007

Best actor.. Jim Broadbent · *Longford* [C4]
Best actress .... Victoria Wood · *Housewife, 49* [ITV1]
Entertainment performance......... Jonathan Ross · *Friday Night With ...* [BBC1]
Comedy performance............................... Ricky Gervais · *Extras* [BBC2]
Single drama .... *Housewife, 49* [ITV1]
Drama series .... *The Street* [BBC1]
Drama serial................................ *See No Evil: The Moors Murders* [ITV1]
Continuing drama .... *Casualty* [BBC1]
Feature .... *The Choir* [BBC2]
Factual series or strand............................ *Ross Kemp on Gangs* [SKY ONE]
Huw Wheldon award for specialist factual ...*Nuremberg: Goering's Last Stand* [C4]
Flaherty award for single documentary .... *Evicted* [BBC1]
Sport.................. *F1: Hungarian Grand Prix – Jenson Button's first win* [ITV1]
News .... *Granada Reports: Morecambe Bay* [ITV1]
Best interactivity .... *Terry Pratchett's Hogfather* [SKY ONE]
Lew Grade award for entertainment.......................... *The X Factor* [ITV1]
Sitcom.................................. *The Royle Family: Queen of Sheba* [BBC1]
International .... *Entourage* [ITV2]
Comedy programme or series .... *That Mitchell & Webb Look* [BBC2]
Pioneer audience award.. *Life on Mars* [BBC1]
Special award.. Andy Harries
Fellowship.. Richard Curtis

BAFTA IN QUOTES

❦ VICTORIA WOOD · It's a relief to win because I was engaged on a no-win, no-fee basis. ❦ ROSS KEMP · I'm rarely speechless, but I am now. ❦ STEPHEN MERCHANT [collecting Ricky Gervais' award on his behalf] · Talk about rubbing salt into the wound. I'm sure he would like me to say I've been robbed, and I would agree. ❦ DAVID MITCHELL · Someone asked me where my suit came from and I very nearly said 'it's none of your business', but people are interested now. ❦ CRAIG CASH · Bloody hell!

REALITY SHOW WINNERS · 2006/07

Channel & show		*winner (prize)*
BBC1	*Strictly Come Dancing*	Mark Ramprakash & Karen Hardy (£1·5m for charity)
ITV1	*X Factor*	Leona Lewis (£1m record contract)
C4	*Celebrity Big Brother*	Shilpa Shetty
ITV1	*Soapstar Superstar*	Antony Cotton (£200,000 for charity)
BBC2	*The Apprentice*	Simon Ambrose (£100k job with Sir Alan Sugar)
BBC1	*Just the Two of Us*	Marti Pellow & Hannah Waterman
BBC1	*Any Dream Will Do?*	Lee Mead (lead role in West End production of *Joseph*)
ITV1	*Dancing on Ice*	Kyran Bracken (a trophy)
ITV1	*Grease is the Word*	Susan McFadden & Danny Bayne (lead roles in *Grease*)
BBC1	*Celebrity Fame Academy*	Tara Palmer-Tomkinson (£780,000 for Comic Relief)
ITV1	*Britain's Got Talent*	Paul Potts (£100,000 & performing at the Royal Variety Show)

TELEVISION IN CRISIS

The integrity of British TV was challenged by a series of scandals in 2007 – which led Culture Secretary James Purnell to conclude in September, 'it has been a bad year for broadcasters'. Below is a brief summary of some of the year's major incidents.

In January, *Celebrity Big Brother* was embroiled in a 'race row' [see p.27]. ❦ In January, Ofcom warned ITV Play after complaints that some of the channel's quiz questions were unreasonably obscure – e.g. answers to 'what items might be found in a woman's handbag?' included 'a balaclava' and 'Rawlplugs'. ❦ In February, Richard Madeley and Judy Finnigan apologised to their viewers, after allegations that some callers to the premium-rate 'You Say, We Pay' phone quiz had not been properly entered. Richard and Judy said they were 'very shocked and also angry' about the problems, and the quiz was suspended pending investigations. ❦ In March, the BBC revealed that *Blue Peter* had faked the results of a phone-in competition. ❦ In April, GMTV apologised for 'errors' in phone-in competitions, after *Panorama* alleged that viewers were encouraged to continue phoning premium rate numbers for entry to competitions even after winners had been selected. Responsibility for the 'irregularities' was accepted by the company providing phone-in quiz services to GMTV. Despite this, in July, the MD of GMTV, Paul Corley, announced his resignation in a move to 'restore trust' in the channel. ❦ In June, Ofcom fined Channel Five a record £300,000 for faking winners on its quiz show *Brainteaser*. ❦ In June, Channel 4 rejected a formal plea from Princes William and Harry, and broadcast controversial images pertaining to the death of their mother, in the documentary *Diana: The Witnesses in the Tunnel*. ❦ In July, the production company RDF apologised to the Queen and the BBC after showing to journalists a trailer for the documentary *A Year With The Queen*. The editing of the trailer out of chronological sequence conveyed the false impression that the Queen had walked out of an Annie Leibovitz photoshoot for *Vanity Fair* 'in a huff'. ❦ In July, the BBC revealed that six programmes had faked phone-in competitions – including flagship shows like *Comic Relief*, *Sport Relief*, and *Children in Need*. In response, BBC Director General Mark Thompson suspended all interactive and phone-in competitions. ❦ A host of other allegations were made and apologies offered for miscounted phone votes and faked scenes in documentaries, trailers, and 'reality' shows. (The naming of the *Blue Peter* cat became a bone of contention.) Some even questioned the ethics of 'noddys' – cut-away shots showing the nodding head of an interviewer, who may or may not be present during the interview. In August, Channel Five News announced it would axe noddys as part of a wider ban on what it called 'traditional – and rather hackneyed – tricks'.

The reaction of the print media was stern (albeit with a dash of Schadenfreude): 'Why should we be expected to go on paying this tax on TV ownership, when Auntie displays all the moral rectitude of Del Boy Trotter?' asked the *Daily Mail*. The reaction of the public was illustrated by an August YouGov poll, which found that 48% of the population 'do not trust [TV] very much to tell the truth', and 79% of those who entered TV phone-in competitions would not do so again.

GENE HUNTISMS

In April 2007, more than 7m tuned-in to the final episode of BBC1's hit time-travel police drama *Life on Mars*. Bigoted 1970s cop Gene Hunt stole the show (and many hearts) with his politically incorrect one-liners, a selection of which are below:

'You great soft, sissy, girlie, nancy, French, bender, Man United supporting poof!'

'Anything happens to this motor and I come over your houses and stamp on all your toys. Got it?'

'He's got fingers in more pies than a leper on a cookery course'

'I think she's as fake as a tranny's fanny'

'The dealers are so scared we're more likely to get Helen Keller to talk … All in all, this investigation is going the speed of a spastic in a magnet factory'

'She's as nervous as a very small nun at a penguin shoot'

In April 2007, Chris Keates of the National Association of Schoolmasters and Union of Women Teachers raised concerns that programmes like *Life on Mars* may encourage bullying. She worried that children may not understand that some views expressed in the show were no longer acceptable.

FILMS ON TV

Below is a breakdown of the feature films broadcast on network television in 2006:

Channel	*number of film slots*	*number of UK film slots*	*UK films as % of total*	*recent UK films*†	*recent UK as % of total*
BBC1	367	80	21·8	30	8·2
BBC2	397	103	25·9	20	5·0
ITV1	183	38	20·8	9	4·9
C4	580	181	31·2	42	7·2
Five	484	36	7·4	4	0·8
Total	2,011	438	21·8	105	5·2

† Released in cinemas since 1999. Over the last ten years the number of films shown on terrestrial television has decreased 28%, from 2,807 to 2,011. [Sources: DGA Metrics; UK Film Council RSU]

MOST-PAUSED TV

Sharon Stone's 'flashing' scene in *Basic Instinct* is the most-paused televisual moment – according to a June 2007 survey for Freeview. The top five paused moments are:

Sharon Stone uncrossing and crossing her legs .... *Basic Instinct* (1992)
Geoff Hurst's controversial goal .... World Cup final (1966)
Del Boy Trotter falling through the bar.................... *Only Fools & Horses* (1989)
Maradona's 'Hand of God' against England........ World Cup quarter final (1986)
John Prescott punching an egg-thrower........... General election campaign (2001)

DA-NOTICES

The Defence Advisory (DA) Notice system is a voluntary arrangement that mediates between news organisations seeking to publish stories involving national security, and the interests of national security itself. The system is overseen by the Defence Press & Broadcasting Advisory Committee (DPBAC) [of senior civil servants and representatives of the media], which monitors the five 'Standing DA-Notices':

DA-NOTICE 01 ... *military operations, plans, and capabilities*
DA-NOTICE 02 ... *nuclear and non-nuclear weapons and equipment*
DA-NOTICE 03 ... *ciphers and secure communications*
DA-NOTICE 04 ... *sensitive installations and home addresses*
DA-NOTICE 05 ... *UK security and intelligence services and special services*

These notices request the media not to publish material that might jeopardise the security of the UK, its allies, or members of the security services (e.g. DA-Notice 02 requests advice be sought before publishing 'detailed security arrangements for the storage, transport and development of nuclear weapons and associated fissile materials'.) DA-Notices carry no power greater than persuasion, though editors remain bound by the Official Secrets Act. The scope of the Notices was relaxed in 2000, but recent events have renewed their purpose. For example, days after 9/11, the Secretary of the DPBAC asked the media to be circumspect even when publishing conjecture on future military operations, noting that 'informed speculation may become very close to the truth'.

BRITISH PRESS AWARDS 2007

National paper ... *The Observer*
Political journalist ... Patrick Wintour · *The Guardian*
Show business ... Fiona Cummins · *Daily Mirror*
Columnist ... Polly Toynbee · *The Guardian*
Feature writer ... Michael Tierney · *The Herald*
Interviewer ... Jan Moir · *Daily Telegraph*
Sports journalist ... Ian Ridley · *Mail on Sunday*
Reporter ... Sheila McNulty · *Financial Times*
Scoop ... 'John Prescott's Affair' by Stephen Moyes · *Daily Mirror*
Front page ... 'My Affair: By Prezza' · *Daily Mirror*
Team ... Cash for Honours · *The Sunday Times*

BLOGGING CODE OF CONDUCT

In March 2007, Tim O'Reilly [see p.198] and other prominent bloggers called for a blogging 'code of conduct' to be compiled, in response to a series of alarming messages and online death threats targeting the popular American blogger Kathy Sierra. Among other stipulations, O'Reilly suggested that bloggers not say anything online they wouldn't say in person, and mooted an end to anonymous posting. The code was still being hotly debated online at the time of writing.

FREE NEWSPAPERS WORLDWIDE

The worldwide circulation of free daily newspapers has increased 137% between 2001–05, from 12m copies a day to 28m. Below are the world's top 5 free dailies:

Title	*country*	*circulation*
Leggo [I read]	Italy	1,050,000
Metro	UK	977,000
Que! [That!]	Spain	964,000
20 Minutos	Spain	920,000
Metro	Italy	850,000

The number of free daily titles in 2005 for selected countries is tabulated below:

Country	*No. titles 2005*	*Adult population*	*No. titles/adult pop.*
Canada	30	25,885,000	1·2
USA	34	213,453,000	0·2
Rep. Korea	9	36,344,000	0·2
France	8	48,911,000	0·2
Germany	3	70,576,000	<0·1
Ireland	3	3,262,000	0·9
Spain	23	37,084,000	0·6
UK	8	47,391,000	0·2

[Source: World Association of Newspapers, World Press Trends 2006]

PAID-FOR DAILY PAPERS · TITLES & CIRCULATION

Newspaper circulation is in decline worldwide, with only Africa and Asia bucking the trend and reporting a growth in circulation in 2005. Despite this, most regions reported a rise in the number of newspapers, with 10,104 titles on sale worldwide:

Number of titles	2001	2002	2003	2004	2005	%±†
Africa	266	273	285	297	308	+15·8
America, North	2,000	1,946	1,945	1,947	1,939	–3·1
America, South	807	852	939	960	970	+20·2
Asia	3,765	3,622	4,347	4,237	4,522	+20·1
Australia & Oceania	88	86	85	84	85	–3·4
Europe	2,004	2,205	2,253	2,306	2,280	+13·8
Circulation, dailies (m)						
Africa	2·8	2·8	2·9	3·1	3·1	+11·6
America, North	61·5	60·9	60·8	60·3	58·7	–4·5
America, South	12·0	11·2	10·7	10·9	11·2	–7·3
Asia	246·8	248·4	267·6	278·2	283·4	+14·9
Australia & Oceania	3·8	3·8	3·8	3·8	3·7	–3·0
Europe	96·8	95·2	93·2	91·3	90·7	–6·3

† % change 2001–05. A worldwide June 2007 poll by Harris International indicated the key reason why people do not read newspapers is lack of time. [Source: WAN, World Press Trends 2006]

THE PULITZER PRIZE · JOURNALISM · 2007

In his 1904 will, Joseph Pulitzer made provision for the establishment of the Pulitzer Prizes to 'promote excellence'. Some of the 2007 Journalism prizes included:

PUBLIC SERVICE AWARD
The Wall Street Journal for its '*creative and comprehensive probe into backdated stock options for business executives that triggered investigations, the ouster of top officials and widespread change in corporate America*'

BREAKING NEWS REPORTING
The Oregonian staff for its '*skillful and tenacious coverage of a family missing in the Oregon mountains, telling the tragic story both in print and online*'

INTERNATIONAL REPORTING
The Wall Street Journal staff for its '*sharply edged reports on the adverse impact of China's booming capitalism on conditions ranging from inequality to pollution*'

EXPLANATORY REPORTING
Kenneth R. Weiss, Usha Lee McFarling, & Rick Loomis of the *Los Angeles Times* for their '*richly portrayed reports on the world's distressed oceans, telling the story in print and online, and stirring reaction among readers and officials*'

JOURNALIST DEATHS

At least 1,000 journalists have been killed around the world in the past 10 years, according to a survey released in 2007 by the International News Safety Institute. Surprisingly, only a quarter died covering wars and armed conflicts; the majority were killed in peacetime, often covering news in their own countries. According to the report, their killers were frequently hostile authorities or criminals intent on silencing press coverage. 90% of the murders have not been solved. The countries with the most deaths were Iraq (138), Russia (88), Colombia (72), the Philippines (55), and Iran (54). Below is a breakdown of journalist deaths since 1997:

Employer	
Press	435
TV	279
Radio	162
News agency	62
Unknown	56
Online	6

Context of death	
Peacetime	731
International armed conflict	167
National armed conflict	102

Peacetime deaths by topic of coverage†	
Corruption	97
Politics	46
Insurgency	39
Civil unrest	21
Investigating drugs	21
Terrorism	14
Investigating crime	14
Investigating paramilitary	4

† 325 deaths were unspecified. 150 also died in accidents. Remaining deaths were in wartime.

Figures include all news media personnel, including those drivers, translators, &c. working alongside journalists. 876 of the 1,000 killed 1996–2006 were journalists, media owners, or those working in an editorial capacity, while 97 were support workers (drivers, &c.), and 27 held unspecified occupations.

UK RADIO HALL OF FAME

The Radio Academy, a body that 'exists to celebrate excellence in all aspects of UK radio', oversees the UK Radio Hall of Fame. In 2006, the following were inducted:

Al Read · Anna Raeburn · Barry Alldis · Betty Marsden
Brian Matthew · Eamonn Andrews · Hattie Jacques · Jimmy Clitheroe
Jimmy Savile · John Timpson · Linda Smith · Pete Murray

THE SONY AWARDS · 2007

For twenty-five years, the Sony Radio Academy Awards have rewarded excellence in British radio with bronze, silver, or gold awards. Some of the 2007 golds were:

Breakfast show	The Today Programme [BBC Radio 4]
Music radio personality of the year	Chris Evans [BBC Radio 2]
Music broadcaster of the year	Colin Murray [BBC Radio 1]
Entertainment award	The Chris Evans Show [BBC Radio 2]
Speech broadcaster	Eddie Nestor [BBC London 94·9]
News journalist	John Humphrys [BBC Radio 4]
Digital station of the year	Gaydar Radio
Station of the year UK	Classic FM

DAB BRANDS

The UK was the first country to broadcast a wide range of radio stations via Digital Audio Broadcasting (DAB). The increased bandwidth allowed the creation of many new stations, some of which are available only on DAB, such as BBC 6 Music and Gaydar. Below is a breakdown of stations in the DAB radio market in 2005:

77% *former analogue stations*	23% *digital-only stations*

[Source: Goldmedia]

HOW WE LISTEN TO THE RADIO

A survey released by Sony to mark the 25th anniversary of the Sony Awards in April 2007 revealed that people now listen to the radio across a variety of platforms:

Platform	*% using*
Traditional radio	82
Through television	42
Digital radio	36
Internet	30
MP3/music player	21
Mobile phone	12

[Figures are for adult listeners only]

Internet radio was the most popular among those aged 35–44, with 41% listening in this fashion.

NOTABLE DESERT ISLAND DISCS · 2007

Castaway	*luxury*	favourite Desert Island Disc
Anthony Horowitz	a fountain pen, ink, and paper	*She's Always a Woman (Billy Joel)*
Lady Natasha Spender	a grand piano	*String Quintet in G Minor (Mozart)*
Edna O'Brien	a vault of very good white wine	*The Foggy Dew (The Chieftains with Sinead O'Connor)*
Ann Daniels	a bar of soap	*Sweet Dreams (Are Made of This) (Eurythmics)*
Brian Aldiss	a banjo	*Old Rivers (Walter Brennan)*
Neil Tennant	a DVD projector & DVDs	*I Don't Want to Hear it Anymore (Dusty Springfield)*
Paul Abbott	a writing pad and pencils	*Town Called Malice (The Jam)*
Grayson Perry	lots of good pens and paper	*Prophecies (Philip Glass)*
Andrew Neil	a wind-up radio	*Violin Concerto in D Major (Tchaikovsky)*
J.P. Donleavy	a long-handled spoon to make dressings	*Emperor Concerto (Beethoven)*
Andy Kershaw	lots of lavatory paper	*Hupenyu Hwangu (Bhundu Boys)*
Jo Brand	a church organ	*Oh England, My Lionheart (Kate Bush)*
Prof. Raymond Tallis	a video of his family	*String Quintet in C Major (Schubert)*
Ben Helfgott	some weights for weight-training	*Nessun Dorma (Puccini)*
Joanna Lumley	a video camera and film	*Symphony No. 7 in A Major (Beethoven)*
Greg Dyke	a guitar and instructions on how to play it	*Like a Rolling Stone (Bob Dylan)*
Paul McKenna	a collage of photos of family, friends, and partner	*Movin' On Up (Primal Scream)*
Prof. Sir Tom Blundell	a combined heat and power micro-unit	*Wednesday Night Prayer Meeting (Charles Mingus)*
Yoko Ono	her life for the next 30 years	*Beautiful Boy (John Lennon)*
Christy Moore	a set of Uilleann pipes	*Taimse Im' Chodladh (traditional)*
Ricky Gervais	a vat of Novocaine	*Lilywhite (Cat Stevens)*
Wangari Maathai	a large basket of fruit	*I Can't Complain (Patti LaBelle)*
Simon Russell Beale	the daily Araucaria crossword	*Symphony No. 4 in B Flat Major (Beethoven)*
Oliver Postgate	a comfortable bed	*When the Saints Come Marching In (traditional)*
Thomas Keneally	a can of caviar, a spoon, and a tin opener	*Herz und Mund und Tat und Leben (Bach)*
Andrew Davies	an endless supply of Mojitos	*Hiawatha Rag (Chris Barber Band Box)*

—CYBER-DISSIDENTS & ENEMIES OF THE INTERNET—

In November 2006, Reporters Without Borders, an organisation campaigning for journalistic freedom and against censorship, released its annual list of 'internet enemies' – countries with repressive internet policies that restrict 'freedom of expression' and enforce website filtering. Egypt appeared on the list for the first time; Nepal, Libya, and the Maldives were removed. The internet's 13 enemies were:

Belarus · Burma · China · Cuba · Egypt · Iran · North Korea
Saudi Arabia · Syria · Tunisia · Turkmenistan · Uzbekistan · Vietnam

As the internet becomes more open to user-generated content, so restrictive regimes have become concerned about the subversive potential of blogs, chatrooms, instant messaging, and the like. A number of states have developed techniques to monitor their subjects – including Cuba, which has installed spyware in cybercafé computers to shutdown web browsers if certain prohibited words are entered. Infamously, the Chinese government has pressurised companies like Google, Yahoo!, and Microsoft to facilitate censorship by blocking key words relating to Taiwanese independence and the Dalai Lama. When censorship fails, repressive regimes take more drastic action. Reporters Without Borders estimated that, as of February 2007, at least 60 'cyber-dissidents' were incarcerated in jails worldwide:

Country	*cyber-dissidents*
China	50
Vietnam	4
Syria	2
Tunisia	1
Egypt	1
Iran	1
Libya	1
Total incarcerated	60

In May 2007, a report by Open Net Initiative [ONI] indicated that 25 out of 41 countries surveyed imposed some form of content filtering. The study suggested that in 2002 only a handful of countries practised 'state-mandated net filtering', but by 2007 this had grown to at least 25. ONI hoped their report might make filtering more transparent. Evidence of filtering was found in: Azerbaijan, Bahrain, Burma/Myanmar, China, Ethiopia, India, Iran, Jordan, Libya, Morocco, Oman, Pakistan, Saudi Arabia, Singapore, South Korea, Sudan, Syria, Tajikistan, Thailand, Tunisia, Turkmenistan, United Arab Emirates, Uzbekistan, Vietnam, and Yemen.

ONLINE NEWSPAPER READERSHIP

In April 2007, online newspaper readership figures were published for the first time by the Audit Bureau of Circulations. Only the *Guardian*, *Telegraph*, *Times*, and *Sun* made their figures public. Unique monthly user figures for March 2007 were:

Website	*monthly unique users*
guardian.co.uk	15,093,058
timesonline.co.uk	8,048,029
thesun.co.uk	7,797,032
telegraph.co.uk	7,392,803

[Source: ABCe · Users 01·03·07–31·03·07]

When the figures were released, guardian.co.uk was quick to point out that they 'contradicted recent claims by the *Telegraph* group that its site was "Britain's No. 1 quality newspaper website".'

MAJOR BRITISH NEWSPAPERS

Title	*editorial address*	*phone*	*editor*	*circulation*	*readership*	*cost*	*owner*	*founded*
Sun	1 Virginia St, Wapping, London E98 1SN	020 7782 4000	Rebekah Wade	3,043,351	7,840,000	35p	N	1911
Daily Mail	Northcliffe Ho., 2 Derry St, London W8 5TT	020 7938 6000	Paul Dacre	2,294,929	5,253,000	45p	A	1896
Daily Mirror	1 Canada Sq., Canary Wharf, London E14 5AP	020 7293 3000	Richard Wallace	1,554,610	3,844,000	40p	T	1903
Daily Telegraph	111 Buckingham Palace Rd, London SW1W 0DT	020 7538 5000	Will Lewis	894,258	2,177,000	70p	H	1855
Daily Star	10 Lower Thames St, London EC3R 6EN	0871 434 1010	Dawn Neesom	778,249	1,620,000	35p	S	1978
Daily Express	10 Lower Thames St, London EC3R 6EN	0871 434 1010	Peter Hill	765,967	1,742,000	40p	S	1900
Times	1 Virginia St, Wapping, London E98 1XY	020 7782 5000	Robert Thomson	636,777	1,730,000	70p	N	1785
Financial Times	1 Southwark Bridge, London SE1 9HL	020 7873 3000	Lionel Barber	452,767	394,000	130p	P	1888
Guardian	119 Farringdon Rd, London EC1R 3ER	020 7278 2332	Alan Rusbridger	371,754	1,239,00	80p	G	1821
Evening Standard	Northcliffe Ho., 2 Derry St, London W8 5TT	020 7938 6000	Veronica Wadley	273,537	773,000	50p	A	1827
Independent	191 Marsh Wall, London E14 9RS	020 7005 2000	Simon Kelner	245,466	767,000	70p	I	1986
News of the World	1 Virginia St, Wapping, London E98 1SN	020 7782 1001	Colin Myler	3,270,753	8,378,000	85p	N	1843
Mail on Sunday	Northcliffe Ho., 2 Derry St, London W8 5TT	020 7938 6000	Peter Wright	2,274,551	5,985,000	140p	A	1982
Sunday Mirror	1 Canada Sq., Canary Wharf, London E14 5AP	020 7293 3000	Tina Weaver	1,377,534	4,210,000	90p	T	1915
Sunday Times	1 Virginia St, Wapping, London E98 1XY	020 7782 5000	John Witherow	1,221,590	3,543,000	200p	N	1821
Sunday Express	10 Lower Thames St, London EC3R 6EN	0871 434 1010	Martin Townsend	744,902	2,039,000	130p	S	1918
People	1 Canada Sq., Canary Wharf, London E14 5AP	020 7293 3000	Mark Thomas	729,715	1,756,000	85p	T	1881
Sunday Telegraph	111 Buckingham Palace Rd, London SW1W 0DT	020 7538 5000	Ian MacGregor	655,047	1,905,000	180p	H	1961
Observer	119 Farringdon Rd, London EC1R 3ER	020 7278 2332	Roger Alton	451,363	1,445,000	180p	G	1791
Daily Star Sunday	10 Lower Thames St, London EC3R 6EN	0871 434 1010	Gareth Morgan	381,241	984,000	80p	S	2002
Independent on Sun.	191 Marsh Wall, London E14 9RS	020 7005 2000	Tristan Davies	209,418	808,000	180p	I	1990
Scotland on Sunday	108 Holyrood Rd, Edinburgh EH8 8AS	0131 620 8620	Les Snowdon	72,041	288,000	130p	J	1988

Ownership: [N]ews Corporation · Northern & [S]hell Media · [P]earson · Press [H]oldings Ltd · [A]ssociated Newspapers · [G]uardian Media Group · [J]ohnston Press [I]ndependent News & Media · [T]rinity Mirror · Circulation: ABC [May 2007] · Readership: NRS [March 2007] · Founded dates relate to the paper's earliest incarnation.

Music & Cinema

Movies are so rarely great art that if we cannot appreciate the great trash we have very little reason to be interested in them.
— PAULINE KAEL (1919–2001)

UK NUMBER ONES · 2006–07

W/ending	*weeks*	*artist*	song
16·09·06	4	Scissor Sisters	*I Don't Feel Like Dancin'*
14·10·06	1	Razorlight	*America*
21·10·06	2	My Chemical Romance	*Welcome To The Black Parade*
04·11·06	1	McFly	*Star Girl*
11·11·06	1	Fedde Le Grande	*Put Your Hands Up For Detroit*
18·11·06	1	Westlife	*The Rose*
25·11·06	1	Akon feat. Eminem	*Smack That*
02·12·06	4	Take That	*Patience*
24·12·06	4	Leona Lewis	*A Moment Like This*
27·01·07	5	Mika	*Grace Kelly*
03·03·07	1	Kaiser Chiefs	*Ruby*
10·03·07	2	Take That	*Shine*
23·03·07	1	Sugababes *vs* Girls Aloud	*Walk This Way*
31·03·07	3	The Proclaimers feat. Brian & Andy	*(I'm Gonna Be) 500 Miles*
21·04·07	1	Timbaland/Nelly Furtado/Justin Timberlake	*Give It To Me*
28·04·07	3	Beyoncé & Shakira	*Beautiful Liar*
19·05·07	1	McFly	*Baby's Coming Back/Transylvania*
26·05·07	10	Rihanna feat. Jay-Z	*Umbrella*
04·08·07	2	Timbaland feat. D.O.E./Keri Hilson	*The Way I Are*
18·08·07	1	Robyn feat. Kleerup	*With Every Heartbeat*
25·08·07	1	Kanye West	*Stronger*
08·09·07	≥3	Sean Kingston	*Beautiful Girls*

UK ONLY ALBUM CHART

In January 2007 – for the first time since the chart was established in 1956 – all the top 10 best-selling albums were by artists from the UK. The top ten albums were:

1 ... The View · *Hats Off To The Buskers*
2 .. The Good, The Bad, & The Queen *The Good, The Bad, & The Queen*
3 ...... Amy Winehouse · *Back to Black*
4 .... James Morrison · *Undiscovered*
5 .... The Fratellis · *Costello Music*
6 .... Snow Patrol · *Eyes Open*
7 .... Razorlight · *Razorlight*
8 .... Keane · *Under the Iron Sea*
9 .... Lily Allen · *Alright, Still*
10 .... Paolo Nutini · *These Streets*

[Source: The Official UK Charts Company]

GLOBAL BEST-SELLING ALBUMS · 2006

Album	*artist*	*publisher*
High School Musical	Cast soundtrack	Walt Disney/Universal/EMI
Stadium Arcadium	Red Hot Chili Peppers	Warner
Love	The Beatles	EMI
Back to Bedlam	James Blunt	Warner
FutureSex/LoveSounds	Justin Timberlake	Sony BMG
B'Day	Beyoncé	Sony BMG
U2 18 Singles	U2	Universal
Me and My Gang	Rascal Flatts	Lyric Street/Hollywood/&c.
Siempre	Il Divo	Sony BMG
Amore	Andrea Bocelli	Universal

[Sources: International Federation of the Phonographic Industry · Physical albums; not downloads]

BEST-SELLING BACK CATALOGUES

Rumours circulated in 2007 that the Beatles would join artists like the Doors and Elton John in releasing their back catalogue in downloadable form. In March 2007, HMV revealed the best-selling back catalogues by CD sales and downloads:

Purchased on CD	*position*	*downloaded*
The Beatles	1	Take That
AC/DC	2	Kylie Minogue
Muse	3	Pink Floyd
Rod Stewart	4	Michael Jackson
Metallica	5	Linkin Park
Pink Floyd	6	Eminem
Oasis	7	Queen
Madonna	8	Guns N' Roses
Michael Jackson	9	David Bowie
Eagles	10	Abba

REVAMPED UK SINGLES CHART

From 1 January 2007, all singles downloaded legitimately from the internet contributed to the official weekly UK singles chart – regardless of whether the track was available as a 'hard copy'. As a result, a number of singles no longer in the shops re-entered the chart – most notably *Chasing Cars* by Snow Patrol which re-entered at No. 9 (it reached No. 6 when first released in July 2006). Following a concerted campaign by Radio 1 DJ Chris Moyles, the enchanting Billie tune *Honey To The Bee* – originally released in 1999 – re-entered the chart at No. 17 in January 2007.

HMV dropped the official singles chart from its stores (after more than 40 years), stating that a chart that counted downloads was 'not appropriate for the purpose of merchandising [CD] singles'.

INFLUENCES ON UK MUSIC

Online music retailer eMusic conducted a poll in December 2006 to discover who was deemed a good or bad influence on the UK music industry. The results were:

Good influences	*Bad influences*
John Peel	Simon Cowell & The X Factor
Alan McGee†	Stock, Aitken & Waterman
Jools Holland	Steps
Michael Eavis‡	The Spice Girls

† Formed Creation Records; discovered Oasis. ‡ Dairy farmer who founded the Glastonbury Festival.

THE BRIT AWARDS · 2007

The 27th Brit Awards were broadcast live for the first time since 1989 (when Mick Fleetwood and Samantha Fox hosted, with hilarious consequences). The 2007 event was compèred by hirsute comedian Russell Brand, whose banter about friendly fire deaths in Iraq provoked boos from the audience and complaints from viewers.

British male .... James Morrison
British female .... Amy Winehouse
British group .... Arctic Monkeys
British album .... Arctic Monkeys · *Whatever People Say I Am, That's What I'm Not*
British single[1] .... Take That · *Patience*
British live act[2] .... Muse
British breakthrough act[3] .... The Fratellis
International male .... Justin Timberlake
International female .... Nelly Furtado
International album .... The Killers · *Sam's Town*
International group .... The Killers
International breakthrough act[4] .... Orson
Outstanding contribution to music .... Oasis

[1] Voted by ITV viewers of the live show. [2] Voted by BBC Radio 2 listeners.
[3] Voted by BBC Radio 1 listeners. [4] Voted by MTV viewers.

THE BRIT AWARDS IN QUOTES: AMY WINEHOUSE · Thank you very much. I'm glad my Mum and Dad are here. I just put on my sexiest dress and hoped. ❦ LILY ALLEN · [on being told by a fan she should have won one of her four nominations] I fucking know! ❦ NOEL GALLAGHER · Thank you very much. It's been a fucking pleasure. ❦ JOSS STONE · [on Robbie entering rehab] Big love to Robbie Williams for going through what he's going through. He is strong and inspired. ❦ RUSSELL BRAND · Amy Winehouse – her surname's beginning to sound like a description of her liver. · Can you honestly say that if someone gave you an envelope with a photo of the Queen's privates in it you wouldn't have a look? ❦ JAMES MORRISON · I really did not expect this – I tried to think of a speech but didn't want to pre-empt losing. ❦

UK MUSIC HALL OF FAME · 2006

Channel 4 launched its UK Music Hall of Fame in 2004. In 2006, a panel of music industry executives, performers, and journalists inducted the following artists:

Prince · James Brown · Brian Wilson · Bon Jovi · Rod Stewart
Led Zeppelin · Dusty Springfield · Sir George Martin (honorary)

CELEBRITY BANDS

In January 2007, Steven '*Under Siege*' Seagal and his band Thunderbox began the UK leg of a world tour to promote their album *Mojo Priest.* This tour drew attention to the range of celebrities who have played or still perform with a band, including:

Celeb	band
Kevin Bacon	*The Bacon Brothers*
Russell Crowe	*The Ordinary Fear of God*[1]
Jared Leto	*30 Seconds to Mars*
Jeff Goldblum	*The Mildred Snitzer Orch.*
Bruce Willis	*The Accelerators*
Keanu Reeves	*Dogstar*
Gary Sinise[2]	*Lt Dan Band*
Jamie Oliver	*Scarlet Division*
Tony Blair	*Ugly Rumours*
Dennis Quaid	*The Sharks*
Billy Bob Thornton	*Tres Hombres*
Alan Fletcher[3]	*Waiting Room*
Juliette Lewis	*The Licks*

[1] Renamed from *Thirty Odd Foot of Grunts* (still TOFOG). [2] Played Lt Dan Taylor in *Forrest Gump*. [3] Karl Kennedy in *Neighbours*.

The song *BBQ*, from Seagal's latest album, contains the following lyric: 'But baby we're cool/We're cool like a polar bear/When you see my new girlfriend/You gonna have to change your underwear'.

ROCK & ROLL HALL OF FAME

Artists become eligible to enter the American 'Rock & Roll Hall of Fame' 25 years after their first record release. In 2007, the following musicians were inducted:

Grandmaster Flash and the Furious Five (Grandmaster Flash, Cowboy, Kidd Creole, Melle Mel, Raheim, Mr Ness/Scorpio)
R.E.M. (Bill Berry, Peter Buck, Mike Mills, Michael Stipe)
The Ronettes (Veronica 'Ronnie' Spector, Estelle Bennett, Nedra Talley)
Patti Smith · Van Halen (Michael Anthony, Sammy Hagar, David Lee Roth, Alex Van Halen, Eddie Van Halen)

CHRISTMAS NUMBER ONE · 2006

For the second year running, the winner of ITV's X Factor achieved the Christmas No. 1. Leona Lewis's *A Moment Like This* raced to the top of the charts, becoming the fastest-selling download song of the year. Take That dropped to 2nd spot after 4 weeks at the top with *Patience*; McFly hit No. 3 with *Sorry's Not Good Enough.*

THE EUROVISION SONG CONTEST · 2007

In March 2007, the *Making Your Mind Up* final was broadcast to allow the public to choose which of these six acts would represent Britain at the May Eurovision:

Hawkins & Brown – *They Don't Make 'Em Like They Used To*
Cyndi – *I'll Leave My Heart* · Brian Harvey – *I Can* · Big Brovaz – *Big Bro Thang*
Liz McClarnon – *(Don't It Make You) Happy!* · Scooch – *Flying the Flag*

Obeying its instinct for high camp europop, the British public voted for Scooch.

Ladbrokes' odds for Eurovision winner
Ukraine 5/2 · Serbia 4/1 · Sweden 5/1 · Belarus 5/1 · Russia 9/1

THE FINAL · 12·05·07 · HELSINKI, FINLAND

The 52nd Eurovision turned more surreal than usual, when the existence of some form of Eastern European block-vote emerged. Eyebrows were raised when the top 16 Eurovision places were filled by countries all of which lay east of the Adriatic Sea. Serbia was awarded the maximum 12 points by Bosnia & Herzegovina, Croatia, Macedonia, Montenegro, Slovenia, and Hungary. Similarly, Ukraine was given 12 points by the Czech Republic, Latvia, Poland, Belarus, and Georgia. Malta admitted that the only reason they awarded the UK 12 points was as a protest against this Eastern European stitch-up. However, not even Malta's charity could rescue Scooch, who (with Ireland's 7) garnered just 19 votes to come 22nd out of 24. (Inevitably, Scooch's poor showing prompted some to question why the UK remains amongst the most generous funders of Eurovision.) The top 3 were:

Country	*artist*	song	*score*
Serbia	Marija Serifovic	*Molitva*	268
Ukraine	Verka Serduchka	*Dancing Lasha Tumbai*	235
Russia	Serebro	*Song#1*	207

WOGANISMS OF NOTE

'Let the dance macabre commence!' ❦ 'Who knows what hellish future lies ahead? Actually, I do, I've seen the rehearsals.' ❦ 'All-white, belt-buckles, and thrusting trousers.' ❦ 'This must have seemed like a tremendously good idea at the time.' ❦ 'Now, I don't know about you, but I can remember when all Russian girls had moustaches.' ❦ 'There is a lot of tempestuous head-shaking and scarf-waving.' ❦ 'I don't know if we'll ever overcome the block-voting that has become such a part of Eurovision ... do we care? Let's just take part!'

SONG LYRICS OF MERIT

SWEDEN · *Don't call for first aid or the fire brigade, Or the local police 'cause they won't care.* ❦ RUSSIA · *Oh! Don't call me funny bunny, I'll blow your money money, I'll get you to my bad ass spinning for you.* ❦ UKRAINE · *I want to see, Aha ... To dance or not to dance, I want to see, Aha ... It's not a question.* ❦ SERBIA · *I walk around like crazy, Falling in love frightens me, Days are like wounds, Countless and hard to get through.* ❦ TURKEY · *Lovey dovey, lovey dovey, all the time, I got lots of candy to make you mine.* ❦ UK · *Would you like something to suck on for landing, Sir?*

OTHER NOTABLE MUSIC AWARDS · 2007

Awards	prize	*winner*
Kerrang!	*Best British band*	Lostprophets
	Hall of fame	Judas Priest
	Best live band	Enter Shikari
NME	*Best British band*	Muse
	Best solo artist	Jamie T
	Best new band	Klaxons
	God-like genius award	Primal Scream
MTV	*Best video*	Rihanna feat. Jay-Z · *Umbrella*
	Best female	Fergie
	Best male	Justin Timberlake
	Best group	Fall Out Boy
Grammys	*Record of the year*	Dixie Chicks · *Not Ready To Make Nice*
	Album of the year	Dixie Chicks · *Taking The Long Way*
	Song of the year	Dixie Chicks · *Not Ready To Make Nice*
	Best tropical Latin album	G. Santa Rosa · *Directo Al Corazón*
Ivor Novello	*Best song*	*Elusive* · Scott Matthews
	Songwriters of the year	The Feeling
	Most performed work	*I Don't Feel Like Dancin'* · Scissor Sisters
	Best contemporary song	*Rehab* · Amy Winehouse
MOBO	*Best UK male*	Dizzee Rascal
	Best UK female	Amy Winehouse
	Best R&B	Ne-Yo
	Best hip hop	Kanye West
	Best African act	2 Face Idibia
Mojo	*Icon award*	Ozzy Osbourne
	Legend	Ike Turner
	Best song	*Rehab* · Amy Winehouse

THE MERCURY MUSIC PRIZE · 2007

The build-up to the 2007 Mercurys was dominated by lurid allegations about Amy Winehouse's lifestyle. Yet, despite a mesmerising performance on the night, Amy was disappointed. 'Nu rave' group Klaxons gleefully accepted the £20,000 prize for *Myths Of The Near Future,* boasting, 'We have made the most forward-thinking record in I don't know how long … so I think we deservedly beat Amy Winehouse'.

The 2007 Mercury nominees

Amy Winehouse .... *Back to Black*
Arctic Monkeys .... *Favourite Worst Nightmare*
Basquiat Strings with Seb Rochford ... *Basquiat Strings*
Bat for Lashes .... *Fur & Gold*
Dizzee Rascal.......... *Maths + English*
Fionn Regan .... *The End of History*
Jamie T................ *Panic Prevention*
The Young Knives.... *Voices of Animals & Men*
Maps .... *We Can Create*
New Young Pony Club .... *Fantastic Playroom*
The View .... *Hats Off to the Buskers*

GROWTH IN ONLINE MUSIC SALES

The UK is currently the largest consumer of online music in Europe, and is predicted to account for 40% of total European online music revenues by 2010. The trend for downloading music has been fuelled in part by the growth in sales of personal digital audio (MP3) players – not least iPods. According to a report by Screen Digest for the European Commission, published in October 2006, the uptake of personal MP3 players across Western Europe has grown significantly since 2002:

MP3 players sold	*2002*	*2003*	*2004*	*2005*
France	55,000	250,000	1,550,000	4,130,000
Germany	106,000	870,000	3,160,000	7,840,000
Italy	16,000	59,000	433,000	1,875,000
Spain	14,000	82,000	1,041,000	2,581,000
UK	78,000	288,000	1,663,000	4,796,000

In 2005, the European online music market generated revenue of €120·8m – or €0·26 per inhabitant. Below are online music revenues, by country, during 2005:

Country	*€m*	*€/inhabitant*
UK	42·1	0·70
Germany	31·7	0·38
France	11·2	0·18
Italy	5·6	0·10
Netherlands	5·1	0·31
Sweden	4·8	0·53
Spain	4·1	0·09
Ireland	1·0	0·25
Greece	0·2	0·02

[Source: European Cmsn, 2006.] The UK is the largest market in Europe for downloading tracks to mobile phones; in 2005, UK revenues from such downloads hit €28·2m, or €0·47 per person. ❦ Digital Rights Management (DRM) is technology that prevents unauthorised copying and sharing of digital goods like music and films. In 2007, DRM became one of the most talked-about issues in the music industry, as major players sought to maximise sales while protecting their copyrights. Until May 2007, all music purchased via Apple's iTunes was enveloped, in the words of Apple CEO Steve Jobs, by 'special and secret' DRM software that restricted the copying and playing of digital tracks. However, in February 2007, Jobs penned an open letter declaring that Apple would 'embrace' an end to DRM if music publishers made such a move possible. In response, EMI announced in April that it would sell its entire digital catalogue DRM-free on iTunes and elsewhere. Optimistically, Jobs said he expected that half the iTunes catalogue would be sold DRM-free by the end of 2007. In August 2007, Universal announced it would sell songs DRM-free for a 6-month trial period, though not on iTunes.

MUSIC DISTRIBUTION · UK

Below is a ranking of record companies by their UK sales from January–July 2007:

Record company	*% sales*
Universal	31·9%
Independents	25·5%
Sony BMG	16·6%
EMI	15·7%
Warner	10·3%

[Source: IFPI · *The Times*] Figures released by the BPI in July 2007 revealed that 90% of all singles are now sold via internet download. However, nearly all album sales (96·5%) are still in CD format.

CD PIRACY

The 2006 Piracy Report of the International Federation of the Phonographic Industry (IFPI) estimated that 37% of all CDs purchased worldwide in 2005 were pirated – amounting to 1·2bn CDs, with a total market value of $4·5bn. In the same year, the IFPI estimated 20bn tracks were illegally downloaded or swapped on the web. The IFPI report suggested that the bulk of piracy currently takes place in three distinct ways, although three new methods were increasingly prevalent.

Current methods of piracy

CD-R PIRACY · using a CD burner attached to a PC; currently the most common method of piracy.

PRESSED · employing professional CD-making equipment to create multiple copies.

INTERNET PIRACY · downloading and sharing of tracks over the internet.

Newer methods of piracy

LAN FILE SHARING · sharing tracks through a Local Area Network, e.g. at a university campus or business.

DIGITAL STREAM RIPPING · converting streamed radio or webcasts into individual MP3 files.

MOBILE PIRACY · transferring music phone-to-phone via Bluetooth.

The IFPI report also identified ten 'priority countries' in which piracy had become a serious problem. These countries are ranked below by their 'physical piracy level' – the number of pirated hard-copy CDs sold as a percentage of the total market:

Physical piracy level	
Indonesia	88%
China	85%
Russia	67%
Mexico	65%
Greece	50%
Brazil	40%
Italy	26%
Spain	22%
Canada	—
S Korea	—

Bulgaria, Pakistan, Taiwan, and Ukraine all warranted 'special focus' status.

DIGITAL MUSIC WORLDWIDE

Record company revenues from worldwide digital sales nearly doubled between 2005 and 2006, from $1·1bn to *c.*$2bn, according to the International Federation of the Phonographic Industry. Digital sales grew from 5·5% of total industry sales in 2005 to *c.*10% in 2006, and the IFPI forecasts that digital sales will account for 25% of all music sales by 2010. Other figures on the global digital music market:

	2005	2006	*% change*
Tracks available for download†	2m	4m	+100%
Single tracks downloaded	420m	795m	+89%
Subscription service users	2·8m	3·5m	+25%
3G cell phone subscriptions‡	90m	137m	+52%
Portable player sales (iPod &c.)	84m	120m	+43%

† Songs on 500 leading online services in 40 countries. ‡ Third-generation mobile phone technology, which allows for advanced services such as music and video downloads. [Source: IFPI, Jan 2007]

APPLAUSE AT CONCERTS

In recent years, commentators have debated an evolution in the unwritten rules governing applause at classical music concerts. Since *c.*1900, it has been customary for listeners to hold their applause until the end of the final movement, lest they break the concentration of performers. Applause at other times has been met by glares (or worse) from fellow patrons and conductors. Yet, nowadays, 'premature clapping' is an increasingly frequent occurrence – and one that has been embraced by those who worry that an overly stuffy atmosphere discourages younger fans. In September 2006, the internationally renowned conductor Leonard Slatkin penned an essay entitled *To Clap or Not to Clap?*, in which he encouraged audiences to applaud whenever they felt so moved, whether or not the final movement had ended. An October 2006 poll on the music blog *Adaptistration* discovered that 74% felt audiences should 'feel free to applaud after a movement if they wish', so long as a conductor can make it clear when applause should be held. Inevitably, there remain some who detest premature clapping as a distraction, while others argue that an applause-free experience can easily be enjoyed for free in one's living room.

Audiences at Milan's La Scala opera house need no encouragement in expressing their feelings about a performance. In December 2006, the 'Loggionisti', fanatical opera buffs who sit in La Scala's upper gallery, heckled tenor Roberto Alagna so aggressively during the first act of *Aïda* that he stalked offstage. (His understudy, Antonello Palombi, was rushed onto the stage in his jeans.) The La Scala audience expressed warmer feelings towards tenor Juan Diego Flórez, whose 2007 performance of the aria 'Ah! mes amis' from Donizetti's *La fille du régiment* drew so much applause that the conductor was forced to ask him to sing it again – breaking a 70-year-old rule at La Scala forbidding encores.

CLASSICAL SOUNDTRACKS

Classic FM listeners voted for their favourite classical film soundtracks in 2007:

[1] Lord of the Rings, *Fellowship of the Ring* (Howard Shore)
[2] Gladiator, *Earth* (Hans Zimmer) · [3] Schindler's List, *Main Theme* (John Williams)
[4] Star Wars, *Theme* (John Williams) · [5] Out of Africa, *Main Title* (John Barry)

THE CLASSICAL BRITS · 2007

Best album .... Paul McCartney · *Ecce Cor Meum*
Singer of the year .... Anna Netrebko · *Russian Album & Violetta*
Contemporary composer award .... John Adams · *The Dharma at Big Sur/ My Father Knew Charles Ives*
Young British performer .... Ruth Palmer · *Shostakovich Violin Concerto No. 1*
Recording of the year .... Berlin Philharmonic & Sir Simon Rattle · *The Planets*
Soundtrack composer .... George Fenton · *Planet Earth*
Instrumentalist .... Leif Ove Andsnes · *Horizons*
Critics' award .... Rene Jacobs · *La Cler*
Lifetime achievement .... Dr Vernon Handley CBE

CLASSIC FM HALL OF FAME · 2007

Each year the radio station *Classic FM* compiles a 'Hall of Fame', reflecting its listeners' 300 favourite classical pieces. In 2007, a British composer, Ralph Vaughan Williams, topped the chart for the first time in the poll's 11-year history. Below are the top 10 favourite classical pieces for 2007 (2006 places in brackets):

1 ... Ralph Vaughan Williams ... *The Lark Ascending* ... [3]
2 ... Edward Elgar ... *Cello Concerto in E minor* ... [7]
3 ... Sergei Rachmaninov ... *Piano Concerto No. 2 in C minor* ... [2]
4 ... Wolfgang Amadeus Mozart ... *Clarinet Concerto* ... [1]
5 ... Ludwig van Beethoven ... *Piano Concerto No. 5 in E flat (The Emperor)* ... [4]
6 ... Edward Elgar ... *Enigma Variations* ... [9]
7 ... Max Bruch ... *Violin Concerto No. 1 in G minor* ... [5]
8 ... Ludwig van Beethoven ... *Symphony No. 6 in F Major (Pastoral)* ... [6]
9 ... Ludwig van Beethoven ... *Symphony No. 9 in D minor (Choral)* ... [8]
10 .. Ralph Vaughan Williams ... *Fantasia on a Theme by Thomas Tallis* .. [11]

QUEEN'S MEDAL FOR MUSIC

The Queen's Medal for Music is awarded annually to those who have a 'major influence on the musical life of the nation'. The nomination process is overseen by a committee under the chairmanship of the Master of the Queen's Music†, currently Sir Peter Maxwell Davies. Established in 2005, the award was first presented to the conductor Sir Charles Mackerras. Welsh opera singer BRYN TERFEL accepted the 2006 award in July of that year, at a special BBC Prom in honour of the Queen's 80th birthday. ❦ Terfel was born in 1965 near Caernarfon, in rural N Wales, and was performing on stage from the age of three. He studied at the Guildhall School of Music and Drama and achieved his big break by winning the Lieder Prize at the Cardiff Singer of the World competition in a struggle against Dmitri Hvorostovsky, dubbed the 'Battle of the Baritones'. Terfel has now sung in every major opera house in the world, with signature roles that include Figaro in Mozart's *Marriage of Figaro*, and the eponymous hero of Verdi's *Falstaff*. Terfel is well known as a concert performer, with appearances at the Last Night of the Proms and the Rugby World Cup, and he has had two best-selling 'crossover' albums of show tunes by Rodgers & Hammerstein and Lerner & Loewe. ❦ Terfel also runs an annual festival at Faenol, NW Wales, to which he invites guest artists from the classical music world to perform. In addition to numerous other accolades, Terfel was awarded a CBE in the 2003 New Year Honours.

† The musical equivalent of the Poet Laureate. The leader of the Court's musicians was known as the 'Master of the King's [or Queen's] Musick' and was responsible for the band of royal musicians. Henry VIII's band had '15 trumpets, 3 lutes, 3 rebecks, 3 tamborets, a harp, 2 viols, 9 sackbuts, a fife and 4 drumslades'. The 'k' of 'Musick' was dropped during the reign of King George V, when Edward Elgar was appointed Master of the King's Music in 1924. Nowadays, Masters of the Queen's Music hold their post for a decade, and can choose to compose works for Royal or State occasions.

SOME CLASSICAL ANNIVERSARIES · 2008

2008 marks two major classical music anniversaries: the 150th anniversary of the birth of Italian opera composer GIACOMO PUCCINI (22·12·1858), and the 170th anniversary of the untimely death, at the age of 31, of Austrian composer FRANZ SCHUBERT (19·11·1828). Other notable classical music anniversaries in 2008 are:

b. 1658	Giuseppe Torelli
b. 1678	Antonio Vivaldi
d. 1708	John Blow
b. 1838	Georges Bizet
d. 1868	Gioacchino Rossini
b. 1908	Olivier Messiaen
b. 1908	Geirr Tveitt
b. 1908	Herbert von Karajan
b. 1918	Leonard Bernstein
d. 1918	Claude-Achille Debussy
d. 1958	Ralph Vaughan Williams
d. 1958	Artur Rodziński

YOUNG MUSICIAN OF THE YEAR · 2006

Mark Simpson, a 17-year-old clarinettist from West Derby, was named BBC Young Musician of the Year in May 2006. The judges – chaired by conductor Marin Alsop – were won over by Simpson's performance of Carl Nielsen's *Clarinet Concerto*.

TOP TEN EUROPEAN ORCHESTRAS

Ten European classical music magazines, including *Gramophone* (UK) and *Fono Forum* (Germany), were asked to rank the best orchestras in Europe. The results were published in October 2006 by the French magazine *Le Monde de la Musique*.

1	Vienna Philharmonic Orchestra
2	Royal Concertgebouw, Amsterdam
3	Berlin Philharmonic Orchestra
4	London Symphony Orchestra
5	Dresden Staatskapelle
6	Bavarian Radio Symphony Orch.
7	Gewandhaus Orchestra, Leipzig
8	St Petersburg Philharmonic Orch.
9	Czech Philharmonic Orchestra
10	Philharmonia Orchestra, London

ROYAL PHILHARMONIC SOCIETY AWARDS · 2007

BBC Radio 3 listeners' award	Miah Persson
Chamber-scale composition	Richard Causton · *Phoenix*
Concert series and festivals	Spitalfields Festival (summer and winter)
Conductor	Vladimir Jurowski
Education	PLAY.Orchestra
Ensemble	Britten Sinfonia
Instrumentalist	Michael Collins
Large-scale composition	Jonathan Harvey · *... towards a pure land*
Opera	Opera North · *Peter Grimes*
Singer	John Mark Ainsley
Young artist	Kate Royal

THE BBC PROMS · 2007

The 2007 Proms were the twelfth and final to be directed by Nicholas Kenyon, who promised to 'cover the whole waterfront', with an ambitious programme designed to celebrate 80 years of the BBC's involvement with the concerts. Eyebrows were raised at the inclusion of some populist performances (an evening of show tunes sung by Michael Ball), but Prommers had more than enough traditional fare (Elgar's 150th anniversary, the centenary of W.H. Auden's birth) to keep them happy. Kenyon will be replaced as director in 2008 by Roger Wright, the Controller of BBC Radio 3.

PROM 72 · THE LAST NIGHT OF THE PROMS · 8·9·2007

Antonín Dvořák .... *Overture 'Othello'*
Sergei Rachmaninov .... *Vocalise*
Maurice Ravel .... *Tzigane*
Thomas Adès .... *The Storm (opening scene from The Tempest)*
Edward Elgar .... *The Spirit of England – The Fourth of August*
Vincenzo Bellini .... *La sonnambula (closing scene)*
Julius Fučík .... *Entrance of the Gladiators*
Franz Léhar .... *Giuditta – 'Meine Lippen sie küssen so heiss'*
Manuel Ponce (arr. Jascha Heifetz) .... *Estrellita*
Richard Strauss .... *Morgen!*
Edward Elgar ...... *Pomp and Circumstance March No. 1 –'Land of Hope and Glory'*
Henry Wood (arr. Bob Chilcott) .... *Fantasia on British Sea Songs*
Hubert Parry (orch. Edward Elgar) .... *Jerusalem*
Henry Wood (arr.) .... *The National Anthem*
Traditional .... *Auld Lang Syne*

Anna Netrebko, soprano; Andrew Kennedy, tenor; Joshua Bell, violin; BBC Symphony Chorus; BBC Symphony Orchestra; Jiří Bělohlávek, conductor.

'HATTOGATE'

When Joyce Hatto died of cancer in June 2006, critics hailed her as 'one of the greatest pianists Britain has ever produced', and lauded the astonishing range of her 119 albums. Yet doubts as to the authenticity of her virtuosic recordings had long simmered, not least because of her retirement from public life. In February 2007, *Gramophone* magazine was contacted by a reader who observed that Apple's iTunes had identified a Hatto recording as belonging to the pianist László Simon. (iTunes automatically identifies music based on its 'mathematical footprint'.) A subsequent investigation by *Gramophone* confirmed that 10 tracks on one of Hatto's albums were in fact recorded by Simon. After further inquiries found more examples of 'borrowing', Hatto's husband (and her sole engineer) admitted to using recordings by others to 'patch' his wife's work – initially to cover her groans of pain while she played. At the time of writing, the British Phonographic Industry had launched its own inquiry, telling *Time* that Hattogate could become 'one of the most extraordinary cases of piracy the record industry has ever seen'. Hatto's widower maintains his only motive was to assure his wife of the critical acclaim denied her by cancer.

SMOKING IN MOVIES

In May 2007, the Motion Picture Association of America (MPAA) warned that movies which 'glamorise smoking or … feature pervasive smoking outside of an historic or other mitigating context may receive a higher rating'. In July, Disney became the first major studio to ban smoking from its films (and 'discourage' it in its adult divisions, Touchstone and Miramax). Subsequently, a number of other studios intimated they would follow suit. ❦ Theorists have traditionally resisted 'magic-bullet' links between media consumption and social behaviour – cautioning against, for example, blaming violent films for violent crime. Yet, the evidence linking tobacco in movies and youth smoking is increasingly compelling. In 2005, *Pediatrics* printed a magisterial review of 40 studies which concluded 'strong empirical evidence indicates that smoking in movies increases adolescent smoking initiation'. In 2007, the Institute of Medicine of the National Academy of Sciences stated that 'studies show a clear dose effect, whereby greater exposure to smoking in the movies is associated with a greater chance of smoking'. According to a 2003 CDC report: current movie heroes are 3–4× more likely to smoke than people in real life; a teen whose favourite star smokes on-screen is significantly more likely to be a smoker; and, bizarrely, US adolescents may see more smoking on-screen than in real life. ❦ One of the most persuasive arguments for smoke-free movies is the precedent set by TV's promotion of 'designated drivers'. In a February 2007 speech to the MPAA, Dr Jay Winsten of the Harvard School of Public Health described how in the late 1980s he asked TV execs and writers to consider 'incorporating a line or two of dialogue to reflect the evolution of a new social norm about drinking-and-driving … and to depict the use of designated drivers'. The response was 'overwhelmingly positive', according to Winsten, who stated that from 1988–89, '160 prime time episodes incorporated the designated driver message'. Polls found 'sharp increases in the use of designated drivers', and Winsten asserted that his campaign contributed to the 25% fall in alcohol-related traffic deaths, 1990–93. Clearly, there are differences between designated drivers and smoking, and between the cultures of TV and Hollywood. Yet Winsten's success shows how media action can wreak good. ❦ Although some were disappointed that the MPAA decided not to R-rate all movies featuring smoking, its decision was widely welcomed. The Directors Guild of America said, 'they, like us, are working to find the delicate balance between addressing important health concerns and safeguarding free expression'.

POPCORN & SADNESS

A January 2007 *Journal of Marketing* study found that people watching sad movies may consume more popcorn than those watching happy ones. 38 subjects were asked to view either upbeat *Sweet Home Alabama* (2002) or tearjerker *Love Story* (1970). By the end of the movies, subjects watching *Love Story* were found to have consumed 36% more buttered popcorn that those watching *Sweet Home Alabama*.

UK TOP-GROSSING FILMS · 2006

Film	*UK box office gross (£m)*	*Director*
Casino Royale	55·5	Martin Campbell
Pirates of the Caribbean: Dead Man's Chest	52·5	Gore Verbinski
The Da Vinci Code	30·4	Ron Howard
Ice Age II	29·6	Carlos Saldanha
Borat	24·1	Larry Charles
Night at the Museum	20·8	Shawn Levy
X-Men 3	19·2	Brett Ratner
Happy Feet	18·9	George Miller
Cars	16·5	John Lasseter
Superman Returns	16·1	Bryan Singer
Mission: Impossible 3	15·5	J.J. Abrams
The Devil Wears Prada	14·0	David Frankel
Chicken Little	13·5	Mark Dindal
Over the Hedge	13·2	Tim Johnson

[Source: UK Film Council/Nielsen EDI · Box office gross as at 4 March 2007]

STUDIO MARKET SHARE · 2006

	Distributor	*total gross ($bn)*	*market share*	*No. 2006 movies*
1	Sony/Columbia	1·7	18·6%	27
2	Buena Vista	1·5	16·2%	19
3	20th Century Fox	1·4	15·2%	24
4	Warner Bros.	1·1	11·6%	21
5	Paramount	0·9	10·3%	16

[Source: Box Office Mojo]

CULTURE TEST FOR BRITISH FILMS

Since 1 January 2007, all films made in the UK must satisfy a 'culture test' before they become eligible for tax concessions. The Department for Culture, Media, and Sport, backed by the European Commission, announced the test would 'measure the extent of a film's British cultural character' by assessing, for example, where the film is set. Films are required to score ≥16 out of 31 points in these four areas:

		points available
Cultural content	the subject matter of the film	16
Cultural contribution	representation of British culture	4
Cultural hubs	how much is made in the UK?	3
Cultural practitioners	are the main cast and crew from the EU?	8

In 2006, 50 indigenous UK films were made: a 35% rise on 2005, when 37 were made. There were 57 UK film co-productions in 2006, and total film spending increased by 48% to £840·1 million.

79TH ACADEMY AWARD WINNERS · 2007

Comedian Ellen DeGeneres gave a low-key, safe, and unpretentious performance when she became only the second woman to single-handedly host the Academy Awards. Predictions that the 79th Oscars would be lucky for Helen Mirren† and eight-time nominee Martin Scorsese were proved right. And the winners were …

Leading actor	Forest Whitaker · *The Last King of Scotland*
Leading actress	Helen Mirren · *The Queen*
Supporting actor	Alan Arkin · *Little Miss Sunshine*
Supporting actress	Jennifer Hudson · *Dreamgirls*
Best picture	*The Departed*
Directing	Martin Scorsese · *The Departed*
Animated feature	George Miller · *Happy Feet*
Art direction	Eugenio Caballero & Pilar Revuelta · *Pan's Labyrinth*
Cinematography	Guillermo Navarro · *Pan's Labyrinth*
Costume design	Milena Canonero · *Marie Antoinette*
Doc. feature	Davis Guggenheim · *An Inconvenient Truth*
Doc. short subject	Yang & Lennon · *The Blood of Yingzhou District*
Film editing	Thelma Schoonmaker · *The Departed*
Foreign language film	Florian Henckel von Donnersmarck · *The Lives of Others*
Make-up	David Martí & Montse Ribé · *Pan's Labyrinth*
Music (score)	Gustavo Santaolalla · *Babel*
Music (song)	Melissa Etheridge *I Need to Wake Up* · *An Inconvenient Truth*
Short film (animated)	Torill Kove · *The Danish Poet*
Short film (live)	Ari Sandel · *West Bank Story*
Sound mixing	Michael Minkler, Bob Beemer, & Willie Burton · *Dreamgirls*
Sound editing	Alan Robert Murray & Bub Asman · *Letters from Iwo Jima*
Visual effects	Knoll, Hickel, Gibson, & Hall *Pirates of the Caribbean: Dead Man's Chest*
Screenplay (adapted)	William Monahan · *The Departed*
Screenplay (original)	Michael Arndt · *Little Miss Sunshine*
Honorary award	Ennio Morricone

† As the odds reached 1/66 for Helen Mirren to win the Best Actress Oscar, bookies William Hill paid out £50,000 ahead of the ceremony. Ladbrokes also stopped taking bets on the actress's victory.

NOTABLE QUOTES ❦ FOREST WHITAKER · I want to thank the people of Uganda who helped this film have a spirit. ❦ HELEN MIRREN · For 50 years and more, Elizabeth Windsor has maintained her dignity, her sense of duty, and her hair-style. She's had her feet planted firmly on the ground, her hat on her head, her handbag on her arm, and she has weathered many, many storms, and I salute her courage and her consistency. ❦ MARTIN SCORSESE · Could you double-check the envelope? ❦ ELLEN DEGENERES · No one knows who's going to win, unless you're British, and then you know you have a good shot. ❦ AL GORE · People all over the world, we need to solve the climate crisis. It's not a political issue. It's a moral issue ❦ GEORGE MILLER (director of animated film *Happy Feet*) · I asked my kids, 'What should I say?' They said, 'Thank all the men for wearing penguin suits.' ❦

OSCAR NIGHT FASHION · 2007

Star	dress	*designer*
Nicole Kidman	*bright red, halter-necked, oversize shoulder bow*	Balenciaga
Reese Witherspoon	*indigo, strapless, scalloped layers*	Nina Ricci
Cate Blanchett	*charcoal, crystal mesh with single strap*	Armani Privé
Gwyneth Paltrow	*peach, multi-pleated, fish-tailed dress*	Zac Posen
Kate Winslet	*pistachio silk dress, draped single strap*	Valentino
Naomi Watts	*pale lemon strapless, empire-line, dropped sleeves*	Escada
Helen Mirren	*pale gold lace V-neck, full patterned skirt*	Christian Lacroix
Penélope Cruz	*nude fitted bodice with full ruched organza skirt*	Versace
Jennifer Lopez	*Grecian-style empire line, with jewelled boat neck*	Marchesa
Jennifer Hudson	*dark brown silk dress with gold bolero*	Oscar de la Renta

THE ACADEMY & OSCAR VOTING

The Academy of Motion Picture Arts and Sciences was formed in 1927 as a non-profit organisation to promote the film industry. Academy membership is divided into 15 branches: actors; animators and short-film makers; art directors and costume designers; cinematographers; composers; documentary filmmakers; directors; executives; editors; make-up artists; producers; PR specialists; sound technicians; visual effect artists; and writers. Membership is by invitation, and candidates must be sponsored by at least two members from the branch to which they are applying; anyone nominated for an Oscar is automatically considered for membership. The Academy currently has *c.*6,500 members – *c.*25% of whom are actors. ❦ One of the greatest privileges of membership is the right to vote on the annual Academy Awards. In January each year, members are asked to nominate, in rank, up to five candidates for each award in their branch (e.g. only actors are allowed to nominate for the Best Actor categories); additionally, every member is entitled to nominate up to five movies for Best Picture. The five most popular candidates in each category are selected using a system of proportional representation, whereby any candidate with 20% of nominations will go through. In the second round of voting, all Academy members are sent a ballot with the five nominations in each category. Members can only vote once for each award, and the nominees with the most votes win the Oscar†. This complex and highly secretive voting process is run by the accountants PricewaterhouseCoopers. In 2007, PwC partners Brad Oltmanns and Rick Rosas were the only two people to know the winners before the envelopes were opened live on stage‡.

† Votes have been tied on two occasions: in 1932, the Best Actor Oscar was shared by Wallace Beery and Frederic March; and in 1968, Barbra Streisand and Katharine Hepburn were presented with Best Actress Oscars. ‡ As a precautionary measure, one of these partners carries a duplicate set of winning envelopes and travels to the ceremony in a separate car, on a secret route. As an additional safeguard, the partner memorises the names of all of the winners – no mean feat, given the number – just in case.

JAMES BOND AND DRINKING

James Bond is forever associated with his order of 'a vodka martini – shaken, not stirred' and, as a result, he has become something of a poster boy for the cocktail. However, heroic research by atomicmartini.com proved that over the course of the 22 Bond films, 007 is more commonly seen quaffing champagne (35 times) than vodka martinis (22 times). The drink-per-film average for each 007 is shown below:

Bond	*films*	*drinks*	*drink/film*
Daniel Craig	1	12	12·0
George Lazenby	1	7	7·0
Sean Connery	7	36	5·1
Timothy Dalton	2	10	5·0
Pierce Brosnan	4	20	5·0
Roger Moore	7	29	4·1
Total	22	114	5·2

Over the course of 22 films, Bond averages one drink every 24·3 minutes. 007 also carelessly placed 7 orders that he either did not receive or did not drink, including: 2 martinis, 2 bottles of champagne (Dom Perignon, naturally), a bourbon with water, a Sazerac, and a bottle of Budweiser. (Sazerac is the name of a venerable cognac; an 18-year-old rye; and a foul-tasting cocktail comprising rye, brandy, and absinthe.) For further analysis of the vodka martini, see *Schott's Food & Drink Miscellany*.

MOST RENTED FILMS

Below are the most rented films of all time in the UK, according to the *Guardian*:

1. *Four Weddings and a Funeral* (1994)
2. *Dirty Dancing* (1987)
3. *Basic Instinct* (1992)
4. *Crocodile Dundee* (1986)
5. *Gladiator* (2000)
6. *Sister Act* (1992)
7. *Forrest Gump* (1994)
8. *The Sixth Sense* (1999)
9. *Home Alone* (1990)
10. *Ghost* (1990)

FILM GUILDS AND SOCIETIES

Film guilds exist to promote high standards throughout the movie industry and to encourage technological and artistic development. Most have no trade union alliances – instead, guild membership is achieved through nomination and approval by a committee. Listed below are some of the most notable UK film guilds:

Guild/Film Society	*abbreviation*	*members*
The Guild of British Camera Technicians	GBCT	460
The British Society of Cinematographers	BSC	350
The Guild of British Film and Television Editors	GBFTE	60
The Guild of Location Managers	GLM	100
The Association of Motion Picture Sound	AMPS	340
The Guild of Stunt and Action Coordinators	GSAC	—
The British Film Designers Guild	BFDG	100
The Directors Guild of Great Britain	DGGB	—
The Casting Directors Guild of Great Britain	CDG	110

MOVIE AWARDS OF NOTE

BAFTAs 2007 · *bafta.org*

Best film .... *The Queen*
Best British film .... *The Last King of Scotland*
Best actor in a leading role .... Forest Whitaker · *The Last King of Scotland*
Best actress in a leading role .... Helen Mirren · *The Queen*
Best actor in a supporting role .... Alan Arkin · *Little Miss Sunshine*
Best actress in a supporting role .... Jennifer Hudson · *Dreamgirls*

MTV MOVIE AWARDS 2007 · *mtv.com*

Best performance .... Johnny Depp · *Pirates of the Caribbean: Dead Man's Chest*
Best movie .... *Pirates of the Caribbean: Dead Man's Chest*
Best villain .... Jack Nicholson · *The Departed*
Best fight .... Gerard Butler *vs* 'The Über Immortal' · *300*
Best kiss .... Will Ferrell & Sacha Baron Cohen · *Talladega Nights*

GOLDEN GLOBES 2007 · *hfpa.org*

Best dramatic film .... *Babel*
Best dramatic actor .... Forest Whitaker · *The Last King of Scotland*
Best dramatic actress .... Helen Mirren · *The Queen*
Best director .... Martin Scorsese · *The Departed*
Best actor in musical or comedy .... Sacha Baron Cohen · *Borat*
Best actress in musical or comedy .... Meryl Streep · *The Devil Wears Prada*

BRITISH INDEPENDENT FILM AWARDS 2006 · *bifa.org.uk*

Best British film .... *This is England*
Best actor .... Tony Curran · *Red Road*
Best actress .... Kate Dickie · *Red Road*
Richard Harris award for outstanding achievement .... Jim Broadbent

GOLDEN RASPBERRIES 2007 · *razzies.com*

Worst picture .... *Basic Instinct 2*
Worst actor .... Shawn & Marlon Wayans · *Little Man*
Worst actress .... Sharon Stone · *Basic Instinct 2*

EMPIRE AWARDS 2007 · *empireonline.co.uk*

Best actor .... Daniel Craig · *Casino Royale*
Best actress .... Penélope Cruz · *Volver*
Best director .... Christopher Nolan · *The Prestige*
Best British film .... *United 93*
Best film .... *Casino Royale*

EVENING STANDARD BRITISH FILM AWARDS 2007

Best film .... *United 93*
Best actor .... Daniel Craig · *Casino Royale*
Best actress .... Dame Judi Dench · *Notes on a Scandal*
Most promising newcomer .... Paul Andrew Williams · *London to Brighton*

'THREE-QUELS'

The summer of 2007 was all about the 'three-quel' – a neologism coined to describe the third episode in a movie franchise. Key three-quels released in 2007 included:

Spider-Man 3 · *Shrek the Third* · *Pirates of the Caribbean: At World's End*
Ocean's Thirteen · *Rush Hour 3* · *Resident Evil: Extinction*
The Bourne Ultimatum

BLOCKBUSTERS

The term *blockbuster* was first used to describe a class of bombs dropped by the British Royal Air Force during WWII. These extremely heavy, vastly powerful bombs were capable of destroying an entire block of buildings at a time. (The 4,000lb blockbuster was first dropped on Emden, Germany in 1941; the 12,000lb blockbuster on Germany's Dortmund–Ems Canal in 1943.) The term has evolved to describe anything of great size or power, but is most frequently applied to entertainment productions such as books, plays, museum exhibits, and especially movies. (Extremely successful prescription medications are also sometimes called *blockbuster* drugs; in music, the term *chartbuster* was coined to describe a best-selling song or group. The term's meaning in US real-estate circles is less pleasant; see below.) ❦ The first blockbuster film is generally said to be Steven Spielberg's *Jaws* (1975), which grossed $260m and (by some accounts) inaugurated the tradition of summer blockbuster thrillers. According to the Internet Movie Database, a movie is generally said to be a blockbuster once it grosses $100m in North America. The UK Film Council's exclusive club of films that grossed >£50m in the UK include:

Title	*UK Box office £*	*year released*
Titanic	69,025,646	1998
Harry Potter and the Philosopher's Stone	66,096,060	2001
The Lord of the Rings: The Fellowship of the Ring	63,009,288	2001
The Lord of the Rings: The Return of the King	61,062,348	2003
The Lord of the Rings: The Two Towers	57,600,094	2002
Casino Royale	55,504,945	2006
Harry Potter and the Chamber of Secrets	54,780,731	2002
Pirates of the Caribbean: Dead Man's Chest	52,515,550	2006
The Full Monty	52,232,058	1997
Star Wars Episode 1: The Phantom Menace	51,063,811	1999

Blockbusting was a US real-estate practice in which estate agents or speculators triggered neighbourhood turnover through the exploitation of racial prejudice. The term is associated with the 1940s and 1950s, when some estate agents used questionable tactics to convince white home-owners of growing black encroachment (for instance, hiring blacks to drive through the neighbourhood). After property owners sold their houses at devalued prices, agents would profit by charging high prices to re-sell the homes to blacks, who often faced few other housing choices. ❦ A *bonkbuster* is a genre of novel noted for its sexual escapades. A *bronco buster* is one who breaks horses; a *baby buster* is one born during a time of low birth rate (the opposite of a *baby boomer*). *Filibuster* has an entirely different etymology.

HOLLYWOOD WALK OF FAME

In 1960, the Hollywood Chamber of Commerce created the *Hollywood Walk of Fame* by placing some 2,500 blank stars along (and around) Hollywood Boulevard. To date, approximately 2,317 of these stars have been occupied. Each year, the Hollywood Walk of Fame Committee considers the nominations for this honour. The stars are divided into five categories, each with its own symbol:

Symbol	*for*
Record	singers & songwriters
Film camera	film stars & directors
Television set	television stars
Microphone	radio stars
Theatrical masks	stage performers

Some of the celebrities presented with a star in 2007 (at a cost of *c.*$25,000) were:

Michael Caine · Matt Damon · Jamie Foxx · John Goodman
Michele Pfeiffer · Robert Altman · Erik Estrada · Kiefer Sutherland
Barbara Walters · Mariah Carey · Sean 'Diddy' Combs
The Doors · Leann Rimes · Shania Twain · Sir Tim Rice

FILM-BLUFFS

Since 37% of 18–24-year-olds judge people according to which films they like, it is unsurprising that many have become dedicated 'film-bluffs'. An April 2007 poll by myfilms.com suggested that 17% of men lie about the movies they have seen. Below are the films that Britons pretend to have seen, and those they really watch:

Britons claim to have seen …	Britons actually watch …
Schindler's List · *The Da Vinci Code* *The Godfather* · *Apocalypse Now* *Shawshank Redemption*	*The Sound of Music* · *Ghost* *Dirty Dancing* · *Love Actually* *Harry Potter* films

BEST NUDE SCENES

Every year the infamous 'Mr Skin' (and his team of self-styled screen nudity experts) award the best nude scene in film. Below are Mr Skin's top nude scenes of 2006:

Salma Hayek & Colin Farrell	*Ask the Dust*
Gretchen Mol	*The Notorious Betty Page*
Brittany Daniel	*Rampage: The Hillside Strangler Murders*
Bai Ling	*Edmond*
Jennifer Aniston	*The Break-Up*

Mr Skin also awards the rather alarming 'Anatomy Awards' to the 'finest moments in female nudity' in film and TV each year. In 2007, Salma Hayek won 'Best Breasts' for her appearances in *Ugly Betty* and *Ask the Dust*, while the Most Shocking Nudity was presented to the cuddly Rosie O'Donnell in *Nip/Tuck*. Best Skinny Dip was awarded to Kelly Brook for her saucy swim in the flop film *Three*.

FILM FESTIVAL PRIZES · 2007

Sundance · World Dramatic Grand Jury Prize [JAN] ...... *Sweet Mud* · Dror Shaul
Berlin · Golden Bear [FEB] .... *Tuya's Wedding* · Wang Quan'an
Tribeca · Best Narrative Feature [APR] .... *My Father My Lord* · David Volach
Cannes · Palme d'Or [MAY] .... *4 Months, 3 Weeks & 2 Days* · Cristian Mungiu
Moscow · Golden St George [JUN] .... *Travelling with Pets* · Vera Storozheva
Edinburgh · Audience Award [AUG] .... *We Are Together* · Paul Taylor
Montreal · International Film Critics Award [AUG]. *Samira's Garden* · Latif Lahlou
Venice · Golden Lion [SEP] .... *Se, Jie (Lust, Caution)* · Ang Lee
Toronto · People's Choice Award [SEP] ...... *Eastern Promises* · David Cronenberg
London · Sutherland Trophy [OCT '06] .... *Red Road* · Andrea Arnold

WORST FILM OF ALL TIME

An MSN Movies poll asked 12,000 Britons to name the worst films of all time:

1	*Spice World*	5	*Hostel*	9	*Catwoman*
2	*Titanic*	6	*Anaconda*	10	*Stop! Or My Mom Will Shoot*
3	*Grease 2*	7	*Batman & Robin*		
4	*Waterworld*	8	*Gigli*		[Source: MSN, Jan. 2007]

SOME MOVIE TAGLINES OF NOTE

At the end of the world, the adventure begins .... *Pirates of the Carib.: World's End*
Charming. Magnetic. Murderous .... *The Last King of Scotland*
Who's ready for thirds? .... *Shrek the Third*
Tradition prepared her. Change will define her .... *The Queen*
The greatest battle lies within .... *Spider-Man 3*
A family on the verge of a breakdown .... *Little Miss Sunshine*
All you have to do is dream .... *Dreamgirls*
Lies. Betrayal. Sacrifice. How far will you take it?...................... *The Departed*
What are the odds of getting even? 13 to one....................... *Ocean's Thirteen*
Innocence has a power evil cannot imagine .... *Pan's Labyrinth*
If you want to be understood ... listen .... *Babel*
Let them eat cake.. *Marie Antoinette*
WARNING: May cause toe-tapping .... *Happy Feet*
This summer Jason Bourne comes home .... *The Bourne Ultimatum*
All bets are off.. *Resident Evil: Extinction*
A global warning.. *An Inconvenient Truth*
The rebellion begins .... *Harry Potter and the Order of the Phoenix*
This summer they're kicking it in Paris .... *Rush Hour 3*
Their war. Our world .... *Transformers*
There are worlds beyond our own.............................. *The Golden Compass*
See our family. And feel better about yours .... *The Simpsons Movie*
Come watch my movie film.. *Borat*

THE ORACLE OF BACON

The University of Virginia's computer science department has developed an algorithm based on the enduring game 'six degrees of Kevin Bacon'. The game tests which actors can be linked to Kevin Bacon within six career moves. (For example, Keira Knightley is two moves away from Kevin Bacon, since she was in *Love Actually* (2003) with Colin Firth, who was in *Where the Truth Lies* (2005) with Kevin Bacon.) The algorithm (or 'Oracle of Bacon') employs the >800,000 Internet Movie Database (IMDb) records to create a map that tracks the shortest path from one actor to another, and calculates a 'Bacon Number' indicating how many actors are linked to Kevin in 0–8 moves. Naturally, these Bacon Numbers are constantly changing; as of January 2007, the breakdown of actors by Bacon Number was:

Bacon No.	*No. people*
0	1†
1	1,920
2	173,757
3	517,654
4	129,381
5	9,147
6	931
7	96
8	17

† Naturally, only 1 person can be zero moves from Kevin Bacon: Kevin himself. The average *Bacon Number* is currently 2·968.

The database can also be used to calculate the 'centre of the Hollywood Universe', which is the actor who can be linked to the most other performers in the least moves. In January 2007 the top 5 were: Rod Steiger (average 2·67), Christopher Lee (2·68), Dennis Hopper (2·69), Donald Sutherland (2·70), and Harvey Keitel (2·70).

The concept of 'six degrees of separation' was popularised by psychologist Stanley Milgram (1933–84), who used the American postal service to test the 'small world theory' that the world is more interconnected than it seems. ❦ A similar principle has been applied to the late Hungarian mathematician Paul Erdös (1913–96), who was a prolific contributor to academic journals. The Erdös Number is used to describe the 'collaborative distance' between academics. Inevitably, someone with much time on their hands has merged the Bacon Number with the Erdös Number to create the hybrid (and deliciously obscure) Erdös–Bacon. This allows academics who have appeared in a film *and* published a paper that links to Erdös to claim an Erdös–Bacon Number (Stephen Hawking apparently has an Erdös–Bacon number of 3.)

IMDb PLOT KEYWORDS

The Internet Movie Database (IMDb) classifies every film with a list of plot 'keywords'. Below is a selection of recent movies with some of their keywords:

Movie	*some plot keywords*
Borat	racist, on the road, male frontal nudity, retardation, homophobia
X-Men 3	presumed dead, prison escape, surprise after end credits, blue fur
Casino Royale	shot in the head, super-villain, lost love, gadget, henchmen
The Da Vinci Code	monk, secret passage, albino, religion, twist at the end
The Queen	royalty, London, England, critically acclaimed, based on fact
Little Miss Sunshine	pageant, car trouble, quirky, dysfunctional, loser
An Inconvenient Truth	glacier, presidential election, Armageddon, humanity, hope

Books & Arts

The secret of the arts is to correct nature.
— VOLTAIRE (François-Marie Arouet) (1694–1778)

NOBEL PRIZE IN LITERATURE

The 2006 Nobel Prize in Literature was awarded to ORHAN PAMUK (1952–),

who in the quest for the melancholic soul of his native city has discovered new symbols for the clash and interfacing of cultures

Turkish writer Orhan Pamuk is celebrated for novels that explore themes of identity through an examination of the transformation of modern Turkey. Writing in the *Guardian*, Margaret Atwood said of Pamuk's award, 'it would be difficult to conceive of a more perfect winner for our catastrophic times'. ❦ In February 2005, Pamuk attracted worldwide media attention when the Turkish government tried to prosecute him for comments that they alleged were an 'insult to Turkishness'. During an interview with a Swiss newspaper, Pamuk stated that 'thirty thousand Kurds and a million Armenians were killed in these lands, and nobody but me dares to talk about it'. The case against him was only dropped after international outcry over freedom of speech. Pamuk's criticisms of his country's past meant that Turkish reaction to his win was ambivalent – many rejoiced in the recognition of Turkish literature while others questioned his 'Turkishness', suggesting his flirtation with controversy signified a dissident nature. ❦ Pamuk used his experiences of growing up in Turkey – a simultaneously secular and Muslim society that straddles Europe and Asia – to inform his work. He drew on personal experiences for his first novel, *Cevdet Bey Ve Oğullari* (1982; Cevdet Bey and His Sons), a work that chronicled the increasing Western influences on traditional Ottoman family life. But Pamuk came to international attention with his third novel, *Beyaz Kale* (1985; The White Castle, 1992), which established his reputation as a novelist who liked to play with identities, a theme that he revisited in his subsequent novel *Kara Kitap* (1990; The Black Book, 1995). His highly acclaimed 2000 novel *Benim Adim Kirmizi* (My Name is Red) won the prestigious and lucrative IMPAC Dublin Award in 2003. ❦ After Pamuk's Laureate was announced, the Swedish Academy faced accusations that it was abandoning literature for politics – a reference both to Pamuk's recently politicised position, and Harold Pinter's award in 2005 (which he used as a platform to attack American foreign policy). Despite a reputation in some quarters as a political agitator, Pamuk claims he has no partisan agenda, describing himself as principally a writer of fiction.

ODDEST BOOK TITLE OF THE YEAR · 2006

The Diagram Group's *Oddest Book Title of the Year* has been contested annually since 1978. The award is administered by *The Bookseller*, and voted on by members of the book trade. The 'oddest' title of 2006, and the runners-up, are given below:

The Stray Shopping Carts of Eastern North America: A Guide to Field Identification
Julian Montague [WINNER]

Tattooed Mountain Women and Spoon Boxes of Daghestan
R. Chenciner, G. Ismailov, M. Magomedkhanov & A. Binnie

Better Never to Have Been: The Harm of Coming into Existence
David Benatar

How Green Were the Nazis?
T. Zeller, F. Bruggemeier & M. Cioc

D. Di Mascio's Delicious Ice Cream: D. Di Mascio of Coventry, an Ice Cream Company of Repute, with an Interesting and Varied Fleet of Ice Cream Vans
Roger De Boer

Proceedings of the Eighteenth International Seaweed Symposium
R. Anderson, J. Brodie, E. Onsoyen & A. Critchley

BULWER-LYTTON FICTION CONTEST

In 1982, the Department of English and Comparative Literature at San José State University created a literary contest in honour of E.G.E. Bulwer-Lytton (1803–73), who infamously opened his book *Paul Clifford* with 'It was a dark and stormy night'. The contest rewards the best 'bad' opening line to an imaginary novel. The 2007 winner was Jim Gleeson, a 47-year-old media technician, whose entry was:

Gerald began – but was interrupted by a piercing whistle which cost him ten percent of his hearing permanently, as it did everyone else in a ten-mile radius of the eruption, not that it mattered much because for them 'permanently' meant the next ten minutes or so until buried by searing lava or suffocated by choking ash – to pee.

TOP 10 BEST-SELLING UK BOOKS · 2006–07

Harry Potter and the Deathly Hallows .... J.K. Rowling
The Sound of Laughter .... Peter Kay
The Interpretation of Murder .... Jed Rubenfeld
Why Don't Penguins' Feet Freeze? .... New Scientist
The Devil Wears Prada .... Lauren Weisberger
The Island .... Victoria Hislop
Cook with Jamie: My Guide to Making You a Better Cook .... Jamie Oliver
The Dangerous Book for Boys .... Hal & Conn Iggulden
Anybody Out There? .... Marian Keyes
Guinness World Records: 2007 .... —

[August 2006–August 2007. Source: Nielsen BookScan ©]

BAD SEX IN FICTION PRIZE · 2006

Each year the *Literary Review* awards its 'Bad Sex in Fiction' prize to a novel that features the most 'inept, embarrassing and unnecessary' sex scene. The 2006 winner was IAIN HOLLINGSHEAD, for his fine début novel, *Twenty Something*:

She's wearing a short, floaty skirt that's more suited to July than February. She leans forward to peck me on the cheek, which feels weird, as she's never kissed me on the cheek before. We'd kissed properly the first time we met. And that was over three years ago. But the peck on the cheek turns into a quick peck on the lips. She hugs me tight. I can feel her breasts against her chest. I cup my hands round her face and start to kiss her properly. She slides one of her slender legs in between mine. Oh Jack, she was moaning now, her curves pushed up against me, her crotch taut against my bulging trousers, her hands gripping fistfuls of my hair. She reaches for my belt. I groan too, in expectation. And then I'm inside her, and everything is pure white as we're lost in a commotion of grunts and squeaks, flashing unconnected images and explosions of a million little particles.

OTHER BOOK PRIZES OF NOTE · 2007

Carnegie Medal	Meg Rosoff · *Just In Case*
Kate Greenaway Medal	Mini Grey · *The Adventures of the Dish & the Spoon*
Commonwealth Writers' Prize	Lloyd Jones · *Mister Pip*
Forward Prize: best poetry collection [2006]	Robin Robertson · *Swithering*
Guardian children's fiction [2006]	Philip Reeve · *A Darkling Plain*
First book award	Yiyun Li · *A Thousand Years of Good Prayers*
Orange prize	Chimamanda Ngozi Adichie · *Half of a Yellow Sun*
Samuel Johnson Prize for non-fiction	Rajiv Chandrasekaran *Imperial Life in the Emerald City*
T.S. Eliot Prize for poetry [2006]	Seamus Heaney · *District and Circle*
Costa Book of the Year & First Novel [2006]	Stef Penney · *The Tenderness of Wolves*
Children's prize	Linda Newbery · *Set in Stone*
Biography	Brian Thompson · *Keeping Mum*
Poetry	John Haynes · *Letter to Patience*
Novel	William Boyd · *Restless*
Nestlé (formerly Smarties) Prize [2006]: 5 & under	Cressida Cowell & Neal Layton *That Rabbit Belongs to Emily Brown*
6–8	Daren King · *Mouse Noses on Toast*
9–11	Julia Golding · *The Diamond of Drury Lane*
Pulitzer Prize: Fiction	Cormac McCarthy · *The Road*
Poetry	Natasha Trethewey · *Native Guard*
British Book Awards: Author of the year	Richard Dawkins
Book of the year	Conn & Hal Iggulden · *The Dangerous Book for Boys*
Newcomer of the year	Victoria Hislop · *The Island*
Sports book of the year	Steven Gerrard · *Gerrard: My Autobiography*
Somerset Maugham Award	Horatio Clare · *Running to the Hills*
	James Scudamore · *The Amnesia Clinic*
Impac	Per Petterson · *Out Stealing Horses*

MAN BOOKER PRIZES

The 2006 (£50,000) Man Booker Prize was awarded to KIRAN DESAI for *The Inheritance of Loss* (Hamish Hamilton). The shortlisted novels for the 2007 prize are:

Author	Title	Publisher
Nicola Barker	*Darkmans*	Fourth Estate
Anne Enright	*The Gathering*	Jonathan Cape
Mohsin Hamid	*The Reluctant Fundamentalist*	Hamish Hamilton
Lloyd Jones	*Mister Pip*	John Murray
Ian McEwan	*On Chesil Beach*	Jonathan Cape
Indra Sinha	*Animal's People*	Simon & Schuster

The biannual International Man Booker was presented in June 2007 to 'the father of modern African literature' – Nigerian novelist and poet, CHINUA ACHEBE.

NATION'S FAVOURITE BOOKS

Pride & Prejudice, *Lord of the Rings*, and *Jane Eyre* were voted the overall top three favourite books in a poll for World Book Day 2007. The top books, by sex, were:

Male favourites		Female favourites
The Lord of the Rings, J.R.R. Tolkien	1	*Pride & Prejudice*, Jane Austen
Nineteen Eighty-four, George Orwell	2	*Jane Eyre*, Charlotte Brontë
The Bible	3	*To Kill a Mockingbird*, Harper Lee
To Kill a Mockingbird, Harper Lee	4	*The Bible*
Crime & Punishment, Dostoyevsky	5	*The Lord of the Rings*, J.R.R. Tolkien
Pride & Prejudice, Jane Austen	6	*His Dark Materials*, Philip Pullman
Catch-22, Joseph Heller	7	*Little Women*, Louisa M. Alcott
His Dark Materials, Philip Pullman†	8	*Rebecca*, Daphne du Maurier
Grapes of Wrath, John Steinbeck	9	*Tess of the D'Urbervilles*, Thomas Hardy
Catcher in the Rye, J.D. Salinger	10	*Harry Potter* series, J.K. Rowling

† In June 2007, Pullman's trilogy won the Carnegie of Carnegies when it was voted 'the best winner of the annual Carnegie medal'. The public vote was held to celebrate the medal's 70th anniversary.

LITERARY CITIES

Edinburgh was ranked the most literary city in the UK, in a May 2007 survey for SkyArts. Based on local authority investment, the number of libraries and bookshops, and the percentage of pupils achieving good grades, the ranked cities were:

1	Edinburgh	6	Liverpool	11	Sheffield
2	Belfast	7	Cardiff	12	Glasgow
3	Brighton	8	Leeds	13	Bristol
4	Newcastle-upon-Tyne	9	Manchester	14	Birmingham
5	London	10	Plymouth	15	Nottingham

LITERATURE & MEMORY

In 2006, a group of psychiatrists and literary scholars led by Dr Harrison Pope of Harvard offered $1,000 to the first person who found an account of 'repressed memory' written prior to 1800. The group theorised that if repressed memory was a natural function of the human brain, it should appear in literature before becoming a fashionable plot device *c.*1800. To qualify, the account had to describe a healthy, lucid adult with amnesia for a specific traumatic event. In a paper published in December 2006, the researchers said that none of the responses offered met their criteria, giving these explanations for frequently cited memory lapses in literature:

Euripides' Heracles	simple delirium
Shakespeare's Hotspur in *Henry IV, Part I*	'ordinary forgetfulness'
Sophocles' Oedipus	infantile amnesia
The Arthurian knight Ivain	simple delirium
Shakespeare's King Lear	simple delirium
Adam & Eve post-Eden	non-specific amnesia

CHILDREN'S LAUREATE

In June 2007, Michael Rosen was announced as Children's Laureate, a two-year post rewarding an outstanding children's writer or illustrator. Previous holders of the prestigious title include Jacqueline Wilson, Quentin Blake, and Michael Morpurgo.

C20th ERA-DEFINING NOVELS

Guardian readers voted *Nineteen Eighty-Four* the 'definitive book of the C20th', in June 2007. Below are the top 10 era-defining books, listed in order of publication:

Heart of Darkness (1902)	Joseph Conrad
The Ragged Trousered Philanthropists (1914)	Robert Tressell
The Great Gatsby (1925)	F. Scott Fitzgerald
Brave New World (1932)	Aldous Huxley
The Grapes of Wrath (1939)	John Steinbeck
The Diary of a Young Girl (1947)	Anne Frank
Nineteen Eighty-Four (1949)	George Orwell
The Catcher in the Rye (1951)	J.D. Salinger
Catch-22 (1961)	Joseph Heller
Bridget Jones's Diary (1996)	Helen Fielding

READING TIME

According to a July 2007 University of Manchester study, the average amount of time Britons spend reading each day rose from 22 minutes in 1975 to 27 minutes in 2000, and a greater number of readers read for >1 hour a day than did in 1975.

POPULAR CLASSICS

The five most popular 'classic' books sold in the UK during 2006 were:

1 .... Leo Tolstoy · *War and Peace*
2 .... *The Tibetan Book of the Dead*
3 .... *The Poems of Thomas Hardy*
4 .... *Classic Fairy Tales*
5 ... Truman Capote · *Summer Crossing*

[Nielsen BookScan/*The Bookseller*]

UNDERGROUND BOOKS

Below are the books most and least likely to impress ladies on the Tube, according to a May 2007 *play.com* poll:

'TURN-ON' TITLES
Romeo & Juliet · Shakespeare
The Intelligent Investor · B. Graham
The Alchemist · Paolo Coelho

'TURN-OFF' TITLES
Tricks of the Mind · Derren Brown
My Side · David Beckham
Harry Potter series · J.K. Rowling

GUILTY READS

In January 2007, a Costa Coffee survey revealed that 85% of the British have a favourite 'guilty pleasure' author. Below are the authors the reading public are loathed to admit to enjoying:

1 .... Stephen King
2 .... J.K. Rowling
3= .... John Grisham
3= .... Dan Brown
4= .... Danielle Steel
4= .... Catherine Cookson
5 .... Terry Pratchett

MEDAL FOR POETRY

James Fenton received the Queen's Gold Medal for Poetry in April 2007 for his collection, *Selected Poems*. Born in Lincoln in 1949, Fenton studied at Magdalen College, Oxford, where he won the Newdigate Prize for poetry whilst still an undergraduate. He was Oxford Professor of Poetry between 1994–99, and is a fellow of the Royal Society of Literature.

UNFINISHED READS

A 2007 Teletext poll revealed the books that readers most often leave unfinished:

FICTION
Vernon God Little · D.B.C. Pierre
Harry Potter & the Goblet of Fire
J.K. Rowling
Ulysses · James Joyce
Captain Corelli's Mandolin
Louis de Bernières
Cloud Atlas · David Mitchell
The Satanic Verses · Salman Rushdie
The Alchemist · Paulo Coelho
War & Peace · Leo Tolstoy
The God of Small Things · Arundhati Roy
Crime & Punishment · Dostoyevsky

NON-FICTION
The Blunkett Tapes · David Blunkett
My Life · Bill Clinton
My Side · David Beckham
Eats, Shoots & Leaves · Lynne Truss
Wild Swans · Jung Chang
Easy Way to Stop Smoking · Allen Carr
The Downing Street Years
Margaret Thatcher
I Can Make You Thin · Paul McKenna
Jade: My Autobiography · Jade Goody
Why Don't Penguins' Feet Freeze?
New Scientist

PUBLIC LIBRARIES

The Chartered Institute of Public Finance and Accountancy (in association with the Museums, Libraries, and Archives Council) annually compiles statistics on UK public library usage. The 2007 report revealed that in 2005/06 there were 13·5m active borrowers, who made 342·2m visits to the 3,474 public libraries. In the same period, government grants to libraries decreased by 5·1%, and the majority (*c*.75%) of library income derived from fees, charges, and other receipts from the public. Below is a comparison of public library expenditure from 2000/01 and 2004/05:

Type of book (*£m*)	*2000/01*	*2004/05*
Reference	12·5	11·2
Adult fiction	26·6	30·3
Adult non-fiction	21·6	22·1
Children's	14·4	15·3
TOTAL BOOKS	75·2	79·0
Talking books	5·0	8·2
Videos/DVDs	4·9	8·6

In 2004–05, 41% of library users were male; 11% of library users were aged over 75 and only 1% was under 14. The employment status of library users is shown below:

Status	%
Retired	38·2
Full-time job	22·8
Part-time job	15·1
Housewife/husband	9·9
Self-employed	5·5
Full-time student	5·2
Unemployed	5·1
Perm. sick/disabled	3·4
Part-time student	3·3
Other	1·8

[Source: CIPFA, 2006]

According to the Library and Information Statistics Unit, there were 590 mobile libraries operating in the UK in 2005 (down from 692 in 1995). They provide 'a service to small and isolated rural settlements', and their stock usually contains a variety of fiction titles, audiobooks, videos, and DVDs.

LIBRARY LENDING

The Public Lending Right (PLR) pays authors 'royalties' when their books are borrowed from public libraries. Payments are calculated using an annually reviewed Rate per Loan which, in 2007, was 5·98p per loan (5·57p in 2006) – although the maximum that any one author can receive per year is £6,600. Below are the top ten 'most borrowed' authors from public libraries in 2005–06:

1 ... Jacqueline Wilson (1)
2 ..... James Patterson (4)
3 .... Josephine Cox (2)
4 .... Danielle Steel (3)
5 .... Ian Rankin (8)
6 .... Janet & Allan Ahlberg (6)
7 .... Mick Inkpen (5)
8 .... Roald Dahl (9)
9 .... John Grisham (7)
10 ...... Nora Roberts (15)

[2004–5 results in brackets]

Below are the authors most borrowed from libraries during the decade 1996–2006:

Author	*no. loans (m)*
Catherine Cookson	25
Danielle Steel†	18
R.L. Stine	18
Josephine Cox	15
Jacqueline Wilson	13
Janet & Allan Ahlberg	12
Dick Francis	12
Roald Dahl	10
Agatha Christie	10
Jack Higgins	10

† Steel's 68 novels have sold 560 million copies since 1981.

THE TURNER PRIZE · 2006

Founded in 1984, the Turner Prize is awarded each year to a British artist (defined, somewhat loosely, as an artist working in Britain or a British artist working abroad) under 50, for an outstanding exhibition or other presentation in the twelve months prior to each May. The winner receives £25,000 – and three runners-up £5,000.

On being awarded the 2006 Turner Prize, German artist Tomma Abts at once became the first woman to win since Gillian Wearing in 1997, the first painter to win since Chris Ofili in 1998, and the very first female painter ever to win the prize. The recognition of an unassuming abstract painter was regarded by many as a 'return to basics', following many years in which controversy and personality had dominated the contest. Since the Turner Prize seems to delight in stimulating fierce debate as to the meaning and merit of modern art, critics and tabloids alike seemed slightly deflated that a relatively neutral and clearly 'artistic' artist had won. ❦ Tomma Abts was born in 1967 in Kiel, Germany, but moved to London in 1994, just as the Young British Artist (YBA) movement was coalescing. Abts says she creates her abstract, angular paintings without source materials and with no sense of how a work will turn out. As if to highlight their seemingly random, organic creation, Abts arbitrarily titles her paintings from a German dictionary of first names. After experimenting with canvas size early in her career, Abts settled on a uniform size of 48×38cm, onto which she adds layers of colour, allowing geometric forms to take shape. Abts describes her works as 'a concentrate of the many paintings underneath'. ❦ The Tate commented that Abts' winning exhibitions in Basel and London 'revealed her rigorous and consistent approach to painting. Through her intimate and compelling canvases, she builds on and enriches the language of abstract painting.' ❦ A small group of artists, who call themselves Stuckists and describe themselves as 'anti the pretensions of conceptual art', protested outside the prize ceremony, calling for the resignation of the Tate's director, Nicholas Serota. The Stuckists' leader, Charles Thomson, tried to dismiss Abts' work as 'silly little meaningless diagrams that make 1950s wallpaper look profound'.

Tomma Abts

Year	*previous winner*				
'92	Grenville Davey	'96	Douglas Gordon	'01	Martin Creed
'93	Rachel Whiteread	'97	Gillian Wearing	'02	Keith Tyson
'94	Antony Gormley	'98	Chris Ofili	'03	Grayson Perry
'95	Damien Hirst	'99	Steve McQueen	'04	Jeremy Deller
		'00	Wolfgang Tillmans	'05	Simon Starling

2007 NOMINATIONS

It was announced in May 2007 that the following four artists are shortlisted for the 2007 Turner Prize, the winner of which will be announced on 3 December:

installation artist Mark Wallinger · *photographer & film-maker* Zarina Bhimji
installation artist Mike Nelson · *sculptor & installation artist* Nathan Coley

THE GULBENKIAN PRIZE · 2007

The £100,000 Gulbenkian Prize is the UK's richest prize for innovative and challenging museums and galleries. In 2007, the prize was awarded to *Pallant House Gallery* in Chichester. The other award finalists were: *Kelvingrove Art Gallery and Museum,* Glasgow; *Kew Palace,* London; and *Weston Park Museum,* Sheffield.

TOP EXHIBITIONS · 2006

The *Art Newspaper*'s annual figures for the most popular art exhibitions in the world illustrate the continuing success of shows in Japan – where, in 2006, five of the world's top ten exhibitions were held. Below are the most popular art exhibitions of 2006 around the world – and in London – by the number of daily visitors:

GLOBAL TOP TEN

2006 exhibition	*museum*	*daily attendance*
The Price Collection: Jakuchu	Tokyo National	6,446
Leonard Foujita	Nat. Museum of Modern Art, Tokyo	6,324
Klimt, Schiele, Moser, Kokoschka	Grand Palais, Paris	6,297
Shaping Faith: Jap. Buddhist Statues	Tokyo National	6,296
Munch: The Modern Life of the Soul	Museum of Modern Art, NY	6,184
Faith & Syncretism	Tokyo National	6,039
Ingres, 1780–1867	Louvre, Paris	5,448
Tutankhamen & the Pharaohs	Museum of Art, Fort Lauderdale	5,443
Chinese & Japanese Calligraphy	Tokyo National	5,383
M. Beckmann: Watercolours & Pastels	Guggenheim Museum, Bilbao	5,278

LONDON TOP TEN

Kandinsky: the Path to Abstraction	Tate Modern	2,700
China: Three Emperors, 1662–1795	Royal Academy of Arts	2,105
BP Portrait Award	National Portrait Gallery	2,081
Henri Rousseau	Tate Modern	2,073
Degas, Sickert & Toulouse-Lautrec	Tate Britain	2,008
Photographic Portrait Prize	National Portrait Gallery	1,960
Icons & Idols	National Portrait Gallery	1,938
Modigliani & His Models	Royal Academy of Arts	1,886
Uncertain States of America	Serpentine Gallery	1,857
Summer Exhibition	Royal Academy of Arts	1,744

BECK'S FUTURES PRIZE

The Beck's Futures prize was launched in 2000 with the aim of rewarding innovations in contemporary art. Despite being the richest prize in modern art, it was abandoned in 2007 over fears that it 'wasn't very cool any more'. Instead, Beck's is working in collaboration with the Institute of Contemporary Arts to develop 'an ambitious new prize for emergent artists', to be launched in 2008.

— WHERE TO SEE MAJOR WORKS OF ART IN THE UK —

Work	Artist	Location
The Hay Wain	Constable	National Gallery, London
Christ of St John of the Cross	Dalí	Kelvingrove Art Gallery, Glasgow
Napoleon Crossing the Alps	Delaroche	Walker Art Gallery, Liverpool
My Bed	Emin	Saatchi Gallery, London
Girl With a White Dog	Freud	Tate Britain, London
St Christopher	Jordaens	The Ulster Museum, Belfast
Angel of the North	Gormley	Gateshead
Coming from the Mill	Lowry	Salford Museum and Art Gallery
Alison Lapper Pregnant	Quinn	Trafalgar Square, London
Self-Portrait (1661)	Rembrandt	Kenwood House, London
Massacre of the Innocents	Rubens	National Gallery, London
Rouen Cathedral: Setting sun	Monet	National Museum of Wales, Cardiff
An Old Woman Cooking Eggs	Velázquez	National Gallery, Edinburgh
Hylas and the Nymphs	Waterhouse	Manchester Art Gallery

ART PARTICIPATION

45·6% of UK adults participate in at least one artistic activity once a week or more, according to the 2007 National Survey of Culture, Leisure, & Sport. The majority of adults (58·9%) who participate in the arts are aged 16–24. Below are the most popular types of artistic activity, by percentage of UK adults participating:

Artistic activity	*% participation*
Buying original/handmade crafts	16·0
Painting, drawing, or sculpture	13·3
Textile crafts	13·0
Computer art	11·6
Playing an instrument (for pleasure)	11·5
Photography as art	9·2
Dance (excluding fitness & ballet)	8·4
Buying original art	7·3
Wood crafts	4·8
Crafts (excluding textile and wood)	4·7
Writing poetry	4·3
Singing to an audience	4·2
Writing stories or plays	3·5
Playing an instrument (to an audience)	3·4
Writing music	2·6
Making films or videos as art	2·2
Rehearsing/performing in a play	2·1
Ballet	0·5
Rehearsing/performing in opera	0·5

STENDHAL SYNDROME

Stendhal Syndrome is a malady in which travellers are 'overcome' after viewing art of great beauty. It was first identified in the late 1970s by Italian psychiatrist Graziella Magherini. Sufferers experience disorientation, dizziness, palpitations, sweating, and a sense of alienation or paranoia; symptoms can last for two to eight days, and cures include bed rest and a return to routine. The putative illness is named after the French writer (born Marie-Henri Beyle), who (as he noted in his diary) felt such 'ecstasy' upon viewing the frescoes in Florence's Church of Santa Croce that his heart began to beat irregularly and he felt the life 'ebbing out' of him. Since 1979, Dr Magherini has treated over 100 cases of the syndrome in Florence alone.

MOST VISITED MUSEUMS

The following VisitBritain figures show the top ten most visited museums in 2005:

Museum	*visits in 2005 (m)*
British Museum†	4·5
National Gallery	4·2
Tate Modern	3·9
Natural History Museum	3·1
Science Museum	2·0
Victoria & Albert	1·9
Tate Britain	1·7
National Portrait Gallery	1·5
Royal Observatory	0·8
National Railway Mus., Yorkshire	0·8

† Houses *c.*13m objects in 75,000m².

INTERNATIONAL MUSEUM SPENDING

Data released by the Art Fund in November 2006 revealed meagre spending on new acquisitions by British museums and galleries compared to their international counterparts. New York's Metropolitan Museum topped the Art Fund chart, spending £53·4m in 2004/05, including £26·3m on Duccio's *Madonna and Child.*

Museum (2004–05)	*acquisitions*	*total income*
The Met, New York	£53·4m	£137·8m
MoMA, New York	£20·0m	£75·3m
Louvre, Paris	£16·8m	£115·2m
The Getty, California†	*c.*£10·5m	*c.*£142·2m
Rijksmuseum, Amsterdam	£9·7m	£48·3m
National Gallery, London	£6·3m	£39·8m
Tate (all UK sites)	£4·8m	£88·8m
V&A, London	£1·3m	£66·1m
British Museum, London	£0·8m	£57·8m

† The Getty declined to confirm their spending. The figures cited are approximate and are taken from various newspaper reports, including the *New York Times.* ❦ An Art Fund publication in May 2006 indicated that 60% of UK museums reported they had allocated no funds to purchase new works.

THE MOST POWERFUL PEOPLE IN ART

ArtReview's 5th 'Power 100' list of the most powerful people in the art world (in 2006) saw Damien Hirst slip from first place to eleventh. The 10 most powerful were:

1 .. François Pinault .. *owner of Christie's*
2 .. Larry Gagosian .... *dealer/gallerist*
3 .. Nicholas Serota ... *museum director*
4 .. Glenn D. Lowry .. *museum director*
5 .. Sam Keller .... *art fair director*
6 .. Eli Broad .... *collector*
7 .. Charles Saatchi .... *collector/gallerist*
8 .. M. Slotover & A. Sharp .. *publishers*
9 .. Bruce Nauman .... *artist*
10. Jeff Koons .... *artist*

Google ranked 100th because of its ubiquity as a web gateway. *ArtReview* noted that the web itself was a vital source of art information, with photo sites (e.g. Flickr) becoming 'viable exhibition areas'.

TOP TEN ARTISTS BY REVENUE · 2006

Artprice annually publishes a ranking of artists based on the income their works generate at auction. In 2006, Pablo Picasso ranked 1st for the 10th year in a row:

#	*Artist ('05 rank)*	*2006 sales ($)*
1	Pablo Picasso (1)	339·2m
2	Andy Warhol (2)	199·4m
3	Gustav Klimt (359)	175·1m
4	Willem de Kooning (7)	107·4m
5	Amedeo Modigliani (21)	90·7m
6	Marc Chagall (6)	89·0m
7	Egon Schiele (47)	79·1m
8	Paul Gaugin (67)	62·3m
9	Henri Matisse (13)	59·7m
10	Roy Lichtenstein (11)	59·7m

[Source: artprice.com]

Below are the artistic 'movements' that have posted the sharpest gains in price over the past 10 years, according to the annual *Artprice* ranking of sales at auctions:

Cologne Group · 1980s & 1990s; examples include Mike Kelley & Christopher Wool
Arte Povera · founded in 1967 in Italy, natural materials, refused to see art as products
English Pop Art · bright colours, synthetic materials, and expressive forms
Contemporary Indian Art · current stars include Tyeb Mehta & Subodh Gupta
Minimal Art · 1960s movement focused on creating new experiences of space and time
The London School · stars include Lucian Freud, Francis Bacon, and Frank Auerbach
Canada's Group of Seven · early C20th; love of landscapes & colour

UK'S FAVOURITE ARTISTS

In November 2006, the Great Art Fair, the UK's largest art show, asked 500 British artists to name their favourite artistic talent. Listed below are the top ten:

Lucian Freud
Howard Hodgkin
David Hockney
J.M.W. Turner
Antoni Tapies
Rembrandt
Jack Vettriano
Barbara Rae
Frank Auerbach
Vincent Van Gogh
[Damien Hirst received just one vote]

LE RÊVE & THE 'TERRIBLE NOISE'

In September 2006, Las Vegas casino developer Steve Wynn agreed to sell Picasso's *Le Rêve* to a hedge fund billionaire for $139m – a deal that would have made the painting the most expensive artwork in history. Disastrously, while showing the painting to friends several days later, Wynn – raising his hand to make a point – jabbed his elbow backwards and ripped the canvas. According to the writer Nora Ephron, who was present at the time, witnesses heard a 'terrible noise' and saw a silver-dollar-sized hole trailed by two 3"-sized rips. 'Thank God it was me,' Wynn reportedly said, later calling the accident 'the world's clumsiest and goofiest thing to do'. (According to the *New Yorker*, Wynn suffers from the eye disease *retinitis pigmentosa*, which damages peripheral vision.) Understandably, the sale was cancelled: Wynn later decided to keep the painting following a $90,000 restoration.

THE CRITICAL YEAR · 2006–07

{OCT 2006} · *Monty Python's Spamalot,* written by python Eric Idle and John Du Prez, starred Tim Curry; Benedict Nightingale of the *Times* thought the production 'less a satire on chivalry, war and things medieval and more a parody of Broadway musicals, complete with sexy girls dancing in a Camelot that doubles as a casino'. ❦ The National Gallery's *Velázquez* exhibition stunned the *Guardian*'s Jonathan Jones, who considered it 'the most sensual, emotional and intellectual art event for some time'. ❦ James Powell's production of *Dirty Dancing* opened to mixed reviews at the Aldwych. The *Guardian*'s Lyn Gardner was bemused at this 'straightforward frame-by-frame recreation of the movie experience', and Dominic Cavendish of the *Telegraph* noted that 'No one is likely to have the time of their lives here'. {NOV} · Jeremy Sams's revival of Rodgers and Hammerstein's *The Sound of Music* featured a Maria chosen via the reality-TV show *How do you Solve a Problem like Maria?*. In the *Independent*, Paul Taylor applauded the winner, Connie Fisher, as 'enchantingly fresh and ardent and she sings with a voice that can range from piping purity to soft tenderness'. The *Times*'s Benedict Nightingale thought she gave 'a fine singing and even acting performance'. ❦ *Sleeping Beauty* at the Royal Opera impressed the *Guardian*'s Judith Mackrell with its choice of Lauren Cuthbertson as lead actress, but failed to 'see her pitched against a Prince with a maverick streak to match her own'. {DEC} · Tate Liverpool hosted *Bad Art for Bad People,* a retrospective of Jake and Dinos Chapman. In the *Times,* Rachel Campbell-Johnston decided 'It's like walking into the laboratory of some crazed horror-movie scientist, watching art history being fed into his mad postmodern machine'. ❦ Marianne Elliott's Cuban-set production of *Much Ado About Nothing* produced a sultry Beatrice and Benedick. In the *Guardian,* Michael Billington was delighted by 'its ability to capture the ecstasy at the heart of Shakespearean comedy and … [it] should be running for a year'. {JAN 2007} · The ENB's *Alice in Wonderland* featured a 'patchwork' score of music by Tchaikovsky, but was, according to the *Independent*'s Jenny Gilbert, let down by some of the designs: 'the crucial down-the-rabbit-hole sequence is badly bodged, a mess of undulating panels, flapping fabric and a light at the end of the tunnel that looks disconcertingly like the Eye of Sauron'. ❦ Fiona Shaw took to the stage for Deborah Warner's production of Samuel Beckett's *Happy Days* at the Lyttelton. In the *Guardian* Michael Billington found 'a brilliant naturalistic performance conceived very much in terms of Shaw's own stage persona'. In the *Telegraph,* Charles Spencer agreed that a 'superbly in-form Fiona Shaw' delivered 'the dramatist's potent stage poetry to perfection'. {FEB} · An impressive retrospective of Gilbert and George opened at Tate Modern to great acclaim. In the *Guardian,* Charlotte Higgins said as a 'big, generous, grimy, often moving experience, it reveals the artists as almost heroic figures in our culture'. ❦ The Wales Millennium Centre, Cardiff, staged David Pountney's take on Mussorgsky's *Khovanshchina* to much acclaim. The WNO production thrilled the *Times*'s Richard Morrison, who found that 'the crowd

Gilbert & George

THE CRITICAL YEAR · 2006–07 cont.

scenes are particularly spectacular, with the WNO chorus in thrilling voice and onstage trumpets adding to the thrill'. ❦ Controversy surrounded Daniel 'Harry Potter' Radcliffe's nude scene in Shaffer's revived *Equus* at the Gielgud. Despite the hoo-ha, Radcliffe managed to impress the *Telegraph*'s Charles Spencer, who said he 'brilliantly succeeds in throwing off the mantle of Harry Potter, announcing himself as a thrilling stage actor of unexpected range and depth'. Likewise, David Lister in the *Independent* said Radcliffe 'acquits himself well', and 'cuts a compelling figure'. {MAR} · Darko Tresnjak's *Merchant of Venice*, set in the glitzy world of contemporary Wall Street, failed to convince the *Independent*'s Paul Taylor, who found it had 'a dated air'. He thought the whole concept 'fundamentally shaky', but was impressed by F. Murray Abraham's Shylock who 'exudes a self-respect lacking in the sniggering, coke-snorting Christian bankers'. ❦ The *Surreal Things* exhibition at the V&A was warmly received by the *Times*'s Rachel Campbell-Johnston, who discovered 'an anarchic efflorescence of all that is fantastical, surprising, bizarre and disturbing, dreamlike, shocking and funny – and sometimes downright ridiculous'. {APR} · *Menopause the Musical* by Jeanie Linders was critically panned when it opened at the Shaw Theatre, London. Nigel Reynolds of the *Telegraph* was far from impressed: '… [it] is so intellectually lightweight it makes the average mag for teenage girls look like the collected works of Wittgenstein. It's garbage, and that's me being chivalrous'. {MAY} · 27 body casts were erected atop buildings around central London in *Event Horizon* – part of Antony Gormley's much anticipated and critically acclaimed exhibition at the Hayward Gallery. A further highlight was *Blind Light* – an 8·5×10m glass box filled with disorientating clouds of misty fog. The *Telegraph*'s Richard Dorment found the piece 'incredibly effective', and liked the idea 'of an artist making a work that is not about seeing but about not seeing'. ❦ Michael Billington of the *Guardian* was charmed by Andrew Upton's 'sparkling' new translation of Gorky's *Philistines* at the Lyttelton, which he judged to be a 'beautifully naturalistic production'. {JUN} · The £12·5m musical adaptation of Tolkien's *Lord of the Rings* opened to mixed reviews, with the *Independent*'s Paul Taylor finding some of the characters' ordeals 'over almost before they've begun'. Taylor concluded that 'viewed as a piece of musical drama, this show is unlikely to blow you away'. ❦ Damon Albarn's 'opera', *Monkey: Journey to the West*, opened at the Palace, Manchester, to rave reviews. Richard Morrison of the *Times* considered it 'a piece of music theatre of the most spectacular kind'. {JUL} · Marianne Elliott's revival of Shaw's *Saint Joan* was well received. In the *Telegraph*, Charles Spencer observed that Joan is 'waging her own jihad', and lauded Anne-Marie Duff's performance in the title role as providing 'life, vitality and certainty … that persuades you why so many were prepared to follow Joan'. {AUG} · Alan Cumming starred in Euripedes' *Bacchae* at the Edinburgh Festival and, according to Billington in the *Guardian*, gave Dionysus, 'a flirty, sportive, sexually equivocal human form'.

Antony Gormley

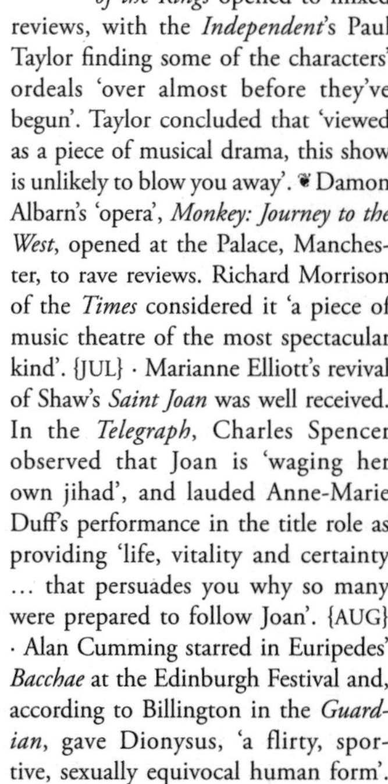

THEATRE'S MOST INFLUENTIAL

According to *The Stage*, the most influential people in UK theatre in 2006 were:

	Person (s)	role · *company*
1=	David Ian	producer · *Live Nation*
1=	Andrew Lloyd Webber	impresario · *Really Useful Group*
3	Cameron Mackintosh	producer · *Delfont Mackintosh Theatres*
4	Howard Panter/Rosemary Squire	MDs · *Ambassador Theatre Group*
5	Nica Burns/Max Weitzenhoffer	chief executive/chairman · *Nimax*
6	Michael Boyd	artistic director · *Royal Shakespeare Company*
7	Nicholas Hytner	artistic director · *National Theatre*
8	Jude Kelly	artistic director · *South Bank Centre*
9	Bill Kenwright	producer · *Bill Kenwright Ltd*
10	Michael Grandage	artistic director · *Donmar Warehouse*

WEST END'S LONGEST RUNNING SHOWS

In October 2006, after 21 years, *Les Misérables* became the longest running musical in London. Below are the longest running shows currently on in the West End:

Show	*Author*	*Duration (years)*
The Mousetrap	Agatha Christie	54
Les Misérables	Boublil/Schönberg/Kretzmer	21
The Phantom of the Opera	Andrew Lloyd Webber & Charles Hart	20
Blood Brothers	Willy Russell	18
The Woman in Black	Susan Hill & Stephen Mallatratt	18

According to the latest (2003) West End Theatre Report, 92% of theatregoers were white, and 65% were female. Below are the geographic origins of theatregoers:

Origin of audience member	%
London	37
Elsewhere in UK	36
North America	17
Europe	7
Elsewhere	4

LAURENCE OLIVIER AWARDS OF NOTE · 2007

Best actor	Rufus Sewell · *Rock 'N' Roll*
Best actress	Tamsin Greig · *Much Ado About Nothing*
Best new play	*Blackbird* · David Harrower
Best new musical	*Caroline, or Change* · Tony Kushner & Jeanine Tesori
Best new comedy	*The 39 Steps* · Patrick Barlow
Best actor (musical)	Daniel Evans · *Sunday in the Park with George*
Best actress (musical)	Jenna Russell · *Sunday in the Park with George*
Best director	Dominic Cooke · *The Crucible*
Outstanding musical production	*Sunday in the Park with George*

REVIEW QUOTES & SHARPING

'Sharping' is the practice of taking passages from critical reviews out of context to puff a theatrical production – an age-old ruse that might be threatened by EU law. The April 2007 Unfair Commercial Practices Directive, more commonly applicable to shops than the stage, could theoretically be employed to punish impresarios who deliberately misrepresent the sentiment of a review to the extent that the ticket-buying public is misled. Below are some examples of sharping par excellence:

I couldn't help feeling that, for all the energy, razzmatazz and technical wizardry, *the audience had been shortchanged*
– *Observer* on *Sinatra*

If it's an all-out retro romp *you want, this only fitfully delivers*
– *Times* on *Saturday Night Fever*

It is both irresistible *and true to say that St George and the Dragon drags on*
– *TimeOut* on *The Unholy & Illustrious History of George & the Dragon*

Frank Loesser's great musical from 1950 is hilarious ... *Grandage's production often falls somewhat flat*
– *Independent on Sunday* on *Guys & Dolls*

Perennially popular entertainment *... now seems to drift rather aimlessly from anecdote to reminiscence*
– *Evening Standard* on *Jeffrey Bernard is Unwell*

[Sources: *Times, Evening Standard, Stage*]

In 1961, Broadway producer David Merrick (aka the 'Abominable Showman') persuaded members of the public who had the same names as famous NY theatre critics, to pen rave reviews of his show.

PERFORMING NUDE

In February 2007, Daniel 'Harry Potter' Radcliffe performed nude (for about ten minutes) in a revival of Peter Shaffer's *Equus.* Just months later, Ian McKellan briefly stripped bare for the title role in Shakespeare's *King Lear*. According to the *Guardian*, other notable, mobile†, nude performances in UK theatre have included:

Year	Performer	Play	Author
1968	Maggie Wright	*Dr Faustus*	Christopher Marlowe
1968	Ensemble	*Hair*	Rado, Ragni & MacDermot
1971	Diana Rigg & Keith Michell	*Abelard & Heloise*	Ronald Millar
1971	Team of rugby players	*The Changing Room*	David Storey
1994	Stephen Dillane	*Hamlet*	William Shakespeare
1997	Ian Holm	*King Lear*	William Shakespeare
1998	Nicole Kidman	*The Blue Room*	David Hare
2000	Kathleen Turner	*The Graduate*	Terry Johnson
2006	Ensemble	*Cabaret*	Kander & Ebb
2007	Daniel Radcliffe	*Equus*	Peter Shaffer
2007	Ian McKellan	*King Lear*	William Shakespeare

† Until 1968, plays were censored by the Lord Chamberlain, who permitted nudes to appear on stage so long as they remained motionless – as occurred, for many years, at Soho's Windmill Theatre.

CLOWNS & CLOWNING

In autumn 2007, the French university Lyons II began offering a one-year, postgraduate course entitled 'Art of the Clown'. Students are taught anthropology, sociology, and economics (in case they 'go on to manage a troupe'), and are then instructed in practical clowning at the *House of Circus and Clown Arts*. ❦ The three traditional varieties of clown are the 'whiteface', the 'Auguste', and the 'character' clown. The whiteface is the oldest of the clown forms, and is characterised by a pure white face and neck, a bald head, and, very often, a ruff and pointed hat. The Auguste, whose role tends to be that of general buffoon and pie-in-face receiver, can usually be identified by his large, ill-fitting clothing, bulbous nose, and brightly coloured wig. Character clowns are the most realistic and tend to be usually based on characters like the 'sad tramp' or the 'happy hobo'. The archetypal character clown was Charlie Chaplin's 'Little Tramp' from *The Kid* (1921). ❦ On the first Sunday in February each year, a church service is held for all UK clowns in memory of 'the father of modern clowns', Londoner Joseph Grimaldi [1778–1837]. Clowns attend the service at Holy Trinity Church, Dalston, East London, in full 'motley and slap', and can often be persuaded to perform for the public afterwards.

FUNNIEST ONE-LINERS

The funniest film 'one-liners' – according to an April 2007 survey by Sky Movies:

Infamy! Infamy!
They've all got it in for me!
KENNETH WILLIAMS, *Carry on Cleo*

He's not the Messiah,
he's a very naughty boy.
TERRY JONES, *Life of Brian*

– Surely you can't be serious.
– I am serious ... and don't
call me Shirley.
LESLIE NIELSEN, *Airplane!*

Remember you're fighting for
this woman's honour, which is
probably more than she ever did.
GROUCHO MARX, *Duck Soup*

Don't knock masturbation,
it's sex with someone I love.
WOODY ALLEN, *Annie Hall*

Do you have a licence for your minkey?
PETER SELLERS
Return of the Pink Panther

CRITICS' CIRCLE AWARDS · 2007

Best new play .... *Rock 'N' Roll* · Tom Stoppard
Best musical .... *Caroline, or Change* · Tony Kushner & Jeanine Tesori
Best actor .... Rufus Sewell · *Rock 'N' Roll*
Best actress .... Kathleen Turner · *Who's Afraid of Virginia Woolf?*
Best Shakespearean performance .... Tamsin Greig · *Much Ado About Nothing*
Most promising newcomer .... Connie Fisher · *The Sound of Music*
Best director .... John Tiffany · *Black Watch*

IF.COMEDDIES · 2007

Edinburgh Fringe's comedy awards, the if.comeddies, were presented in August 2007. The £8,000 prize went to Australian comedian Brendon Burns for his 'edgy' show, *So I Suppose This Is Offensive Now*. Tom Basden was named Best Newcomer.

WINNER & NOMINEES 2007

BRENDON BURNS	*So I Suppose This Is Offensive Now*
Andrew Lawrence	*Social Leprosy for Beginners and Improvers*
Andrew Maxwell	*Waxin'*
Ivan Brackenbury's	*Hospital Radio Roadshow*
Pappy's Fun Club	*Pappy's Fun Club*

VICTORIAN JOKE BOOK

The personal joke book of Thomas Lawrence (*c.*1820–96), long considered one of the finest Victorian clowns, was discovered in January 2007. His gags included:

What's the difference between a rowing boat and Joan of Arc? One is made of wood and the other is Maid of Orleans.

You know I'm very fond of the ladies – I say bless those wives that fill our lives, With little bees and honey, They ease life's shocks, they mend our socks – But can't they spend the money.

Bad husbands are like bad coals – they smoke, they go out, and they don't keep the pot boiling.

– Have you seen my girlfriend's bonnet, I gave her that?
Have you seen her jacket, I gave her that. Have you seen her eyes?
– Yes, they were both black.
– Yes, I gave her those.

BRITISH COMEDY AWARDS · 2006

Best TV comedy actor	Stephen Merchant · *Extras*
Best TV comedy actress	Catherine Tate · *Catherine Tate Xmas Special*
Best comedy entertainment personality	Harry Hill
Best male newcomer	Russell Brand
Best female newcomer	Charlotte Church
Best new TV comedy	*Star Stories*
Best TV comedy	*Peep Show*
Best comedy entertainment programme	*Harry Hill's TV Burp*
Best international comedy TV show	*Curb Your Enthusiasm*
Best stage comedy	*Little Britain*
Best comedy film	*Wallace & Gromit: The Curse of the Were-Rabbit*
Best live stand-up tour	Jimmy Carr
Ronnie Barker writer of the year	Sacha Baron Cohen, Dan Mazer, Anthony Hines & Peter Bayhnam · *Borat*
Outstanding contribution to entertainment	Chris Tarrant

THE 'SIZE ZERO' DEBATE

Excessively thin models were banned from the catwalks of Madrid Fashion Week in September 2006 by the Spanish Association of Fashion Designers. The Spanish define excessively thin as having a Body Mass Index (BMI) of less than 18 [see p.103] – which effectively disqualified *c*.30% of the models scheduled to participate in the shows. Coming as it did in the midst of a fierce debate on the influence of skinny models on eating disorders, Madrid's decision reverberated throughout the fashion industry and press. In early 2007, the organisers of Milan Fashion Week followed Madrid's lead, requiring all models to have a BMI ≥18. Taking a somewhat more measured line, the British Fashion Council, which runs London Fashion Week, wrote to designers requesting that they use only 'healthy-looking girls' over the age of 16. ❦ Inevitably (given an excuse to show images of beautiful models) the media pounced on this story, labelling it the 'size zero' debate. (A name which makes little sense, given that this American size, equivalent to a UK size 4, is not sold in most British shops.) In May 2007, the British Fashion Council set up a 'model health inquiry' to inform the debate. A panel of designers and models, chaired by Lady Kingsmill, was charged with examining issues like: the age of models; the prevalence of drug and alcohol abuse; and the industry's use of very thin girls. In their final September 2007 report, the inquiry made 14 non-binding recommendations for London Fashion Week including: banning models aged <16 from the catwalks, and encouraging models to provide a medical certificate 'attesting their good health'. ❦ Keen to take a populist approach (and aware that the vast majority of their customers have BMIs far greater than 18), a range of companies distanced themselves from 'size zero' models. John Lewis announced they would use only 'normal-sized' models in their advertising, and Unilever vowed not to use 'size zero' models in the promotion of any of their brands – which include Lynx, Dove, and PG Tips.

READY-TO-WEAR FASHION WEEKS

NEW YORK
February & September
Who shows: *Ralph Lauren, Vera Wang, Diane Von Furstenberg, Calvin Klein, Zac Posen, Oscar de la Renta, Michael Kors, Donna Karan*

LONDON
February & September
Who shows: *Aquascutum, Ben de Lisi, Paul Smith Women, Nicole Farhi, Marc by Marc Jacobs, Betty Jackson, Marios Schwab, Gareth Pugh*

MILAN
February & September/October
Who shows: *Gucci, Armani, Prada, Dolce & Gabbana, Moschino, Versace, Roberto Cavalli, Max Mara, Burberry Prorsum, Fendi*

PARIS
February/March & October
Who shows: *Stella McCartney, Chanel, Vivienne Westwood, Jean Paul Gaultier, John Galliano, Issey Miyake, Christian Dior, Chloé, Lanvin*

According to *Vogue*, some key trends for Autumn/Winter 2007/08 include: cinched waist; ladylike skirts; midi-skirts and dresses; black with more black; the skirt suit; military chic; chunky knits; metallics; opulence and luxe; thigh-slimming slim-fit dresses; purple hues; and lovely quilted coats.

CELEB FASHION LINES

Below is a selection of fashion ranges 'designed' by 'celebrities' during 2007:

Celeb	*designed for*
Kate Moss	Topshop
Madonna	H&M
Lily Allen	New Look
Kelly Brook	New Look underwear
Scarlett Johansson	Reebok
Kylie Minogue	H&M swimwear
Paul Weller	Ben Sherman

When Kate Moss's collection went on sale in April 2007, the Oxford Street Topshop implemented a range of measures to avoid an undignified scrum. Colour-coded wristbands were issued to ensure that only 150 shoppers were allowed into the store at any one time; each shopper was given just 20 minutes to browse; and no one was allowed to purchase more than 5 items.

FASHION MUSES

Designer	*muse*
Marc Jacobs	Sofia Coppola
Karl Lagerfeld	Lady Amanda Harlech
John Galliano	Eva Green
Philip Treacy	Isabella Blow
Valentino	Georgina Brandolini
Roberto Cavalli	Eva Cavalli
Zac Posen	Natalie Portman
Matthew Williamson	Sienna Miller

Inevitably, designers can be fickle in their choice of muse.

HOUSE DESIGNERS

Aquascutum	Michael Hertz
Balenciaga	Nicolas Ghesquiere
Burberry	Christopher Bailey
Chanel	Karl Lagerfeld
Chloé	Paolo Melim Andersson
Christian Dior	John Galliano
Fendi	Karl Lagerfeld
Givenchy	Riccardo Tisci
Gucci	Frida Giannini
Lanvin	Alber Elbaz
Louis Vuitton	Marc Jacobs
Marni	Consuelo Castiglioni
Missoni	Angela Missoni
Prada	Miuccia Prada
Yves Saint Laurent	Stefano Pilati

ELLE STYLE AWARDS

Best	*winner*
Actor	Jude Law
Actress	Thandie Newton
Film	*Volver*
TV show	Ugly Betty
British music act	Amy Winehouse
British band	Razorlight
Style icon	Madonna†
Model	Naomi Campbell
British designer	Giles Deacon
Int. designer	Stella McCartney
H&M young designer	Gareth Pugh
Fashion photographer	Giles Bensimon

† The 'Queen of Pop' was later branded 'mutton dressed as lamb' by Peaches Geldof.

BRITISH FASHION AWARDS · 2006

Designer of the year	Giles Deacon
Best menswear designer	Kim Jones
Best accessories designer	Stuart Vevers for Mulberry
Best new designer	Marios Schwab
Red carpet designer	Vivienne Westwood
Best model	Kate Moss
Outstanding achievement in fashion	Joan Burstein

NIJINSKY AWARDS · 2006

The biennial Nijinsky Awards honour the best in international dance. In 2006, German Marco Goecke was honoured as Emerging Choreographer, and Lifetime Achievement awards went to French dancer Gil Roman, Spanish dancer Ana Laguna, and American dancers and choreographers Trisha Brown and John Neumeier. Brown is the artistic director of the Trisha Brown Dance Company in New York, and Neumeier has been artistic director of the Hamburg Ballet since 1973. The awards were presented by Princess Caroline of Hanover at the Monte Carlo Opera House, where legendary dancer Vaslav Nijinsky (after whom the awards are named) often performed early in the last century. Winners received trophies modelled after Rodin's 1912 bronze of Nijinsky dancing *L'Après-midi d'un faune*.

PERFORMANCE ATTENDANCE BY TYPE

During the 2003–04 season, West End theatregoers aged 15 and over attended the following types of performance at least once in the previous twelve months:

Performance type	% ♂	% ♀
Musical	66	69
Play	50	49
Entertainment	23	21
Dance	22	27
Opera	21	18
Other	12	11
None or 1st visit	14	14

[Source: The Society of London Theatre]

NATIONAL DANCE AWARDS · 2006

The Critics' Circle National Dance Awards are judged and presented by the critics and journalists involved in reviewing dance productions. The awards aim to celebrate the diversity of dance in Great Britain. The winners in 2006 included:

Outstanding achievement	Ivor Guest · dance historian and writer
Best male dancer	Carlos Acosta†
Best female dancer	Miyako Yoshida · *Royal Ballet*
Audience award	*Northern Ballet Theatre & Independent Ballet Wales*
Dance UK industry award	Val Bourne CBE
Best choreography: classical	Alexei Ratmansky · *The Bright Stream*
– modern	Wayne McGregor · *Amu*
– musical theatre	Twyla Tharp
Emerging artist: modern	Alexander Varona
– classical	Steven McRae · *Royal Ballet*
Company prize for outstanding repertoire: modern	*Phoenix Dance Theatre*
– classical	*Les Ballets Trockadero de Monte Carlo*
Best foreign dance company	*The Bolshoi Ballet*
Working Title *Billy Elliot* award	Brad Corben & Joseph Poulton
Patron's award	*Strictly Come Dancing*

† For performances with his own company and as Principal Guest Artist with The Royal Ballet.

PRITZKER ARCHITECTURE PRIZE

The international Pritzker Architecture Prize honours living architects who have created structures that contribute to the beauty and functionality of the built environment. In 2007, the Pritzker was awarded to Lord Richard Rogers, whose works include the Pompidou Centre, Lloyd's of London, the Millennium Dome, and Heathrow's Terminal 5. The winner receives a $100,000 prize and a medallion.

THE STIRLING PRIZE · 2006

The 11th Royal Institute of British Architects [RIBA] Stirling Prize was awarded, in October 2006, to Richard Rogers Partnership for the New Area Terminal at Barajas Airport, Madrid. The judges said 'the building is robust enough to withstand the results of minor battles lost in terms of signage and shopping, the simplicity and clarity of the architectural ambition being all-dominant'. The specifications:

Client	AENA	Architect	Richard Rogers Prtshp
Structural engineer	Anthony Hunt Associates/TPS, with OTEP/HCA	Co-architect	Estudio Lamela
Façade engineer	Arup	Total cost	€1,238m
Completion	2006	Main terminal length	1,200m
Year of full operation	2010	Total aeroplane stands	62
Gross internal area	760,000,000m²	Car park spaces	9,000
		Annual passenger no. (2010)	35m

The other buildings and architects shortlisted for the £20,000 Stirling prize were:

Brick House, London	Caruso St John Architects
Phaeno Science Centre, Wolfsburg	Zaha Hadid Architects and Mayer Bährle Freie Architekten BDA
Evelina Children's Hospital, London	Hopkins Architects
Idea Store, Whitechapel, London	Adjaye/Associates
National Assembly for Wales, Cardiff	Richard Rogers Partnership

During the research for her book *How To Be a Happy Architect*, Irena Bauman, a design advisor to the government, discovered some criticism of the Stirling Prize. A few of the winning buildings, although aesthetically pleasing, proved to be less than perfectly functional in practice. For example, the Laban dance centre in east London wowed the judges in 2003 with its use of light, yet the centre has since been criticised by some for being too light and hot in the summer and too cold in the winter.

BLUE PLAQUES

There are currently more than 800 'blue plaques' in London marking 'where the great and the good have penned their masterpieces, developed new technologies, lived or died'. Subjects must have been dead for at least 20 years (or have passed the 100th anniversary of their birth) and must have a surviving London building associated with them. The clay plaques are usually 2" thick and 19·5" in diameter.

THE ARCHAEOLOGICAL YEAR 2006–07

{OCT} · A 100m year old fossilised insect encased in amber was discovered in Burma. Because the fossil has features of wasps and bees, it was proposed as the missing link between the two insects. {NOV} · Scientists discovered the remains of *Dunkleosteus terrelli* – a sea creature thought to have lived *c*.400m years ago. The scientists suggested that the creature could bring its jaws together with a force of *c*.5,000kg – a bite four times more powerful than that of the *Tyrannosaurus rex*. {DEC} · The fossils of a gigantic new species of dinosaur, which lived *c*.150m years ago, were uncovered in Spain. At 30–37m long from head to tail, the *Turiasaurus riodevensis* is thought to be the largest animal ever to have roamed Europe. {JAN 2007} · The fossilised remains of >69 species were found at the bottom of a cave on Nullarbor Plain, Australia, where they are thought to have fallen 400,000–800,000 years ago. Amongst the finds were 8 previously unknown kangaroo species, and the first complete skeleton of a marsupial lion. ❦ Excavations at Durrington Walls revealed traces of a large settlement that may have housed those who constructed the nearby monument, Stonehenge. {FEB} · A previously unknown Roman coin was rediscovered in a stash of money deposited in a Newcastle bank vault in the C18th. Minted in 32BC, the coin depicts Antony and Cleopatra in profile – though it does little to justify Cleopatra's legendary reputation for beauty. {MAR} · Palaeontologists in Montana, USA, discovered a new dinosaur, *Oryctodromeus cubicularis*, which they suspect may have lived in burrows. {APR} · The bone fragments of one of the earliest modern humans were discovered in a cave in China. The bones are thought to be *c*.42,000 years old. ❦ Researchers discovered that remains thought to be relics of Joan of Arc were, in fact, bones from an Egyptian mummy and a cat. {MAY} · Archaeologists in Ephesus, Turkey, announced the discovery of what they suspected was a graveyard for gladiators. One of the most convincing pieces of evidence (apart from three gravestones depicting gladiators) was the unearthing of skeletons that displayed healed injuries consistent with (3-pronged) trident wounds. ❦ After 30 years of searching, Israeli archaeologists claimed to have found the ancient tomb of King Herod at Herodium, near Jerusalem. {JUN} · Researchers at the Royal Veterinary College, London, used computer modelling to suggest that the *Tyrannosaurus rex*, usually perceived as a fearsome hunter, was in fact a clumsy beast, hampered by its long tail, with a top speed of only 15–25mph. ❦ The remains of a hitherto unknown giant penguin were discovered on the south coast of Peru. Thought to have inhabited the tropical waters of the Pacific Ocean some 36m years ago, the penguin stood 1·5m high and sported a beak 18cm long. {JUL} · A very well-preserved baby mammoth was found frozen in the Siberian permafrost. The specimen was in such good condition that scientists hoped to extract usable DNA. {AUG} · An ancient forest of 8m-year-old cypress trees was discovered in an open-cast coal mine in NE Hungary. It is hoped analysis of the trees might offer an insight into the Earth's climate 8m years ago. ❦ Evidence from NASA's satellites indicated that the temple complex of Angkor, Cambodia, covered *c*.3,000 sq km.

TREASURE HUNTERS

The Treasure Act (1996) requires that all treasure found in England, Wales, or N Ireland be reported to the District Coroner (treasure is defined as coins or gold/silver objects over 300 years old). According to the Dept of Culture, Media, & Sport's latest annual Treasure Report (Oct 2006), 506 finds of treasure were reported in 2004, up from 79 in 1997. All items reported as treasure must be taken to a local museum for examination; those considered of value are referred to the British Museum, which decides whether it, or any other museum, wishes to acquire them†. As the table below shows, most treasure in 2004 was unearthed by 'metal detectorists':

Method of discovery	*finds*	*%*
Metal detecting	469	92·7
Archaeological find	25	4·9
Chance find	12	2·4

Charted below is the number of finds submitted in 2004, by period and outcome:

Period of object(s)	*acquired*	*disclaimed*	*not treasure*	*pending*	*total*
Bronze Age	24	7	3	1	35
Iron Age	12	2	–	–	14
Roman	35	35	1	1	72
Early Medieval	47	26	2	–	75
Medieval	45	63	2	–	110
Post-Medieval	66	62	5	–	133
C18–20th	–	–	43	–	43
Not known	2	11	11	–	24
Total	231	206	67	2	506

† Should a museum wish to acquire an object, a coroner will hold an inquest to ascertain if the find is treasure. If the find is declared treasure, it is taken to the British Museum or National Museums & Galleries of Wales where it is valued by the independent Treasures Valuation Committee, which also calculates the reward. This reward is then paid to the finder (or shared between finder and landowner if such an agreement is in place) within 1 year (provided the finder did not break the law in unearthing the artefact). If the find is deemed treasure but no museum wishes to acquire it, the Secretary of State disclaims the find, and the objects are returned to the finder. ❦ One of the most impressive finds in 2004 was a Viking hoard discovered in a Cheshire field by metal detectorist Steve Reynoldson. A battered lead box contained a twisted silver rod, an ingot, and 21 silver bracelets. In return for this booty, Reynoldson was rewarded with £28,000 to share with the landowner.

WORLD MONUMENT WATCH LIST

Below are the UK and Ireland's most 'endangered architectural and cultural sites':

UK	IRELAND
Mavisbank House, Scotland	Vernon Mount, Cork
Richhill House, Armagh City, NI	Tara Hill, Meath
St Peter's College, Scotland	
Wilton's Music Hall, London	

[Source: 2008 World Monuments Watch List]

Sci, Tech, Net

Every great advance in science has issued from a new audacity of imagination.
— JOHN DEWEY (1859–1952)

POLONIUM-210

Alexander Litvinenko's alleged murder in London in 2006 [see p.27] gave media exposure to the little-known element Polonium (Po). Reports quickly surfaced that Litvinenko had died from radioactive poisoning and, within days, traces of the highly toxic isotope Polonium-210 had been found in more than 12 locations in London, Moscow, and Hamburg, and on 4 aircraft. Hundreds of people with elevated levels of Po-210 have since been traced. ❦ Polonium was the first element to be discovered as a consequence of its radioactivity. It was isolated in 1898 by Marie and Pierre Curie, during their analysis of the radioactive ore 'pitchblende'. Provisionally called Radium F, the element was renamed Polonium to draw attention to the political plight of Marie's homeland, Poland, which was then under the partitioned rule of Russia, Prussia, and Austria. ❦ Po is an extremely rare and highly toxic metallic element found in uranium ores at a quantity of *c.*0·1g per ton. Po has 34 isotopes (more than any other element), all of which are radioactive. The most widely used of these isotopes – Po-210 – occurs in nature at very low levels (all humans carry harmless traces). However, in sufficient quantities, Po-210 emits enough gamma particles to produce a blue glow and, according to the CDC, the alpha particles it emits 'carry high amounts of energy that can damage or destroy genetic material in cells inside the body'. By weight, Po-210 is 250bn times more toxic than cyanide; a dose smaller than a grain of salt is fatal. ❦ In the industrial world, Po-210 is used as a heat source for satellite power supplies, a trigger for nuclear weapons, and as a means of eliminating static. (It is also found in cigarettes; according to a *NYT* article by Prof. Robert Proctor, 'pack and a half smokers are dosed to the tune of about 300 chest X-rays' a year.) ❦ The British Health Protection Agency notes that 'Po-210 only represents a radiation hazard if it is taken into the body – by breathing it in, by taking it into the mouth, or if it gets into a wound. It is not a radiological hazard as long as it remains outside the body. Most traces of it can be eliminated through handwashing, or washing machine and dishwasher cycles'. ❦ Because of Po-210's rarity, toxicity, and difficulty of extraction, it became clear that Litvinenko's death was unlikely to have been accidental. As Prof. Goodhead of the UK's Medical Research Council told the BBC, 'to poison someone, much larger amounts are required and this would have to be man-made, perhaps from a particle accelerator or a nuclear reactor'. Inevitably, speculation as to the origin of the Po-210 that killed Litvinenko focused on Russia [see p.32].

84 209
4,2,5
–
527
9.3
Po
$[Xe].4f^{14}.5d^{10}.6s^{2}.6p^{4}$
Polonium

THE WORLD'S WORST SOUND

Professor Trevor Cox, an acoustics expert at Salford University, spent a year researching the world's worst sounds. Cox posted clips of 34 objectionable noises online, which were rated by 1·1m visitors. The sounds voted most unpleasant were:

1	vomiting	6	badly played violin
2	microphone feedback	7	whoopee cushion
3	wailing babies	8	an argument in a soap opera
4	train wheels scraping on tracks	9	hum of mains electricity
5	a squeaky see-saw	10	a Tasmanian devil

The Jan 2007 survey revealed that men found the sound of babies crying more repellent than women; Prof. Cox suggested that – through evolution – women might have become habituated to this sound.

LONG BETS

The Long Bets Foundation, an educational charity dedicated to improving long-term thinking, operates a website that allows anyone with $50 to post a 'societally or scientifically important' prediction concerning an event at least 2 years into the future. Bets (minimum $200) can be placed on the prediction, and the winner's spoils are donated to a charity of his or her choosing. Some notable bets include:

By 2029 no computer, or 'machine intelligence', will have passed the Turing Test†. $20,000

The US men's soccer team will win the World Cup before the Red Sox win the World Series. $2,000

At least one human alive in the year 2000 will still be alive in 2150. $2,000

The first discovery of extraterrestrial life will be some place other than on a planet or on a satellite of a planet. $2,000

In a Google search of five keywords or phrases representing the top five news stories of 2007, weblogs will rank higher than the *New York Times* website. $2,000

[Source: longbets.org]

† British mathematician Alan Turing devised the Turing Test in 1950 to address the question of whether machines can think. A machine will be said to pass the test when a human conversing with it via a text-only system cannot tell whether their interlocutor is another human or a machine.

ONLINE FEARS

64% of web users avoid some online activities because of security concerns, according to a 2006 Int. Telecommunications Union study. The greatest fears are:

Theft of personal information	26%	Spam	8
Viruses & worms	25	Disturbing content	4
Spyware	19	Being diverted to 'bad sites'	3
Scams & fraud	13	Other	2

NOBEL PRIZES IN SCIENCE · 2006

THE NOBEL PRIZE IN PHYSICS

John C. Mather,
NASA Goddard Space Flight Center, Maryland

George F. Smoot,
University of California, Berkeley

'for their discovery of the blackbody form and anisotropy of the cosmic microwave background radiation'

Mather and Smoot's research confirmed fundamental predictions proposed by the Big Bang theory. Their research used detailed measurements of cosmic microwave background radiation (CMB), gleaned from NASA's COBE satellite, to reveal an 'echo' of the vast explosion, or Big Bang, said to have formed the universe. Mather demonstrated that CMB followed the 'blackbody' curve, a pattern in the energy spectrum predicted to result from the first light in the universe. Smoot noted tiny variations, or 'anisotropies', within the CMB, that represented very faint traces of the formation of the earliest structures in the expanding universe.

THE NOBEL PRIZE IN CHEMISTRY

Roger D. Kornberg,
Stanford University

'for his studies of the molecular basis of eukaryotic transcription'

Kornberg developed a detailed picture of molecular-level transcription – a vital part of the process by which cells construct proteins from DNA. Kornberg's research focused on eukaryotes – organisms whose cells have a defined nucleus – a group that includes humans. Understanding how transcription works has great medical potential, since disturbances in the transcription process can cause diseases like cancer.

THE NOBEL PRIZE IN PHYSIOLOGY OR MEDICINE

Andrew Z. Fire, *Stanford University*

Craig C. Mello, *University of Massachusetts Medical School*

'for their discovery of RNA interference – gene silencing by double-stranded RNA'

Fire and Mello identified RNA interference – a process that regulates the flow of genetic information – used by the body to defend itself against viral infections. The discovery has opened up new fields of research in the study of gene functionality which, in turn, has the potential to advance the treatment of viruses and cancers by allowing scientists to target and shut down harmful genes.

ROYAL SOCIETY PRIZE FOR SCIENCE BOOKS · 2007

Daniel Gilbert · *Stumbling on Happiness* (Knopf)

THE ABEL PRIZE & COPLEY MEDAL

The Abel Prize was created in memory of Norwegian mathematician Niels Henrik Abel (1802–29), who is justly famous for proving that the general quintic equation is unsolvable algebraically. In 2007, the Abel Prize was awarded to Srinivasa S.R. Varadhan, from New York's Courant Institute of Mathematical Sciences, for his 'fundamental contributions to probability theory and in particular for creating a unified theory of large deviations'. The Abel Prize is worth *c.*$1 million. ❦ In November 2006, Professor Stephen Hawking was awarded the Copley Medal for his outstanding contribution to theoretical cosmology. Presented by the Royal Society, the Copley is the world's oldest prize for scientific achievement. First awarded in 1731, it has previously been won by such scientific luminaries as Justus von Liebig, Charles Darwin, Michael Faraday, Albert Einstein, and Louis Pasteur.

IG NOBEL PRIZE

Ig Nobel prizes are awarded for scientific 'achievements that cannot or should not be reproduced'. Some of the esteemed honours presented in 2006 include:

ORNITHOLOGY · Ivan R. Schwab (University of California, Davis) and the late Philip R.A. May (University of California, LA) *for their work into why woodpeckers do not get headaches.*

LITERATURE · Daniel Oppenheimer (Princeton University) *for his timely report entitled 'Consequences of Erudite Vernacular Utilized Irrespective of Necessity: Problems with Using Long Words Needlessly'.*

PHYSICS · Basile Audoly and Sebastien Neukirch (Université Pierre et Marie Curie, Paris) *for their investigation into why dry spaghetti, when bent, often breaks into more than two pieces.*

CHEMISTRY · Antonio Mulet, José Javier Benedito, and José Bon (University of Valencia, Spain) and Carmen Rosselló (University of Illes Balears, Mallorca, Spain) *for their joint study entitled 'Ultrasonic Velocity in Cheddar Cheese as Affected by Temperature'.*

MATHEMATICS · Nic Svenson and Piers Barnes (The Australian Commonwealth Scientific and Research Organisation) *for their tireless exploration into how many photographs must be taken to ensure no one in a group picture has their eyes closed.*

[Source: improb.com]

DARWIN AWARDS

The annual Darwin Awards '*salute the improvement of the human genome by honouring those who accidentally kill themselves in really stupid ways*'. In 2006, this posthumous accolade went to Jason Ackerman and Sara Rydman, both 21, from Lake View, South Florida. The two students managed to pull down and crawl inside a massive, helium-filled promotional balloon, which was advertising apartments. The hapless due died from oxygen starvation while attempting to get a 'buzz' from the gas.

THE EDGE ANNUAL QUESTION · 2007

The online magazine *Edge* annually invites notable scientists and intellectuals to answer one probing question, usually with fascinating results. Below is a selection of the 160 responses to the 2007 question, 'What are you optimistic about? Why?':

It has never been a better time to have autism · Simon Baron-Cohen (psychologist)

The evaporation of the powerful mystique of religion · Daniel Dennett (philosopher)

The acceptance of the reality of global warming has shown us the greatest and widest ranging market failure ever seen · Brian Eno (artist, composer, producer)

Truth prevails. Sometimes, technology helps · Xeni Jardin (technology journalist)

Shortening sleep will prolong conscious life · Marcel Kinsbourne (psychologist)

The decline of violence · Steven Pinker (psychologist)

The tools for cultural production and distribution are in the pockets of 14-year-olds Howard Rheingold (communications expert)

THE IMPORTANCE OF NAMES

Research by David Figlio, Professor of Economics at the University of Florida, suggested that a girl's name can dictate whether or not she will go on to study maths or physics after the age of 16. The study, published in May 2007, indicated that girls with particularly feminine names (as judged by a linguistic test), such as Anna, Emma, or Isabella, were less likely to study traditionally masculine subjects than girls with less feminine names, such as Ashley, Alex, or Grace. The study, conducted on twins, also revealed that those with 'lower-status' names, or names with unusual spellings, often performed less well in tests than a more traditionally named sibling.

THE SCIENCE OF PROCRASTINATION

In January 2007, psychologist Piers Steel published the results of his 10-year analysis of procrastination. The study includes a formula designed to predict whether a person will procrastinate in a specific situation. According to Steel, the desire to finish a task (rather than procrastinate) is based on the following four factors:

$$\textit{Desire to finish} = \frac{\text{(E)xpectation of success} \times \text{(V)alue of completing the task}}{\text{(I)ndividual's sensitivity to delay} \times \text{(D)eadline of the task}}$$

Steel hopes that his formula (named Temporal Motivational Theory) may be able to help model complex systems of human motivation, such as the behaviour of stock markets and even nations. Sadly, TMT does not offer a solution to the problem of procrastination, which 'chronically' affects *c*.15–20% of adults. Steel notes that in light of this issue, 'continued research into procrastination should not be delayed'.

(Apropos of nothing, in April 2007, scientists at Leeds University developed a formula for the 'perfect' bacon butty. The ideal sandwich is: 2–3 rashers of back bacon, cooked under a preheated grill for 7 mins at 240°C, which are then placed between 2 slices of farmhouse bread, 1–2cm thick.)

15 GREATEST MEDICAL BREAKTHROUGHS

In January 2007, the *British Medical Journal* shortlisted 15 contenders for the title of 'greatest medical breakthrough since 1840' (the year the *BMJ* was first published):

Anaesthesia........ *developed in the 1800s by John Snow, symbol of humanitarianism*
Antibiotics............*the wonder drugs first discovered in 1929 by Alexander Fleming*
Chlorpromazine........................ *unlocking psychosis for paranoid schizophrenics*
Computers .... *transcending our limits*
Discovery of DNA's structure .... *by James Watson and Francis Crick in 1953*
Evidence-based medicine............................. *increasing, not dictating, choice*
Germ theory ....*understanding of hygiene has extended life expectancy*
Imaging .... *X-rays and scans revealed the world within*
Immunology .... *made magic bullets and organ transplants possible*
Oral rehydration therapy .... *simple solution for saving lives after diarrhoea*
The pill............... *allowing women to choose when or whether to become pregnant*
Risks of smoking............. *2 landmark studies from 1950s revealed harmful effects*
Sanitation ....*greater awareness revolutionised public health*
Tissue culture ....*allows cells to be grown on industrial scale to create vaccines, &c.*
Vaccines .... *saved millions of lives and eradicated diseases like smallpox*

11,000 votes were cast in an online poll to select which breakthrough was the most valuable. The overall winner (with 1,765 votes) was 'sanitation'. Oddly, most medical professionals chose 'anaesthesia', whereas the public voted for 'antibiotics'.

THE MOST DANGEROUS PATHOGENS

The most dangerous pathogens (disease-causing micro-organisms) are generally those that can survive outside the body for the longest period of time. According to research by Paul Ewald and Bruno Walther, the most dangerous pathogens are:

Pathogen	*deaths per 100,000*	*days survival outside body*
Smallpox	10,000	885
Tuberculosis	5,000	244
Diphtheria	200	370
Whooping cough	100	12
Pneumonia	36	29
Influenza	10	14
Measles	7	4
Mumps	5	1

[Source: P.W. Ewald & B. Walther, *Biological Reviews*, vol. 79, p.849 · *New Scientist*]

THE BEST SCIENCE BOOK EVER WRITTEN

The British Royal Institution debated the best scientific read in October 2006. The shortlist included: Richard Dawkins, *The Selfish Gene* (1976); Primo Levi, *The Periodic Table* (1975); Konrad Lorenz, *King Solomon's Ring* (1952); and Tom Stoppard, *Arcadia* (1993). Primo Levi's tale of life as a Jew in Mussolini's Italy recounted through scientific metaphor was judged to be the best science book ever written.

SOME NOTABLE SCIENTIFIC RESEARCH · 2006–07

{OCT 2006} · Scientists from the Children's Hospital in Boston, MA discovered that after a heart attack, a rat's heart can be stimulated to recover by injecting 2 drugs: 'p38 MAP kinase inhibitor' and 'fibroblast growth factor 1'. It is hoped that similar re-growth and repair might be replicated in humans. ❦ A report published in the *Proceedings of the National Academy of Sciences* proposed that elephants have self-awareness – a human trait previously found only in great apes and bottlenose dolphins. The elephants were observed inspecting their reflections in a large mirror placed in their enclosure at the Bronx Zoo, suggesting that they recognised their own images. {NOV} · A study into cot death published in the *Journal of the American Medical Association* suggested that the condition might be caused by a brain abnormality, raising hopes that those at risk could be identified and treated. ❦ Researchers at the Pasteur Institute in Paris isolated 'opiorphin' – a new pain-killer found in men's saliva. Results of rat trials suggested that opiorphin could be up to 6 times more powerful than morphine. {DEC} · An Australian study published in *Neuropsychology* indicated that left-handed people could think more quickly than right-handers when performing certain tasks. {JAN 2007} · American scientists reported in *Nature Biotechnology* that they had discovered a new way to harvest stem cells without using controversial lab-grown human embryos. The new technique involves extracting amniotic fluid from pregnant women and cultivating the cells in a lab. ❦ The Roslin Institute announced it had genetically modified chickens to lay eggs containing proteins that could be used to make cancer-treating drugs. {FEB} · Andrew Oswald, professor of economics at the University of Warwick, mooted that being awarded a Nobel Prize might increase one's life expectancy by up to 2 years. Oswald compared the life spans of male Nobel laureates and nominees, and suggested that a higher social status helped the winners live longer. ❦ Researchers at the Medical Research Council Prion Unit developed a therapy that restored to health mice that had shown early signs of Creutzfeldt-Jakob disease (CJD). It was hoped that a version of this therapy, which blocks production of normal prions, might be developed for humans. {MAR} · A team of researchers at London's Hammersmith Hospital discovered that the hormone kisspeptin, which triggers fertility in teenage girls, could be used to boost fertility in older women. ❦ The American company Ventria Bioscience was granted preliminary approval to grow rice that had been genetically modified to produce human proteins. The crop will be used to develop medicines for the treatment of diarrhoea in children. ❦ Research published in *Biological Psychiatry* suggested that oxytocin, a hormone linked to social behaviour, could aid 'emotional recognition'. A study indicated that men were significantly better at judging the 'emotion' of sets of photographed human eyes after sniffing oxytocin than before. ❦ A US-led team developed a genetically modified malaria-resistant mosquito. Since these GM mosquitoes outlived their malaria-carrying cousins, it was hoped that they might flourish in the wild and help eradicate the deadly

NOTABLE SCIENTIFIC RESEARCH · 2006–07 cont.

disease. {APR} · An international team of researchers writing in *Nature Biotechnology* revealed that they had developed a method to convert one blood-group type to another. ❦ German scientists announced they had formed immature sperm cells from human bone marrow, which might offer some hope to infertile men. ❦ Research published in *Science* indicated a genetic link to obesity. The identification of a possible 'fat gene' might explain why some can eat a healthy diet yet still struggle with their weight. ❦ American scientists published the results of a trial in which 15 young patients diagnosed with type 1 diabetes were given stem cell treatment. 13 of the volunteers were able to stop their daily insulin injections – some for more than 3 years after the experimental treatment began. {MAY} · Three separate medical teams announced that they had successfully completed scar-free abdominal surgery by entering the patient's body through the mouth. 'Natural orifice transluminal endosurgery' (NOTES) involves putting a flexible camera and surgical instruments down a patient's throat to reach the abdominal cavity. NOTES also reduces recovery time significantly. ❦ Researchers at the University of California discovered an abnormally high number of people diagnosed with lupus living in houses built on a disused oil field in New Mexico. The findings suggested that environmental triggers, like pollution, might in part be responsible for the autoimmune disease. ❦ Dutch scientists at the University of Groningen suggested that some people might simply be more accident-prone than others. Reviewing 79 studies on accidents, they concluded that 1 in 29 people are, inexplicably, 50% more likely to suffer a mishap than those in the general population. Sadly, the research did not identify any particularly clumsy 'types'. {JUN} · Research led by Professor James Surmeier, reported in *Nature* online, indicated that the drug isradipine, normally used to treat high blood pressure, could help to control Parkinson's disease. ❦ University of Sheffield research on opposite-sex twins indicated that the influence of the male's testosterone in the womb could reduce the female twin's fertility. ❦ Norwegian researchers writing in *Science* reported that eldest children tend to have higher IQs – perhaps because the eldest get more undivided parental attention at a formative age. {JUL} · Research by the University of Arizona revealed that, on average, women speak 16,215 words a day, and men speak 15,669 – fuelling the debate that women are by far the more talkative sex. ❦ Scientists at King's College London suggested that those with many moles on their skin were more likely to age well. ❦ The *Proceedings of the National Academy of Sciences* reported that genetically modified goats have been bred with a drug in their milk that serves as an antidote to nerve agents like sarin and VX. ❦ US scientists reported in *Nature* that they had used deep brain stimulation to rouse a patient in a minimally conscious state. A 38-year-old man, who had suffered a serious head injury six years previously, was able to speak, chew, and swallow after electrical pulses had stimulated his brain. {AUG} · A study in the *BMJ* indicated that US abstinence programs did not reduce the incidence of underage or unprotected sex.

SOLVING THE FERMI PARADOX?

The Fermi Paradox has been summed up thus: 'if the age and size of the universe suggest the existence of extra-terrestrials, how come we haven't had any contact with the little green men?' Or, more pithily, 'where is everybody?' The paradox is named after the Nobel Prize-winning atomic physicist Enrico Fermi (1901–54), who first posed the question (as well as giving us the *fermi*: a measure equal to 10^{-15}m). In January 2007, Rasmus Bjork, of Copenhagen's Niels Bohr Institute, suggested that the size of space might hold the answer. Bjork calculated that if 64 probes were sent into the alien-friendly 'galactic habitable zone', travelling at 1,000 times the speed of NASA's current Cassini mission, it would still take *c.*10bn years to search just 0·4% of the stars. Bjork held out some hope that radio telescopes might shorten the search, but he explained that until aliens 'can develop an exotic form of transport that gets them across the galaxy in two weeks, it's still going to take millions of years to find us'.

PLANETARY EVENTS 2008

3 January	Perihelion: Earth is at orbital position closest to Sun
7 February	annular solar eclipse: visible from Antarctica, Australia, & NZ
21 February	total lunar eclipse: visible from Americas, Europe, & Africa
24 February	Saturn at opposition: closest approach to Earth
20 March	Equinox: Sun passes northward over Equator at 05:48 GMT
20 June	Solstice: Sun directly above Tropic of Cancer at 23:59 GMT
4 July	Aphelion: Earth is at orbital position farthest from Sun
9 July	Jupiter at opposition
1 August	total solar eclipse: visible from Canada, Russia, & China
16 August	partial lunar eclipse: visible from Asia, Europe, Africa, & Australasia
13 September	Uranus at opposition
22 September	Equinox: Sun passes southward over Equator at 15:44 GMT
21 December	Solstice: Sun directly above Tropic of Capricorn at 12:04 GMT

GEIPAN & ALIEN SIGHTINGS

In February 2007, the French space agency CNES published online its archive of >6,000 eyewitness reports of possible UFO sightings. These sightings have been collected since 1977 by GEIPAN (*Groupe d'études et d'informations sur les phénomènes aérospatiaux non-identifiés*), which investigates UFO reports, and attempts to provide plausible scientific explanations. GEIPAN classifies the various sightings thus:

Unidentified	*unidentified due to insufficient data*	*probably identified*	*conclusively identified*
28%	30%	33%	9%

GEIPAN's website includes advice on what to do if you think you see a UFO: 'firstly, ask yourself are you really observing a UFO'. If so, 'write down the details as quickly and accurately as you can', including date, time, and location of sighting; shape, size, and colour of object; and any noise it makes.

KEY SPACE MISSIONS OF 2007

MARS RECONNAISSANCE ORBITER (MRO) · NASA's MRO arrived at Mars on 10 March 2006, with a mission to explore the history of water on the Red Planet, and investigate whether water has been present long enough to have sustained life. A February 2007 report, based on early findings from the most powerful telescopic camera ever sent to Mars, suggested that liquid or gas may previously have flowed through cracks in underground rocks on the planet.

CASSINI-HUYGENS · A joint ESA and NASA project to study Saturn and its moons. Previously only two of Saturn's moons – Titan and Enceladus – were thought to be geologically active. However, in June 2007, new data from Cassini suggested otherwise. Scientists noted that Tethys and Dione were expelling particles into the surrounding atmosphere, indicating that they too were geologically alive.

ROSETTA · Orbiter launched by ESA in March 2004 with the aim of reaching the comet Churyumov-Gerasimenko by 2014. During February 2007, Rosetta performed a 'swingby' of Mars, capturing stunning images of the planet and its moon, Phobos.

THEMIS · A mission composed of 5 satellites launched by NASA in February 2007. The satellites were dispersed around Earth to study the cause of auroras in the atmosphere. By examining the Northern Lights and similar phenomena, scientists hope to learn more about the functioning of Earth's magnetosphere.

STEREO · The international Solar TErrestrial RElations Observatory, launched in October 2006, uses twin satellite observatories to trace energy and matter flowing between the Sun and Earth. In April 2007, the STEREO team released the first 3-D pictures of the Sun which, it is hoped, may improve understanding of solar physics, and allow scientists to learn more about space weather forecasting.

COROT · A French-led satellite mission launched in December 2006 to search for potentially habitable planets. In May 2007, COROT's telescope identified its first new planet, a giant world similar to Jupiter but hotter and at least 1·3 times larger. The massive planet – named Corot-exo-1b – is 1,500 light-years from Earth in the constellation Monoceros.

NASA's CENTENNIAL CHALLENGES · SPACE GLOVE

In 2005, NASA set a series of Centennial Challenges in an attempt to encourage innovation in the design of materials for space exploration [see *Schott's Almanac 2006*]. One of the original challenges offered $250,000 to the first person who successfully created a space glove that maximised movement while maintaining protection. In May 2007, Peter Homer, an engineer from Maine, USA, became the first person to win one of NASA's Centennial Challenges, when he was awarded $200,000 for his home-made space glove. Homer used a standard rubber glove as his base, and created the Dacron-coated design on his dining room table. (Homer sourced most of his materials from eBay.) The remaining $50,000 went unclaimed, since there were no takers for the challenge to create a 'mechanical counter-pressure glove'.

SOME INVENTIONS OF NOTE · 2006–07

{OCT 2006} · A team at Duke University, USA, performed a series of successful tests on a device that creates an 'invisibility cloak'. The gizmo, constructed from 'metamaterial', succeeded in deflecting microwaves around a small copper cylinder and restoring them on the other side – as if they had passed directly through the object. {NOV} · The Italcementi Group developed a titanium dioxide coating for buildings that can destroy smog in the surrounding atmosphere. The coating is being used in paints, plaster, and other building materials. {DEC} · Toshiba developed plastic 'paper' that can be reused up to 500 times. The technology utilises heat-sensitive pigments that switch from white to black at one temperature, and from black to white at another, allowing work to be printed and later erased. ❦ Brinker Technology of Aberdeen adapted the principle of blood clotting to develop a system to fix leaking pipes. Small polymer cube blobs are added 'upstream' of a leak, from where they travel to form a temporary fix. {JAN 2007} · Electrolux invented a pair of shoes that 'hoover' while you walk. The Dustmate shoe (or Shoover, as it is more aptly known) has a small rechargeable vacuum engine in its sole, which sucks up dust as you perambulate. {FEB} · 6 blind patients had their eyesight partially restored by a prototype 'bionic eye'. The device, developed at the Californian Doheny Eye Institute, is implanted onto the retina, from where it receives images from a tiny camera mounted onto a pair of glasses. {MAR} · Dutch inventors produced an aerodynamic windproof umbrella that will not turn inside out during gales. An asymmetric design allows the brolly to withstand winds up to gale force 10. ❦ American engineering graduate John Cornwell developed a robotic fridge that can eject chilled cans of beer to thirsty drinkers waiting across the room. ❦ The US Army developed vehicles fitted with V-shaped steel undersides to deflect the blast from roadside bombs &c. Tests in Iraq proved the design to be highly effective – after 200 sorties, no soldiers had been killed. ❦ British engineers developed a gadget which could cut the energy consumption of fridges by up to 30%. The 'e-cube' overrides the fridge's thermostat to judge the temperature of the *food* and not the *air* inside a fridge. (The air temperature will temporarily rise whenever the door is opened, forcing normal sensors to activate the cooling mechanism needlessly.) {MAY} · Nokia applied for a US patent for a system that can warn cell phone users when lightning is striking nearby. {JUN} · The US Army developed a remote-controlled robot which could retrieve injured soldiers from the theatre of war. The Battlefield Extraction-Assist Robot (BEAR) can lift >135kg while traversing bumpy terrain, and should be ready for field tests in 5 years' time. ❦ Italy's National Research Council developed a pill that expands in the stomach and sates the appetite. It is hoped that this pill, manufactured from hydrogel, could be used to help the obese shed those pounds. {JUL} · Scientists at Southampton University produced a tiny generator that is powered by natural vibrations alone. The generator could be used in situations where battery replacement is impossible, problematic, or awkward – such as in cardiac pacemakers.

INTERNATIONAL PATENTS

The World Intellectual Property Organisation received *c.*145,300 applications for international patents in 2006, an increase of 6·4% since 2005. The Patent Cooperation Treaty (PCT) allows inventors to file just one application which provides protection for their invention in a number of countries simultaneously. The industry sectors with the most patents published in 2006 were: telecommunications (10·5%), pharmaceuticals (10·4%), and information technology (10·4%). The countries and companies applying for the most PCT patents in 2006 were:

Most international applications

Country	*est. 2006 applications*
1 .. United States	49,555
2 .. Japan	26,906
3 .. Germany	16,929
4 .. Republic of Korea	5,935
5 .. France	5,902
6 .. UK	5,045

Most company applications

Company	*country*	*applications*
Philips Elec.	Netherlands	2,495
Matsushita	Japan	2,344
Siemens	Germany	1,480
Nokia	Finland	1,036
Bosch	Germany	962

(No UK company made the top 50)

Northeast Asian countries accounted for 25·3% of all PCT patent filings in 2006.

CELEBRITY PATENTS

In December 2006, Google released a Patent Search feature that allows users to sift through the *c.*7 million patents registered at the US Patent and Trademark Office, 1790–mid-2006. Fairly quickly, curious users began to search for patents registered by celebrities and, in January 2007, the blog Ironic Sans compiled a list. A selection appears below, along with information provided by the USPTO:

Jamie Lee Curtis · INFANT GARMENT 'A disposable infant garment' which includes 'moisture-proof pockets' for 'one or more clean-up wipers'.
[Patent 4753647, filed 1987]

Edward Van Halen · MUSICAL INSTRUMENT SUPPORT · 'A supporting device for stringed musical instruments' which permits 'total freedom of the player's hands', allowing for 'new techniques and sounds previously unknown'.
[Patent 4656917, filed 1985]

Marlon Brando · DRUMHEAD TENSIONING DEVICE · Fiendishly complex design for drum tension adjuster.
[Patent 6812392, filed 2002]

Julie Newmar · PANTYHOSE SHAPING BAND FOR CHEEKY DERRIERE RELIEF · 'Pantyhose wherein a panty portion is made of a semielastic fabric'. 'An elastic shaping band is attached to the rear panty portion ... and fits between the wearer's buttocks to delineate the wearer's derriere in cheeky relief'.
[Patent 3914799, filed 1974]

Michael Jackson · METHOD & MEANS FOR CREATING ANTI-GRAVITY ILLUSION · 'A system for allowing a shoe wearer to lean forwardly beyond his centre of gravity by virtue of wearing a specially designed pair of shoes' that contain 'a specially designed heel slot'.
[Patent 5255452, filed 1992]

SCI, TECH, NET WORDS OF NOTE

SAT TAGS · GPS satellite markers that track the whereabouts of animals (or product shipments) in the wild. *Also* GEOSLAVERY · using technology (such as GPS tracking and biometric scanning) to track the location and activity of workers (or prisoners).

NETROOTS · online grass-roots support for a political candidate.

CROWDSOURCING · where companies use the expertise and resources of the online community to solve a problem.

GOOGTUBE · the entity formed by the merger of Google and YouTube.

FLOG · a 'fake blog' run by a company or marketing department posing as a real-life consumer.

FOLKSONOMY · user-generated index to online content, created by linking descriptive TAGs to content. *Hence* TAGGING · adding descriptive tags to online content to aid searching.

UPGRAGE · 'upgrade rage' experienced by those installing *Windows Vista* &c.

EXERGAMING · the unlikely combination of computer games and exercise.

SITELETS *or* MICROSITES · temporary sites dedicated to a niche subject, or set up in response to a particular event.

ZERO WASTE · [1] using sophisticated recycling to minimise or eliminate waste; [2] factoring after-use recycling into the manufacture of a product.

HAFNIUM · a metal used to make nuclear reactors that is expected to revolutionise micro-chip technology.

INFOMANIA · inability to concentrate on a single task because of interruptions from email, phones, IMs, &c.

GLOBISH · a simplified form of English that uses basic syntax and 1,500 words; codified by Jean-Paul Nerrière, a retired IBM VP, to facilitate communication.

DRM · Digital Rights Management – technology used to control copyrighted digital material, like songs and movies.

WILF · unlikely neologism for aimlessly surfing the net; supposedly from 'What Was I Looking For?'.

DDOS · Distributed Denial of Service, where websites are overwhelmed by malicious visits that crash servers, cut bandwidth, and render sites inoperable. In May 2007, Russia was accused of launching a DDOS attack on Estonia.

GREAT FIREWALL OF CHINA · attempt by Beijing to control the internet.

LIFECASTING · web-casting all of one's activities – 24 hours a day.

CYBER-VETTING · using the web to assess the (inter)NET REP(utation) of potential employees/employers/lovers.

BUCCANERD · internet pirates whose booty is copyright films, music, or software. *Yarrrr!*

NERDCORE · a 'hardcore nerd'. *Also* NERD RAPTURE · the ecstasy of 'gadget freaks' when confronted by objects like Apple's iPhone – known as THE GOD MACHINE or THE JESUS PHONE.

MACOLYTE · one who worships at the altar of all things Apple.

SCI, TECH, NET WORDS OF NOTE cont.

PODSLURPING · illicit copying of data to a portable storage device (e.g. iPod).

HACTIVISTS · hacker activists who (ab)use the web as a weapon.

VC² · Viewer-Created Content. *Also* UGC · User Generated Content.

ECO-ANXIETY · concern over environmental doomsday scenarios, and the damage done by one's carbon footprint.

'meh' · a dismissive online shrug.

NPs · the New Puritans who eschew hedonism, consumerism, &c., to live a simpler, greener, and more ethical life.

BLOGOLA · fees/bribes paid to bloggers.

TWITTER · a micro-blogging site that one updates via text message.

TIME SHIFTING · using TiVo, SKY+, podcasts, &c., to consume media at a time (and location) of one's choosing.

WITRICITY · wireless electricity that could be used to power a laptop over a room-sized distance.

DIGERATI · elite members of online communities and the computer industry; from DIGital litERATI.

NETWORK PROMISCUITY · tendency for users of social networking sites (Facebook, MySpace, Bebo, &c.) – and websites more generally – to spread their membership widely. *Also* FACE vs SPACE · the 'war' between Facebook and MySpace. *Also* FACEHOOKED · an addiction to Facebook. *Also* FACE-BLOCKING · where companies ban their employee access to Facebook &c.

EARCON · a branding 'audio icon'.

SNAKE-OIL SALESMEN · EasyJet's term for unscrupulous carbon-offset traders.

RED RING OF DEATH · flashing red lights on the Xbox 360 console, which indicate a major hardware failure. *Also* BRICKING · because the broken Xbox is as much use as a brick. *Also* COFFINS · the boxes used to return consoles.

MEGANICHE · based on the idea that, because of the sheer scale of the web, even a relatively rococo subject area can attract significant web traffic.

TRIPLE BOTTOM LINE · the aspiration that companies will take into account People, Planet, and Profit when judging the success of a project.

NATURE DEFICIT DISORDER · where kids are strangers to Mother Nature.

MOST HATED WEB WORDS

A June 2007 survey for the Lulu Blooker Prize asked web users the words most likely to make them 'wince, shudder or want to bang your head on the keyboard'.

1 .... folksonomy†
2 .... blogosphere
3 .... blog
4 .... netiquette
5 .... blook
6 .... webinar
7 .... vlog
8 ..... social networking
9 .... cookie
10 .... wiki

† Coined by Thomas Vander Wal in 2002. [See p.194]

CONSOLE TIMELINE

'72 .... first home console, *Magnavox Odyssey*
'75 .... *Atari Pong* launched
'75 ... improved *Magnavox Odyssey* 100 & 200
'76 .... *Atari Super Pong* released
'76 ... *Coleco Telstar*, first to use AY-3-8500 chip
'76 ..... first programmable system – *Channel F*
'77 .... *Atari 2600* first to use plug-in cartridges
'77 .... the *Telstar Alpha* launched
'77 ...... *Odyssey 4000* released; 8 colour games
'79 .... *Atari 400* released, first 8-bit
'80 .... Mattel's *Intellivision*, first 16-bit
'80 .... Namco released *Pac-Man*
'82 .... *Atari 5200* released
'82 ... *ColecoVision* feat. *Donkey Kong* launched
'82 .... *ZX Spectrum* launched in UK
'82 .... PC *Commodore 64* entered market
'83 .... Nintendo launched *Famicom* (later *NES*) in Japan
'85 .... *Amiga 1000*, first multi-media PC
'85 ... *Tetris* first developed to be played on PC
'85/6. Nintendo's *NES* launched in US/Europe
'86 .... *Atari 7800* competed with Nintendo
'86 .... *Sega Master System* launched
'87 .... the first *Final Fantasy* game came out
'89 .... *Sega Mega Drive*, first 16-bit console
'89 .... Nintendo *Gameboy*, first handheld
'89 .... Atari launched colour handheld *Lynx*
'91 ...... Nintendo released *Super NES* in USA
'93 .... Atari's *Jaguar* flopped
'93 ..... innovative shoot 'em up *Doom* released
'95 ... Sega *Saturn* bt *PlayStation* to release first
'95 ... Sony *PlayStation* launched in US/Europe
'97 .... *Nintendo 64* last cartridge-based console
'97 .... *PlayStation*'s 20 millionth unit sold
'98 .... *Grand Theft Auto* debut
'99 .... Sega *Dreamcast*, first internet enabled
'00 .... Sony *PlayStation 2* launched & sold out
'00 .... PC game *The Sims* released
'01 ... Nintendo *GameCube*, interactive gaming
'01 .... Microsoft *XBox*, built-in hard-drive
'01 .... Sega stopped making consoles
'04 ..... Nintendo *DS*, handheld with 2 screens
'05 .... portable Sony *PSP* launched
'05 ...... Microsoft *Xbox 360*, online capability
'06 .... Sony *PlayStation 3*, HD games
'06 .... Nintendo *Wii*, wireless controller

BEST-SELLING VIDEO GAMES

In January 2007, the *Independent* compiled a list of the best-selling video game franchises of all time, confirming the market domination of Japanese developers. The top franchises are:

Title	*developer*	*units*
Mario	Nintendo	193m
Pokémon	Nintendo	155m
Final Fantasy	Square Enix	68m
Madden NFL	EA	56m
The Sims	Maxis/EA	54m
Grand Theft Auto	Rockstar	50m
Donkey Kong	Nintendo	48m
Legend of Zelda	Nintendo	47m
Sonic the Hedgehog	Sega	44m
Gran Turismo	Sony	44m

Nielsen/NetRatings said that, in March 07, 37% of US adults online owned a games console.

VIRTUAL BAD DRIVERS

Frequent players of racing video games are more likely to be aggressive drivers, according to a German study published by the *Journal of Experimental Psychology* in March 2007. The research supports the theory that 'media-primers', such as video games, can affect how people react in real life [see p.148]. To win racing games, players are encouraged to break the law (driving on pavements, at high speed, crashing into other gamers, and so on) – thereby linking risk-taking with feelings of exhilaration. The study indicated that these links were particularly strong in young males who, after playing racing games, reported taking greater risks on the road in real life. It was suggested that those who played virtual racing games less frequently were more cautious drivers.

WEBBY AWARDS

Awarded by the International Academy of Digital Arts and Sciences, the Webby Awards reward excellence in web design, innovation, and functionality. Below is a selection of the winners at the 11th annual awards in 2007:

Activism .... *greenpeace.org/apple*
Best homepage .... *sony.com*
Best practices .... *flickr.com*
Best writing .... *howstuffworks.com*
Blog – political .... *truthdig.com*
Community .... *flickr.com*
Education .... *howstuffworks.com*
Fashion .... *zoozoom.com*
Humour .... *theonion.com*
Lifestyle .... *bp.com/carbonfootprint*
Magazine .... *mediastorm.org*
Movies .... *panslabyrinth.com*
Music .... *last.fm*
News .... *bbc.co.uk/news*
Newspaper .... *guardian.co.uk*
Politics .... *opensecrets.org*
Sports .... *thereggiebushproject.com*

NET POPULATION

747 million people (aged >15) used the internet in January 2007 – according to comScore Networks. Below are the countries with the most internet users:

MILLION INTERNET USERS (≥15)

Country	*Jan 06*	*Jan 07*	*change*
USA	150·9	153·4	+2%
China	72·4	86·8	+20%
Japan	51·5	53·7	+4%
Germany	31·2	32·2	+3%
UK	29·8	30·1	+1%
S Korea	24·3	26·4	+8%
France	23·7	24·6	+4%
India	15·9	21·1	+33%
Canada	18·3	20·4	+11%
Italy	16·0	18·1	+13%
World	676·9	746·9	+10%

DOMAIN NAMES

By 2006, 120m Top Level Domain (TLD) names had been registered – 65m of which were .com or .net. Top Level Domain country codes (ccTLD), of which there are >240 globally, also experienced growth, especially in registrations in China (.cn). Below are the ccTLDs with the most registrations:

1	.de	Germany
2	.uk	United Kingdom
3	.eu	European Union
4	.nl	Netherlands
5	.cn	China
6	.it	Italy
7	.ar	Argentina
8	.us	United States
9	.br	Brazil
10	.ch	Switzerland

[Source: VeriSign · Zooknic, 2007]

WEBLOG AWARDS

The Weblogs are independent awards, nominated and voted for by the public. Some of the winners in 2007 were:

Best new blog .... *saynotocrack.com*
Group blog .... *lifehacker.com*
Writing .... *waiterrant.net*
Blog design .... *uk.gizmodo.com*
Topical .... *postsecret.blogspot.com*
Best-kept secret . *thepioneerwoman.com*
Humorous .... *gofugyourself.typepad.com*
Blog of the year . *postsecret.blogspot.com*

BLOOKER PRIZE

The 'Blooker Prizes' reward books that started life as blogs. The top prize (£5,000) in 2007 went to former US soldier Colby Buzzell's wartime account: *My War: Killing Time in Iraq.*

WEB 2·0 &c.

'Web 2·0' refers to the perception that the net has shifted from being an information source to a 'participatory web', in which users contribute and collaborate via blogs, wikis, social networking, and other user-focused environments. ('Web 2·0' was apparently coined in 2004 by Dale Dougherty, during a brainstorming session for O'Reilly Media.) Although in some cases enabled by technological progress, Web 2·0 is not a hardware or software development so much as a 'set of principles and practices' that prioritize collective intelligence. As noted by Susannah Fox and Mary Madden in a report for the Pew Internet Project, Web 2·0 replaces 'the authoritative heft of traditional institutions with the surging wisdom of crowds'. A September 2005 essay by Tim O'Reilly attempted to map some of the axiomatic differences between Web 1·0 and Web 2·0 [see right]. ❦ While frequently derided as conceptually (and otherwise) problematic, the ubiquity of the phrase 'Web 2·0' may be taken as a sign of its usefulness. Many offshoots have developed, including: 'Travel 2·0' [traveller 'empowerment' via discussion forums &c. – *USA Today*]; 'Library 2.0' ['user-friendly' information flows at modernised libraries – *Information Today*]; and 'Gaming 3·0' [console games featuring dynamic, user-generated content – *BusinessWeek.com*]. Splendidly, a 2005 *Economist* article expressed fears of a 'Bubble 2·0', whereby an excess of hype, and a paucity of sound business models, could precipitate a second tech bubble, with stock market consequences similar to those seen in the 1990s.

O'Reilly's 'Web 1·0 *vs* Web 2·0'

Web 1·0	*Web 2·0*
Britannica Online	Wikipedia
Personal websites	blogging
Page views	cost per click
Publishing	participation
Content management systems	wikis
Directories	tagging
DoubleClick	Google AdSense
Taxonomy	folksonomy

ONLINE CONTENT SPEND

The average online Briton spent £36 on streaming or downloading audio and video content from the net in 2006. Men spent 40% more than women, averaging £3·58 a month (compared to £2·57). The average monthly spend, by age, in 2006 was:

Age	*£/month*
16–24	5·34
25–34	3·57
35–44	3·08
45–54	2·78
>55	1·85

About 75% of online Britons have listened to music via the internet. Tabulated below are the most popular genres of audio content, by method of consumption:

Streaming		*Downloading*		*Podcasting*	
Music	55%	Music	38%	Music	26%
News	22%	Comedy	10%	Comedy	5%
Comedy	18%	Books	7%	Books	4%

[Source: Nielsen/NetRatings]

INTERNET APPLICATIONS

Internet applications are downloadable programs operated via the internet, such as those that run games, instant messaging and VOIP. Below are the most popular:

Application	*unique audience (m)*
MSN Messenger	14·7
Windows Media Player	14·0
RealPlayer	7·9
Apple QuickTime	7·1
iTunes	5·6
Yahoo! Messenger	3·0
Skype	2·3
Google Earth	1·7
AOL Companion	1·4
LimeWire	1·3

[Source: Nielsen/NetRatings · 2007]

25·3m Britons used an internet application in November 2006, according to Nielsen/NetRatings. On average, Britons spend 3·5 hours each month using these applications, although some gaming sites proved much more popular (or, addictive). UK users of Pacific Poker play for an average of 10 hours 17 minutes a month.

MALWARE

MALWARE (MALicious softWARE) is that which is specifically designed to infiltrate and harm computers. The category includes TROJAN HORSES (that contain harmful programs), WORMS (self-replicating programs), VIRUSES (that distribute copies of themselves), and SPYWARE (that surreptitiously collects user data). According to IT security firm Sophos, 30% of all malware is written in China, and 14·2% in Brazil. In 2006, the top ten countries hosting malware on the web were:

Country	%
USA	34·2
China	31·0
Russia	9·5
Netherlands	4·7
Ukraine	3·2
France	1·8
Taiwan	1·7
Germany	1·5
Hong Kong	1·0
Korea	0·9
Others	10·5

According to the Sophos 2007 security report, the amount of image spam sent in 2006 increased from 18·5% in January to 35·1% in December. Image spam eschews text in order to escape detection by anti-spam filters. The images are often placed one on top of another to create 'noise' that further complicates the message, and makes each one unique. Despite some efforts to reduce the problem, the US was the worst nation for relaying spam in 2006. The top spamming countries were:

Country	%
USA	22·0
China (inc. HK)	15·9
South Korea	7·4
France	5·4
Spain	5·1
Poland	4·5
Brazil	3·5
Italy	3·2
Germany	3·0
UK	1·9
Others	28·0

Named after a section of the penal code in Nigeria where many such scams originate, '419 scams' typically offer large amounts of money in an attempt to extract either confidential information or cash. Disguises used by scammers in 2006 included a 19-year-old who claimed to have discovered a herbal cure for AIDS, and a dying KGB agent claiming to hold the secrets to the JFK assassination.

STN SIGNIFICA

Some (in)significa(nt) Sci, Tech, Net footnotes to the year. ❦ Princeton announced the closure of its ESP lab, the Princeton Engineering Anomalies Research laboratory, after 28 years. The lab claimed modest results but suffered a degree of ridicule. ❦ The Chinese government forced online gaming companies to install anti-addiction software, limiting those under 18 to just three consecutive hours of play per day. ❦ Google banned ads for websites that provide essay, dissertation, and thesis-writing services. Google also blacklisted sites with 'unacceptable content' – such as advertising for weapons, prostitution, drugs, tobacco, and 'miracle cures'. ❦ Parents in the UK use the internet to spy on their children, according to research by helpline Parentline Plus. 41% of parents admitted checking their computer to see which sites their children had visited, and 25% admitted to reading their children's private emails. ❦ The Maldives became the first country to open an embassy in *Second Life*. Later, Kan Suzuki became the first Japanese politician to open an office in the virtual world. ❦ The ultra-violent video game *Manhunt 2* was banned by censors in the UK, who criticised its 'casual sadism' and 'unremitting bleakness'. ❦ According to Screen Digest, the market value of Massively Multiplayer Online Games (MMOGs) reached $1bn outside Asia; *World of Warcraft* was the most popular subscription game, accounting for 54% of the market [see p.243]. ❦ Sony apologised to Church of England officials after Manchester Cathedral was featured in the video game *Resistance: Fall of Man*. The offending scene used the Cathedral as the site of a bloody shoot-out between a US soldier and a fright of aliens. ❦ Research by the School of Information Sciences at UC Berkeley indicated that Facebook users tended to come from wealthier homes and were more likely to have attended college than users of MySpace. ❦ Human rights organisation Privacy International published a ranking of web companies' handling of personal data. Google ranked worst for privacy, because of the large quantity of user data it compiles, and the absence – according to Privacy International – of a coherent privacy policy. Google said the findings were based on numerous 'inaccuracies and misunderstandings' about its services. ❦ A study by human resources firm Croner revealed that 39% of UK bloggers admitted to posting online damaging or derogatory details about their workplace. ❦ The Electronic Sports World Cup grand final was held in Paris in July 2007. More than 750 eager gamers qualified from around the world to compete in games such as *Quake 4*, *Warcraft 3*, and *Pro Evolution Soccer 4*. The prize money totalled $200,000. ❦ Research by WebFetch revealed significant variances in results from different search engines, indicating the limitations of relying on one search engine alone. Comparing Google, Yahoo!, MSN, and Ask, WebFetch found only 0·6% of 776,435 first-page search results were the same across the 4 different engines. ❦ In July 2007, the BBC launched its iPlayer, which allows users to download a range of BBC programmes for free. Programmes are currently available for up to 7 days after broadcast, and can be stored on the iPlayer for up to 30 days.

EUROPEAN INTERNET ACTIVITY

According to Mediascope Europe, in a typical 5-day week in 2006, 53% of Europeans used the web (40% in 2005). A breakdown of net usage is given below:

Country	*% weekday use*
Norway	80
Netherlands	76
Sweden	75
Denmark	72
UK†	61
France	56
Germany	51
Belgium	50
Spain	47
Italy	32

† 74% of UK internet use is personal; 26% is work-related. On average, UK users spend 11·3 hours per week online.

Below are the most visited website genres in Europe, by percentage of users viewing:

Genre (% viewing)	*2005*	*2006*
Search engines	84	88
Email	76	85
News	57	63
Travel	52	53
Local information	45	51
Banking & finance	47	50
Holidays	49	49
Music	41	47
Shopping	42	38
Auction	35	36
Health	26	32

ONLINE DATING & LIES

The suspicion that the internet provides the perfect forum for embellishment and re-invention was confirmed in February 2007 by research proving that most people lie on their online dating profile. Jeff Hancock at New York's Cornell University took 40 male and 40 female New York singletons and diligently assessed their physiques. Hancock found that nine out of ten participants had lied at least once on their forms – most commonly about their weight. Inevitably, all the women that lied about their weight claimed to be lighter than they were; in contrast, men were more likely to overstate their height. Fortunately, the fibs were mostly minor and unlikely to be noticed in any face-to-face meetings. The average difference between profile and reality was: 6lbs in weight, ⅓ of an inch in height, and 5 months in age.

PENETRATION OF TECHNOLOGY IN THE EU

The % of European households with access to various technologies in 2006:

Country (% access to)	*computer*	*internet*	*broadband*
France	55·8	49·0	19·6
Germany	76·0	66·3	17·0
Ireland	58·0	51·0	9·1
Italy	57·0	45·4	14·5
Spain	55·0	43·0	14·5
UK	73·0	61·1	20·8

[Source: Screen Digest 2006 · PC & internet penetration/household, broadband penetration/capita]

TOTAL ONLINE SPENDING · UK

Verdict Research revealed that British consumers' online spending had increased 33·4% between 2005 and 2006. It was predicted that by 2011 online sales would be worth £28·1bn, which is *c*.8·9% of the UK's total retail sales. UK online spending:

Year	Spending	Year	Spending	Year	Spending
1997	£100m	2001	£3·2bn	2005	£8·2bn
1998	£400m	2002	£3·8bn	2006	£10·9bn
1999	£1bn	2003	£5bn	[Figures relate to physical	
2000	£1·8bn	2004	£6·4bn	goods. Tickets &c. not inc.]	

L33T SPEAK

'Leet speak' is an internet slang language in which certain letters, usually vowels, are replaced by numbers and symbols to form a code. It was originally developed in the 1980s by hackers, but is now more commonly used in chat rooms and by online gamers. Leet speak has also been used to circumvent filters that bar certain words (e.g. porn has become pr0n). In its most simple form, just four vowels are replaced (A=4, E=3, I=1, O=0), so the word 'leet' becomes l33t. Although leet speak is based on the English language, there are many phrases and words unique to it. According to the BBC, some of the most commonly used leet speak words and phrases are:

Leet	*meaning*
0wn3d	to have been beaten
w00t	used as a term of victory
13wt	treasure; a misspelling of 'loot'
h4x0r	hacker
d34d	dead
f00	fool
ph33r	fear (e.g. 'ph33r m3!')
j00	you (e.g. 'j00 d34d f00')
m3	me

Because of its flexibility, a much more sophisticated form of the language – known as 'ultra leet' – has evolved. Ultra leet uses a complete alphabet of numbers and symbols – so, for example, the word 'leet' becomes '|_337'. The ultra leet alphabet is:

<table>
<tr><td>A</td><td>B</td><td>C</td><td>D</td><td>E</td><td>F</td><td>G</td><td>H</td><td>I</td><td>J</td><td>K</td><td>L</td><td>M</td><td>N</td><td>O</td><td>P</td><td>Q</td><td>R</td><td>S</td><td>T</td><td>U</td><td>V</td><td>W</td><td>X</td><td>Y</td><td>Z</td></tr>
<tr><td>4</td><td>|3</td><td>C</td><td>|)</td><td>3</td><td>|=</td><td>6</td><td>|-|</td><td>1</td><td>_|</td><td>|<</td><td>|_</td><td>|\/|</td><td>||</td><td>0</td><td>|></td><td>Q</td><td>|2</td><td>5</td><td>7</td><td>|_|</td><td>\/</td><td>|/|</td><td>><</td><td>`/</td><td>Z</td></tr>
</table>

ECO-FRIENDLY ELECTRONICS

Greenpeace ranked the green credentials of a range of electronics manufacturers in April 2007, rating their recycling policies and the levels of toxicity of their products. Below are the company rankings, along with their scores from 10 (best) to 1 (worst):

Company	*score*
Lenovo	8·0
Nokia	7·3
Sony Ericsson	7·0
Dell	7·0
Samsung	6·3
Motorola	6·3
Fujitsu-Siemens	6·0
Hewlett-Packard	5·6
Acer	5·3
Toshiba	4·3
Sony	4·0
LGE	3·6
Panasonic	3·6
Apple	2·7

Travel & Leisure

One half of the world cannot understand the pleasures of the other.
— JANE AUSTEN (1775–1817)

HEELYS

According to the manufacturer, Heelys are 'sneakers with a single stealth wheel in each heel that allow "heelers" to walk, roll, and grind their way across streets, school campuses and skate parks'. The shoes are protected by a slew of patents, including one that covers the stance adopted by heelers: 'feet staggered, toes up and heels gliding'. Since 2000, Heelys have established themselves as playground favourites in >60 countries, selling >9m pairs. Despite some financial commentators warning that Heelys may be too faddy for long-term investment, in 2006 Heelys Inc. posted net sales of $188·2m (an increase of 328% on 2005) and, according to AP, the company has a market capitalisation of close to $1bn. ❦ The 'shoes that roll' were the brainchild of Roger Adams, who was born in 1954 in Tacoma, Washington, where his parents owned the Adams-Tacoma Roller Bowl – the largest roller-skating rink in the Pacific Northwest. As a child, Adams worked at the rink repairing skates. However, the idea for Heelys only came to him in his forties, when he was disillusioned with his work as a mental-health supervisor and 'burned out' by the divorce from his wife of 21 years. As he told *MSNBC* 'if there was one thing that started it – it was a mid-life crisis'. Adams created the first ever Heely by eviscerating a pair of Nikes with a hot butter knife and implanting skateboard wheels. ❦ Inevitably, Heelys (and the copy-cats that have rolled onto their bandwagon) have attracted safety concerns. The US pressure group World Against Toys Causing Harm included Heelys amongst its list of 10 'worst toys' of 2006 – and the boxes in which Heelys come caution 'there is no way to heel and/or grind without running the risk of serious bodily harm, including head injury, spinal injury, or even death'. A number of medical professionals have warned of the risks of wearing Heelys, and many schools and shopping centres have banned wheeled shoes for reasons of public safety. More soberly, the Royal Society for the Prevention of Accidents recommends purchasing the safety gear listed on the Heely website. ❦ Stung by stories blaming their shoes for causing accidents, the Heelys Inc. website contains 'safety rules of thumb' and advice on 'common courtesy' – 'crowded public areas are not good places for heeling'. Indeed, in April 2007, Heelys published the results of an independent analysis of 2 million US Consumer Production Safety Cmsn reports on product-related injuries from 2001–06. This analysis rather splendidly concluded that 'wheeled footwear is safer than nearly all other popular sports with the exception of table tennis, billiards, and bowling'.

STREET NAMES & CLASS

Research by Richard Webber, of University College London, suggests that road names can indicate the social class of residents. Webber analysed 745,000 road names in the United Kingdom, cross-referencing them with data used by banks and financial services companies to judge wealth by postcode. This database, released in October 2006, suggested that the wealthiest live in roads with names like 'Badgers Wood', whereas the least well off lived in roads with names like 'Frederick Street'.

Road name beginnings		*Road name endings*	
Most well off residents	*Least well off residents*	*Most well off residents*	*Least well off residents*
Badgers	Frederick	Wood	Street
Copse	Midland	Common	Walk
Firs · Highlands	Smith · Arthur	Chase · Orchard	Square · Path

UK MOTORWAYS

M1 ... London – Yorkshire
M2 ... London – Faversham
M3 ... London – Southampton
M4 ... London – South Wales
M5 ... Birmingham – Exeter
M6 ... Catthorpe – Carlisle
M8 ... Edinburgh – nr. Greenock
M9 ... Edinburgh – Dunblane
M10 ... St Albans spur
M11 ... London – Cambridge
M18 ... Rotherham – Goole
M20 ... London – Folkestone
M23 ... London – Gatwick
M25 ... London orbital
M26 ... M20 – M25 spur
M27 ... Southampton bypass
M32 ... M4 – Bristol spur
M40 ... London – Birmingham
M41 ... London – West Cross
M42 ... Birmingham – Measham
M45 ... Dunchurch spur
M48 ... Severn Bridge
M49 ... Avonmouth – Severn Crossing
M50 ... Ross spur
M53 ... Chester – Birkenhead
M54 ... M6 – Telford
M55 ... Preston – Blackpool
M56 ... Manchester – Chester
M57 ... Liverpool outer ring
M58 ... Liverpool – Wigan
M60 ... Manchester ring road
M61 ... Manchester – Preston
M62 ... Liverpool – Hull
M65 ... Calder Valley
M66 ... Bury easterly bypass
M67 ... Manchester Hyde – Denton
M69 ... Coventry – Leicester
M73 ... Maryville – Mollinsburn
M74 ... Glasgow – Gretna
M77 ... Ayr Road route
M80 ... Stirling – Haggs
M90 ... Inverkeithing – Perth
M180 ... South Humberside
M181 ... Bottesford – Scunthorpe
M271 ... Upton – Totton
M275 ... Hilsea – Portsmouth
M602 ... Eccles – Manchester
M606 ... Cleckheaton – Bradford
M621 ... Leeds southern motorway
M876 ... M80 – Kincardine Bridge

NORTHERN IRELAND

M1 ... Belfast – Dungannon
M2 ... Belfast – Antrim/Ballymena
M3 ... Belfast Cross – Harbour Bridge
M5 ... M2 – Greencastle
M12 ... M1 – Craigavon
M22 ... Antrim – Randalstown

HOUSEHOLDS WITH REGULAR USE OF CAR(S)

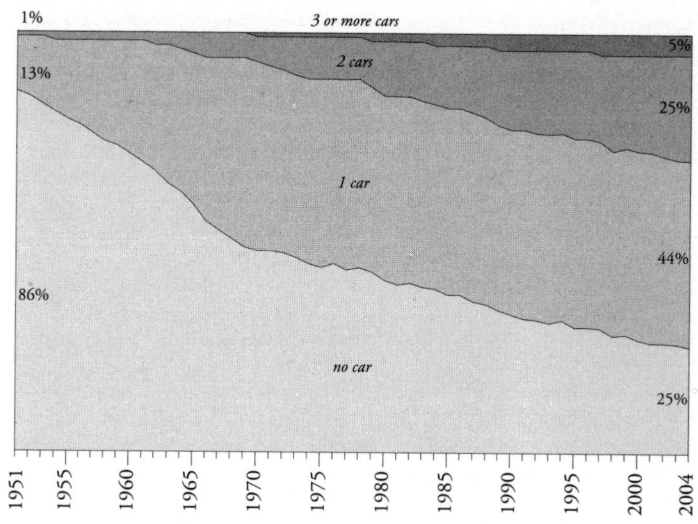

WEARING SEAT BELTS

The rate of seat belt wearing in the UK was shown by a TRL survey in April 2006:

% wearing	*Drivers*			*Front-seat passengers*				*Rear-seat passengers*			
Age	17–29	30–59	>60	0–13	14–29	30–59	>60	0–13	14–29	30–59	>60
♂	92	90	94	97	89	91	94	94	62	48	75
♀	95	97	96	98	94	96	97	95	72	71	78

SPEED LIMITS & SPEEDING

Below is a breakdown of car speeds on various types of roads in Britain, in 2006:

30mph *speed zone*	
<20mph	7%
20–29	43
30–34	30
35–39	15
40–44	4
45–49	1
>50	0

average speed · 30mph

Dual carriageway 70mph	
<30mph	0%
30–39	0
40–49	3
50–59	15
60–64	15
65–69	19
70–79	34
>80	13

average speed · 69mph

Motorway 70mph	
<50mph	3%
50–59	12
60–64	12
65–69	17
70–74	20
75–79	17
80–89	16
>90	3

average speed · 71mph

VEHICLE COLLISIONS

A study released by the Highways Agency in February 2007 found that 4×4 cars (SUVs) are more likely to overturn than other vehicles. However, collisions in 'Chelsea tractors' are less likely to result in serious injury, as illustrated below:

FORM OF LOSS OF CONTROL (%)							INJURIES BY SEVERITY (%)			
no loss of control	*skid*	*skid & overturn*	*jack-knife*	*jack-knife & o/turn*	*overturn*		*uninjured*	*slight*	*serious*	*fatal*
83·4	13·1	2·1	0	0	1·4	Car	38·3	54·7	6·2	0·7
83·2	11·1	2·7	0·2	0·3	2·5	SUV	50·2	43·8	5·5	0·5
87·5	9·7	1·5	0	0	1·3	MPV†	42·6	51·8	5·0	0·6
88·9	8·3	0	0	0	2·8	Motorhome	75·0	19·4	5·6	0
86·9	10·3	1·3	0·1	0	1·4	Others‡	41·8	49·7	7·9	0·6

† Multi-Purpose Vehicle; people carriers, e.g. the Renault Espace. ‡ This category will contain some vehicles from the other groups where information about their make and model was unavailable.

MOBILE PHONES & DRIVING

In February 2007, new penalties came into force for driving while using a mobile phone. The maximum fixed penalty was doubled to £60, and up to three points can be added to an offender's licence. In 2005, 13 deaths and 400 injuries were attributed to drivers using hand-held mobile phones. ❦ A study published by the Transport Research Laboratory in April 2007, indicated that talking on the phone while driving was more distracting than chatting to passengers or adjusting the radio. Hands-free phones fared no better: when 30 volunteers drove an 11 mile route in a simulator, those chatting on the phone were much more likely to miss road signs.

CONTRIBUTORY FACTORS IN ROAD ACCIDENTS

Department for Transport figures released in September 2006, illustrated the factors that most commonly contributed to traffic accidents in Great Britain during 2005:

FATAL ACCIDENTS

Contributory factor	*% of accidents*
Loss of control	35
Careless, reckless, or in a hurry	18
Failed to look properly	17
Going too fast for conditions	17
Exceeding speed limit	12
Poor turn/manoeuvre	12
Failed to judge other's path/speed	10
Impaired by alcohol	9

ALL ACCIDENTS

Contributory factor	*% of accidents*
Failed to look properly	32
Failed to judge other's path/speed	18
Careless, reckless, or in a hurry	16
Poor turn/manoeuvre	15
Loss of control	14
Going too fast for conditions	12
Slippery road	10
Pedestrian failed to look properly	9

OBJECTS HIT DURING ROAD ACCIDENTS

Data from the DfT (Road Casualties Great Britain, 2005 Annual Report) showed the objects hit during single vehicle accidents, on all types of roads, during 2005:

Object hit | type of accident	*fatal %*	*serious %*	*slight %*	*all (No.)*
None	1·5	18·4	80·1	41,110
Road sign or traffic signal	3·2	17·4	79·4	1,561
Lamp post	3·6	18·4	78·0	1,871
Telegraph or electricity pole	2·6	16·7	80·7	804
Tree	7·1	24·0	68·9	3,445
Bus stop or shelter	5·6	15·4	79·0	162
Crash barrier	2·8	15·1	82·2	2,409
Submerged	15·2	24·2	60·6	33
Entered ditch	1·8	18·1	80·0	1,846
Other permanent objects	2·5	18·2	79·3	6,553
Total (number)	1,293	11,058	47,445	59,796

MODE OF TRAVEL BY AGE

National Travel Survey figures show the journeys made (by age and mode) in 2005:

Mode (%) age	*<17*	*17–20*	*21–29*	*30–39*	*40–49*	*50–59*	*60–69*	*>70*
Car driver	0	24·2	43·1	56·1	61·5	58·1	49·4	38·5
Car passenger	54·8	24·9	15·5	11·8	11·3	13·8	18·0	21·7
Bus and coach	6·5	15·9	7·8	4·2	3·6	3·9	6·3	10·3
Walk	33·2	24·4	23·7	21·4	17·7	19·5	22·5	23·9
Bicycle	1·7	1·9	1·5	1·5	1·3	1·1	1·0	1·1
Other	3·8	8·6	8·5	5·1	4·6	3·6	2·7	4·5

[Source: Department for Transport, National Travel Survey 2005, Great Britain data]

SEX IN CARS

68% of British adults have had sex in a car, according to a survey conducted in October 2006 by yesinsurance.co.uk. The ten most popular 'passion wagons' were:

1 .... Volvo Estate†
2 .... Mercedes Benz Sprinter Van
3 .... VW Camper Van
4 .... BMW 3 Series Saloon
5 .... Ford Escort
6 .... Audi TT
7 .... Land Rover Discovery
8 .... Porsche Carrera
9 .... VW Golf
10 .... Ford Focus

† The Volvo Estate was first introduced by the Swedish company in 1953. The car was originally called the Duet because it was designed to be 'two cars in one', uniting practicality and pleasure, as well as work and leisure. Since 1953, over 4m Volvo Estates have been sold. Volvo is Latin for 'I roll'.

BLACK CABS AND THE 'KNOWLEDGE'

All licensed London black cab drivers must have 'the Knowledge of London', an encyclopaedic command of the area within a 6 mile (or 9·65km) radius of Charing Cross†, as well as a broad knowledge of Greater London. To acquire the Knowledge, aspirant cabbies study the 'Blue Book' which catalogues the 320 routes (or 'runs') on which they will be examined. Runs consist of a start and end point (e.g. the Public Carriage Office to the British Museum) and – for each run – all 'knowledge boys' are expected to know:

· *the shortest route between the points*
· *points of interest along the route*
· *points of interest in a ¼ mile radius 'dumb-bell' at the end of either point*
· *the shortest reverse route*

Candidates have up to 6 months to learn the first 80 runs in the 'Blue Book', and a further 18 months to learn the remaining 240. Examinations for the Knowledge are run by the Public Carriage Office, and take the form of a complex series of written exams and oral 'appearances', as well as a driving test, a medical assessment, and a criminal record check. ❦ On average, it takes 34 months for an applicant to do the Knowledge and pass the exams. In 2005/06, there were 21,681 black cabs in London and 24,661 licensed drivers. (A brand new TX4 black cab costs *c.*£27,000–£35,000.) ❦ Specialist Knowledges exist for the 9 suburban areas of Greater London; drivers with Suburban licences may only ply for hire within the sectors they have passed.

When the Knowledge was introduced in 1865 it clearly caused some consternation, as the *Journal of the Social Arts* noted in 1869: 'the examination as to the driver's knowledge of town was a great obstacle to many men, for the oldest driver in London might be completely puzzled when examined in that way'. † Charing Cross has served as the traditional centre point of London since 1290, when Queen Elinor died and King Edward decreed that twelve crosses be erected to mark her funeral procession from Lincoln to Westminster Abbey. The final cross was erected near Trafalgar Square, from where all official distances to and from the capital (as well as the scope of the black cab Knowledge) are still calculated.

MOBILES LEFT IN TAXIS

A Pointsec survey of 2,000 taxi drivers in 11 cities worldwide, in November 2006, identified the items most frequently left in taxis. The survey revealed that, in the preceding 6 months, 54,872 mobile phones, 4,718 PDAs, 3,179 laptops, and 923 USB memory sticks had been left in London taxis alone. The number of mobiles left in taxis in cities around the world, over a period of 6 months, are shown below:

City	*lost mobiles*
London	54,872
Mumbai	32,970
Sydney	6,440
Washington DC	6,102
Berlin	6,100
Oslo	3,640
Helsinki	3,023
San Francisco	2,754
Frankfurt	1,647
Munich	1,485
Stockholm	1,192

BICYCLES AND CYCLING

The number of cyclists in London has risen by 83% since 2000, according to May 2007 data from the Greater London Authority. There are an estimated 480,000 journeys made by bicycle across the capital every day. Despite this growth in cycling, the number of cyclists killed or seriously injured on London's roads has fallen by 28% since 2000. ❦ In April 2007, a report by Halifax Home Insurance revealed that a bicycle is stolen every 71 seconds in England. Nearly 440,000 bicycles were reported stolen in 2006, 90% of which had been purloined when left locked up in a public space. The ten worst bicycle theft hotspots in England during 2006 were:

Central London	York	Brighton
Kingston-upon-Thames	Oxford	Portsmouth
Cambridge	Richmond &	Nottingham
Bristol	Twickenham	[Source: Halifax Insurance]

A report by Transport for London's road safety unit, obtained by the *Times* in April 2007, indicated that cyclists who broke the law and jumped red lights were safer than those who stayed in cycle lanes. It seems that by waiting at the lights many cyclists risk being hit by lorries who fail to see them. The risk is greater for female cyclists – 86% of women cyclists killed in London between 1999–2004 were hit by a lorry; for male cyclists the figure was 47%. The unpublished study suggested that women were at a greater risk from being hit by lorries because they were more likely to obey red traffic lights. By 'jumping' red lights, (male) cyclists were less likely to fall victim to a lorry driver's blind spot.

THE VATICAN'S 10 COMMANDMENTS OF DRIVING

In June 2007, the Vatican's Pontifical Council for the Pastoral Care of Migrants and Itinerant People released a 36-page document entitled *Guidelines for the Pastoral Care of the Road.* While the guide noted the opportunities and benefits of driving (visiting the sick, for example), it also warned against the 'psychological regression' that cars can produce, and offered the following ten 'driving commandments':

1	*you shall not kill*
2	*the road shall be a means of communion between people and not of mortal harm*
3	*courtesy, uprightness, and prudence will help you deal with unforeseen events*
4	*be charitable and help your neighbour in need, especially victims of accidents*
5	*cars shall not be an expression of power and domination, and an occasion of sin*†
6	*charitably convince the young and not so young not to drive when they are not in a fit condition to do so*
7	*support the families of accident victims*
8	*bring guilty motorists and their victims together, at the appropriate time, so that they can undergo the liberating experience of forgiveness*
9	*on the road, protect the more vulnerable party*
10	*feel responsible toward others*

† According to Reuters, when asked at a news conference to explain how a car could become an occasion of sin, Cardinal Renato Martino suggested, 'when a car is used as a place for sin' [see p.207].

AIR PASSENGER DUTY INCREASE

On 1 February 2007, the doubling of Air Passenger Duty (APD) (announced in Brown's December 2006 Pre-Budget Report) came into effect. Most passengers flying in February had to pay the extra duty, despite booking their tickets before Brown's statement. The increased duty, added to all tickets, is intended to discourage flying and counteract its environmental effects. The new rates of APD are below:

Economy European flights (including internal UK flights)	£10
Business and first class European flights	£20
Economy long-haul flights	£40
Business and first class long-haul flights	£80

A February 2007 report by Oxford University's Centre for the Environment cast doubt on the effectiveness of 'green taxes' on curbing air travel emissions. The research indicated that high income groups who contributed most to greenhouse gas emissions from travel would simply absorb price increases rather than modify their travelling habits. The study recommended the use of awareness campaigns specifically to target the worst offending group – i.e. men who earned >£40,000 a year.

AIRCRAFT IN SERVICE · 2005

There were 952 aircraft in service in the UK in 2005 – up from 700 in 1995:

Carrier	*aircraft*
British Airways	232
EasyJet	98
BMI	58
Thomsonfly	42
Flybe	35
First Choice Airways	32
Virgin Atlantic	32
My Travel Airways	29
Monarch	28

[Not all carriers listed. Source: Civil Aviation Authority]

AMERICA'S 'NO-FLY' LIST

The USA's Transportation Security Administration (TSA) maintains a 'No-Fly' list of passengers prohibited from boarding aircraft. Developed after 9/11, the list includes the name, nationality, date of birth, and passport number of individuals who may pose a 'threat to civil aviation', based on intelligence from the FBI and CIA. The TSA also maintains a 'Selectee' list of those who must pass through extensive screening before boarding. The exact number on the 'No-Fly' list is classified, but estimates vary from 50,000–350,000. The FBI admitted that, as of 2004, the List had caused some 350 Americans to be delayed or denied boarding. The 'No-Fly' list has prompted numerous complaints from those given 'false positives', according to TSA logs. One such example was the British folk singer Cat Stevens, who changed his name to Yusuf Islam after becoming a Muslim in the 1970s. He was prevented from entering the US in 2004 after his name was discovered on the 'No-Fly' list.

In January 2007, it was announced that the 'No-Fly' list was being reviewed in a process the TSA hoped would halve the number of people listed by 2008. The Homeland Security Department also began a complaints system for those who consider they have been added to the list erroneously.

THE ENVIRONMENTAL IMPACT OF FLYING

The British public does not believe that the airline industry is doing enough to minimise rising CO_2 levels or counteract global warming. A Populus/*Times* survey, in April 2007, asked the public which group they thought bore the greatest responsibility for the environmental impact of flying. The survey results are below:

Most responsible	%
Airlines	35
Passengers	18
Government	18
Aircraft makers	17
Oil companies	13

CABIN BAGGAGE RESTRICTIONS

Stringent airline cabin baggage restrictions have been in place since August 2006, after the police foiled an alleged terrorist plot to bomb transatlantic flights. At the time of writing, baggage allowances were as follows: each passenger is allowed one item of hand luggage (maximum dimensions: length 56cm, width 45cm, depth 25cm). Passengers may carry only small quantities of liquids, but each must be in a separate container of not more than 100ml. The liquids must be presented at the security check in a single, transparent, resealable plastic bag (approximately 20×20cm). Liquids allowed include: all drinks, soups, syrups, lotions, creams, perfume, make-up, toothpaste, hair products, hair and shower gel, and pressurised containers. Essential medicines (like diabetic kits) which have been verified as authentic are allowed; baby food and milk are allowed on board, but only if tasted by an accompanying passenger. At the time of going to press these restrictions were under review, and readers were advised to consult baa.com before travelling.

SLEEPING IN AIRPORTS

In 1996, Canadian Donna McSherry created *The Budget Traveller's Guide to Sleeping in Airports* [sleepinginairports.net], based on her experiences as a fiscally challenged young person. Since then, thousands have contributed tips, tricks, and airport reviews, providing fodder for McSherry's periodic best and worst airport awards. Below are the site's five best and worst airports in which to sleep, as of May 2007:

BEST ('Golden Pillow Award')	WORST ('Poopy Airport Award')
Singapore Changi Airport	*Jackson Airport (Papua New Guinea)*
Amsterdam Airport Schiphol	*Mumbai Airport*
Athens International Airport	*Cairo International Airport*
Auckland International Airport	*O'Hare International Airport (Chicago)*
Helsinki-Vantaa (Finland)	*Indira Gandhi Intl Airport (Delhi)*

Some of the many tips on sleepinginairports.net: always have a backup plan; bring an emergency airport survival kit including an inflatable pool raft, toilet paper, and Post-it notes (if traveling solo, write the time you need to be awake on a note and stick it to yourself); always act innocent; dress in layers; arrival lounges tend to be more comfortable than departure lounges; if someone puts out their hand asking for a bribe, thank them, smile, then shake their hand – or pretend to speak Klingon.

TRAIN STATION ASSAULTS

In January 2007, the British Transport Police released figures showing the number of assaults at UK railway stations. The 10 most dangerous stations in '05–'06 were:

Railway station	*number of assaults*
Leeds	159
London Victoria	71
London Waterloo	53
London Bridge	45
Birmingham New Street	40
Wimbledon	39
Clapham Junction	35
London King's Cross	32
London Liverpool Street	31
Cardiff Central	30

[Bickley, Kent, was the most vandalised station]

TRANSPORT FARES

BBC research indicated that Britons spend 15% of their disposable income on transport – 3·8% of which goes on fares. In January 2007, the price of UK rail travel increased by an average of 4·3% (more than 1% above inflation). According to the union the Transport Salaried Staffs' Association (TSSA), the rail journey from London to Manchester costs 55p per mile compared to 17p per mile for the journey from Paris to Calais. Other European fares, according to the TSSA, include:

Route	*miles*	*£ cost*	*p/mile*
London–Newcastle	288	112	39
Berlin–Bonn	365	63	17
Madrid–Barcelona	387	63	16

In January 2007, Mayor of London Ken Livingstone increased cash fares on London's underground and buses by 33% – a price increase that made London the most expensive public transport capital in the world. London Liberal Democrats released comparative price figures for underground rail in several capital cities:

City	*Single (£)*	*Daily (£)*	*Monthly (£)*
London	4·00	6·60	89·10
London (Oyster card)	1·50	6·60	89·10
Tokyo	1·51	3·07	72·87
Berlin	1·41	3·91	45·11
New York	1·07	3·50	40·51
Paris	0·96	5·65	35·30

LONDON CONGESTION CHARGE

GENERAL INFORMATION	
Current price	£8 per day
Operating times	7am–6pm
Days of operation	Mon–Fri

HOW TO PAY	
Online	www.cclondon.com
Phone	0845 900 1234
Text message (SMS)	81099

On 19 February 2007, the zone was extended westwards to cover most of the boroughs of Kensington and Chelsea, and Westminster. The £8 charge must be paid by midnight on the day of travel.

TRAIN PUNCTUALITY

Regional		*% trains on time*
Arriva Trains Wales	(88·4)	90·9
Central Trains	(85·1)	86·2
First Gt Western. West	(89·4)	82·5
First ScotRail	(89·5)	88·7
Gatwick Express	(92·6)	88·3
Island Line	(97·8)	97·3
Merseyrail	(93·3)	93·2
Northern Rail	(89·4)	89·5

Long-distance		*% trains on time*
First Great Western	(78·6)	75·6
GNER	(88·4)	81·9
Midland Mainline	(96·1)	93·7
ONE (InterCity)	(85·5)	84·5
TransPennine Express	(87·3)	91·2
Virgin Cross Country	(86·4)	84·9
Virgin West Coast	(89·3)	83·8

London & SE		*% trains on time*
c2c	(93·1)	93·8
Chiltern Railways	(93·9)	92·9
First Capital Connect	(N/A)	88·2
First Gt Western. Link	(86·6)	85·6
ONE	(89·8)	88·3
Silverlink	(92·4)	90·8
South Eastern	(90·0)	88·7
South West Trains	(92·2)	90·0
Southern	(90·9)	88·5
Thameslink	(90·5)	—
WAGN	(92·7)	—

Figures from Q4 2006/07, figures in brackets are Q4 2005/06. Long-distance trains are deemed 'on time' if within 10 mins of timetabled arrival time; London & regional trains within 5 mins. [Source: Office of Rail Regulation 2006–07]

STRESS RELIEF FOR COMMUTERS

Tactics for dealing with the stresses and strains of the daily commute were explored by researchers from Nottingham Trent University. The study, presented to the Applied Positive Psychology Conference in April 2007, revealed that the problems which most vexed commuters were: lack of space, loud music, delays, and obnoxious smells. Nine coping strategies were identified to lessen the horrors of commuting:

1 .... singing or talking to yourself
2 .... planning the day ahead
3 ..working on laptop, writing, reading
4 .... emotion-focused coping†
5 .... seek counselling
6 .... listen to audio book or music
7 .... chew gum, snack, or chat
8 .... smoke, or drink alcohol
9 .... meditate or pray

† vent anger or eye-up attractive commuters

LONDON STATION DESTINATION GUIDE

Charing Cross .... *serves* South & South-east
Euston .... Midlands, North-west of England & Scotland
King's Cross .... Midlands, North of England & Scotland
Liverpool Street .... East of England & East Anglia · Stansted Express
Marylebone .... Chilterns
Paddington .... West of England & Wales · Heathrow Express
St Pancras .... East Midlands & Yorkshire · Eurostar
Victoria .... South & South-east · Gatwick Express
Waterloo .... South & South-west

TOP EXPAT LOCATIONS

A study by the Institute for Public Policy Research, released in December 2006, indicated that nearly one in ten British citizens lives abroad. 5·5m British-born people reside overseas, suggesting a high rate of departure that is compensated for by an equally high rate of immigration into the UK. The top British expat locations are:

Country	*resident Britons*
Australia	1,300,000
Spain	761,000
United States	678,000
Canada	603,000
Ireland	291,000
New Zealand	215,000
South Africa	212,000
France	200,000

UK HOLIDAY HABITS

A survey by Virgin Holidays in January 2007 revealed how bad the British are at escaping the office. Britons confessed to the following bad habits while on holiday:

Contacted work while on holiday	56%
Took work on holiday with them	40
Checked their work email while on holiday	38
Were irritated by their partner's work-related conversations	29
– of whom, asked their partner to not talk about work	26
Were willing to alter their holiday plans for work	39
Made and received work calls while on holiday	♂ 30 · ♀ 18
Took a laptop with them on holiday	♂ 17 · ♀ 8

28% of women felt their partners placed more importance on work than on their relationship. ❦ A survey released by David Lloyd Leisure in April 2007 indicated that nearly one in ten injure themselves trying to get fit for a holiday. Men were nearly twice as likely to suffer injury than women, mainly because they neglected to warm-up properly. Britons spend >£2·9bn a year on home exercise equipment, despite nearly one in five admitting to using the equipment once, or not at all.

ITEMS LOST IN HOTELS

In January 2007, Travelodge compiled an inventory of all the items in the lost property offices of their hotels. The things most often mislaid (or abandoned) were:

1	mobile phones and chargers
2	toiletries
3	clothes
4	shoes
5	books
6	hen/stag night 'accessories'
7	jewellery
8	laptops
9	electrical gadgets
10	false teeth and limbs

A Travelodge survey in March 2007 revealed that 57% of solitary travellers felt lonely sleeping without their partners, that 28% resorted to hugging a pillow for comfort, and that 20% of men (and only 15% of women) admitted to cuddling a teddy bear. In response, the chain piloted the 'Cuddillow' – a 2' 6" bespoke cuddling pillow that could be hired from the reception of some of their hotels.

TOP BRITISH ATTRACTIONS

Free admission	*visits*	*Charged admission*	*visits*
Blackpool Pleasure Beach	5·7m	Tower of London	2·1m
Tate Modern	4·9m	St Paul's Cathedral	1·6m
British Museum	4·8m	Kew Gardens	1·4m
The National Gallery	4·6m	Edinburgh Castle	1·2m
Natural History Museum	3·8m	Chester Zoo	1·2m
Science Museum	2·4m	Eden Project	1·2m
V&A Museum	2·4m	Canterbury Cathedral	1·0m

[Source: Association of Leading Visitor Attractions, 2006] In February 2007, ALVA announced that visitor figures were back on track after the July 2005 London bombings caused tourists to stay away.

PORTABLE LAVATORY REQUIREMENTS

The Event and Labor Services department at Stanford University has calculated the number of portable lavatories required for events of different size and duration. For example, an event for 1,000 lasting 6 hours needs 8 lavatories. The department does warn: 'consider other factors such as whether food and beverages are being served'.

People	*1 hr*	*2hrs*	*3hrs*	*4hrs*	*5hrs*	*6hrs*	*7hrs*	*8hrs*	*9hrs*	*10hrs*
0–500	*loos*=4	4	4	6	6	6	8	8	8	8
1,000	4	6	6	6	6	8	8	8	8	12
2,000	4	8	8	8	8	12	12	12	12	16
3,000	8	8	10	10	10	12	16	16	20	20
4,000	8	8	12	12	16	16	20	24	24	28
5,000	12	12	12	16	20	30	30	30	30	34
6,000	12	12	16	16	20	30	30	36	36	40
7,000	12	12	16	20	30	32	40	40	52	52
8,000	12	12	20	24	32	32	40	44	52	54
9,000	16	16	24	28	40	40	52	52	60	64
10,000	16	16	28	40	40	52	52	60	60	72

BEACH LITTER

The Marine Conservation Society's annual *Beachwatch* survey (April 2007) revealed that the amount of litter on Britain's beaches has increased by more than 90% since 1994. The survey indicated that, on average, two pieces of litter could be found per metre of beach. The items of litter most commonly found on beaches were:

Pieces of plastic 1–50cm	13·2%	Plastic caps/lids	5·4%
Cotton bud sticks	8·6%	Rope	4·3%
Pieces of plastic <1cm	6·2%	Cigarette stubs	4·2%
Crisp/sweet/lolly wrappers	5·6%	Plastic drink bottles	3·9%
Polystyrene pieces	5·5%	Fishing net	3·3%

VISITS TO ATTRACTIONS · ENGLAND

Most of those who visited English attractions in 2005 were adults, according to data from VisitBritain; the most popular attractions for children were farms. The table below shows the percentage of adult and child visitors to various attractions:

Attraction	*adults (%)*	*children*
Workplaces†	80	20
Historic houses/castles	80	20
Gardens	79	21
Other historic properties	78	22
Places of worship	76	24
Museums/art galleries	70	30
Visitor/heritage centres	70	30
Steam/heritage railways	67	33
Wildlife attractions/zoos	64	36
Country parks	62	38
Leisure/theme parks	57	43
Farms	52	48
Other	73	27

† Workplaces include operating industrial or craft attractions, vineyards etc.
[Source: Survey of Visits to Visitor Attractions England, 2005, VisitBritain]

NEWLY INSCRIBED WORLD HERITAGE SITES · 2007

Cultural Properties: Bordeaux, Port of the Moon, France
Central University City Campus of UNAM, Mexico
Gamzigrad-Romuliana, Palace of Galerius, Serbia
Gobustan Rock Art Cultural Landscape, Azerbaijan
Iwami Ginzan Silver Mine and landscape, Japan
Kaiping Diaolou and Villages, China · Lavaux Vineyard terraces, Switzerland
Mehmed Paša Sokolović Bridge, Višegrad, Bosnia and Herzegovina
Samarra archaeological city, Iraq · Sydney Opera House, Australia
The old town of Corfu, Greece · Twyfelfontein or /Ui-//aes, Namibia
The Parthian Fortresses of Nisa, Turkmenistan
The Red Fort Complex, India · The Rideau Canal, Canada
The Richtersveld Cultural and Botanical Landscape, South Africa
Mixed site (both Cultural and Natural): Lopé-Okanda, Gabon
Natural Properties: Jeju Volcanic Island and Lava Tubes, Korea
Primeval Beech Forests of the Carpathians, Slovakia/Ukraine
Rainforests of the Atsinanana, Madagascar
South China Karst, China · Teide National Park, Spain
Extensions approved for: Jungfrau-Aletsch-Bietschhorn, Switzerland

The Arabian Oryx Sanctuary became the first site to be removed from the UNESCO World Heritage list owing to Oman's 'failure to preserve the outstanding universal value of the Sanctuary.'

GREAT BRITAIN · ORDNANCE SURVEY DATA

Most northerly point .... Out Stack, North of Unst in Shetland HP613203
Most southerly point .... Pednathise Head, Isles of Scilly SV839053
Most easterly point ....Lowestoft Ness TM556937
Most westerly point...................... Gob a' Ghaill, Outer Hebrides NA055015
Furthest point from sea...................SK 257144 · East of Church Flatts Farm, *c.*1 mile south-east of Coton in the Elms, Derbyshire

Highest point · England.................. Scafell Pike in Cumbria, 978m (3,210ft)
— Scotland ....Highland Ben Nevis, 1,343m (4,406ft)
— Wales.................................... Gwynedd Snowdon, 1,085m (3,560ft)
— Northern Ireland .... County Down Slieve Donard, 850m (2,789ft)
— Isle of Man...Snaefell, 621m (2036ft)

The Ordnance Survey defines the remotest point to be the point farthest from a metalled road. In mainland Britain, this point is calculated to be on the hillside of Ruadh Stac Beag, between Letterewe Forest and Fisherfield Forest [NH 02550 77010] which is 11km (7mi) from the A832. [Source: Ordnance Survey · Crown ©]

ROUGH GUIDE'S WORLD WONDERS

To mark a quarter-century of publishing its celebrated guidebooks, in May 2007 *Rough Guide* published a guide to the 25 ultimate world wonders and experiences:

Salt flats of Salar de Uyuni, Bolivia · Uluru or Ayers Rock, Australia
Pyramids at Giza, Egypt · Drifting down the Amazon
'Fairy chimneys' & caves of Cappadocia, Turkey · Grand Canyon, Arizona, USA
Petra, the city carved from stone in the Jordanian desert · Machu Picchu, Peru
Gaudí's *Sagrada Familia*, Barcelona · Perito Moreno glacier, Patagonia
Sistine Chapel, Rome · Trekking in the Himalayas
Angkor Wat, Cambodia · The canals and palaces of Venice
Taking a camel train across the Sahara · The Great Wall of China
Victoria Falls, Zambia and Zimbabwe · Paddling in the Barrier Reef, Belize
Taj Mahal, India · Maya ruins of Mexico and Guatemala
Stone giants of Easter Island · Grand Mosque, Djenné, Mali
The temptations of Las Vegas · The Forbidden City, China
Itaipú, the world's biggest dam, Paraguay and Brazil

The *Rough Guide*'s 25 wonders and experiences of Britain and Ireland were: Edinburgh Festival · Pembrokeshire Coast Path Walk · Punting on the Cam · Guinness in Dublin · Borrowdale, the Lake District · Durham Cathedral · New Forest cycling · Belfast murals · Surfing in Newquay · Tobermory, Isle of Mull · Hiking in Snowdonia · York · Notting Hill Carnival · Skellig Michael, off SW Ireland · Balti Triangle, Birmingham · Clubbing in London · Walking on Dartmoor · Scotland's West Highlands Railway · Sun rise on the winter solstice at Brú na Bóinne Neolithic site in Ireland · Football at Old Trafford · Back roads of Connemara · Walking from St Paul's to Tate Modern · Holkham Beach, Norfolk · Conwy Castle, Wales · Glastonbury Festival.

CHILDREN'S BEST AND WORST THINGS

A survey, released in December 2006 by Luton First, revealed what children ≤10 considered to be the *very best* and *very worst* things in the whole wide world ever:

The very best things		*the very worst things*
Being a celebrity	1	killing people
Good looks	2	wars
Being rich	3	drunk people
Being healthy	4	bullies
Pop music	5	illness
Families	6	smoking
Friends	7	stealing
Nice food	8	divorce
Watching films	9	being fat
Heaven/God	10	dying

The children were also asked to name the most famous person in the world. They chose: [1] God [2] President Bush [3] Madonna [4] Jesus [5] Father Christmas [6] The Queen [7] Tony Blair [8] Simon Cowell [9] Sharon Osbourne [10] Britney Spears

MEMBERSHIP OF YOUTH ORGANISATIONS

The table below shows UK membership of selected youth organisations in 2005:

Organisation	Members	Organisation	Members
Clubs for young people	400,000	Army Cadets	45,000
Brownie Guides	249,000	Combined Cadet Force	42,000
Cub Scouts	134,000	Air Cadets	33,000
Guides	126,000	Explorer Scouts	26,000
Scouts	99,000	Girls Brigade	26,000
Beaver Scouts	97,000	Nat. Fed. of Young Farmers	21,000
Young Men's Christian Assoc.	85,000	Snr Section (e.g. Ranger Guides)	20,000
Rainbow Guides	82,000	Sea Cadets	13,000
Boys Brigade	57,000	Scout Network	4,000

[Source: Social Trends 37: 2007 edition & various, Crown ©]

TOY OF THE YEAR

Every January since 1965, the Toy of the Year Award has been presented by the Toy Retailer's Association to celebrate the top market performers. The overall 2006 winner was DR WHO CYBERMAN MASK. Some other category winners included:

Category	*winner*		
Girl	Nintendog Trick Trainer pups	Game	*Deal or No Deal* board-game
Boy	Dr Who figures	Innovation	Butterscotch Pony
		Craze	Shoot Out cards

MISS GREAT BRITAIN 2007

Rachael Tennant, a 19-year-old oil industry worker from Aberdeen, was crowned Miss Great Britain 2007 after wowing judges at London's Grosvenor House Hotel. The bizarre judging panel included racing pundit John McCririck, Christine 'Battleaxe' Hamilton, aristocrat Lord Charles Brockett, Aussie paparazzo Darryn Lyons, and *Zoo* editor Ben Todd. Rachael has light blonde shoulder-length hair, stands 5' 7" tall, and boasts vital statistics of 32·25·32. As Miss GB, Rachael won:

a speaking part in a Hollywood film · a modelling contract · £5,000 in clothes
a photoshoot with Zoo *magazine · automatic entry into a Miss World contest*

GUILTY PLEASURES

A host of intellectuals confided their 'guilty pleasures' to *Guardian* journalist Philip Oltermann in February 2007. A selection of their censurable delights follows:

ANTONY BEEVOR (historian)
Blind Date
'Its true awfulness and the glimpses of young macho-macha life in this country proved utterly gripping'

ELAINE SHOWALTER (academic)
Trinny & Susannah
'Despite their posh accents, brusque manner and seemingly effortless elegance, Trinny and Susannah had an overall respect and affection for other women'

STEVE JONES (biologist)
estate agents
'I dream about houses that I could never afford to buy'

ANTHONY GIDDENS (sociologist)
American wrestling on cable TV
'The programme is politically incorrect in more or less every way one could think of'

STEVEN PINKER (psychologist)
rock lyrics
'Dylan's "God said to Abraham, kill me a son" is a perfect example of a benefactive double-object dative construction'

A.C. GRAYLING (philosopher)
boxing
'Boxing should be banned, of course…'

RICHARD DAWKINS (scientist)
computer programming
'It was a classic addiction: prolonged frustration, occasionally rewarded by a briefly glowing fix of achievement'

NAOMI WOLF (writer)
Star magazine
'Even though it is 90% escapism for me, I do tell myself it shines a light on what the id of the culture is obsessing about: why Paris Hilton, right now?'

GARDEN OF THE YEAR

The 2006 Historic Houses Association – Christie's Garden of the Year Award, was presented to BOURTON HOUSE GARDEN in Gloucestershire. The three acre garden combines 'flamboyant borders' with 'a myriad of magically planted pots'.

THE CHELSEA FLOWER SHOW

The following gardens were awarded top prizes at the 2007 Chelsea Flower Show:

Best show garden .... *a space garden on Mars* · Bradstone
Best chic garden.................................. *a private basement garden* · Helios
Best city garden .... *a small, sheltered garden in Moscow* · Harpak Group
Best courtyard garden .... *an old farmyard garden* · A.W. Gardening Services
Best roof garden.......objets trouvés *used as plant containers* · Anthony Samuelson
President's award.. UK Horticulture

PROPERTY DEVALUING PLANTS

The 10 plants most likely to put people off buying a property are apparently these:

Plant	*% put off*
Leylandii	71
Ivy	67
Pampas grass	55
Conifer trees	50
Wisteria	49
Magnolias	47
Privet	36
Geraniums	31
Bamboo	29
Carnations	18

[Source: UKTV Gardens 2007]

BRITAIN IN BLOOM

The Royal Horticultural Society's 'Britain in Bloom' 2006 category winners were:

Category	*winner*
Champion of champions	Alness
City	Aberdeen
Lrg.town/sml. city (12–35k)	Perth
– (35–100k)	Shrewsbury
Town	Brightlingsea
Small town	St Martin's Parish (Guernsey)
Large village	Broughshane (N.I.)
Village	Norton in Hales
Urban regeneration	Seedley & Langworthy
Urban community	Starbeck
Coastal category	Scarborough
Floral award (discretionary)	Shrewsbury

MOST COMMON GARDEN BIRDS · UK

Each January, the Royal Society for the Protection of Birds asks the public to spend an hour spotting birds in their gardens. In 2007, 400,000 participated in the *Big Garden Birdwatch*, counting more than 6·5m birds. The most common are below:

1	house sparrow
2	starling
3	blue tit
4	blackbird
5	chaffinch
6	collared dove
7	woodpigeon
8	great tit
9	robin
10	greenfinch

[The 2007 Birdwatch twitch took place 27–28 January]

Some of the more unusual birds spotted include the black-throated thrush (which, in January, is usually in Asia), an American robin, red kites, little egrets, kingfishers, choughs, and black redstarts.

UK'S FOOD HABITS

The Food Standards Agency annually surveys British attitudes towards food. The 2007 survey revealed a growing concern with healthy eating and food provenance. Below is a breakdown of where *most* or *some* of household food shopping is done:

Type of shop	*(%) most*	*some*
Large supermarkets	63	8
Supermarket chain local	30	15
Small grocery/corner shops	2	39
Local specialist shops	2	25
Over the internet	2	3
Street markets	0	13
Farmers' markets	0	10
Farm shops	0	12

[FSA *Consumer Attitudes to Food*, Feb 2007]

Respondents were also asked how frequently they ate the following types of food:

Frequency (%)	*home-made*	*partly prepared*	*fully prepared*	*take-away*
Most days	63	20	8	1
A few times/week	24	35	18	4
About once a week	7	19	21	17
A few times/month	4	16	31	58
Never	2	11	22	18

40% admitted to snacking between meals the day before the survey. The most popular snacks were: fresh fruit (40%); biscuits or cakes (28%); crisps and savoury snacks (20%); chocolate bars (16%); and bread or toast (8%). ❦ Sainsbury revealed the number of items purchased during an average supermarket visit fell from 42 to 39 between 2006–7; a reduction in junk food sales accounted for the fall.

HYBRID FRUITS

Created by selective cross-breeding, hybrid fruits now form part of a $100m industry in America alone. (One of the leading hybrid fruiterers, Zaiger's Genetics of California, has patented >200 new fruits.) Examples of hybrid fruits include:

Fruit	*mix of*
Aprium	apricot & plum
Boysenberry	raspberry, blackberry, & loganberry
Grapefruit	pomelo & sweet orange
Jostaberry	blackcurrant & gooseberry
Loganberry	raspberry & blackberry
Nectaplum	nectarine & plum
Peacotum	peach, apricot, & plum
Pluot	plum & apricot
Tangelo	tangerine & grapefruit
Tayberry	raspberry & blackberry

THE EU & SUPERFOODS

On 1 July 2007, the European Union introduced new legislation to prevent food manufacturers from labelling products as 'superfoods' unless the claim could be substantiated. Foods like salmon, blueberries, and spinach had all been widely marketed as 'superfoods' due to their high-nutrient content. From July, manufacturers were permitted to use the term only if the health claims had been clinically verified.

THE WORLD'S TOP TABLES

Restaurant Magazine's 2007 survey of the world's finest tables listed the following:

El Bulli	Girona, Spain	*Bras*	Laguiole, France
The Fat Duck	Bray, UK	*Mugaritz*	San Sebastián, Spain
Pierre Gagnaire	Paris, France	*Le Louis XV*	Monte Carlo, Monaco
French Laundry	California, US	*Per Se*	New York, US
Tetsuya's	Sydney, Australia	*Arzak*	San Sebastián, Spain

NEW UK MICHELIN STARS · 2007

The *Michelin Guide* was first published in 1900 by the Michelin Tyre Company. A three-star rating system is employed on a deceptively simple set of criteria: [*] 'A very good restaurant in its category'; [**] 'Excellent cooking, worth a detour'; [***] 'Exceptional cuisine, worth a special trip'. In reality, the award of one Michelin star confers instant recognition; two stars confer fame; and three stars are the culinary equivalent of a Nobel prize. The following gained UK stars in 2007:

**	*Petrus*	Wilton Place, London SW1	020 7235 1200
**	*The Vineyard at Stockcross*	Newbury, Berkshire	01635 528 770
*	*Christophe*	Guernsey	01481 230 725
*	*Atlantic*	Jersey	01534 744 101
*	*Glenapp Castle*	Ballantrae, Scotland	01465 831 212
*	*The Kitchin*	Edinburgh, Scotland	0131 555 1755
*	*The Crown at Whitebrook*	Monmouth, Wales	01600 860 254
*	*The Harrow*	Marlborough, Wiltshire	01672 870 871
*	*The Abbey*	Penzance, Cornwall	01736 330 680
*	*Seaham Hall*	Seaham, Durham	01915 161 400
*	*La Noisette*	Sloane Street, London SW1	020 7750 5000
*	*Benares*	Berkeley Square, London W1	020 7629 8886
*	*Arbutus*	Frith Street, London W1	020 7734 4545
*	*L'Atelier de Joel Robuchon*	West Street, London WC2	020 7010 8600
*	*Chapter One*	Dublin, Ireland	353 1 873 2266

In June '07, C&D Assurance offered restaurants insurance to guard against losing a Michelin star.

MOST EATEN MEALS

The average Briton is capable of making just 4½ different meals, according to a 2007 poll for Loyd Grossman sauces. Below are the meals the British eat most often:

Meal	*number eaten in a lifetime*		
Spaghetti Bolognese	2,960	Fish and chips	2,089
Stew	2,612	Steak and chips	1,741
Sausage and mash	2,264	Chilli con carne	1,567
		Burger and chips	1,045

RESTAURANT EMBARRASSMENT

In January 2007, the Ashburton Cookery School, Devon, revealed the following survey results into British attitudes when ordering food and wine in restaurants:

% of diners	*Yes*	*No*	*d/k*
Do you feel awkward tasting wine at the table?	76	20	4
Do you know what corked wine tastes like?	62	14	24
Would you ever send back wine if it was unsatisfactory?	46	35	19
Would you ever send back food if it was unsatisfactory?	22	63	15
Would you be dissuaded from ordering an item if you were unsure about how to pronounce it?	71	29	0
As host, have you ever ordered cheaper items, in the hope that your guests would follow suit?	55	32	13
During a business meeting, have you ever chosen food or wine that you did not want, to impress others?	65	24	11
During a business meeting, have you ever ordered the same food and drink as others to match them?	34	66	0

Also revealed by the survey are those factors that govern people's choice of wine:

Prior knowledge	*price*	*random choice*	*other*
22%	42	14	22

GOOD HOUSEKEEPING FOOD AWARDS

Some winners of *Good Housekeeping* magazine's annual food awards in 2007 were:

Favourite regional food† .... Yorkshire pudding
Favourite wine under £10 .... Jacob's Creek
Favourite store-cupboard ingredient .... Lea & Perrins Worcestershire sauce
Favourite indulgent food .... Green & Black's chocolate
Best healthy eating product .... Yeo Valley organic fat free natural yogurt
Favourite TV food programme .... Rick Stein's cookery series
Favourite supermarket .... Waitrose
Best time-saving ingredient .... Jus-Rol pastry
Sexiest food .... chocolate
Best organic product .... Yeo Valley organic yogurt
Favourite soft drink .... Bottlegreen cordials
Favourite new product‡ .... St James cheese
Outstanding contribution to food .... Joanna Blythman (journalist)

† Runners-up included the Cornish pasty and the Melton Mowbray pork pie. ‡ Voted for by an expert panel that included Prue Leith, Aggie Mackenzie, *GH* editor Louise Chunn, and Fergus Henderson. In March 2007, the Vegetarian Society announced that Guinness had won the Imperfect World Award. The prize highlights a product that vegetarians lust after but cannot consume, because the recipe or production process uses animal products (Guinness is made using swim bladders of fish).

CRUFTS BEST IN SHOW · 2007

The 2007 Crufts Best in Show was Tibetan terrier *Araki Fabulous Willy*, handled by Larry Cornelius. The winning pair were presented with the famous Keddell Memorial trophy, and won £100 and a year's supply of Pedigree Chum (worth £1,500). Confusingly, Tibetan terriers are not true 'terriers'; they were given the name by European travellers. In Tibet, this breed of dogs is known as Dhoki Apso.

Scruffts is an annual, national competition for crossbreeds that includes the categories Child's Best Friend, Golden Oldie, Most Handsome Dog, and Prettiest Bitch. Entry to each class costs just £1.

DANGEROUS DOGS

According to the British Veterinary Association the ownership, breeding, or sale of the following breeds of dog is banned in the UK by the Dangerous Dogs Act (1991):

Pit Bull Terrier · Japanese Tosa · Dogo Argentino · Fila Braziliero

MOST ABANDONED BREEDS

Battersea Dogs & Cats Home released figures in October 2006 which showed that far more pedigree dogs were taken in by the Home (4,908) than mongrels (2,990). Listed below are the pedigree breeds most commonly abandoned by their owners:

Breed	*abandoned*
Staffs bull-terrier	169
Mongrel	73
Jack Russell	72
German shepherd	53
Labrador	49
Rottweiler	31
Border collie	24

[Figures from Sept. 2006]

Rabbits are the most commonly abused pets in Britain, according to 2006 figures from the RSPCA. *c.*35,000 rabbits are abandoned by their owners each year, perhaps because keeping rabbits can cost £4,000 over an average 8-year life. In April 2007, the RSPCA announced that 9,500 pets were abandoned in 2006 (40% more than in 2005). In 2006, *c.*3,000 cats were rescued by the RSPCA.

THE SUPREME CAT SHOW · 2006

The annual Supreme Cat Show is organised by the Governing Council of the Cat Fancy (GCCF). To be eligible, a cat must first have qualified by winning a certificate at an ordinary GCCF championship show. All breeds recognised by the GCCF may take part in the Supreme shows – and there is a special category for non-pedigree cats. A knock-out competition selects the Supreme Kitten, the Supreme Adult, and the Supreme Neuter, who then battle it out to be crowned the Supreme Exhibit. The 2006 Supreme Cat Show was held at Birmingham's NEC on 25 November. The Supreme Exhibit was awarded to Supreme UK and Imperial Grand Champion GRIZABELLA OHBLADI OHBLADA, a female Black Smoke Devon Rex owned by Mr and Mrs J.A. Boucher, and bred by Mrs I. Challis.

RAT POPULATION

Rat numbers in the UK have reached record levels, according to the 2006 National Rodent Survey published by the National Pest Technicians Association (NPTA) in January 2007. In 2006, it was estimated that Londoners were never more than 18 metres from a rat; by 2007 this distance had shrunk to just 14 metres. Tabulated below is the year-on-year increase in the rat and mouse populations within the UK:

Year *(% increase in population)*	*Brown rat*	*House mouse*	*Summer rat*
1998–99	18%	-2·0%	31%
1999–2000	24%	-7·0%	30%
2000–01	29%	-7·5%	48%
2001–02	32%	-8·5%	52%
2002–03	34%	-8·5%	59%
2003–04	26%	-1·5%	47%
2004–05	39%	12·5%	69%

The UK rat population is estimated to be 70m, more than one rat for every person in the population.

FAMOUS HORSES &c.

A survey by animal welfare charity Brooke revealed Britain's best-known equidae:

Red Rum 45%
Black Beauty 33%
Shergar 23%
Desert Orchid 16%
Muffin the Mule ... 13%
Donkey from *Shrek* . 9%
Eeyore 8%

[Source: Brooke, April 2007]

BEST & WORST CELEB DOG OWNERS

According to *New York Dog* magazine, Tinseltown's best and worst dog owners are:

BEST *owner & pet*	WORST *owner & pet*
Oprah Winfrey & 'Solomon'	Britney Spears & 'Bit Bit'
Tori Spelling & 'Mimi La Rue'	Paris Hilton & 'Tinkerbell'
Nicollette Sheridan & 'Oliver'	Serena Williams & 'Jackie'

HEALTH BENEFITS OF PET OWNERSHIP

The health benefits of keeping pets were explored in research published in the *British Journal of Health Psychology* in January 2007. Dr Deborah Wells of Queen's University Belfast, reviewed a number of studies and concluded that pet owners were on average healthier than non-owners. However, it seems that owning a cat was less beneficial than owning a dog. In general, dog owners had lower rates of blood pressure and cholesterol – perhaps because owning a dog reduces levels of stress, provides companionship, and encourages regular constitutional 'walkies'.

ANIMALS IN THE NEWS · 2007

Some of the year's more unusual animal stories. ❦ A riding school in Ireland was forced to postpone its Christmas party after Gus, a camel, went on a rampage, eating 200 mince pies and downing six cans of Guinness. ❦ The lives of two dolphins were saved by the world's tallest man, after they swallowed fragments of plastic liner from around their pool. Bao Xishun, a Mongolian herdsman who stands 2·36m (7'9") tall, used his 1·06m-long arms (41·7") to extract the plastic from the dolphins' stomachs. ❦ A 'rogue' elephant (nicknamed Osama bin Laden) was shot dead after he trampled to death 14 people in India. ❦ A German pensioner was awarded a contract to supply giant rabbits to North Korea, after he bred Robert, a 23·1lb monster. The North Koreans said they wanted to improve 'meat production'. ❦ In Tallahassee, Florida, an unnamed duck managed to survive being shot in the wing and leg and being locked in a fridge for two days. The lucky duck managed also to survive two heart attacks during surgery at the Goose Creek Animal Sanctuary. ❦ A Chilean flamingo named Florence went missing after a gust of wind blew her out of her enclosure at Drusillas Park, Sussex. Her fox-ravaged remains were found two weeks later. ❦ Mozart, a male iguana at Antwerp's Aquatopia, had his penis amputated after suffering permanent tumescence for over a week. (Fortunately, male iguanas have two penises.) ❦ A sloth named Mats was banished to Duisburg Zoo after failing to cooperate in an experiment. Scientists at the University of Jena had been trying to entice Mats to the top of a pole for three years, but the sloth consistently refused to budge. ❦ Fishermen in New Zealand caught a colossal squid that weighed 450kg (992lbs); it was the largest specimen ever caught intact. ❦ For the first time in 30 years, two snowy owls were sighted together in the UK. Hopes of the birds mating on the Isle of Lewis were dashed after it was discovered that both owls were male. ❦ One lane of a highway in Taiwan was closed so that more than a million milkweed butterflies might safely cross the road during their seasonal migration. ❦ Two labradors, Lucky and Flo, proved so successful at sniffing out pirated DVDs in Malaysia that crime bosses put a price on their heads. It was thought that 50,000 Ringgit (*c.*£7,000) was offered for each dead dog. ❦ Knut, a polar bear rejected by his parents, achieved celebrity status at Berlin Zoo, after animal rights' campaigners argued that he should be euthanized because hand-rearing would domesticate him. Knut later appeared on the cover of *Vanity Fair*. ❦ A Sudanese man was forced to 'marry' a goat named Rose, with whom he had been caught acting 'improperly'. Sadly, Rose passed away sometime later, after choking on a plastic bag while scavenging. ❦ Thousands of Japanese were tricked into buying lambs disguised as poodles – Japan's latest must-have accessory. The scam was uncovered when one owner complained that her 'poodle' neither barked nor ate dog food. ❦ The belief that seahorses are monogamous was shattered by researchers who found that most are promiscuous, indiscriminate, and (in roughly 37% of encounters) homosexual. ❦ Three elderly ladies from Seaham, County Durham, knitted 50 woollen pullovers to help penguins stricken by an oil slick in Tasmania.

Money

I'd trade it all for a little more.
— CHARLES MONTGOMERY BURNS (*c.*1881–)

MONEY IN CIRCULATION

Note	*featured personality*	*notes issued in 2007*	*size mm*	*circulation value 2007*
£5	Elizabeth Fry	106m	135×70	£1,100m
£10	Charles Darwin	323m	142×75	£5,886m
£20	Edward Elgar/A. Smith	328m	149×80	£23,740m
£50	Sir John Houblon	13m	156×85	£6,705m
Others†	—	—	—	£1,018m
Total	—	770m	—	£38,449m

† Includes higher-value notes used for internal transactions. [Source: Bank of England]

Coin	*issued in 2005*
GOLD · Sovereign	45,542
Half Sovereign	30,299
SILVER · 4p Maundy	1,685
3p Maundy	1,685
2p Maundy	1,685
1p Maundy	1,685
NICKEL BRASS · £2	15,331,500
£1	68,138,000
CUPRO-NICKEL · £5†	101,106,000
50p	30,254,500
20p	81,356,250
10p	66,836,000
5p	210,012,000
BRONZE · 2p	131,133,000
1p	378,752,000

† Includes special editions
[Source: Royal Mint]

On 13 March 2007, the Bank of England announced the release of a new £20 note featuring a portrait of the Scottish political economist Adam Smith (1723–90). The £20 note is the most common of all of the 4 denominations: *c.*1·3bn 'twenties' were in circulation at the start of 2007, representing 55% of all notes by volume, and 64% by value. The new £20 notes, which over the next two years will replace those featuring Edward Elgar, have a range of sophisticated security measures to fox counterfeiters, viz: raised print; a holographic strip; a 'see-through' pound sign that becomes visible when held to the light; and an enhanced watermark. (Additional 'covert' security features were not made public by the Bank [see p.232].) ❦ Although Adam Smith appears on some Scottish £50 notes, he is the first Scotsman to feature on a note issued by the Bank of England. Smith's best known work, *An Inquiry into the Nature and Causes of the Wealth of Nations* (1776), proposed a laissez-faire model of enterprise, and famously stated 'there is no art which one government sooner learns of another than that of draining money from the pockets of the people'.

In March 2007, Iran issued an 'atomic banknote'– a 50,000 rial note featuring a 'nuclear' logo.

BUDGET 2007 · KEY POINTS

Gordon Brown announced a surprise 2p cut in the basic rate of income tax in the final minutes of his 11th (and last) Budget on 21 March 2007. The cut was seen as an attempt to wrong-foot both the Tories and any potential competition for the post-Blair leadership of the Labour party (and country). Some of the key measures presented in the Budget are below (others are detailed elsewhere in this section):

Income tax	basic rate cut from 22p to 20p from April 2008 10p starter rate abolished; top-rate threshold raised to £43,000 from 2009
Stamp duty	zero-carbon homes under £500,000 exempt
Inheritance tax	threshold raised from £285,000 to £350,000 by 2010
Corporation tax	cut from 30% to 28%; small company tax raised by 3p
Small businesses	offered up to £3,000 to pay for training of new staff
Housing	£18m for the Low Carbon Buildings programme
Education	spending to increase to £64bn in 2008, and £74bn in 2010
National insurance	cut-off point raised from £34,840 to £43,000
Capital gains	tax exemption to rise to £9,200; £18,400 for couples in 2008
ISAs	cash limit increased to £3,600; equity limit increased to £7,200
Science	investment to rise from £5bn to £6·3bn by 2010–11
Transport	fuel duty to rise by 2p per litre
Biofuel	20p differential to be extended until 2010
Road tax	top rate to rise to £400, with £35 off for fuel-efficient cars
Air travel	no VAT on air travel
Child benefit	to rise from £17·45 a week to £20 a week for first child by 2010
Nursery education	free nursery education extended to 15 hours a week
Lone parent bonus	£40 bonus for the first 12 months in work
Nicotine replacement products	VAT cut from 17·5% to 5% for 12 months
Landfill tax	to increase by £8 per tonne per year
Africa	£50m to help protect the world's second largest rainforest
R&D tax credit	credits to increase by £100m
Health	NHS to receive an extra £8bn
Armed forces	an extra £400m for troops in Iraq and Afghanistan
Counter-terrorism	an extra £86·4m for the intelligence and security services
Pensioners	tax-free allowance to rise to £10,000 by 2011 for over-75s
Pensioner homes	grants of £300–£4,000 for insulation and central heating
Personal allowance	to be raised to £1,180 for pensioners from April 2008
Internet gambling	duty to rise to 15%

BUDGET 2007 BOOZE 'n' FAGS

Typical unit	*budget*
Pack 20 cigarettes	+11p
Pack 5 cigars	+4p
25g rolling tobacco	+11p
25g pipe tobacco	+7p
Pint beer	+1p
175ml glass wine	+1p
75cl bottle wine	+5p
Sparkling wine	+7p
Spirits	*frozen*
Cider	+1p
Sparkling cider	+5p

BUDGET 2007 · REACTION & MISC

David Cameron *'It's not a tax cut, it's a tax con'* · Sir Menzies Campbell *'It is an income tax cut for the wealthy dressed up as a tax cut for the poor'* · Daily Mail '*What Gord giveth, Gord taketh away*' · Independent *'2p, or not 2p?'* · Sun *'Reasons 2p cheerful'*

Brown's speech lasted 48 minutes; he talked at a rate of 147 words per minute.

Budget word count			
Tax.............63	Family(-ies).... 18	Environmental. 11	Stability..........6
Child(ren)..... 41	Carbon 14	Growth........ 11	Africa............2
Invest(-ment).. 36	Education 14	Inflation....... 10	Iraq..............1
	Increase(d)..... 12	Pensioners.......8	Prime Minister..1

COMPUTERISED CONDENSATION

When Brown's speech (7,049 words) is entered into the Auto Summarize feature of *Microsoft Word* and reduced to *c.*1% of the original (3 sentences), the result is:

In the last year investment has grown by 6%, business investment by 7%, with inward investment up 10%. Now, alongside North America, Britain has the G7's fastest growing business investment – rising in real terms by 48% since 1997 – and overall investment rising to 17·5% of our national income. Education spending rising as a share of national income from 4·5% in 1997 – increasing to 5·6 % in 2010.

In 2007, Brown's tie was hot-pink paisley; in 2006, lavender; in 2005, red; in 2004, lilac; in 2003, orange & red; in 2002, blue/pink spots; in 2001, red; in 2000, purple spots; and 1997–99, red.

LOST PENNIES

Since the penny was introduced in 1971, *c.*650m 1 penny pieces have gone missing. Research commissioned by Chevrolet suggested that *c.*75% of Londoners were too embarrassed to pick up a stray penny from the pavement (despite the fact that this act has traditionally been considered lucky). The best places to find a lost penny are:

Location	*value of lost pennies*
On the street	£26m
In handbags and suitcases	£11m
In the car	£7·8m
Down the back of sofas	£5·9m
In clothes and shoes	£3·9m
In the washing machine	£3·3m
In the supermarket	£2·6m
On public transport	£2m
Inside vacuum cleaners	£1·3m
Down the drain	£650,000

[Source: Chevrolet, April 2007]

Originally, the silver Anglo-Saxon penny coin was worth one-twelfth of a shilling. Later, Henry III struck gold pennies which were worth 20 silver pennies. Copper pennies were first minted in 1797 in Birmingham; copper was replaced with bronze in 1860. The modern 1p coin was introduced into general circulation on 15 February 1971 when the UK adopted decimal currency. Initially made from bronze, rising metal prices prompted the introduction of a copper-plated steel penny in 1992. (Their steel core makes new pennies magnetic.) There are now an estimated 10·6m 1ps in circulation.

INCOME TAX · 2007–08

Income tax was first levied in 1799 by Pitt the Younger as a 'temporary measure' to finance the French Revolutionary War. The initial rate was 2 shillings in the pound. The tax was abolished in 1816, only to be re-imposed in 1842 by Robert Peel (again temporarily) to balance a fall in customs duties. By the end of the C19th, income tax was a permanent feature of the British economy. The current rates are:

Income tax allowances	2006–07	2007–08
Personal allowance	5,035	5,225
Personal allowance (65–74)	7,280	7,550
Personal allowance (>75)	7,420	7,690
Income limit for age-related allowances	20,100	20,900
Married couple's allowance (born before 6·4·1935)	6,065	6,285
Married couple's allowance (aged ≤75)	6,135	6,365
Minimum amount of married couple's allowance	2,350	2,440
Blind person's allowance	1,660	1,730

The rate of relief for the continuing married couple's allowance, maintenance relief for people born before 6 April 1935, and for the children's tax credit, remains 10%.

Income tax rates	*threshold*	%
Starting rate	£0–2,230	10
Basic rate	£2,231–34,600	22
Higher rate	>£34,600	40

Payment bands 0%	10%	22%	40%
Personal allowance	*from* 0–2,230	*from* 2,231–34,600	*after* 34,600

The 10% starting rate includes SAVINGS income. Where an individual has savings income in excess of the starting rate limit they will be taxed at 20% up to the basic rate limit, and at the higher rate for income above the basic rate limit. The tax rates for dividends are 10% for income up to the basic rate limit, and 32·5% thereafter.

STAMP DUTY

The thresholds below (in £) represent the 'total value of consideration' of the deal. The rate that applies to any given transfer applies to the whole value of that deal.

rate %	*Residential* not *in a disadvantaged area*	*Residential in a disadvantaged area*	*Non-residential*
0	0–125,000	0–150,000	0–150,000
1	125,001–250,000	150,001–250,000	150,001–250,000
3	250,001–500,000	250,001–500,000	250,001–500,000
4	>500,001	>500,001	>500,001

The rate of stamp duty on the transfer of SHARES and SECURITIES is set at 0·5%.

NATIONAL INSURANCE · 2007–08

Although National Insurance dates from 1911, modern funding of social security was proposed by Beveridge and established by the National Insurance Act (1946).

Lower earnings limit, primary Class 1	£87/w
Upper earnings limit, primary Class 1	£670/w
Primary threshold	£100/w
Secondary threshold	£100/w
Employees' primary Class 1 rate	11% of £100–£670/w · 1% >£670/w
Employees' contracted-out rebate	1·6%
Married women's reduced rate	4·85% of £100–£670/w · 1% >£670/w
Employers' secondary Class 1 rate	12·8% on earnings above £100/w
Employers' contracted-out rebate, salary-related schemes	3·7%
Employers' contracted-out rebate, money-purchase schemes	1·4%
Class 2 rate	£2·20/w
Class 2 small earnings exception	£4,635/y
Special Class 2 rate for share fishermen	£2·85/w
Special Class 2 rate for volunteer development workers	£4·35/w
Class 3 rate	£7·80/w
Class 4 lower profits limit	£5,225/y
Class 4 upper profits limit	£34,840/y
Class 4 rate	8% of £5,225–£34,840/y · 1% >£34,840/y

CAPITAL GAINS TAX

Annual exemptions 2007–08 Individuals &c. = £9,200 · Other trustees = £4,600

The amount chargeable to Capital Gains Tax is added onto the top of income liable to income tax for individuals, and is charged to CGT at the following levels:

Below the Starting Rate limit	10%
Between the Starting Rate and Basic Rate limits	20%
Above the Basic Rate limit	40%

Capital gains arising on disposal of a 'principal private residence' remain exempt.

CORPORATION TAX ON PROFITS

2007–08	*£ per year*
Small companies' rate: 20%	0–300,000
Marginal small companies' relief	300,001–1,500,000
Main rate: 30%	>1,500,001

For companies with 'ring fence' profits (income and gains from oil extraction and oil rights in the UK), the small companies' rate of tax on those profits remains at 19% for the '07/'08 financial year.

METHODS OF PAYMENT

The figures for non-cash transactions since 1991 illustrate the trends in how UK households and businesses make payments – and a decline in the passing of cheques:

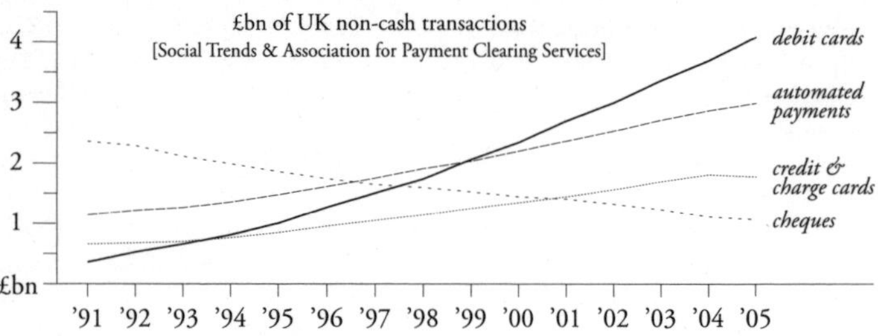

COUNTERFEIT MONEY

According to the Bank of England, banknotes are becoming harder to counterfeit because of increasingly sophisticated security measures. Bank of England notes include: a watermark of the Queen; metal thread that is 'windowed' to appear as a series of silver dashes; a foil hologram; micro lettering under or behind the Queen's portrait; and a fluorescent feature that is visible only under ultraviolet light. Notwithstanding these safeguards, in 2005 the number of counterfeit banknotes removed from circulation increased 53% (from 2004), to approximately 505,000 notes. This rise was blamed on 'home forgers' who use PCs and laser printers to produce passable reproductions. Tabulated below are the denominations and numbers of forged Bank of England notes taken out of circulation in 2005:

Note	*number seized*				
£5	6,000	£10	7,000	£50	5,000
		£20	487,000	Total	505,000

The European Central Bank's annual report shows that the number of counterfeit euro notes removed from circulation peaked in 2003 and, since then, the number has remained stable, with about 49,000 fakes recovered each month. The table below shows the denominations and numbers of fake euro notes seized 2005–06:

Note	*number seized*				
€5	5,860	€20	212,080	€200	11,720
€10	29,170	€50	268,160	€500	8,720
		€100	50,300	Total	586,010

In consultation with the Central Bank Counterfeit Deterrence Group (CBCDG), a consortium of the world's Central Banks, the latest version of Adobe Photoshop will not allow users to scan or manipulate the latest banknotes of many major currencies. The design of newer banknotes contains a pattern of five circles that is detected by the image processing software which then blocks user access. On the Smith £20 note the circles are within a cluster of yellow dots; on euro notes they appear as a constellation of stars. Inevitably, computer users have found ways to circumvent these restrictions.

WORLD'S RICHEST CITIES

The richest cities in the world in 2005, ranked by Gross Domestic Product, were:

City	*GDP ($)*
Tokyo	1·2tr
New York	1·1tr
Los Angeles	639bn
Chicago	460bn
Paris	460bn
London	452bn
Osaka/Kobe	341bn
Mexico City	315bn
Philadelphia	312bn
Washington, DC	299bn

[PricewaterhouseCoopers]

INCOME TAX PAYABLE · 2006–07

Annual income (£)	*No. of taxpayers (m)*	*Total tax liability (£m)*	*Average rate of tax (%)*	*Average amount of tax (£)*
5,035–7,499	2·7	306	1·8	114
7,500–9,999	3·4	1,390	4·7	411
10,000–14,999	6·0	6,990	9·4	1,170
15,000–19,999	4·9	10,800	12·7	2,200
20,000–29,999	6·4	24,000	15·2	3,720
30,000–49,999	4·5	29,000	17·5	6,540
50,000–99,999	1·5	24,500	25·3	16,800
100,000–199,999	0·4	14,500	31·3	41,500
200,000–499,999	0·1	9,930	34·2	99,500
500,000–999,999	0·02	4,350	35·4	239,000
≥£1,000,000	0·006	4,750	34·2	734,000
ALL INCOMES	29·7m	£131,000	17·9%	£4,390

[Total annual income of the individual for income tax purposes including earned and investment income. Figures relate to taxpayers only. In this context, tax reductions refer to allowances given at a fixed rate, for example Married Couple's Allowance. Source: HM Revenue & Customs, Crown ©]

DRUGS & MONEY

A staggering 100% of euro notes in Ireland tested positive for cocaine, according to a study conducted in January 2007 by Dublin City University. Greater quantities of the drug were discovered on higher denomination bills, though it was thought that only 5% of euro notes were likely to have been actually used for 'snorting'. (The remaining 95% were suspected to have been cross-contaminated in wallets and pockets.) ❦ In Spain, 94% of euros tested positive for cocaine – at an average of 25·18 micrograms of coke per note. ❦ The mysterious 2006 phenomenon of crumbling euro notes in Germany was blamed on users of crystal methamphetamine. The sulphates used in the manufacture of the drug form sulphuric acid when mixed with sweat, which then renders the notes brittle and susceptible to disintegration.

HOUSE PRICES AGAINST INCOME

Below are Nationwide's gross house price to earnings ratios for first time buyers. They show that, in 2007, buyers in London spent 6·9× the average London wage on a first time property (4·7× in 1983); and across the UK, the average first time buyer spent 5·3× the average UK wage on a property (2·7× in 1983).

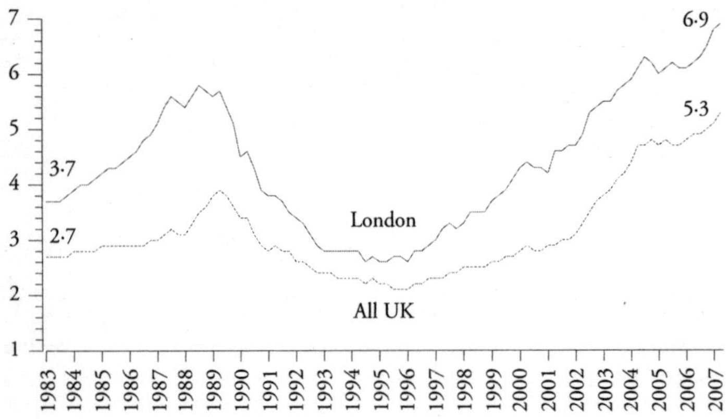

COUNCIL TAX BANDS · 2007–08

ENGLAND	*value £*
A	≤40,000
B	40,001–52,000
C	52,001–68,000
D	68,001–88,000
E	88,001–120,000
F	120,001–160,000
G	160,001–320,000
H	>320,001

WALES	*value £*
A	≤44,000
B	44,001–65,000
C	65,001–91,000
D	91,001–123,000
E	123,001–162,000
F	162,001–223,000
G	223,001–324,000
H	324,001–424,000
I	>424,001

SCOTLAND	*value £*
A	≤27,000
B	27,001–35,000
C	35,001–45,000
D	45,001–58,000
E	58,001–80,000
F	80,001–106,000
G	106,001–212,000
H	>212,001

SIGNS OF PROSPERITY

According to an ING Direct poll of 200 estate agents, areas need to show at least 6 of the following 10 'prosperity signs' before they can be considered 'on the up':

Ethnic cuisine
Graffiti disappearing
Crowded public transport
Better school results
Thicker telephone directories

More burglar alarms
Planning notices appear
More skips and scaffolding
More traffic wardens
Neighbourhood Watch schemes

THE SUNDAY TIMES RICH LIST · 2007

No.	*Billionaire* (UK)	*age*	*£ billion*	*activity*	*last year*
1	Lakshmi Mittal	56	19·3	steel	1
2	Roman Abramovich	41	10·8	industry, football	2
3	Duke of Westminster	55	7·0	property	3
4	Sri & Gopi Hinduja	71, 67	6·2	industry, finance	7
5	David Khalili	61	5·8	art, property	99
6	Hans Rausing & family	81	5·4	packaging	4
7	Philip & Christina Green	55, 57	4·9	retail	5
8	John Fredriksen	62	3·5	shipping	10
9	David & Simon Reuben	68, 65	3·5	property	8
10	Jim Ratcliffe	54	3·3	chemicals	45=

WORLDWIDE PERSONAL WEALTH

The richest 2% of adults own >50% of *global* household wealth, according to the World Distribution of Household Wealth report, released in December 2006. The study, produced by the World Institute for Development Economics Research of the United Nations University (UNU-WIDER), included every country in the world, and measured all aspects of household wealth, including financial assets, debt, property, and land. The research highlighted the global inequality of wealth distribution, where just a handful of countries account for 90% of the world's household wealth. Below is a breakdown of where the world's wealthiest 1% live:

USA	37%	Italy	4%	Spain	1%
Japan	27%	Germany	4%	Switzerland	1%
UK	6%	Canada	2%	Taiwan	1%
France	5%	Netherlands	2%	*Rest of the world*	10%

To be among the 37m people in the richest 1% of the world, you require assets of >$500,000. In 2000, the average wealth per person was $127,000 in the UK, and $144,000 in the USA.

FORBES MAGAZINE RICH LIST · 2007

No.	*Billionaire* (Worldwide)	*age*	*$ billion*	*activity*	*last year*
1	William Gates III	51	56·0	Microsoft	1
2	Warren Buffett	76	52·0	investing	2
3	Carlos Slim Helu	67	49·0	telecoms	3
4	Ingvar Kamprad & family	80	33·0	Ikea	4
5	Lakshmi Mittal	56	32·0	Mittal Steel	5
6	Sheldon Adelson	73	26·5	casinos	14
7	Bernard Arnault	58	26·0	LVMH	7
8	Amancio Ortega	71	24·0	Zara clothing	23
9	Li Ka-Shing	78	23·0	investing	10
10	David Thomson & family	49	22·0	media	–

CONFIDENCE IN PROFESSIONS · UK & EUROPE

Below is a comparison of UK and European consumer confidence in a range of different professions, according to the 2007 *Reader's Digest* Trusted Brands survey:

% with a great deal of trust or quite a lot of trust		*profession*	*% with not very much trust or no trust at all*	
Europe	*UK*		*Europe*	*UK*
92	95	airline pilots	6	5
17	8	car salesmen	80	91
85	91	doctors	15	9
38	39	financial advisers	58	59
24	10	football players	74	89
29	13	journalists	68	87
50	59	judges	47	40
45	48	lawyers	52	51
56	54	meteorologists	42	45
86	94	nurses	12	6
60	74	police	39	26
7	7	politicians	92	93
53	69	priests/church ministers	45	31
50	48	taxi drivers	48	51
77	82	teachers	21	17

DEMANDING WORKERS

British employees came second in a global rank of 'demanding workers' compiled by FDS International in May 2007. However, despite receiving better pay than many nationalities and working fewer hours than most, the French proved the most dissatisfied of the 23 nations polled. The top ten countries for 'whinginess' were:

'Overall whinginess' ranking		*% unhappy with pay*	*average income (£)*	*% unhappy with hours*	*average hours/w*
1	France	43	30,540 [9th]	34	34·5 [12th]
2 =	UK	40	32,690 [4th]	35	36·4 [6th]
2 =	Sweden	35	31,420 [6th]	38	35·7 [8th]
3	USA	38	41,950 [1st]	31	39·6 [4th]
4 =	Australia	30	30,610 [8th]	44	34·8 [11th]
4 =	Portugal	42	19,730 [13th]	57	39·1 [5th]
5 =	Canada	35	32,220 [5th]	28	31·9 [14th]
5 =	Greece	40	23,620 [12th]	38	39·8 [2nd]
6	Poland	55	13,490 [14th]	45	39·8 [3rd]
7 =	Germany	33	29,210 [10th]	28	34·5 [13th]
7 =	Spain	41	25,820 [11th]	28	35·2 [9th]
8	Japan	38	31,410 [7th]	25	42·2 [1st]
9	Switzerland	18	37,080 [3rd]	33	36·1 [7th]
10	Norway	23	40,420 [2nd]	24	34·9 [10th]

INTEREST RATES & THE MPC

Since 1997, the Monetary Policy Committee (MPC) has been responsible for setting UK interest rates. Charted below are the base rate changes since Nov 2003:

Date	*change*	*rate*
05·07·07	+0·25	5·75%
10·05·07	+0·25	5·50%
11·01·07	+0·25	5·25%
09·11·06	+0·25	5·00%
03·08·06	+0·25	4·75%
04·08·05	–0·25	4·50%
05·08·04	+0·25	4·75%
10·06·04	+0·25	4·50%
06·05·04	+0·25	4·25%
05·02·04	+0·25	4·00%
06·11·03	+0·25	3·75%

CHARITY DONATIONS

The top 500 charities in the UK received £10·9bn in donations in 2006. The *Charity Trends 2007* report released by the Charities Aid Foundation in July 2007 listed the UK charities with the largest income from voluntary donations in 2006:

Charity	*voluntary income*
Cancer Research UK	£297m
Oxfam	£176m
British Red Cross	£115·7m
Royal Nat. Lifeboat Inst.	£108·4m
Save the Children (UK)	£95·6m

COST OF SCAMS

3·2m people are affected by scams each year, at a total cost to victims of £3·5bn, according to the Office of Fair Trading. The most common types of scam are shown below, with the average cost to each victim, and the overall annual cost in 2006:

£/victim	Type	*cost (£m)*
5,660	*High risk investment*	490
5,000	*African fee fraud*[1]	340
4,240	*Property investor*	160
3,030	*Holiday club*[2]	1,170
1,900	*Foreign lottery*	260
1,810	*Loan scams*	190
930	*Pyramid schemes*	420
530	*Career opportunity*	30
240	*Clairvoyant mailings*[3]	40
240	*Work at home*	70
170	*Internet dialler*[4]	60
160	*Prize draw*	60
110	*Matrix schemes*[5]	10
90	*Miracle health*	20
80	*Premium rate telephone*	80

[1] Victims are persuaded to give their bank details in order to receive large amounts of money from Africa. Their bank accounts are then cleared. [2] Having won a 'free holiday', victims then have to pay for flights and extras – and do not get to go where they want, when they want. [3] Recipients receive a letter promising predictions that will 'change their lives forever', provided they pay a fee. [4] Consumers accidentally use software that connects them to the internet using an expensive telephone line. [5] Victims are placed on a waiting list for a 'valuable free gift' if they spend >£20 on the scammer's website. Those at the top of the list only receive their 'gift' when a further 100 people have spent enough to be signed up.

The average age of scam victim was 47; 26% were 35–44, and 13% were over 65. ❦ 71% caught by miracle health scams were women; 72% of risky investment scam victims were men. ❦ 30% of victims said they fell for scams because it was unexpected and they were 'caught off guard'. [Source: OFT]

GLASS CEILINGS &c.

The 'glass ceiling' is an unofficial (metaphorically invisible) barrier to promotion, usually 'hit' by women, the disabled, members of ethnic minorities, or those who for whatever reason do not match the (unspoken) requirements of an organisation. In 1991, the US Department of Labor defined the glass ceiling as 'those artificial barriers based on attitudinal or organisational bias that prevent qualified individuals from advancing upward in their organisation into management-level positions'. The *Oxford English Dictionary* traces the first use of the phrase to an *Adweek* article in 1984, and since then, a number of spin-off phrases have been coined:

Stained-glass ceiling.................................. *a barrier to those in the Church*
Celluloid ceiling† .... *a barrier to those in the film industry*
Marble ceiling.. *a barrier to those in politics*
Paper ceiling........................... *a barrier to those in newspapers or publishing*
Grass ceiling.................................... *a barrier to those in the field of sport*
Glass elevator ...*where some are unfairly promoted over those whose careers are 'stuck'*
Pink plateau.......................................*a barrier to homosexuals in any field*

† In a 2006 analysis, Dr Martha Lauzen noted that 'in 2005, women comprised 17% of all directors, executive producers, producers, writers, cinematographers, and editors working on the top 250 domestic grossing films. This is the same percentage of women employed in these roles in 1998'. ❦ Over the last five years there has been a 40% fall in women holding senior management positions within the UK's 350 biggest companies, according to PricewaterhouseCoopers. The March 2007 report suggested women took themselves off the career ladder before they hit the glass ceiling, as a result of the cost of childcare and increasing female entrepreneurship and self-employment.

STRESS-FREE WORKING

In 2007, *New Scientist* analysed research into office stress and offered six tips, viz:

CREATE A GOOD SPACE · *from the physical to the psychological, even the flow of people through the office can affect stress.*

RAISE YOUR STATUS · *research found that 'the lower a man's "grade" the more likely he was to die young'.*

BE SOCIAL · *'social support from work colleagues will help lower stress levels'.*

DON'T BE TOO SOCIAL · *'sociability to the point of not getting anything done is stressful'.*

LEARN TO SWITCH OFF† · *'so-called "psychological detachment" from the office has been associated with less fatigue, more positive mood and fewer days off work'.*

MODERN STRESS-BUSTING‡ · *'try yoga, deep breathing or lunchtime walks'.*

† In one study, a respondent asked if it was 'normal' for her husband to put his BlackBerry on the pillow next to them when they made love. ‡ A Tokyo company allows its workers to stroke cats during their breaks; in New York, MetroNaps sell 15 minutes in a sleep pod for $14; and tests at the Monell Chemical Senses Centre discovered that women feel less tense after sniffing sweat from armpits.

MOST TRUSTED UK BRANDS · 2007

Category	*most trusted brand*
Airline	British Airways
Car hire	Hertz
Chocolate/confectionery	Cadbury
Coffee	Nescafé
Deodorant	Sure
Food retailer	Tesco
Hay fever remedy	Piriton
Household cleaner	Flash
Indigestion remedy	Rennie
Margarine/butter	Flora
Mortgage lender	Halifax/BOS
Motoring organisations	AA
Optician	Specsavers
Pet food	Whiskas
Sun care	Nivea
Tea	PG Tips†
Toothpaste	Colgate
Utility company	British Gas

[Source: *Reader's Digest*, 2007 Trusted Brand Survey] † The PG Tips chimps were dropped as the 'face' of PG in 2002, bringing to an end the longest running British TV ad campaign. Despite this, the chimps were chosen as the nation's favourite ad characters in 2003.

UNPAID OVERTIME

According to January 2007 data from the Trades Union Congress, UK workers undertake an average of 7 hours and 6 mins unpaid overtime a week – equivalent to £4,800/year. Below is a regional breakdown of this unpaid work:

Area	*average unpaid overtime*	*£/year*
England	7h 11m	4,786
N Ireland	7h 12m	4,298
Wales	7h 6m	4,224
Scotland	6h 30m	4,151

[The average length of unpaid overtime in London was 7h 36m/week, £7,070/year.]

2008 ISSUE COINS

The Queen graciously gave approval to the Chancellor of the Exchequer's recommendations that the following special coins be issued during 2008:

· A Crown piece to celebrate the 60th birthday of the Prince of Wales · A Crown piece to celebrate the 450th anniversary of the accession of Elizabeth I · £2 coin to mark the 100th anniversary of the London Olympic Games in 1908

ADVERTISED JOBS

Below are the jobs most frequently advertised by ad-spend (Jan–Sept 2006), according to Nielsen Media Research:

PRIVATE SECTOR JOBS

Job title	*ad expenditure (£)*
Lawyer	34,285
Teacher	14,790
Admin Officer (general)	12,140
Driver	12,139
Rep/Salesman	11,080
Chef	8,463
Trainee/school leaver	8,354
Sales Manager	8,305
Sales Exec	7,676
Architect	7,446

PUBLIC SECTOR JOBS

Job title	*ad expenditure (£)*
Teacher	37,512
Lecturer/Snr Lecturer/Reader	23,335
Head of Dept/Dean (education)	21,777
Admin Officer (general)	12,908
Headship/Principal	9,102
Professor/Chair	8,520
Director	7,992
Board Member	7,911
Educational Research Fellow	6,270
Educational Research Assoc.	4,139

[Figures relate to job adverts in the press]

FINANCIAL SNAP-SCHOTT · 2007

Item (£)	*09·2006*	*09·2007*
Church of England · marriage service (excluding certificate)	218·00	240·00
– funeral service (excluding burial and certificate)	87·00	93·00
Season ticket · Arsenal FC (2007/8; centre, E & W upper tiers)	1,825·00	1,825·00
– Grimsby Football Club (2007/8; Upper Carlsberg)	323·00	342·00
Annual membership · MCC (full London member)	344·00	344·00
– Stringfellows, London	600·00	600·00
– Groucho Club, London (+35; London member)	500·00	550·00
– Trimdon Colliery & Deaf Hill Workmen's Club	3·50	3·50
– The Conservative Party (>22)	15·00	25·00
– The Labour Party (those in work)	39·00	36·00
– The Liberal Democrats (minimum required)	6·00	9·00
– UK Independence Party	20·00	20·00
– Royal Society for the Protection of Birds (adult)	31·00	32·00
Annual television licence† · colour	131·50	135·50
– black & white	44·00	45·50
Subscription, annual · *Private Eye*	24·00	28·00
– *Vogue*	28·50	39·00
– *Saga Magazine*	19·95	19·95
New British Telecom line installation	124·99	124·99
Entrance fee · Thorpe Park (12+ 'thrill seeker' purchased on the day)	28·50	32·00
– Buckingham Palace State Rooms (adult)	14·00	15·00
– Eden Project, Cornwall (adult, day)	13·80	14·00
'Pint of best bitter' · Railway Inn, Yelverton, Devon	2·20	2·50
– Railway Inn, Banff, Scotland	—	2·50
– Railway Inn, Trafford, Manchester	1·90	1·80
– Railway Inn, Coleshill, Birmingham	2·40	2·40
– Railway Tavern, Globe St, London, E2	—	2·00
Fishing rod licence · Salmon and Sea Trout (full season)	65·00	66·50
List price of the cheapest new Ford (Ford Ka 1·3i 'on the road')	7,090·00	7,095·00
British Naturalisation (includes ceremony fee)	268·00	655·00
Manchester United home shirt (2007/8 season)	39·99	39·99
Tea at the Ritz, London (afternoon, per person)	35·00	36·00
Kissing the Blarney Stone (admission to Blarney Castle) [€8]	5·40	5·00
Hampton Court Maze (adult)	3·50	3·50
Ordinary London adult single bus ticket (cash)	1·50	2·00
Mersey Ferry (adult return)	2·15	2·20
Passport · new, renewal, or amendment (3 week postal service)	51·00	66·00
Driving test (practical + theory; cars, weekday)	70·00	77·00
Driving licence (first · car, motorcycle, moped)	38·00	45·00
NHS dental examination (standard)	15·50	15·90
NHS prescription charge (per item)	6·65	6·85
Moss Bros three-piece morning suit hire (weekend, basic 'Lombard')	49·00	45·00
FedEx Envelope (≤0·5kg) UK–USA	44·41	52·55

† The blind concession is 50%. Those ≥75 may apply for a free licence.

—RPI 'BASKET' CHANGES—

Some 2007 changes to the RPI basket:

items removed · vegetable oil; Brie; Brussels sprouts; child's Wellington boots; men's leather boots; gemstone cluster ring; portable colour television; VHS video recorder; portable CD radio cassette; 35mm compact camera; decorative outdoor plant pot; blank/prerecorded VHS cassette; photographic develop and print, &c.

items added · olive oil; pro-biotic drink; courgettes; broccoli; shower head; electric fan; credit card charges; mortgage fees; mobile downloads; diamond solitaire ring; toothbrush; satellite navigation system; flat panel television; digital (DAB) radio; recordable DVD; photographic digital processing, &c.

—RECENT CPI/RPI DATA—

CPI & RPI % change over 12 months:

Year	*month*	CPI	RPI
2007	Aug	1·8	4·1
	Jul	1·9	3·8
	Jun	2·4	4·4
	May	2·5	4·3
	Apr	2·8	4·5
	Mar	3·1	4·8
	Feb	2·8	4·6
	Jan	2·7	4·2
2006	Dec	3·0	4·4
	Nov	2·7	3·9
	Oct	2·4	3·7
	Sep	2·4	3·6
	Aug	2·5	3·4
	Jul	2·4	3·3
	Jun	2·5	3·3
	May	2·2	3·0
	Apr	2·0	2·6
	Mar	1·8	2·4

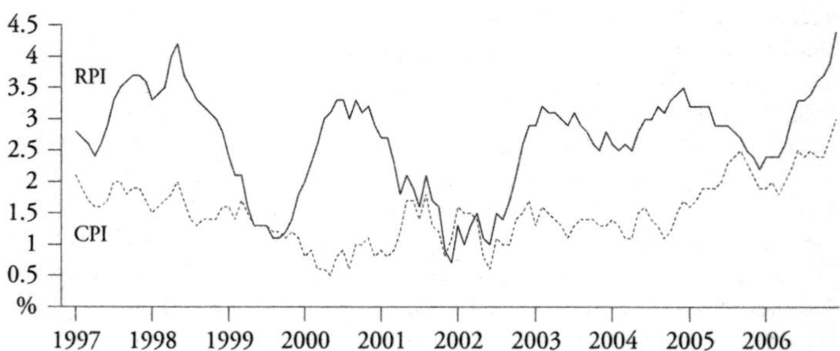

SPARE CASH

17% of Britons claimed to have no money left after paying their basic living expenses, according to an ACNielsen study in 2006. Of the 40 countries surveyed, Portugal had the highest percentage of people who claimed to have no spare cash:

Country	*% with no spare cash*
Portugal	23
United States	22
United Kingdom	17
Canada	16
France	16
Turkey	16
Hungary	15
Germany	15
Global average	13

POSTAL PRICING IN PROPORTION

Category	*size (mm)*	*thickness (mm)*	*weight (g)*	*1st*	*2nd*
Letter	≤240×165	≤5	0–100	34p	24p
Large Letter	≤353×250	≤25	0–100	48p	40p
			101–250	70p	60p
			251–500	98p	83p
			501–750	142p	120p
Packet	>353 long or >250 wide	or >25	0–100	109p	92p
			101–250	138p	120p
			251–500	184p	152p
			501–750	238p	192p
			751–1,000	292p	230p
			1,001–1,250	425p	—

Items >1,250g will cost an extra 75p for each additional 250g or part thereof.

AIRMAIL RATES

AIRMAIL	*Letters* Europe	*Zone* 1	*Zone* 2
Postcards	0·48	0·54	0·54
≤10g	0·48	0·54	0·54
≤20	0·48	0·78	0·78
≤40	0·69	1·17	1·24
≤60	0·90	1·58	1·74
≤80	1·10	2·00	2·24
≤100	1·31	2·42	2·74
≤120	1·52	2·83	3·23
≤140	1·73	3·25	3·72

To find a postcode call
08456 039 038
For further information see
royalmail.com

Small packets		*Printed papers*	
Europe	*Z 1/2*	*Europe*	*Z 1/2*
1·19	1·58	1·03	1·50
1·31	1·80	1·12	1·72
1·44	2·02	1·23	1·95

Recorded Signed For = postage + 70p · Special Delivery (9am) = £9·35 for up to 100g
A universal stamp can be used to send letters up to 40g to Europe (60p), or worldwide (£1·12)

ROYAL MAIL STAMPS OF 2007

9 Jan........The Beatles
1 Feb........Sea Life
13 Feb........Sky at Night
1 Mar........World of Invention
22 Mar...Abolition of the Slave Trade
23 Apr........Celebrating England
15 May........Beside the Seaside
17 May........Wembley
3 Jul........Grand Prix
17 Jul........Harry Potter
26 Jul........Scouts
4 Sep........Birds
20 Sep........British Army Uniforms
16 Oct........Royal Diamond Wedding
6 Nov........Christmas 2007
8 Nov........Lest We Forget

As pioneers of the philatelic system, the UK is the only country exempt from having to display its name on its international stamps.

VIRTUAL CURRENCY

Inside the virtual worlds of Massively Multiplayer Online Role-Playing Games (MMORPGs), players use virtual currency to buy and sell objects like houses, weapons, spells, &c. And, as MMORPGs gain subscribers and stature, increased interest (and regulatory attention) has focused on these virtual currency transactions. Although most game publishers explicitly prohibit users from trading 'game gold' for real-world money, many players have chosen to sell virtual currency online, whether through third-party brokers or via peer-to-peer exchanges. Until 2007, eBay was a primary source for trading virtual currency, but in January of that year the company announced it would no longer allow the sale of any virtual property, citing the complex legal issues surrounding the ownership of virtual goods†. In February 2007, Chinese regulators banned the exchange of 'QQ coins' (issued by the country's main provider of instant-messaging) for real money, amid concerns the coins were being used to purchase illicit services (in 2006, China's Central Bank had said the coins were so widespread they threatened to affect the value of the yuan). ❦ Below are some virtual currency exchange rates against the US dollar. Amounts listed represent the units of virtual currency purchasable for $1, as of March 28, 2007:

Game	*currency unit*	*$1=*
Anarchy Online	credits (Atlantean – RK1)‡	3,831,417·62
City of Heroes	influence	413,564·92
Dark Age of Camelot	platinum (Galahad – Hibernia)	1·47
Dungeons & Dragons	platinum	12,515·64
EVE Online	isk	8,503,401.36
EverQuest	platinum	3,770·73
EverQuest II	gold (Befallen – Good)	43·25
Final Fantasy XI	gil (Unicorn)	24,987·50
Guild Wars	gold	12,510·42
Lineage II	adena (Devianne)	81,338·75
Second Life	Linden dollar	270
Star Wars Galaxies	credit	1,240,694·78
World of Warcraft (EU)	gold (Lothar – Horde)	21·26
World of Warcraft (US)	gold (Frostmourne – Alliance)	4·72

† Notably, 'online reality phenomenon' *Second Life* was exempt from the eBay ban. The makers of *Second Life*, Linden Labs, encourage the sale of their virtual currency for real-world money. In October 2005, *Second Life* even launched its own online currency exchange, LindeX, allowing users and the public to trade Linden dollars for US dollars. Regulatory and fraud controls are used to keep the Linden dollar stable. *Entropia Universe* also encourages the exchange of its virtual currency (the Project Entropia Dollar, PED) for real money; game currency can be withdrawn from real-world ATMs through use of a special card. In fact, virtual property may be increasingly valuable – in April 2007, the BBC reported on research by security firm Symantec suggesting that access to a *World of Warcraft* account was more valuable to criminals than a stolen credit card. ‡ In some games, currency values differ from server to server. In such cases, one server has been chosen arbitrarily and noted in brackets. The list is intended for illustrative purposes, and is not exhaustive.

[Sources: IGE; *Second Life*; GameUSD.com; UMMO Letters. Linden dollar exchange rate as of December 8, 2006, via CNN.]

ISLAMIC FINANCE

Sharia law decrees that money is simply a medium of exchange with no intrinsic value, and that Muslims are forbidden to charge *Riba* [interest or usury] since it leads to *zulm* [injustice]. The Qur'an states in verses 278–9 of Surah 2, al-Baqara:

'O you who believe! Fear Allah, and give up what remains of your demand for usury, if you are indeed believers.' 'If you do it not, take notice of war from Allah and His Messenger: but if you turn back, you shall have your capital sums; deal not unjustly, and you shall not be dealt with unjustly.'

Sharia law also prohibits dealing in anything *Haram* [unlawful] (e.g. pornography, gambling, alcohol, pork, &c.) or *Bay' al-Gharar* [risky] (e.g. goods sold deceitfully). While Islamic finance existed throughout the Middle Ages, its recent popularity dates back to the first Islamic banks founded in the 1960s, with steady growth since then. And, as Islam has expanded alongside globalised capitalism, *Fuqhas* [Islamic jurists] have examined classical texts to create acceptable Islamic analogues of conventional financial products (bank accounts, loans, mortgages, &c.). Since Sharia prohibits the charging of interest, Islamic finance has developed a range of models that operate by sharing risk and reward, including:

IJARA · a form of leasing, where the bank purchases an item and rents it to the customer for an agreed time and price. The bank retains ownership of the item, and reclaims it at the end of the leasing period. A similar model is IJARA-WA-IQTINA, except the customer is able to purchase the item at the end of the contract. A form of IJARA with diminishing MUSHARAKA [see right] allows for large investments, such as the purchase of property; for example, where the ownership of a house is gradually shifted from bank to customer with every transfer of capital over and above rental payments.

MUSHARAKA · a joint venture where profits sharing is agreed in advance, but repayment of losses may only be in proportion to the sum invested.

MUDARABA · an investment model in which the customer invests money and the bank invests expertise. Profits are shared and, in the event of a loss, no fees are charged.

MURABAHA · a form of credit where the bank purchases an item and re-sells it to the customer on a deferred basis, adding a mutually agreed margin of profit for the bank (reward for risk).

Estimating the popularity of *halal* [lawful] financial products is problematic – not least because the market is growing. However, according to the Financial Services Authority, in 2006, 'assets controlled by Islamic banks at the global level are reported to be \$200–\$500bn and are growing at a pace of 10–15% per year'. ❦ In Britain, the popularity of Islamic finance has seen the growth of Islamic banks, and the development of *halal* products by many of the high street banks. Over a number of years, the Treasury has sought to develop Britain as a centre for Islamic finance and, as Chancellor, Gordon Brown introduced measures in successive Budgets to facilitate and regulate Sharia compliant insurance, investment, mortgages, bonds (*sukuk*) and other financial products. Further measures are expected in future Budgets.

ECONOMIC INDICATORS OF NOTE

Indicator	2006	2005	2004	2003	2002	2001	2000	1999	1998	1997	1996	(...) 1986
FTSE 100 share index	5,941	5,168	4,520	4,030	4,566	5,541	6,348	6,313	5,667	4,695	3,845	1,679
Dow Jones Industrial Average	11,409	10,548	10,317	8,994	9,226	10,189	10,735	10,465	8,626	7,441	5,743	—
CBI business optimism survey	-8·0	-18·5	6·5	-7·5	-3·2	-27·0	-3·0	-7·0	-33·8	0·0	1·8	—
RPI inflation (% year-on-year)	3·2	2·8	3·0	2·9	1·6	1·8	2·9	1·6	3·4	3·1	2·4	3·4
Real GDP (% year-on-year)	2·8	1·8	3·3	2·8	2·1	2·4	3·8	3·0	3·4	3·1	2·8	4·0
Average mortgage rate (%)	5·17	5·21	4·96	4·71	5·03	6·05	6·79	6·47	7·76	7·08	6·73	11·9
Number of taxpayers (million)	30·6	30·3	28·5	28·9	28·6	29·3	27·2	26·9	26·2	25·7	25·8	23·7
Highest rate of income tax (%)	40	40	40	40	40	40	40	40	40	40	40	60
Employment rate (%)	74·6	74·7	74·8	74·7	74·4	74·6	74·4	73·8	73·3	72·7	71·8	—
Unemployed (millions)	0·9	0·9	0·9	0·9	0·9	1·0	1·1	1·2	1·3	1·6	2·1	3·1
Unemployment rate (%)	2·9	2·7	2·7	3·0	3·1	3·1	3·6	4·1	4·5	5·3	6·9	10·5
Growth in consumer credit (% year-on-year)	7·6	12·5	14·2	14·9	15·9	13·4	14·5	15·8	17·2	17·1	15·9	—
Credit cards in issue (millions)	67·4	70·6	71·4	66·4	60·4	53·9	49·7	43·5	40·1	36·6	32·5	N/A
Outstanding credit card balance (£bn)	66·1	67·5	63·8	54·2	47·5	40·7	35·6	29·7	24·6	19·3	15·7	—
Mortgage loan approvals (thousands)	1,234	1,195	1,253	1,370	1,423	1,258	1,122	1,146	1,036	1,190	1,078	—
Housing transactions (thousands)	1,348	1,531	1,793	1,345	1,588	1,458	1,431	1,470	1,347	1,440	1,243	1,795
Halifax house price (% change year-on-year)	8·3	5·7	18·3	22·4	17·4	8·5	9·8	7·2	5·4	6·3	4·5	11·0
Change in average earnings (%)	4·1	4·1	4·3	3·4	3·5	4·5	4·5	4·8	5·2	4·3	3·5	8·1
Lending secured on houses (£bn)	344·9	288·4	291·4	277·4	220·8	160·1	119·8	114·7	89·4	77·2	71·7	N/A
Properties repossessed (%)	0·19	0·13	0·07	0·07	0·11	0·14	0·20	0·27	0·31	0·31	0·40	0·30
New car registrations (thousands)	2,340	2,444	2,599	2,646	2,682	2,578	2,337	2,242	2,262	2,157	2,018	—
US Dollar/GB Pound ($/£)	1·84	1·82	1·83	1·64	1·50	1·44	1·52	1·62	1·66	1·64	1·56	1·47
Euro/GB Pound (€/£) [pre-1999 estimated]	1·47	1·46	1·47	1·45	1·59	1·61	1·64	1·52	(1·49)	(1·45)	(1·21)	(1·48)
Gold price per Troy ounce (£)	328	245	223	222	206	188	184	172	177	202	249	251
Oil US Dollar/barrel (Brent spot price)	65·2	54·6	38·3	28·9	25·0	24·5	28·7	17·9	12·8	19·1	20·6	14·5

[Sources: Bank of England; ONS; Halifax Building Society; Council of Mortgage Lenders; HM Treasury; British Bankers' Association · Many figures have been rounded]

COLOUR TRADEMARKS

Colour trademarks may be granted to brands when a particular hue can be proven to have iconic associations with a certain product or service. Such colour marks are limited to a specific range of products – a practice intended to prevent befuddled consumers mistaking one brand for another, while ensuring that one company does not dominate any part of the colour spectrum. For example, Heinz enjoys exclusivity in its distinctive turquoise only for its delicious baked beans. Since trademark law is not standardised internationally, rules differ from region to region. So, while Cadbury has protection for its purple packaging in Great Britain and New Zealand, the Australian courts ruled that the company did not have 'an exclusive reputation in the use of this dark purple colour in connection with chocolate'. The European Court of Justice recommends that colour trademark applicants give the trademark office both a description of the colour and the relevant shade from an internationally accepted colour-coding system, such as Pantone. For example:

Company	*colour*	*Pantone*
Tiffany	robin egg blue	1837
Orange	orange	151
UPS	brown	N/A
BP	green	348C
Deutsche Telekom	magenta	N/A
Cadbury	purple	N/A
Heinz baked beans	turquoise	N/A
Kodak	yellow	123
Veuve Clicquot	orange	137C

As branding develops in sophistication, and brands become increasingly globalised, the legal and technical issues surrounding trademarks become more complex. For example, in 2003 the European Court of Justice ruled that sounds might be trademarked – if they could be represented in an intelligible and objective way, such as through musical notation. This paved the way for advances in so-called 'sonic logos' or 'earcons'. Increasingly, courts are being asked to give protection to a range of sensory trademarks, including gustatory [taste], tactile [touch], and olfactory [smell].

UK ENERGY CONSUMPTION

Below is a comparison of energy consumption by final users in 1970 and 2005:

	domestic	*other*	*transport*	*industry*
1970	25·5%	12·5	19·5	42·5
2005	29·5%	12·5	37	21

And a comparison of final energy consumption by fuel type in 1970 and 2005:

	petroleum	*gas*	*solid fuels*	*electricity*
1970	47%	10·5	31	11·5
2005	44·5%	34·5		18·5

In 2005, solid fuels accounted for just 1·5%; a further 1% (not shown) was attributed to 'other'. In June 2007, a survey by Energy Experience revealed that two-thirds of Britons claim not to have enough electric plug sockets in their homes. According to the National House Building Council, all new 3-bedroom homes must have at least 38 sockets. [Source: DTI Digest of UK Energy Statistics 2006]

IMMIGRATION & WORK

According to the Home Office, 137,035 work permit holders and their dependants arrived in the UK in 2005 – the majority (*c*.33%) were from India. Most immigrants come to the UK for the purpose of work, as is shown by 2004 OECD figures:

Purpose of entry to (%)	*work*	*accompanying family of workers*	*family re-unification or formation*	*humanitarian*	*other*
Australia	32	30	26	10	1
France	12	–	68	7	13
Germany	19	12	33	7	29
UK	42	19	15	17	6
USA	8	9	66	8	10

OECD figures compare the employment rate of native and foreign-born residents:

Employed (%)	*native* ♂	*native* ♀	*foreign-born* ♂	*foreign-born* ♀
Australia	81	66	76	58
France	69	58	67	48
Germany	70	58	64	47
Ireland	75	56	74	54
UK	78	67	73	55
USA	73	65	80	56

[Source: 2007 OECD Factbook · 2004 figures, rounded up to nearest whole number]

GAMBLING

65% of British adults (*c*.25·9m people) engaged in at least one form of gambling in the prior 12 months, according to the May 2007 report *Taking Part: National Survey of Culture, Leisure, & Sport.* Most, 37·4%, engaged in just 1 form of gambling; 16% engaged in 2; and 11·7%, ≥3. Below are rates of participation in various activities:

Participated during past 12 months	%
National Lottery	57·0
Bets on horse racing	12·2
Scratchcards	10·3
Other lottery	6·9
Gaming/fruit machines	6·7
Bingo tickets	5·9
Bets on events (football; elections)	3·3
Bets on dog racing	3·1
Football pools or 'fixed odds'	3·1
Table games (roulette, cards, dice)	2·7
Private bets	2·3
Other types†	0·6

[† include raffles, internet/TV gambling, &c.]

Gender	*% gamble*
Male	68
Female	62
Qualification	*% gamble*
None	68
Other/unknown	68
Below A-levels	69
Trade apprentice	76
A-levels and above	61

Ethnicity	*% gamble*
White	68
Mixed	55
Asian	39
Black	46
Other	47
Area type	*% gamble*
Urban	65
Rural	66

Religion	*% gamble*
No religion	65
Christian	68
Buddhist	48
Hindu	52
Muslim	28
Sikh	59
Other religion	56

[Source: DCMS]

Parliament & Politics

I used to say that politics was the second lowest profession
and I have come to know that it bears a great similarity to the first.
— RONALD REAGAN (1911–2004)

THE HOUSE OF COMMONS

House of Commons, London, SW1A 0AA
Switchboard: 020 7219 3000 · www.parliament.uk

STATE OF THE PARTIES · as at 12 September 2007

Party	Seats	Party	Seats
Labour	353	Independent	2
Conservative	195	Independent Labour	1
Liberal Democrat	63	Ulster Unionist	1
Scottish National Party	6	Respect	1
Plaid Cymru	3	Speaker (Michael Martin)	1
Democratic Unionist	9	Deputy Speakers	3
Sinn Féin [seats not taken]	5	TOTAL	646
Social Democratic & Labour	3	GOVERNMENT MAJORITY	69

Oldest MP .... Ian Paisley [DUP; North Antrim] *b.*06·04·26
Youngest MP .... Jo Swinson [Lib Dem; East Dunbartonshire] *b.*05·02·80
Largest majority .... 19,519; Thomas Clarke [Lab; Coatbridge, Chryston & Bellshill]
Smallest majority .... 37; Laura Moffatt [Lab; Crawley]

'FRIT'

The word 'frit', derived from the verb 'fright', means to be afraid or terrified. It is apparently of Lincolnshire or Black Country origin – and the *Oxford English Dictionary* traces an early use of the word to John Clare who, in 1821, wrote 'The coy hare squats nestling in the corn, Frit at the bow'd ear tott'ring o'er her head'. This archaic term has special meaning in the House of Commons, where it is hurled as a term of abuse – especially by Tory members. It seems that the term's popularity in the House derives from an exchange in April 1983, when Denis Healey accused Margaret Thatcher of planning a 'cut and run' election in June. Thatcher (who likely learned the term during her childhood in Grantham) venomously replied:

Oh, the Right Honourable Gentleman is afraid of an election is he? Really? Fraid, frightened, frit! Couldn't take it! Couldn't stand it! Oh-ho! If I was going to cut and run I'd have gone after the Falklands. Frightened! Frightened! Inflation is lower than it has been for thirteen years; a record the Right Honourable Gentleman couldn't begin to touch.

ADDRESSES TO BOTH HOUSES OF PARLIAMENT

In May 2007, Bertie Ahern addressed both Houses of Parliament, becoming the first Taoiseach and the 33rd individual (excluding reigning UK monarchs) so to do. The House of Commons lists those to whom both Houses of Parliament have listened:

Date	*speaker*	position/reason
23·03·39	Albert Lebrun	*President of France*
21·10·42	Field Marshal Jan Christiaan Smuts	*Prime Minister of South Africa*
11·05·44	Mackenzie King	*Prime Minister of Canada*
17·05·45	King George VI	*on the occasion of victory in Europe*
21·08·45	King George VI	*on the occasion of victory in World War II*
09·03·50	Vincent Auriol	*President of France*
26·10·50	King George VI	*opening of the new House of Commons Chamber*
22·10·54	Haile Selassie	*Emperor of Ethiopia*
24·04·56	Marshal Nikolai Bulganin	*PM of the Soviet Union (USSR)*
	Nikita Khrushchev	*First Secretary of the Communist Party of USSR*
07·04·60	General Charles de Gaulle	*President of France*
22·06·65	Queen Elizabeth II	*700th Anniversary of de Montford's parliament*
28·04·66	U Thant	*Secretary-General of the United Nations*
09·02·67	Alexei Kosygin	*Prime Minister of USSR*
28·04·69	Giuseppe Saragat	*President of the Italian Republic*
03·03·70	Willy Brandt	*Chancellor of West Germany*
23·06·76	Valéry Giscard d'Estaing	*President of France*
04·05·77	Queen Elizabeth II	*Queen's Silver Jubilee address*
08·06·82	Ronald Reagan	*President of the United States of America*
24·10·84	François Mitterrand	*President of France*
18·12·84	Mikhail Gorbachev	*Gen. Sec. of the Communist Party of USSR*
23·01·86	Shimon Peres	*Prime Minister of Israel*
28·04·86	King Juan Carlos	*King of Spain*
02·07·86	Dr Richard Von Weizsäcker	*President of West Germany*
20·07·88	Queen Elizabeth II	*tercentenary of the Bill of Rights*
08·05·89	Daniel Ortega	*President of Nicaragua*
24·10·90	Francesco Cossiga	*President of the Italian Republic*
10·11·92	Boris Yeltsin	*President of the Russian Federation*
28·04·93	Dr Mário Soares	*President of Portugal*
05·05·93	Nelson Mandela	*Foreign and Commonwealth Affairs Committee*
07·12·93	Mikhail Gorbachev	*Inter-Parliamentary Union*
06·05·95	Queen Elizabeth II	*50th Anniversary of Victory in Europe Day*
29·11·95	Bill Clinton	*President of the United States of America*
15·05·96	Jacques Chirac	*President of France*
11·07·96	Nelson Mandela	*President of South Africa*
16·07·96	Dalai Lama	*all-party group on Tibet*
29·10·98	Dr Carlos Menem	*President of the Argentine*
06·07·00	John Howard	*Prime Minister of Australia*
30·04·02	Queen Elizabeth II	*Queen's Golden Jubilee address*
08·05·07	Kofi Annan	*former Secretary-General of the United Nations*
15·05·07	Bertie Ahern	*Taoiseach, Republic of Ireland*

BRITISH PRIME MINISTERS

Year	Prime Minister	Party
2007	Gordon Brown	L
1997	Tony Blair	L
1990	John Major	C
1979	Margaret Thatcher	C
1976	James Callaghan	L
1974	Harold Wilson	L
1970	Edward Heath	C
1964	Harold Wilson	L
1963	Alec Douglas-Home	C
1957	Harold Macmillan	C
1955	Sir Anthony Eden	C
1951	Winston Churchill	C
1945	Clement Attlee	L
1940	Winston Churchill	N/C
1937	Neville Chamberlain	N/C
1935	Stanley Baldwin	N/C
1931	Ramsay MacDonald	N
1929	Ramsay MacDonald	L
1924	Stanley Baldwin	C
1924	Ramsay MacDonald	L
1923	Stanley Baldwin	C
1922	Andrew Bonar Law	C
1916	David Lloyd George	Co
1908	Herbert Asquith	Li & Co
1905	H. Campbell-Bannerman	Li
1902	Arthur Balfour	C
1895	Marquess of Salisbury	C
1894	Earl of Rosebery	Li
1892	William Gladstone	Li
1886	Marquess of Salisbury	C
1886	William Gladstone	Li
1885	Marquess of Salisbury	C
1880	William Gladstone	Li
1874	Benjamin Disraeli	C
1868	William Gladstone	Li
1868	Benjamin Disraeli	C
1866	Edward Stanley	C
1865	John Russell	Li
1858	Viscount Palmerston	Li
1858	Edward Stanley	C
1855	Viscount Palmerston	Li
1852	G. Hamilton-Gordon	C
1852	Edward Stanley	C
1846	John Russell	W
1841	Sir Robert Peel	T
1835	William Lamb	W
1834	Sir Robert Peel	T
1834	Arthur Wellesley	T
1834	William Lamb	W
1830	Charles Grey	W
1828	Arthur Wellesley	T
1827	Frederick Robinson	T
1827	George Canning	T
1812	Robert Jenkinson	T
1809	Spencer Perceval	T
1807	William Bentinck	T
1806	William Grenville	W
1804	William Pitt [The Younger]	T
1801	Henry Addington	T
1783	William Pitt [The Younger]	T
1783	William Bentinck	T
1782	William FitzMaurice	W
1782	C. Watson-Wentworth	W
1770	Frederick Lord North	T
1767	Augustus Fitzroy	W
1766	William Pitt [The Elder]	W
1765	C. Watson-Wentworth	W
1763	George Grenville	W
1762	John Stuart	T
1757	T. Pelham-Holles	W
1756	William Cavendish	W
1754	T. Pelham-Holles	W
1743	Henry Pelham	W
1742	Spencer Compton	W
1721	Sir Robert Walpole	W

Whig · Liberal · Tory · Labour · Conservative · National · Coalition

SEXIEST POLITICIAN

In *NW* magazine's January 2007 poll of the world's 100 sexiest men, David Cameron climbed to 87 (he was 92nd in 2006). Gordon Brown made a brooding début at 97.

GORDON BROWN'S FIRST CABINET

Greater than usual speculation surrounded Gordon Brown's first Cabinet, not least because his pledge to 'build a government that uses all the talents' led him to approach (and be rebuffed by) a number of Lib Dems – including Paddy Ashdown. In the event, Brown's changes were sweeping (only SoS Defence was unchanged), non-partisan (Blairites and Brownites got top jobs), and relatively deftly handled. Appointments of note included former Chief Whip Jacqui Smith becoming the first female Home Secretary, and David Miliband becoming the youngest Foreign Secretary since 1977. A number of positions were overhauled, including the Dept for Education & Skills which was split into Children, Schools & Families and Innovation, Universities, & Skills. Brown's Cabinet was notable also for containing the first ever married couple (Ed Balls & Yvette Cooper), and the first brothers since 1919 (David & Ed Miliband). As predicted, Brown did not appoint a Deputy PM.

Prime Minister; First Lord of the Treasury.......... Gordon Brown
Chancellor of the Exchequer.......... Alistair Darling
SoS Foreign & Commonwealth Affairs.......... David Miliband
SoS Justice; Lord Chancellor.......... Jack Straw
SoS the Home Department.......... Jacqui Smith
SoS Defence; SoS Scotland.......... Des Browne
SoS Health.......... Alan Johnson
SoS Environment, Food & Rural Affairs.......... Hilary Benn
SoS International Development.......... Douglas Alexander
SoS Business, Enterprise & Regulatory Reform.......... John Hutton
Leader of the Commons; Minister for Women.......... Harriet Harman
SoS Work & Pensions; SoS Wales.......... Peter Hain
SoS Transport.......... Ruth Kelly
SoS Communities & Local Government.......... Hazel Blears
Parliamentary Secretary to the Treasury; Chief Whip.......... Geoff Hoon
SoS Children, Schools, & Families.......... Ed Balls
Minister for Cabinet Office; Chancellor of the Duchy of Lancaster... Ed Miliband
SoS Culture, Media, & Sport.......... James Purnell
SoS Northern Ireland.......... Shaun Woodward [unpaid]
Leader of the House of Lords; Lord President of the Council..... Baroness Ashton
Chief Secretary to the Treasury.......... Andy Burnham
SoS Innovation, Universities, & Skills.......... John Denham

Also attending Cabinet

Minister for the Olympics and London & South East.......... Tessa Jowell
Lords Chief Whip; Captain of the Gentlemen-at-Arms.......... Lord Grocott
Attorney General.......... Baroness Scotland of Asthal
Minister for Housing.......... Yvette Cooper
Minister for Africa, Asia, & UN.......... Sir Mark Malloch Brown†

Gordon Brown's promise of an inclusive 'big tent' approach was in part fulfilled by a number of appointments outside Cabinet, including: former Met Police chief Lord Stevens as International Security Adviser; former CBI chief Sir Digby Jones as Trade Promotion Minister; and former Navy chief Sir Alan West as Security Minister. † Previously, United Nations Deputy Secretary-General.

POLITICAL PLAIN-SPEAKERS

The perception that politicians are evasive has been supported by research conducted in April 2007 by psychologist Geoff Beattie at Manchester University. Beattie studied every television interview given by ten prominent politicians over a period of three weeks and analysed their responses. The politicians' answers were classified thus: *direct* – a full answer to the question asked; *intermediate* – a partial answer; and *non response* – refusal to answer the question, or an irrelevant response. On average, the ten politicians gave direct replies to questions only 45·6% of the time.

Non response	%
John Reid	44
Tony Blair	42
John Prescott	39
Patricia Hewitt	32
Gordon Brown	32
Sir Menzies Campbell	30
David Davis	23
David Cameron	16·7
William Hague	16·7
Nick Clegg	10·3

Direct response	%
David Davis	57
Sir Menzies Campbell	54
Nick Clegg	51·7
David Cameron	47·2
William Hague	47·2
Gordon Brown	47
Patricia Hewitt	46
Tony Blair	40
John Prescott	39
John Reid	36

A June 2007 survey by the Sutton Trust revealed that 38% of politicians in 2007 were privately educated (compared to 46% in 1974). 42% of politicians in 2007 attended Oxbridge, down from 62% in 1974. The profession with most Oxbridge graduates in 2007 was the judiciary (78%).

FORMS OF ADDRESS

In the chamber of the Commons, Members refer to each other not by name but by formal title. (The aim is both to depersonalise sometimes heated debate and to emphasise that MPs do not sit as individual citizens, but as representatives of their constituents.) Most MPs are referred to as 'the Honourable Member for [their constituency]' – however, there are a number of exceptions to this convention:

Position	*formal title*
Generic, of the same party	my Honourable Friend
Generic, of a different party	the Honourable Member Opposite
Privy councillor	the Right Honourable
Member with a courtesy title	the Noble Lord, the Member for
Irish peer	the Honourable Baronet
Practising lawyer	Honourable and Learned†
Member of the armed forces	Honourable and Gallant†

† The Select Committee on Modernisation of the House of Commons recommended abandoning these titles in a report in March 1998, though they are still to be heard from time to time. ❦ Despite belonging to different parties, Conservative MP Nicholas Soames and Labour MP Tony Banks would regularly refer to each other as 'my Honourable Friend' because of a long, close personal friendship.

WOMEN IN POLITICS WORLDWIDE

Women continue to struggle against inequality, according to a UN report released in December 2006: *The State of the World's Children 2007: Women & Children, the Double Dividend of Gender Equality.* The study concluded that women's lack of access to education and employment contributed to their poverty and disenfranchisement. Symptomatic of this gender divide is women's lack of representation at government level. Attitudes towards female politicians may go some way to explain this inequality. The chart below shows the percentage of the public (by region) who agreed or strongly agreed that men make better political leaders than women:

Region	*% agreeing that men make better politicians*
Middle East & North Africa	77
Sub-Saharan Africa	59
South Asia	58
East Asia & Pacific	55
Latin America & Caribbean	35

Women are under-represented in every national parliament worldwide. 10 countries have no female MPs at all, and in 40 other countries women account for less than 10% of parliamentarians. Below is the global average of women in government:

In parliament.......17% | Female ministers...14% | Heads of govt.......6%

The following Inter-Parliamentary Union table shows the countries with the highest percentage of women (in a lower house or single chamber), as of 31·10·2006:

Country		*elections*	*% ♀*
1	Rwanda	09·2003	48·8
2	Sweden	09·2006	47·3
3	Costa Rica	02·2006	38·6
4	Finland	03·2003	38·0
5	Norway	09·2005	37·9
6	Denmark	02·2005	36·9
7	Netherlands	01·2003	36·7
8	Cuba	01·2003	36·0
8 =	Spain	03·2004	36·0
10	Argentina	10·2005	35·0
(15	Germany	09·2005	31·8)
(50	UK	05·2005	19·7)
(67	USA	11·2004	15·2)

[Sources: UN *State of the World's Children 2007*; World Values Survey; Inter-Parliamentary Union]

MOST IMPORTANT ISSUES FACING BRITAIN

According to an Ipsos Mori poll, the most important issues facing Britain today are:

Issue	*% spontaneously stating*
Crime/law & order	30
Race relations/immigration	18
NHS/hospitals	6
Defence/foreign affairs	12
Education/schools	3
Economy/economic situation	3
Housing	3

[Source: Ipsos Mori, August 2007]

THE SCOTTISH PARLIAMENT

The current state of parties (as at 12 September 2007)

Number of MSP*s*	*Constituency*	*Regional*	*Total*
Scottish National Party	21	26	47
Scottish Labour	37	9	46
Scottish Conservative	3	13	16
Scottish Liberal Democrat	11	5	16
Scottish Green Party	0	2	2
Independent	0	1	1
Presiding Officer (Alex Fergusson)	1	0	1

THE NATIONAL ASSEMBLY FOR WALES

The current state of parties (as at 12 September 2007)

Number of AM*s*	*Constituency*	*Regional*	*Total*
Labour	24	2	26
Plaid Cymru	7	8	15
Conservative	5	7	12
Liberal Democrat	3	3	6
Independent	1	0	1
Presiding Officer (Lord Dafydd Elis-Thomas)	1	0	1

THE NORTHERN IRELAND ASSEMBLY

The current state of parties (as at 12 September 2007)

DUP	36	SDLP	16	Green Party	1
Sinn Féin	28	Alliance	7	Independent	1
Ulster Unionists	18	PUP	1	Speaker: William Hay	

Elections for the Northern Ireland Assembly were held on 7 March 2007. The total electorate was 1,107,904, and the turnout was 63·5%. The NI Assembly was restored on 8 May 2007 [see p.30].

THE LONDON ASSEMBLY

The current state of parties (as at 12 September 2007)

Conservative	9	Liberal Democrat	5	One London Group	2
Labour	7	Green	2	(June 2004 turnout, 36·6%)	

Mayoral and Assembly elections will be held on 1 May 2008. At the time of writing, although he had not yet been selected, Boris Johnson's bid to oust Ken Livingstone was the focus of media attention.

THE HOUSE OF LORDS

State of the parties (as at 2 July 2007)

Conservative	204
Labour	211
Liberal Democrat	77
Crossbench	205
Bishops	26
Other	12
Total	735

12 Peers on leave of absence are excluded.

Archbishops and Bishops	26 [0]
Life Peers under the Appellate Jurisdiction Act 1876	26 [1]
Life Peers under the Life Peerages Act 1958	603 [139]
Peers under the House of Lords Act 1999	92 [3]

[Numbers within brackets indicate the number of women included in the figure.]

REFORM & THE HOUSE OF LORDS

Labour's controversial plans to reform the House of Lords hit yet another impasse in March 2007, when the Commons voted for an upper chamber that was 100% elected and, days later, the Lords voted for one that was 100% appointed. Both Houses were presented with a series of options for reform on which to vote:

HOUSE OF COMMONS (vote 7·3·07)	*composition of Lords* [*appointed:elected*]	HOUSE OF LORDS (vote 14·3·07)
defeated 196–375	fully appointed	approved 361–121
no vote	80:20	defeated without vote
no vote	60:40	defeated without vote
defeated 155–418	50:50	defeated 46–409
defeated 178–392	40:60	defeated 45–392
approved 305–267	20:80	defeated 114–336
approved 337–224	fully elected	defeated 122–326

Additionally, the Commons voted 391–111 to remove the remaining 92 hereditary peers.

None of these votes changed the law, nor were they binding on the government – which at the time of writing was considering further consultation. ❦ In its 1983 manifesto, the Labour party promised to 'take action to abolish the undemocratic House of Lords as quickly as possible'. However, by 1997 the (now 'New Labour') manifesto promised to create a 'modern House of Lords', via a two-stage process: first, ending the right of hereditary peers to sit and vote, and second, reforming the composition and powers of the House of Lords. In 1999, after considerable debate, Labour's first stage of reform removed all but 92 of the hereditary peers. Since then, the Labour government has reasserted its commitment to 'further long-term reform of the House of Lords'. However, despite all of the three main parties embracing the need to complete the second stage of reform, consensus between the parties and the Houses has proved elusive. In 2003, seven options for change were all rejected by MPs. The current stalemate on reform – focusing as it does on whether Lords are appointed or elected, and the powers they enjoy – looks likely to be exacerbated by the controversy surrounding allegations of 'cash for peerages' [see p.29].

'MOST FANCIABLE' MPs

Below are the 'most fanciable' MPs of 2007, according to the Valentine's Day blog of Sky News political editor Adam Boulton. (2006 positions and ages in parentheses.)

1 (–)	Julie Kirkbride (46)	CON
2 (1)	Caroline Flint (45)	LAB
3 (–)	Nick Clegg (39)	LD
4 (9)	Theresa May (50)	CON
5 (–)	Shahid Malik (39)	LAB
6 (–)	Dawn Butler (37)	LAB
7 (6)	Lynne Featherstone (55)	LD
8 (–)	Angus MacNeil (36)	SNP
9 (–)	Nadine Dorries (48)	CON
10 (–)	Ed Vaizey (37)	CON

MPs' FAVOURITE FILMS

175 Members of Parliament voted for their favourite films in December 2006 – with *Casablanca* the cross-party winner. The top 5 films are shown below, by party:

LABOUR	CONSERVATIVE	LIBERAL DEMOCRAT
Casablanca	*Casablanca*	*Casablanca*
Star Wars	*One Flew Over the Cuckoo's Nest*	*Saving Private Ryan*
One Flew Over the Cuckoo's Nest	*Carry On Up the Khyber*	*Star Wars*
Brassed Off	*Gone with the Wind*	*Austin Powers: Goldmember*
Citizen Kane	*Zulu*	*Life of Brian*

MPs' TRAVEL EXPENSES

Details of MPs' travel expenses were made public in 2007, following a two-year Freedom of Information campaign by Norman Baker MP. The top claimants are:

Air travel		
Alistair Carmichael	LD	£34,347
Eric Joyce	LAB	30,578
Angus MacNeil	SNP	19,919
Gregory Campbell	DUP	17,733
Peter Robinson	DUP	16,126

Car mileage†		
Janet Anderson	LAB	16,612
Laurence Robertson	CON	12,015
Stephen O'Brien	CON	9,878
Eric Joyce	LAB	9,647
Daniel Kawczynski	CON	8,866

Rail travel		
Alan Milburn	LAB	16,782
John Grogan	LAB	13,934
Ann Cryer	LAB	12,668
Sir Gerald Kaufman	LAB	12,434
Phil Willis	LD	11,753

Taxi and car hire		
Richard Bacon	CON	5,685
Stephen Dorrell	CON	4,933
John Thurso	LD	4,717
John Grogan	LAB	4,063
Nigel Evans	CON	3,430

[Period: Apr '05–Mar '06] †Based on 40p/mile for the first 10,000 miles and 25p thereafter. ❦ The top air fare claimants had constituencies in remote locations like Orkney, Shetland, and N Ireland. ❦ MPs could claim 20p/mile for bicycle travel; the most claimed was £230, by Jeremy Corbyn (LAB).

THE CONSERVATIVES' 12 GREAT PEOPLE

As part of a review into the way in which history is taught in schools, the Conservative party published, in December 2006, a list of twelve people who had helped to shape Britain's institutions. The list, compiled with the help of academics, was intended to inspire schoolchildren and maintain Britain's 'national identity':

Individual	*dates*	institution
Saint Columba	521–597	*Christianity in Britain*
Alfred the Great	849–899	*the Kingdom of England*
Henry II	1133–89	*the common law*
Simon de Montfort	1208–65	*parliament*
James IV	1443–1513	*the Kingdom of Scotland*
Thomas Gresham	1519–79	*the stock market*
Oliver Cromwell	1599–1658	*the British army*
Isaac Newton	1643–1727	*the Royal Society*
Robert Clive	1725–74	*the British Empire*
Sir Robert Peel	1778–1850	*the police*
Millicent Fawcett	1847–1929	*universal suffrage*
Aneurin Bevan	1897–1960	*the National Health Service*

POLITICIANS' HEROES

In 2007, Communicate Research asked more than 150 MPs to nominate a hero:

Hero	*nominations*
Nelson Mandela	27
Margaret Thatcher	12
Winston Churchill	11
Tony Blair	7†
Aneurin Bevan	6
Benjamin Disraeli	4
Harold Wilson	4
Mikhail Gorbachev	4
Barbara Castle	4
Clement Attlee	3
Gordon Brown	3

[January 2007] † One of Blair's nominees was a Conservative. David Cameron received only one nomination, as did Jed Bartlet, the fictitious US President played by Martin Sheen in *The West Wing*.

E-PETITIONS

In November 2006, the government introduced an online service allowing the public to create, sign, and deliver petitions directly to Number 10. These e-petitions proved extremely popular – by April 2007 there were 7,296 petitions listed on the website. To date, the most popular (with over 1·8m 'signatures') has been a petition against road pricing. Below is a selection of the e-petitions online in September 2007:

Intervene in Zimbabwe · Repeal the Hunting Act · Scrap the BBC licence fee
Change organ donation from opt in to opt out · Make Jeremy Clarkson PM
Ignore the petition to repeal the Hunting Act · Make smoking whilst driving illegal · Withdraw from the European Union · Ban plastic shopping bags
Stop claiming there is consensus on climate change [see p.22; see also petitions.pm.gov.uk]

PARLIAMENTARY SALARY & ALLOWANCES

Members of Parliament	
Members' Parliamentary salary	£60,675 (from 1·4·2007)
Staffing allowance (maximum)	£90,505
Incidental Expenses Provision (IEP)	£21,339
IT equipment (centrally provided)	worth *c.*£3,000
London supplement (for inner London seats)	£2,812
Additional costs allowance (for those with seats outside London)	£23,083
Winding Up Allowance (maximum)	£37,281
Car mileage, first 10,000 miles	40p per mile
— thereafter	25p per mile
Motorcycle allowance	24p per mile
Bicycle allowance	20p per mile

The House of Commons decided that the annual pay award for MPs and Ministers in 2007 should be a one-off increase, as opposed to the staggered increase of 2006.

Position	*1·4·2007*
Prime Minister†	£128,174
Cabinet Minister†	£76,904
Cabinet Minister (Lords)	£104,386
Minister of State†	£39,893
Minister of State (Lords)	£81,504
Parliamentary Under Secretary†	£30,280
Parliamentary Under Secretary (Lords)	£70,986
Government Chief Whip†	£76,904
Government Deputy Chief Whip†	£39,893
Government Whip†	£25,673
Leader of the Opposition†	£70,497
Leader of the Opposition (Lords)	£70,986
Opposition Chief Whip†	£39,893
Speaker†	£76,904
Attorney General	£109,201
Lord Chancellor	elects to receive the salary of Lords Cabinet Ministers

† Ministers in the Commons additionally receive their salaries as MPs (as above).

Backbench Peers	
Subsistence	Day £79·50 · Overnight £159·50
Office secretarial allowance	£69 per sitting day and <40 additional days
Travel	as for MPs
Spouses/children's expenses	6 return journeys per year
Lords' Ministers and paid office holders	
Ministers' night subsistence allowance	£35,090 for those with a second home in London
London supplement	£1,667 except those with official residence &c.
Secretarial allowance	£5,192
Spouses/children's expenses	15 return journeys per year

SALARIES FOR DEVOLVED LEGISLATURES &c.

Scottish Parliament 2007–08	*1·4·2007*
Member of the Scottish Parliament (MSP)	£53,091
First Minister†	£76,907
Scottish Minister†	£39,897
Junior Scottish Minister†	£24,989
Presiding Officer†	£39,897

† additionally receive their salaries as MSPs (as above).

National Assembly for Wales 2007–08	*additional salary*	*total salary*
Assembly Member (AM)	—	£46,496
Assembly First Minister	£76,996	£123,492
Assembly Minister	£39,939	£86,435
Presiding Officer	£39,939	£86,435
Leader of the largest non-cabinet party	£39,939	£86,435
AMs who are also MPs or MEPs		£15,499

Northern Ireland Assembly	*total salary*
Members of the Legislative Assembly (MLA)	£43,101
Presiding Officer	£43,901

These salaries have applied since the Assembly was restored on 8 May 2007 (it had been suspended since 14 October 2002). Prior to this MLA's were paid only for the work carried out in their constituency.

European Parliament 2007–08	*total salary*
UK Members of the European Parliament	as MPs

Members of Parliament who are also members of a devolved legislature receive the full parliamentary salary (see above) and one third of the salary due to them for their other role. Since 2004, Westminster MPs are ineligible to serve additionally as MEPs. The devolved legislatures control their own expenses and allowances.

London Assembly 2007–08	*total salary*
Member of the London Assembly (MLA)	£50,582
Mayor of London	£137,579
Deputy Mayor	£90,954

MP'S SALARIES & NO CONFIDENCE VOTES

On 23 May 2007, the then Health Secretary, Patricia Hewitt, survived a Commons vote of 'no confidence' over her management of the NHS. The Tories moved 'that the salary of the Secretary of State for Health should be reduced by £1,000', which is parliamentary code for censuring a minister and obliging them to resign. The motion was defeated by a majority of 63. The House of Commons Library gives one example of a similar vote of no confidence from June 1895, when the Opposition called for the salary of the Secretary of War to be cut by £100. The motion was carried by a majority of 7, and the Liberal Government actually decided to resign.

POLITICAL EPITAPHS

In January 2007, a headstone was erected at the grave of Labour MP Robin Cook (1946–2005). Referring to Cook's passionate and eloquent opposition to the war in Iraq, the epitaph reads: *I may not have succeeded in halting the war, but I did secure the right of Parliament to decide on war.* Other notable political epitaphs include:

THOMAS JEFFERSON
1743–1826
Here was buried Thomas Jefferson, author of the Declaration of American Independence, of the statute of Virginia for religious freedom, and father of the University of Virginia.

CLEMENT ATTLEE
1883–1967
For twenty years leader of the Labour Party.

KARL MARX
1818–83
Workers of all lands unite. The philosophers have only interpreted the world in various ways; the point is to change it.

JOHN QUINCY ADAMS
1767–1848
This is the last of Earth! I am content!

MARTIN LUTHER KING, JR
1929–68
Free at last! Free at last! Thank God Almighty, we are free at last!

HAROLD WILSON
1916–95
Tempus Imperator Rerum (Time Commands All Things)

Winston Churchill (1874–1965) proposed for himself: *'I am ready to meet my Maker. Whether my Maker is prepared for the great ordeal of meeting me is another matter.'* It is not on his headstone.

HUNDRED DAYS

Gordon Brown's accession to Prime Minister [see pp.16–17] was accompanied by much discussion of his first '100 days' of power. The phrase has been used on a number of occasions to describe the first three 'honeymoon' months of a new administration – during which it is assumed that radical reforms may be accomplished with less than usual opposition. The phrase seems to have originated in 1815 to describe the period 20 March–28 June – between Napoleon's escape from Elba and the second restoration of Louis XVIII following England's victory at Waterloo. The *Oxford English Dictionary* credits Louis de Chabrol de Volvic, Prefect of Paris, with coining the phrase in a speech to the king: '*Cent jours se sont écoulés depuis le moment fatal où votre majesté quitta sa capitale*'. The archives of the *Times* indicate that a range of figures have had their first '100 days' scrutinised, including: LBJ, Richard Nixon, JFK†, Harold Wilson, Margaret Thatcher, Arthur Scargill, and Tony Blair. Most famous, however, are Franklin D. Roosevelt's initial '100 days' as President in 1933, during which he pioneered the economic and political reforms of the 'New Deal'.

† John F. Kennedy's Presidency (20·01·1961–22·11·1963) is occasionally referred to as the '1,000 days'. Incidentally, George Canning ('The Zany of Debate') was Prime Minister for only 119 days before succumbing to pneumonia on August 8, 1827. Canning was buried in Westminster Abbey.

POLITICAL WORDS OF THE YEAR

Some of the words and phrases that have featured in the political discourse of 2007:

BLAIRAQ · the *Independent*'s headline verdict on Tony Blair's legacy.

AB · After Blair. *Also* ABG or ABB · Anyone But Gordon/Brown.

STALINIST RUTHLESSNESS · according to a senior civil servant, Brown's management style – which was also described by an ULTRA-BLAIRITE as manifesting GESTAPO TACTICS.

BIG CLUNKING FIST · Blair's curious allusion to Brown.

MRS ROCHESTER · description of Brown, coined by Frank Field, and deployed at PMQs by David Cameron. [In Charlotte Brontë's *Jane Eyre,* Mrs Bertha Rochester was Mr Rochester's first wife, whom he kept in secret at the top of his house. She was a violent, cunning lunatic, who attacked, among others, her own brother. She died by setting the house on fire and throwing herself off the roof.]

BROWN'S BOUNCE · Gordon's honeymoon as PM [see pp.17, 251, 260].

CHANGE · the relentless leitmotiv of Brown's accession; he used the word 8 times in a 353-word speech during his first statement as PM outside the door of Number 10. Brown also spoke of the MORAL COMPASS bestowed upon him by his parents.

More BULLDOG than POODLE · headline in the *Washington Post* in July, after Brown's first meeting as PM with George W. Bush. Bush said of Brown, 'He's not the dour Scotsman … he's actually a HUMOROUS SCOTSMAN'.

MILIBANDWAGON · pressure on David Miliband to stand against Brown. *Also* MILIBAND OF BROTHERS · David and Ed in the Cabinet [see p.251].

SHAM CAM · Nickname for Cameron, based on a perception that he lacks political substance. In the *Observer,* Andrew Rawnsley asked, 'Could Cameron turn out to be the Tories' Kinnock?'.

DAVID CAMERON'S CONSERVATIVE PARTY · the unusually personal wording on the ballot papers at the July Ealing Southall by-election. The Tory candidate, Tony Lit, came 3rd, behind Labour and the Lib Dems.

ETONOCRACY · nickname for the Tories under the leadership of (Old Etonian) David Cameron.

DECONTAMINATION STRATEGY · supposedly Cameron's first goal: to rid the Tories of their NASTY PARTY tag.

DEAD-IN-THE-WATER-DAVE · verdict on Cameron's decision to visit Rwanda during the UK floods in July [see p.26].

BOJO · Nickname for Boris Johnson MP, who is standing to represent the Conservatives at the May 2008 Mayor of London election. (Boris's full name is Alexander Boris de Pfeffel Johnson – or 'Al' to his family.) Johnson was also called 'a type of Norman Tebbit in a clown's uniform' by the pressure group Compass, which in August published a detailed dossier claiming that Johnson was 'a member of the hard Tory right'.

I DON'T THINK WE'LL MISS YOU · Cherie's Parthian comment to the press pack, as the Blairs exited Downing St.

GENERAL ELECTION BREAKDOWN 1979–2005

Date	3·5·79	9·6·83	11·6·87	9·4·92	1·5·97	7·6·01	5·5·05
Winning party	Con	Con	Con	Con	Lab	Lab	Lab
Seat majority	43	144	102	21	179	167	67
PM	Thatcher	Thatcher	Thatcher	Major	Blair	Blair	Blair
Leader of Op.	Callaghan	Foot	Kinnock	Kinnock	Major	Hague	Howard
Lib (Dem) leader	Steel	Steel	Steel	Ashdown	Ashdown	Kennedy	Kennedy
Conservative							
Seats	339	397	375	336	165	166	198
Votes (m)	13·70	13·01	13·74	14·09	9·60	8·36	8·78
Share of votes (%)	43·9	42·4	42·2	41·9	30·7	31·7	32·4
% of seats	53·4	61·1	57·8	51·6	25·0	25·2	30·5
Labour							
Seats	268	209	229	271	418	412	355
Votes (m)	11·51	8·46	10·03	11·56	13·52	10·72	9·55
Share of votes (%)	36·9	27·6	30·8	34·4	43·2	40·7	35·2
% of seats	42·4	32·2	35·2	41·6	63·6	62·7	55·2
Liberal Democrat (&c.)							
Seats	11	23	22	20	46	52	62
Votes (m)	4·31	7·78	7·34	6·00	5·24	4·81	5·99
Share of votes (%)	13·8	25·4	22·6	17·8	16·8	18·3	22·0
% of seats	1·7	3·5	3·4	3·1	7·0	7·9	9·6
Monster Raving Loony							
Candidates	–	11	5	22	24	15	19
Average vote (%)	–	0·7	0·7	0·6	0·7	1·0	–
Lost deposits	–	11	5	22	24	15	19
Women MPs	19	23	41	60	120	118	127
– as %	3·0	3·5	6·3	9·2	18·2	17·9	19·7
Turnout (%)	76·0	72·7	75·3	77·7	71·4	59·4	61·4
– England (%)	75·9	72·5	75·4	78·0	71·4	59·2	61·3
– Wales (%)	79·4	76·1	78·9	79·7	73·5	61·6	62·6
– Scotland (%)	76·8	72·7	75·1	75·5	71·3	58·2	60·8
– N. Ireland (%)	67·7	72·9	67·0	69·8	67·1	68·0	62·9
Postal vote (%)	2·2	2·0	2·4	2·0	2·3	5·2	14·6
Spoilt ballots (%)	0·38	0·17	0·11	0·12	0·30	0·38	0·7
– av./constituency	186	79	57	61	142	152	291
Deposit to stand	£150	£150	£500	£500	£500	£500	£500
– threshold (%)	12½	12½	5	5	5	5	5

Some figures (e.g. that of a winning party's majority) are disputed. Source: House of Commons.

EARLY DAY MOTIONS

Early Day Motions (EDMs) are those 'tabled' by MPs calling for a debate on a specific topic. EDMs must be in the form of a single-sentence resolution (starting with 'That') no longer than 250 words; they may not incorporate unparliamentary language or irony, and must not criticise MPs, Peers, judges, or Royalty unless they are explicitly motions of censure. Since most EDMs stand no chance of being debated (let alone becoming or amending law), they are primarily used to raise public and parliamentary awareness of a subject. Up to 6 MPs may sponsor an EDM, after which other MPs may add their signature in support. According to the Commons Information Office, in an average session most EDMs get a handful of signatures, 70–80 get >100, and 6–7 get >200. Since 1939, only 67 EDMs have attracted >300 signatures. EDMs cover a bewildering diversity of topics, some serious, some personal, some downright bizarre. For example, the motion which led to the fall of the government in 1979 started as EDM 351, tabled by Margaret Thatcher. However, in May 2007, EDM 1453 proposed: *That this House believes that voting in the Eurovision Song Contest has become a joke, as countries vote largely on narrow nationalistic grounds or for neighbour countries rather than the quality of the song, and that such narrow voting is harmful to the relationship between the peoples of Europe; and calls for the BBC to insist on changes to the voting system or to withdraw from the contest.* [see p.140]

THE 'RED PHONE'

During a visit to China in March 2007, Chairman of the Joint Chiefs of Staff General Peter Pace announced that Washington and Beijing were considering an emergency hotline between the leaders of the two countries. Such hotlines tend to be known as 'red phones', after the US–Russia link established in 1963, following the potentially disastrous failures of communication during the 'Cuban missile crisis'. (For example, it reportedly took the US *c.*12 hours to receive and decode Khrushchev's first settlement message, and the Soviet ambassador later disclosed that he handed messages to a bicycle courier, who in turn sent them via Western Union.) The 'red phone' was actually used for the first time in 1967, when it helped prevent the Six Day War from escalating into a global conflict. ❦ Initially, the 'red phone' consisted of a set of teleprinters connected via transatlantic cable. In the 1970s the teleprinters were replaced with actual phones and, later, satellite communication lines and facsimile transmission. Why the phone is 'red' is the subject of some speculation. Moscow apparently called their side of the connection 'the red telephone' – though whether this was because of its actual colour, the urgency of its function, or a humorous allusion to political ideology, is unclear. To this day, operators reportedly continue to send a coded message every hour for maintenance purposes, and are said to enjoy testing their colleagues' skills with texts such as favourite chilli recipes and (from the Russians) tricky passages from Dostoevsky.

Ironically, there has never been a red phone in the Oval Office. The phone has been black (pre-Kennedy, Nixon–Ford, Bush 41–43), turquoise (Kennedy–Johnson), and white (Carter–Reagan). In April 2007, it was disclosed that China and Japan had discussed the establishment of their own 24-hour hotline to guard against 'unexpected eventualities'. [Sources: BBC; *Time*; CNN; *CDI Russia Weekly*]

TRIDENT

On 13 March 2007, the Labour government survived a backbench revolt and secured the renewal of Trident – Britain's nuclear deterrent – by 409 votes to 161. Tony Blair, a supporter of CND in his earlier political life, was forced to rely on Tory votes after 95 Labour MPs attempted to delay the decision and, when this delay failed, 88 voted against the principle of renewal. 4 junior members of the government resigned in protest, and further resignations were only prevented by allowing some MPs to abstain. This rebellion, the largest on a domestic issue since 1997, was seen as further defining 'New Labour' as distinct from 'old Labour', which has long campaigned for nuclear disarmament. (Other Blairite policies that required Tory support were the Iraq war in 2003, and school trusts in 2006.) ❦ Considerable speculation surrounded the timing of the vote, which was called within months of Blair's expected resignation. The government insisted that a decision was urgently required, since the existing missile system would need to be replaced in the 2020s, and the development of new missiles would take *c.*17 years. However, some suggested that the vote, certain to be difficult for any Labour leader, was pursued by Blair to save his successor embarrassment. The Tories were quick to capitalise on Labour's discomfort, claiming that 'old Labour' was resurgent as Blair's leadership drew to a close.

Britain's nuclear deterrent has three components – submarines, missiles, and warheads. The Royal Navy has 4 Vanguard-class submarines (*Vanguard*, *Victorious*, *Vigilant*, and *Vengeance*) which operate at a posture known as 'Continuous At Sea Deterrence', where one submarine is on armed patrol 24 hours a day, 365 days a year. Since the end of the Cold War, all the missiles are targeted at remote points in the sea, and the 'notice to fire' has been extended to several days. (To ensure full availability, each sub has two crews, known as 'Port' and 'Starboard'). The boats are capable of circumnavigating the world underwater, and regularly patrol for several months at a time. Each sub is fitted with 16 Trident II D5 missiles – manufactured in the US by Lockheed Martin. The missiles are 44ft (13m) long; they weigh 130,000lb (48,500kg); and cost *c.*£16·8m each. D5s have a range of >4,600 miles (7,400km), and each is capable of delivering up to 12 nuclear warheads. The warheads themselves are made in Britain by the Atomic Weapons Establishment in Aldermaston.

The March 2007 vote involved two of Trident's components: the construction of new subs and a plan to extend the life of the D5 missiles. The cost of these programmes was estimated to be £15–£20bn over 30 years – or 3% of the current annual defence budget. (A decision to replace the warheads was expected to be taken in the next parliament, although the government committed itself to cutting the UK's stockpile by 20%.) ❦ Two issues were central to the controversy over Trident's renewal: Britain's obligations under the Non-Proliferation Treaty and other agreements, and the role of a nuclear deterrent in a post Cold War world. Despite vociferous opposition, the government insisted that 'renewing our minimum nuclear deterrent is fully consistent with all our international obligations'. And, Tony Blair stated, 'the notion of unstable, usually deeply repressive and anti-democratic states, in some cases profoundly inimical to our way of life, having a nuclear capability, is a distinct and novel reason for Britain not to give up its capacity to deter'.

STATE DEPT & MISINFORMATION

The website of the US Dept of State contains a section dedicated to 'Identifying Misinformation' and debunking conspiracy theories, urban legends, and the like. The site is maintained by the Department's 'counter-misinformation officer', who 'has 13 years of experience in this area'. Inevitably, a significant part of the site addresses the many conspiracy theories relating to the 9/11 attacks, including:

'The World Trade Centre (WTC) twin towers were destroyed by controlled demolitions.'

'No plane hit the Pentagon on 9/11. Instead, it was a missile fired by elements "from inside the American state apparatus".'

'The planes that hit the WTC towers were remotely controlled.'

'WTC building 7 was destroyed by a controlled demolition.'

'United Airlines flight 93, which crashed in Pennsylvania, was shot down by a missile.'

'Insider trading in the stocks of United Airlines and American Airlines just before September 11 is evidence of advance knowledge of the plot.'

'4,000 Jews failed to show up for work at the WTC on September 11.'

'Al-Qaeda is not responsible for the September 11 attacks.'

Each of these 'prevalent myths' is systematically addressed and rebutted by the State Dept, using published reports and eyewitness statements. Additionally, the website offers tips for identifying misinformation – much of which, it notes, is directed against the US military or intelligence community – 'a favourite villain in many conspiracy theories'. Journalists and news consumers are advised always to ask:

Does the story fit the pattern of a conspiracy theory? [*'Conspiracy theories are rarely true, even though they have great appeal and are often widely believed. In reality, events usually have much less exciting explanations.'*]

Does the story fit the pattern of an 'urban legend'? [*'Is the story startlingly good, bad, amazing, horrifying, or otherwise seemingly "too good" or "too terrible" to be true? Urban legends, which often circulate by word of mouth, email, or the Internet, are false claims that are widely believed because they put a common fear, hope, suspicion … into story form.'*]

Does the story contain a shocking revelation about a highly controversial issue? [*'Any highly controversial issue or taboo behaviour is ripe material for false rumours and urban legends.'*]

Is the source trustworthy? [*'Certain websites, publications, and individuals are known for spreading false stories.'*]

What does further research tell you? [*'The only way to determine whether an allegation is true or false is to research it as thoroughly as possible.'*]

A number of other myths are refuted by the State Dept, including: the US will invade Venezuela in an operation supposedly entitled 'Plan Balboa'; the AIDS virus was created by the US military to be used as a biological weapon; Americans kidnap children from the Third World and murder them for their body parts; and so on.

PROSCRIBED TERRORIST GROUPS

The organisations below are currently proscribed under UK legislation, and are consequently outlawed within the UK. 44 international terrorist organisations are proscribed under the Terrorism Act 2000, of which 2 are proscribed as glorifying terrorism under powers introduced in the Terrorism Act 2006. Additionally, 14 organisations in Northern Ireland are proscribed under previous legislation.

17 November Revolutionary Org. [N17] · formed in 1974 to oppose the Greek military Junta, its stance was initially anti-Junta and anti-US.

Abu Nidal Org. [ANO] · aims to destroy Israel; hostile to states supporting Israel.

Abu Sayyaf Group [ASG] · aims appear to include the establishment of an Islamic state in the S Philippine island of Mindanao.

Al-Gama'at al-Islamiya [GI] · aims to replace the Egyptian government with an Islamic state.

Al Gurabaa · splinter group of Al-Muajiroon that glorifies acts of terrorism.

Al Ittihad Al Islamia [AIAI] · aims to establish a radical Sunni Islamic state in Somalia, and to regain the Ogaden region of Ethiopia as Somalian; suspected of aiding al-Qaeda.

Al-Qaeda · inspired and led by Osama Bin Laden; aims to expel Western forces from Saudi Arabia, destroy Israel, and end Western influence in the Muslim world.

Ansar Al Islam [AI] · opposes the influence of the US in Iraqi Kurdistan and the relationship of the KDP and PUK to Washington.

Ansar Al Sunna [AS] · aims to expel all foreign influences from Iraq and create a fundamentalist Islamic state.

Armed Islamic Group (Groupe Islamique Armée) [GIA] · aims to create an Islamic state in Algeria.

Asbat Al-Ansar (League of Partisans or *Band of Helpers)* · aims to enforce strict Islamic law within Lebanon and elsewhere.

Babbar Khalsa [BK] · a Sikh movement that aims to establish an independent Khalistan within the Punjab region of India.

Baluchistan Liberation Army [BLA] · seeks an independent nation encompassing the Baluch areas of Pakistan, Afghanistan, and Iran.

Egyptian Islamic Jihad [EIJ] · aims to replace Egyptian government with an Islamic state. Now, also allied to Osama Bin Laden.

Euskadi ta Askatasuna (Basque Homeland and Liberty) [ETA] · seeks the creation of an independent state comprising the Basque regions of both Spain and France.

Groupe Islamique Combattant Marocain [GICM] · aims to replace the governing Moroccan monarchy with a caliphate.

Hamas Izz al-Din al-Qassem Brigades · aims to end Israeli occupation in Palestine.

Harakat-Ul-Jihad-Ul-Islami [HUJI] · fights for accession of Kashmir to Pakistan and aims to spread terror throughout India.

Harakat-Ul-Jihad-Ul-Islami (Bangladesh) [HUJI-B] · aims to create an Islamic regime in Bangladesh.

Harakat-Ul-Mujahideen/Alami [HUM/A] & *Jundallah* · reject all forms of democracy; aim for a caliphate based on Sharia law and accession of all Kashmir to Pakistan.

PROSCRIBED TERRORIST GROUPS cont.

Harakat Mujahideen (HM) · seeks independence for Indian-administered Kashmir.

Hizballah External Security Org. · committed to the 'liberation' of Palestinian territories.

Hezb-E Islami Gulbuddin [HIG] · aims to make Afghanistan an Islamic state.

International Sikh Youth Federation [ISYF] · aims to create an independent state of Khalistan for Sikhs within India.

Islamic Army of Aden [IAA] · aims to replace the Yemeni government with an Islamic state following Sharia law.

Islamic Jihad Union [IJU] · aims to replace the Uzbek regime with an Islamic democracy.

Islamic Movement of Uzbekistan [IMU] · aims to establish an Islamic state in Uzbekistan.

Jaish e Mohammed [JEM] · seeks to remove Indian control of Kashmir.

Jeemah Islamiyah [JI] · aims to create a unified Islamic state in Singapore, Malaysia, Indonesia, and the Southern Philippines.

Khuddam Ul-Islam [KUL) & *Jamaat Ul-Furquan* [JUF] · aim for Pakistani control of Kashmir, an Islamist state in Pakistan; the destruction of India and the USA, &c.

Kongra Gele Kurdistan (PKK) · seeks an independent Kurdish state in SE Turkey.

Lashkar e Tayyaba [LT] · seeks independent Islamic Kashmir.

Liberation Tigers of Tamil Eelam [LTTE] · aims for a separate Tamil state in Sri Lanka.

Mujaheddin e Khalq [MEK] · Iranian dissidents based in Iraq.

Palestinian Islamic Jihad – Shaqaqi [PIJ] · aims to create an independent Islamic Palestine.

Revolutionary Peoples' Liberation Party – Front (Devrimci Halk Kurtulus Partisi – Cephesi) (DHKP–C] · aims to establish a Marxist–Leninist regime in Turkey.

Teyre Azadiye Kurdistan [TAK] · Kurdish terrorist group operating in Turkey.

Salafist Group for Call and Combat (Groupe Salafiste pour la Prédication et le Combat) [GSPC] · aims to create an Islamic state in Algeria.

Saved Sect or *Saviour Sect* · Al-Muajiroon splinter that glorifies acts of terrorism.

Sipah-E Sahaba Pakistan (SSP), (Aka Millat-E Islami Pakistan (MIP), Lashkar-E Jhangvi (LeJ) · aims to turn Pakistan into a Sunni state under Sharia law.

Libyan Islamic Fighting Group [LIFG] · aims to create an Islamic state in Libya.

Jammat-ul Mujahideen Bangladesh [JMB] · Bangladeshi terror group.

Tehrik Nefaz-e Shari'at Muhammadi [TNSM] · anti-coalition forces in Afghanistan.

PROSCRIBED IRISH GROUPS

Continuity Army Council · Cumann na mBan · Fianna na hEireann Irish National Liberation Army Irish People's Liberation Organisation Irish Republican Army · Loyalist Volunteer Force · Orange Volunteers Red Hand Commando · Red Hand Defenders · Saor Eire · Ulster Defence Association · Ulster Freedom Fighters Ulster Volunteer Force

[Source & descriptions: Home Office]

THE EUROPEAN UNION

The European Union (EU) has its roots in the European Coal & Steel Community (ECSC), formed in 1951 between Belgium, France, Germany, Italy, Luxembourg, and the Netherlands, who united to co-operate over production of coal and steel: the two key components of war. Since then, through a series of treaties, Europe as an economic and political entity has developed in size, harmonisation, and power. For some, the expansion in EU membership [see below] and the introduction of the euro (in 2002) are welcome developments in securing co-operation and peace; for others, the growth of the EU is a threat to the sovereignty of member nations.

MAJOR EU INSTITUTIONS

European Parliament · the democratic voice of the people of Europe, the EP approves the EU budget; oversees the other EU institutions; assents to key treaties and agreements on accession; and, alongside the Council of Ministers, examines and approves EU legislation. The EP sits in Strasbourg and Brussels, and its members are directly elected every 5 years.

Council of the EU · the pre-eminent decision-making body, the Council is made up of ministers from each national government. The Council meets regularly in Brussels to decide EU policy and approve laws, and every three months Presidents and PMs meet at European Councils to make major policy decisions.

European Commission · proposes new laws for the Council and Parliament to consider, and undertakes much of the EU's day-to-day work, such as overseeing the implementation of EU rules. Commissioners are nominated by each member state, and the President of the Commission is chosen by the national governments. It is based in Brussels.

European Court · ensures EU law is observed and applied fairly, and settles any disputes arising. Each state sends a judge to the Court in Luxembourg.

EU MEMBERSHIP

Country	*entry*	*members*
Belgium France Germany Italy Luxembourg Netherlands	1952	6
Denmark Ireland UK	1973	9
Greece	1981	10
Portugal Spain	1986	12
Austria Finland Sweden	1995	15
Cyprus Czech Rep. Estonia Hungary Latvia Lithuania Malta Poland Slovakia Slovenia	2004	25
Romania Bulgaria	2007	27
Turkey *Croatia*	*in accession talks*	
Serbia *Bosnia* *Montenegro* *Albania* *Macedonia*	*potential candidates*	

UK OPINION ON THE EU

The latest Eurobarometer Survey (Autumn 2006) shows just how Eurosceptic the UK is. Charted below are UK opinions on the EU, and the UK's rank in the EU25:

Position	%	*rank*
Agree that the UK has benefited from EU membership	39	25th
Think that UK membership of the EU is a good thing	34	25th
Have a positive view of the EU	28	25th
Trust the European Commission	25	25th
Trust the European Parliament	25	25th
Feel the EU is going in the right direction	25	24th
Believe [erroneously] that the EU has 15 members	34	12th
Claim to understand how the EU works	40	16th
Tend to trust the EU	26	25th
Support the proposed EU Constitution	40	–
– further enlargement of the EU	36	21st
– a common EU foreign policy	48	25th
– a common EU defence and security policy	57	23rd
Think crime should be addressed nationally [i.e. outside EU]	69	1st
– immigration	63	3rd
– environmental issues	42	5th

EU'S 50TH BIRTHDAY CAKES

On 25 March 1957, the Treaty of Rome was signed, creating the European Economic Community (now the European Union). To celebrate 50 years of this Treaty, all 27 member states were asked to bake two cakes traditional to their country for a party in Berlin. Below is a brief description of some of these European birthday cakes:

Cake	*country*	description
Tikvenik	Bulgaria	*pastry made with sweet pumpkin*
Banitsa	Bulgaria	*pastry with brined goat's cheese filling*
Savarin	France	*cake ring soaked in rum and filled with cream*
Tarte tatin	France	*caramelised apple tart*
Frankfurter Kranz	Germany	*crown-shaped cake filled with buttercream*
Kirschsahnetorte	Germany	*cherry cream cake*
Porter cake	Ireland	*fruit cake with Guinness*
Orange cake	Ireland	*orange cake*
Ciambellone tradizionale	Italy	*ring-shaped butter cake*
Tiramisu	Italy	*soft sponge cake with coffee cream cheese*
Tarta de Santiago	Spain	*almond cake*
Roscón de Reyes	Spain	*traditional ring-shaped Christmas cake*
Pehtranova potica	Slovenia	*cake flavoured with tarragon and nuts*
Prekmurska gibanica	Slovenia	*strudel with poppy seeds, curd cheese, & apple*
Hot cross bun	UK	*traditional Easter spiced bun*
Eccles cake	UK	*rich fruity flaky pastry*

THE EURO

NOTES & COINS IN CIRCULATION

Coin	*number*	*total value €*
€ 2	3,542m	7,084m
€ 1	5,309m	5,309m
50¢	4,430m	2,215m
20¢	7,353m	1,470m
10¢	9,250m	925m
5¢	11,420m	571m
2¢	13,229m	264m
1¢	16,069m	161m
TOTAL	70,602m	17,999m

Note	*number*	*total value €*
€500	423m	211,658m
€200	152m	30,333m
€100	1,099m	109,852m
€50	3,885m	194,259m
€20	2,173m	43,460m
€10	1,753m	17,530m
€5	1,294m	6,470m
TOTAL	10,779m	613,562m

[Source: European Central Bank, 03·07]

Coins	*common side design*
€2, €1	EU map before enlargement of 2004
50¢, 20¢, 10¢	individual EU countries before enlargement of 2004
5¢, 2¢, 1¢	Europe in relation to Africa and Asia

Note	*colour*	*size (mm)*	*architecture*
€5	grey	120×62	Classical
€10	red	127×67	Romanesque
€20	blue	133×72	Gothic
€50	orange	140×77	Renaissance
€100	green	147×82	Baroque/Rococo
€200	yellow	153×82	C19th iron/glass
€500	purple	160×82	C20th modern

CURRENT CIRCULATION OF THE EURO

OFFICIAL CURRENCY
Belgium, Germany, Greece, Spain, France, Ireland, Italy, Luxembourg, the Netherlands, Austria, Portugal, Finland, Slovenia
[Malta & Cyprus intend to join in 01·01·08]

DE FACTO CURRENCY
Andorra, Kosovo, Montenegro

SPECIAL ARRANGEMENTS
Monaco, the Vatican City, San Marino

OVERSEAS TERRITORIES
Guadeloupe, French Guiana, Martinique, Mayotte, Réunion, Saint Pierre and Miquelon, French Southern & Antarctic Territories

Charted below is the value of the pound against the euro and dollar, since 1999:

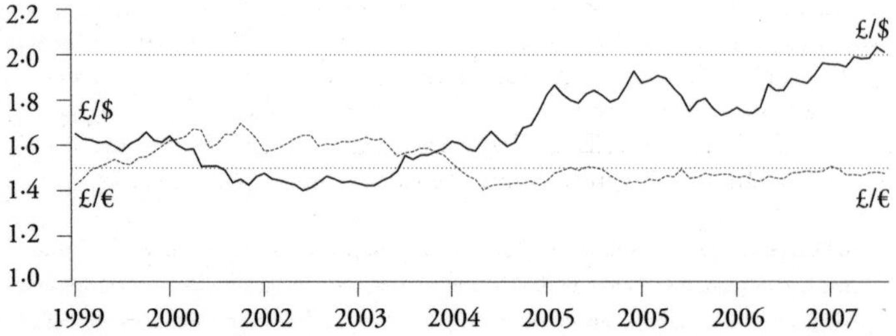

NEW COUNTRY GROUPINGS

A profusion of formal country groupings exist across the world – from the UN, the G8, and Nato to OPEC, the Paris Club, and the African Union [see *Schott's Almanac* 2008]. Recently, however, a range of informal terms have been popularised to describe emerging spheres of economic, political, or military influence and power:

BRIC
Brazil, Russia, India, China
from this group, a number of terms have developed
BRIMC = BRIC + Mexico
BRICS = BRIC + South Africa
BRICA = BRIC + the Arab Gulf Cooperation Council (GCC) states: Saudi Arabia, Kuwait, UAE, Oman, Bahrain, and Qatar
BRICET = BRIC + Eastern Europe and Turkey

G8+5
G8 nations (Canada, France, Germany, Italy, Japan, Russia, UK, & US) + Brazil, China, India, Mexico and South Africa

CHINDIA
China and India

FOUR ASIAN TIGERS
Hong Kong, Singapore, South Korea, and Taiwan

EU8+2
recent EU members [see p.268]
Czech Republic, Estonia, Hungary, Latvia, Lithuania, Poland, Slovakia and Slovenia + Bulgaria and Romania

NEXT ELEVEN (N-11)
Bangladesh, Egypt, Indonesia, Iran, Mexico, Nigeria, Pakistan, Philippines, Turkey, Vietnam, and South Korea

THE COMMONWEALTH

The Commonwealth of Nations is a voluntary association of 53 sovereign states – all of which, excepting Mozambique, have experienced British rule. The Commonwealth has no formal constitution; its goal is to promote 'democracy and good governance, respect for human rights and gender equality, the rule of law, and sustainable economic and social development'. The Commonwealth Nations are:

Antigua & Barbuda* · Australia* · Bahamas* · Bangladesh · Barbados* Belize* · Botswana · Brunei Darussalam · Cameroon · Canada* · Cyprus Dominica · Fiji Islands† · The Gambia · Ghana · Grenada* · Guyana · India Jamaica* · Kenya · Kiribati · Lesotho · Malawi · Malaysia · Maldives · Malta Mauritius · Mozambique · Namibia · Nauru · New Zealand* · Nigeria · Pakistan Papua New Guinea* · St Kitts & Nevis* · St Lucia* · St Vincent* · Samoa Seychelles · Sierra Leone · Singapore · Solomon Islands* · South Africa Sri Lanka · Swaziland · Tanzania · Tonga · Trinidad & Tobago Tuvalu* · Uganda · United Kingdom · Vanuatu · Zambia

In December 2003, Zimbabwe withdrew its membership after its suspension was not lifted.
* The Queen is not only Queen of the UK and its overseas territories, but also of these realms.
† Fiji's military regime was suspended from the Councils of the Commonwealth on 8·12·06

Establishment & Faith

A king is a thing men have made for their own sakes, for quietness' sake.
Just as in a family one man is appointed to buy the meat.
— JOHN SELDEN (1584–1654)

THE SOVEREIGN

ELIZABETH II
by the Grace of God, of the United Kingdom of Great Britain and Northern Ireland and of her other Realms and Territories Queen, Head of the Commonwealth, Defender of the Faith

Born at 17 Bruton Street, London W1, on 21 April 1926, at *c.*2·40am
Ascended the throne, 6 February 1952 · Crowned, 2 June 1953

ORDER OF SUCCESSION

The Prince of Wales · Prince William of Wales · Prince Henry of Wales
The Duke of York · Princess Beatrice of York · Princess Eugenie of York
The Earl of Wessex · The Lady Louise Windsor · The Princess Royal
Mr Peter Phillips · Miss Zara Phillips · Viscount Linley [&c...]

The eldest son of the monarch is heir to the throne followed by his heirs. After whom come any other sons of the monarch and their heirs, followed by any daughters of the monarch and their heirs. Roman Catholics are barred from succession under the Act of Settlement (1701).

THE UNION FLAG

Government buildings are obliged to fly the Union Flag on these days:

BD Countess of Wessex	20 Jan
Queen's Accession	6 Feb
BD Duke of York	19 Feb
St David's Day (Wales)	1 Mar
Commonwealth Day	13 Mar
BD Earl of Wessex	10 Mar
BD The Queen	21 Apr
St George's Day (England)	23 Apr
Europe Day	9 May
Coronation Day	2 Jun
BD Duke of Edinburgh	10 Jun
Official BD The Queen	14 Jun
BD Duchess of Cornwall	17 Jul
BD The Princess Royal	15 Aug
Remembrance Day	11 Nov
BD Prince of Wales	14 Nov
Queen's Wedding Day	20 Nov
St Andrew's Day (Scotland)	30 Nov

Also, the Opening & Prorogation of Parliament

On the days listed above, the Union Flag should be flown from 8am to sunset.

ENGLISH MONARCHS

The monarchy is the oldest profession in the world.
— CHARLES, PRINCE OF WALES (1948–)

Danish Line

Svein Forkbeard 1014
Canute the Great 1016–35
Harald Harefoot 1035–40
Hardicanute 1040–42
Edward the Confessor 1042–66
Harold II 1066

Norman Line

William the Conqueror 1066–87
William II Rufus 1087–1100
Henry I Beauclerc 1100–35
Stephen 1135–54
Henry II Curtmantle 1154–89
Richard I Coeur de Lion 1189–99
John (Lackland) 1199–1216
Henry III 1216–72
Edward I 1272–1307
Edward II 1307–27
Edward III 1327–77
Richard II 1377–99

Plantagenet, Lancastrian Line

Henry IV 1399–1413
Henry V 1413–22
Henry VI 1422–61, 1470–71

Plantagenet, Yorkist Line

Edward IV 1461–70, 1471–83
Edward V 1483
Richard III Crookback 1483–85

House of Tudor

Henry VII Tudor 1485–1509
Henry VIII 1509–47
Edward VI 1547–53
Lady Jane Grey .... [9 days] 1553
Mary I Tudor 1553–58
Elizabeth I 1558–1603

House of Stuart

James I 1603–25
Charles I 1625–49

Commonwealth & Protectorate

Oliver Cromwell 1649–58
Richard Cromwell 1658–59

House of Stuart, Restored

Charles II 1660–85
James II 1685–88

House of Orange and Stuart

William III, Mary II 1689–1702

House of Stuart

Anne 1702–14

House of Brunswick, Hanover

George I 1714–27
George II 1727–60
George III 1760–1820
George IV 1820–30
William IV 1830–37
Victoria 1837–1901

House of Saxe-Coburg-Gotha

Edward VII 1901–10

House of Windsor

George V 1910–36
Edward VIII 1936
George VI 1936–52
Elizabeth II .... 1952– *Whom God Preserve*

MONARCH MNEMONIC

Willy, Willy, Harry, Stee, Harry, Dick, John, Harry III. I, II, III Neds, Richard II, Harrys IV, V, VI... then who? Edwards IV, V, Dick the bad, Harrys (twain) & Ned the lad, Mary, Bessie, James the vain, Charlie, Charlie, James again ... William & Mary, Anne Gloria, 4 Georges, William & Victoria; Edward VII next & then George V in 1910; Edward VIII soon abdicated: George the VI was coronated; After which Elizabeth who is our Queen until her death.

ROYAL FINANCES

The Queen receives income from public funds to meet expenditure that relates to her duties as Head of State and the Commonwealth. This derives from 4 sources:

Source (year ending 31 March)	2006	2007
The Queen's Civil List	£11·2m	£12·2m
Parliamentary Annuities	£0·4m	£0·4m
Grants-in-Aid	£20·3m	£20·6m
Expenditure met directly by Government Departments and the Crown Estate	£5·5m	£4·1m
TOTAL	£37·4m	£37·3m

ROYAL FAMILY ENGAGEMENTS

Mr Tim O'Donovan compiled a list of official engagements undertaken by the Royal Family during 2006 – as reported in the pages of the Court Circular:

	Official visits, openings, &c	*Receptions, lunches, dinners, &c*	*Other, e.g. investitures, meetings*	*Total official engagements UK*	*Total official engagements abroad*
The Queen	92	69	219	380	45
Duke of Edinburgh	134	150	69	353	53
Prince of Wales	164	104	159	427	73
Duchess of Cornwall	110	46	6	162	50
Duke of York	101	71	40	212	234
Earl of Wessex	107	82	34	223	195
Countess of Wessex	113	43	26	182	53
Princess Royal	305	102	84	491	104
Duke of Gloucester	145	36	31	212	26
Duchess of Gloucester	74	17	18	109	18
Duke of Kent	138	45	18	201	28
Princess Alexandra	69	31	25	125	—

ROYAL CONGRATULATIONS

The tradition of sending messages of royal congratulations to subjects on certain auspicious days was inaugurated in 1917 by George V, who sent telegrams to those celebrating their 60th wedding anniversary or 100th birthday. Nowadays, on request, the Queen sends congratulatory cards, via the Royal Mail, to citizens of Her Realms or UK Overseas Territories, on the following celebratory occasions:

WEDDING ANNIVERSARIES	BIRTHDAYS
60th, 65th, & 70th anniversaries and then every year thereafter	100th & 105th birthdays and then every year thereafter

YEOMAN WARDERS & WARDRESSES

It was announced in January 2007 that Moira Cameron had become the first female Yeoman Warder of the Tower of London. The Yeoman Warders (aka Beefeaters†) were formed by Henry VII in 1485 to guard prisoners and protect the Crown Jewels. They are instantly recognisable in their ceremonial garb of scarlet and gold robes, red stockings, white ruff, and black patent shoes; yet, they are more often to be found sporting a more informal navy blue and red-trimmed uniform. Yeoman Warders must serve at least 22 years as senior non-commissioned officers in the forces before they can be considered for the post. There are currently 38 Warders; their duties include guarding the Crown Jewels, giving guided tours, attending to the gates, and ensuring the requisite six ravens‡ are present at the Tower at all times.

† It is not known how Yeoman Warders came to be called 'Beefeaters'. Some attribute the nickname to their ruddy appearance, others to evidence that they were paid partly in meat. Records from 1813 reveal that the daily ration for 30 men was a proteinaceous 24lb of beef, 18lb of mutton, and 16lb of veal. ‡ Legend has it that were the ravens ever to leave the Tower of London, the White Tower would fall and with it the Kingdom. Supposedly, to ensure this calamity was avoided, Charles II (1630–85) decreed that there should never be fewer than 6 ravens resident at the Tower. However, in 2004 it was revealed that the raven legend might be a slice of Victorian whimsy. The Tower of London's official historian, Dr Geoff Parnell, studied 1,000 years of records and found that references to ravens could be traced back only to the late-C19th. Parnell also discovered that on occasion – as during the Blitz – the Tower had been bereft of its requisite unkindness of ravens without serious consequences. ❦ There are currently eight ravens at the Tower: Gwylum, Thor, Hugine, Munin, Branwen, Bran, Gundulf, and Baldrick. They are tended by Yeoman Warder Ravenmaster Derrick Coyle.

THE WAY AHEAD GROUP

In April 2007, the *News of the World* reported that Prince William's (temporary?†) split from Kate Middleton had been formalised at a meeting of the Way Ahead Group at Windsor Castle. Prince William was quoted as saying 'I don't want any more commitment, I don't want to get married just yet. What should I do?' The Queen was reported to have answered, 'Don't rush down the aisle – we don't want another Diana'. ❦ The Way Ahead Group [WAG] was established by the Royal family several years before the death of Diana, Princess of Wales, to safeguard the future of the monarchy through modernisation. Chaired by the Queen, the WAG comprises members of the Royal family (the Duke of Edinburgh, the Prince of Wales, the Duke of York, the Princess Royal, &c.) and senior courtiers. According to various reports, the WAG has pioneered a number of reforms, including: volunteering that the Queen pay tax; opening Buckingham Palace to the public to pay for the post-fire restoration of Windsor Castle; creating the Royal website; reducing the cost of Royal travel; trimming the scope of the Civil List; and so on. In 2002, the veteran 'royal watcher' Robert Lacey told CNN that the WAG even discussed changing the law of primogeniture to allow the sovereign's first-born to accede to the throne.

[† At the time of writing, the somewhat on–off William–Kate relationship appeared to be back on.]

THE QUEEN'S CHRISTMAS BROADCAST 2006

'I have lived long enough to know that things never remain quite the same for very long. One of the things that has not changed all that much for me is the celebration of Christmas. … The birth of Jesus naturally turns our thoughts to all new-born children and what the future holds for them. The birth of a baby brings great happiness – but then the business of growing up begins. It is a process that starts within the protection and care of parents and other members of the family – including the older generation. … But the pressures of modern life sometimes seem to be weakening the links which have traditionally kept us together as families and communities. As children grow up and develop their own sense of confidence and independence in the ever-changing technological environment, there is always the danger of a real divide opening up between young and old, based on unfamiliarity, ignorance or misunderstanding. … The wisdom and experience of the great religions point to the need to nurture and guide the young, and to encourage respect for the elderly. … It is very easy to concentrate on the differences between the religious faiths and to forget what they have in common – people of different faiths are bound together by the need to help the younger generation to become considerate and active citizens. And there is another cause for hope that we can do better in the future at bridging the generation gap. As older people remain more active for longer, the opportunities to look for new ways to bring young and old together are multiplying. As I look back on these past twelve months, marked in particular for me by the very generous response to my eightieth birthday, I especially value the opportunities I have had to meet young people. I am impressed by their energy and vitality, and by their ambition to learn and to travel. It makes me wonder what contribution older people can make to help them realise their ambitions. I am reminded of a lady of about my age who was asked by an earnest little grand-daughter the other day "Granny, can you remember the Stone Age?" Whilst that may be going a bit far, the older generation are able to give a sense of context as well as the wisdom of experience which can be invaluable. Such advice and comfort are probably needed more often than younger people admit or older people recognise. … I wish you all a very happy Christmas together.

the pressures of modern life sometimes seem to be weakening the links which have traditionally kept us together as families and communities

[The Queen's 2006 Christmas Message was available, for the first time, as a podcast.]

When the Queen's Christmas broadcast is entered into Microsoft Word's 'Auto Summarize' feature and is condensed down to two sentences, the result is:

As older people remain more active for longer, the opportunities to look for new ways to bring young and old together are multiplying. It makes me wonder what contribution older people can make to help them realise their ambitions.

C4's ALTERNATIVE CHRISTMAS BROADCAST

In 1993, Channel 4 initiated its 'alternative' Christmas speech (broadcast at the same time as the Queen's), during which those outside the 'establishment' are asked to broadcast an iconoclastic festive communiqué. Below are the selected speakers:

1993........Quentin Crisp (1908–99), gay icon, author of *The Naked Civil Servant*
1994................Rev Jesse Jackson, Baptist preacher and civil rights campaigner
1995............Brigitte Bardot (Camille Javal), celebrated actress and sex-symbol
1996............................ mimic Rory Bremner as Diana, Princess of Wales
1997....Belfast schoolgirl Margaret Gibney, with a plea for an end to the Troubles
1998 .... parents of murdered schoolboy Stephen Lawrence, Doreen & Neville
1999................................Ali G – comic creation of Sacha Baron Cohen
2000...................Helen Jeffries, mother of Zoe, a 14-year-old victim of CJD
2001..........................Genelle Guzman, survivor of the 9/11 WTC attack
2002................ Sharon Osbourne, *X Factor* judge, manager and wife of Ozzy
2003.................................... *Wife Swap*'s Barry and Michelle Seabourn
2004.............Marge Simpson – to celebrate C4's broadcasting of *The Simpsons*
2005.......................celebrity chef and school food campaigner, Jamie Oliver
2006..Khadijah†

† Channel 4 joined the debate over the wearing of the veil by Muslims [see p.290] by asking Khadijah Ravat, a 33-year-old Islamic teacher who wears the Niqab, to make the 2006 alternative Christmas broadcast. However, in response to pressure from inside and outside the Muslim community, Ravat withdrew. Channel 4 replaced Ravat with an anonymous Muslim woman – named only as Khadijah – who had converted to Islam *c.*10 years previously. While wearing the Niqab, Khadijah criticised MP Jack Straw's earlier comments on the veil, claiming they 'weren't particularly helpful to Muslims'.

GIFTS TO THE ROYAL FAMILY

Detailed guidelines govern the 'acceptance, classification, retention, and disposal' of gifts to members of the Royal family. These ensure 'no gifts, including hospitality or services, should be accepted which would, or might appear to, place the member of the Royal family under any obligation to the donor', while balancing 'any offence that might be caused' by declining an offer. Gifts are classified as OFFICIAL or PERSONAL – the former are 'received in an official capacity in the course of official duties in support of, and on behalf of The Queen'; the latter are subject to the normal tax rules. Below are some official gifts received by the Royals in 2006:

Three medals dedicated to the history of Lithuania · One painting of two horses by the Latvian artist, Ivars Heinrihsons · *The Hidden and Forbidden History of Latvia Under Soviet and Nazi Occupations 1940–91* (Vol 14) · Sculpture of a basketball player in a wheelchair (bronze/resin on wooden plinth) · Sculpture of a tree made from Brazilian wood · Toy Porsche for Lady Louise · Hoylake Bruichladdich Links single malt from Bruichladdich Distillery Co., Ltd · Cufflinks from the Ukraine–British Chamber of Commerce · Robe, whip, and hat from the President of Kazakhstan · Spatula from the Textile Institute of Ulaanbaatar.

WHO'S NEW IN WHO'S WHO

Published annually since 1849, *Who's Who* is one of the most respected biographical reference books in the world. When, during WWII, paper rationing threatened its publication, Churchill personally intervened to ensure the book continued to be printed. Below are some of those who were added to the 2007 edition (those who have died during the year enter the companion *Who Was Who*):

David Aaronovitch *columnist*
Piers Adams *virtuoso recorder player*
Roger Allam *actor*
Benedict Allen *author, adventurer*
David Arnold *film composer*
David Backhouse *sculptor*
Kevin Bakhurst *Ctrlr.* BBC *News 24*
John Banville *writer*
Lionel Barber *Editor,* FT
Trajan Basescu *President, Romania*
Prof. Susan Bassnett *writer, academic*
Jan Beaney *textile artist, author*
Bob 'the cat' Bevan *writer, comedian*
Sanjeev Bhaskar *actor, writer*
Josep Borrell Fontelles *President, European Parliament*
Julia Bracewell *Chair, sportscotland*
Tom Bradby *Political Ed.* ITV *News*
Karen Bruce *choreographer, director*
John Bryant *Editor-in-chief,* Telegraph
Anibal Cavaco Silva *President, Portugal*
Ian Cheshire *CEO B&Q*
Leonard Cohen *writer, composer*
Giles Coren *columnist*
Peter Duncan *Chief Scout*
Noel Edmonds *TV presenter*
Andrew Festing *painter*
Claire Fox *Dir. Institute of Ideas*
Helen Fraser *MD Penguin*
Frank Gardner *BBC correspondent*
Muriel Gray *presenter, broadcaster*
Bonnie Greer *writer*
Charles Hazlewood *conductor*
Philip Hobbs *racehorse trainer*
Jonathan Ive *Senior VP, Apple*
Alison Jackson *artist, photographer*
Akram Khan *dancer, choreographer*
Denis Lawson *actor, director*
Paul Lewis *financial journalist*
David McDonald (Tennant) *actor*
Chris McLaughlin *Ed.* Tribune
Claire Martin *jazz singer, presenter*
Stephen Mear *choreographer*
John Micklethwait *Ed.* The Economist
Kate Mosse *novelist, broadcaster*
Grayson Perry *artist in ceramics*
Jay Rayner *journalist*
John Rocha *fashion designer*
Jenny Seagrove *actress*
Jon Sopel *TV presenter*
Toby Stephens *actor*
Susie Symes *Museum of Immigration*
Veronica Tennant *ballet dancer, writer*
Rosemary Thew *CEO DSA*
William Tuckett *principal guest artist, Royal Ballet*
Richard Wallace *Ed.* Daily Mirror
Paul Watkins *cellist, conductor*
Jasmine Whitbread *Chief Executive Save the Children*
John Wonnacott *artist*
Edward Young *asst. Private Secretary to the Queen*
Elias Zerhouni *Dir. Nat. Inst. Health*

A few recreations – PIERS ADAMS 'conspiracy research (9/11, moon landings, JFK, etc)' · BRENDA BILLINGTON 'returning purchases to clothes shops' · PROF. KENNETH BOOTH 'watching sport, and thinking of what might have been, reading obituaries, and thinking of what will be' · SHUNA LINDSAY 'building wooden replica model warships, collecting dolphins' · WILLIAM TUCKETT 'playing with my cats, compulsively buying DVDs, fighting addiction to Bendicks Bittermints (unsuccessfully)' · PROFESSOR JONATHAN SHEPHERD 'building blast furnaces'.

SOME HONOURS OF NOTE · 2007

New Year's Honours

KNIGHT BACHELOR

James Dyson .... entrepreneur
Michael Holroyd .... biographer
John Scarlett .... ex-Chief MI6
George Shearing .... jazz pianist

DBE

Evelyn Glennie .... percussionist
Ann Leslie .... journalist

CBE

Kevin Cahill. Chief Exec Comic Relief
Stephen Carter ..... Chief Exec Ofcom
Imogen Cooper .... pianist
Gareth Edwards .... rugby player
Peter Greenaway .... film director
Margaret Howell ...... fashion designer
Penelope Keith .... actress
Christopher Logue .... poet, writer
Alexander McCall Smith .... writer
John Rutter ..... composer, conductor
Hilary Spurling .... biographer
Rod Stewart .... musician
Colin Thubron .... travel writer

OBE

Christopher Beale .... Chair IoD
Linda Bennett .... founder LK Bennett
Mike Golding .... yachtsman
Sally Greene .... Old Vic theatre
Hugh Laurie .... actor
Steven Pimlott . theatre, opera director
Ian Woosnam .... golfer

MBE

Brian Barron ...... BBC correspondent
Johnny Briggs .... actor
Shirley Collins ...... folk singer, writer
Steven Gerrard .... footballer
John Grey shoe shiner, Virgin Atlantic
Ricky Hatton .... boxer
Zara Phillips .... equestrian
June Sarpong .... TV presenter
Faye White .... Arsenal Ladies Cpt

Queen's Birthday Honours

GCB

Robin Janvrin ... Private Sec to Queen

CB

Stephen Aldridge .... PM Strategy Unit

KNIGHT BACHELOR

Ian Botham .... cricketer
John Hegarty .... advertising
Salman Rushdie† .... writer

DBE

Carolyn Emma Kirkby . classical singer

CBE

Christiane Amanpour .... CNN
Shami Chakrabarti .... Liberty
Michael Eavis ... founder Glastonbury
Barry Humphries .... entertainer
Betty Jackson .... designer
Stephen Poliakoff .... writer
David Starkey .... historian

OBE

Barbara Taylor Bradford .... writer
Nicky Clarke .... hairdresser
Dick Clement .... screenwriter
Joe Cocker .... singer
Ryan Giggs .... footballer
Ian La Frenais .... screenwriter
Peter Sallis .... actor

MBE

Dee Caffari .... yachtswoman
Teddy Sheringham .... footballer

† Rushdie's knighthood reignited the controversy surrounding allegations of 'blasphemy' in his 1988 novel *The Satanic Verses*. Iran and Pakistan denounced the honour as a 'provocative act', and protests were held in Britain and in many Islamic countries. ❦ In June 2007, Sir Tim Berners-Lee, the 'inventor' of the world wide web, was presented with the Order of Merit.

THE RED POPPY

A symbol of Christ's blood in medieval art, the red poppy is now recognised across the Commonwealth as a sign of military sacrifice and remembrance. The poppy's associations with warfare derive from the flower's ability to thrive in the churned soil of WWI battlefields in Belgium and northern France. (As Lord Haig wrote in 1921, the poppy is 'the tribute which Nature has placed on the graves of thousands of our gallant dead'.) Canadian doctor and serviceman John McCrae (1872–1918) immortalised the significance of the poppy in his celebrated poem: *In Flanders Fields* 'the poppies blow Between the crosses row on row, That mark our place; and in the sky The larks, still bravely singing, fly Scarce heard amid the guns below'. ❦ Soon after the Great War, artificial poppies were manufactured and sold in France to support children scarred by the fighting. In 1921, this idea was adopted by Lord Haig and his newly established charity for ex-servicemen, the British Legion. The first 'poppy day' was held on Remembrance Day 1921 and, as the *Times* reported, was an instant success: 'The poppy had an official price of 3d., but none who bought had regard for that figure. In Smithfield Market before breakfast time the petals of a single poppy were sold for £5 each. In the City, at Lloyds, on the Stock Exchange … the collectors' boxes were filled with notes and cheques. In every big shop in the West-end, in the hotels and restaurants and clubs, on the steps of public buildings, the poppy was bought and sold. There was a vendor at every suburban station, and if a passenger escaped into his train without a flower it was only to buy one as soon as he alighted at his destination'. In this first year, an estimated 8 million poppies were sold. 84 years later, in 2005, £24·7m was raised from the sale of 36m poppies, 107,000 wreaths and 750,000 remembrance crosses.

In 1933, the Women's Co-operative Guild introduced an alternative white 'peace poppy', to honour the dead while rejecting the glorification of war. These white poppies proved immediately controversial: some women lost their jobs for wearing them, and the British Legion denounced them as 'an insult to the Flanders poppy and all it stands for'. (Although white poppies have never proved as popular as red, their sales in 1986 were given an inadvertent fillip by Margaret Thatcher when she expressed her 'deep distaste' for them.) ❦ In November 2006, Channel 4 newsreader Jon Snow was criticised for refusing to wear a poppy on television. In a blog, Snow defended his position, denouncing the pressure to conform as 'poppy fascism', and noting, 'I am begged to wear an Aids ribbon, a breast cancer ribbon, a Marie Curie flower … You name it, from the Red Cross to the RNIB, they send me stuff to wear, and I don't. And in those terms, and those terms alone, I do not and will not wear a poppy.'

ON FLIRTING DURING DINNER

When you are seated next to a LADY,
you should be only POLITE during the *first course*;
you may be GALLANT in the *second*;
but you must not be TENDER till the DESSERT.

ESTATES OF THE REALM

The Estates of the Realm are those classes within the body politic with administrative powers. The original Estates of England, as represented in Parliament, were:

1st – CLERGY · 2nd – BARONS & KNIGHTS · 3rd – COMMONS

after some adjustment these became

1st – LORDS SPIRITUAL · 2nd – LORDS TEMPORAL · 3rd – COMMONS

According to the redoubtable *Oxford English Dictionary*, the Fourth Estate has been used to refer to the PRESS, since Henry Fielding wrote in 1752 'None of our political writers … take notice of any more than three Estates, namely, Kings†, Lords, and Commons … passing by in silence that very large and powerful body which form the Fourth Estate in this community'. Famously, Thomas Carlyle reported that while Edmund Burke was speaking in the Commons, he referred to the Press Gallery, declaring, 'Yonder sits the Fourth Estate, more important than them all'.

† Fielding, it seems, was making a common error in supposing that three Estates of the Realm were the Crown, the House of Lords, and the House of Commons. ❦ In 1875, smaller landowners were also referred to as the Fourth Estate. ❦ A number of institutions have been dubbed the Fifth Estate, including publicans (1876), women (1912), cinema (1918), the BBC, radio, television, trades unions, quangos, universities, philanthropic trusts, opinion polls, independent research centres, and most recently 'citizen media' – notably bloggers. ❦ The Scottish tradition of Estates differs.

A MAXIM OF GOOD MANNERS

In PRIVATE watch your *thoughts* · In your FAMILY watch your *temper*
In your BUSINESS watch your *avarice* · In SOCIETY watch your *tongue*

ON INTRODUCTIONS

With the exception of reigning Sovereigns (including the Pope), Presidents, and Cardinals, introductions made between strangers should abide by these four rules:

Youth is introduced to *age* – 'Teddy Sheringham, may I present Theo Walcott?'

Men are introduced to *women* – 'Dame Edna, this is Count Victor Grezhinski.'

Lower ranks are introduced to *higher* – 'Captain Mainwaring, this is Private Pike.'

Individuals are introduced to *groups* – 'Take That, this is Robbie Williams.'

Traditionally, the so-called English Rule was 'the roof is an introduction' – by which all guests 'under the roof' of a common host might feel at liberty to initiate conversation with their fellow guests without waiting for any formal introduction.

AN ELEMENTARY GUIDE TO FORMS OF ADDRESS

Personage	*envelope*	*start of letter*	*verbal address*
The Queen	The Queen's Most Excellent Majesty†	Madam/May it please your Majesty	Your Majesty/Ma'am
The Duke of Edinburgh	HRH The Duke of Edinburgh†	Sir	Your Royal Highness/Sir
The Queen Mother	Her Majesty Queen —— The Queen Mother†	Madam	Your Majesty/Ma'am
Royal Prince	HRH The Prince ——, (The Prince of ——)†	Sir	Your Royal Highness/Sir
Royal Princess	HRH The Princess (of) ——†	Your Royal Highness	Your Royal Highness/Madam
Royal Duke	HRH The Duke of ——†	Your Royal Highness	Your Royal Highness/Sir
Royal Duchess	HRH The Duchess of ——†	Your Royal Highness	Your Royal Highness/Madam
Duke	His Grace the Duke of ——	My Lord Duke/Dear Duke	Your Grace/Duke
Duchess	Her Grace the Duchess of ——	Dear Madam/Dear Duchess	Your Grace/Duchess
Marquess	The Most Honourable The Marquess of ——	My Lord/Dear Lord ——	My Lord/Lord ——
Marchioness	The Most Honourable The Marchioness of ——	Madam/Dear Lady ——	Madam/Lady ——
Earl	The Rt Hon The Earl of ——	My Lord/Dear Lord ——	My Lord/Lord ——
Earl's wife	The Rt Hon The Countess of ——	Madam/Dear Lady ——	Madam/Lady ——
Countess	The Rt Hon The Countess of ——	Madam/Dear Lady ——	Madam/Lady ——
Viscount	The Rt Hon The Viscount ——	My Lord/Dear Lord ——	Lord ——
Viscount's wife	The Rt Hon The Viscountess ——	Madam/Dear Lady ——	Lady ——
Baron	The Rt Hon Lord ——	My Lord/Dear Lord ——	Lord ——
Baron's wife	The Rt Hon Lady ——	My Lady/Dear Lady ——	Lady ——
Baroness	The Rt Hon The Lady (*or* The Baroness) ——	My Lady/Dear Lady ——	Madam/Lady ——
Baronet	Sir Bertie Wooster Bt (*or* Bart)	Dear Sir Bertie	Sir Bertie
Baronet's wife	Lady ——	Dear Madam/Dear Lady ——	Lady ——
Knight of an Order	Sir Bertie Wooster (*and order*)	Dear Sir Bertie	Sir Bertie
Knight Bachelor	Sir Bertie Wooster	Dear Sir Bertie	Sir Bertie
Knight's wife	Lady ——	Dear Madam/Dear Lady ——	Lady ——
Dame	Dame ——	Dear Madam/Dear Dame ——	Dame ——

AN ELEMENTARY GUIDE TO FORMS OF ADDRESS cont.

Personage	*envelope*	*start of letter*	*verbal address*
Life Peer	The Rt Hon Lord —— (of ——)	My Lord/Dear Lord ——	Lord ——
Life Peeress	The Rt Hon The Lady (*or* Baroness) —— (of ——)	My Lady/Dear Lady ——	Lady ——
Archbishop	The Most Rev & Rt Hon the Lord Archbishop of ——	Dear Archbishop	Your Grace/Archbishop
Bishop	((The Rt Rev) (and Right Hon)) The Bishop of ——	Dear Bishop	Bishop
Lord Chancellor	The Rt Hon The Lord Chancellor	*by rank*	*by rank*
Prime Minister	The Rt Hon The Prime Minister PC MP	Dear Prime Minister	Prime Minister/Sir
Deputy PM	The Rt Hon The Deputy Prime Minister PC MP	Dear Deputy Prime Minister	Deputy Prime Minister/Sir
Chancellor of the Exchequer	The Rt Hon The Chancellor of the Exchequer PC MP	Dear Chancellor	Chancellor/Sir
Foreign Secretary	The Rt Hon The SoS for Foreign & Comwth Affairs	Dear Foreign Secretary	Foreign Secretary/*by rank*
Home Secretary	The Rt Hon The SoS for the Home Department	Dear Home Secretary	Home Secretary/*by rank*
Secretary of State	The Rt Hon The SoS for ——	Dear Secretary of State	Secretary of State/*by rank*
Minister	(The Rt Hon) Bertie Wooster Esq. (PC) MP	Dear Minister	Minister/*by rank*
MP‡	Bertie Wooster Esq. MP	Dear Mr Wooster	Mr Wooster
MP Privy Councillor	The Rt Hon Bertie Wooster PC MP	Dear Mr Wooster	Mr Wooster
Privy Councillor	The Rt Hon Bertie Wooster PC	Dear Mr Wooster	Mr Wooster
High Court Judge	The Hon Mr Justice ——	Dear Sir ——/Dear Judge	Sir/My Lord/Your Lordship
Ambassador (British)	His Excellency —— HM Ambassador to ——	*by rank*	Your Excellency
Lord Mayor	The Rt Hon the Lord Mayor of ——	My (Dear) Lord Mayor	Lord Mayor
Mayor	The Worshipful Mayor of ——	(Dear) Mr Mayor	Mr Mayor

It is hard to overstate the complexity of 'correct' form which (especially in the legal and clerical fields, as well as Chivalry) can become extremely rococo, and is the subject of considerable dispute between sources. Consequently, the above tabulation can only hope to provide a very elementary guide. ❦ Readers interested in the correct formal styling of the wives of younger sons of Earls, for example, are advised to consult specialist texts on the subject. † It is usual to address correspondence to members of the Royal Family in the first instance to their Private Secretary. ‡ A similar styling is used for Members of the European Parliament [MEP]; Scottish Parliament [MSP]; National Assembly for Wales [AM]; and Northern Ireland Assembly [MLA]. From the moment Parliament is dissolved there are no Members of Parliament, and consequently the letters MP should not be used. By convention medical doctors are styled Dr ——, whereas surgeons use the title Mr ——; many gynaecologists, although surgeons, are styled Dr.

THE DIPLOMATIC SERVICE

The origins of modern diplomacy can be traced back to C13th northern Italy, where city states like Milan and Venice exchanged ambassadors to improve relations and facilitate trade. As relationships between European countries became increasingly important, major states began to post ambassadors permanently at overseas courts. In 1487, Spain sent to England the first permanent representative. The 1815 Congress of Vienna formalised the previously ad hoc system of diplomatic rank and precedence, a system that often soured international relations when one country received only low-ranking officials from another. The diplomatic hierarchy was:

Ambassador, Papal Nuncio, or High Commissioner .... *represents head of state*
Minister Plenipotentiary.................. *in charge of legations rather than embassies*
Minister .... *lowest rank of diplomatic mission chief*
Chargé d'Affaires............ *temporary head of mission, in absence of more senior staff*

With the formation of the UN after WWII, it became increasingly unacceptable for countries to treat others as diplomatically inferior. As a consequence, most legations were upgraded to embassies, and most embassies were headed by ambassadors. Rules relating to the treatment and status of ambassadors and their staff were formalised by the 1961 Vienna Convention, which created diplomatic immunity[†] and exemptions from taxation. Traditionally, the credentials of ambassadors are held in a sealed letter signed by the sovereign or head of state, which grants them powers of negotiation. ❦ The United Kingdom diplomatic service currently has: 46 High Commissions to Commonwealth countries[‡]; 107 Embassies; 10 Missions to international organisations (like the UN); 38 posts staffed entirely by locally engaged staff; 220 Honorary Consulates; and 3 unstaffed posts (as of 2003, in Baghdad, Mogadishu, and Monrovia). Although the UK maintains diplomatic relations with most countries, she does not formally recognise Taiwan as a state.

† To ensure independence, diplomats are exempt from the criminal, civil, and administrative jurisdiction of their host country. Consequently, diplomats and their immediate family cannot be arrested, have their homes searched, be called as a witness, or prosecuted. In exceptional cases a country may waive the immunity of their diplomats. A host country may also declare a visiting diplomat *persona non grata* and expel them without explanation or appeal.

‡ A diplomatic mission in a Commonwealth country is a High Commission and the head of mission is a High Commissioner. They have the same status and perform the same functions as Embassy and Ambassador respectively. ❦ In January 2007, Sweden announced that it would open an Embassy in the virtual world of Second Life [see *Schott's Almanac 2008*]. The Embassy is aimed solely at promoting tourism, and has no powers to issue passports or visas.

MOUSTACHES AND THE ARMY

'If a moustache is worn, it is to be trimmed and not below the line of the lower lip. Beards and whiskers are only to be worn with authority, which will usually be granted only on medical or religious grounds, or where tradition permits. The appearance of the beard and whiskers is to be neat and tidy.' [Queen's Regulations 1975]

COURT STRUCTURE IN ENGLAND & WALES

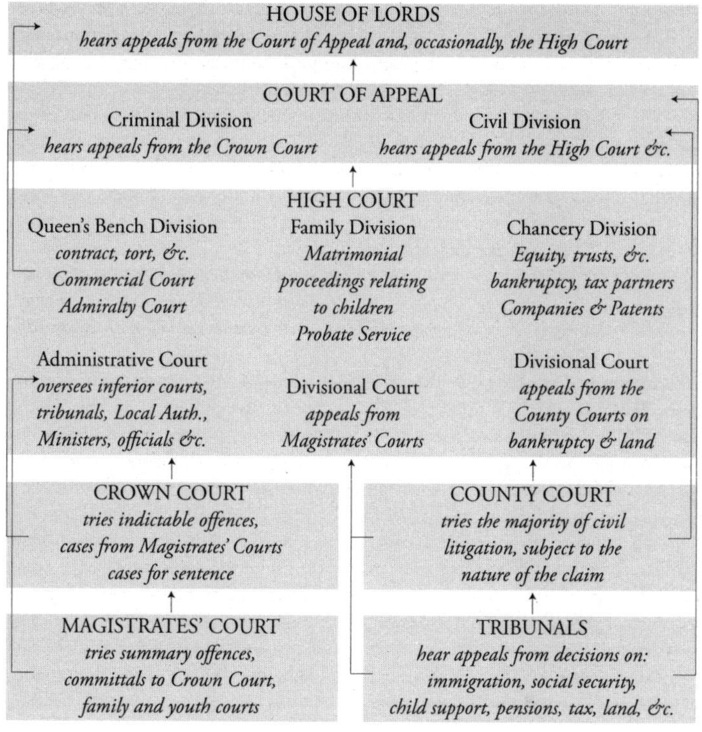

[Source: The Court Service · Crown ©]

ATTRACTIVE DEFENDANTS & JURORS

Jurors are less likely to find attractive defendants guilty – according to research presented to the British Psychological Society in March 2007. Researchers from York and Bath Spa Universities gave 96 volunteers a transcript of a fictional mugging and a photograph of the defendant and asked them for a verdict, the extent of the defendant's guilt, and the sentence that should be passed. Regardless of the ethnicity of the volunteer, less attractive defendants were more likely to be judged guilty, and 'ugly' black defendants were the most likely to be given a harsh sentence. ❦ Research by Cheryl Thomas for the Ministry of Justice published in June 2007 suggested that jurors show greater leniency towards ethnic minorities. The study simulated 27 trials and varied the ethnic mix of the jury, defendant, and victim. The resulting data suggested that jurors of all races showed greater leniency to ethnic minority defendants. Thomas speculated that jurors were attempting to correct a perceived bias in the criminal justice system. However, despite this apparent tendency, the *verdicts* in the trials were not significantly affected by the race of the defendant.

NATO MILITARY SPENDING & FORCES

[Source: Nato] *(Iceland has no forces)*	*Defence spending* (% of GDP) 1985–89 (average)	2006	*Effective annual strength of armed forces* (No., % of labour force) 1985	1990	1995	2000	2006
Belgium	2·7	1·1	107k (2·8%)	106k (2·7%)	47k (1·2%)	42k (1·0%)	39k (0·9%)
Bulgaria	NA	2·4	NA	NA	NA	NA	43k (1·6%)
Canada	2·1	1·2	83k (0·9%)	87k (0·9%)	70k (0·7%)	59k (0·5%)	64k (0·5%)
Czech Republic	NA	1·8	NA	NA	NA	52k (1·4%)	26k (0·7%)
Denmark	2·0	1·4	29k (1·4%)	31k (1·4%)	27k (1·3%)	24k (1·1%)	21k (1·0%)
Estonia	NA	1·6	NA	NA	NA	NA	5k (1·0%)
France	3·7	2·4	560k (2·7%)	548k (2·6%)	502k (2·3%)	394k (1·8%)	356k (1·6%)
Germany	3·0	1·3	495k (2·3%)	545k (2·5%)	352k (1·3%)	319k (1·0%)	245k (0·7%)
Greece	5·1	3·0	201k (6·1%)	201k (5·7%)	213k (5·7%)	205k (5·1%)	139k (3·3%)
Hungary	NA	1·2	NA	NA	NA	50k (1·5%)	23k (0·7%)
Italy	2·2	1·7	504k (2·5%)	493k (2·4%)	435k (2·2%)	381k (1·8%)	309k (1·4%)
Latvia	NA	1·5	NA	NA	NA	NA	5k (0·5%)
Lithuania	NA	1·2	NA	NA	NA	NA	11k (0·9%)
Luxembourg	0·8	0·6	1·2k (0·9%)	1·3k (0·9%)	1·3k (0·9%)	1·4k (0·8%)	1·4k (0·7%)
Netherlands	2·7	1·5	103k (2·0%)	104k (1·8%)	67k (1·2%)	52k (0·9%)	50k (0·7%)
Norway	2·9	1·5	36k (2·3%)	51k (2·9%)	38k (2·3%)	32k (1·8%)	20k (1·0%)
Poland	NA	1·9	NA	NA	NA	191k (1·5%)	150k (1·2%)
Portugal	2·5	1·6	102k (2·6%)	87k (2·1%)	78k (1·8%)	68k (1·5%)	39k (0·9%)
Romania	NA	2·0	NA	NA	NA	NA	75k (1·0%)
Russian Federation	NA	2·8	NA	NA	?	?	?
Slovak Republic	NA	1·7	NA	NA	NA	NA	19k (1·0%)
Slovenia	NA	1·7	NA	NA	NA	NA	7k (0·8%)
Spain	2·1	1·2	314k (2·7%)	263k (2·1%)	210k (1·6%)	144k (1·1%)	127k (0·7%)
Turkey	3·3	3·0	814k (4·7%)	769k (4·0%)	805k (3·8%)	793k (3·6%)	499k (2·2%)
United Kingdom	4·5	2·3	334k (1·9%)	308k (1·7%)	233k (1·3%)	218k (1·1%)	206k (1·0%)
United States	6·0	3·8	2,244k (2·9%)	2,181k (2·6%)	1,620k (1·9%)	1,483 (1·5%)	1,355k (1·3%)

UK SERVICE RANKS

service	ROYAL NAVY	ROYAL MARINES†	ARMY	ROYAL AIR FORCE	NATO
OFFICERS	Admiral of the Fleet	—	Field Marshal	Marshal of the RAF	OF-10
	Admiral	General	General	Air Chief Marshal	OF-9
	Vice-Admiral	Lieutenant General	Lieutenant General	Air Marshal	OF-8
	Rear Admiral	Major General	Major General	Air Vice-Marshal	OF-7
	Commodore	Brigadier	Brigadier	Air Commodore	OF-6
	Captain	Colonel	Colonel	Group Captain	OF-5
	Commander	Lieutenant Colonel	Lieutenant Colonel	Wing Commander	OF-4
	Lieutenant Commander	Major	Major	Squadron Leader	OF-3
	Lieutenant	Captain	Captain	Flight Lieutenant	OF-2
	Sub-Lieutenant	Lieutenant/2nd Lieutenant	Lieutenant/2nd Lieutenant	Flying Officer/Pilot Officer	OF-1
	Midshipman	—	Officer Cadet	Officer Designate	OF-(D)
OTHER RANKS	Warrant Officer Class 1	Warrant Officer Class 1	Warrant Officer Class 1	Warrant Officer	OR-9
	Warrant Officer Class 2	Warrant Officer Class 2	Warrant Officer Class 2	—	OR-8
	Chief Petty Officer	Colour Sergeant	Staff Sergeant	Flight Sergeant/Chief Technician	OR-7
	Petty Officer	Sergeant	Sergeant	Sergeant	OR-6
	Leading Rate	Corporal	Corporal	Corporal	OR-4
	—	—	Lance Corporal	—	OR-3
	Able Rating	Marine	Private (Class 1–3)	Junior Technician / Leading & Senior Aircraftman	OR-2
	—	—	Private (Class 4)/Junior	Aircraftman	OR-1

[Source: DASA] The Naval rank of Warrant Officer Class 2 was introduced in 2004. † The Royal Marines were established in 1664 as a corps of sea soldiers to be raised and disbanded as required. In 1755, they became a permanent part of the Navy, trained as soldiers and seamen to fight and to maintain discipline on ships. The Royal Marines gained their tough fighting reputation during the capture of Gibraltar in 1704, and have since played a decisive role in military deployments across the world.

THE BRITISH PASSPORT

It is estimated that, as of May 2006, 38·68m adults and 8·99m children held a valid British passport. Passports are issued at the discretion of the government, and British citizens do not have a legal right to one – unless they are British Nationals Overseas [see p.99]. ❦ The first British passports were issued by the Privy Council between 1540–1685. Initially, each passport was personally signed by the monarch, but since 1794 all passports have been granted by the Secretary of State. During WWI, nation states became increasingly concerned to establish the identity of their citizens, and so the requirement for passports became more common. The British Nationality and Status of Aliens Act (1914) defined the modern British passport as a one page document containing a photograph of the holder and a physical description (including useful details such as shape of face, complexion, and size of facial features). By 1920, the League of Nations agreed on a book-format passport for member states, resulting in a new 32-page blue British passport. Over the years various changes – such as laminated photos and watermarked paper – have been introduced to make passports more difficult to forge. In 1985, the EU agreed that all member states' passports should have burgundy covers embossed with both the name of the issuing country and the European Union. As a result of recent concerns over identity theft, the latest British passports now contain some biometric data. (The EU has ruled that by August 2006 facial biometric data be included, and by July 2009 fingerprint biometrics.) Facial recognition maps extrapolated from the passport photo, and personal details normally recorded on page 31 of the passport (such as date and place of birth) are stored on a chip implanted in the document. ❦ Since British passports are issued in the name of Her Majesty, the Queen does not possess one, although all other members of the Royal family do – including the Duke of Edinburgh. ❦ From April 2007 face-to-face interviews were introduced for first-time passport applicants, to combat fraud – which costs the UK an estimated £1·7bn a year. ❦ Below is the number of passports issued each year:

British Passport Wording

Her Britannic Majesty's Secretary of State Requests and requires in the Name of Her Majesty all those whom it may concern to allow the bearer to pass freely without let or hindrance, and to afford the bearer such assistance and protection as may be necessary.

Year	*passports issued*
2004	6·1m
2003	5·5m
2002	5·4m
2001	5·7m
2000	5·5m
1999	5·6m
1998	4·9m
1997	4·7

[Source: UKPS; figures do not include passports issued abroad]

In February 2007, the National Audit Office raised concerns that the new biometric 'e-passports', of which 4m have been issued so far at a cost of £66 each, might fail after just 2 years. The microchips that hold personal data have only a 2-year warranty, and had not been tested to see whether they could withstand frequent travel. ❦ In March 2007, the Home Office admitted that the Identity and Passport Service had received 16,500 fraudulent applications between October 2005 – September 2006. Despite various safeguards, it was estimated that *c.*10,000 passports were issued to fraudsters.

ENGLISH CHURCH CENSUS

6·3% of the population regularly worship at one of the estimated 37,501 churches in England – according to the 2005 English Church Census, undertaken by Christian Research. 83% of English churchgoers were white, 10% black, and 7% other non-white ethnic groups. (Church attendance amongst blacks was greater than three times their proportion in the general population.) A breakdown of English churches in 2005, by denomination and congregation, is tabulated below:

Denomination	*number of churches*	*average people in congregation*	*average age of congregation*	*% of all churchgoers*
Roman Catholic	3,656	244	44	28
Anglican	16,247	54	49	28
Methodist	5,999	48	55	9
Pentecostal	2,227	129	33	9
Baptist	2,386	107	43	8
Independent	2,281	84	42	6
'New'	1,307	140	34	6
Utd Reformed Church	1,470	48	55	2
Orthodox	317	81	40	1
Other	1,611	63	44	3
ALL	37,501	99·8	43·9	100%

A 2007 report by the Von Hugel Institute, Cambridge, indicated that Catholicism is likely to overtake Anglicanism as the dominant UK religion, as a consequence of Catholic migration from countries such as Poland. Attendance at Mass, especially in areas of London, has recently grown significantly.

CHURCH WEDDINGS

There were 57,200 church weddings in 2005 – 200 more than in 2004. The most important factors in choosing a church wedding over a civil service were:

Reason	%
To have a 'proper' wedding	75
Convenience of location	69
Significance of specific church	60
Personal religious belief	56
Church exterior or setting	55
The spiritual or sacred ambience	55
A specific vicar	53
The music/choir/bell-ringing	49
The church interior	47
Desire to personalise the service	47
Family's religion	46
The marriage preparation sessions organised by the church	36

[Source: Church of England, Henley Centre, January 2007] ❦ A survey conducted for the Asian Wedding Exhibition 2007 revealed that 72% of British Asian weddings have more than 300 guests, and *c.*30% cost more than £30,000. Over 1,000 British Muslim, Hindu, and Sikh men and women were questioned about their views on marriage and weddings. 52% of respondents indicated that they would consider marrying outside their religion, and 77% felt the ideal age to marry was between 26–29 years old. Just over half (56%) said they would live with their partner before marriage, and 64% revealed they would live with their extended family once they were married.

THE VEIL

In October 2006, Jack Straw (then Leader of the Commons and former Home Secretary) expressed reservations about Muslims wearing the veil. While defending the right of women to wear what they chose, he asks that constituents visiting his surgery in Blackburn (where *c*.25% are Muslim) consider removing their veils, so that he can speak to them 'face-to-face'. The controversy Straw's comment provoked highlighted tensions between sections of the Islamic community and the secular society, and demonstrated the complexity of public opinion in regard to religious symbols. When, in November 2006, a British Airways employee was asked to remove or conceal a Christian cross that hung from her necklace, the *News of the World* commissioned an ICM poll on the subject, and discovered:

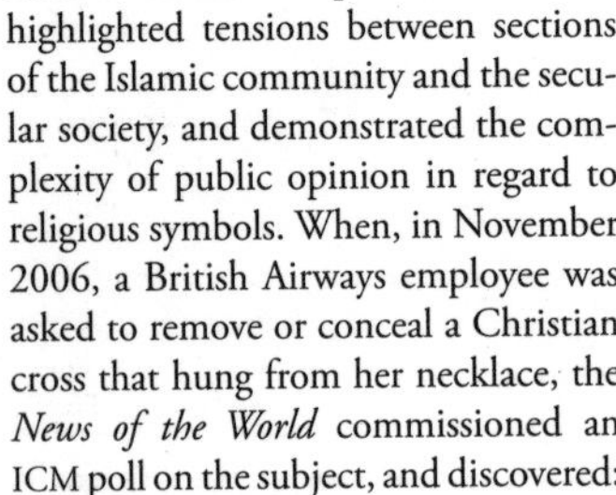

Acceptable in the workplace	*% agree*
Small cross on a necklace	92
A turban	85
A veil or headscarf	67

A host of recent cases have tested Jack Straw's assertion that veils are 'a visible sign of separation and of difference'. In November 2006, the Lord Chief Justice announced an inquiry into the wearing of veils in court after a trial was halted when a legal advisor refused to remove her veil. Some months later, a magistrate withdrew from a case in which a defendant wore her full veil. Also in November 2006, a classroom assistant was sacked by her Church of England school for refusing to remove her veil in class – a tribunal later ruled that she had not faced discrimination. In February 2007, a 12-year-old lost a legal challenge to her school's ban on full-face veils. A month later the government announced that schools could ban garments that prevented eye-to-eye contact. ❦ Akin with many faiths, followers of Islam are obliged to be modest in their dress. Traditionally, Muslim men cover themselves from navel to knee. As for women, Surah 24:31 of the Koran says, '*And say to the believing women that they should lower their gaze and guard their modesty; that they should not display their beauty and ornaments except what (must ordinarily) appear thereof; that they should draw their veils over their bosoms and not display their beauty*'. However, the extent that this and other passages obligate Muslim women to wear veils is hotly debated within Islam – not least because of the gradations of modesty that different veils afford. ❦ The *Hijab* is usually a simple scarf, wrapped around the head and neck, that leaves the face exposed. The *Niqab* covers all of the head and face, leaving exposed only the eyes (though some will also wear an eye-veil). The *Burqa* covers the entire head, face, and body, leaving just a fine mesh through which the wearer can see. ❦ In May 2007 the *Economist* noted, 'in every corner of the Muslim world, female attire is stirring strong emotions' – citing poles of opinion from Iran, where women are not safe on the streets without the *Hijab*, to Turkey, where civil servants are banned from covering their hair at work. However, as Islam grows in popularity and power, the borders of the so-called 'Muslim world' become ever more diffuse. Thus, the debate over the veil, and the associated debates over tolerance, integration, human rights, and the rights of women, are likely to become ever more pertinent.

RELIGION & FAITH: RECENT SURVEY DATA

Below are some selected results from recent surveys into faith, religion, and belief:

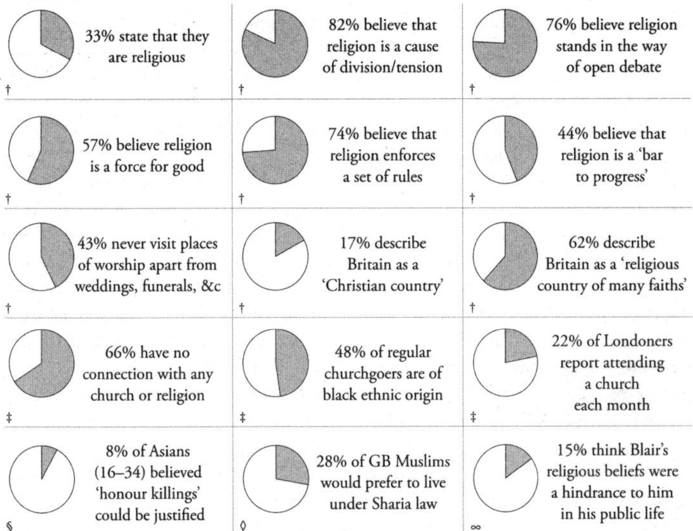

33% state that they are religious †
82% believe that religion is a cause of division/tension †
76% believe religion stands in the way of open debate †
57% believe religion is a force for good †
74% believe that religion enforces a set of rules †
44% believe that religion is a 'bar to progress' †
43% never visit places of worship apart from weddings, funerals, &c †
17% describe Britain as a 'Christian country' †
62% describe Britain as a 'religious country of many faiths' †
66% have no connection with any church or religion ‡
48% of regular churchgoers are of black ethnic origin ‡
22% of Londoners report attending a church each month ‡
8% of Asians (16–34) believed 'honour killings' could be justified §
28% of GB Muslims would prefer to live under Sharia law ◊
15% think Blair's religious beliefs were a hindrance to him in his public life ∞

[Key to sources: † = ICM *Guardian* poll Dec 2006 of British adults. ‡ = Tearfund poll Apr 2007 of UK 16+. § = ICM BBC Asian Network Aug 2006. ◊ = Policy Exchange, GB Muslims Jan 2007. ∞ BPIX/*Observer* May 2007]

THE 4 GODS OF AMERICAN BELIEF

2006 research from Baylor University, Texas, indicated that Americans tended to believe in one of four types of God, which they described in the following manner:

Authoritarian · God is very involved in people's 'daily lives and world affairs'; God will punish those who are unfaithful; God is responsible for economic and natural disasters. (31% of US believe)

Benevolent · God is involved in daily life but is not angry or wrathful, and is mostly a positive force. (23% believe)

Critical · God observes the world and is unhappy with it, but does not get involved in daily affairs; 'divine justice may not be of this world'. (16% believe)

Distant · God is not involved in the world and is not angry, but is rather a 'cosmic force which sets the law of nature in motion'. (24% believe)

The study found that women tend to believe in an *authoritarian* or *benevolent* God, while men believe in a *critical* or *distant* God. Easterners were found to believe in a *critical* God, Southerners an *authoritarian* God, Midwesterners a *benevolent* God, and Westerners a *distant* God. Lower incomes and levels of education were generally correlated with more engaged views of God, while those with college degrees or incomes >$100,000 tended towards a *distant* God, or were atheists.

BENEDICT XVI & LIMBO

In April 2007, after a three-year study by the Vatican's International Theological Commission, Pope Benedict XVI abolished the state of limbo. The Roman Catholic concept of limbo was first introduced by medieval theologians to explain the fate of innocent infants who died unbaptised. (The word derives from the Latin *in limbo* – referring to limbo's position 'on the edge' of hell, where those who die without sin but before baptism rest.) Two forms of limbo were traditionally distinguished: *limbus patrum*, for the souls of Old Testament prophets and holy people who died before Christ's salvation; and *limbus infantium*, for babies who died before being baptised. The Theological Commission said in their report that, 'grace has priority over sin and the exclusion of innocent babies from heaven does not seem to reflect Christ's special love for the little ones'. However, the Commission warned that their conclusions did not question 'original sin', and should not be interpreted so as 'to negate the necessity of baptism or delay the conferral of the sacrament'.

BELONGING TO A RELIGION

A breakdown of religious belief is provided by the British Social Attitudes survey, which asked 'do you regard yourself as belonging to any particular religion?'. The table below reveals the percentage of Britons who claimed to belong to a particular religion. 53·5% claimed to be Christian, 6·3% other, and 39·9% were of no religion:

Christian	%	*Non-Christian*	%
Church of England/Anglican	26·6	Islam/Muslim	2·6
Christian – no denomination	9·6	Hindu	1·2
Roman Catholic	9·2	Jewish	0·8
Presbyterian/Church of Scotland	3·3	Sikh	0·8
Baptist/Methodist	3·3	Buddhist	0·3
United Reformed Church	0·4	Other non-Christian	0·6
Other Christian	1·5	No religion	39·9

[Source: Social Trends 2007 Crown ©; British Social Attitudes Survey; 'don't knows' were excluded]

THE MOTHERS' UNION TEN COMMANDMENTS

The Mothers' Union is a Christian organisation with 3·6m members worldwide. In October 2006, the Union published a booklet entitled *Fair Enough?* which proposed ten modern 'commandments' to aid the poor and fight climate change:

[1] Turn off the television and other electrical equipment at the mains. [2] Use energy-efficient light bulbs. [3] Use computers less. [4] Turn down the central heating by one degree centigrade. [5] Reduce plane travel. [6] Use public transport. [7] Buy second-hand clothes and other goods. [8] Switch to ethically registered banks and investments. [9] Use local shops which stock Fairtrade, vegetarian, and organic produce. [10] Re-use and recycle everything where possible.

REASONS TO ATTEND CHURCH

An estimated 7·6 million adults in the UK attend church each month, according to research by Christian development agency Tearfund, published in April 2007. A further 3 million who have either stopped attending or have never been to church would consider going if they were invited. Tearfund asked infrequent or non-churchgoers what would motivate them to attend church services in the future:

Nothing would motivate them	63%
If a family member started going	9%
If someone personally invited them	8%
Difficult personal circumstances (e.g. illness, bereavement, &c.)	7%
If a friend started going	5%
An external event (e.g. war, disaster, death of a well-known person, &c.)	4%
An invitation from the church	3%
If the church ran a course to learn more about Christianity (e.g. Alpha)	1%

THE SEVEN SINS OF ENGLAND

In May 2007, Channel 4 aired an exploration of the 'seven sins of England', to analyse the roots and endurance of 'historical chavvery'. These seven sins were:

BINGE-DRINKING · SLAGGISHNESS · CONSUMERISM
HOOLIGANISM · VIOLENCE · RUDENESS · BIGOTRY

TEMPLETON PRIZE

The Canadian philosopher Charles Taylor won the 2007 *Templeton Prize for Progress Toward Research or Discoveries About Spiritual Realities*. A professor at Northwestern University in Illinois and professor emeritus at McGill University in Montreal, Taylor has focused on the need to address the spiritual dimensions of human existence, particularly when considering social problems such as bigotry and violence. 'We have somehow to break down the barriers between our contemporary culture of science and disciplined academic study … on one hand, and the domain of spirit, on the other', he said during the award's announcement on 14 March, 2007, at the Church Center for the United Nations in New York. The award was later presented by Prince Philip at a private ceremony at Buckingham Palace on 2 May, 2007. ❦ Sir John Templeton founded his eponymous prize in 1972 'to encourage and honor the advancement of knowledge in spiritual matters'. The prize (currently $1·5m) is said to be the largest annual monetary prize of any kind given to an individual. Templeton stipulated its value always be greater than the Nobel Prize, to 'underscore that research and advances in spiritual discoveries can be quantifiably more significant than disciplines recognised' by the Nobel committees. Previous Templeton winners have included Mother Teresa (1973), Billy Graham (1982), and Alexander Solzhenitsyn (1983).

NEW SAINTS

A Roman Catholic saint is one who has been declared worthy of 'public veneration' throughout the Church. Canonization is a lengthy and complex procedure, often spanning centuries, which depends on evidence of a candidate's exceptional sanctity, as well as proof of several miracles. (Canonization is distinct from beatification, in which the Church grants permission to venerate an individual with the titular suffix 'Blessed', but only within a particular diocese or other specified area.) Pope Benedict XVI canonized the following saints between October 2006–June 2007:

RAFAEL GUÍZAR VALENCIA
(1878–1938 · § 15·10·2006)
A Mexican priest persecuted by the revolutionary movement, he founded a religious newspaper in 1911, and was elected Bishop of Veracruz in 1919. There he helped victims of a massive earthquake, and later operated a Mexico City seminary in secret for 15 years.

FILIPPO SMALDONE
(1848–1923 · § 15·10·2006)
Known for his work among the deaf-mutes of Italy, he founded several institutes throughout the country; his Lecce institute became the basis for the Congregation of the Salesian Sisters of the Sacred Hearts. He later worked with blind children, orphans, and the abandoned.

ROSA VENERINI
(1656–1728 · § 15·10·2006)
Dedicated to the education of women as a means of cultural, spiritual, and moral improvement, she founded 'the first public school for girls in Italy', in Viterbo in 1685, and went on to found 40 more schools before her death.

THEODORE GUÉRIN
(1798–1856 · § 15·10·2006)
A French nun who led the missionary Sisters of Providence to Indiana in 1840, where she founded several schools, including Saint Mary-of-the-Woods College (now the oldest Catholic college for women in the US).

FR. ANTÔNIO DE SANT'ANA GALVÂO
(1739–1822 · § 11·5·2007)
A Franciscan monk who founded Our Lady of the Conception of Divine Providence in 1774, and the St Clare Friary in Sorocaba, São Paulo, in 1811. The Church reportedly credits him with 5,000 miracle cures.

GEORGE PRECA
(1880–1962 · § 3·6·2007)
A Maltese priest who founded the Society of Christian Doctrine (a group of evangelical lay people), and was known for spreading the gospel throughout the Maltese Islands.

SIMON OF LIPNICA
(*c.*1435–82 · § 3·6·2007)
A Polish preacher who fearlessly ministered to the sick during Krakow's plague epidemic in 1482–83, before himself succumbing.

FR. CHARLES OF ST ANDREW
(1821–93 · § 3·6·2007)
A Passionist priest known as the 'Saint of Mt Argus', he worked in England and Ireland and was known both for his great virtue and his miraculous cures.

MARIE EUGENIE OF JESUS MILLERET
(1817–98 · § 3·6·2007)
Dedicated to education and social issues, she founded the Religious of the Assumption in Paris in 1839. The congregation is still active.

The death of John Paul II prompted immediate calls of '*Santo Subito*' ['saint now'] in St Peter's Square. On 9 May 2005, Benedict XVI formally waived the usual five-year waiting period so that the processes of collecting evidence supporting beatification and canonization could begin immediately. In April 2007, the Vatican announced that the beatification process for JPII was 'advancing rapidly'.

TWO MINUTE SILENCE

On 8 May 1919, Australian journalist Edward George Honey wrote to the *London Evening News* (under the pseudonym Warren Foster) proposing a dignified silence to mark those who had died in the Great War. The idea apparently piqued the curiosity of King George V who, on 7 November 1919, issued the following proclamation:

TO ALL MY PEOPLE

BUCKINGHAM PALACE

Tuesday next, November 11, is the first anniversary of the Armistice, which stayed the world-wide carnage of the four preceding years and marked the victory of Right and Freedom. I believe that my people in every part of the Empire fervently wish to perpetuate the memory of that Great Deliverance, and of those who laid down their lives to achieve it. To afford an opportunity for the universal express of this feeling it is my desire and hope that at the hour when the Armistice came into force, the eleventh hour of the eleventh day of the eleventh month, there may be, for the brief space of two minutes, a complete suspension of all our normal activities. During that time, except in the rare cases where this may be impractical, all work, all sound, and all locomotion should cease, so that, in perfect stillness, the thoughts of every one may be concentrated on reverent remembrance of the Glorious Dead. No elaborate organisation appears to be necessary. At a given signal, which can easily be arranged to suit the circumstances of each locality, I believe that we shall all gladly interrupt our business and pleasure, whatever it may be, and unite in this simple service of Silence and Remembrance.

GEORGE R.I.

A leader in the *Times* welcomed the King's aspiration: 'We can conceive no service worthier, or so sure to touch the inmost feeling of the British race. The idea of this momentary elevation of the hearts and minds of all above their daily cares and pleasures in one communion of what all, indeed, feel, but none can utter, has a majestic simplicity native to their character and their habits'. ❦ George V's choice of a two minute silence may or may not have been original – some attribute the idea to the S African politician Sir Percy Fitzpatrick (1862–1931) – but this duration was not chosen at whim. Edward Honey's letter originally proposed a five minute silence, and it was this idea that George V reportedly tested when he invited Honey to Buckingham Place to watch a rehearsal by Grenadier Guards. Clearly, the display of highly trained soldiers standing to attention for five minutes was enough to convince the King that his people needed a less daunting target. ❦ In recent years, some have looked askance at what they perceive to be an 'inflation' in silence. They argue extending the two minute silence undermines its symbolism and invites unedifying comparisons of human tragedy. However, if recent commemorations are anything to go by, it seems that two minute silences are nowadays considered insufficient:

USA, 2005 · *to commemorate the 2003 death of 7 Columbia astronauts* ...... 3 mins
Worldwide, 2006 · *to commemorate the SE Asian tsunami* .... 3 mins
N Ireland Assembly, 1998 · *1st anniversary of the Omagh bombing* .... 4 mins
Spain, 2005 · *1st anniversary of the Madrid train bombings* .... 5 mins
Spain, 2004 · *one day after the Madrid train bombings* .... 10 mins
Iraq, 2007 · *1st anniversary of the Askariya Shrine bombing, Samarra* .... 15 mins

Sport

I think there'll be a few tears. — TIM HENMAN [see p.315]

CRICKET WORLD CUP 2007

The 2007 Cricket World Cup, hosted by the West Indies, was derided as a dull affair that dragged on too long – it took 47 days for the 16 teams to play 51 games. Matters were not helped when Ireland beat Pakistan, nor when Pakistan and India failed to make the Super 8s. For many, though, the cricket was overshadowed by the tragic death of Pakistan's coach Bob Woolmer, and the lengthy and sometimes bizarre police investigation that followed [see p.27]. ❦ In the end, Australia were hailed as worthy champions who consistently out-played their opponents to make their 3rd consecutive World Cup victory appear inevitable. Their rain-delayed final against Sri Lanka should have been dominated by Adam Gilchrist (who made 149 off 104 balls), but it ended in farce when bad light stopped play with 3 overs left. The Aussies began their celebrations, only for the umpires to declare that play would resume. In near darkness, the players gamely returned to the field, scarcely able to see bat or ball. ❦ Even the chief executive of the International Cricket Council, Malcolm Speed, admitted that the tournament may not have lived up to expectations, noting 'it was disappointing there were not a great number of matches that stayed in the mind'. Some criticised the organisers' decision to sell tickets at a price that many local fans could not afford. Those that did purchase tickets were banned from bringing flags or musical instruments, creating a decidedly dull and un-Caribbean atmosphere. All agreed that the next tournament (India in 2011) needed to be a shorter and more exciting affair. ❦ Under the captaincy of Michael Vaughan, England failed to reach the semi-finals, succumbing to South Africa in a woeful 9-wicket defeat. (This was the 4th consecutive occasion that England had failed to reach the latter stages of the competition.) Many blamed the batting order for England's inability to grasp any early advantages – citing Vaughan's frequent early dismissals. Matters were not helped when Andrew Flintoff was dismissed from his vice-captaincy after spending a wild night carousing, which culminated in an undignified capsized pedalo – dubbed the '*Fredalo*' affair. 'I'm embarrassed and ashamed. It shouldn't have happened', Flintoff said, 'there was water involved and a pedalo as well. But I don't want to go into detail. I don't think my life was in danger'. In typical fashion, England produced a thrilling display in their final game against the Windies when there was nothing to play for: Kevin Pietersen hit a 90-ball century, and the game was won by just 1 wicket. ❦ In the wake of England's poor performance, and her 5–0 Ashes whitewash [see p.309], coach Duncan Fletcher resigned.

Bob Woolmer

CRICKET WORLD CUP 2007 · RESULTS TABLE

SEMI-FINAL

24·04·07 · *Jamaica*
Sri Lanka *vs* New Zealand

Sri Lanka won the toss

Sri Lanka: 289 for 5 (50·0 overs)
New Zealand: 208 all out (41·4 overs)

Sri Lanka won by 81 runs

FINAL

28·04·07 · *Barbados*
Australia *vs* Sri Lanka

Australia won the toss

Australia: 281 for 4 (38·0 overs)
Sri Lanka: 215 for 8 (36·0 overs)

Australia won by 53 runs

SEMI-FINAL

25·04·07 · *St Lucia*
Australia *vs* South Africa

South Africa won the toss

S Africa: 149 all out (43·5 overs)
Australia: 153 for 3 (31·3 overs)

Australia won by 7 wickets

Super Eight · *Antigua*

Australia *bt* West Indies	*by* 103r
New Zealand *bt* West Indies	*by* 7w
Australia *bt* Bangladesh	*by* 10w
New Zealand *bt* Bangladesh	*by* 9w
Sri Lanka *bt* England	*by* 2r
Australia *bt* England	*by* 7w

Super Eight · *Guyana*

South Africa *bt* Sri Lanka	*by* 1w
England *bt* Ireland	*by* 48r
Sri Lanka *bt* West Indies	*by* 113r
South Africa *bt* Ireland	*by* 7w
Bangladesh *bt* South Africa	*by* 67r
New Zealand *bt* Ireland	*by* 129r

Super Eight · *Grenada*

South Africa *bt* West Indies	*by* 67r
Sri Lanka *bt* New Zealand	*by* 6w
New Zealand *bt* South Africa	*by* 5w
Australia *bt* Sri Lanka	*by* 7w
Sri Lanka *bt* Ireland	*by* 8w
Australia *bt* New Zealand	*by* 215r

Super Eight · *Barbados*

England *bt* Bangladesh	*by* 4w
Australia *bt* Ireland	*by* 9w
Ireland *bt* Bangladesh	*by* 74r
South Africa *bt* England	*by* 9w
West Indies *bt* Bangladesh	*by* 99r
England *bt* West Indies	*by* 1w

Group A
St Kitts & Nevis

1st Australia · 2nd South Africa
3rd Netherlands · 4th Scotland

Australia *bt* Scotland	*by* 203r
South Africa *bt* Netherlands	*by* 221r
Australia *bt* Netherlands	*by* 229r
South Africa *bt* Scotland	*by* 7w
Netherlands *bt* Scotland	*by* 8w
Australia *bt* South Africa	*by* 83r

Group B
Trinidad

1st Sri Lanka · 2nd Bangladesh
3rd India · 4th Bermuda

Sri Lanka *bt* Bermuda	*by* 243r
Bangladesh *bt* India	*by* 5w
India *bt* Bermuda	*by* 257r
Sri Lanka *bt* Bangladesh	*by* 198r
Sri Lanka *bt* India	*by* 69r
Bangladesh *bt* Bermuda	*by* 7w

Group C
St Lucia

1st New Zealand · 2nd England
3rd Kenya · 4th Canada

Kenya *bt* Canada	*by* 7w
New Zealand *bt* England	*by* 6w
England *bt* Canada	*by* 51r
New Zealand *bt* Kenya	*by* 148r
New Zealand *bt* Canada	*by* 114r
England *bt* Kenya	*by* 7w

Group D
Jamaica

1st West Indies · 2nd Ireland
3rd Pakistan · 4th Zimbabwe

West Indies *bt* Pakistan	*by* 54r
Ireland *tied* Zimbabwe	tie
Ireland *bt* Pakistan	*by* 3w
West Indies *bt* Zimbabwe	*by* 6w
Pakistan *bt* Zimbabwe	*by* 93r
West Indies *bt* Ireland	*by* 8w

BATTLE OF THE SURFACES

In May 2007, a bizarre tennis match in Mallorca pitted the skills of Roger 'King of Grass' Federer against Rafael 'King of Clay' Nadal. For *c.*2½† hours Federer (Wimbledon champion for 4 consecutive years, with an unbeaten run of 48 wins on grass) fought Nadal (French Open champion, with 72 straight wins on clay) on a half-grass, half-clay court specially constructed for this one-off match at a cost of £800,000. Nadal eventually emerged victorious, with a winning score of 7–5, 4–6, 7–6 (12–10). Previously, Federer and Nadal had faced each other only ten times:

World rank		*nationality*	*born*	*turned pro*	*handed*	*wins by surface* hard	clay	grass
1	FEDERER	Swiss	8·8·1981	1998	right	2	0	1
2	NADAL	Spanish	3·6·1986	2001	left	2	5	0

† To allow the players enough time to change into footwear appropriate for the different ends, the time allowed for the change-over was extended from the usual 90 seconds to two minutes.

THE WORLD SERIES OF POKER

Jerry Yang, a social worker from Temecula, CA, came from behind to win the 38th annual World Series of Poker. The final kicked off at noon, 17 July 2007, with Yang positioned 8th out of 9. By 4am the next day, only Yang and Canadian Tuan Lam remained. Yang beat Lam's paired queens with a straight, to take the $8·25m prize.

In January 2007, a jury at Snaresbrook Crown Court ruled that poker was a game of luck, not skill.

TOP RUNNING MOMENTS

In January 2007, health and fitness website realbuzz.com asked readers to vote for their top moment in the history of running. The top ten memorable moments were:

Runner	*year*	*event*	*% vote*
Paula Radcliffe	2005	relieved herself during the London Marathon	28
Roger Bannister	1954	ran the first sub-4-minute mile	27
Coe & Ovett	1980	800m & 1,500m rivalry at the 1980 Olympics	20
Budd & Decker	1984	3,000m rivalry at the Los Angeles Olympics	8
Jesse Owens	1936	took 4 golds at 'Hitler's Olympics' in Munich	4
Jim Peters	1954	marathon runner collapsed 11 times in final lap†	3
Sally Gunnell	1992	epic 400m hurdles final at the Barcelona Olympics	3
Carl Lewis	1984	took 4 golds at the Los Angeles Olympics	3
Emil Zatopek	1952	took gold the first time he ran a marathon	3
Ben Johnson	1988	stripped of his 100m gold for failing a drugs test	1

† Peters was suffering from heatstroke and dehydration as he entered the stadium with a 17-minute lead. Just 200m from the finish he collapsed for the last time and was carried off. He never raced again.

SWIMMING THE AMAZON

52-year-old Slovenian Martin Strel broke a world record in 2007 by swimming the entire length of the Amazon. At an average of 52 miles a day, it took Strel 66 days to swim the 3,272-mile river. He wore only a wetsuit for the perilous attempt, during which he dodged piranhas, tackled crocodiles, and overcame nausea, diarrhoea, and sunstroke. A seasoned marathon swimmer, Strel had previously conquered the Danube in 2000 (1,776 miles), the Mississippi in 2001 (2,348 miles) and the Yangtze in 2004 (3,900 miles). He completed the Amazon swim to raise awareness of the plight of the rain forest, saying 'I hope people remember this rain forest is our friend and stop destroying it. Most importantly, remember that it is never too late'.

LONDON MARATHON · 2007

On Sunday 22 April 2007, *c*.36,000 took part in the 27th London Marathon.

♂ *race results*		♂ *wheelchair race results*	
M. Lel [KEN]	2h 7m 41s	D. Weir [GBR]	01·30·49
A. Goumri [MOR]	02·07·44	K. Fearnley [AUS]	01·30·50
F. Limo [KEN]	02·07·47	S. Mendoza [MEX]	01·33·47

♀ *race results*		♀ *wheelchair race results*	
Chunxiu Zhou [CHI]	02·20·38	S. Woods [GBR]	01·50·40
G. Wami [ETH]	02·21·45	F. Porcellato [ITA]	01·59·46
C. Tomescu-Dita [ROM]	02·23·55	S. Piercey [GBR]	02·41·18

The temperature reached a record 23·5°C, making 2007 the hottest London Marathon ever run. Despite this 35,674 out of 36,391 runners completed the race, the greatest number of finishers ever.

– OTHER MARATHONS OF NOTE · 2006/07 –

BERLIN	*first run* 1974	NEW YORK	*first run* 1970
2006 · Sep 24	sunny, warm	2006 · Nov 5	fresh, cloudy
♂	H. Gebrselassie [ETH] · 2:05:56	♂	M. dos Santos [BRZ] · 2:09:58
♀	G. Wami [ETH] · 2:21:34	♀	J. Prokopcuka [LAT] · 2:25:05
Purse	$340,000	Purse	>$700,000

CHICAGO	*first run* 1977	BOSTON	*first run* 1897
2006 · Oct 22	cold, gusty winds	2007 · Apr 16	very windy, rainy
♂	R. K. Cheruiyot [KEN] · 2:07:35	♂	R. K. Cheruiyot [KEN] · 2:14:13
♀	B. Adere [ETH] · 2:20:42 NR	♀	L. Grigoryeva [RUS] · 2:29:18
Purse	$650,000	Purse	$575,000

In 2006, the 'big five' marathons (all those listed above) joined to create the body 'World Marathon Majors'. The World Marathon Majors Series was then announce: a competition including all the Majors as well as the IAAF World Marathon Championships and the Olympic marathon. The inaugural series began with Boston's 2006 run, and will end in New York in November 2007.

UEFA WOMEN'S CUP

In April 2007, Arsenal Ladies became the first British club ever to win the UEFA Women's Cup. Arsenal faced the Swedish side Umea IK, Europe's only full-time professional women's team, who were hoping to win the trophy for a record third time. In the first leg, at Sweden's Gammliavallen Stadium, a tense 90-minute standoff was finally ended with a decisive goal by Arsenal Ladies defender Alex Scott. A crowd of 3,467 then pitched up at Borehamwood FC's Meadow Park to witness the second leg, in which Arsenal doggedly held Umea IK to a goalless draw to take the title.

EUROPEAN XI vs MANCHESTER UTD

To commemorate the 50th anniversary of the Treaty of Rome and the creation of the European Union, a team of Europe's best players took on Manchester United at Old Trafford in March 2007. Cristiano Ronaldo dazzled for United as they beat the European XI 4–3. The players who made up the European XI squad are below:

S. Canizares (Valencia) · G. Zambrotta (Barcelona) · I. Campo (Bolton)
R. Ayala (Valencia) · P. Christanval (Fulham) · M. Materazzi (Inter Milan)
J. Carragher (Liverpool) · E. Abidal (Lyons) · D. Stefanovic (Portsmouth)
A. Mancini (AS Roma) · S. Giannakopoulos (Bolton) · A. Pirlo (AC Milan)
S. Gerrard (Liverpool) · G. Gattuso (AC Milan) · K. Kallström (Lyons)
F. Malouda (Lyons) · B. Zenden (Liverpool) · H. Larsson (Helsingborg)
R. Fowler (Liverpool) · Z. Ibrahimovic (Inter) · E. Diouf (Bolton) · G. Coupet (Lyons)

THINKING ABOUT FOOTBALL

A study of Premiership football fans revealed that the average supporter thinks about football 80 times a day (once every 12 mins). The May 2007 Virgin Money research illustrated the number of times each day fans thought about their team:

Sheffield U.	110	Man. Utd.	71	Aston Villa	62	Fulham	57
Charlton	104	Newcastle	70	Tottenham	61	Bolton	57
Chelsea	90	Arsenal	69	Middlesbr'gh	59	Wigan	57
Liverpool	81	Reading	67	Blackburn	58	Watford	51
West Ham	79	Portsmouth	63	Man. City	57	Everton	43

THE WORLD CUP & DOMESTIC VIOLENCE

The Home Office released statistics in October 2006 that appeared to show a surge in domestic violence on days when England played World Cup matches. On average, reports of domestic violence increased 25% on England match days; they rose by 31·4% on the day England beat Paraguay 1–0. This marked spike in reports of domestic violence appears to be linked to watching England play, since, by comparison, on the day of the France/Italy final, reports increased by only 4·6%.

SPORTS NEWS IN BRIEF

· PISTORIUS & THE IAAF ·

At a July 2007 Golden League meet in Rome, Paralympian double amputee Oscar Pistorius came 2nd in the 400m against able-bodied athletes. Described as the 'fastest thing on no legs', Pistorius' ambition is to compete at the Olympics – but to achieve this, he must first gain permission from the International Association of Athletics Federations. The IAAF have questioned whether the carbon fibre blades Pistorius uses give him an unfair advantage by lengthening his stride to unhuman proportions. The technical and ethical issues surrounding this decision have proved complex, and many have questioned whether allowing Pistorius to compete would set a precedent for able-bodied athletes to use similar technologies. At the time of writing, Pistorius had agreed to undergo stringent biomechanical tests, so that the IAAF could assess whether such use of prosthetics was 'fair'.

· THE TEVEZ SAGA ·

The question of who owned striker Carlos Tevez troubled several Premier League clubs in 2006/07. West Ham supposedly signed Tevez in August 2006, but reportedly failed to declare, when registering him, that a 3rd party (Media Sports Investment/Just Sports Inc.) owned his economic rights. In April 2007, West Ham was fined £5·5m for the omission, but the Premier League did not dock points from the club – much to the chagrin of Sheffield Utd, who had been relegated. West Ham announced that any 3rd-party agreement with MSI/JSI had been 'torn up', paving the way for the club to sell Tevez to the highest bidder – which proved to be Man. Utd. However, this transfer stalled after the ownership of Tevez again proved unclear. In August 2007, MSI paid West Ham *c*.£2m to release Tevez, and the protracted loan-transfer to Man Utd was completed. In the end, the controversial and convoluted Tevez transfer prompted the Premier League to tighten rules on 3rd-party player ownership.

· BOWLED WARNEY ·

Master leg spinner and *Wisden* Cricketer of the Century, Shane Warne retired from Test cricket in January 2007, after a 15-year, 3,154-run, and unsurpassed 708-wicket career. Many contend that Warne, the larger than life, mullet-sporting, and hard-living Melburnian, saved the art of spin bowling from near extinction. He is reputed to have a dozen different deliveries – introducing a whole generation to the 'flipper', the 'slider', and the 'zooter'. Warne bowled the unplayable 'ball of the century' to Mike Gatting in the 1993 Ashes series, was Man-of-the-Match at the 1999 World Cup final, and played a vital role in Australia's 06/07 Ashes whitewash [see p.309].

· FORMULA ONE 'SPYGATE' ROW ·

On 13 September 2007, McLaren was punished with the largest fine in sport history, for allegedly using leaked Ferrari technical data. The World Motor Sport Council docked all McLaren's points in the constructors' championship, and fined it a staggering $100m (£50m). McLaren's only relief was that its championship-leading drivers Lewis Hamilton and Fernando Alonso did not forfeit points. McLaren principal Ron Dennis commented, 'I do not accept that we deserved to be penalised or to have our reputation damaged in this way'. At the time of writing, McLaren was reported to be considering an appeal against the ruling.

DEATH OF THE TOUR

'DEATH NOTICE: the Tour de France died on 25 July, 2007, at the age of 104, after a long illness ...' — *France Soir* (26/7/07)

The Tour's Grand Départ from London on 7 July, and its journey across southeast England, attracted 4m cheering spectators and launched the gruelling race with optimism and verve. But after 17 days, pre-race favourite Alexandre Vinokourov tested positive for a blood transfusion, obliging him and his Astana team-mates to withdraw. Vinokourov disputed the results but said he did not want to 'waste time' proving his innocence. Just 24 hours later, the Cofidis team withdrew after Cristian Moreni tested positive for testosterone. At this point, it seemed that victory was assured for race leader Michael Rasmussen. However, Rasmussen was sacked by his team after it emerged that he had repeatedly failed to provide accurate details of his whereabouts for the purpose of pre-Tour drug testing – leaving the competition in chaos. All involved deny any wrongdoing. ❦ Though some journalists and riders called for the Tour to be abandoned, pressure from advertisers and sponsors ensured the show stayed on the road. Eventually, Spaniard Alberto Contador was declared the winner of the 2007 Tour – though for many the race was irreparably tainted. It remains to be seen whether *France Soir*'s funereal prediction proves accurate.

PARTICIPATING IN SPORT

Below are the top sports, games, and activities participated in by English adults:

Activity (%)	♂	♀
Indoor swimming/diving	13	18
Health, fitness, gym	13	13
Recreational cycling	12	6
Snooker, pool, billiards	13	3
Keep-fit, aerobics	4	10
Outdoor football	12	1
Golf, pitch and putt	9	1
Jogging or running	7	3
Tenpin bowling	4	3
Darts	6	2

[Source: *Taking Part: The National Survey of Culture, Leisure and Sport* · DCMS 2005/06]

THE LAUREUS AWARDS · 2007

The Laureus World Sporting Academy encourages the 'positive and worthwhile in sport', presenting awards to athletes in all disciplines. The 2007 winners were:

World sportsman of the year .... Roger Federer (tennis)
World sportswoman of the year .... Yelena Isinbayeva (pole-vault)
World team of the year .... Italian men's football team
World breakthrough of the year .... Amélie Mauresmo (tennis)
Comeback of the year .... Serena Williams (tennis)
Sportsperson with a disability .... Martin Braxenthaler (Alpine skiier)
Action sportsperson of the year .... Kelly Slater (surfing)
Lifetime achievement award .... Franz Beckenbauer

BBC SPORTS PERSONALITY OF THE YEAR · 2006

I'm actually shaking. People have said to me 'have you prepared a speech?', and I was like 'no'. – I wasn't expecting it at all. It's amazing, thanks to all the voters, it's just amazing to be here with all these amazing sports people.
— ZARA PHILLIPS

Sports personality of the year .... Zara Phillips†
Team of the year .... St Helens (rugby league)
Overseas personality .... Roger Federer
Coach of the year .... Daniel Anderson (St Helens)
Lifetime achievement .... Björn Borg
Young personality .... Theo Walcott (Arsenal)
Unsung hero .... Val Hanover (North Shropshire Special Olympics Club)
Helen Rollason award 'for courage and achievement in the face of adversity' .... Paul Hunter
Special award .... David Walliams‡

† Zara Phillips won the award 35 years after her mother, Princess Anne, took the title. Phillips was rewarded for holding both the European and World three-day eventing titles concurrently, a feat achieved by only three others. On the day of the award, Zara courted controversy by becoming the first Royal to appear in an advert, after posing for pictures endorsing Land Rover. ‡ Walliams' Channel swim, the 23rd fastest out of 1,200 crossings, raised £1m for Sports Relief – prompting calls for him to win the Sports Personality of the Year. It is thought that the BBC were less than keen for a comedian to scoop the prestigious prize, and so presented him with a Special Award instead.

WORLD DARTS CHAMPIONSHIPS

Raymond van Barneveld claimed his first PDC World Championship in January 2007 after defecting from the BDO. 'Barney' faced 13-time world champion Phil 'The Power' Taylor in the final, a match-up hoped for by all. Taylor started strongly and took a 3–0 lead, but Barney fought back and levelled the match at 6–6. With the pressure mounting, both players missed vital shots, forcing a sudden-death play-off. After a tense 3hr 10min match, van Barneveld finally landed the double 20 he required to take the trophy and the £100,000 purse. Taylor conceded that it was probably the best match he had contested in his 18-year career.

The final of the 30th BDO World Championship at the Lakeside Country Club was a David and Goliath affair. House-husband and 500–1 outsider, Phil 'Nixy' Nixon (for whom it had taken 20 attempts to qualify for the competition) was pitted against England captain and No.1 seed Martin 'Wolfie' Adams. At first, the contest looked set to be a whitewash as Adams confidently raced to a 6–0 lead. Yet, Nixon rallied in an extraordinary fashion, finding his form to take 6 consecutive sets and putting the match even at 6–6. With just one set to play, Adams regained his composure and claimed the £70,000 title with a double 20.

The Professional Darts Corporation split from the British Darts Organisation in 1992, claiming they wanted to 'take the sport to a new level'. The organisations now compete to secure the top players.

THE PREMIERSHIP · 2006/07

Team	*won*	*drew*	*lost*	*goals for*	*goals against*	*goal difference*	*points*
Manchester Utd	28	5	5	83	27	56	89
Chelsea	24	11	3	64	24	40	83
Liverpool	20	8	10	57	27	30	68
Arsenal	19	11	8	63	35	28	68
↑ CHAMPIONS LEAGUE ↑							
Tottenham	17	9	12	57	54	3	60
Everton	15	13	10	52	36	16	58
Bolton	16	8	14	47	52	–5	56
↑ UEFA CUP ↑							
Reading	16	7	15	52	47	5	55
Portsmouth	14	12	12	45	42	3	54
Blackburn	15	7	16	52	54	–2	52
Aston Villa	11	17	10	43	41	2	50
Middlesbrough	12	10	16	44	49	–5	46
Newcastle	11	10	17	38	47	–9	43
Manchester City	11	9	18	29	44	–15	42
West Ham	12	5	21	35	59	–24	41
Fulham	8	15	15	38	60	–22	39
Wigan Athletic	10	8	20	37	59	–22	38
↓ RELEGATION ↓							
Sheffield Utd	10	8	20	32	55	–23	38
Charlton	8	10	20	34	60	–26	34
Watford	5	13	20	29	59	–30	28

Top scorer	Didier Drogba (Chelsea): 20 goals
Most clean sheets	Chelsea: 22

In May 2007, Arsenal Ladies won a record quadruple. The team not only won the Women's Premier League title for the 4th time, but also took the FA Cup, League Cup, and UEFA Cup [see p.300].

OTHER DIVISIONS – UP & DOWN

Up	*2006/07*	*Down*
Sunderland, Birmingham Derby	*Championship*	Southend, Luton Leeds
Scunthorpe, Bristol City Blackpool	*League One*	Chesterfield, Bradford Rotherham, Brentford
Walsall, Hartlepool Swindon, Bristol Rovers	*League Two*	Boston United Torquay
Dagenham & Redbridge Morecambe	*Conference*	St Albans, Southport Tamworth, Altrincham

FA CUP

19 May 2007 · Wembley Stadium
Attendance: 89,826
CHELSEA 1–0 MAN UTD (AET)
Referee: Steve Bennett [GBR]

THE KEY MOMENTS

7 ..... no penalty given for alleged Wes Brown handball
21 .... Drogba shot wide
31 .... Van der Sar saved Lampard shot
37 ..... Lampard long shot over the bar
41 .... Rooney wide shot offside
45 .. Joe Cole subbed for Arjen Robben
46 .... Giggs shot saved by Cech
57 .... Giggs effort over the bar
64 ..... Rooney ran at goal, Cech saved
78 .. drop-ball restart after minor fracas
90 ... 0–0 at full time, extra time added
104 .... Giggs 'goal' disallowed for foul on Chelsea keeper Cech
115 .... Drogba GOAL for Chelsea

CHAMPIONS LEAGUE

23 May 2007 · Olympic Stad., Athens
Attendance: 74,000
AC MILAN 2–1 LIVERPOOL
Referee: Herbert Fandel [GER]

THE KEY MOMENTS

9 .... Pennant shot saved by Dida
16 ...... shot by Kaka blocked by Reina
23 ..... Gerrard shot high over the bar
27 .... Alonso's long shot just wide
31 .... Riise's powerful shot over the bar
40 .... Gattuso yellow card
45 ..... Pirlo shot deflected off Inzaghi, GOAL for Milan
54 .... Jankulowski booked
59 .... Mascherano booked
61 .... Carragher booked
63 .... weak Gerrard shot saved
82 .. Inzaghi rolled ball into net, GOAL
84 .... Dida saved Crouch long shot
88 ... Kuyt headed GOAL for Liverpool

DELOITTE FOOTBALL MONEY LEAGUE · 2005/06

The Deloitte Football Money League is based on club income, including: ticket sales, television revenue, and merchandising, but does not factor in players' wages or transfer fees. Manchester United held the top spot for 8 years until it was deposed by Real Madrid in the 2004/05 season. The world's wealthiest clubs by revenue are:

Club	*£m*
Real Madrid	202
Barcelona	179·1
Juventus	173·7
Man Utd	167·8
AC Milan	165
Chelsea	152·8
Inter Milan	142·8
Bayern Munich	141·5
Arsenal	133
Liverpool	121·7

[Deloitte: 2005/06]

SOME FOOTBALL AWARDS OF NOTE · 2006/07

FIFA world player of the year .... Fabio Cannavaro [Real Madrid/Italy]
European footballer of the year .... Fabio Cannavaro [Real Madrid]
Prof. Footballers' Assoc. player of the year .... Cristiano Ronaldo [Man. Utd]
PFA young player award .... Cristiano Ronaldo [Man. Utd]
PFA special merit award .... Sir Alex Ferguson [Man. Utd]
Football Writers' Assoc. player of the year .... Cristiano Ronaldo [Man. Utd]
FA women's football awards: players' player of the year .... Kelly Smith [Arsenal]
LMA manager of the year .... Steve Coppell [Reading]

HOME NATIONS' FOOTBALL RECORD · 2006/07

Date		*result*		*type*	*venue*
07·10·06	Denmark	0–0	N Ireland	ECQ	Parken Stad., Copenhagen
07·10·06	Wales	1–5	Slovakia	ECQ	Millennium Stadium, Cardiff
07·10·06	Scotland	1–0	France	ECQ	Hampden Park, Glasgow
07·10·06	England	0–0	FYR Mac.	ECQ	Old Trafford, Manchester
11·10·06	N Ireland	1–0	Latvia	ECQ	Windsor Park, Belfast
11·10·06	Ukraine	2–0	Scotland	ECQ	Olympic Stadium, Kiev
11·10·06	Wales	3–1	Cyprus	ECQ	Millennium Stadium, Cardiff
11·10·06	Croatia	2–0	England	ECQ	Maksimir Stad., Zagreb
14·11·06	Wales	4–0	Liechtenstein	F	Racecourse Grnd, Wrexham
15·11·06	Netherlands	1–1	England	F	Amsterdam Arena, Amsterdam
06·02·07	N Ireland	0–0	Wales	F	Windsor Park, Belfast
07·02·07	England	0–1	Spain	F	Old Trafford, Manchester
24·03·07	Liechtenstein	1–4	N Ireland	ECQ	Rheinpark Stadium, Vaduz
24·03·07	Rep. Ireland	1–0	Wales	ECQ	Croke Park, Dublin
24·03·07	Scotland	2–1	Georgia	ECQ	Hampden Park, Glasgow
24·03·07	Israel	0–0	England	ECQ	Ramat Gan Stad., Tel Aviv
28·03·07	N Ireland	2–1	Sweden	ECQ	Windsor Park, Belfast
28·03·07	Wales	3–0	San Marino	ECQ	Millennium Stadium, Cardiff
28·03·07	Italy	2–0	Scotland	ECQ	Stadio San Nicola, Bari
28·03·07	Andorra	0–3	England	ECQ	Olympic Stadium, Barcelona
26·05·07	Wales	2–2	New Zealand	F	Racecourse Grnd, Wrexham
30·05·07	Austria	0–1	Scotland	F	Gerhard Hanappi Stad., Vienna
01·06·07	England	1–1	Brazil	F	Wembley Stadium†, London
02·06·07	Wales	0–0	Czech Rep.	ECQ	Millennium Stadium, Cardiff
06·06·07	Estonia	0–3	England	ECQ	A. Le Coq Arena, Tallinn
06·06·07	Faroe Is.	0–2	Scotland	ECQ	Svangaskard Stadium, Toftir
22·08·07	Bulgaria	0–1	Wales	F	Naftex Stadium, Bulgaria
22·08·07	England	1–2	Germany	F	Wembley Stadium, London
22·08·07	N Ireland	3–1	Liechtenstein	ECQ	Windsor Park, Belfast
08·09·07	England	3–0	Israel	ECQ	Wembley Stadium, London
08·09·07	Latvia	1–0	N Ireland	ECQ	Skonto Stadium, Riga
08·09·07	Scotland	3–1	Lithuania	ECQ	Hampden Park, Glasgow
08·09·07	Wales	0–2	Germany	ECQ	Millennium Stadium, Cardiff
12·09·07	England	3–0	Russia	ECQ	Wembley Stadium, London
12·09·07	France	0–1	Scotland	ECQ	Parc des Princes, Paris
12·09·07	Iceland	2–1	N Ireland	ECQ	Laugardalsvöllur, Reykjavik
12·09·07	Slovakia	2–5	Wales	ECQ	Anton Malatinsky, Trnava

KEY: F – Friendly · ECQ – European Champ. Qualifier. · † In May 2007, after a 7-year redevelopment, the new Wembley Stadium finally re-opened to host the FA Cup final [see p.305]. The legendary ground was built in 1923 (in just 300 days), to house the British Empire Exhibition. Soon after, the stadium became the home of British football, hosting every FA Cup final from 1923–2000. After Australian firm Multiplex won the contract to rebuild the stadium, delay after delay saw the price inflate to £800m. Many mourned the passing of Wembley's iconic white towers, but as the new 133m steel arch took shape, looming over the north London skyline, most agreed it was suitably impressive.

WORLD SWIMMING CHAMPIONSHIPS · 2007

American Michael Phelps won a record 7 golds at Melbourne's swimming World Championships in March 2007. Phelps's efforts helped the American team top the medal table by some margin, with 40 medals. The British team were left frustrated after winning just 2 silver and 3 bronze medals†. Selected results follow:

	Event	*winner*	*record*	*time*
♀	50m backstroke	Leila Vaziri [USA]	WR	28·16
♂	100m backstroke	Aaron Peirsol [USA]	WR	52·98
♀	100m backstroke	Natalie Coughlin [USA]	WR	59·44
♂	200m freestyle	Michael Phelps [USA]	WR	1:43·86
♀	200m freestyle	Laure Manaudou [FRA]	WR	1:55·52
♂	200m backstroke	Ryan Lochte [USA]	WR	1:54·32
♂	200m butterfly	Michael Phelps [USA]	WR	1:52·09
♂	200m medley	Michael Phelps [USA]	WR	1:54·98
♂	400m medley	Michael Phelps [USA]	WR	4:06·22
♀	400m medley	Kathryn Hoff [USA]	WR	4:32·89
♀	4×100m medley	Australia	WR	3:55·74
♂	4×200m freestyle	USA	WR	7:03·24
♀	4×200m freestyle	USA	WR	7:50·09

Key: WR – World Record · † British swimming Performance Director Bill Sweetenham resigned in September 2007; the controversial Australian's leadership saw Team GB's results improve markedly.

CYCLING WORLD TRACK CHAMPIONSHIPS · 2007

Great Britain topped the medal table at the World Track Cycling Championships in Mallorca, Spain, in March 2007. The eleven British medallists are listed below:

	Event	*name*	*medal*	*time*
♂	1,000m time trial	Chris Hoy	G	1:00·99
♂	1,000m time trial	Jamie Staff	B	1:02·074
♂	Keirin†	Chris Hoy	G	–
♂	Keirin	Ross Edgar	B	–
♀	Keirin	Victoria Pendleton	G	–
♀	Sprint	Victoria Pendleton	G	11·879
♂	Individual pursuit	Bradley Wiggins	G	–
♀	Individual pursuit	Rebecca Romero	S	03·196
♂	Team pursuit	Great Britain	G	3:57·468
♀	Team sprint	Great Britain	G	33·63
♂	Team sprint	Great Britain	S	43·832

Key: Gold · Silver · Bronze · † In the bizarre Japanese cycling event Keirin, 6–8 sprint cyclists jostle for position while following a pace-setting moped (the 'derny') for the opening laps of an 8-lap race. With *c*.2 laps to go, the derny veers off, and the cyclists sprint pell-mell to the finish. ❦ Australia's Anna Meares set a new world record of 33·588s, when she took Gold in the 500m time-trial.

WORLD BOXING CHAMPIONS · AT 12·9·2007

Weight	WBC	WBA	IBF	WBO
Heavy	Maskaev [KAZ]	Chagaev [UZB]	Klitschko [UKR]	S Ibragimov [RUS]
Cruiser	Mormeck [FRA]	Mormeck [FRA]	Cunningham [USA]	Maccarinelli [GBR]
Light heavy	Dawson [USA]	Drews [CRO]	Woods [GBR]	Erdei [HUN]
Super middle	Kessler [DEN]	Kessler [DEN]	Berrio [COL]	Calzaghe [GBR]
Middle	Taylor [USA]	Sturm [GER]	Abraham [AUS]	Taylor [USA]
Light middle	*vacant*	Alcine [CAN]	Spinks [USA]	Dzinziruk [UKR]
Welter	Mayweather [USA]	Cotto [PUR]	Cintron [PUR]	Williams [USA]
Light welter	Witter [GBR]	Rees [GBR]	Malignaggi [USA]	Torres [COL]
Light	David Diaz [USA]	Juan Diaz [USA]	Julio Diaz [MEX]	Juan Diaz [USA]
Super feather	Marquez [MEX]	Valero [PAN]	Fana [RSA]	Guzman [DOM]
Feather	Chi [KOR]	John [INA]	Guerrero [USA]	Luevano [USA]
Super bantam	R Marquez [MEX]	Caballero [PAN]	Molitor [CAN]	De Leon [MEX]
Bantam	Hasegawa [JAP]	Sidorenko [UKR]	Perez [NCA]	Peñalosa [PHI]
Super fly	Mijares [MEX]	Munoz [VEN]	*vacant*	Montiel [MEX]
Fly	Naito [JAP]	Sakata [JAP]	Donaire [PHI]	Narvaez [ARG]
Light fly	Sosa [MEX]	Reveco [ARG]	Solis [MEX]	Calderon [PUR]
Straw	Kyowa [JAP]	Niida [JAP]	Condes [PHI]	*vacant*

The Ring magazine, the self-proclaimed 'bible of boxing', creates a ranking of the best boxers across all weight divisions, which many boxing fans regard as an authoritative source of the best 'pound-for-pound' boxers in the world. At 10/9/2007, *The Ring* top 10 were: [1] Floyd Mayweather (Welterweight); [2] Manny Pacquiao (Super Featherweight); [3] Juan Manuel Marquez (Super Featherweight); [4] Bernard Hopkins (Light Heavyweight); [5] Israel Vazquez (Super Bantamweight); [6] Winky Wright (Middleweight); [7] Rafael Marquez (Super Bantamweight); [8] Joe Calzaghe (Super Middleweight); [9] Ricky Hatton (Light Welterweight); [10] Miguel Cotto (Welterweight).

WISDEN CRICKETER OF THE YEAR

In 2007, the *Wisden* Cricketer of the Year was awarded to Paul Collingwood [ENG], Monty Panesar [ENG], Mark Ramprakash [ENG], Mohammad Yousuf [PAK], and Mahela Jayawardene [SRI]. The *Wisden* Leading Cricketer in the World was presented to the unique Sri Lankan spin bowler Muttiah 'Murali' Muralitharan.

TWENTY20 CUP FINAL DAY · 2007

Seam bowler Ryan McLaren was named Man of the Match, after his impressive haul (3 for 22) helped Kent Spitfires take the Twenty20 title at Edgbaston by 4 wickets. Gloucestershire Gladiators were held to 146–8, allowing Kent to achieve victory with 3 balls to spare, thanks to Darren Stevens's 30 runs off 21 balls.

Semi-final 1	Gloucestershire (152–2) *bt* Lancashire (148–6) by 8 wickets
Semi-final 2	Kent (141–5) *bt* Sussex (140) by 5 wickets
Cup Final	Kent (147–6) *bt* Gloucestershire (146–8) by 4 wickets

THE 2006/07 ASHES

1st Test · Brisbane
23–27 Nov, 2006
Australia won the toss

Australia	602 for 9
England	157 all out
Australia	202 for 1
England	370 all out

Australia won by 277 runs
MOTM · Ricky Ponting

Harmison opened the 1st Test with a disastrous wide to Langer; he compounded this error with 4 boundaries off his first 2 overs, before being banished to fielding duty. Impressive batting from Ponting and Langer gave Australia a daunting lead. With the tourists' bowlers floundering, it took the batting partnership of Pietersen and Collingwood to restore some pride. But, England were simply outplayed.

2nd Test · Adelaide
1–5 Dec, 2006
England won the toss

England	551 for 6
Australia	513 all out
England	129 all out
Australia	168 for 4

Australia won by 6 wickets
MOTM · Ricky Ponting

Flintoff bravely opted to declare at 551 for 6 at the end of the 2nd day – the largest-ever declared first innings total for a team which then went on to lose the match. England's collapse was spectacular, but not as spectacular as the Australians' play. Warne's relentlessly brilliant bowling destroyed England's batting, and the resulting loss was widely viewed as a catastrophe and an embarrassment for England.

3rd Test · Perth
14–18 Dec, 2006
Australia won the toss

Australia	244 all out
England	215 all out
Australia	527 for 5
England	350 all out

Australia won by 206 runs
MOTM · Michael Hussey

England were initially enlivened by Panesar's Ashes début – and Monty did not disappoint, taking 5 wickets in an innings. Yet the Aussies remained tight: Hussey seemed impossible to dismiss, and Warne took 4 wickets in the 2nd innings, to take his career total to 699. England never got a chance to seize the initiative, and Australia joyously took back the Ashes at the earliest opportunity in the Series.

4th Test · Melbourne
26–30 Dec, 2006
England won the toss

England	159 all out
Australia	419 all out
England	161 all out

Australia won by an innings and 99 runs
MOTM · Shane Warne

Australia sapped the last vestiges of England's pride by taking the 4th Test in just 3 days. Accurate and reliable bowling from Lee, Clark, and Warne forced England's batsmen into making mistakes. The relentless skill of the home side appeared to befuddle England, and only Monty Panesar was able to offer the Barmy Army anything to cheer about. The dissection of England's poor performance continued.

5th Test · Sydney
2–6 Jan, 2007
England won the toss

England	291 all out
Australia	393 all out
England	147 all out
Australia	46 for 0

Australia won by 10 wickets
MOTM · Stuart Clark
MOTS · Ricky Ponting

Australia easily out-played England in the final Test, securing the first 5–0 whitewash for 86 years. Warne, McGrath, and Langer produced play fitting for their final outing as international players. Australia needed just 46 runs in their 2nd innings, which Langer and Hayden achieved with ease in just 10·5 overs, confirming the overwhelming superiority of the Australian side.

RUGBY UNION SIX NATIONS · 2007

Date		*result*		*venue*
03·02·07	Italy	3–39	France	Stadio Flaminio
03·02·07	England	42–20	Scotland	Twickenham
04·02·07	Wales	9–19	Ireland	Millennium Stadium
10·02·07	England	20–7	Italy	Twickenham
10·02·07	Scotland	21–9	Wales	Murrayfield
11·02·07	Ireland	17–20	France	Croke Park
24·02·07	Scotland	17–37	Italy	Murrayfield
24·02·07	Ireland	43–13	England	Croke Park
24·02·07	France	32–21	Wales	Stade de France
10·03·07	Scotland	18–19	Ireland	Murrayfield
10·03·07	Italy	23–20	Wales	Stadio Flaminio
11·03·07	England	26–18	France	Twickenham
17·03·07	Italy	24–51	Ireland	Stadio Flaminio
17·03·07	France	46–19	Scotland	Stade de France
17·03·07	Wales	27–18	England	Millennium Stadium

FINAL TABLE 2007						TOTAL HONOURS EVER		
points	*w*	*d*	*l*	*pd*	*country*	*triple crowns*	*grand slams*	*titles*
8	4	0	1	69	France	n/a	8	16
8	4	0	1	65	Ireland	9	1	10
6	3	0	2	4	England	23	12	25
4	2	0	3	−53	Italy	n/a	0	0
2	1	0	4	−27	Wales	18	9	23
2	1	0	4	−58	Scotland	10	3	14

HEINEKEN EUROPEAN CUP FINAL · 2007

LEICESTER 9–25 LONDON WASPS · 20·05·07 · Twickenham
Leicester – *penalty goals*: Goode (3) · Wasps – *tries*: Reddan, Ibañez
penalty goals: King (4); *dropped goal*: King

81,076 fans watched Wasps win their 2nd Heineken Cup in 3 years, preventing Leicester from securing the treble (Premiership, Anglo-Welsh, and European Cup).

INTERNATIONAL RUGBY BOARD AWARDS · 2006

International player of the year .... Richie McCaw [NZL]
International team of the year .... New Zealand
International coach of the year .... Graham Henry [NZL]
International sevens team of the year .... Fiji
International sevens player of the year .... Uale Mai [SAM]
International women's personality of the year .... Margaret Alphonsi [ENG]
IRB Hall of Fame inductees .... William Webb Ellis & Rugby School

RUGBY LEAGUE CHALLENGE CUP · 2007

ST HELENS 30–8 CATALANS DRAGONS
25·08·07 · WEMBLEY STADIUM

St Helens – *tries*: Roby, Gardner (2), Wellens, Clough · *conversions:* Long (5)
Catalans Dragons – *tries*: Khattabi, Murphy

84,241 boisterous spectators turned out to watch St Helens retain the Challenge Cup. A combination of staunch defending and the stifling heat meant neither side scored for the first half hour; a stunning solo effort by Saints' James Roby broke the deadlock. The Catalans did well to reach the final, considering the French side was formed only 2 years ago; yet the experience of St Helens ultimately prevailed.

MAN OF STEEL · 2006

In 2006, St Helens full-back Paul Wellens was presented with the Man of Steel prize, awarded by sports journalists to the most outstanding player in Rugby League's Super League. Wellens is the fifth St Helens player to win in seven years.

GOLF MAJORS · 2007

♂	*course*	*winner*	*score*
MASTERS	Augusta, Georgia	Zach Johnson [USA]	+1
US OPEN	Oakmont, Pennsylvania	Angel Cabrera [ARG]	+5
THE OPEN	Carnoustie†, Scotland	Padraig Harrington‡ [IRL]	–7
USPGA	Southern Hills, Oklahoma	Tiger Woods [USA]	–8
♀			
KRAFT NABISCO	Mission Hills, California	Morgan Pressel [USA]	–3
LPGA	Havre de Grace, Maryland	Suzann Pettersen [NOR]	–14
US OPEN	Pine Needles, North Carolina	Cristie Kerr [USA]	–5
BRITISH OPEN	St Andrews, Scotland	Lorena Ochoa [MEX]	–5

† Carnoustie began to be called 'Carnasty' after the course proved particularly problematic in 1999. Apparently, recent modifications to the course might result in a new nickname: 'Carnicey'. ‡ By winning the Open, Padraig Harrington became the first European since Paul Lawrie in 1999 to win a Major, and the first Irishman in 60 years to win the Open. In September 2007, Tiger Woods won his 60th career title after equalling the course record at Cog Hill, IL, to win the BMW Championship.

RBS SHOT OF THE YEAR

The 2006 RBS Shot of the Year was awarded to Paul Casey for his amazing hole-in-one during the Ryder Cup. Casey holed the shot from 213 yards on the 14th with a four iron, helping him and partner David Howell beat Stewart Cink and Zach Johnson at the K Club. Casey won £2,000 to donate to the charity of his choice.

SOME ATHLETICS WORLD RECORDS OF NOTE

	Event	*set by*	*when*	*record*
♂	100m	Asafa Powell [JAM]	2007	9·74s†
♀	100m	Florence Griffith-Joyner [USA]	1988	10·49s
♂	110m hurdles	Xiang Liu [CHN]	2006	12·88s
♀	100m hurdles	Yordanka Donkova [BUL]	1988	12·21s
♂	200m	Michael Johnson [USA]	1996	19·32s
♀	200m	Florence Griffith-Joyner [USA]	1988	21·34s
♂	400m	Michael Johnson [USA]	1999	43·18s
♀	400m	Marita Koch [GDR]	1985	47·60s
♂	400m hurdles	Kevin Young [USA]	1992	46·78s
♀	400m hurdles	Yuliya Nosova [RUS]	2003	52·34s
♂	800m	Wilson Kipketer [DEN]	1997	1:41·11
♀	800m	Jarmila Kratochvílová [TCH]	1983	1:53·28
♂	1,500m	Hicham El Guerrouj [MAR]	1998	3:26·00
♀	1,500m	Yunxia Qu [CHN]	1993	3:50·46
♂	Mile	Hicham El Guerrouj [MAR]	1999	3:43·13
♀	Mile	Svetlana Masterkova [RUS]	1996	4:12·56
♂	5,000m	Kenenisa Bekele [ETH]	2004	12:37·35
♀	5,000m	Meseret Defar [ETH]	2007	14:16·63
♂	10,000m	Kenenisa Bekele [ETH]	2005	26:17·53
♀	10,000m	Junxia Wang [CHN]	1993	29:31·78
♂	Marathon	Paul Tergat [KEN]	2003	2:04·55
♀	Marathon	Paula Radcliffe [GBR]	2003	2:15·25
♂	High jump	Javier Sotomayor [CUB]	1993	2·45m
♀	High jump	Stefka Kostadinova [BUL]	1987	2·09m
♂	Long jump	Mike Powell [USA]	1991	8·95m
♀	Long jump	Galina Christiakova [URS]	1988	7·52m
♂	Triple jump	Jonathan Edwards [GBR]	1995	18·29m
♀	Triple jump	Inessa Kravets [UKR]	1995	15·50m
♂	Pole vault	Sergey Bubka [UKR]	1994	6·14m
♀	Pole vault	Yelena Isinbayeva [RUS]	2005	5·01m
♂	Shot put	Randy Barnes [USA]	1990	23·12m
♀	Shot put	Natalya Lisovskaya [URS]	1987	22·63m
♂	Discus	Jürgen Schult [GDR]	1986	74·08m
♀	Discus	Gabriele Reinsch [GDR]	1988	76·80m
♂	Hammer	Yuriy Sedykh [URS]	1986	86·74m
♀	Hammer	Tatyana Lysenko [RUS]	2007	78·61m†
♂	Javelin	Jan Zelezny [CZE]	1996	98·48m
♀	Javelin	Osleidys Menéndez [CUB]	2005	71·70m
♂	Decathlon	Roman Sebrle [CZE]	2001	9,026pts
♀	Heptathlon	Jackie Joyner-Kersee [USA]	1988	7,291pts
♂	4×100m relay	USA	1992	37·40s
♀	4×100m relay	Germany [GDR]	1985	41·37s
♂	4×400m relay	USA	1998	2:54·20
♀	4×400m relay	USSR	1988	3:15·17

[Records correct as of 19·09·07 · † = awaiting ratification]

WORLD ATHLETICS CHAMPIONSHIPS · 2007

USA topped the medals table at Osaka, but team GB had much to be proud of after exceeding their target (3 medals, 14 finalists) to achieve 5 medals and 13 finalists:

Men	*event*	*Women*
Tyson Gay [USA] 9·85s	100m	Veronica Campbell [JAM] 11·01s
Xiang Liu [CHI] 12·95s	110/100m hurdles	Michelle Perry [USA] 12·46s
Tyson Gay [USA] 19·76s CR	200m	Allyson Felix [USA] 21·81s
Jeremy Wariner [USA] 43·45s	400m	Christine Ohuruogu [GBR] 49·61s
Kerron Clement [USA] 47·61s	400m hurdles	Jana Rawlinson [AUS] 53·31s
Alfred Kirwa Yego [KEN] 1:47·09s	800m	Janeth Jepkosgei [KEN] 1:56·04s
Bernard Lagat [USA] 3:34·77s	1,500m	Maryam Yusuf Jamal [BRN] 3:58·75s
Bernard Lagat [USA] 13:45·87s	5,000m	Meseret Defar [ETH] 14:57·91s
Kenenisa Bekele [ETH] 27:05·90s	10,000m	Tirunesh Dibaba [ETH] 31:55·41s
Donald Thomas [BAH] 2·35m	high jump	Blanka Vlašic [CRO] 2·05m
Irving Saladino [PAN] 8·57m	long jump	Tatyana Lebedeva [RUS] 7·03m
Reese Hoffa [USA] 22·04m	shot put	Valerie Vili [NZL] 20·54m
Tero Pitkämäki [FIN] 90·33m	javelin	Barbora Špotáková [CZE] 67·07m
Gerd Kanter [EST] 68·94m	discus	Franka Dietzsch [GER] 66·61m
Ivan Tsikhan [BLR] 83·63m	hammer	Betty Heidler [GER] 74·76m
Nelson Évora [POR] 17·74m NR	triple jump	Yargelis Savigne [CUB] 15·28m
Brad Walker [USA] 5·86m	pole vault	Yelena Isinbaeva [RUS] 4·80m
Roman Sebrle [CZE] 8,526pts	dec-/heptathlon	Carolina Kluft [SWE] 7,032pts
USA 37·78s	4×100m relay	USA 41·98s
USA 2:55·56s	4×400m relay	USA 3:18·55s

THE EUROPEAN ATHLETICS CUP · 2007

In June 2007, France's men and Russia's women won the European Athletics Cup in Munich for the second year running. The cup is contested annually by national teams – each fielding one representative per event, who accumulates points for their team (8 points for 1st to 1 point for 8th). At the close of competition, the lowest-scoring 2 teams are relegated. The results of the 2007 European Cup were:

♂	*country*	*points*	♀	*country*	*points*
1	France	116	1	Russia	127
2	Germany	116	2	France	107
3	Poland	110	3	Germany	94·5
4	Great Britain & NI	101	4	Poland	89
5	Russia	93	5	Ukraine	81
6	Greece	70	6	Belarus	80
7	Ukraine†	58·5	7	Greece†	75
8	Belgium†	53·5	8	Spain†	64·5

† These teams will be relegated into the lower leagues for the 2008 European Cup. · Great Britain's women's team secured promotion back to the top flight by winning 12 out of 20 events in their league.

WIMBLEDON WINNERS · 2007

MEN'S SINGLES
Roger Federer [SUI]
bt Rafael Nadal [ESP]
7–6 (9–7), 4–6, 7–6 (7–3), 2–6, 6–2

'I was drained mentally and physically. It was a huge occasion, the record was on the line.'
ROGER FEDERER
on matching Björn Borg's record five consecutive Wimbledon wins.

LADIES' SINGLES
Venus Williams [USA]
bt Marion Bartoli [FRA]
6–4, 6–1

MEN'S DOUBLES
Arnaud Clement [FRA]
& Michael Llodra [FRA]
bt Bob Bryan [USA]
& Mike Bryan [USA]
6–7 (5–7), 6–3, 6–4, 6–4

LADIES' DOUBLES
Cara Black [ZIM]
& Liezel Huber [RSA]
bt Katarina Srebotnik [SLO]
& Ai Sugiyama [JPN]
3–6, 6–3, 6–2

MIXED DOUBLES
Jamie Murray [GBR]
& Jelena Jankovic [SRB]
bt Jonas Bjorkman [SWE]
& Alicia Molik [AUS]
6–4, 3–6, 6–1

BOYS' SINGLES
Donald Young [USA]
bt Vladimir Ignatic [BLR]
7–5, 6–1

GIRLS' SINGLES
Urszula Radwanska [POL]
bt Madison Brengle [USA]
2–6, 6–3, 6–0

BOYS' DOUBLES
Daniel Lopez [ITA]
& Matteo Trevisan [ITA]
bt Roman Jebavy [CZE]
& Martin Klizan [SVK]
7–6 (7–5), 4–6, [10]–[8]

GIRLS' DOUBLES
Anastasia Pavlyuchenkova [RUS]
& Urszula Radwanska [POL]
bt Misaki Doi [JPN]
& Kurumi Nara [JPN]
6–4, 2–6, [10]–[7]

WIMBLEDON 2007 PRIZE MONEY & MISC.

Round (No. prizes)	*singles*†
Winner (1)	£700,000
Runner-up (1)	£350,000
Semi-final (2)	£175,000
Quarter-final (4)	£88,550
4th round (8)	£47,250
3rd round (16)	£27,050
2nd round (32)	£16,325
1st round (64)	£10,000

For the first time, the prize money was equal for both men and women in 2007.
† Winnings for doubles are different.

No. GB men in 1st round [2006]	[10] 7
No. GB men in 2nd round	[5] 1
No. GB women in 1st round	[5] 5
No. GB women in 2nd round	[2] 1
Tim Henman out in	R2
Fastest serve ♂	A. Roddick 144mph
Fastest serve ♀	V. Williams 126mph
Most aces ♂	R. Federer (85 in 7 matches)
Most aces ♀	M. Krajicek (45 in 5)
Total attendance	444,810

THE DAVIS CUP

The Davis Cup began in 1900 and now involves 134 countries, of which only 16 qualify to play in the World Group. The rest fight it out in continental leagues in an effort to gain promotion into the elite World Group – to which, by beating Croatia, Britain secured her entry in September. Below are Britain's results for '07:

6–8 April · Europe–Africa Zone Group 1, 2nd round
National Exhibition Centre, Birmingham (surface: indoor)
Great Britain *bt* Netherlands 4–1

Andy Murray [GBR] *bt* Raemon Sluiter [NED] 6–3, 7–5, 6–2
Tim Henman [GBR] *bt* Robin Haase [NED] 7–6 (7–4), 6–3, 7–6 (7–4)
Jamie Murray & Greg Rusedski [GBR]
bt Robin Haase & Rogier Wassen [NED] 6–1, 3–6, 6–3, 7–6 (7–5)
Robin Haase [NED] *bt* Jamie Murray [GBR] 4–6, 7–6 (7–0), 6–2
Tim Henman [GBR] *bt* Igor Sijsling [NED] 6–2, 6–3

21–23 Sept · World Group Play-offs
All England Lawn Tennis Club, London (surface: grass)
Great Britain *bt* Croatia 4–1

Andy Murray [GBR] *bt* Marin Cilic [CRO] 3–6, 6–4, 6–2, 4–6, 6–3
Tim Henman [GBR] *bt* Roko Karanusic [CRO] 6–4, 6–3, 6–3
Jamie Murray & Tim Henman [GBR]
bt Marin Cilic & Lovro Zovko [CRO] 4–6, 6–4, 7–6 (7–3), 7–5
Andy Murray [GBR] *bt* Roko Karanusic [CRO] 6–4, 7–6
Marin Cilic [CRO] *bt* Jamie Baker [GBR] 6–4, 6–4

'Tiger Tim' Henman retired from professional tennis on 22 September 2007. In a 13-year career, he won 11 ATP Tour titles, reached 6 Grand Slam semi-finals (4 at Wimbledon), ranked 4th in the world, and was Britain's finest male player since Fred Perry. On his day, Henman's serve-and-volley game could beat the very best. But since he never reached a Grand Slam final and, painfully, never won Wimbledon, the 'Henmaniacs' on 'Henman Hill' grew used to disappointment ['*Come on Tim!*']. (For their part, the media never got used to Henman's reserved public persona.) It seems likely that the very British perception that Tiger Tim never lived up to his promise will, over time, be outshone by his considerable achievements.

TENNIS GRAND SLAM TOURNAMENTS · 2007

Event	*month*	*surface*	♂ *winner*	♀
Australian Open	Jan	Rebound Ace	Roger Federer	Serena Williams
French Open	May/Jun	clay	Rafael Nadal	Justine Henin
Wimbledon	Jun/Jul	grass	Roger Federer	Venus Williams
US Open	Aug/Sep	cement	Roger Federer	Justine Henin

FORMULA ONE TEAMS & DRIVERS · 2007

McLaren Mercedes................Fernando Alonso [ESP] & Lewis Hamilton [GBR]
Renault........................Giancarlo Fisichella [ITA] & Heikki Kovalainen [FIN]
Ferrari................................Felipe Massa [BRA] & Kimi Räikkönen [FIN]
Honda.............................Rubens Barrichello [BRA] & Jenson Button [GBR]
BMW Sauber..........................Nick Heidfeld [GER] & Robert Kubica [POL]
Toyota.................................Ralf Schumacher [GER] & Jarno Trulli [ITA]
Red Bull............................David Coulthard [GBR] & Mark Webber [AUS]
Williams..............................Nico Rosberg [GER] & Alexander Wurz [AUT]
Toro Rosso .Vitantonio Liuzzi [ITA] & (S. Speed [USA]) *replaced by* Sebastian Vettel [GER]
Spyker . (Christijan Albers [NED]) *replaced by* Sakon Yamamoto [JAP] & Adrian Sutil [GER]
Super Aguri.........................Takuma Sato [JAP] & Anthony Davidson [GBR]

FORMULA ONE WORLD CHAMPIONSHIP · 2007

Date	*Grand Prix*	*track*	*winning driver*	*car*
18·03·07	Australian	Albert Park	Kimi Räikkönen	Ferrari
08·04·07	Malaysian	Sepang	Fernando Alonso	McLaren
15·04·07	Bahrain	Sakhir	Felipe Massa	Ferrari
13·05·07	Spanish	Catalunya	Felipe Massa	Ferrari
25·05·07	Monaco	Monte Carlo	Fernando Alonso	McLaren
10·06·07	Canada	Gilles-Villeneuve	Lewis Hamilton	McLaren
17·06·07	USA	Indianapolis	Lewis Hamilton	McLaren
01·07·07	French	Magny-Cours	Kimi Räikkönen	Ferrari
08·07·07	British	Silverstone	Kimi Räikkönen	Ferrari
22·07·07	European†	Nürburgring	Fernando Alonso	McLaren
05·08·07	Hungarian	Hungaroring	Lewis Hamilton	McLaren
26·08·07	Turkish	Istanbul Park	Felipe Massa	Ferrari
09·09·07	Italian	Monza	Fernando Alonso	McLaren
16·09·07	Belgian	Spa	Kimi Räikkönen	Ferrari
30·09·07	Japanese	Fuji Speedway		
07·10·07	Chinese	Shanghai Int. Circuit		
21·10·07	Brazilian	Interlagos		

† First race of the season in which rookie Lewis Hamilton did not finish on the podium.

SUPERBIKES, RALLY & MOTORSPORT

Isle of Man TT (Senior) [2007]........................John McGuinness (HM Plant)
Isle of Man TT (Supersport Junior) [2007]..............Ian Hutchinson (HM Plant)
Moto GP [2006]...Nicky Hayden (Honda)
British Superbikes [2006].................................Ryuichi Kiyonari (Honda)
World Superbikes [2006]....................................Troy Bayliss (Ducati)
World Rally [2006]......................................Sébastien Loeb (Citroën)
Le Mans [2007]...............Franck Biela, Emanuele Pirro, Marco Werner (Audi)
Indie 500...Dario Franchitti (Dallara-Honda)

888.COM WORLD SNOOKER CHAMPIONSHIP · 2007

1998 World Champion John Higgins emerged victorious over qualifier Mark Selby in a match that persisted for a gruelling 12 hours, and ended later than any other Crucible final (at 12:54am). Despite 'the Wizard of Wishaw' (Higgins) beginning the final day with a 12–4 overnight lead, the 'Jester from Leicester' (Selby) staged a remarkable comeback to win all 6 frames of the afternoon session. The next 4 frames were evenly split, before Selby won the 27th – after a 55-minute fight that included a 21-minute battle for the yellow. Higgins recovered his form in the midnight hour, taking the final 4 frames with ease, and managing a 129 break in the 30th.

THE FINAL · FRAME-BY-FRAME
John Higgins [SCO] 18–13 Mark Selby [ENG]

DAY ONE				DAY TWO			
Frame	*tally*			*Frame*	*tally*		
73–25	1–0	86–5	5–3	36–73	12–5	63–70	13–11
58–32	2–0	75–0 (75)	6–3	0–110 (109)	12–6	75–2	14–11
19–95	2–1	85–9 (70)	7–3	36–65 (65)	12–7	22–82	14–12
25–76 (67)	2–2	101–24 (100)	8–3	4–74 (62)	12–8	54–77	14–13
10–132 (116)	2–3	70–61	9–3	0–66	12–9	71–33	15–13
97–0 (97)	3–3	59–75 (58 *JH*)	9–4	48–72	12–10	57–43 (57)	16–13
98–11	4–3	98–0	10–4	81–40	13–10	129–1 (129)	17–13
		78–55 (53 *JH*)	11–4			78–1 (78)	18–13
		116–0 (106)	12–4				

2007 was the 30th anniversary of the tournament at the Crucible. ❦ Snooker journalist and commentator Clive Everton had covered every day of snooker at every World Championship since 1977, but was forced to miss the 2007 final after he slipped and fell in his hotel room, breaking his hip.

THE AMERICA'S CUP

The America's Cup yacht race is considered the oldest contested trophy in sports history. The first race was staged in 1851 when the *America* (owned by the New York Yacht Club) triumphed over 14 British boats (representing the Royal Yacht Squadron) in a race around the Isle of Wight†. The original trophy was donated to the New York Yacht Club‡ under a 'Deed of Gift,' which stated that it must remain a 'perpetual challenge cup for friendly competition between nations'. Nowadays, the Cup (known affectionately as the 'Auld Mug') is contested by its current holder and the winner of the Louis Vuitton Cup. By tradition, each race is hosted by the Cup's previous victor. However, since the last winners, Alinghi, hailed from landlocked Switzerland, the 2007 race was held in Valencia, Spain. (This was the first race to be held in Europe since the original contest in 1851.) Team Alinghi retained their title, for the Société Nautique de Genève yacht club, by defeating Emirates Team New Zealand 5–2 in a seven-race final. Alinghi won the last race by just a second.

† Famously, when Queen Victoria inquired which yacht had been runner-up, she was told: 'Your Majesty, there is no second'. ‡ Until the Cup was won by Australia in 1983, the New York Yacht Club remained unbeaten for 25 challenges over 132 years – the longest winning streak in sports history.

READY RECKONER OF OTHER RESULTS · 2006/07

AMERICAN FOOTBALL · Superbowl	Indianapolis Colts *bt* Chicago Bears 29–17
ANGLING · National Coarse Ch. Div.1	Garbolino Ossett 15·83kg
BADMINTON · World Ch.	Nova Widianto & Lilyana Nastir [INA] *bt* Zheng Bo & Gao Ling [CHN] 21–16, 21–14
English National Ch.	Nick Kidd *bt* Nathan Rice 21–15, 21–15
BASEBALL · World Series [2006]	St Louis Cardinals *bt* Detroit Tigers 4–1
BASKETBALL · NBA finals	San Antonio Spurs 4–0 Cleveland Cavaliers
BBL Trophy final	Plymouth Raiders 74–65 Newcastle Eagles
THE BOAT RACE	Cambridge *bt* Oxford [by 1¼ lengths, in 17min 49s]
BOG SNORKELLING · World Championships	Joanne Pitchforth 1min 35·18s
BOWLS · WIBC World Indoor Singles	Mervyn King *bt* Gary Pitschou 8–7, 9–6
CHEESE ROLLING · Cooper's Hill	♂ Jason Crowther [WAL] ♀ Jemima Bullock [NZL]
CHESS · British Championship	Jacob Aagaard [SCO] 8·5pts
COMPETITIVE EATING · Int. Hot Dog Eating†	Joey Chestnut [USA] [66 in 12 minutes]
World Nettle Eating Championship	Paul Collins [ENG] 17 metres raw leaves
CRICKET · Test series – England *vs* West Indies	won 3–0
NatWest Series	West Indies *bt* England 2–1
Test Series – England *vs* India	lost 0–1
NatWest Series	England *bt* India 4–3
NatWest Twenty20	West Indies *drew* England 1–1
NatWest Women's Series	New Zealand *bt* England 3–2
Friends Provident Trophy	Durham *bt* Hampshire by 125 runs
County Championship	Sussex
CYCLING · Tour de France	Alberto Contador [see p.302]
Tour of Britain	Romain Feillu [FRA]
DARTS · Ladbrokes W. Ch. [PDC]	Raymond Van Barneveld *bt* Phil Taylor [see p.303]
Lakeside World Championship [BDO]	Martin Adams *bt* Phil Nixon [see p.303]
ELEPHANT POLO · World Championships	Angus Estates *bt* National Parks of Nepal
ENDURANCE RACES · Marathon des Sables	Lahcen Ahansal [MAR] 17:25·06 Laurence Fricotteaux [FRA] 23:28·21
Devil o' the Highlands	♂ John Kennedy 6:31·18 · ♀ Helen Johnson 7:07·53
EQUESTRIANISM · Badminton	Headley Britannia *ridden by* L. Fredericks [AUS] 39·6 pen
Burghley	Parkmore Ed *ridden by* William Fox-Pitt [GBR] 45·8 pen
FOOTBALL · FA Cup Women's	Arsenal Ladies 6–0 Leeds United Ladies
UEFA Cup	Sevilla 2–2 Espanyol (AET; 3–1 penalties)
Community Shield	Manchester United 1–1 Chelsea (AET; 3–0 penalties)
Carling Cup	Chelsea 2–1 Arsenal
Johnstone's Paint Trophy	Doncaster 3–2 Bristol (AET)
Premier League	Manchester United
Championship	Sunderland
League 1	Scunthorpe
League 2	Walsall
Scottish Premier League	Celtic
Scottish Cup	Celtic 1–0 Dunfermline
Copa América	Brazil 3–0 Argentina
Asian Cup	Iraq 1–0 Saudi Arabia

— READY RECKONER OF OTHER RESULTS · 2006/07 cont. —

FORMULA ONE · World Drivers' Champion [2006]	Fernando Alonso · Renault
GOLF · Women's World Cup of Golf	Paraguay (–9)
Solheim Cup	USA 16–12 Europe
Walker Cup	USA 12½ –11½ GB & Ireland
GREYHOUND RACING · Blue Square Greyhound Derby	Westmead Lord
GYMNASTICS · Acrobatic Gymnastics World Cup Finals	
Mixed pairs	Revaz Gurgenidze/Tatiana Okulova [RUS] 29·052
Women's pairs	Kristina Maraziuk/Natalia Kakhntuk [BLR] 28·630
Men's pairs	Konstantin Pilipchuk/Alexei Dudchenko [RUS] 28·661
HORSE RACING	
Grand National	Silver Birch *trained by* Gordon Elliott *ridden by* Robbie Power
Vodafone Epsom Derby	Authorized *trained by* Peter Chapple-Hyam *ridden by* Frankie Dettori
Cheltenham Gold Cup	Kauto Star *trained by* Paul Nicholls *ridden by* Ruby Walsh
1,000 Guineas	Finsceal Beo *trained by* Jim Bolger *ridden by* Kevin Manning
2,000 Guineas	Cockney Rebel *trained by* Geoff Huffer *ridden by* Oliver Peslier
The Oaks	Light Shift *trained by* Henry Cecil *ridden by* Ted Durcan
St Leger	Lucarno *trained by* John Gosden *ridden by* Jimmy Fortune
ICE HOCKEY · Stanley Cup	Anaheim Ducks *bt* Ottawa Senators, 4–1
PARACHUTING · FAI World Cup Formation Skydiving 8-way	France, 204pts
RUGBY LEAGUE · Super League [2006]	St Helens
Challenge Cup	St Helens 30–8 Catalans Dragons
League Leaders' Shield	St Helens
World Club Challenge	St Helens 18–14 Brisbane Broncos
RUGBY UNION · Guinness Premiership	Gloucester
Guinness Premiership Championship	Gloucester 16–44 Leicester Tigers
EDF Energy Anglo-Welsh Cup	Ospreys 35–41 Leicester
Magners Celtic League	Ospreys
Heineken Cup	London Wasps 25–9 Leicester Tigers
European Challenge Cup	Clermont Auvergne 22–16 Bath
Varsity Match [2006]	Cambridge 15–6 Oxford
RUNNING · Great North Run [2006]	♂ Hendrick Ramaala [RSA] 1:01·00
	♀ Berhane Adere [ETH] 1:10·14
SNOOKER · Saga Insurance Masters	Ronnie O'Sullivan 10–3 Ding Junhui
SQUASH · Super Series	R. Ashour [EGY] *bt* G. Gaultier [FRA] 11–10 (2–0), 11–8, 4–11, 11–4
SUMMER X GAMES · Skateboarding Big Air	Bob Burnquist 95·66pts
Skateboard Street	♂ Chris Cole ♀ Marisa Dal Santo
Moto X Freestyle	Adam Jones 94·40pts
BMX Park	Daniel Dhers 91·66pts
BMX Big Air	Kevin Robinson 95·33pts
TENNIS · Australian Op.	Roger Federer [SUI] *bt* F. Gonzalez [CHI] 7–6 (7–2), 6–4, 6–4
	Serena Williams [USA] *bt* Maria Sharapova [RUS] 6–1, 6–2
French Open	Rafael Nadal [ESP] *bt* Roger Federer [SUI] 6–3, 4–6, 6–3, 6–4
	Justine Henin [BEL] *bt* Ana Ivanovic [SRB] 6–1, 6–2
US Open	Roger Federer [SUI] *bt* Novak Djokovic [SRB] 7–6 (7–4), 7–6 (7–2), 6–4
	Justine Henin [BEL] *bt* Svetlana Kuznetsova [RUS] 6–1, 6–3

† Defeated, six-time champ Takeru Kobayashi complained of severe 'jaw arthritis' before the event.

Ephemerides

God sees their sins ... and in his Ephemerides
his Journals, he writes them downe.
— JOHN DONNE (1572–1631)

2008

Roman numerals............. MMVIII	Indian (Saka) year......1930 (Mar 21)
Regnal year[1] ....56th (6 Feb)	Sikh year ... 340 Nanakshahi Era (Mar 14)
Dominical Letter[2]................... FE	Jewish year ....5769 (Sep 30)
Epact[3] XXII	Roman year [AUC] ......2761 (Apr 21)
Golden Number (Lunar Cycle)[4] ..XIV	Masonic year.................6008 AL[5]
Chinese New Year....Rat 4706 (Feb 7)	Knights Templar year........ 890 AO[6]
Hindu New Year.......2064 (Mar 22)	Baha'i year................165 (Mar 21)
Islamic year..............1429 (Jan 10)	Queen bee colour ....red

[1] The number of years from the accession of a monarch; traditionally, legislation was dated by the Regnal year of the reigning monarch. [2] A way of categorising years to facilitate the calculation of Easter. If 1 January is a Sunday, the Dominical letter for the year will be A, if 2 January is a Sunday, it will be B, and so on. [3] The number of days by which the solar year exceeds the lunar year. [4] The number of the year (1–19) in the 19-year Metonic cycle; it is used in the calculation of Easter, and is found by adding 1 to the remainder left after dividing the number of the year by 19. [5] Anno Lucis, the 'Year of Light' when the world was formed. [6] Anno Ordinis, the 'Year of the Order'.

ON CHARACTER & THE EYES

The *long, almond-shaped* eye with *thick eyelids* covering nearly half of the pupil, when taken in connection with the full brow, is indicative of GENIUS, and is often found in artists, literary and scientific men. It is the eye of TALENT, or IMPRESSIBILITY. The *large, open, transparent* eye, of whatever colour, is indicative of ELEGANCE, of TASTE, of REFINEMENT, of WIT, of INTELLIGENCE. *Weakly marked eyebrows* indicate a FEEBLE CONSTITUTION and a tendency to MELANCHOLIA. *Deep sunken* eyes are SELFISH, while eyes in which the *whole iris shows* indicate ERRATICISM, if not LUNACY. *Round* eyes are indicative of INNOCENCE; *strongly protuberant* eyes of WEAKNESS of both MIND and BODY. Eyes *small and close together* typify CUNNING, while those *far apart and open* indicate FRANKNESS. The normal distance between the eyes is the width of one eye; a distance greater or less than this intensifies the character supposed to be symbolised. *Sharp angles*, turning down at the corners of the eyes, are seen in persons of ACUTE JUDGMENT and PENETRATION. *Well-opened steady* eyes belong to the SINCERE; *wide staring* eyes to the IMPERTINENT. [Anonymous, *c.*1830?]

RED-LETTER DAYS

Red-letter days are those days of civil and ecclesiastical importance – so named because they were marked out in red ink on early religious calendars. (The Romans marked unlucky days with black chalk, and auspicious days with white.) When these days fall within law sittings, the judges of the Queen's Bench Division sit wearing scarlet robes. The Red-letter days in Great Britain are tabulated below:

Conversion of St Paul	25 Jan
Purification	2 Feb
Accession of HM the Queen	6 Feb
Ash Wednesday	1 Mar
St David's Day	1 Mar
Annunciation	25 Mar
BD HM the Queen	21 Apr
St Mark	25 Apr
SS Philip & James	1 May
St Matthias	14 May
Ascension	25 May
Coronation of HM the Queen	2 Jun
BD HRH Duke of Edinburgh	10 Jun
St Barnabas	11 Jun
Official BD HM the Queen†	14 Jun
St John the Baptist	24 Jun
St Peter	29 Jun
St Thomas	3 Jul
St James	25 Jul
St Luke	18 Oct
SS Simon & Jude	28 Oct
All Saints	1 Nov
Lord Mayor's Day†	8 Nov
BD HRH the Prince of Wales	14 Nov
St Andrew's Day	30 Nov

(† *the date of each varies by year*)

FINGERNAILS AS AN INDICATION OF CHARACTER

A *white mark* on the nail bespeaks MISFORTUNE.
Pale or *lead-coloured* nails indicate MELANCHOLY people.
Broad nails indicate a GENTLE, TIMID, and BASHFUL nature.
Lovers of KNOWLEDGE and LIBERAL SENTIMENTS have *round nails.*
People with *narrow nails* are AMBITIOUS and QUARRELSOME.
Small nails indicate LITTLENESS of MIND, OBSTINACY and CONCEIT.
CHOLERIC, MARTIAL men, delighting in WAR, have *red and spotted nails.*
Nails *growing into the flesh* at the points or sides indicate LUXURIOUS TASTES.
People with *very pale nails* are subject to much INFIRMITY of the FLESH
and PERSECUTION by NEIGHBOURS and FRIENDS. [Anon]

KEY TO SYMBOLS USED OVERLEAF

[★BH]	UK Bank Holiday
[◕]	Clocks change (UK)
[❦]	Hunting season (traditional)
[ND]	National day
[NH]	National holiday
[ID 1900]	Independence day
[BD1900]	Birthday
[†1900]	Anniversary of death
[§ *patronage*]	Saint's Day
[WA 1900]	Wedding anniversary
[AD 1900]	Admission day [US States]
☺/◑	New/full moon [GMT]
[☄]	Annual meteor shower
[UN]	United Nations day
[◉]	Eclipse
[£]	Union Flag to be flown (UK)

Certain dates are subject to change, estimated, or tentative at the time of printing.

JANUARY

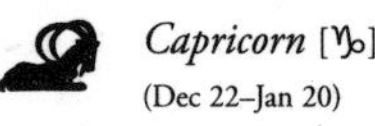

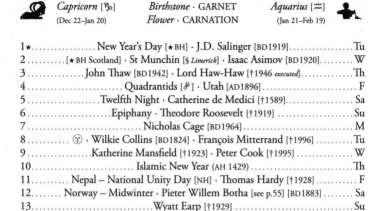

Capricorn [♑] (Dec 22–Jan 20)	*Birthstone* · GARNET *Flower* · CARNATION	*Aquarius* [♒] (Jan 21–Feb 19)

1★ ... New Year's Day [★BH] · J.D. Salinger [BD1919] ... Tu
2 ... [★BH Scotland] · St Munchin [§ *Limerick*] · Isaac Asimov [BD1920] ... W
3 ... John Thaw [BD1942] · Lord Haw-Haw [†1946 *executed*] ... Th
4 ... Quadrantids [☄] · Utah [AD1896] ... F
5 ... Twelfth Night · Catherine de Medici [†1589] ... Sa
6 ... Epiphany · Theodore Roosevelt [†1919] ... Su
7 ... Nicholas Cage [BD1964] ... M
8 ... ○ · Wilkie Collins [BD1824] · François Mitterrand [†1996] ... Tu
9 ... Katherine Mansfield [†1923] · Peter Cook [†1995] ... W
10 ... Islamic New Year (AH 1429) ... Th
11 ... Nepal – National Unity Day [NH] · Thomas Hardy [†1928] ... F
12 ... Norway – Midwinter · Pieter Willem Botha [see p.55] [BD1883] ... Sa
13 ... Wyatt Earp [†1929] ... Su
14 ... Edmond Halley [†1742] · Cecil Beaton [BD1904] ... M
15 ... Edward Gibbon [†1794] ... Tu
16 ... André Michelin [BD1853] · Eric Liddell [BD1902] ... W
17 ... St Anthony of Egypt [§ *basket-makers*] · James Earl Jones [BD1931] ... Th
18 ... Cary Grant [BD1904] · Jane Horrocks [BD1964] ... F
19 ... St Henry of Finland [§ *Finland*] · Stefan Edberg [BD1966] ... Sa
20 ... Presidential Inauguration Day, USA · St Sebastian [§ *archers, soldiers, & athletes*] ... Su
21 ... USA – Martin Luther King Jr Day · Placido Domingo [BD1941] ... M
22 ... ◐ · Sir Alf Ramsey [BD1920] ... Tu
23 ... St John the Almsgiver · Rutger Hauer [BD1944] ... W
24 ... Hadrian [BD AD76] ... Th
25 ... Scotland – Burns' Night · Conversion of St Paul · St Dwyn [§ *lovers*] ... F
26 ... Australia – Australia Day [NH] · Andrew Ridgeley [BD1963] ... Sa
27 ... Holocaust Memorial Day · Giuseppe Verdi [†1901] ... Su
28 ... Sir Francis Drake [†1596] · Jackson Pollock [BD1912] ... M
29 ... St Julian the Hospitaller [§ *innkeepers and boatmen*] ... Tu
30 ... Franklin D. Roosevelt [BD1882] ... W
31 ... Anna Pavlova [BD1881] · Norman Mailer [BD1923] ... Th

French Rev. calendar	*Pluvôse* (rain)	Dutch month	*Lauwmaand* (chilly)
Angelic governor	*Gabriel*	Saxon month	*Wulf-monath* (wolf)
Epicurean calendar	*Marronglaçaire*	Talismanic stone	*Jasper*

❦ The Latin month *Ianuarius* derives from *ianua* ('door'), since it was the opening of the year. It was also associated with *Janus*, the two-faced Roman god of doors and openings who guarded the gates of heaven. Janus could simultaneously face the year just past and the year to come. ❦ *If January Calends be summerly gay, 'Twill be winterly weather till the calends of May.* ❦ *Janiveer – Freeze the pot upon the fier.* ❦ *He that will live another year, Must eat a hen in Januvere.* ❦ On the stock market, the *January Effect* is the trend of stocks performing especially well that month. ❦

FEBRUARY

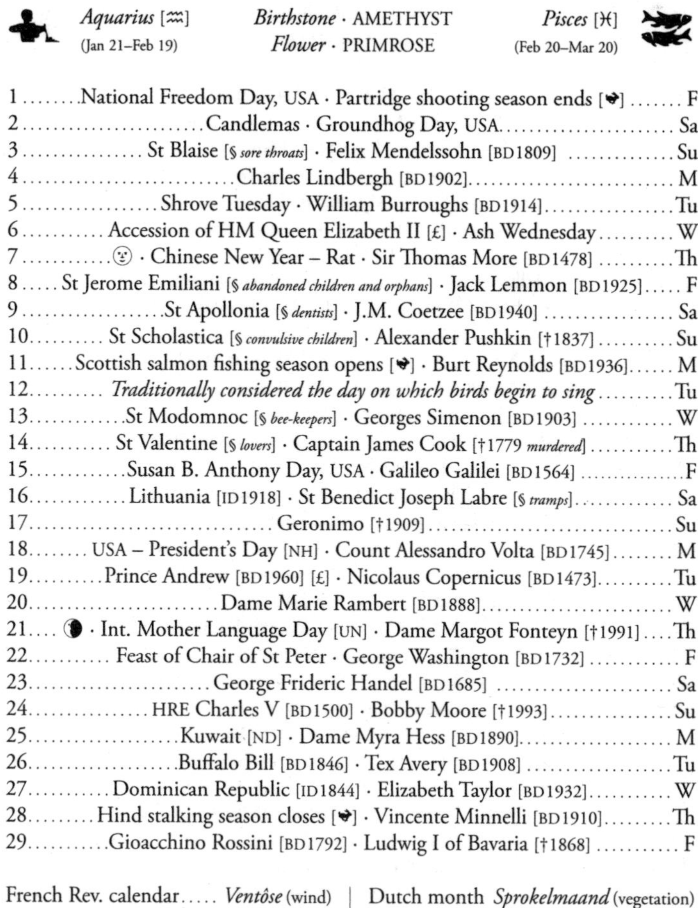

Aquarius [♒] (Jan 21–Feb 19)	*Birthstone* · AMETHYST *Flower* · PRIMROSE	*Pisces* [♓] (Feb 20–Mar 20)

1 .... National Freedom Day, USA · Partridge shooting season ends [🐦] .... F
2 .... Candlemas · Groundhog Day, USA .... Sa
3 .... St Blaise [§ *sore throats*] · Felix Mendelssohn [BD1809] .... Su
4 .... Charles Lindbergh [BD1902] .... M
5 .... Shrove Tuesday · William Burroughs [BD1914] .... Tu
6 .... Accession of HM Queen Elizabeth II [£] · Ash Wednesday .... W
7 .... ☺ · Chinese New Year – Rat · Sir Thomas More [BD1478] .... Th
8 ..... St Jerome Emiliani [§ *abandoned children and orphans*] · Jack Lemmon [BD1925] ..... F
9 .... St Apollonia [§ *dentists*] · J.M. Coetzee [BD1940] .... Sa
10 .... St Scholastica [§ *convulsive children*] · Alexander Pushkin [†1837] .... Su
11 ...... Scottish salmon fishing season opens [🐦] · Burt Reynolds [BD1936] ...... M
12 .... *Traditionally considered the day on which birds begin to sing* .... Tu
13 .... St Modomnoc [§ *bee-keepers*] · Georges Simenon [BD1903] .... W
14 .... St Valentine [§ *lovers*] · Captain James Cook [†1779 *murdered*] .... Th
15 .... Susan B. Anthony Day, USA · Galileo Galilei [BD1564] .... F
16 .... Lithuania [ID1918] · St Benedict Joseph Labre [§ *tramps*] .... Sa
17 .... Geronimo [†1909] .... Su
18 .... USA – President's Day [NH] · Count Alessandro Volta [BD1745] .... M
19 .... Prince Andrew [BD1960] [£] · Nicolaus Copernicus [BD1473] .... Tu
20 .... Dame Marie Rambert [BD1888] .... W
21 .... ◐ · Int. Mother Language Day [UN] · Dame Margot Fonteyn [†1991] .... Th
22 .... Feast of Chair of St Peter · George Washington [BD1732] .... F
23 .... George Frideric Handel [BD1685] .... Sa
24 .... HRE Charles V [BD1500] · Bobby Moore [†1993] .... Su
25 .... Kuwait [ND] · Dame Myra Hess [BD1890] .... M
26 .... Buffalo Bill [BD1846] · Tex Avery [BD1908] .... Tu
27 .... Dominican Republic [ID1844] · Elizabeth Taylor [BD1932] .... W
28 .... Hind stalking season closes [🐦] · Vincente Minnelli [BD1910] .... Th
29 .... Gioacchino Rossini [BD1792] · Ludwig I of Bavaria [†1868] .... F

French Rev. calendar ..... *Ventôse* (wind)	Dutch month *Sprokelmaand* (vegetation)
Angelic governor .... *Barchiel*	Saxon month .... *Solmonath* (Sun)
Epicurean calendar .... *Harrengsauridor*	Talismanic stone .... *Ruby*

❦ Much mythology and folklore considers February to have the bitterest weather: *February is seldom warm.* ❦ *February, if ye be fair, The sheep will mend, and nothing mair; February, if ye be foul, The sheep will die in every pool.* ❦ *As the day lengthens, the cold strengthens.* ❦ The word 'February' derives from the Latin *februum* – which means cleansing or purification, and reflects the rituals undertaken by the Romans before spring. ❦ Having only 28 days in non-leap years, February was known in Welsh as '*y mis bach*' – the little month. ❦ February is traditionally personified in pictures either by an old man warming himself by the fireside, or as 'a sturdy maiden, with a tinge of the red hard winter apple on her hardy cheek'. ❦

MARCH

Pisces [♓] (Feb 20–Mar 20)	*Birthstone* · BLOODSTONE *Flower* · JONQUIL	*Aries* [♈] (Mar 21–Apr 20)

1	St David [§ *Wales*] · Trout fishing season begins [🐟]	Sa
2	Mother's Day · Howard Carter [†1939 *curse of the mummy?*]	Su
3	Doll's Festival, Japan · Fatima Whitbread [BD1961]	M
4	Patsy Kensit [BD1968] · John Candy [†1994]	Tu
5	St Piran [§ *tin miners*] · Rex Harrison [BD1908]	W
6	Ghana [ID1957] · George Formby [†1961]	Th
7	○ · St Felicity & St Perpetua of Carthage [§ *mothers separated from their children*]	F
8	Women's Rights & Int. Peace Day [UN] · Kenneth Grahame [BD1859]	Sa
9	Victoria 'Vita' Sackville-West [BD1892]	Su
10	Prince Edward [BD1964] [£] · Commonwealth Day	M
11	Lawrence Llewelyn-Bowen [BD1965]	Tu
12	Jack Kerouac [BD1922] · Anne Frank [†1945]	W
13	William H. Macy [BD1950]	Th
14	St Matilda [§ *parents with many children*] · Karl Marx [†1883]	F
15	Maine [AD1820] · Aristotle Onassis [†1975]	Sa
16	Palm Sunday · St Urho [§ *Finnish immigrants in America*]	Su
17	St Patrick's Day [§ *Ireland*] · World Maritime Day [UN]	M
18	Wilfred Owen [BD1893] · Luc Besson [BD1959]	Tu
19	Dr David Livingstone [BD1813]	W
20	First Day of Spring · Maundy Thursday	Th
21	◐ · Good Friday · Holi (Spring Festival)	F
22	World Day for Water [UN] · Sir Anthony Van Dyck [BD1599]	Sa
23	Easter · World Meteorological Day [UN] · Sir Steve Redgrave [BD1963]	Su
24★	Easter Monday [★BH] · St Dunchad [§ *Irish sailors*] · William Morris [BD1834]	M
25	Annunciation Day · Claude Debussy [†1918]	Tu
26	Robert Frost [BD1874] · Tennessee Williams [BD1911]	W
27	Burma – Army Day · Mariah Carey [BD1970]	Th
28	King George I [BD1660] · Sir Dirk Bogarde [BD1921]	F
29	Norman Tebbit [BD1931]	Sa
30	BST begins [●] · Rolf Harris [BD1930] · Warren Beatty [BD1937]	Su
31	René Descartes [BD1596] · Al Gore [BD1948]	M

French Rev. cal. ..... *Germinal* (budding)	Dutch month .... *Lentmaand* (spring)
Angelic governor .... *Machidiel*	Saxon month..... *Hrèth-monath* (rough)
Epicurean calendar.... *Oeufalacoquidor*	Talismanic stone .... *Topaz*

❦ The first month of the Roman year, March is named for Mars, the god of war but also an agricultural deity. ❦ The unpredictability of March weather leads to some confusion (*March has many weathers*), though it is generally agreed that March *comes in like a lion, and goes out like a lamb*. Yet, because March is often too wet for crops to flourish, many considered *a bushel of Marche dust* [a dry March] *is worth a ransom of gold*. ❦ March hares are 'mad' with nothing more than lust, since it is their mating season. ❦ The *Mars* bar is named after its creator Frank Mars. ❦

APRIL

Aries [♈] (Mar 21–Apr 20)

Birthstone · DIAMOND
Flower · SWEET PEA

Taurus [♉] (Apr 21–May 21)

1 ... April Fool's Day [except in Scotland] · Roebuck season opens [❦] ... Tu
2 ... Hans Christian Andersen [BD1805] ... W
3 ... *traditional day for well-dressing in Droitwich* ... Th
4 ... Senegal [ID1960] · Linus Yale [BD1821] ... F
5 ... Pocahontas & John Rolfe [WA1614] · Bette Davis [BD1908] ... Sa
6 ... ☺ · Richard the Lionheart [†1199] ... Su
7 ... World Health Day [UN] · William Wordsworth [BD1770] ... M
8 ... Buddha, Siddhartha Gautama [BD563BC] · Vivienne Westwood [BD1941] ... Tu
9 ... Sir Francis Bacon [†1626] · Hugh Hefner [BD1926] ... W
10 ... Joseph Pulitzer [BD1847] ... Th
11 ... St Stanislaw of Krakow [§ *Poland*] · Primo Levi [†1987 *suicide*] ... F
12 ... St Zeno [§ *Verona*] · Sugar Ray Robinson [†1989] ... Sa
13 ... Baisakhi Mela (Nanakshahi Calendar) · Catherine de Medici [BD1519] ... Su
14 ... Julie Christie [BD1940] · Julian Lloyd-Webber [BD1951] ... M
15 ... Emma Thompson [BD1959] · Samantha Fox [BD1966] ... Tu
16 ... Madame Marie Tussaud [†1850] · Spike Milligan [BD1918] ... W
17 ... J.P. Morgan [BD1837] · Eddie Cochran [†1960] ... Th
18 ... Zimbabwe [ID1980] · Thor Heyerdahl [†2002] ... F
19 ... First Seder Night · Lord Byron [†1824] · Charles Darwin [†1882] ... Sa
20 ... ◑ · First Day of Passover (Pesach) · Joan Miró [BD1893] ... Su
21 ... Queen Elizabeth [BD1926] [£] · Charlotte Brontë [BD1816] · Lyrids [☄] ... M
22 ... Henry Fielding [BD1707] · Vladimir Nabokov [BD1899] ... Tu
23 ... St George [§ *England*] · World Book & Copyright Day [UN] ... W
24 ... Anthony Trollope [BD1815] · Wallis Simpson [†1986] ... Th
25 ... Australia & New Zealand – Anzac Day · St Mark [§ *notaries*] ... F
26 ... Rudolf Hess [BD1894] · Charles Francis Richter [BD1900] ... Sa
27 ... Sierra Leone [ID1961] · St Zita [§ *bakers*] · Socrates [†399BC *poisoned*] ... Su
28 ... Oskar Schindler [BD1908] · Saddam Hussein [BD1937] ... M
29 ... Daniel Day Lewis [BD1957] · Alfred Hitchcock [†1980] ... Tu
30 ... Stag stalking season closes [❦] · Adolf Hitler [†1945 *suicide*] ... W

French Rev. calendar ... *Floréal* (blossom)
Angelic governor ... *Asmodel*
Epicurean calendar ... *Petitpoisidor*

Dutch month ... *Grasmaand* (grass)
Saxon month ... *Easter-monath*
Talismanic stone ... *Garnet*

❦ April, T.S. Eliot's 'cruellest month', heralds the start of spring and is associated with new growth and sudden bursts of rain. ❦ Its etymology might derive from the Latin *aperire* ('to open') – although in Old English it was known simply as the *Eastre-monath*. ❦ *April with his hack and his bill, Plants a flower on every hill.* ❦ The custom of performing pranks and hoaxes on April Fool's Day (or *poisson d'avril* as it is known in France) is long established, although its origins are much disputed. ❦ According to weather folklore, *If it thunders on All Fools' day, it brings good crops of corn and hay*. Usually, cuckoos will first appear in the *Times* around 8 April. ❦

MAY

Taurus [♉] (Apr 21–May 21) | *Birthstone* · EMERALD | *Flower* · LILY OF THE VALLEY | *Gemini* [♊] (May 22–Jun 22)

1 .... May Day · Ascension Day · Joseph Heller [BD1923] .... Th
2 .... Donatella Versace [BD1955] · Oliver Reed [†1999] .... F
3 .... World Press Freedom Day [UN] · James Brown [BD1933] .... Sa
4 .... Tito [†1980] .... Su
5★. ☺ · [★BH] May Day Bank Holiday · Karl Marx [BD1818] · Eta Aquarids [✐]. M
6 .... Rudolph Valentino [BD1895] · Tony Blair [BD1953] .... Tu
7 .... Gary Cooper [BD1901] · Edwin Herbert Land [BD1909] .... W
8 .... VE Day · Paul Gauguin [†1903] .... Th
9 .... Europe Day – European Union · J.M. Barrie [BD1860] .... F
10 .... St Catald [§ *invoked against plagues, drought, & storms*] .... Sa
11 .... Whit Sunday · Spencer Perceval [†1812 *assassinated*] .... Su
12 .... Dante Gabriel Rossetti [BD1828] · Burt Bacharach [BD1929] .... M
13 .... Garland Day – Dorset · Chet Baker [†1988] .... Tu
14 .... Paraguay [ND] · Henry John Heinz [†1919] .... W
15 .... International Day of Families [UN] · Pierre Curie [BD1859] .... Th
16 .... Liberace [BD1919] · Jim Henson [†1990] .... F
17 .... Ascension · Dennis Hopper [BD1936] .... Sa
18 .... International Museum Day · Dame Margot Fonteyn [BD1919] .... Su
19 .... St Yves [§ *lawyers & Brittany*] · T.E. Lawrence [†1935] .... M
20 ..... ◐ · Honoré de Balzac [BD1799] · Dame Barbara Hepworth [†1975] ..... Tu
21 .... Leo Sayer [BD1948] .... W
22 .... Int. Day for Biological Diversity [UN] · Laurence Olivier [BD1907] ...... Th
23 ...... John D. Rockefeller [†1937] · Marvellous Marvin Hagler [BD1954] .... F
24 .... Gabriel Fahrenheit [BD1686] .... Sa
25 .... Jordan [ID1946] · Miles Davis [BD1926] .... Su
26★ .... [★BH] · Sir Matt Busby [BD1909] · Zola Budd [BD1966] .... M
27 .... John Calvin [†1564] · Henry Kissinger [BD1923] .... Tu
28 .... Ethiopia [ND] · Ian Fleming [BD1908] .... W
29 .... International Day of United Nations Peacekeepers [UN] .... Th
30 .... St Walstan [§ *agriculture*] · Henry VIII & Jane Seymour [WA1536] .... F
31 .... The Visitation of the Blessed Virgin Mary · Clint Eastwood [BD1930] .... Sa

French Rev. cal.	*Prairial* (meadow)	Dutch month	*Blowmaand* (flower)
Angelic governor	*Ambriel*	Saxon month	*Trimilchi* [see below]
Epicurean calendar	*Aspergial*	Talismanic stone	*Emerald*

❦ Named after *Maia*, the goddess of growth, May is considered a joyous month, as Milton wrote: 'Hail bounteous May that dost inspire Mirth and youth, and warm desire'. ❦ However, May has long been thought a bad month in which to marry: *Who weds in May throws it all away.* ❦ Anglo-Saxons called May *thrimilce*, since in May cows could be milked three times a day. ❦ May was thought a time of danger for the sick; so to have *climbed May hill* was to have survived the month. ❦ Kittens born in May were thought weak, and were often drowned. ❦

JUNE

Gemini [♊] (May 22–Jun 22)	*Birthstone* · PEARL *Flower* · ROSE	*Cancer* [♋] (Jun 23–Jul 23)

1	Kentucky [AD1792] · John Drinkwater [BD1882]	Su
2	Coronation of Elizabeth II [1953] [£] · Thomas Hardy [BD1840]	M
3	○ · St Kevin [§ *blackbirds*] · Josephine Baker [BD1906]	Tu
4	Kaiser Wilhelm II [†1941]	W
5	World Environment Day [UN] · Adam Smith [BD1723]	Th
6	D Day (1945) · Captain Robert Falcon Scott [BD1868]	F
7	Malta [ND] · Dean Martin [BD1917] · E.M. Forster [†1970]	Sa
8	St Medard [§ *good weather, prisoners, & toothache*]	Su
9	Feast of Weeks (Shavuot) · Cole Porter [BD1891]	M
10	HRH Prince Philip [BD1921] [£] · Judy Garland [BD1922]	Tu
11	Paul McCartney & Heather Mills [WA2002]	W
12	Russia [ID1990] · Gregory Peck [†2003]	Th
13	St Anthony of Padua [§ *horses, mules, & donkeys*] · Harriet Beecher Stowe [BD1811]	F
14	HM the Queen's Official Birthday (provisional) [£]	Sa
15	Father's Day · Edvard Grieg [BD1843]	Su
16	Freshwater fishing season opens [🐟] · Blooms day (*Ulysses*)	M
17	St Botulph [§ *agricultural workers*] · John Wesley [BD1703]	Tu
18	◐ · Seychelles [ND] · Delia Smith [BD1941]	W
19	Salman Rushdie [BD1947]	Th
20	Longest Day · First Day of Summer · Catherine Cookson [BD1906]	F
21	St Aloysius Gonzaga [§ *youth*] · Jean-Paul Sartre [BD1905]	Sa
22	Prunella Scales [BD1932] · Meryl Streep [BD1949]	Su
23	Midsummer Eve · Vespasian [†AD79]	M
24	Midsummer Day · Mick Fleetwood [BD1942]	Tu
25	Slovenia [ID 1991] · George Orwell [BD1903]	W
26	United Nations Charter Day [UN] · Tony Hancock [†1968]	Th
27	Vera Wang [BD1949] · Isabelle Adjani [BD1955]	F
28	Mel Brooks [BD1926]	Sa
29	St Paul [§ *authors*] · Fatty Arbuckle [†1933]	Su
30	St Theobald [§ *bachelors*]	M

French Rev. cal.	*Messidor* (harvest)	Dutch month	*Zomermaand* (Summer)
Angelic governor	*Muriel*	Saxon month	*Sere-monath* (dry)
Epicurean calendar	*Concombrial*	Talismanic stone	*Sapphire*

❦ June is probably derived from *iuvenis* ('young'), but it is also linked to the goddess *Juno*, who personifies young women. In Scots Gaelic, the month is known as *Ian t-òg-mhìos*, the 'young month'; and in Welsh, as *Mehefin*, the 'middle'. ❦ According to weather lore, *Calm weather in June, Sets corn in tune.* ❦ To 'june' a herd of animals is to drive them in a brisk or lively manner. ❦ It has been claimed that 'June is the reality of the Poetic's claims for May'. ❦ In parts of South Africa the verb 'to june-july' is slang for shaking or shivering with fear – because these months, while summer in the north, are midwinter in the south. ❦

JULY

Cancer [♋] (Jun 23–Jul 23)	*Birthstone* · RUBY *Flower* · LARKSPUR	*Leo* [♌] (Jul 24–Aug 23)

1	Canada – Canada Day [NH] · Somalia [ND]	Tu
2	Amelia Earhart [†1937 *disappeared over the Pacific*]	W
3	☺ · Tom Cruise [BD1962] · Jim Morrison [†1971]	Th
4	USA – Independence Day [NH] · Louis Armstrong [BD1901]	F
5	Cape Verde [ID1975] · Sir Thomas Stamford Raffles [†1826]	Sa
6	Kenneth Grahame [†1932] · Sylvester Stallone [BD1946]	Su
7	Gustav Mahler [BD1860] · Marc Chagall [BD1887]	M
8	John D. Rockefeller [BD1839]	Tu
9	Edward Heath [BD1916] · David Hockney [BD1937]	W
10	Camille Pissarro [BD1830] · Arthur Ashe [BD1943]	Th
11	World Population Day [UN] · St Benedict [§ *inflammatory diseases*]	F
12	Kiribati [ID1979] · Yul Brynner [BD1915]	Sa
13	St Margaret [§ *expectant mothers*]	Su
14	[★ BH N. Ireland] · France – Bastille Day · Gustav Klimt [BD1862]	M
15	St Swithin's Day · Rembrandt [BD1606]	Tu
16	Feast of Our Lady of Mount Carmel · Roald Amundsen [BD1872]	W
17	Duchess of Cornwall [BD1947] [£] · Adam Smith [†1790]	Th
18	◐ · Richard Branson [BD1950] · Nick Faldo [BD1957]	F
19	Edgar Degas [BD1834]	Sa
20	St Wilgefortis [§ *difficult marriages*] · Sir Edmund Hillary [BD1919]	Su
21	Belgium [ND] · Baron von Reuter [BD1816]	M
22	St Mary Magdalene [§ *hairdressers & repentant women*]	Tu
23	Michael Foot [BD1913] · Montgomery Clift [†1966]	W
24	Simon Bolivar Day – Venezuela & Ecuador · Alexandre Dumas [BD1802]	Th
25	St James [§ *labourers*] · Charles Macintosh [†1843]	F
26	St Ann [§ *women in labour*] · George Bernard Shaw [BD1856]	Sa
27	St Aurelius [§ *orphans*]	Su
28	Beatrix Potter [BD1866] · Delta Aquarids (South) [☄]	M
29	St Martha [§ *cooks*] · Mama Cass Elliot [†1974]	Tu
30	Emily Brontë [BD1818] · Otto von Bismarck [†1898]	W
31	St Ignatius of Loyola [§ *those on spiritual exercises*]	Th

French Rev. cal.	*Thermidor* (heat)	Dutch month	*Hooymaand* (hay)
Angelic governor	*Verchiel*	Saxon month	*Mæd-monath* (meadow)
Epicurean calendar	*Melonial*	Talismanic stone	*Diamond*

❦ July was originally called *Quintilis* (from *Quintus* – meaning 'fifth'), but it was renamed by Mark Anthony to honour the murdered Julius Caesar, who was born on 12 July. ❦ *A swarm of bees in May is worth a load of hay; A swarm of bees in June is worth a silver spoon; But a swarm of bees in July is not worth a fly.* ❦ *If the first of July be rainy weather, 'Twill rain mair or less for forty days together.* ❦ *Bow-wow, dandy fly – Brew no beer in July.* ❦ July used to be known as the thunder month, and some churches rang their bells in the hope of driving away thunder and lightning. ❦

AUGUST

Leo [♌] (Jul 24–Aug 23) · *Birthstone* · AGATE · *Flower* · GLADIOLUS · *Virgo* [♍] (Aug 23–Sep 23)

1 . ☺ · Stag & buck stalking seasons begin [❥] · St Alphonsus [§ *confessors, theologians*] F
2 .... Louis Bleriot [†1936] · Wes Craven [BD1939] .... Sa
3 ....Tony Bennett [BD1926] .... Su
4 .... [★BH Scotland] · Queen Mother [BD1900] · Percy Bysshe Shelley [BD1792] ... M
5 ....Oyster Day, UK · Richard Burton [†1984] .... Tu
6 ....Delta Aquarids (North) [✐] · Barbara Windsor [BD1937] .... W
7 .... Labour Day – Western Samoa · St Cajetan [§ *the unemployed*] .... Th
8 .... Nigel Mansell [BD1953] .... F
9 .... International Day of the World's Indigenous People [UN] .... Sa
10 .... Herbert Hoover [BD1874] · Antonio Banderas [BD1960] .... Su
11 ....Edith Wharton [†1937] · Jackson Pollock [†1956]............... M
12 .... Glorious Twelfth – grouse season begins [❥] · Perseids [✐] .... Tu
13 ....William Caxton [BD1422] · H.G. Wells [†1946]................ W
14 .... Pakistan [ID1947] · René Goscinny [BD1926] .... Th
15 ....VJ Day (1945) · Assumption Day · Princess Anne [BD1950] [£]........ F
16 .... ◐ · St Stephen the Great [§ *bricklayers*] · Bela Lugosi [†1956]........... Sa
17 ....Robert De Niro [BD1943] · Ira Gershwin [†1983] .... Su
18 .... Robert Redford [BD1937] .... M
19 .... Afghanistan [ID1919] · Gabrielle 'Coco' Chanel [BD1883] .... Tu
20 ....St Oswin [§ *the betrayed*] · Don King [BD1931]................... W
21 ....Hawaii [AD1959] · Christopher Robin Milne [BD1920]............ Th
22 ....Henri Cartier-Bresson [BD1908] .... F
23 ....Louis XVI [BD1754] · Rudolph Valentino [†1926].............. Sa
24 ....Ukraine [ID1991] · George Stubbs [BD1724] .... Su
25★ ....[★BH] · Ivan 'the Terrible' [BD1530] · Gene Simmons [BD1949] .... M
26 .... St Adrian of Nicomedia [§ *arms dealers, soldiers, & plagues*] .... Tu
27 ....Earl Mountbatten [†1979 *assassinated*] · Samuel Goldwyn [BD1882]....... W
28 ....Sir John Betjeman [BD1906]......................... Th
29 .... St John the Baptist [§ *convulsive children*] · Edmond Hoyle [†1769] .... F
30 .... ☺ · Dennis Healey [BD1917] · Cameron Diaz [BD1972] .... Sa
31 .... Malaysia [ND] · Caligula [BD AD12] .... Su

French Rev. cal. .... *Fructidor* (fruits)
Angelic governor .... *Hamaliel*
Epicurean calendar .... *Raisinose*

Dutch month ..... *Oogstmaand* (harvest)
Saxon month...... *Weod-monath* (weed)
Talismanic stone .... *Zircon*

❦ Previously called *Sextilis* (as the sixth month of the old calendar), August was renamed in 8BC, in honour of the first Roman Emperor, Augustus, who claimed this month to be lucky, as it was the month in which he began his consulship, conquered Egypt, and had many other triumphs. ❦ *Greengrocers rise at dawn of sun, August the fifth – come haste away, To Billingsgate the thousands run, Tis Oyster Day! Tis Oyster Day!* ❦ *Dry August and warme, Dothe harvest no harme.* ❦ *Take heed of sudden cold after heat.* ❦ *Gather not garden seeds near the full moon.* ❦ *Sow herbs.* ❦

SEPTEMBER

Virgo [♍] (Aug 23–Sep 23)	*Birthstone* · SAPPHIRE *Flower* · ASTER	*Libra* [♎] (Sep 24–Oct 23)

1 .... Partridge shooting season opens [❦] · Libya [ND] .... M
2 .... First Day of Ramadan · Vietnam [ND] .... Tu
3 .... Charlie Sheen [BD1965] · Ho Chi Minh [†1969] .... W
4 .... St Ida of Herzfeld [§ *widows*] .... Th
5 .... Rin Tin Tin [BD1918] · George Lazenby [BD1939] .... F
6 .... Swaziland [ND] · King James II [†1701] .... Sa
7 .... Queen Elizabeth I [BD1533] · Buddy Holly [BD1936] .... Su
8 .... International Literacy Day [UN] · Nativity of Blessed Virgin Mary ...... M
9 .... Japan – Chrysanthemum Day · Count Leo Tolstoy [BD1828] .... Tu
10 .... St Nicholas of Tolentino [§ *sick animals*] · Colin Firth [BD1960] .... W
11 .... New Year – Ethiopia · O. Henry [BD1862] .... Th
12 .... Barry White [BD1944] .... F
13 .... St John Chrysostom [§ *orators*] · Tupac Shakur [†1996] .... Sa
14 .... Exaltation of the Holy Cross · Hicham el Guerrouj [BD1974] .... Su
15 .... ◐ · Battle of Britain Day · Honduras [ND] .... M
16 .... International Day for the Preservation of the Ozone Layer [UN] .... Tu
17 .... Tobias Smollett [†1771] .... W
18 .... Chile [ND] · Greta Garbo [BD1905] .... Th
19 .... St Januarius [§ *blood banks*] · James Garfield [†1881] .... F
20 .... Alexander the Great [BD 356BC] · Sir James Dewar [BD1842] .... Sa
21 .... International Day of Peace [UN] · Larry Hagman [BD1931] .... Su
22 .... First Day of Autumn · Fay Weldon [BD1931] .... M
23 .... Sigmund Freud [†1939] · Bruce Springsteen [BD1949] .... Tu
24 .... Guinea-Bissau [ID1973] · Jim Henson [BD1936] .... W
25 .... St Cadoc of Llancarvan [§ *cramps*] .... Th
26 .... St Cosmas & St Damian [§ *pharmacists & doctors*] · Béla Bartók [†1945] .... F
27 .... Meat Loaf [BD1947] .... Sa
28 .... Brigitte Bardot [BD1934] · Arthur 'Harpo' Marx [†1964] .... Su
29 .... ☺ · Michaelmas Day · Émile Zola [†1902] .... M
30 .... Jewish New Year (AM 5769) (Rosh Hashanah) .... Tu

French Rev. cal. ... *Vendémiaire* (vintage)	Dutch month .... *Herstmaand* (Autumn)
Angelic governor .... *Uriel*	Saxon month ...... *Gerst-monath* (barley)
Epicurean calendar .... *Huîtrose*	Talismanic stone .... *Agate*

❦ September is so named as it was the seventh month in the Roman calendar. ❦ *September blows soft, Till the fruit's in the loft. Forgotten, month past, Doe now at the last.* ❦ *Eat and drink less, And buy a knife at Michaelmas.* ❦ To be 'Septembered' is to be multihued in autumnal colours, as Blackmore wrote: 'His honest face was Septembered with many a vintage'. ❦ Poor Robin's Almanac (1666) states 'now *Libra* weighs the days and nights in an equal balance, so that there is not an hairs breadth difference betwixt them in length; this moneth having an R in it, Oysters come again in season'. ❦ The Irish name *Meán Fómhair* means 'mid-autumn'. ❦

OCTOBER

Libra [♎] (Sep 24–Oct 23)	*Birthstone* · OPAL *Flower* · CALENDULA	*Scorpio* [♏] (Oct 24–Nov 22)

1 ...... Int. Day of Older Persons [UN] · Pheasant shooting season opens [❦] .... W
2 .... End of Ramadan (Eid al-Fitr) · Julius 'Groucho' Marx [BD1890] .... Th
3 .... Germany [ND] · Gore Vidal [BD1925] .... F
4 .... Lesotho [ND] · Janis Joplin [†1970] .... Sa
5 .... International Teachers' Day [UN] · Kate Winslet [BD1975] .... Su
6 .... Children's Day [UN] · Elizabeth Taylor & Larry Fortensky [WA1991] ..... M
7 .... St Sergius [§ *Syria*] .... Tu
8 .... Betty Boothroyd [BD1929] · Paul Hogan [BD1939] .... W
9 .... Day of Atonement (Yom Kippur) · Brian Blessed [BD1937] .... Th
10 .... Taiwan [ND] · Harold Pinter [BD1930] .... F
11 .... St Gummarus [§ *glove-makers*] · Eleanor Roosevelt [BD1884] .... Sa
12 .... Spain [ND] · James Ramsay MacDonald [BD1866] .... Su
13 .... Milton S. Hershey [†1945] · Marie Osmond [BD1959] .... M
14 .... ◐ · Feast of Tabernacles (Succoth) · Errol Flynn [†1959] .... Tu
15 .... P.G. Wodehouse [BD1881] · Mata Hari [†1917 *executed*] .... W
16 .... World Food Day [UN] · St Hedwig [§ *brides*] .... Th
17 ..... Int. Day for the Eradication of Poverty [UN] · Evel Knievel [BD1938] ...... F
18 .... Alaska Day, USA · Martina Navratilova [BD1956] .... Sa
19 .... Philip Pullman [BD1946] .... Su
20 .... St Acca [§ *learning*] · Elfriede Jelinek [BD1946] .... M
21 .... St Hilarion [§ *hermits*] · Orionids [☄] · Jack Kerouac [†1969] .... Tu
22 .... Catherine Deneuve [BD1943] · Sir Kingsley Amis [†1995] .... W
23 .... St John of Capistrano [§ *jurors*] · Dame Anita Roddick [BD1942] .... Th
24 .... United Nations Day [UN] · Christian Dior [†1957] .... F
25 .... Kazakhstan [ND] · Georges Bizet [BD1838] .... Sa
26 .... BST ends [●] · Alfred the Great [†899] · Bob Hoskins [BD1942] .... Su
27 .... Turkmenistan [ND] · Dylan Thomas [BD1914] .... M
28 .. ☺ · First Day of Diwali (Festival of Lights) · St Simon the Zealot [§ *sawyers*] . Tu
29 .... Turkey [ND] · Joseph Goebbels [BD1897] .... W
30 .... St Marcellus the Centurion [§ *concientious objectors*] .... Th
31 .... Hallowe'en · John Keats [BD1795] .... F

French Rev. cal.	*Brumaire* (fog; mist)	Dutch month	*Wynmaand* (wine)
Angelic governor	*Barbiel*	Saxon month	*Win-monath* (wine)
Epicurean calendar	*Bécassinose*	Talismanic stone	*Amethyst*

❦ October was originally the eighth month of the calendar. ❦ *Dry your barley land in October, Or you'll always be sober.* ❦ October was a time for brewing, and the month gave its name to a 'heady and ripe' ale: 'five Quarters of Malt to three Hogsheads, and twenty-four Pounds of Hops'. Consequently, *often drunk and seldom sober falls like the leaves in October.* ❦ In American politics, an *October surprise* is an event thought to have been engineered to garner political support just before an election. ❦ Roman Catholics traditionally dedicated October to the devotion of the rosary. ❦

NOVEMBER

Scorpio [♏] (Oct 24–Nov 22) · *Birthstone* · TOPAZ · *Flower* · CHRYSANTHEMUM · *Sagittarius* [♐] (Nov 23–Dec 21)

1 .... All Saints' Day · Hind and doe stalking season opens [❤] .... Sa
2 .... All Souls' Day · St Eustachius [§ *firefighters*] .... Su
3 .... Annie Oakley [†1926] · John Barry [BD1933] .... M
4 .... St Charles Borromeo [§ *learning and the arts*] · Felix Mendelssohn [†1847] ..... Tu
5 .... Guy Fawkes' Night · Taurids [☄] · Vivien Leigh [BD1913] .... W
6 .... St Leonard of Noblac [§ *against burglars*] .... Th
7 .... Leon Trotsky [BD1879] .... F
8 .... Bram Stoker [BD1847] · Gordon Ramsay [BD1966] .... Sa
9 .... Remembrance Sunday [£] · Dylan Thomas [†1953] .... Su
10 .... St Tryphon [§ *gardeners*] .... M
11 .... Remembrance Day · USA – Veterans Day · Angola [ID 1975] .... Tu
12 .... Friedrich Hoffmann [†1742] · Elizabeth Gaskell [†1865] .... W
13 ..... ◐ · Robert Louis Stevenson [BD1850] · Whoopi Goldberg [BD1955] ..... Th
14 .... Prince Charles [BD1948] [£] · Joseph McCarthy [BD1908] .... F
15 .... St Albert the Great [§ *scientists*] · Sir William Herschel [BD1738] .... Sa
16 ...... Int. Day for Tolerance [UN] · St Gertrude the Great [§ *souls in purgatory*] ...... Su
17 .... Leonids [☄] · Martin Scorsese [BD1942] .... M
18 .... St Odo of Cluny [§ *rain*] · Marcel Proust [†1922] .... Tu
19 .... Monaco [ND] · Charles I [BD1600] .... W
20. Queen Elizabeth II & Prince Philip [WA1947] [£] · Robert Kennedy [BD1925] Th
21 .... Presentation of the Blessed Virgin Mary in the Temple .... F
22 .... George Eliot [BD1819] · Mae West [†1980] .... Sa
23 .... St Felicity [§ *martyrs*] .... Su
24 .... John Knox [†1572] · Billy Connolly [BD1942] .... M
25 .... Andrew Carnegie [BD1835] · Yukio Mishima [†1970 *seppuku*] .... Tu
26 .... St John Berchmans [§ *altar boys & girls*] .... W
27 .... ☺ · USA – Thanksgiving · Bruce Lee [BD1940] .... Th
28 .... East Timor [ND] · Manolo Blahnik [BD1942] .... F
29 .... Giacomo Puccini [†1924] · Graham Hill [†1975] .... Sa
30 .... St Andrew [§ *Scotland & Russia*] · Mark Twain [BD1835] .... Su

French Rev. calendar .... *Frimaire* (frost)
Angelic governor .... *Advachiel*
Epicurean calendar .... *Pommedetaire*

Dutch month .. *Slaghtmaand* [see below]
Saxon month ...... *Wind-monath* (wind)
Talismanic stone .... *Beryl*

❦ Originally, the ninth (*novem*) month, November has long been associated with slaughter, hence the Dutch *Slaghtmaand* ('slaughter month'). The Anglo Saxon was *Blotmonath* ('blood' or 'sacrifice month'). ❦ A dismal month, November has been the subject of many writers' ire, as J.B. Burges wrote: 'November leads her wintry train, And stretches o'er the firmament her veil Charg'd with foul vapours, fogs and drizzly rain'. ❦ Famously, Thomas Hood's poem *No!* contains the lines 'No warmth, no cheerfulness, no healthful ease ... No shade, no shine, no butterflies, no bees, No fruits, no flowers, no leaves, no birds, —— November!' ❦

DECEMBER

Sagittarius [♐] (Nov 23–Dec 21)

Birthstone · TURQUOISE
Flower · NARCISSUS

Capricorn [♑] (Dec 22–Jan 20)

Day		
1	World AIDS Day [UN] · Stephen Poliakoff [BD 1952]	M
2	Kyrgyzstan [ND] · Marquis de Sade [†1814]	Tu
3	International Day of Disabled Persons [UN] · Pierre-Auguste Renoir [†1919]	W
4	St Ada [§ *nuns*] · John Gay [†1732]	Th
5	Thailand [ND] · José Carreras [BD 1946]	F
6	St Nicholas [§ *bakers & pawnbrokers*] · Anthony Trollope [†1882]	Sa
7	Pearl Harbor Day, USA · St Ambrose [§ *protector of bees & domestic animals*]	Su
8	The Immaculate Conception · Jim Morrison [BD 1943]	M
9	Kirk Douglas [BD 1916] · John Malkovich [BD 1953]	Tu
10	Nobel Prizes awarded · Human Rights Day [UN]	W
11	St Damasus [§ *archaeologists*]	Th
12	◐ · Edvard Munch [BD 1863] · Pennsylvania [AD 1787]	F
13	Japan – Soot Sweeping Day · Donatello [†1466]	Sa
14	Geminids [☄] · St Agnellus [§ *invoked against invaders*]	Su
15	National Bill of Rights Day, USA · Frankie Dettori [BD 1970]	M
16	Kazakhstan [ID 1991] · Glenn Miller [†1944 *missing, presumed dead*]	Tu
17	Sow Day – Orkney · Sir Humphrey Davy [BD 1778]	W
18	International Migrants Day [UN] · Steven Spielberg [BD 1946]	Th
19	Leonid Brezhnev [BD 1906]	F
20	St Ursucinus of Saint-Ursanne [§ *against stiff neck*]	Sa
21	Shortest Day · First Day of Winter	Su
22	First Day of Chanukah · Beatrix Potter [†1943]	M
23	Ursids [☄] · Japan [ND]	Tu
24	Christmas Eve · William Makepeace Thackeray [†1863]	W
25	Christmas Day [NH] · Charlie Chaplin [†1977]	Th
26 ★	[★BH] Boxing Day [NH] · St Stephen [§ *stonemasons & horses*]	F
27	☺ · St John [§ *Asia Minor*] · Johannes Kepler [BD 1571]	Sa
28	Childermass · Dame Maggie Smith [BD 1934]	Su
29	Islamic New Year (AH 1430) · Rasputin [†1916 *assassinated*]	M
30	Our Lady of Bethlehem · Tiger Woods [BD 1975]	Tu
31	New Year's Eve · Scotland – Hogmanay	W

French Rev. calendar	*Nivôse* (snow)	Dutch month	*Wintermaand* (Winter)
Angelic governor	Hanael	Saxon month	*Mid-Winter-monath*
Epicurean calendar	*Boudinaire*	Talismanic stone	*Onyx*

❦ *If the ice will bear a goose before Christmas, it will not bear a duck afterwards.* ❦ Originally the tenth month, December now closes the year. ❦ *If Christmas Day be bright and clear there'll be two winters in the year.* ❦ The writer Saunders warned in 1679, 'In December, Melancholy and Phlegm much increase, which are heavy, dull, and close, and therefore it behoves all that will consider their healths, to keep their heads and bodies very well from cold'. ❦ Robert Burns splendidly wrote in 1795, 'As I am in a complete Decemberish humour, gloomy, sullen, stupid'. ❦

ANNIVERSARIES OF 2008

25th Anniversary (1983)
Wearing seat belts became compulsory in the UK ❦ Epsom Derby winning horse, Shergar, kidnapped

50th Anniversary (1958)
Sir Edmund Hillary reached the South Pole ❦ The Jim Henson Company founded, as Muppets Inc. ❦ *My Fair Lady* opened in London's West End

75th Anniversary (1933)
The Blaine Act effectively ended prohibition in the US ❦ Adolf Hitler appointed Chancellor of Germany ❦ The *Inverness Courier* reported the first modern sighting of the Loch Ness monster ❦ *King Kong* premiered in New York

100th Anniversary (1908)
The Territorial Army founded ❦ Butch Cassidy and the Sundance Kid supposedly killed in Bolivia ❦ Henry Ford produced the first Ford *Model T*

150th Anniversary (1858)
The Virgin Mary appeared to shepherdess Bernadette Soubirous at Lourdes ❦ Big Ben, the bell inside the Palace of Westminster Tower, cast.

200th Anniversary (1808)
Beethoven conducted at the premiere of his Fifth Symphony, in Vienna ❦ The first Covent Garden Theatre Royal destroyed by fire ❦ The Rum Rebellion took place in New South Wales, Australia

250th Anniversary (1758)
Halley's comet appeared for the first time since its discovery ❦ The British indecisively engaged the French fleet at the Battle of the Bay of Bengal

500th Anniversary (1508)
Michelangelo started work on the ceiling of the Sistine Chapel

700th Anniversary (1308)
Edward II married Isabella of France

FRENCH NOTEPAPER TRADITIONS

According to the 1891 edition of *Brewer's Historic Notebook*, an attempt was made in French Society (during the ?C18th) to create a formal etiquette concerning notepaper. Different coloured writing paper was to be used for each day of the week:

Day	*notepaper colour*
Sunday	delicate mauve
Monday	pale green
Tuesday	pink
Wednesday (an unlucky day)	sombre grey
Thursday	blue
Friday	white
Saturday	straw-colour

BRITISH SUMMER TIME

BST starts and ends at 1am on these Sundays (*'spring forward – fall back'*):
2008 .... clocks forward 1 hour, 30 March · clocks back 1 hour, 26 October
2009 .... clocks forward 1 hour, 29 March · clocks back 1 hour, 25 October
2010 .... clocks forward 1 hour, 28 March · clocks back 1 hour, 31 October

ST JOHN'S STAIRWAY TO HEAVEN

St John Climacus (*c.*570–649) was a Greek ascetic whose treatise on monastic virtue – *Klimax tou paradeisou* (Ladder of Paradise) – enumerated 30 steps to Paradise:

· PARADISE ·

FAITH, HOPE, CHARITY

PEACE OF GOD

PRAYER *without ceasing*

SOLITUDE

INNER LIGHT

Death of the NATURAL MAN

SINGLE-MINDEDNESS, or ONLY ONE AFFECTION, and that FOR GOD

Abandonment of FALSE HUMILITY and DOUBT

PRIDE *utterly crushed out*

SELF-GLORIFICATION *cast out*

Conquest of FEAR

WATCHFULNESS; the ETERNAL LAMP *burning*

PSALMODY

Death of the CARNAL MIND

POVERTY, or *loss* of the LOVE OF ACCUMULATING

CHASTITY

TEMPERANCE

Conquest of INDOLENCE of MIND and BODY

Restraint of EXAGGERATION and FALSE REPRESENTATION

SILENCE

Shunning SLANDER and IDLE TALK

Forgiveness of INJURIES

EQUANIMITY

SORROW, *the seed of joy*

Constant thought of DEATH

PENITENCE

OBEDIENCE

Giving up FATHER and MOTHER

Giving up all EARTHLY GOOD and HOPE

Renouncement of THE WORLD

· THE WORLD ·

MELODY OF SINGING BIRDS

The melody of singing birds was traditionally ranked as follows:

The NIGHTINGALE first,
then the LINNET, TITLARK, SKYLARK, and WOODLARK.
The MOCKING BIRD has the greatest powers of imitation,
the ROBIN and GOLDFINCH are superior in vigorous notes.

QUARTER DAYS

Quarter Days are those days traditionally employed to divide the year for legal, financial, or contractual purposes such as tenancies, interests, rents, &c. They are:

QUARTER DAYS – *England & Wales*
25 March (Lady Day) · 24 June (Midsummer Day)
29 September (Michaelmas) · 25 December (Christmas Day)

QUARTER DAYS – *Scotland*
2 February (Candlemas Day) · 15 May (Whitsuntide)
1 August (Lammas) · 11 November (Martinmas)

TRADITIONAL CATHOLIC EPOCHS

Traditionally, the Catholic Church divided the history of man into 6 epochs, viz:

1	Adam to Noah
2	Noah to Abraham
3	Abraham to David
4	David to the Babylonian Captivity
5	captivity of Judah to Christ's birth
6	birth of Christ to the world's end

'MONTH WITH NO NEW MOON'

The Gregorian calendar was introduced into Britain in September 1752 – the days of which ran 1, 2, 14, 15, 16, 17, 18, 19, 20, 21, 22, 23, 24, 25, 26, 27, 28, 29, and 30. The first quarter moon of this September fell on the 15th, at one o'clock in the afternoon, and the full moon fell on the 23rd. The annihilation of 3rd to 13th days of September 1752 led it to be known as 'the month with no new moon'.

SEVEN BODIES IN ALCHEMY

Body	*alchemical equivalent*
The Sun	GOLD
The Moon	SILVER
Mars	IRON
Mercury	QUICKSILVER
Saturn	LEAD
Jupiter	TIN
Venus	COPPER

NOTABLE CHRISTIAN DATES · 2008

Epiphany · *manifestation of the Christ to the Magi* .... 6 Jan
Presentation of Christ in the Temple (Candlemas) .... 2 Feb
Ash Wednesday · *1st day of Lent* .... 6 Feb
Good Friday · *Friday before Easter; commemorating the Crucifixion* .... 21 Mar
Easter Day (Western churches) · *commemorating the Resurrection* .... 23 Mar
The Annunciation · *when Gabriel told Mary she would bear Christ* .... 25 Mar
Easter Day (Eastern Orthodox) · *commemorating the Resurrection* .... 27 Apr
Rogation Sunday · *the Sunday before Ascension Day* .... 27 Apr
Ascension Day · *commemorating the ascent of Christ to heaven* .... 1 May
Pentecost (Whit Sunday) · *commemorating the descent of the Holy Spirit* .... 11 May
Trinity Sunday · *observed in honour of the Trinity* .... 18 May
Corpus Christi · *commemorating the institution of the Holy Eucharist* .... 22 May
All Saints' Day · *commemorating all the Church's saints collectively* .... 1 Nov
Advent Sunday · *marking the start of Advent* .... 30 Nov
Christmas Day · *celebrating the birth of Christ* .... 25 Dec

A few other terms from the Christian Calendar:

Bible Sunday .... 2nd in Advent
Black/Easter Monday .... the day after Easter
Collop/Egg Monday .... 1st before Lent
Egg Saturday .... day prior to Quinquagesima
Fig/Yew Sunday .... Palm Sunday
Holy Saturday .... before Easter
Holy Week .... before Easter
Low Sunday .... Sunday after Easter
Maundy Thursday .... day before Good Friday
Mothering Sunday .... 4th in Lent
Palm Sunday .... before Easter
Passion Sunday .... 5th in Lent
Plough Monday .... after Epiphany
Quadragesima .... 1st Sunday in Lent
Quinquagesima .... Sunday before Lent
Refreshment .... 4th Sunday in Lent
Septuagesima .... 3rd Sunday before Lent
Sexagesima .... 2nd Sunday before Lent
Shrove Tuesday ('pancake day') .... before Lent
Shrovetide .... period preceding Lent
St Martin's Lent .... Advent
Tenebrae .... last 3 days of Holy Week

CHRISTIAN CALENDAR MOVEABLE FEASTS

Year	*Ash Wednesday*	*Easter Day*	*Ascension*	*Pentecost*	*Advent Sunday*
2008	6 Feb	23 Mar	1 May	11 May	30 Nov
2009	25 Feb	12 Apr	21 May	31 May	29 Nov
2010	17 Feb	4 Apr	13 May	23 May	28 Nov
2011	9 Mar	24 Apr	2 Jun	12 Jun	27 Nov
2012	22 Feb	8 Apr	17 May	27 May	2 Dec
2013	13 Feb	31 Mar	9 May	19 May	1 Dec
2014	5 Mar	20 Apr	29 May	8 Jun	30 Nov
2015	18 Feb	5 Apr	14 May	24 May	29 Nov
2016	10 Feb	27 Mar	5 May	15 May	27 Nov
2017	1 Mar	16 Apr	25 May	4 Jun	3 Dec
2018	14 Feb	1 Apr	10 May	20 May	2 Dec
2019	6 Mar	21 Apr	30 May	9 Jun	1 Dec

NOTABLE RELIGIOUS DATES FOR 2008

HINDU

Makar Sankrant · *Winter festival* .... 14 Jan
Vasant Panchami · *dedicated to Saraswati and learning* .... 11 Feb
Maha Shivaratri · *dedicated to Shiva* .... 6 Mar
Holi · *spring festival of colours dedicated to Krishna* .... 21/22 Mar
Varsha Pratipada (Chaitra) · *Spring New Year* .... 6 Mar
Hindu New Year & Ramayana Week .... 6 Apr
Rama Navami · *birthday of Lord Rama* .... 14 Apr
Hanuman Jayanti · *birthday of Hanuman, the Monkey God* .... 20 Apr
Raksha Bandhan · *festival of brotherhood and love* .... 16 Aug
Janmashtami · *birthday of Lord Rama* .... 24 Aug
Ganesh Chaturthi · *birthday of Lord Ganesh* .... 3 Sep
Navarati & Durga-puja · *celebrating triumph of good over evil* .... *starts* 30 Sep
Saraswati-puja · *dedicated to Saraswati and learning* .... *starts* 6 Oct
Dassera (Vijay Dashami) · *celebrating triumph of good over evil* .... 9 Oct
Diwali (Deepvali) · *New Year festival of lights* .... 28 Oct
New Year .... 29 Oct

JEWISH

Purim (Feast of Lots) · *commemorating defeat of Haman* .... 21 Mar
Pesach (Passover) · *commemorating exodus from Egypt* .... 20 Apr
Shavuot (Pentecost) · *commemorating revelation of the Torah* .... 9 Jun
Tisha B'Av · *day of mourning* .... 10 Aug
Rosh Hashanah (New Year) .... 30 Sep
Yom Kippur (Day of Atonement) · *fasting and prayer for forgiveness* .... 9 Oct
Sukkoth (Feast of Tabernacles) · *marking the time in wilderness* .... 14 Oct
Simchat Torah · *9th day of Sukkoth* .... 21 Oct
Chanukah · *commemorating re-dedication of Jerusalem Temple* .... 22 Dec

ISLAMIC

Eid al-Adha · *celebrating the faith of Abraham* .... 9 Dec
Al Hijra (New Year) .... 10 Jan
Ashura · *celebrating Noah leaving the Ark, and the saving of Moses* .... 19 Jan
Milad Al-Nabi · *birthday of Muhammad* .... 20 Mar
Ramadan · *the month in which the Koran was revealed* .... *starts* 2 Sep
Eid al-Fitr · *marks end of Ramadan* .... 1 Oct

SIKH

Birthday of Guru Gobind Singh · *founder of the Khalsa* .... 5 Jan
Sikh New Year (Nanakshahi calendar) .... 14 Mar
Hola Mahalla · *festival of martial arts* .... 22 Mar
Vaisakhi (Baisakhi) · *founding of the Khalsa* .... 13 Apr
Birthday of Guru Nanak (founder of Sikhism) .... 14 Apr
Martyrdom of Guru Arjan .... 16 Jun
Diwali · *festival of light* .... 28 Oct
Martyrdom of Guru Tegh Bahadur .... 24 Nov

NOTABLE RELIGIOUS DATES FOR 2008 cont.

BAHA'I

Nawruz (New Year)	21 Mar	Day of the Covenant	26 Nov
Ridvan	21 Apr	Ascension of Abdu'l-Baha	28 Nov
Declaration of the Báb	23 May	*World Religion Day*	21 Jan
Ascension of Baha'u'llah	29 May	*Race Unity Day*	11 Jun
Martyrdom of the Báb	9 July	*World Peace Day*	21 Sep
Birth of the Báb	20 Oct	*In addition, the eve of each of the*	
Birth of Baha'u'llah	12 Nov	*nineteen Baha'i months is celebrated.*	

JAIN

Mahavira Jayanti · *celebrates the day of Mahavira's birth* ..... 18 Apr
Paryushan · *time of reflection and repentance* ..... 28 Aug
Diwali · *celebrated when Mahavira gave his last teachings and attained ultimate liberation* .. 28 Oct
New Year ..... 29 Oct
Kartak Purnima · *time of pilgrimage* ..... Oct/Nov

BUDDHIST

Parinivana Day · *marks the death of the Buddha* ..... 8 Feb
Losar · *Tibetan New Year* ..... 8 Feb
Sangha Day (Magha Puja Day) · *celebration of Buddhist community* ..... 25 Mar
Wesak (Vesak) · *marks the birth, death & enlightenment of the Buddha* ..... 20 May
Dharma Day · *marks the start of the Buddha's teaching* ..... 18 Jul

RASTAFARIAN

Ethiopian Christmas	7 Jan	Birthday of Marcus Garvey	17 Aug
Ethiopian Constitution	16 Jul	Ethiopian New Year's Day	11 Sep
Birthday of Haile Selassie	23 Jul	Crowning of Haile Selassie	2 Nov

PAGAN

Imbolc · *fire festival anticipating the new farming season* ..... 2 Feb
Spring Equinox · *celebrating the renewal of life* ..... 20 Mar
Beltane · *fire festival celebrating Summer and fertility* ..... 1 May
Summer Solstice (Midsummer; Litha) · *celebrating the sun's power* ..... 20 Jun
Lughnasadh · *harvest festival* ..... 1 Aug
Autumn Equinox (Harvest Home; Mabon) · *reflection on the past season* ..... 22 Sep
Samhain (Hallowe'n; All Hallows Eve) · *Pagan New Year* ..... 31 Oct
Winter Solstice (Yule) · *celebrating Winter* ..... 21 Dec

CHINESE LUNAR NEW YEAR · 7 Feb

[Every effort has been taken to validate these dates. However, readers should be aware that there is a surprising degree of debate and dispute. This is caused by the interplay of: regional variations; differing interpretations between religious authorities; seemingly arbitrary changes in dates when holidays conflict; avoidance of days considered for one or other reason inauspicious; as well as the inherent unpredictability of the lunar cycle. Many festivals, such as Jewish holidays, start at sundown on the preceding day.]

PUBLIC & BANK HOLIDAYS

England, Wales, & N. Ireland	2008	2009	2010
New Year's Day	1 Jan	1 Jan	1 Jan
[NI *only*] St Patrick's Day	17 Mar	17 Mar	17 Mar
Good Friday	21 Mar	10 Apr	2 Apr
Easter Monday	24 Mar	13 Apr	5 Apr
Early May Bank Holiday	5 May	4 May	3 May
Spring Bank Holiday	26 May	25 May	31 May
[NI *only*] Battle of the Boyne	14 July	13 Jul	12 Jul
Summer Bank Holiday	25 Aug	31 Aug	30 Aug
Christmas Day	25 Dec	25 Dec	27 Dec
Boxing Day	26 Dec	28 Dec	28 Dec

Scotland	2008	2009	2010
New Year's Day	1 Jan	1 Jan	1 Jan
2nd January	2 Jan	2 Jan	4 Jan
Good Friday	21 Mar	10 Apr	2 Apr
Early May Bank Holiday	5 May	4 May	4 May
Spring Bank Holiday	26 May	25 May	31 May
Summer Bank Holiday	4 Aug	3 Aug	2 Aug
Christmas Day	25 Dec	25 Dec	27 Dec
Boxing Day	26 Dec	28 Dec	28 Dec

These are the expected dates of holidays; some are subject to proclamation by the Queen.

BELGIAN DRINKING LEGENDS

In the C18th, it was said that Belgian labourers spent a quarter of their wages on drink; on ordinary days they took 6 drams, on festal days more. The drams were:

The *Worm-killer*	5:30am	The *Digester*	2:00pm
The *Eye-opener*	8:00am	The *Soldier*	5:00pm
The *Whip*	11:00am	The *Finisher*	7:30pm

TRADITIONAL WEDDING ANNIVERSARY SYMBOLS

1st	Cotton	10th	Tin	35th	Coral
2nd	Paper	11th	Steel	40th	Ruby
3rd	Leather	12th	Silk, Linen	45th	Sapphire
4th	Fruit, Flowers	13th	Lace	50th	Gold
5th	Wood	14th	Ivory	55th	Emerald
6th	Sugar	15th	Crystal	60th	Diamond
7th	Wool, Copper	20th	China	70th	Platinum
8th	Pottery	25th	Silver	75th	Diamond
9th	Willow	30th	Pearl		

American symbols differ.

PHASES OF THE MOON · MMVIII

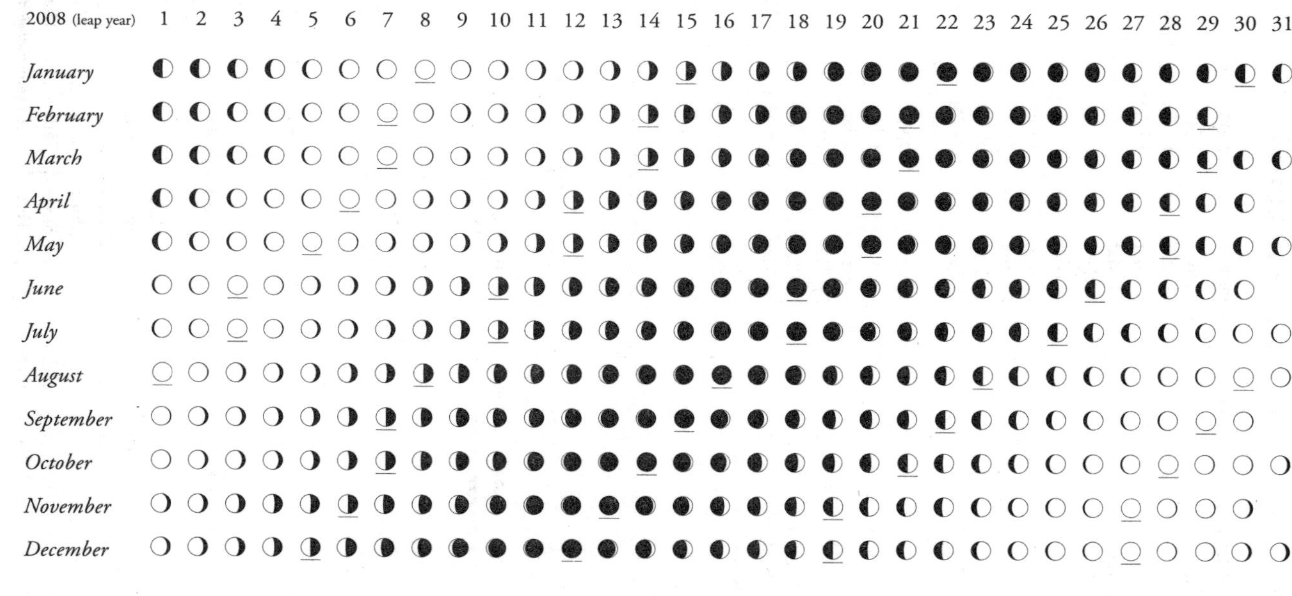

Key: New Moon · First Quarter · Full Moon · Last Quarter · Dates are based on Universal Time (Greenwich Mean Time)

CHRISTMAS DAY 1684 & SOVEREIGNS

On Christmas Day 1684, all of the eight British sovereigns listed below were alive:

Richard Cromwell	4·10·1626–12·7·1712
Charles II	29·5·1630–6·2·1685
James II	14·10·1633–16·9·1701
William III	4·11·1650–19·3·1702
Mary II	30·4·1662–28·12·1694
Anne	6·2·1665–1·8·1714
George I	28·5·1660–11·6·1727
George II	10·11·1683–25·10·1760

FURTHER GEM SYMBOLISM

Moss agate	health, prosperity, and long life
Amethyst	prevents violent passions
Bloodstone	courage, wisdom, and firmness in affection
Chrysolite	frees from evil passions and sadness
Emerald	ensures true love, discovers false
Diamonds	innocence, faith, and virgin purity; friends
Garnet	constancy and fidelity in every engagement
Opal	sharpens the sight and faith of the possessor
Pearl	purity; gives clearness to physical and mental sight
Ruby	corrects evils resulting from mistaken friendship
Sapphire	repentance; frees from enchantment
Sardonyx	ensures conjugal felicity
Topaz	fidelity and friendship; prevents bad dreams
Turquoise	ensures prosperity in love

CANONICAL HOURS

The eight traditional Canonical hours of the Catholic Church are tabulated below:

Matins (Nocturnes)	*midnight–daybreak*
Lauds	*daybreak*
Prime	*6:00am (1st hour of the day)*
Tierce	*9:00am (3rd hour of the day)*
Sexte	*midday (6th hour of the day)*
Nones	*3:00pm (9th hour of the day)*
Vespers	*sunset*
Compline	*bedtime*

END OF THE WORLD

In 1566, Nostradamus predicted that the world would come to an end when:

GOOD FRIDAY falls on *St George's Day* (23rd April),
EASTER SUNDAY falls on *St Mark's Day* (25 April),
and CORPUS CHRISTI falls on *John the Baptist's Day* (24 June)

This coincidence came about in AD 45, 140, 387, 482, 577, 672, 919, 1014, 1109, 1204, 1421, 1451, 1546, 1666, 1734, 1886, and 1945, and still the world turns.

ON CHARACTER & THE FACE

Straight lips, firmly closed, RESOLUTION. *Large ears* denote GENEROSITY. *Thick lips* indicate GENIUS and CONSERVATISM. *Large dilating nostrils* are a sign of POETIC TEMPERAMENT & A SENSITIVE NATURE. *A long forehead* denotes LIBERALITY. *Arched eyebrows*, GOOD ANCESTRY & AMIABILITY. *A bold, projecting Roman nose* indicates ENTERPRISE. *Delicate nose*, GOOD NATURE. A *large nose*, STRENGTH OF WILL and CHARACTER. *Lips slightly curved upward at the ends* indicate a FINE SENSE OF HUMOUR. *Soft round cheeks* denote GENTLENESS & AFFECTION; *dimples in the cheeks*, ROGUERY; *in the chin*, one who FALLS EASILY IN LOVE. *A broad chin* denotes FIRMNESS. *An eye that looks one cheerfully and frankly in the face* shows HONESTY & FAITHFULNESS. [Anonymous, *c.*1830?]

BEES & THE MONTHS

A swarm of bees in May
Is worth a load of hay;
A swarm of bees in June
Is worth a silver spoon;
A swarm of bees in July
Is not worth a fly.

THE CUCKOO'S YEAR

In April the cuckoo shows his bill;
In May he sings all day;
In June he alters his tune;
In July away he'll fly;
In August go he must.

A WOMAN'S CHANCE TO MARRY

'Every woman has some chance to marry. It may be one to fifty, or it may be ten to one that she will. Representing her entire chance at one hundred at certain points of her progress in time, it is found to be in the following ratio'

Woman's age	*likelihood of marriage*
15–20 years	14½%
20–25 years	52%
25–30 years	18%
30–35 years	15½%
35–40 years	3¾%
40–45 years	2¾%
45–50 years	¾ of 1%
50–56 years	⅛ of 1%
>60 years	1/10 of 1% (or 1 in 1,000)

[Source: *The Handy Cyclopedia of Things Worth Knowing*, Joseph Trienens, 1911]

TRADITIONAL COLOUR COORDINATION

Yellow contrasts with .... purple, russet, and auburn
Red contrasts with .... green, olive, and drab
Blue contrasts with .... orange, citrine, and buff
Yellow harmonises with .... orange, green, citrine, russet, buff, and drab
Red harmonises with .... orange, purple, russet, citrine, auburn, and buff
Blue harmonises with .... purple, green, olive, citrine, drab, and auburn

—ANON'S ALPHABET OF WRITERLY ADVICE (c.1911)—

A word out of place spoils the most beautiful thought. – VOLTAIRE

Begin humbly. Labour faithfully. Be patient. – ELIZABETH STUART PHELPS

Cultivate accuracy in words and things; amass sound knowledge; avoid affectation; write all topics which interest you. – F.W. NEWMAN

Don't be afraid. Fight right along. Hope right along. S.L. CLEMENS

Every good writer has much idiom; it is the life and spirit of Language. – W.S. LANDOR

Follow this: If you write from the heart, you will write to the heart. – BEACONSFIELD

Genius may begin great works, but only continued labour completes them. – JOUBERT

Half the writer's art consists in learning what to leave in the ink-pot. – STEVENSON

It is by suggestion, not cumulation, that profound impressions form on the imagination. – LOWELL

Joy in one's work is an asset beyond the valuing in mere dollars. – C.D. WARNER.

Keep writing, and profit by criticism. Use for a motto Michelangelo's wise words: 'Genius is infinite patience'. – L.M. ALCOTT

Lord, let me never tag a moral to a story, nor tell a story without a meaning. – VAN DYKE

More failures come from vanity than carelessness. – JOSEPH JEFFERSON

Never do a 'pot-boiler'. Let one of your best things go to boil the pot. – O. HENRY

Originality does not mean oddity, but freshness. It means vitality, not novelty. – NORMAN HAPGOOD

Pluck feathers from the wings of your imagination, and stick them in the tail of your judgment. – HORACE GREELEY

Quintessence approximates genius. Gather much thought into few words. – SCHOPENHAUER

Revise. Revise. Revise. – E.E. HALE

Simplicity has been held a mark of truth: it is also a mark of genius. – CARLYLE

The first principle of composition of whatever sort is that it should be natural and appear to have happened so. – FREDERICK MACMONNIES

Utilize your enthusiasms. Get the habit of happiness in work. – BEVERIDGE

Very few voices but sound repellent under violent exertion. – G.E. LESSING

Whatever in this world one has to say, there is a word, and just one word, to express it. Seek that out and use it. – DE MAUPASSANT

Yes, yes; believe me, you must draw your pen not once, nor twice, but o'er and o'er again through what you've written, if you would entice The man who reads you once to read you twice. – HORACE

Zeal with scanty capacity often accomplishes more than capacity with no zeal at all. – GEORGE ELIOT

Index

The perfect search engine would understand exactly what you mean and give back exactly what you want.
— LARRY PAGE, co-founder *Google*

10 INFLUENTIAL NON-PEOPLE – BOND, JAMES

BOOKER PRIZES – DA-NOTICES

DAB RADIO – HALL OF FAME, ROCK & ROLL

HALL OF FAME, UK RADIO – MOON, MONTHS

MOON PHASES – PRIZE, BOOKS

PRIZE, FILM FESTIVALS – SUICIDE RATES

—SUMMER TIME, BRITISH – ZIMBABWE STAGFLATION—

ERRATA, CORRIGENDA, &c.

In keeping with many newspapers and journals, *Schott's Almanac* will publish in this section any significant corrections from the previous year. Below are some errata from *Schott's Almanac 2007* – many of which were kindly noted by readers.

[p.25 *of the 2007 edition*] In the second column, Guantánamo was missing its third 'a'. [p.77] Some bizarre typographical mishap meant that CO_2 was printed CO^2. [p.83] A minus sign was omitted from the difference in male and female life expectancy for Vietnam entry; this has been corrected on p.83. [p.145] The Danish composer is Carl August Nielsen (not Neilsen). [p.146] The seating capacity of the Metropolitan Opera was incorrectly given as 2,065. It is, in fact, 3,800 with 95 standing-room places; an additional 35 seats can be added for ballet performances. [p.153] The designer of Rachel Weisz's dress was Narciso (not Narcisco) Rodriguez. [p.247] The US$ to GB£ entry was repeated in error. [p.306] The *Wisden* Leading Cricketer of the Year, won by Andrew Flintoff in 2006, was in fact created in 2004 and can be won any number of times. [p.308] The Six Nations title was erroneously dated 2005, when the table correctly showed the 2006 results. [p.331] The entry on October Surprises incorrectly stated that US hostages in Tehran were released in October 1980; in fact, they were released in January 1981. Considerable debate surrounds the political machinations of the whole episode.

ACKNOWLEDGMENTS

The author would like to thank:

Jonathan, Judith, Geoffrey, & Oscar Schott, Anette Schrag
Benjamin Adams, Richard Album, Joanna Begent, Catherine Best,
Michael Binyon, Martin Birchall, Andrew Cock-Starkey, James Coleman,
Mark Colodny, Aster Crawshaw, Jody & Liz Davies, Peter DeGiglio,
Colin Dickerman, Will Douglas, Miles Doyle, Charlotte Druckman,
Stephanie Duncan, Jennifer Epworth, Sabrina Farber, Kathleen Farrar
Josh Fine, Minna Fry, Alona Fryman, Panio Gianopoulos, Charlotte Hayes,
Mark & Sharon Hubbard, Nick Humphrey, Max Jones, Amy King
Robert Klaber, Maureen Klier, Alison Lang, Jim Ledbetter, Annik LeFa
John Lloyd, Ruth Logan, Josh Lovejoy, Chris Lyon, Sam MacAuslan
Jess Manson, Michael Manson, Sarah Marcus, Sara Mercurio,
Susannah McFarlane, David Miller, Peter Miller, Polly Napper, Ishbel Nicol,
Nigel Newton, Sarah Norton, Cally Poplak, Dave Powell, Alexandra Pringle,
Karen Rinaldi, Pavia Rosati, Joy Ross, David Shipley, Jared Van Snellenberg,
Bill Swainson, Caroline Turner, & Greg Villepique.